Davis Chapman

SAMS Teach Yourself
Visual C++® .NET
in 21 Days

SAMS

201 West 103rd St., Indianapolis, Indiana, 46290 USA

Teach Yourself Visual C++ .NET in 21 Days
Copyright © 2002 by Sams Publishing

International Standard Book Number: 0672321971

Library of Congress Catalog Card Number: 2001087651

Printed in the United States of America

First Printing: December 2001

03   02   01   00   4   3   2   1

Trademarks

All terms mentioned in this book that are known to be trademarks or service marks have been appropriately capitalized. Sams Publishing cannot attest to the accuracy of this information. Use of a term in this book should not be regarded as affecting the validity of any trademark or service mark.

Warning and Disclaimer

Every effort has been made to make this book as complete and as accurate as possible, but no warranty or fitness is implied. The information provided is on an "as is" basis. The author and the publisher shall have neither liability nor responsibility to any person or entity with respect to any loss or damages arising from the information contained in this book or from the use of the programs accompanying it.

ASSOCIATE PUBLISHER
Linda Engelman

ACQUISITIONS EDITOR
Laurie McGuire
Linda Scharp

DEVELOPMENT EDITOR
Susan Shaw Dunn

MANAGING EDITOR
Charlotte Clapp

PROJECT EDITORS
Natalie Harris
Sheila Schroeder

PRODUCTION EDITOR
Tony Reitz

COPY EDITOR
Linda Seifert

INDEXER
Sharon Shock

PROOFREADER
Harvey Stanbrough

TECHNICAL EDITORS
Tony Davis
Erik Thompson

TEAM COORDINATOR
Lynne Williams

MEDIA DEVELOPER
Dan Scherf

INTERIOR DESIGNER
Gary Adair

COVER DESIGNER
Aren Howell

PAGE LAYOUT
Plan-it Publishing

Contents at a Glance

Contents

About the Author

DAVIS CHAPMAN first began programming computers while working on his Masters Degree in Music Composition. While writing applications for computer music, he discovered that he enjoyed designing and developing computer software. It wasn't long before he came to the realization that he stood a much better chance of eating if he stuck with his new-found skill and demoted his hard-earned status as a "starving artist" to a part-time hobby. Since that time, Davis has focused on the art of software design and development, with a strong emphasis on the practical application of Client/Server and Web/Internet technologies. Davis was the lead author for *Building Secure Applications with Visual Basic, Sams Teach Yourself Visual C++ 6 in 21 Days, Web Development with Visual Basic 5* and *Building Internet Applications with Delphi 2*. Davis was also a contributing author on *MFC Programming with Visual C++ 6 Unleashed, Special Edition Using Active Server Pages*, and *Running a Perfect Web Site, Second Edition*. He has been a consultant working and living in Dallas, Texas, for the past 12 years. Davis can be reached at davis@chaperada.net.

About the Technical Editors

TONY DAVIS is the co-founder and President of MillenniSoft, Inc. a turnkey software development and consulting company in Dallas, Texas. He has been a business application software architect, designer, and developer for over 14 years specializing in C++ Windows client/server applications.

ERIK THOMPSON works as a senior software engineer specializing in C++, COM, ATL and the middle-tier. He has been working with computers since the mid '80s. When he isn't coding for work, he can be found on *The Code Project* as an editor and writing articles about new technologies or areas of interest. Erik lives in Redmond, Washington.

Dedication

As always, this is dedicated to my beautiful wife, Dore, and the rest of my family. Next year, we'll have a summer vacation. I promise.

Acknowledgments

There are many people who deserve credit for helping this book reach the bookstore shelves. Linda Sharp deserves credit for getting the whole project off the ground. Laurie McGuire also deserves kudos for picking it up from Linda and managing the project. I know I made life tough for Laurie from time to time, so she also deserves credit for being patient with me throughout this project. Thanks to Susan Dunn, Tony Reitz, and the rest of the editing team for all the hard work that they put in. I've seen enough of what the editors have to do to know that I don't want to trade jobs with you. Thanks also to Tony Davis and Erik Thompson for keeping me honest and never hesitating to let me know when I don't know what I'm talking about. You both did a great job of tech editing this book, even diving into the source code to uncover undocumented aspects that I'd missed. Finally, I'd like to thank my wife and family for being patient with me as I virtually ignored them throughout summer vacation slaving over a hot computer (in the Texas heat, no less).

Tell Us What You Think!

As the reader of this book, *you* are our most important critic and commentator. We value your opinion and want to know what we're doing right, what we could do better, what areas you'd like to see us publish in, and any other words of wisdom you're willing to pass our way.

As an associate publisher for Sams, I welcome your comments. You can fax, e-mail, or write me directly to let me know what you did or didn't like about this book—as well as what we can do to make our books stronger.

Please note that I cannot help you with technical problems related to the topic of this book, and that due to the high volume of mail I receive, I might not be able to reply to every message.

When you write, please be sure to include this book's title and author as well as your name and phone or fax number. I will carefully review your comments and share them with the author and editors who worked on the book.

Fax: 317-581-4770

E-mail: feedback@samspublishing.com

Mail: Linda Engelman
            Sams Publishing
            201 West 103rd Street
            Indianapolis, IN 46290 USA

Introduction

Welcome to Visual C++. Over the next 21 days, you will learn how to use the features that Microsoft has built into its C++ development environment to enable you to create very advanced applications for the Windows operating system, as well as get an introduction into building applications for Microsoft's new .NET platform. When Microsoft's developers first came up with the idea behind Visual C++, they decided to take their world-class C++ compiler and create a development environment and tool set that would enable developers to create Windows applications with a level of ease and speed that was previously unheard of. Since that first version, Microsoft has continued to improve the tools that are a part of Visual C++ to make it even easier to create Windows applications. As Microsoft has introduced new technologies into the Windows platforms, it has also introduced tools into the Visual C++ suite to make it easy to integrate these new technologies into your applications.

If you are new to C++, don't worry. I've tried to make it easy for you to learn the C++ programming language while also learning how to build applications using the Visual C++ tools. Although I can't provide as thorough a guide to the C++ programming language as in a book dedicated to the language itself, I've tried to explain how the language works throughout the book.

C++ Sidebar: Help with Programming Specifics

As you go through the book, you'll find specially identified sections dedicated to various aspects of the C++ programming language that you are seeing in the example code. If you already know the C++ programming language and are reading this book to learn the Visual C++ tool, you can skip these sections.

MFC Note: Quick Focus on Classes

If you've looked at previous versions of this book, you might notice that I've extensively rewritten a good part of it. My goal with this new version is not just to introduce you to and guide you through the various tools and resources you will use to build applications with Visual C++, but also to include a great deal more detail about the various options available to you with each feature that's covered.

I've even included special sections focusing more deeply on the classes used to implement certain areas of functionality. Like the special sections on the C++ programming languages, you can easily skip these sections on the Microsoft Foundation Classes

(MFC) class library and return to them at a later time, as you are ready to dig deeper under the covers of Visual C++. This way, you'll be able to get a lot of use out of this book long after the initial 21 days.

How This Book Is Organized

This book is organized in weeks, with each set of seven days set off into a part unto itself. However, even though the book is organized in weeks, the topics aren't necessarily organized that way.

At the end of each day's lesson, you'll find a short quiz and one or two exercises to help make sure that you learned the topic you were studying. Don't worry—just in case you need the answers to the quizzes and some guidance when building the exercises, the solutions are provided in Appendix A, "Answers to Quiz Questions."

The first week covers the basics of building applications with Visual C++. You'll learn how to use designers to design your application windows. You'll learn how to use various controls available to you as a Windows application developer. You'll also learn a lot about the Visual C++ development environment and the tools that it makes available to you.

By the time you begin the second week, you'll be doing more and more programming, as the topics become more involved. You'll still be using the Visual C++ tools to construct your applications, but the programming code will be getting a little more involved. You'll also start learning about more advanced topics, such as displaying graphics and creating SDI and MDI applications. Toward the end of the second week, you'll begin to work with databases.

In the third week, you'll learn how to create and use your own ActiveX controls. You'll also learn how to build multitasking applications, which perform multiple tasks at a time. Finally, you'll learn some of the basics of using Visual C++ with Microsoft's new .NET platform, and how it affects your approach to designing and programming applications.

After you finish the third week, you'll be ready to tackle the world of Windows programming with Visual C++. You'll have the skills and know-how required to build most Windows applications available today.

Conventions Used in This Book

While you read this book, you'll probably notice a couple of conventions that make it easier for you to learn the topic being discussed.

All the source code in this book is shown in a monospaced font (see Listing 0.1 for an example). This includes all source code from the applications that you will be building and illustrations of how various functions can be used. Syntax variables that you need to replace with an appropriate value appear in monospace italic. Whenever you add new code or change code in a function with other code already there, the code lines that you need to add or change are highlighted in boldfaced text and have a special Input icon in the margin next to them.

INPUT **LISTING 0.1** Some Sample Code

```
void main()
{
// if you are adding or changing code in an existing code
// snippet, I will point out the lines by making them boldfaced.
}
```

You can identify special information by looking for these graphic elements:

ANALYSIS This icon identifies text that explains the code preceding it.

NEW TERM This icon indicates a new term that's defined and explained in a paragraph. The term being defined is formatted in *italic*.

Note Notes offer a deeper explanation of a topic or explain interesting or important points. They also provide more information that may help you avoid problems or that you should consider when using the described features.

Tip Tips offer advice or suggest easier or alternative methods of doing something.

Caution Cautions alert you to possible problems or hazards and advise you on how to avoid or fix them.

Enough said! You didn't buy this book to read about this book. You bought this book to learn how to use Visual C++ to build Windows applications, so flip the page and start programming...

WEEK 1

At a Glance

Welcome to the world of Visual C++! Over the next three weeks, you'll learn to build various applications using this extremely flexible and complete programming tool. Each day you'll learn a different area of functionality and how to use it in your applications. Every area of functionality will be accompanied with a hands-on sample application that you will build yourself. There's not a more effective way of learning new technologies than to work with them yourself. Learning by doing—that's what you'll do as you make your way through this book.

Over the course of the first week, you'll learn several basics involved in building applications with Visual C++. This starts on the first day as you learn about and become familiar with the Visual C++ development environment by building a simple application.

On Day 2, "Debugging Your Application," you'll learn some valuable tools and techniques for debugging the applications that you build with Visual C++. You'll learn how to add special debugging macros to help expose possible bugs in your application before giving the application to users. You'll also learn how to use the integrated debugger in the Visual Studio Integrated Development Environment (IDE) and how you can use it to find and correct problems in your code.

1

2

3

4

5

6

7

Note

Why learn how to debug your programs before you've written any? Because learning how to debug and step through your code enables you to watch your code in action, and gain a better understanding of how it works. Also, once you move beyond applications with only one or two lines of code, bugs are likely to sneak in, and you need to know how to find and correct them when they do.

On Day 3, "Using Controls in Your Application," you'll begin learning more about the specifics of building applications in Visual C++. You'll learn about the standard controls used in Windows applications, how you can place and configure these on an application window, and how you can interact with them.

On Day 4, "Integrating Mouse and Keyboard to Allow User Interaction," you'll learn how your applications can react to mouse and keyboard events. You'll see how you can determine where the mouse is in your application space. You'll also learn how to determine what keys the user is pressing on the keyboard and how you can react to these user actions.

On Day 5, "Working with Timers," you'll learn how to work with timers in a Visual C++ application. You'll learn how to have two or more timers running at the same time and how you can tell them apart.

On Day 6, "Adding Dialogs to Your Application for User Feedback," you'll see how you can add additional windows to your application and how you can use them to get information from the user. You'll see how you can use built-in dialogs to ask the user simple questions and how you can build your own custom dialogs to get more detailed information.

On Day 7, "Creating Menus for Your Application," you'll see how you can call functions in your application from menus that you've added to your application.

That will end the first week of this book. At that time, you can look back over what you've learned during the week and think about all you can do with what you've learned when you build applications. So, without further ado, jump in and get started.

DAY 1

Building Your First Application in the Visual C++ Development Environment

Welcome to *Sams Teach Yourself Visual C++.NET in 21 Days*. Over the next three weeks, you will learn how to build a wide variety of applications with Microsoft's Visual C++. What's even better is that you'll learn how to create these types of applications by building them yourself. As you read this book, you will gain actual programming experience using Visual C++. So let's get started!

Note   One of the first distinctions that you need to understand is that the Visual
C++ programming language is separate from the Visual Studio Integrated
Development Environment (IDE). Whatever mention is made of the tools
and editors is referring to the Visual Studio IDE. If what you bought is just
Visual C++, and not the whole Visual Studio bundle, you are still working in
the Visual Studio IDE. This is the development environment and tool set
used by all the programming languages included in Visual Studio. In short,
over the next 21 days, you'll be working with the Visual Studio tools and
editors, but the programming code that will be generated by the Visual
Studio tools and that you will be typing in yourself, is the Visual C++ programming language. It's important to understand the separation of these
two, as you can use other tools to work with the Visual C++ programming
language, and you can use the Visual Studio tools to program in other programming languages.

Today, your focus will be on learning about the Visual Studio development environment
and some of the tools that it provides for building applications. Although Visual C++
provides more tools than you would probably use in any one application development
effort—even more than you could possibly learn to use in a single day—I limit the focus
to the primary tools that you will use throughout this book, as well as in just about every
application you build with Visual C++. Today, you'll learn about the following:

- The primary areas of the Visual C++ development environment
- How to build the basic infrastructure for your applications using the Application
  Wizard
- How to use the Dialog Painter to paint dialog windows, much in the same way that
  you can build windows with Visual Basic, PowerBuilder, or Delphi
- How to attach functionality to your application windows using the Properties pane

Touring the Visual C++
Development Environment

Before you begin a quick tour around the Visual C++ development environment, start
Visual C++ on your computer so that you can see firsthand how each area is arranged
and how to change and alter that arrangement yourself.

After Developer Studio (the Microsoft Visual development environment) starts, you see a
window that looks like Figure 1.1. Each area has a specific purpose in the Developer

Studio environment. You can rearrange these areas to customize the Developer Studio environment so that it suits your particular development needs.

FIGURE 1.1

The Visual C++ opening screen.

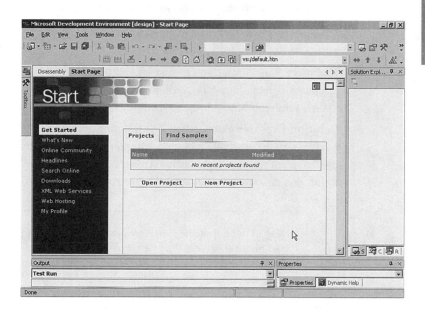

Note

The startup screen for Visual Studio has changed on a monthly basis during the beta process. As a result, the final startup screen that you see with your version of Visual Studio .NET or Visual C++ .NET may be different from the one in the above figure.

Caution

The browser startup screen, as well as certain other functions within the Visual Studio environment, generate and execute scripts on your computer. If you have an anti-virus product installed on the same machine as Visual Studio .NET or Visual C++ .NET, you may be presented with potential virus warnings when these scripts are executed.

The Solution Explorer

When you start Visual C++ for the first time, an area on the right side of the IDE looks as though it's taking up a lot of real estate and providing little to show for it. This area, known as the Solution Explorer, is your key to navigating the various pieces and parts of your development projects. The Solution Explorer is similar to the Project Explorer in previous versions of Visual Basic, Visual InterDev, and Visual J++. The panes in this group allow you to view the parts of your application in three different ways:

- **Class Pane** allows you to navigate and manipulate your source code on a C++ class level.
- **Resource Pane** allows you to find and edit each of the various resources in your application, including dialog window designs, icons, and menus (this will not be visible until you have a project open).
- **Solution Explorer Pane**, labeled as Solution Explorer, allows you to view and navigate all the files that make up your application. Eventually, you'll see how you can have multiple projects open at one time as a solution. When you get to this point, you can navigate between the projects within the Solution Explorer.

 Note

Keep in mind that the starting collection of panes in this region is only the starting arrangement. You can drag any of the initial three views to other areas of the IDE, as well as add panes to this grouping.

The Output Area

The Output area might not be visible when you start Visual C++ for the first time. After you compile your first application, it appears at the bottom of the Developer Studio environment and remains open until you close it. The Output area is where the Visual Studio IDE initially provides any information that it needs to give you; where you see all the compiler progress statements, warnings, and error messages; and where the Visual C++ debugger displays all the variables with their current values as you step through your code. After you close the Output area, or any of the panes initially grouped within this area, it reopens if Visual C++ has a new message for you.

The Editor Area

The editor area is basically the entire Developer Studio area that's not otherwise occupied by panes, menus, or toolbars. This is the area where you perform all your editing when using Visual C++, where the code editor windows display when you edit C++ source code, and where the window designers display when you design a dialog box. The editor area is even where the icon painter displays when you design the icons for use in your applications.

Menu Bars

The first time you run Visual C++, a couple of toolbars display just below the menu bar. Many other toolbars are available in Visual C++, and you can customize and create your own toolbars. The toolbars that are initially open are the following:

- The Standard toolbar contains most of the standard tools for opening and saving files, cutting, copying, pasting, and various other commands that you will likely find useful.

- A toolbar that contains functions appropriate for the activity that you are performing in the editor area. For instance, when you initially open Visual C++, you'll see the toolbar for navigating the Visual C++ documentation. If you are editing some C++ code, you'll have a toolbar containing functions that you'll frequently use while editing code. If you are designing a dialog window, you'll have a toolbar containing functions for sizing and aligning controls on the dialog.

Rearranging the Developer Studio Environment

The Developer Studio provides two easy ways to rearrange your development environment. The first is by right-clicking your mouse over the toolbar area. This action opens the pop-up menu shown in Figure 1.2, allowing you to turn on and off various toolbars.

FIGURE 1.2

Toolbar on and off menu.

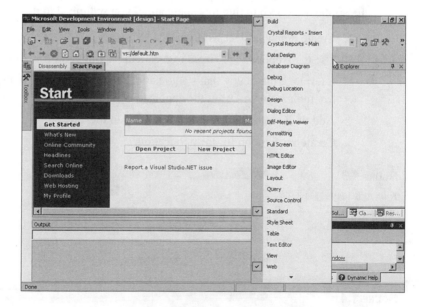

Another way that you can easily rearrange your development environment is to grab the bar of horizontal lines at the left end of any of the toolbars or panes with the mouse. You can drag the toolbars away from where they are docked, making them floating toolbars.

You can drag these toolbars (and panes) to any other edge of the Developer Studio to dock them in a new spot. Even when the toolbars are docked, you can use the docking bar to drag the toolbar left and right to place the toolbar where you want it to be located (or up and down if it's docked on the left or right sides).

Moving the panes about is slightly more involved. In the new Visual Studio IDE, you can separate the various tabs within any pane and make them singular panes, or combine them in new combinations. After you combine two or more panes into a single grouping, the group will have a series of tabs for selecting which pane should be visible.

 Note

On the workspace, Properties, and Output areas, you can use the top bar to drag the entire window around the Developer Studio environment. These windows are docked in the Developer Studio.

Starting Your First Project

For your first Visual C++ application, you are going to create a simple application that presents the user with two buttons, as in Figure 1.3. The first button will present the user with a simple greeting message, shown in Figure 1.4, and the second button will close the application. In building this application, you will need to do the following things:

1. Create a new project workspace.
2. Use the Application Wizard to create the application framework.
3. Rearrange the dialog that's automatically created by the Application Wizard to resemble how you want the application to look.
4. Add the C++ code to show the greeting to the user.
5. Create a new icon for the application.

FIGURE 1.3

Your first Visual C++ application.

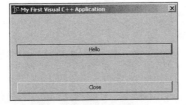

FIGURE 1.4

If the user clicks the first button, a simple greeting is shown.

Creating the Project Workspace

Every application development project needs a project workspace in Visual C++. The workspace includes the directories where the application source code is kept, as well as the directories where the various build configuration files are located. You can create a new project workspace by following these steps:

1. Click Create New Project on the VS.NET Start Page (make sure that the Get Started tab is selected on the left side of the page). This opens the New Project Wizard shown in Figure 1.5.

Tip

If you've closed the Start Page, select View, Web Browser, Show Browser from the menu to reopen the VS.NET Start page.

FIGURE 1.5

The New Project Wizard.

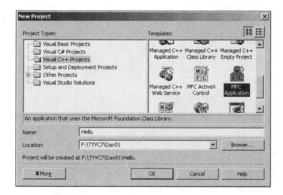

2. In the Project Types tree, select Visual C++ Projects. Select MFC Application in the Templates area on the right side of the New Project dialog. (You will have to scroll down on the right side to expose the MFC Application template.)

3. Type **Hello** in the Name field. This will be the name for the project.

4. Click OK. The New Project Wizard does two things: allocates a project directory (specified in the Location field, but it doesn't actually create the directory until the AppWizard is completed) and then starts the AppWizard.

Using the Application Wizard to Create the Application Shell

The MFC Application Wizard asks you a series of questions about what type of application you are building and what features and functionality you need. It uses this information to create a shell of an application that you can immediately compile and run. This shell provides you with the basic infrastructure that you need to build your application around. You will see how this works as you follow these steps:

1. On the left side of the Wizard, select Application Type. This will provide you with some options for the type of application that you want to build. On the right side, specify that you want to create a Dialog-based application, as shown in Figure 1.6.

FIGURE 1.6

Specifying the application type.

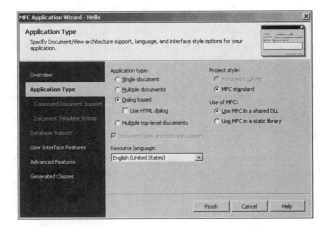

2. On the left side, select User Interface Features. In this area of the Application Wizard, you can specify the look of your main application window. In the field near the bottom of the wizard, delete the project name (Hello) and type in the title that you want to appear in the title bar of the main application window. For this example, type **My First Visual C++ Application**, as in Figure 1.7.

FIGURE 1.7

Specifying the application title.

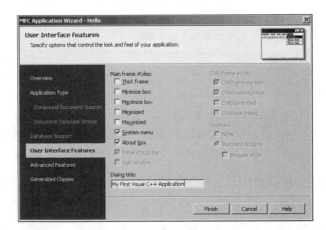

3. Click Finish to let MFC Application Wizard generate your application shell.

4. After the AppWizard generates your application shell, you are returned to the Developer Studio environment. Notice that the solution area now presents you with a tree view of the resources in your application shell, shown in Figure 1.8. You might also be presented with the main dialog window in the editor area of the Developer Studio area.

FIGURE 1.8

Your workspace with a tree view of the project's classes.

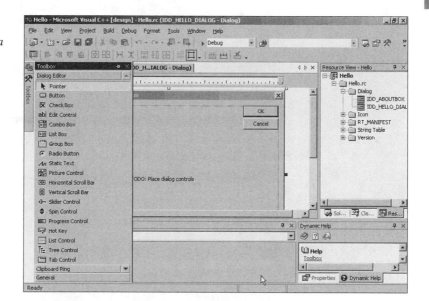

5. Select Build, Build from the menu to compile your application.

6. As the Visual C++ compiler builds your application, you see progress and other compiler messages scroll by in the Output pane. Once your application is built, the Output pane should display a message telling you that there were no errors or warnings (see Figure 1.9).

7. Select Debug, Start to run your application.

8. Your application presents a dialog with a TODO message and OK and Cancel buttons, as shown in Figure 1.10. The title showing on the title bar is the same that you entered back in the Application Wizard, not the name of the application itself. You can click either button to close the application.

FIGURE 1.9

The Output pane displays any compiler errors.

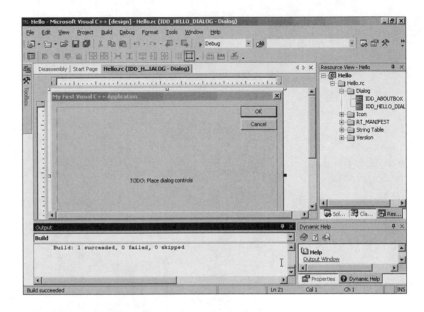

FIGURE 1.10

The unmodified application shell.

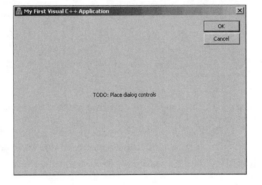

MFC Note: How Windows Applications Work

This section in this and following days explores the Microsoft Foundation Classes (MFC), and how they enable you to build Windows applications quickly and easily. This information isn't necessary for you to know to make it through the book, and can be skipped. You will learn plenty about MFC, and how to build applications using it without reading these sections. However, if you want to understand how things are working below the surface, this is where you'll find that information.

Microsoft Foundation Classes are a series of C++ classes that abstract much of the programming involved in interacting with the Windows operating systems. If you have used other visual programming tools to build Windows applications, like Visual Basic or

1

Delphi, you worked with components that provided you with prepackaged functionality. This is very similar to how MFC works. Just as in Visual Basic, you have a command button that you can place on a window that has various properties that you can adjust to control its look and behavior, MFC has a class—in this case, CButton—that encapsulates the command button functionality.

If you've ever studied how Windows programs are written in C/C++ without using an application framework like MFC, you know that all Windows programs start with a single function called WinMain. This is the starting point of the application, and creates the main window of the application. It then starts a loop receiving event messages that it then passes to the appropriate event handler function in a control or window to process, as shown in Figure 1.11. If there is no appropriate event handler to process the message, it's passed to a default event handler that's controlled by the operating system.

FIGURE 1.11

The raw Windows application processing path.

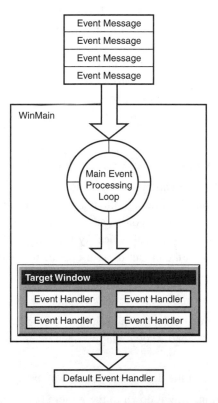

MFC removes most of this part of building Windows applications for you. If you dig deep, you'll find the WinMain function buried deep within the MFC source code. What you do see, if you look at the Class View in the workshop pane, are three classes: CAboutDlg, CHelloApp, and CHelloDlg. The second of these classes, CHelloApp, is derived from the CWinApp class. This class encapsulates much of the WinMain functionality, removing much of the drudgery of Windows application programming from your shoulders. The CWinApp class also contains much of the general application functionality that doesn't really belong in any control or other more specialized object, like functions to read and write application configuration information to the registry database, and command-line parameter processing.

The other two classes, CAboutDlg and CHelloDlg, are both derived from the CDialog class, which is a specialized derivation of the more general-purpose CWnd class. The CWnd class encapsulates most of the window functionality, and the CDialog class focuses on dialog windows. You learn much more about the CDialog class, along with its ancestor CWnd class, in the next few days.

NEW TERM When a class is referred to as being a *derivation* of another class, it means that the first class has inherited the second class. This is also referred to as the second class being an ancestor of the first. What this really means is that the deriving class (the one doing the inheriting) has the ancestor class as part of itself. Without adding any functionality to the derived class, it already has all the functionality in the ancestor class. Because of all the existing functionality inherited from the base/ancestor class, the derived class can focus on how it's different from the ancestor class, greatly reducing the amount of code that has to be written to provide the derived class' functionality.

Designing Your Application Window

Now that you have a running application shell, you need to turn your focus to the window layout of your application. Even though the main dialog window may already be available for painting in the editor area, you should still navigate to find the dialog window in the workspace so that you'll be able to easily find the window in subsequent development efforts. To redesign the layout of your application dialog, follow these steps:

1. Select the Resource View tab in the workspace pane (see Figure 1.12).

2. Expand the resources tree to display the available dialogs. At this point, you can double-click the IDD_HELLO_DIALOG dialog to open the window in the Developer Studio editor area.

3. Click the text displayed in the dialog and delete it by using the Delete key.

4. Select the Cancel button, drag it down to the bottom of the dialog, and resize it so that it's the full width of the layout area of the window, see Figure 1.13.

5. In the Properties pane (on the right side just under the Solution Explorer pane), change the value in the Caption field to &Close.

FIGURE 1.12

The Resource View tab in the workspace pane.

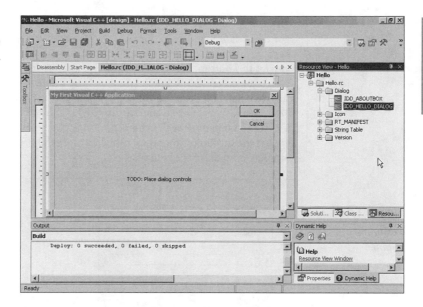

FIGURE 1.13

Positioning the Cancel button.

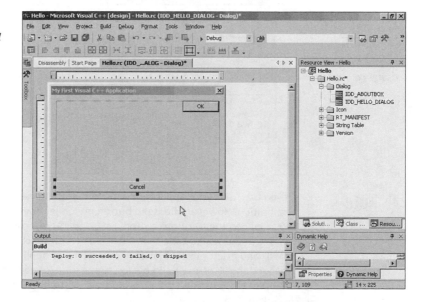

6. Move and resize the OK button to around the middle of the window, as in Figure 1.14.

7. In the Properties area, change the ID value to IDHELLO and the caption to &Hello.

8. Now when you build and run your application, it will look like what you've just designed (see Figure 1.15).

Note

For those of you new to programming Windows applications, the ampersand (&) in the caption specifies that the character following it is the quick
key for this button, menu, or control. In older versions of Windows, you
would see an underline under the C in Close (under certain circumstances,
such as when you have the Alt key pressed, you'll still see the C underlined).
This provides users with a shortcut to trigger this button by pressing the Alt
key at the same time as the character just after the ampersand. This will
trigger the button (or menu, or other control) and provides users with an
alternative to using the mouse.

FIGURE 1.14

*Positioning the OK
button.*

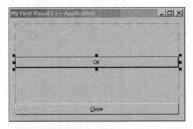

FIGURE 1.15

*Running your
redesigned application.*

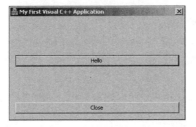

Note

If you play with your application, notice that the Close button still closes the
application. However, the Hello button no longer does anything because
you changed the ID of the button. MFC applications contain a series of
macros in the source code that determine which functions to call based on
the ID and event message of each control in the application. Because you
changed the ID of the Hello button, there is no longer a macro matching
the ID of the button to point to the function to be called when the button
is clicked.

Adding Code to Your Application

You can attach code to your dialog through the Properties pane. You can use the
Properties pane to build the table of Windows messages that the application might

receive, including the functions they should be passed to for processing, which the MFC macros use for attaching functionality to window controls. You can attach the functionality for this first application by following these steps:

1. To attach some functionality to the Hello button, select the Hello button and then select Control Events (the lightning bolt) in the Properties pane (see Figure 1.16).

FIGURE 1.16

Selecting Control Events in the Properties pane.

2. Select BN_CLICKED in the list of messages. The value area beside the event ID should become a combo box. Click the combo arrow, and a function suggestion will appear in the drop-down portion of the combo box. The suggested function will be called OnBnClickedHello (see Figure 1.17). Select this function name from the drop-down area; it will appear in the value area beside the BN_CLICKED event ID. This opens the OnBnClickedHello function in the editor area.

FIGURE 1.17

The suggested event function.

3. Add the code in bold in Listing 1.1 just below the TODO comment line (see Figure 1.18). Be sure to enter the code exactly as shown.

Note

As you are typing code, notice that the editor begins showing function definitions to you. This is a function called IntelliSense. It tries to guess what function or object method/property you are typing and enables you to select the function, method, or property from a list of available functions, etc. This can help prevent typing errors. Once you have the function name entered and type the open parenthesis, the function parameters are listed, with the current one that you are entering highlighted. IntelliSense is intended as a programming aid, so that you know what functions and properties are available and what the parameters are for a function that you are calling. This functionality was first introduced in Visual Basic 5, and then added to Visual C++ 6 a couple of years later.

FIGURE 1.18

*Source code view
where you insert
Listing 1.1.*

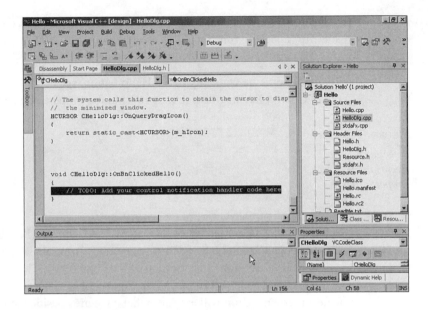

LISTING 1.1   HELLODLG.CPP: The `OnBnClickedHello` Function

```
void CHelloDlg::OnBnClickedHello(void)
{
    // TODO: Add your control notification handler code here
```

```
    // Say hello to the user
    MessageBox("Hello. This is my first Visual C++ Application!");
}
```

4. When you build and run your application, the Hello button should display the message shown in Figure 1.19.

Note

If you get any errors when you try to build your application, make sure that you entered the code exactly as it is in Listing 1.1. C++ is case-sensitive, so a simple thing like not having capitalized the function name correctly will cause an error.

FIGURE 1.19

Now your application will say hello to you.

C++ Sidebar: Function Structure and Syntax

If you already know the C++ programming language and are reading this book to learn the Visual C++ tool, you can skip this section. Whenever you see this section in this and following days, it's devoted to teaching the C++ programming language, syntax, and structure.

If you look at the code in Listing 1.1, be aware of several aspects, as you will be seeing and using them in all the C++ code you write. We'll start with the first line of the listing:

```
void CHelloDlg::OnBnClickedHello(void)
```

This line is part of the function shell created by the Visual C++ Developer Studio. This is the function name and calling syntax. Elsewhere in the code, usually in a header file (signified by the .h file extension), is a declaration for this function, which you'll see on a later day. This code listing is the implementation of the function.

The first word on the line, `void`, is the return value data type. Whenever you see the word `void` used either here or in place of the function arguments (within the parenthesis at the end of the line), it means that there is no return value, or parameters to be passed to the function.

The second word on the line, `CHelloDlg`, is the class that this function is a member of. This is followed by two colons (`::`) and then the function name. Spaces are allowed between these elements, but not between the two colons.

Following the function name is the list of arguments to be passed to the function, enclosed within parentheses. The parentheses always have to be used, even when the function doesn't take any parameters. This is different from languages like earlier versions of Visual Basic, where the parameters are optional if the function doesn't take parameters, or if it's a subroutine and doesn't have a return value.

C++ Rule

When calling functions in C++, the parentheses following the function name must always be included, even when there are no parameters to be passed to the function.

On the next line of the listing, an open brace ({)marks the start of the function body. This is eventually followed by a close brace (}) marking the end of the function body. The braces enclose sections of code in C++, just as in the Java language, and similar to the use of BEGIN and END in Visual Basic and Delphi.

C++ Rule

Function bodies are always enclosed within a pair of braces ({}).

The next line of code, which is the last of the code created by the Developer Studio, starts with two forward slash characters (//). The use of two forward slash characters without anything between them (no spaces, tabs, etc.) indicates that everything following them on that particular line is a comment and is to be ignored by the compiler (unless the slashes are part of a text string). This is one of two methods of commenting your code. The second method is more useful for marking several lines of comments. It consists of a slash followed by an asterisk (/*) to mark the start of the comments, and then the opposite (*/) to mark the end of the comments.

Finally, there are several things to learn about the one line of actual code that you added:

```
MessageBox("Hello. This is my first Visual C++ Application!");
```

First, C++ is case sensitive. Function names and variables must be capitalized exactly as they are declared. This means that the compiler sees the following three function names as being three different function names:

```
MessageBox
```

```
messageBox
```

```
messagebox
```

If you didn't enter the code as shown, and changed the capitalization of the function MessageBox, when you tried to compile your code you would have received an error message stating that the function messagebox is an "undeclared identifier."

C++ Rule

Case matters! C++ is a case-sensitive language.

Following the function name is the function argument enclosed in parentheses, terminated with a semi-colon. Every line in C++ is terminated with a semicolon. The exceptions to this rule are flow-control statements such as if, while, and for, which can be followed by a pair of braces for enclosing multiple lines of code, or a single line which is terminated with a semi-colon. If you didn't put a semi-colon at the end of this line, you would have received an error message stating that you are missing a ; before the closing brace (this error message always points to the line after the line that's actually missing the semi-colon.) Comments are not considered to be code, so don't need to be terminated with a semicolon. However, if you have a comment on the same line as a line of code, you must terminate the line of code with a semicolon before the comment starts.

C++ Rule

Each line of code containing an action to be performed must be terminated with a semicolon (;).

If you made the two mistakes outlined above—not capitalizing the MessageBox function correctly, and not terminating the line with a semicolon—you received two error messages when you tried to build your code (see Figure 1.20). When you double-click one of these error messages, a marker appears next to the line of code where the error was detected (see Figure 1.21).

FIGURE 1.20

Error messages show the mistakes in the code that need to be corrected.

Adding Finishing Touches

Now that your application is functionally complete, you can add a few details to finish the project, such as

- Creating the dialog box icon
- Adding maximize and minimize buttons

FIGURE **1.21**

*Double-clicking an
error message takes
you to the code lines
where the error was
detected.*

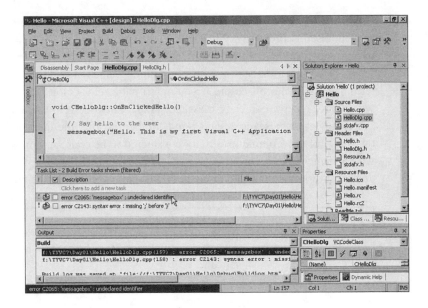

Creating the Dialog Box Icon

If you noticed the icon in the top-left corner of your application window, you saw three
blocks with the letters M, F, and C. What does MFC have to do with your application?
MFC stands for *Microsoft Foundation Classes*. Technically, it's the C++ class library that
your application is built with, but do you want to broadcast that to every user who sees
your application? Most likely not. Edit the application icon to display an image that you
want to represent your application. Follow these steps:

1. In the Resources pane in the Solutions area, expand the icon branch and double-
   click the IDR_MAINFRAME icon (see Figure 1.22). This brings the application icon
   into the editor area of the IDE.

2. By using the painting tools provided, repaint the icon to display an image that you
   want to use to represent your application (see Figure 1.24). You'll need to open the
   colors window by right-clicking in the white space around the icon, and selecting it
   from the context menu that appears (see Figure 1.23).

FIGURE 1.22

The standard MFC icon.

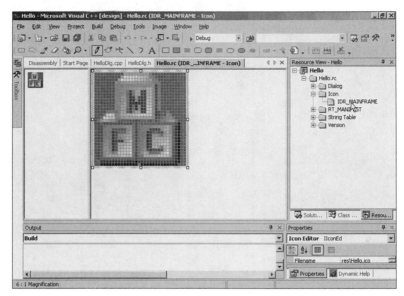

FIGURE 1.23

Opening the colors window.

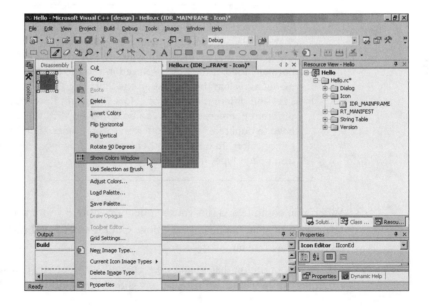

Figure 1.24

*Your own custom icon
for your application.*

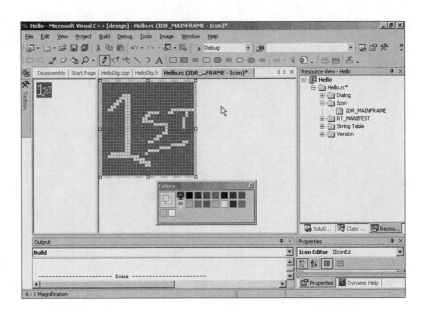

Note

Each icon created in the Developer Studio is actually multiple icons. The one
that initially appears for drawing is 32×32 pixels. This normally appears on
the desktop and in the About window. There is also a 16×16 pixel icon that's
normally used as the icon displayed in the top-left corner of the application
menu, as well as the task list on the Start bar. Other icons have the same
sizes and different number of colors. These are for various situations where
different numbers of colors can be displayed with the icons. You will likely
have to duplicate your custom icon several times in different sizes and number of colors. To open the other icons for drawing, select Image, Current
Icon Image Types from the menu.

3. When you compile and run your application, notice your custom icon in the top-
   left corner of your application window. Click the icon and select About Hello from
   the drop-down menu.

4. On the About dialog that Visual C++ created for you, you can see a large version
   of your custom icon in all its glory, as shown in Figure 1.25.

FIGURE 1.25

Your application's About window.

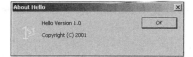

Adding Maximize and Minimize Buttons

In the dialog editor, where you design your application window, you can add the minimize and maximize buttons to the title bar of your application window by following these steps:

1. Select the dialog window itself as though you were going to resize the window.

2. Find the minimize and maximize properties in the Properties pane. Set both of these values to TRUE. Once you turn on the minimize and maximize boxes, you can compile and run your application. The minimize and maximize buttons appear on the title bar (see Figure 1.26).

FIGURE 1.26

The application window with the minimize and maximize buttons.

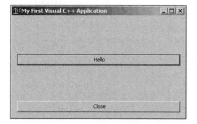

Summary

Today you got your first taste of building applications using Visual C++. You learned about the different areas of the Visual C++ Developer Studio and what function each area serves. You also learned how you can rearrange the Developer Studio environment to suit the way you work. You also learned how you can use the Visual C++ wizards to create an application shell and then attach functionality to the visual components that you place on your application windows.

Q&A

Q. How can I change the title on the message box, instead of using the application name?

A. By default, the message box window uses the application name as the window title. You can change this by adding a second text string to the MessageBox function call. The first string is always the message to be displayed, and the second string is used as the window title. For example, the `OnBnClickedHello` function would look like

```
// Say hello to the user
MessageBox("Hello. This is my first Visual C++ Application!",
           "My First Application");
```

Q. Can I change the text on the About window to give my company name and more detailed copyright information?

A. Yes, the About window is in the Dialogs folder in the Resources View tab of the Workspace pane. If you double-click the `IDD_ABOUTBOX` dialog, the About box will be opened in the dialog designer, where you can redesign it however you want.

Workshop

The Workshop provides quiz questions to help solidify your understanding of the material covered and exercises to provide you with experience in using what you've learned. The answers to the quiz questions and exercises are provided in Appendix A, "Answers to Quiz Questions."

Quiz

1. How do you change the caption on a button?
2. What can you do with the MFC Application Wizard?
3. How do you attach functionality to the click of a button?

Exercise

Add a second button to the About window in your application. Have the button display a different message from the one in the first window.

DAY 2

Debugging Your Application

Nobody's perfect. This rule applies to all programmers. No one writes perfect code the first time. If any programmer claims to write perfect code, he or she is either lying or is an alien from another planet. Since you will never write perfect code with your initial effort, you'll find that you need to know how to use several of the tools provided with Visual C++ to debug your code. This will enable you to find mistakes in your code before you turn your application over to a user.

Today you'll learn about some of the debugging tools that you can use in the fight against bugs. Some are passive tools; you wait for them to detect and tell you about problems. Others are active tools; allowing you to dig around in your application as it's running, watching as the application steps through your code. Today, you'll learn about

- The difference between debug and release builds, and why you'll want to make use of both

- The macros you can include in your C++ code that enable you to sit back and wait for problems to be detected

- The Developer Studio debugger that you can use to step through your code, following how your code processes different situations

What Is Debugging?

In the very early days, computer memory was constructed of electrical relays, not silicon chips. When programs running on one of these computers started to fail, technicians examined the computer to try and determine the problem. What they found was a moth caught in one of the memory relays. An actual bug prevented the proper operation of the programs. This is where the term *bug* came from. Now it's used to label all defects in computer software, whether the defect causes the program or entire OS to crash, or just presents incorrect results.

In the effort to create bug-free applications, most software passes through several phases of debugging, each with different approaches. These phases are

- Initial testing and debugging
- Unit testing
- Integration testing
- Build and regression testing
- Alpha and beta testing
- Release build

Initial Testing and Debugging

Each developer performs this phase of debugging as he/she completes a function or section of code. The developer builds a simple application stub that will call the freshly developed code, and run through it with every possible value and condition combination under which the code may be called. In this phase of testing, it's the developer's responsibility to make sure that every line of code is stepped through under every possible set of conditions to make sure that the functionality is working correctly and that no unforeseen results are produced. This is where most of the logic errors should be caught and eliminated.

Unit Testing

Unit testing is the next phase in the debugging process. Once each developer has completed and tested all the individual pieces of functionality, it's put together into a functional unit. The idea is that this unit will be used as a "black box" where the inputs are known, and the outputs are predictable, but the internal implementation and functionality isn't known or visible from the outside. These units are tested with all possible variations of input, to verify that the unit works correctly and gives the correct output results. During this phase of testing, the developer should be primarily concerned with the unit inputs and outputs, not with the internal logic—unless, that is, the test results determine that there is a problem with the internal logic.

Integration Testing

Integration testing is where two or more units are put together and tested as a whole. This phase of testing is intended to make sure that the units work together, and to detect any problems with their interaction. This is the phase where most of the testing activity is taken over by another team member, and all problems found are reported back to the developer via documented bug reports. These reports describe the nature of the problem and contain as much information as possible for the developer to be able to re-create the problem. All these bug reports are logged and tracked, so those team members can keep track of all problems and the status of each at any given time.

Build and Regression Testing

The build of an application occurs when the entire application is compiled and linked as a whole. This is where any problems with function definitions between units surface, as they usually prevent the successful build of the entire application. This test is performed to make sure the entire application can be compiled and run. One team member is assigned responsibility for this test. Some companies, like Microsoft, have a daily build test for all their development efforts. This means that all the applications being built within the company are built once every day. If any one developer's code breaks the build, that developer is given build responsibility—meaning that person is responsible for the build test every day, at least until a different developer's code breaks the build.

NEW TERM   Once an application is successfully built, it's put through a series of *regression tests*. These are completely scripted tests that are often automated and run overnight. The tests put the application through a series of actions to test known, working functionality. The purpose of these tests is to make sure that no bugs have been introduced into code that is known to work correctly. As the functionality in an application grows, more regression tests are added to test the new functionality. If any bugs are found in an application, they are documented and logged, and the report is given to the appropriate developer, along with the test script so that the developer can reproduce the bug.

Alpha and Beta Testing

NEW TERM   The next two phases of testing puts the application into the hands of users. These users are asked to use the application on a daily basis, and report any and all problems that they encounter. The first of these two phases, *alpha testing*, is where the users are employees of the company developing the application. During the second phase, *beta testing*, outside users are given the application. There's also a gradual increase in the number of users testing the application. During the alpha phase, there may only be a handful of users testing the application, while during the Beta phase, the number of users is gradually increased until there potentially may be hundreds, if not thousands, of users testing the application.

When problems are found during these phases of testing, the problem reports are given to internal testers who try to duplicate the problems, and document the steps required to replicate the bug. Once this is done, the problem report is sent to a committee that rates each problem's seriousness, and then prioritizes the problems. Next, the reports are passed to the individual developers to correct, and the whole series of tests are started again.

Release Build

NEW TERM   Once an application is determined to be ready to release, a *release build* is created. In the release build, all the debugging code is stripped out of the application. The Visual C++ compiler automatically performs the stripping of debugging code. In the normal mode for Visual C++, which is the Debug mode, the compiler inserts all sorts of flags within the compiled code that specify which line of code is being executed. Although this information is read only by the debugger, and isn't executed, it increases the size of the application significantly, and does slow down the execution somewhat (although this is difficult to detect with today's generation of fast processors). The release build also removes the debug-aiding code, which you'll learn about in the next section, and removes a significant amount of code that no longer needs to be compiled.

Once a release build is created, it's run through regression tests to make sure that no program logic was accidentally removed in the build. If this is found to be the case, the affected unit is determined and the developer responsible for the problem code is alerted to the problem. To switch between Debug and Release mode in Visual C++, choose Configuration Manager from the Build menu, then select the desired mode from the combo box on the Configuration Manager dialog as shown in Figure 2.1.

Note   Along with these macros, a lot of debugging code is removed when a release build is created. The machine code also is optimized to speed up the application's execution as well as shrink the size of the resulting file. All of this can introduce subtle—and sometimes not so subtle—bugs into the application. Because these types of bugs sometimes sneak into a release build, corporations still do a large amount of testing of the release build of applications.

FIGURE 2.1

Switching between Debug and Release mode.

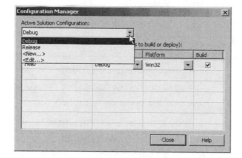

2

Debug-Aiding Code

You can use four macros liberally in your code to verify assumptions and to alert you when problems arise in your application. These macros are executed only with debug builds of your applications. When you make release builds, these macros are removed.

NEW TERM　A *macro* in C++ (as well as in the predecessor C programming language) is a pseudo-function created using the #define pre-compiler directive. Prior to compiling, the macro is replaced by all code used in the macro definition to define the macro functionality. One benefit of using macros is that it allows the designers of MFC to define one implementation of a particular macro for debug builds, and another for release builds.

C++ Sidebar: Pre-Compiler Directives

In the C and C++ programming languages, all source code files are passed through a pre-compiler before compiling the code. The pre-compiler processes some specific directives, expanding the code to be compiled significantly. All pre-compiler directives are recognizable because they start with the pound symbol (#) as the very first character in the line, before any character other than white space. Table 2.1 lists the primary pre-compiler directives.

TABLE 2.1　C/C++ Pre-Compiler Directives

Directive	Description
#include *file_name*	This directive instructs tells the pre-compiler to insert the contents of the specified file at this location. If the file name is between angle brackets (<>), the configured directories are searched for the file specified. If quotes (" ") are used, the path specified with the filename is used to find the file. The path can be either a relative path (from the project directory), or an absolute path (including the drive letter).

TABLE 2.1 continued

Directive	Description
`#define CONSTANT value`	This directive defines a constant value. The constant is normally declared in all uppercase. The pre-compiler replaces every occurrence of the constant with the value before compiling.
`#define CONSTANT(par1)` `➥definition`	This directive defines a macro. The macro is normally declared in all uppercase. The pre-compiler replaces every occurrence of the macro with the definition of the macro prior to compiling. When the pre-compiler processes the macro, it goes through the definition and replaces all occurrences of the parameters with the actual variables or values supplied in each use of the macro.
`#ifdef CONSTANT`	This directive tells the pre-compiler to include the following section of code only if the specified constant has already been defined.
`#ifndef CONSTANT`	This directive tells the pre-compiler to include the following section of code only if the specified constant hasn't been defined.
`#else`	This directive is used with the prior two directives, marking the next section to be included or not depending on whether the condition was met for including the prior section.
`#endif`	This directive marks the end of the sections to be conditionally included or excluded from the code to be compiled.
`#pragma option`	This directive specifies some compiler- or machine-specific option. Many options are available to use with the #pragma directive with most C/C++ compilers. To determine which #pragma options are available with a specific compiler, reference the compiler's documentation (we'll look at some of the #pragma options available in Visual C++ from time to time as we make our way through this book).

Tip

Start working with pre-compiler directives slowly. You should start by using only the #include directive to include needed header files, and the #define directive to define constants. Leave the other directives until you have a bit of experience under your belt; using them can result in confusing and unexpected results if you don't thoroughly think through how and when to use them.

Verifying Assumptions

You can use four macros in your code to test the various assumptions you make while designing and building your applications. These are a series of variations on the first one of these macros, called ASSERT. The syntax for this macro is as follows:

```
ASSERT(bAssumption);
```

The parameter passed into this macro is any Boolean expression that should always evaluate to TRUE. For example, if you have a function with a parameter a that should always be positive in value, you can test it with an ASSERT as follows:

```
ASSERT(a >= 0);
```

If this function is ever called with a negative value passed in the a parameter, ASSERT will display a warning like that shown in Figure 2.2, pointing you to the specific ASSERT that failed.

FIGURE 2.2

An ASSERT alerting you to a problem in your application.

 Never place necessary functionality in the parameter being passed to the ASSERT macro.

When using ASSERT, keep in mind that when you create a release build of your application, all uses of ASSERT are removed from the application. If you have used any program logic in the parameter being passed to this macro, it too will be removed from the application.

Two variations on ASSERT can be used to test classes and objects in your code. The first of these, ASSERT_VALID, is used as follows:

```
ASSERT_VALID(pObject);
```

This version is used to test objects in your application to verify that they are valid, and that there are no problems with the object's internal state. The one parameter passed into this macro is an instantiated C++ object.

Note The ASSERT_VALID macro doesn't work on all C++ objects. The object must be inherited from the CObject base class, and must have overridden the AssertValid member function. For most standard MFC classes, these criteria are met. For testing your own classes, you'll need to keep these require-ments in mind when designing the classes.

The second variation on ASSERT is the ASSERT_KINDOF macro, which is used as follows:

```
ASSERT_KINDOF(classname, pObject);
```

This macro validates that an object is a specific class, or is derived from that specific class. The first parameter is the class name that the second parameter needs to be an instance of.

Note This function can only be used to verify the class of classes that meet other specific criteria; for instance, it has to be a descendent of the CObject class, and must have one of two other macros used in the class declaration. The two macros that the class must use at least one of are DECLARE_DYNAMIC or DECLARE_SERIAL. This is getting well ahead of ourselves, however, if you don't already know the C++ programming language. You might have to refer to this note after you have a more thorough understanding of C++ and the MFC class library.

Like the ASSERT macro, both variations are completely removed from release builds of applications, so don't use these in place of necessary logic. You want to use these macros only for verifying assumptions in your code.

One last variation on the ASSERT macro is uniquely different, yet the same. This is the VERIFY macro. It's used just like the ASSERT macro, as follows:

```
VERIFY(bAssumption);
```

One key difference between the VERIFY and ASSERT macro is that any logic passed as the parameter to the VERIFY macro remains in the application when a release build is made. This means that you can put actual program logic in the parameter to the VERIFY macro, and that logic won't be removed when you make a release build. However, just like the ASSERT macro, the VERIFY macro will only test the expression and alert you if it's FALSE in debug builds of your applications.

Following Flow and Execution

Sometimes you want to know the execution path that your application is taking, or certain things that are going on as it's executing, but you don't want to step through the application line-by-line. What you would really like to do is have a log of when the application reaches or passes certain points of code, and what the state of certain variables are. This is easy to do (adding your own code for writing logging messages to a file) but it's a pain to strip that code when you need to pass the application to someone else.

An easy way to accomplish this logging, without the pain of removing all your logging messages, is by using the TRACE macro. The TRACE macro sends any string message you pass to it to any debug output window you run on the computer the same time your application is running (see Figure 2.3). The syntax for this macro is as follows:

```
TRACE("This is my trace message.\n");
```

FIGURE 2.3

Trace messages from a debugging session.

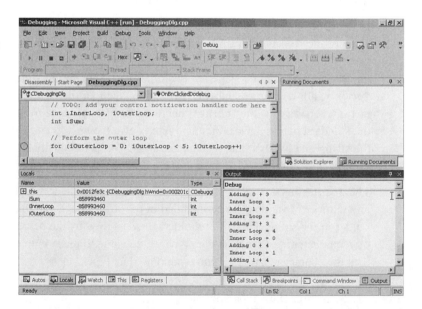

> **Tip**
>
> The TRACE macro works just like the printf function in C, so you can pass it variables to be dynamically added to the message string just as you would with the printf function.

Caution   The output string from the TRACE macro is limited to 512 characters. If the formatted string you pass to the TRACE macro is longer (including the string terminating NULL character), it will trigger an ASSERT.

Just as with the ASSERT macro, all uses of the TRACE macro are automatically removed from release builds.

C++ Sidebar: Formatting Strings

The C programming language was the predecessor to the C++ programming language. C++ was created for the purpose of making an object-oriented version of C. You can still write standard C applications using any C++ compiler, because part of the C++ standard is full support for the C programming language.

In the C programming language, there is a family of string formatting/printing functions. The primary function, printf, is used to format and print strings to the primary output device (this is for character-mode applications that would be running in a DOS window on a Windows system). There are two other variations to this function. The first, fprintf, allows you to send your string message to a file or output device. In fact, the printf version calls the fprintf function, specifying where to send the string as the standard output device. Finally, there is also the sprintf function, which formats the string and places it into a character array. You occasionally still see these functions used in C++ code.

The printf function takes a string as its primary parameter, which can be followed by any number of variables to be included in the string. Each variable must have a placeholder in the string. These placeholders are specified by the percent symbol (%) followed by a character indicating the data type of the value to place in that location. Table 2.2 lists the characters and their corresponding data types.

TABLE 2.2   printf Data Type Specifiers

Placeholders	Data Type
%c	A single-byte character.
%C	A wide or UNICODE character.
%d or %i	Decimal integer data type. This includes integers and longs.
%u	Unsigned integer data type.
%f	Floating-point data types, including doubles and floats.

TABLE 2.2 continued

Placeholders	Data Type
%s	Null-terminated string.
%S	Wide or UNICODE string.
%x	Hexadecimal value (lower-case).
%X	Hexadecimal value (upper-case).
%o	Octal value.
%%	Percent sign. Because the percent sign is used to indicate that the next character in the string is a placeholder for a variable value, you have to include two percent signs in order to include a percent sign in your string.

2

If you need to format a number variable to be a specific number of digits, you can insert the number of digits between the percent and the placeholder character, as follows:

```
printf("This number: %5d is five digits wide.", iNbr);
```

For floating-point numbers, you can also specify the precision by adding a decimal point and the precision following the number specifying the width, as follows:

```
printf("I have %3.2f dollars in my wallet.", fMoney);
```

If the fMoney variable's value was 123.456, the output from the above function call would be:

```
I have 123.46 dollars in my wallet.
```

Normally, when you format numbers, they are printed aligned on the right side. This means that if the fMoney value was 1.234, the output would look like the following:

```
I have    1.23 dollars in my wallet.
```

If you need the number to be aligned on the left side, add a minus sign (–) to the formatting expression:

```
printf("I have %-3.2f dollars in my wallet.", fMoney);
```

The resulting output would look like the following:

```
I have 1.23 dollars in my wallet.
```

If you want the output to include the minus sign if the value is negative, place the plus sign (+) just after the percent sign:

```
printf("I have %+3.2f dollars in my wallet.", fMoney);
```

This will cause a minus sign to be printed if the value of the fMoney variable is negative.

You also can include non-printable characters in the strings by including a backslash followed by the character that represents the non-printable character. This can be used to include tabs, new-lines, carriage-returns, and so on. Table 2.3 lists the primary non-printable characters that you're likely to include.

TABLE 2.3 `printf` Non-Printable Character Specifiers

Placeholders	Description
\n	New-line character. Use this to break a string into multiple lines of text.
\t	Tab character.
\r	Carriage-return. Causes the text to scroll back to the first of the string (but doesn't scroll to the next line).
\\	Backslash character. Because the backslash indicates that the next character in the string is a placeholder for a non-printable character, you have to include two backslash characters to include a single backslash in your string.

The Visual Studio Debugging Tools

For detailed examinations of your code while in use, Visual C++ provides a set of debugging tools that allow you to look at your code on whatever level is appropriate. You have the ability to step through your code and watch what is happening on the inside, or you can observe event messages being passed to your application from the outside. Depending on what your debugging needs are, odds are that the tool you need is already included with Visual C++.

Visual Studio Debugger

The main tool you'll use for debugging your applications will be the integrated debugger that is built into Visual Studio. Using it, you can step through your code, examining how all the variables and data structures are manipulated as your application runs.

Setting Breakpoints

In preparation for debugging an application, you first need to decide where you need to start. You won't normally want to start at the very first line of code and step through the entire application (that's a lot of code to step through). Instead, you'll most likely want to step through just a select portion of the code. You accomplish this by placing a breakpoint in your code.

NEW TERM A *breakpoint* is a location in an application where, while running the application in a debugger, execution is suspended. In other words, the application stops on the line of code with a breakpoint. This enables you to run your application as normal; the breakpoint will stop your application at the point you want to start stepping through the code line by line.

> **Note**
>
> From time to time, you'll have a breakpoint on an invalid line of code, such as a comment or the wrong line in a multi-line statement. On these occasions, when you start your application in the debugger, you'll get a message informing you of this situation. The breakpoints will automatically be moved to the next valid line of code. The application will also go into step mode on the very first line of executable code, deep within MFC.

You can place and remove breakpoints using the F9 key. You can also add breakpoints by choosing New Breakpoint from the Debug menu (you must have a project open to have the Debug menu available). If you use the menu, you'll be presented with a breakpoint properties dialog (see Figure 2.4), in which you can set conditions on when the breakpoint will stop code execution and when it won't.

FIGURE 2.4

The New Breakpoint property dialog.

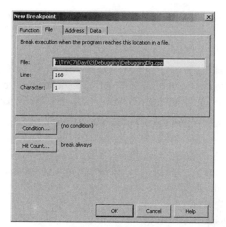

> **Tip**
>
> If you use the Debug menu to add the breakpoint, you'll find it easier to select the File tab to add the breakpoint, as it will add the breakpoint at a particular line in the source code file. On the Function tab, you have to specify the function and the line number within the function where you want the breakpoint.

You can open the Breakpoints pane by selecting Windows and then Breakpoints from the Debug menu. In the Breakpoints pane, you can select a breakpoint to modify the properties of, add new breakpoints, disable or delete breakpoints, or jump to the code location of a particular breakpoint (see Figure 2.5). Table 2.4 lists the toolbar buttons in the Breakpoints pane.

FIGURE 2.5

The Breakpoints pane.

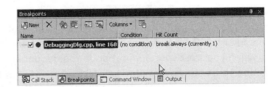

TABLE 2.4   Breakpoint Toolbar Buttons

Button	Description
New Breakpoint	Adds a breakpoint. You need to specify the function or file, as well as the line number within the function or file.
Delete Breakpoint	Deletes the selected breakpoint from the project.
Clear All Breakpoints	Clears and deletes all breakpoints currently set in the project.
Enable/Disable	Enables/disables all breakpoints in the All Breakpoints project. This allows you to disable the breakpoints so that you won't be stopping, without removing the breakpoints from your code.
Go To Source Code	Takes you to the selected breakpoint in the project source code.
Go To Disassembly	Takes you to the selected breakpoint in the assembly code that equates to the machine code that is being executed.
Columns	Displays a list of data columns that you can choose to display in the breakpoints pane.
Properties	Opens the New Breakpoint properties dialog for the selected breakpoint, enabling you to set conditions on when the breakpoint will be triggered.

Stepping Through Code

After you stop your application with a breakpoint, you need to be able to step through the code one (or more) line(s) at a time. Several functions are available for doing this. These functions are all located on the Debug menu, as well as on the Debug toolbar. Table 2.5 lists the buttons for doing this.

TABLE 2.5 Code Stepping Toolbar Buttons

Button	Description
Show Next Line	Highlights the next line of code that will be executed.
Step Into	If the current line of code is a function, the debugger will step into the function; otherwise, it steps to the next line of code in the current function.
Step Over	Steps to the next line of code in the current function. This method of stepping doesn't step into functions, but just executes the function and steps to the next line with the function's results.
Step Out	Steps out of the current function to where the function was called.

Examining Local Variables

Once you start your debugging session, you'll notice a new window under the code editor area of the Visual Studio environment. This is the variables area, where you can watch the values of the variables and objects change as you step through your application. The default display in this area is the Locals view, where all the variables being used on the current line of code, along with those that were used or modified on the previous line of code, are always available, as shown in Figure 2.6.

You will most likely use this mode of viewing the variables in your application. This mode allows you to see all the variables currently being modified and utilized. However, as flexible as this mode is, it's not the only method you'll use to look at your variables.

Watching Specific Variables

Sometimes you need to watch a specific variable or object as you step through your code. You aren't so much concerned with all the other data in your application as you are with this specific variable (or set of variables). It's on these occasions that you need to be able to see the variable's value, even if it's not being used in the current code line.

FIGURE 2.6

The local variables are visible in the Locals window.

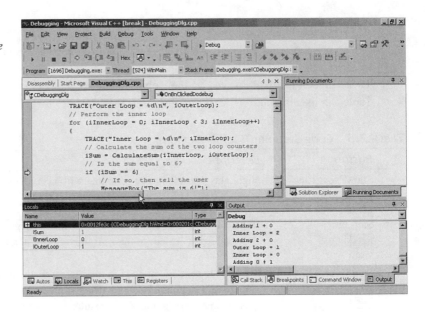

The first way that you can check the current value of a specific variable is to hover the mouse pointer over the variable for a couple of seconds. The Visual Studio debugger will display the current value of the variable in the form of pop-up or fly-by text—much the same as when you leave the pointer over a toolbar button and the name or function of the button appears (see Figure 2.7).

FIGURE 2.7

Use Quick Watch to check a variable's current value.

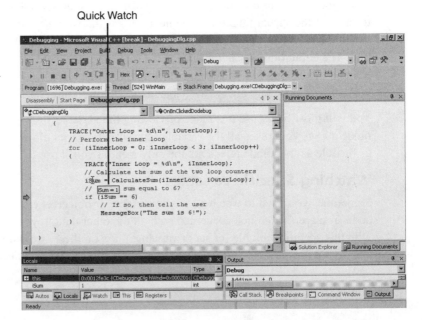

Quick Watch

The other way to watching one or more specific variables is through the Watch pane. If you select the Windows, Watch, Watch 1 from the Debug menu, you'll find a simple table in which you enter variable names into the first column. In the second column, the current value of the variable will be displayed, and the data type in the third (see Figure 2.8).

FIGURE 2.8

The Watch pane lets you watch specific variables and objects.

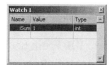

2

Examining the `this` Variable

The far right tab on the variables window provides you with a tree-view of the `this` variable. Through the This window, you can navigate to find any aspect of the current object and see its state and value (see Figure 2.9).

FIGURE 2.9

The This window lets you examine all aspects of the current object.

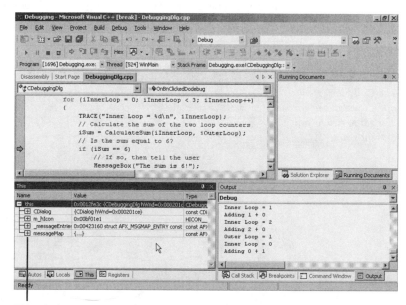

This window

C++ Sidebar: What's `this`?

In C++, the current object the code is executing is always referred to as `this`. It's basically a moving variable that can always be used to refer to the class in which you are writing code. If you were adding functionality to the class for a window and you needed to pass the window to another object, you could pass this as the appropriate parameter in whatever function you were calling in the other object. (In actuality, you'd be passing a pointer to the window, not the actual window, but that's a topic for later in the book.)

Checking the Call Stack

Sometimes you might find yourself in the midst of your code, deep in the heart of your application, and you'll need to see what path was taken to get where you are. You can see this information by using the Call Stack view. The Call Stack view is initially on the lower right side of the Visual Studio (see Figure 2.10). From here, you can see the sequence of function calls, and can click any in the stack to see that place in the code and examine the state of the variables at the time of the function call.

 Note

If function calls listed on the call stack are within compiled objects for which the source code isn't available, you can't go to that location within the source code. Instead, you might find yourself in the middle of a bunch of assembler code, as the debugger takes you to the location in the machine code where the function call was made.

FIGURE 2.10

The Call Stack view allows you to see how you got to where you currently are.

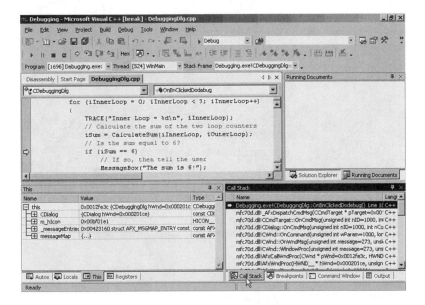

2

> **Tip**
>
> One circumstance that I find myself using the call stack in is when I get an ASSERT error in one of the MFC classes. In this situation, I'll use the Call Stack to see where the application left my code, and determine what my code passed to the MFC code that caused the error.

Spy++

You'll learn about one other debugging tool at this time. This tool is separate from the Visual Studio environment but is distributed with it. The tool, called Spy++, can be found on the Tools menu. What this tool does is allow you to see and record all the event messages sent to a specific application. This application also allows you to see all the windows currently existing on the system you are running, along with the relationships between the windows.

When you first start up Spy++, it will show a tree view of all the currently existing windows running on your computer, as shown in Figure 2.11. You can also look at the current processes or threads to find the window that you are looking for, as shown in Figure 2.12.

> **Note**
>
> When you first open Spy++, you may look at all the windows that it's listing and think that you don't have all those windows open on your computer. Keep in mind is that anything that can receive messages is considered to be a window. All the controls that you place on a dialog window are also "windows." There are also many open windows that aren't shown but still receive messages from the OS, and that shows up in Spy++.

FIGURE 2.11

Spy++ shows the existing windows running on the system.

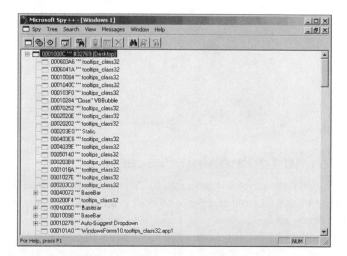

FIGURE 2.12

Various windows can be located via processes or threads.

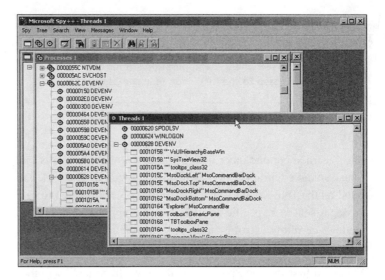

After you locate the window for which you want to see the event messages, select that window, and choose Log Messages from the Spy menu to bring up the dialog in Figure 2.13. In this dialog, you can specify how you want the messages to be captured. Do you want all the messages for the parent application or window? On the other tabs, you can even specify which event messages you do and don't want to see. Once you have configured how you want to see the messages, click OK and Spy++ will start logging the messages received by the window(s) you specified, as shown in Figure 2.14.

FIGURE 2.13

Configuring how to receive event messages.

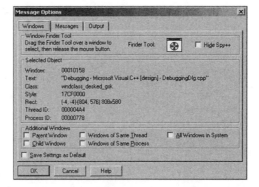

Attaching to Running Processes

One last tool that is useful is built into the Visual Studio environment and allows you to attach the Visual Studio debugger to a running application. Granted, most of the time you want to debug an application you'll start it in the debugger and won't need this tool. However, there are occasions when this tool is very helpful.

FIGURE 2.14

Looking at the messages received by the specified application window.

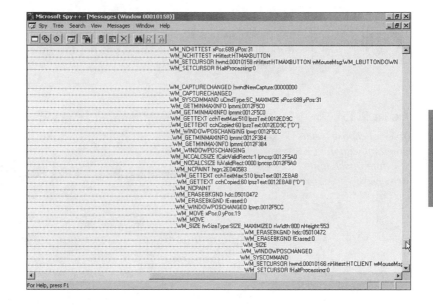

Suppose that you have an application that seems to be stuck in an infinite loop. If you are running it in the debugger, you can simply break its execution and try and determine what the problem is. If not, you need to somehow attach the debugger to this application.

NEW TERM An *infinite loop* is a situation where a loop in your code never stops. It may be a conditional loop where the exit condition is never triggered, or a `for` loop where the counter isn't incremented, or something else of this sort. In short, it's someplace in your code where the application execution gets stuck. If you have one of these in your application, the only thing you can do to end the loop is usually killing the application, losing any processing that the application has already performed.

If you pull down the Debug menu, you'll find a menu entry labeled Processes. If you select this menu entry, you'll be presented with the dialog shown in Figure 2.15. This dialog contains a list of all the processes running on the computer. On this dialog, you can choose the desired application and click the Attach button. This will bring up the dialog shown in Figure 2.16, which allows you to select which debugger you want to use on the application. For your Visual C++ applications, you'll want to use the Native option. If you've built the application as a managed code C++ application (which we'll get to several days down the road), then you may want to take the Common Language Runtime option. Click OK and your application will now be in the debugger and any breakpoints you have will trigger. If you don't have any breakpoints, you can click the Break button and force a breakpoint at the point in the code that your application happens to be.

Tip

> The Debug menu is available only if you have an open project. To walk through the process outlined here, you need to either create a new project, or open an existing project.

FIGURE 2.15

You can choose a running application to which to attach the debugger.

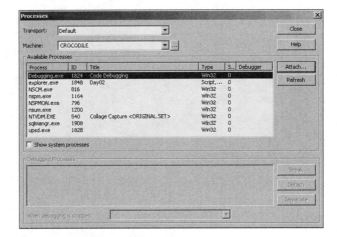

FIGURE 2.16

You can choose which debugger you want to use.

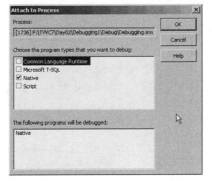

Building a Faulty Application

Now that you know the basic functions of the debugging tools included with Visual Studio, you'll build a buggy application and use the Visual Studio debugger to find and correct problems. If you already know C++, and have experience using debuggers, you can skip the rest of this chapter.

The application that you'll build looks very much like the one you created yesterday. It will have two buttons, one of which closes the application and another that performs some looping and calculating. The main window will look like the one shown in Figure 2.17.

FIGURE 2.17

The finished application.

When the upper button is clicked, the application will perform a couple of nested loops, calling a function to add the counters from the two loops together. When the sum of the two counters reaches the maximum sum possible, a message box will be displayed to inform the user (see Figure 2.18).

FIGURE 2.18

Displaying the message box.

So, to build this application, you need to follow these steps:

1. Create an application shell using the MFC Application Wizard.
2. Redraw the main dialog so that the two buttons are displayed as shown.
3. Add the function to add the two numbers together.
4. Add the event function for the clicked event on the top button.
5. Add code in the clicked event function, performing two nested loops, calling the adding function with each loop.

Creating the Application Shell

The first thing that you'll do is build the application shell and redraw the main dialog. To do this, you'll follow the same steps you performed yesterday, altering only a couple of items.

1. Create a new project, as you did earlier in steps 1–4 of the section "Creating the Project Workspace," naming the project Debugging.
2. Use the MFC Application Wizard to create the application shell, as you did earlier in steps 1–4 in the section "Using the Application Wizard to Create the Application Shell," entering **Code Debugging** in step 2 as the title on the main application window.
3. Redraw your dialog window as you did yesterday in steps 1–7 of the section "Designing Your Application Window."

4. For the OK button, change the ID property to ID_DODEBUG, and the caption property to &Perform Debugging. Your main dialog should look like the one shown in
Figure 2.19.

FIGURE 2.19

*The redesigned main
dialog.*

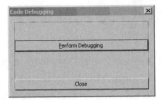

Adding a Function

The next thing that you need to do is add the function that adds the two counters together, and returns the resulting sum. To add this function, perform the following steps:

1. Select Class View pane.

2. Right-click the CDebuggingDlg class (you may need to expand the tree-view to
expose the CDebuggingDlg class).

3. Select Add, Add Function from the context menu (see Figure 2.20).

FIGURE 2.20

*Adding a function to
the dialog class.*

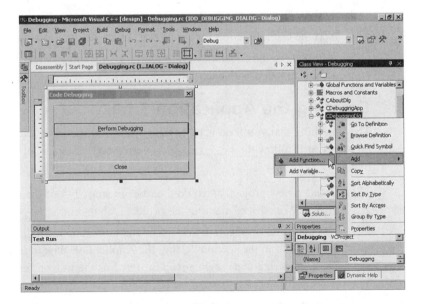

4. In the Add Member Function Wizard, enter **int** for the Return Type, and the name **CalculateSum** for the function name.

5. Enter **int** for the Parameter Type and **iLeftValue** for the Parameter Name and click the Add button. This will place iLeftValue in the Parameter list. Add a second parameter the same way, naming it **iRightValue**. The Add Member Function Wizard should now look like the one in Figure 2.21.

FIGURE 2.21

Adding a function to the dialog class.

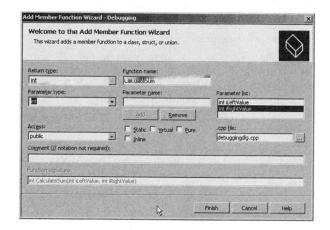

6. Click the Finish button to add the new function.

7. Enter the boldfaced code in Listing 2.1 to the CalculateSum function.

LISTING 2.1   DEBUGGINGDLG.CPP: The CalculateSum Function

```
int CDebuggingDlg::CalculateSum(int iLeftValue, int iRightValue)
{
    int iSum;

    // Add the two parameters together
    iSum = iLeftValue - iRightValue;
    // Return the result
    return iSum;
}
```

INPUT

Note

Yes, the above code is WRONG! You need to have some wrong code in the application so that you have something to debug. To make this code wrong, you specified to subtract the second value from the first rather than add the two values.

C++ Sidebar: C/C++ Operators

C++ has the usual operators for performing addition and subtraction on values. Also, some operators aren't common to other programming languages. Table 2.6 lists the most common operators.

TABLE 2.6   C/C++ Operators

Operator	Description
+	Adds two numbers together
-	Subtracts the second number from the first
*	Multiplies two numbers together
/	Divides the first number by the second
%	Performs modulus division (returns only the remainder)

In addition, there are the assignment operators. These operators assign a value to the variable on the left of the operator. Table 2.7 lists the common assignment operators.

TABLE 2.7   C/C++ Assignment Operators

Operator	Description
=	Equals, straight assignment of the value on the right to the variable on the left
+=	Adds the value on the right to the current value of the variable on the left, assigning the resulting value to the variable on the left
-=	Subtracts the value on the right from the value of the variable on the left, assigning the resulting value to the variable on the left
*=	Multiplies the value on the right with the value of the variable on the left, assigning the resulting value to the variable on the left
/=	Divides the value of the variable on the left by the value on the right, assigning the resulting value to the variable on the left

Now that you know how to perform basic mathematical operations in C++, look at the structure of the function you just added. First notice that the only variable not passed into the function as a parameter is declared on the function's first line. In C++, all variables must be declared before their first use. This could be performed just before the variable's use, even in the same line as the first use, as follows:

```
int iSum = iLeftValue - iRightValue;
```

You declare variables as follows: The first thing in the line is the data type, in this case int (short for integer). Next is a space or tab (or as many spaces as you want), followed by the variable name. When you declare variables, you can declare multiple variables of the same data type in a single line, separating them with a comma, as follows:

```
int iVar1, iVar2, iVar3;
```

C++ Rule

All variables must be declared before their first use.

2

Table 2.8 lists the basic data types built into C++.

TABLE 2.8 The Basic C/C++ Data Types

Data Type	Description
int	Integer
long	Long integer
float	Floating point number
double	A double (large floating point number)
char	Character
bool	A built-in Boolean data type (starting in Visual C++ 5); values can be true or false

Note

The bool data type isn't the same as the BOOL data type that you'll frequently see used. BOOL is defined as an integer, and its value can be TRUE or FALSE. These two Boolean data types aren't interchangeable, and you must be careful which values you use with which.

Although this list isn't complete, it's the primary data types that are built into the language. Most other data types are built from these base types.

The second line of code in the function is a simple mathematical operation, assigning the result to the variable that was declared just prior. The last line is where the result is returned to the calling function using the return keyword. The return keyword is how all function results are returned to the calling function. Its use is always as follows:

```
return somevalue;
```

If the function type is void, you can use the return keyword without any argument, as there shouldn't be any value returned from the function.

C++ Rule

The return keyword is always used to return the result value to the calling function.

Adding the Main Loop

Now comes the final step in preparation for debugging your application. You need to attach an event function to the top button on your dialog, adding the looping code. To do this, perform the following steps:

1. Add the event handling function to the top button as instructed yesterday in steps 1 and 2 of the section "Adding Code to Your Application."

2. Following step 3 from yesterday, select the OnBnClickedDodebug function in the CDebuggingDlg class.

3. Add the boldfaced code in Listing 2.2 to the function shell.

LISTING 2.2   DEBUGGINGDLG.CPP: The OnClickedDodebug Function

```
void CDebuggingDlg::OnBnClickedDodebug(void)
{
    // TODO: Add your control notification handler code here
        int iInnerLoop, iOuterLoop;
        int iSum;

    // Perform the outer loop
    for (iOuterLoop = 0; iOuterLoop < 5; iOuterLoop++)
    {
        // Perform the inner loop
        for (iInnerLoop = 0; iInnerLoop < 3; iInnerLoop++)
        {
            // Calculate the sum of the two loop counters
            iSum = CalculateSum(iInnerLoop, iOuterLoop);
            // Is the sum equal to 6?
            if (iSum = 6)
                // If so, then tell the user
                MessageBox("The sum is 6!");
        }
    }
}
```

INPUT

Note

Again, there is an error in the preceding code. Because today's topic is debugging, this is intentional. The error is in the comparison to see if the iSum value equals 6.

C++ Sidebar: Flow Control

2

The function in Listing 2.2 used two new flow control statements. If you've used any other major programming languages, you probably recognized what these are, but maybe not how they are used in C++. These are the `for` loop (often called a `for...next` loop in other programming languages), and the `if` conditional (often called `if...then` in other languages).

NEW TERM　For the `for` loop, all you have is the `for` statement, which can be followed by a single line of code (if the entire loop functionality can be expressed in a single line), or multiple lines of code (known as a *code block*) enclosed within braces, as follows:

```
for (...)
   single-line functionality;

for (...)
{
   multiple lines of functionality;
}
```

The loop itself is defined within the parenthesis that follow the `for` keyword. This is divided into three statements, each separated by semicolons. The first statement is the loop initialization, where the loop counter is set to its initial value. The second statement is the condition for continuing the loop. The third statement is how to increment the counter each time through the loop. For instance, if you had the following loop defined:

```
for (i = 0; i < 10; i++)
```

it would read as follows:

1. For i equals 0.
2. Loop while i is less than 10.
3. Increment i each time through the loop.

Another thing that might be new to you is how the loop counter is being incremented. There are two operators in the C and C++ programming languages for incrementing and decrementing. To increment, you use two plus symbols (++) either before or after the variable (the location you use is important, but we'll get to that in the next paragraph).

To decrement, you use two minus signs (- -).

Whether you place the increment or decrement in front of or after the variable to be affected depends on how you are using the variable at the time. If the increment or decrement symbol is in front of the variable, the variable is incremented (or decremented) before it's used. If the increment symbol is placed after the variable, the variable is incremented (or decremented) after it's used. To see how this works, let's take the following code example:

```
int a, b, c, d;

a = 1;
b = ++a;
c = 1;
d = c++;
```

In the preceding code, the variable a is incremented prior to assigning its value to variable b. The resulting value of b is 2. On the other hand, variable c is incremented after assigning its value to variable d, resulting in the value of d being 1.

Now, in a for loop, the placement of the increment symbol determines if the counter is incremented as the first action in each loop, or the last. What difference does this make? Well, it affects how many times the loop is executed.

Another thing that may have your curiosity aroused is the counter in both loops that starts at 0. This is accepted practice for C and C++ programming. In the C and C++ languages, all counting starts at 0, not 1. The first position in an array is position 0, not position 1.

The other flow control construct you used is the if construct. The syntax for this is the if keyword, followed by the condition enclosed within parentheses. If there is only one line of code to be executed on this condition, it can immediately follow the if statement. If there are multiple lines of code, they need to be enclosed within braces, as in the following example:

```
if (some condition)
    single-line functionality;

if (some condition)
{
    multiple lines of functionality;
}
```

Unlike with some other programming languages, the condition must always be enclosed within parentheses. There are several basic condition operators that you'll commonly use in this situation, as shown in Table 2.9.

TABLE 2.9   The Basic C/C++ Condition Evaluation Operators

Conditional	Description
==	Is equal (notice that this uses two equal signs, not one)
!=	Not equal
<	Less than
<=	Less than or equal to
>	Greater than
>=	Greater than or equal to

Debugging the Application

At this point, you are ready to start debugging your application. You will compile your application, and then place a breakpoint on the outer loop. Then, you'll start your application and trigger the looping calculations, so that you can step through your code. As you are stepping through the code, you'll correct the errors that you find in the code, as you are debugging it. So, follow these steps:

1. Select Build from the Build menu to compile your application.

2. Place text insertion cursor on the first `for` statement, and press F9.

3. Select Start from the Debug menu to start your application.

| Caution | If you choose the Debug, Start without Debugging menu selection, then you won't be running the application within the debugger. You will need to close the application and restart it using the Debug menu's Start command. |

4. Click the Perform Debugging button on the main dialog of your application. Your application should stop on the breakpoint that you placed in the application.

Debugging the Loops

Because of the way that the two counters are added together, the problem with the `CalculateSum` function won't be apparent the first time through the outer loop. Because of this, you'll first concentrate on the problem with the `OnClickedDebug` function.

If you step through the code using the Step Over button (see Figure 2.22), you'll find that the `if` condition is triggered the very first time through the loop (assuming that you entered the code exactly as it was provided in Listing 2.2). Not only that, but the value of the `iSum` variable jumps from 0 to 6 when evaluating the condition. As you examine the `if` condition, you see the code as follows:

```
if (iSum = 6)
```

FIGURE 2.22

Step through your application with the Step Over function.

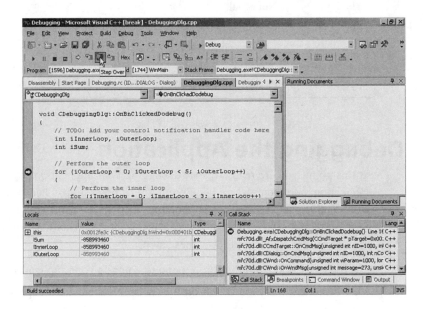

This is one of the easiest problems to code by accident, and also one of the most difficult to see, because the code "looks" right. However, if you think through the C/C++ conditionals, you'll remember that the conditional for "is equal" is two equal symbols, not one. By only having a single equal symbol here, you are assigning the value 6 to the variable `iSum`. Because the new value of the `iSum` variable isn't 0, the condition evaluates to `TRUE`, so the condition is met, and the message box is displayed.

To correct this error, add another equal to the condition, with no white space between the two equal symbols, making this line look as follows:

```
if (iSum == 6)
```

If you continue stepping through the code, you'll see the Visual C++ compiler take a moment to recompile and link your application. This is a capability that has only been available in Visual C++ since the previous version. Before that, you always had to stop the application, make your changes, recompile, and restart your debugging session. Now, you can just make your corrections and continue on.

1. Change the `if` statement, adding a second equals sign.

2. Step to the next line of code. Notice the application being recompiled before continuing on, applying your changes in place.

Caution

Not every change can be automatically re-compiled without stopping the debugging session. Some changes still require stopping the debugging session to recompile, forcing you to restart the debugging session all over again.

2

C++ Sidebar: Boolean Values

In the C and C++ programming languages, the Boolean FALSE is always 0, as there is no native Boolean data type in the C/C++ programming language. Since 0 is FALSE, any non-zero value is automatically evaluated as TRUE. It's common practice in C/C++ to define a Boolean data type where FALSE is defined as 0, and TRUE is defined as 1.

C++ Rule

For the BOOL data type, 0 is always FALSE. Any other value is TRUE. For the bool data type, false and true are represented by a single bit, with false being 0 and true being 1.

Debugging the Calculation

After stepping through the OnClickedDebug function a few more times, (at least until you are into the second time through the outer loop) you'll start to see funny values being returned from the CalculateSum function. It looks like this function is subtracting the outer loop counter from the inner loop counter. This can't be right, they're supposed to be added together! You'll have to switch to the Step Into button to step into the CalculateSum function to see what's going on inside this function, as shown in Figure 2.23.

Once inside the CalculateSum function, you find that the main line of code reads as follows:

```
iSum = iLeftValue - iRightValue;
```

It seems that this function is indeed subtracting the counters instead of adding. You make this correction, changing to code to read as follows:

```
iSum = iLeftValue + iRightValue;
```

Continuing, you don't find any additional problems to be corrected, so you decide to step out of the current function using the Step Out button.

FIGURE 2.23

Stepping into the CalculateSum function.

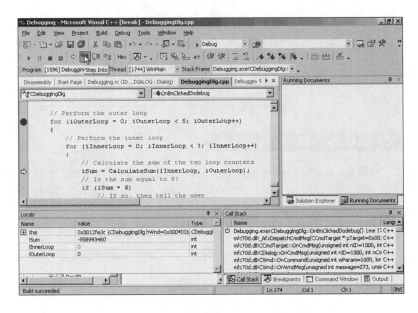

Summary

Today you learned a valuable skill that you will use with all the applications you build using Visual C++. It's a fair estimate that between one third and one half of the time you spend on creating and coding any particular application will actually be spent debugging it. This is an average estimate, so any one application may take much less or much more time to debug. This is also a skill you'll build with practice. Most top-notch programmers developed their skill through practice, not just in coding, but also in debugging their code.

Q&A

Q. Why do I need to make a release build of my application? Why can't I just distribute the debug build?

A. There are two primary reasons why you would want to make and distribute a release build of your application instead of a debug build. First, the release build will be smaller and will run faster. While it may be difficult to notice the performance difference in short routines, if your application performs any lengthy processing, the speed difference makes a noticeable improvement.

The second primary reason for distributing a release build is to protect your "intellectual property." If you distribute a debug build of your application, anyone can run it inside any standard debugger, and can trace their way through your application. Unless you distribute your code with your application, the user will be seeing only the Assembler code version of your application, however, this is sufficient for a lot of advanced programmers to reverse engineer the original source code.

> **Note**
>
> Specialized debuggers are available that enable someone to step through your release build and see the Assembler code. However, these specialized debuggers aren't provided with any C++ development tools, and must be purchased separately.

Q. How does the debugger work? How does it know where in my code the application execution is?

A. In a debug build, the compiler adds extra information that doesn't get executed when running the application. This information is mixed in with the executable code. The information specifies what source code file and line of code each set of machine instructions correlates with. It also contains information about each of the variables in the code, and where each of them is stored in memory while the application is running. This is all information that the debugger uses to display the correct code as you are stepping through your application.

Q. I don't want my breakpoint to be triggered each time that my application hits it. Is there some way of getting it to trigger only when certain values are reached?

A. If you open the Breakpoints pane, you can view the properties of each of your breakpoints. Within the breakpoint properties dialog, you can place conditions on the breakpoint, such as only stopping when a certain variable is equal to a specific value.

Workshop

The Workshop provides quiz questions to help solidify your understanding of the material covered and exercises to provide you with experience in using what you've learned. The answers to the quiz questions and exercises are provided in Appendix A, "Answers to Quiz Questions."

Quiz

1. What three primary stepping commands are used when debugging code?
2. What is the difference between the ASSERT and VERIFY macros?
3. Why would you use the Spy++ tool?

Exercise

Add ASSERT macros to validate the parameters being passed to the CalculateSum function. You need to make sure that the values passed in are greater than or equal to 0. Also add an ASSERT macro to verify that the iSum value is non-negative prior to returning it.

DAY 3

Using Controls in Your Application

Some of the things you will find in just about every Windows application are buttons, check boxes, text fields, and drop-down list boxes. These are known as controls, and many controls are built into the operating system itself. With Visual C++, using these common controls is as easy as placing them on a dialog window with a drag-and-drop window design method. Today you are going to learn

- What the basic controls in Visual C++ are
- How to declare and attach variables to a control
- How to synchronize the values between a control and a variable
- How to specify the order users navigate around your application windows
- How to trigger actions with controls
- How to manipulate and alter the appearance of controls while your application is running

The Basic Windows Controls

Several standard controls are built into the Windows operating system, including sliders, tree and list controls, progress bars, and so on. However, today you will work with a half dozen controls that appear in just about every Windows application:

- Static Text
- Edit Control
- Button
- Check Box
- Radio Button
- Drop-down list box (also known as a Combo Box)

These and other controls are readily available for use in Visual C++ applications. They can be found on the toolbox pane in the Dialog Painter editor in the Developer Studio (see Figure 3.1).

FIGURE 3.1

The standard controls available on the Toolbox pane.

The Static Text Control

You use the static text control to present text to the user. The user won't be able to change the text or otherwise interact with the control. Static text is intended as a read-only control. However, you can easily change the text displayed by the control as your application is running through the code you create for your application.

Key properties for the Static Text control are listed in Table 3.1.

TABLE 3.1 Key Properties for the Static Text Control

Property	Description
ID	Identifies the control. The default value is always IDC_STATIC. If you need to be able to control the Static Text control to change its appearance or text, you need to change its ID property.
Caption	Specifies the text displayed in the Static Text control.
Visible	Indicates whether the control can be seen when the application is running.
Disabled	Indicates that the control should be disabled. When the control is disabled, it appears grayed out. This causes the text in the caption to appear as an outline or indention in the surface of the dialog window.
Tab Stop	Indicates whether users should be able to stop on the control while navigating through the dialog's controls by using the tab key. This is a property that you might not initially consider to belong with a Static Text control. Actually, when you add mnemonics to the captions, this property becomes very important, as the focus will go to the next control in the tab order after the Static Text control.

MFC Note: The CStatic Class

Each of the controls that can be used in a Windows application has a corresponding MFC class. This class encapsulates all the control functionality, providing a simple way of interacting with the control. The class that encapsulates the Static Text control is the CStatic class.

The CStatic class is a descendent of the CWnd class, which is the base class for all of the visual components in a MFC application. The CStatic class is normally used to display text that the user can't interact with.

The Edit Box Control

The edit box is one of the primary tools for allowing the user to enter information that your application needs. It's a control that allows the user to type a specific amount of text, which you can capture and use for whatever purposes you might need it. The edit box accepts plain text only; no formatting is available to the user. Key properties for the Edit Box control are listed in Table 3.2.

TABLE 3.2 Key Properties for the Edit Box Control

Property	Description
ID	Identifies the control. You need to change the ID property so that you can identify and interact with the Edit Box control.

TABLE 3.2 continued

Property	Description
Visible	Indicates whether the control can be seen when the application is running.
Disabled	Indicates that the control should be disabled.
Align Text	Specifies whether the text in the control is aligned to the left or right end, or if it's centered in the control.
Multiline	Specifies whether the text in the control can continue over multiple lines.
Number	Restricts the text entered into an Edit Control to numbers.
Password	Hides any text in the control, displaying asterisks (*) instead.
Tab Stop	Indicates whether users should be able to stop on the control while navigating through the dialog's controls by using the tab key.

MFC Note: The CEdit Class

The Edit Box control is encapsulated in the CEdit class. The CEdit class is a descendent of the CWnd class, and extends the CWnd class by adding various methods for editing and interacting with the text in the control. The CEdit class even contains methods for interacting with the Clipboard, including Copy, Cut, Paste, and Undo, all methods that take no parameters.

The Command Button Control

A command button is a button that the user can press to trigger some action. Command buttons have a textual label to tell users what will happen when they click the button. You also can place an image on the button—alone or along with a textual description—to convey what the button does. Key properties for the Command Button control are listed in Table 3.3.

TABLE 3.3 Key Properties for the Command Button Control

Property	Description
ID	Identifies the control. You need to change the ID property so that you can identify and interact with the Command Button control.
Caption	Specifies the text displayed in the Command Button control.
Visible	Indicates whether the control can be seen when the application is running.
Disabled	Indicates that the control should be disabled. This causes the text in the caption to appear as an outline or indention in the surface of the dialog window.

TABLE 3.3 Key Properties for the Command Button Control

Property	Description
Default Button	Indicates that this control should be triggered if the user presses the Enter key.
Tab Stop	Indicates whether users should be able to stop on the control while navigating through the dialog's controls by using the tab key.

MFC Note: The `CButton` Class

The `CButton` class is the MFC class that encapsulates the Command Button control. This class is a descendent of the `CWnd` class, and encapsulates not just the Command Button control, but also the Check Box and Radio Button controls as well. It's inherited by the `CBitmapButton` class, which allows you to display an image on the button.

You can check and alter the state of a button with the `GetState` and `SetState` methods. You can control the appearance and behavior of the button with the `GetButtonStyle` and `SetButtonStyle` methods.

The Check Box Control

A check box is a square that the user can click to check (×) or uncheck. The check box control is used to turn a particular value on and off. They are basically on/off switches with an occasional third, in-between state. Key properties for the Check Box control are listed in Table 3.4.

TABLE 3.4 Key Properties for the Check Box Control

Property	Description
ID	Identifies the control. You need to change the ID property so that you can identify and interact with the Check Box control.
Caption	Specifies the text that is displayed in the Check Box control.
Visible	Indicates whether the control can be seen when the application is running.
Disabled	Indicates that the control should be disabled. This causes the text in the caption to appear as an outline or indention in the surface of the dialog window.
Tri-state	Indicates that the Check Box has three states instead of the normal two. The third state is disabled, which means that the value of the control is neither TRUE nor FALSE.
Tab Stop	Indicates whether users should be able to stop on the control while navigating through the dialog's controls by using the tab key.

The Radio Button Control

A radio button is a circle that the user can click to fill with a black spot. The radio button is similar to the check box control, but it's used in a group of two or more where only one of the values can be in the on state at a time. You normally use radio buttons in groups of at least two, surrounded by a group box. The group box allows each group of radio buttons to be visually independent, indicating to users that only one radio button in each group can be in the on state at any time. Key properties for the Radio Button control are listed in Table 3.5.

TABLE 3.5   Key Properties for the Radio Button Control

Property	Description
ID	Identifies the control. You need to change the ID property so that you can identify and interact with the Radio Button control.
Caption	Specifies the text that is displayed in the Radio Button control.
Visible	Indicates whether the control can be seen when the application is running.
Disabled	Indicates that the control should be disabled. This causes the text in the caption to appear as an outline or indention in the surface of the dialog window.
Group	Indicates that a control is the first in a group of controls. This property is available for most controls, but it's most important for Radio Buttons. Only the first radio button in a group of radio buttons should have this property set to TRUE.
Auto	Causes the radio button to automatically change state when it's checked. By default, this is set to TRUE.
Left Text	Causes the caption to appear on the left of the radio button. The caption text normally appears on the right of the radio button.
Tab Stop	Indicates whether users should be able to stop on the control while navigating through the dialog's controls by using the tab key.

The Combo Box Control

A combo box, (also known as a drop-down list box) control, is an edit box with a list of available values attached. You use the combo box to provide a list of choices, from which the user may select one value. Sometimes, the user is given the option of typing in his own value when a suitable one isn't provided in the list. Key properties for the Combo Box control are listed in Table 3.6.

TABLE 3.6   Key Properties for the Combo Box Control

Property	Description
ID	Identifies the control. You need to change this property so that you can identify and interact with the Combo Box control.
Caption	Specifies the text displayed in the Combo Box control.
Visible	Indicates whether the control can be seen when the application is running.
Disabled	Indicates that the control should be disabled. This causes the text in the caption to appear as an outline or indention in the surface of the dialog window.
Sort	Controls whether the entries in the drop-down list are sorted.
Type	Specifies the type of combo box to be displayed. Simple, Dropdown (the default), or Drop List. The Simple type displays the list at all times. The Dropdown style only displays the list when the control has focus, either from the user tabbing into the control or clicking on the arrow to drop-down the list. The Drop List type has a static text control in which the current selection is displayed; otherwise, it's the same as the Dropdown type.
Tab Stop	Indicates whether users should be able to stop on the control while navigating through the dialog's controls by using the tab key.

MFC Note: The `CComboBox` Class

The `CComboBox` class encapsulates the Combo Box control. It's a descendent of the `CWnd` class, and is inherited by the `CComboBoxEx` class. The `CComboBoxEx` class provides functionality for including images in the selections in the drop-down list.

The `CComboBox` class provides functions for interacting with the drop-down list. It provides functions for determining and specifying the current selection with the `GetCurSel` and `SetCurSel` methods, along with the `SelectString` and `FindString` methods. It also allows you to add and remove items from the list with the `AddString`, `InsertString`, and `DeleteString` methods. When you need to reset the contents of the list and start again, you can use the `ResetContent` method.

Adding Controls to Your Window

The application you will build today will have a number of controls on a single dialog window (see Figure 3.2). These controls have several functions:

- At the top of the window is an edit field where the user can enter a message that displays in a message box when he or she clicks the button beside the field.
- Below the edit field are two buttons that either populate the edit field with a default message or clear the edit field.
- Below the two buttons is a drop-down list box that contains a list of standard Windows applications. When a user selects one of these programs and then clicks the button beside the drop-down list, the selected program will run.
- Below the combo box are two groups of check boxes that affect the controls you add to the top half of the dialog: the controls for displaying a user message and the controls for running another program.
- The left set of check boxes will enable and disable each group of controls you provide.
- The right set of check boxes will show and hide each group of controls.
- At the bottom of the dialog box is a button that can be clicked to close the application.

FIGURE 3.2

Today's application will use a number of standard controls.

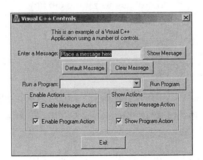

Creating the Application Shell and Dialog Layout

Using what you learned yesterday, create a new application shell and design the application dialog layout as follows:

1. Create a new MFC Application Visual C++ project, calling the project Controls.
2. Use the same settings in the MFC Application Wizard as you used for the past two days; specify the dialog title Visual C++ Controls.
3. After you create the application shell, lay out the main dialog as shown earlier in Figure 3.2.
4. Configure the control properties as specified in Table 3.7.

TABLE 3.7 Property Settings for the Controls on the Application Dialog

Control	Property	Setting
Static Text	Caption	This is an example of a Visual C++ Application using a number of controls.
Static Text	ID	IDC_STATICMSG
	Caption	Enter a &Message:
Static Text	ID	IDC_STATICPGM
	Caption	Run a &Program:
Edit Box	ID	IDC_MSG
Button	ID	IDC_SHWMSG
	Caption	&Show Message
Button	ID	IDC_DFLTMSG
	Caption	&Default Message
Button	ID	IDC_CLRMSG
	Caption	&Clear Message
Button	ID	IDC_RUNPGM
	Caption	&Run Program
Button	ID	IDC_EXIT
	Caption	E&xit
Combo Box	ID	IDC_PROGTORUN
Group Box	Caption	Enable Actions
Group Box	Caption	Show Actions
Check Box	ID	IDC_CKENBLMSG
	Caption	&Enable Message Action
Check Box	ID	IDC_CKENBLPGM
	Caption	E&nable Program Action
Check Box	ID	IDC_CKSHWMSG
	Caption	S&how Message Action
Check Box	ID	IDC_CKSHWPGM
	Caption	Sh&ow Program Action

5. After you place all these controls on the dialog window and configure all their properties, reselect the combo box and find the Data property in the Properties area. Enter the following values, separating them with a semicolon (see Figure 3.3).

- Notepad
- Paint
- Solitaire

FIGURE 3.3

Use the properties pane to add entries in the combo box's drop-down list.

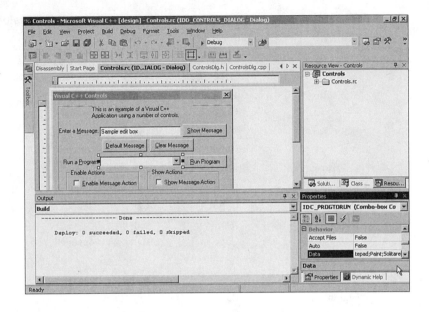

Tip

When adding a combo box control to the window, it's important that you click and drag the area for the control to the size you want the drop-down list to be. After you draw the control on the window, you can resize the width of the control as you would normally expect to do. To resize how far the list drops down, you need to click the arrow, as if you were trying to trigger the drop-down list while the application was running.

Specifying the Control Tab Order

Now that you have all the controls laid out on the window, you need to make sure that the user navigates in the order you want if he or she uses the Tab key to move around the window. You can specify the tab order by following these steps:

1. Select either the dialog window or one of the controls on the window in the editing area of the Developer Studio.

2. Choose Tab Order from the Format menu. By turning on the Tab Order, you see a number beside each of the controls on the window. The numbers indicate the order in which the dialog will be navigated (see Figure 3.4).

FIGURE 3.4

Turning on Tab Order shows the order in which the dialog will be navigated.

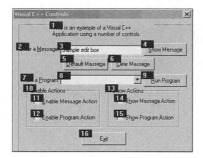

3. Click each number box in the order that you want users to navigate the window. The controls will renumber themselves to match the order in which you selected them.

4. After you specify the tab order, select Tab Order from the Format menu again to return to the layout editor.

> **Note**
>
> Any static text with a mnemonic should appear just before the control that accompanies the text in the tab order. Because the user can't interact with the static text, when the user chooses the mnemonic, the focus will go directly to the next control in the tab order.

A mnemonic is the underlined character in the caption on a button, check box, menu, or other control label. The user can press this underlined character and the Alt key at the same time to go directly to that control or to trigger the clicked event on the control. You specify a mnemonic by placing an ampersand (&) in front of the character to be used as the mnemonic when you type the Caption value. (It's important to ensure that you don't use the same mnemonic more than once on the same window, or set of menus, because the user can get confused when choosing a mnemonic that doesn't result in the action that he or she expects.)

One last thing that you want to do before getting into the details of the application code is check your mnemonics to make certain that there are no conflicts in your controls. Follow these steps:

1. Select the dialog window or one of the controls in the layout editor. Right-click the mouse and select Check Mnemonics.

2. If there are no conflicts in your mnemonics, Visual C++ returns a message box dialog, letting you know that there are no conflicts (see Figure 3.5).

Figure 3.5

The mnemonic checker tells you whether there are conflicts.

3. If any conflicts exist, the dialog indicates the conflicting letter and gives you the option of automatically selecting the first control containing the conflicting mnemonic (see Figure 3.6).

Figure 3.6

You can detect duplicate mnemonics automatically.

Attaching Variables to Your Controls

At this point, if you've programmed using Visual Basic or PowerBuilder, you probably figure that you're ready to start slinging some code. Well, with Visual C++ applications built using MFC, it's not quite the same process. Before you can begin coding, you have to assign variables to each of the controls that will have a value attached—everything except the static text and the command buttons. You will interact with these variables when you write the code for your application. The values that the user enters into the screen controls are placed into these variables for use in the application code. Likewise, any values that your application code places into these variables are updated in the controls on the window for the user to see.

How do you declare these variables and associate them with the controls that you placed on the window? Follow these steps:

1. Select the control to which you want to attach a variable.

2. Right-click the mouse over the control and select Add Variable from the context menu that appears.

3. Select the ID of one of the controls that you need to attach a variable to, such as IDC_MSG. The ID of the selected control should already be selected in the Control ID combo box.

4. Specify Value for the Category.

5. Select the data type for the variable in the Variable type combo box.

6. Enter a name in the Variable Name edit control.

7. Enter a comment to describe the variable, and what it will be used for, in the Comment edit control at the bottom of the dialog (see Figure 3.7). Click Finish to add the variable.

FIGURE 3.7

Adding a variable to a control.

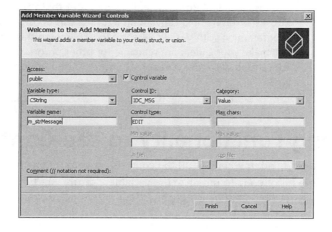

8. Repeat steps 1–7 for all the other controls for which you need to add variables. You should add the variables for your application as listed in Table 3.8.

TABLE 3.8 Variables for Application Controls

Control	Variable Name	Category	Type	Access
IDC_MSG	m_strMessage	Value	CString	public
IDC_PROGTORUN	m_strProgToRun	Value	CString	public
IDC_CKENBLMSG	m_bEnableMsg	Value	BOOL	public
IDC_CKENBLPGM	m_bEnablePgm	Value	BOOL	public
IDC_CKSHWMSG	m_bShowMsg	Value	BOOL	public
IDC_CKSHWPGM	m_bShowPgm	Value	BOOL	public

Note

The BOOL data type isn't included in the list of data types available for use in the Add Member Variable Wizard. However, the bool data type is available. These aren't the same data type. Although bool is now a native data type in C++, a lot of the MFC class library uses the BOOL data type, as MFC predates the addition of bool. Whenever you need to use a data type that's not included in the combo box list for data types, you can enter your own data type into the edit area of the combo box. In this case, enter **BOOL** for the data type rather than select it from the combo box list of data types.

Tip

All these variables are prefixed with m_ because they are class member variables. This is an MFC naming convention. After the m_, a form of Hungarian notation is used, in which the next few letters describe the variable type. In this case, b means Boolean, and str indicates that the variable is a string. You'll see this naming convention in use in this book and other books about programming with Visual C++ and MFC. Following this naming convention will make your code more readable for other programmers; knowing the convention will make it easier for you to read other programmer's code as well.

Attaching Functionality to the Controls

Before you begin adding code to all the controls on your application window, you need to add a little bit of code to initialize the variables, setting starting values for most of them. Do this by following these steps:

1. In the Class View pane, expand the CControlsDlg class and select the OnInitDialog function in the list of member functions.

2. Double-click the OnInitDialog node to be taken to the source code for the OnInitDialog function.

3. Find the TODO marker, which indicates where to begin adding your code, and add the boldfaced code in Listing 3.1.

LISTING 3.1   CONTROLSDLG.CPP—Adding Initialization Code to the OnInitDialog Function

```
BOOL CControlsDlg::OnInitDialog()
{
    CDialog::OnInitDialog();
...
    // Set the icon for this dialog.  The framework does this automatically
    //  when the application's main window is not a dialog
    SetIcon(m_hIcon, TRUE);      // Set big icon
    SetIcon(m_hIcon, FALSE);     // Set small icon

    // TODO: Add extra initialization here
    // Put a default message in the message edit
    m_strMessage = "Place a message here";

    // Set all of the check boxes to checked
    m_bShowMsg = TRUE;
    m_bShowPgm = TRUE;
    m_bEnableMsg = TRUE;
    m_bEnablePgm = TRUE;
```

INPUT

LISTING 3.1   continued

```
// Update the dialog with the values
UpdateData(FALSE);

    return TRUE;  // return TRUE  unless you set the focus to a control
}
```

> **Note**
>
> The OnInitDialog function includes more code than is included in Listing 3.1. I won't include all the code for every function in the code listings throughout this book as a means of focusing on the code that you need to add or modify (and as a means of keeping this book to a reasonable size). You are welcome to look at the code left out of the listings in the book, to learn what it is and what it does, as you build your understanding of MFC and Visual C++.

> **Note**
>
> If you've programmed in C or C++ before, you've noticed that you are setting the value of the m_strMessage variable in a very un–C-like manner. It looks more like how you would expect to set a string variable in Visual Basic or PowerBuilder. That's because this variable is a CString type variable. The CString class enables you to work with strings in a Visual C++ application in much the same way that you would work with strings in other programming languages. However, because this is the C++ programming language, you still need to add a semicolon at the end of each statement.

This initialization code is simple. You are setting an initial message in the edit box that you will use to display messages for the user. Next, you are setting all the check boxes to the checked state. It's the last line of the code you added to this function that you really need to notice.

The UpdateData function is the key to working with control variables in Visual C++. This function takes the data in the variables and updates the controls on the screen with the variable values. It also takes the data from the controls and populates the attached variables with any values changed by the user. This process is controlled by the argument passed into the UpdateData function.

If the argument is FALSE, the values in the variables are passed to the controls on the window. If the argument is TRUE, or left out, the variables are updated with whatever appears in the controls on the window. As a result, which value you pass to this function depends on which direction you need to update.

After you update one or more variables in your code, you need to call UpdateData, passing it FALSE as its argument. If you need to read the variables to get their current value, you need to call UpdateData with a TRUE value before you read any of the variables. You'll get the hang of this as you add more code to your application.

Caution
Be careful where you place the UpdateData function call, plus what value you pass to it. For instance, if you initialize the values of all your variables, and then call UpdateData(TRUE), you'll wipe out the variables' values, replacing them with the controls' values. Likewise, if a user changes the value in one of the controls and then UpdateData(FALSE) is called, the control's value will be changed to the variable's value, erasing what the user had entered.

C++ Sidebar: The Scope Resolution Operator

If you look at the snippet of existing code left in Listing 3.1, you see the following code on the third line:

```
CDialog::OnInitDialog();
```

Based on what you've already seen, this looks like the first line of the function listing, where the class is specified with two colons followed by the function name, as on the first line of code in the listing:

```
BOOL CControlsDlg::OnInitDialog()
```

The first line of the listing is the function name, along with the return type and the class of which the function is a member. The third line is calling the same function in the base class. This is how you call base class functions in C++, by listing the base class name, followed by two colons, and then the function, passing any necessary parameters.

The two colons together with nothing between them is known as the *scope resolution operator* and is used to specify the scope of the function. In the two situations above, it's specifying that the function is a member of the class in front of the two colons. If you have a function with the two colons in front of the function call with no class name, the scope resolution operator indicates that the function is a global function, and not a member of any class.

You can also use the scope resolution operator to define variable scope, although this usage is much rarer than with functions.

Closing the Application

The first thing that you want to take care of is making sure that the user can close your application. Because you deleted the OK and Cancel buttons and added a new button for closing the application window, you need to place code into the function called by the Exit button to close the window. To do this, follow these steps:

1. Use the tabs over the editing area to bring up the dialog window and select the Exit button. Using the Properties pane, add a function for the button on the BN_CLICKED message, as you learned to do in the previous two days. If you've closed the dialog, or closed and reopened the project, use the Resources pane to reopen the dialog.

2. Enter the boldfaced code in Listing 3.2.

LISTING 3.2   CONTROLSDLG.CPP—The OnBnClickedExit Function

```
void CControlsDlg::OnBnClickedExit()
{
    // TODO: Add your control notification handler code here
    // Exit the program
    OnOK();
}
```

INPUT

A single function call within the OnBnClickedExit function closes the Window and exits the application. Where did this OnOK function come from, and why didn't you have to call it in yesterday's application? Two functions, OnOK and OnCancel, are built into the base CDialog class from which your CControlsDlg class is inherited. In the CDialog class, the message map already has the object IDs of the OK and Cancel buttons attached to the OnOK and OnCancel functions so that buttons with these IDs automatically call these functions. If you had specified the Exit button's object ID as IDOK, you wouldn't have needed to add any code to the button unless you wanted to override the base OnOK functionality.

Note

You may be wondering why, in this situation, you didn't need to specify that the OnOK function is in the base CDialog class by calling it as follows:

    CDialog::OnOK();

You didn't need to specify this because this function isn't being overridden in your class. Anytime that you call a function in a base class that hasn't been overridden in a descendent class, you don't need to use the scope resolution operator to specify the class that contains the function.

Showing the User's Message

Showing the message that the user typed into the edit box is easy because it's similar to what you did in yesterday's application. You can add a function to the Show Message button and call the MessageBox function, as in Listing 3.3.

LISTING 3.3   CONTROLSDLG.CPP—Displaying the User's Message

```
void CControlsDlg::OnBnClickedShwmsg()
{
    // TODO: Add your control notification handler code here
    // Display the message for the user
    MessageBox(m_strMessage);
}
```

INPUT

If you compile and run the application at this point, you'll find a problem with this code. It displays the string that you initialized the m_strMessage variable with in the OnInitDialog function. It doesn't display what you type into the edit box. This happens because the variable hasn't been updated with the contents of the control on the window yet. You need to call UpdateData, passing it a TRUE value, to take the values of the controls and update the variables before calling the MessageBox function. Alter the OnBnClickedShwmsg function as in Listing 3.4.

LISTING 3.4   CONTROLSDLG.CPP—The Updated OnBnClickedShwmsg Function

```
void CControlsDlg::OnBnClickedShwmsg()
{
    // TODO: Add your control notification handler code here
    // Update the message variable with what the user entered
    UpdateData(TRUE);

    // Display the message for the user
    MessageBox(m_strMessage);
}
```

INPUT

Now if you compile and run your application, you should be able to display the message you type into the edit box (see Figure 3.8).

Clearing User Messages

If users prefer the edit box to be cleared before they type messages, you can attach a function to the Clear Message button to clear the contents. You can add this function through the Class Wizard in the usual way. The functionality is a simple matter of setting the m_strMessage variable to an empty string and then updating the controls on the window to reflect this. Listing 3.5 shows the code to do this.

FIGURE 3.8

The message entered in the edit box is displayed to the user.

LISTING 3.5 CONTROLSDLG.CPP—The `OnBnClickedClrmsg` Function

```
void CControlsDlg::OnBnClickedClrmsg()
{
    // TODO: Add your control notification handler code here
    // Clear the message
    m_strMessage = "";

    // Update the screen
    UpdateData(FALSE);
}
```

INPUT

Disabling and Hiding the Message Controls

The last thing that you want to do with the message controls is add functionality to the Enable Message Action and Show Message Action check boxes. The first of these check boxes enables or disables the controls dealing with displaying the user message. When the check box is in a checked state, the controls are all enabled. When the check box is in an unchecked state, all those same controls are disabled. Likewise, the second check box shows and hides this same set of controls. Listing 3.6 shows the code for these two functions.

LISTING 3.6 CONTROLSDLG.CPP—The Functions for the Enable and Show Message Actions Check Boxes

```
void CControlsDlg::OnBnClickedCkenblmsg()
{
    // TODO: Add your control notification handler code here
    // Get the current values from the screen
    UpdateData(TRUE);

    // Is the Enable Message Action check box checked?
    if (m_bEnableMsg == TRUE)
    {
        // Yes, so enable all controls that have anything
        // to do with showing the user message
        GetDlgItem(IDC_MSG)->EnableWindow(TRUE);
        GetDlgItem(IDC_SHWMSG)->EnableWindow(TRUE);
        GetDlgItem(IDC_DFLTMSG)->EnableWindow(TRUE);
        GetDlgItem(IDC_CLRMSG)->EnableWindow(TRUE);
```

INPUT

3

LISTING 3.6 continued

```
                 GetDlgItem(IDC_STATICMSG)->EnableWindow(TRUE);
        }
        else
        {
            // No, so disable all controls that have anything
            // to do with showing the user message
            GetDlgItem(IDC_MSG)->EnableWindow(FALSE);
            GetDlgItem(IDC_SHWMSG)->EnableWindow(FALSE);
            GetDlgItem(IDC_DFLTMSG)->EnableWindow(FALSE);
            GetDlgItem(IDC_CLRMSG)->EnableWindow(FALSE);
            GetDlgItem(IDC_STATICMSG)->EnableWindow(FALSE);
        }
    }

    void CControlsDlg::OnBnClickedCkshwmsg()
    {
        // TODO: Add your control notification handler code here
        // Get the current values from the screen
        UpdateData(TRUE);

        // Is the Show Message Action check box checked?
        if (m_bShowMsg == TRUE)
        {
            // Yes, so show all controls that have anything
            // to do with showing the user message
            GetDlgItem(IDC_MSG)->ShowWindow(TRUE);
            GetDlgItem(IDC_SHWMSG)->ShowWindow(TRUE);
            GetDlgItem(IDC_DFLTMSG)->ShowWindow(TRUE);
            GetDlgItem(IDC_CLRMSG)->ShowWindow(TRUE);
            GetDlgItem(IDC_STATICMSG)->ShowWindow(TRUE);
        }
        else
        {
            // No, so hide all controls that have anything
            // to do with showing the user message
            GetDlgItem(IDC_MSG)->ShowWindow(FALSE);
            GetDlgItem(IDC_SHWMSG)->ShowWindow(FALSE);
            GetDlgItem(IDC_DFLTMSG)->ShowWindow(FALSE);
            GetDlgItem(IDC_CLRMSG)->ShowWindow(FALSE);
            GetDlgItem(IDC_STATICMSG)->ShowWindow(FALSE);
        }
    }
```

INPUT

By now, you should understand the first part of these functions. First, you update the variables with the current values of the controls on the window. Next, you check the value of the Boolean variable attached to the appropriate check box. If the variable is TRUE, you want to enable or show the control. If the variable if FALSE, you want to disable or hide the control.

At this point, the code begins to be harder to understand. The first function, GetDlgItem, is passed the ID of the control that you want to change. This function returns a pointer to the control. You can call this function to retrieve a pointer to any of the controls on the window while your application is running. The next part of each command is where a member function of the control object is called. The second function is a member function of the control for which a pointer was returned by the first function.

The second functions in these calls, EnableWindow and ShowWindow, look like they should be used on windows, not controls. Well, yes, they should be used on windows; they happen to be members of the CWnd class, which is a base class of the CDialog class from which your CControlsDlg class is inherited. It just so happens that, in Windows, all controls are themselves windows, completely separate from the window on which they are placed. This allows you to treat controls as windows and to call windows functions on them. In fact, all the control classes are descended from the CWnd class, revealing their true nature as windows.

If you compile and run your application now, you can try the Enable and Show Message Action check boxes. They should work just fine, as shown in Figure 3.9.

FIGURE 3.9

The user message controls can now be disabled.

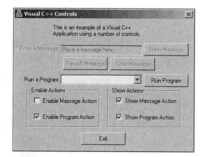

C++ Sidebar: Boolean Expressions

In Listing 3.6, you could have written the if statements slightly differently. Because the Boolean variables that you're checking the value of are, by their very nature, either TRUE or FALSE, you don't really need to compare the value of them to TRUE. Instead, you can just write the if statement as follows:

```
if (m_bEnableMsg)
```

Following this logic, you can do the same thing to various variables where all you need to determine is whether the variable has a value (for example, isn't zero). This is often done when checking pointers to make sure that they point to something. This all assumes that the variable in question was originally initialized to zero, or NULL (defined as zero). For instance, if you wanted to check to see if a value was assigned to an integer variable, you could check using the following:

```
if (iVar != 0)
```

However, you can also use the following:

```
if (iVar)
```

Reversing this logic, you can also check to see if a variable is equal to zero by negating the expression, as follows:

```
if (!iVar)
```

In these situations, the exclamation mark (!) means *not*. So, just as the != is read as "not equal," !iVar is read as "not iVar" or "iVar is equal to zero."

C++ Sidebar: Object Pointers

The next part of the above code listings primarily consist of the same line of code, over and over again. This line of code looks like the following:

```
GetDlgItem(IDC_MSG)->EnableWindow(TRUE);
```

The first function, GetDlgItem, is passed the ID of a control on the dialog window. This function returns a pointer to the control specified. When a function returns a pointer to an object, you can save the pointer in a variable, or, as in this example, use that returned pointer to call a member method of the object to which the pointer points.

NEW TERM   A *pointer* is a reference to an object or variable. It consists of the address in memory where the object or variable is currently located. When you use a pointer, instead of handing the object to the CPU, you are telling the CPU where it can find the object.

When you declare a variable of a certain class, you can call the methods and access the properties and variables in that class by using the dot notation, as follows:

```
CMyObject obj;
obj.Method1();
```

When you are working with a pointer, there are a couple of changes in the syntax. First, a pointer is declared with an asterisk in front of the variable name, as follows:

```
CMyObject *obj;
```

or

```
CMyObject* obj;
```

The first declaration states that the variable obj is a pointer to a CMyObject class. This line could also contain another variable that was an instance of the CMyObject class, as follows:

```
CMyObject *obj, objInstance;
```

The second declaration states that all variables declared on this line are pointers to instances of the CMyObject class.

When using a pointer to access member methods, properties, or variables of an object, always use the -> notation, as follows:

```
obj->Method1();
```

When you have an instance of an object or variable, and you need to initialize a pointer to point to that instance, use the ampersand to get the address of the object:

```
CMyObject objInstance, *pObj;
pObj = &objInstance;
```

An ampersand in front of any variable is read as "the address of," so in the above code, you are setting the value of pObj, which is a pointer, to the address of objInstance, which is an instance of the CMyObject class.

Getting back to the example code, the repeating line of code could be specified as follows:

```
CWnd *pWnd;

pWnd = GetDlgItem(IDC_MSG);
pWnd->EnableWindow(TRUE);
```

However, by taking advantage of the ability to combine functionality in a single line of code, you can shorten this functionality into a single line as in Listing 3.6 by treating the pointer returned from the GetDlgItem function to access the member function EnableWindow for the control specified, as follows:

```
GetDlgItem(IDC_MSG)->EnableWindow(TRUE);
```

Taking the functionality combination capability in C++ even further, the size of the two functions in Listing 3.6 can be reduced by eliminating the if statement, and passing the Boolean variable to the EnableWindow and ShowWindow functions instead of hardcoding the parameter values. This would enable you to take the following code

```
// Is the Enable Message Action check box checked?
if (m_bEnableMsg == TRUE)
{
    // Yes, so enable all controls that have anything
    // to do with showing the user message
```

3

```
    GetDlgItem(IDC_MSG)->EnableWindow(TRUE);
    GetDlgItem(IDC_SHWMSG)->EnableWindow(TRUE);
    GetDlgItem(IDC_DFLTMSG)->EnableWindow(TRUE);
    GetDlgItem(IDC_CLRMSG)->EnableWindow(TRUE);
    GetDlgItem(IDC_STATICMSG)->EnableWindow(TRUE);
}
else
{
    // No, so disable all controls that have anything
    // to do with showing the user message
    GetDlgItem(IDC_MSG)->EnableWindow(FALSE);
    GetDlgItem(IDC_SHWMSG)->EnableWindow(FALSE);
    GetDlgItem(IDC_DFLTMSG)->EnableWindow(FALSE);
    GetDlgItem(IDC_CLRMSG)->EnableWindow(FALSE);
    GetDlgItem(IDC_STATICMSG)->EnableWindow(FALSE);
}
```

and reduce it to the following:

```
// Enable or disable all controls that have anything
// to do with showing the user message
GetDlgItem(IDC_MSG)->EnableWindow(m_bEnableMsg);
GetDlgItem(IDC_SHWMSG)->EnableWindow(m_bEnableMsg);
GetDlgItem(IDC_DFLTMSG)->EnableWindow(m_bEnableMsg);
GetDlgItem(IDC_CLRMSG)->EnableWindow(m_bEnableMsg);
GetDlgItem(IDC_STATICMSG)->EnableWindow(m_bEnableMsg);
```

MFC Note: Member Methods of CWnd

In the CWnd class, which is the base class for all user interface objects in MFC, three member methods were used in Listing 3.6:

- GetDlgItem
- EnableWindow
- ShowWindow

The first of these methods, GetDlgItem, can be used to retrieve a pointer to a child window. The pointer returned is a CWnd pointer. There is one parameter passed to this method, and that is the ID of the child window. This function is normally used to get a pointer to a control on a dialog window, but can be used to get a pointer to any child window.

The second method, EnableWindow, turns on and off the ability for the user to interact with the window for which it's called. It takes a Boolean value as it's only parameter. If the parameter is TRUE, the window will be enabled, allowing user interaction. If the parameter is FALSE, the window or control will be disabled, and the user won't be able to interact with it.

The third method, ShowWindow, is just like the EnableWindow method, only it shows and hides the window or control. It takes a single Boolean value as a parameter, which tells it whether the window or control should be visible.

Running Another Application

The last major piece of functionality to be implemented in your application is for the set of controls for running another program. Earlier you added the names of three Windows applications into the combo box; when you run your application, you can see these application names in the drop-down list. You can select any one of them, and the value area on the combo box is updated with that application name. With that part working as it should, you need only to add code to the Run Program button to actually get the value for the combo box and run the appropriate program. Once you create the function for the Run Program button, add the code in Listing 3.7 to the function.

3

LISTING 3.7 CONTROLSDLG.CPP—Starting Other Windows Applications

```
void CControlsDlg::OnBnClickedRunpgm()
{
    // TODO: Add your control notification handler code here
    // Get the current values from the screen
    UpdateData(TRUE);

    // Declare a local variable for holding the program name
    CString strPgmName;

    // Copy the program name to the local variable
    strPgmName = m_strProgToRun;

    // Make the program name all uppercase
    strPgmName.MakeUpper();

    // Did the user select to run the Paint program?
    if (strPgmName == "PAINT")
        // Yes, run the Paint program
        WinExec("mspaint.exe ", SW_SHOW);

    // Did the user select to run the Notepad program?
    if (strPgmName == "NOTEPAD")
        // Yes, run the Notepad program
        WinExec("notepad.exe ", SW_SHOW);

    // Did the user select to run the Solitaire program?
    if (strPgmName == "SOLITAIRE")
        // Yes, run the Solitaire program
        WinExec("sol.exe ", SW_SHOW);
}
```

INPUT

As you expect, the first thing that you do in this function is call UpdateData to populate the variables with the values of the controls on the window. The next step might seem a little pointless: You declare a new CString variable and copy the value of the combo box to it. Is this really necessary when the value is already in a CString variable?

Well, it depends on how you want your application to behave. The next line in the code is a call to the CString function MakeUpper, which converts the string to all uppercase. If you use the CString variable that is attached to the combo box, the next time UpdateData is called with FALSE as the argument, the value in the combo box is converted to uppercase. Considering that this is likely to happen at an odd time, this is probably not desirable behavior. That's why you use an additional CString in this function.

Once you convert the string to all uppercase, you have a series of if statements that compare the string to the names of the various programs. When a match is found, the WinExec function is called to run the application. Now, if you compile and run your application, you can select one of the applications in the drop-down list and run it by clicking the Run Program button.

Caution

Make sure that you understand the difference in C and C++ between using a single equal sign (=) and a double equal sign (==). The single equal sign performs an assignment of the value on the right side of the equal sign to the variable on the left side of the equal sign. If a constant is on the left side of the equal sign, your program won't compile, and you'll get a nice error message telling you that you can't assign the value on the right to the constant on the left. The double equal sign (==) is used for comparison. It's important to use the double equal sign when you want to compare two values because if you use a single equal sign, you alter the value of the variable on the left. This confusion is one of the biggest sources of logic bugs in C/C++ programs.

Note

The WinExec function is an obsolete Windows function. You should use the CreateProcess function instead. However, the CreateProcess function has a number of arguments that are difficult to understand this early in programming using Visual C++. The WinExec function is still available and is implemented as a macro that calls the CreateProcess function. This allows you to use the much simpler WinExec function to run another application while still using the function that Windows wants you to use.

Another API function that can be used to run another application is the ShellExecute function. This function was originally intended for opening or printing files, but can also be used to run other programs.

Summary

Today, you learned how you can use standard windows controls in a Visual C++ application. You learned how to declare and attach variables to each of these controls and how to synchronize the values between the controls and the variables. You also learned how you can manipulate the controls by retrieving the control objects using their object ID and how you can manipulate the control by treating it as a window. You also learned how to specify the tab order of the controls on your application windows, thus enabling you to control how users navigate your application windows. Finally, you learned how to attach application functionality to the controls on your application window, triggering various actions when the user interacts with various controls. As an added bonus, you learned how you can run other Windows applications from your own application.

Q&A

Q. When I specified the object IDs of the controls on the window, three controls had the same ID—IDC_STATIC. These controls were the text at the top of the window and the two group boxes. The other two static text controls started out with this same ID until I changed them. How can these controls have the same ID, and why did I have to change the ID on the two static texts where I did change them?

A. All controls that don't normally have any user interaction, such as static text and group boxes, are by default given the same object ID. This works fine as long as your application doesn't need to perform any actions on these controls. If you do need to interact with one of these controls, as you did with the static text prompts for the edit box and combo box, you need to give that control a unique ID. In this case, you needed the unique ID to be able to retrieve the control object so you could enable or disable and show or hide the control. You also need to assign it a unique ID if you want to attach a variable to the control so that you could dynamically alter the text on the control.

The application behaves in a somewhat unpredictable way if you try to alter any of the static controls that share the same ID. As a general rule of thumb, you can allow static controls to share the same object ID if you aren't going to alter the controls at all. If you need to perform any interaction with the controls, you need to assign each one a unique object ID.

Q. Is there any other way to manipulate the controls, other than retrieving the control objects using their object IDs?

A. In the Add Member Variable Wizard, you can declare variables for your controls by specifying `Control` for the variable category. This basically gives you an variable that is the control's MFC class, providing you with a direct way of altering and interacting with the control. You can then call all `CWnd` class functions on the control, as you did to enable or disable and show or hide the controls in your application, or you can call the control class methods, enabling you to do things in the code that are specific to that type of control. For example, if you add another variable to the combo box control and specify that it's a Control category variable, you can use it to add items to the drop-down list on the control.

Workshop

The Workshop provides quiz questions to help you solidify your understanding of the material covered and exercises to provide you with experience in using what you've learned. The answers to the quiz questions appear in Appendix A, "Answers to Quiz Questions."

Quiz

1. Why do you need to specify the tab order of the controls on your application windows?

2. How can you include a mnemonic that will take the user to the edit box or combo box?

3. Why do you need to give unique object IDs to the static text fields in front of the edit box and combo boxes?

4. Why do you need to call the `UpdateData` function before checking the value of one of the controls?

Exercises

1. Add code to the Default Message button to reset the edit box to say `Enter a message here`.

2. Add code to enable or disable and show or hide the controls used to select and run another application.

3. Extend the code in the `OnBnClickedRunpgm` function (in Listing 3.7) to allow users to enter their own program names to be run.

DAY 4

Integrating Mouse and Keyboard to Allow User Interaction

Depending on the type of application you are creating, you might need to track what the user is doing with the mouse. You need to know when and where the mouse was clicked, which button was clicked, and when the button was released. You also need to know what the user did while the mouse button was being held down.

You might also need to read the keyboard events. As with the mouse, you might need to know when a key was pressed, how long it was held down, and when it was released.

Today you will learn

- What mouse events are available for use and how to determine which one is appropriate for your application's needs
- How you can listen to mouse events and how to react to them in your Visual C++ application

- What keyboard events are available for use and what actions will trigger each of these events
- How to capture keyboard events and take action based on what the user pressed

Understanding Mouse Events

As you learned yesterday, when you are working with most controls, you are limited to a select number of events that are available in the Class Wizard. When it comes to mouse events, you are limited mainly to click and double-click events. Just looking at your mouse tells you that there must be more to capturing mouse events than recognizing these two. What about the right mouse button? How can you tell if it's been pressed? And what about drawing programs? How can they follow where you drag the mouse?

If you select the dialog window, look at the Messages option in the Properties pane, and then scroll through the list of messages that are available, you will find a number of mouse-related events, which are also listed in Table 4.1. These event messages enable you to perform any task that might be required by your application.

TABLE 4.1 Mouse Event Messages

Message	Description
WM_LBUTTONDOWN	The left mouse button has been pressed.
WM_LBUTTONUP	The left mouse button has been released.
WM_LBUTTONDBLCLK	The left mouse button has been double-clicked.
WM_RBUTTONDOWN	The right mouse button has been pressed.
WM_RBUTTONUP	The right mouse button has been released.
WM_RBUTTONDBLCLK	The right mouse button has been double-clicked.
WM_MBUTTONDOWN	The middle mouse button (on a 3-button mouse) has been pressed.
WM_MBUTTONUP	The middle mouse button (on a 3-button mouse) has been released.
WM_MBUTTONDBLCLK	The middle mouse button (on a 3-button mouse) has been double-clicked.
WM_XBUTTONDOWN	One extended Microsoft Intellimouse button has been pressed.
WM_XBUTTONUP	One extended Microsoft Intellimouse button has been released.
WM_XBUTTONDBLCLK	One extended Microsoft Intellimouse button has been double-clicked.
WM_MOUSEMOVE	The mouse is being moved across the application window space.
WM_MOUSEWHEEL	The mouse wheel is being moved.

Drawing with the Mouse

Today you will build a simple drawing program that uses some of the available mouse events to let the user draw simple figures on a dialog window. This application depends mostly on the WM_MOUSEMOVE event message, which signals that the mouse is moving. You will look at how you can tell within this event function whether the left mouse button is down or up. You will also learn how you can tell where the mouse is in the window. Sounds fairly straightforward, so let's get going. Follow these steps:

1. Create a new MFC Application Visual C++ project, calling the project Mouse.

2. Specify that this project will be a dialog-based application in the MFC Application Wizard.

3. Use the default settings in the MFC Application Wizard for most of the options. Specify Mouse and Keyboard as the application title.

4. Once the application shell is created, remove all controls from the dialog window. This provides the entire dialog window surface for drawing. This step is also necessary so that your application can capture any keyboard events.

 Note

> If there are any controls on a dialog, all keyboard events are directed to the control that currently has input focus—the control that's highlighted or has the cursor visible in it. To be able to capture any keyboard events in a dialog, you have to remove all controls from the dialog.

4

5. Select the dialog window, and then select Messages mode in the Properties pane (see Figure 4.1). Select WM_MOUSEMOVE from the list of messages, and add a function by selecting OnMouseMove from the combo box.

FIGURE 4.1

Selecting the Messages mode in the Properties pane.

6. Add the boldfaced code in Listing 4.1.

LISTING 4.1   The `OnMouseMove` Function

```
void CMouseDlg::OnMouseMove(UINT nFlags, CPoint point)
{
    // TODO: Add your message handler code here and/or call default

    // Check to see if the left mouse button is down
    if ((nFlags & MK_LBUTTON) == MK_LBUTTON)
    {
        // Get the Device Context
        CClientDC dc(this);

        // Draw the pixel
        dc.SetPixel(point.x, point.y, RGB(0, 0, 0));
    }

    CDialog::OnMouseMove(nFlags, point);
}
```

INPUT

Look at the function definition at the top of the listing. You will notice that two arguments are passed into this function. The first of these arguments is a set of flags that is used to determine whether and which mouse button is depressed. This determination is made in the first line of your code with the `if` statement:

```
if ((nFlags & MK_LBUTTON) == MK_LBUTTON)
```

In the first half of the condition being evaluated, the flags are filtered down to the one that indicates that the left mouse button is down. In the second half, the filtered flags are compared to the flag that indicates that the left mouse button is down. If the two match, the left mouse button is down.

> **Tip**
>
> Actually, you can simplify the `if` expression by limiting it to the & operation. When you & the `nFlags` variable with the flag `MK_LBUTTON`, you'll have a positive value if the flag is set, or 0 if not. This can be evaluated as a Boolean in the `if` statement, as follows:
>
> ```
> if (nFlags & MK_LBUTTON)
> ```

The second argument to this function is the location of the mouse. This argument gives you the coordinates on the screen where the mouse currently is. You can use this information to draw a spot on the dialog window.

Before you can draw any spots on the dialog window, you need to get the device context for the dialog window. This is done by declaring a new instance of the `CClientDC` class.

This class encapsulates the device context and most of the operations that can be performed on it, including all screen-drawing operations. In a sense, the device context is the canvas upon which you draw with your application. Until you have a canvas, you can't do any drawing or painting. Once the device context object is created, you can call its SetPixel function, which colors the pixel at the location specified in the first two arguments with the color specified in the third argument. If you compile and run your program, you can see how it allows you to draw on the window surface with the mouse (see Figure 4.2).

FIGURE 4.2

Drawing on the window with the mouse.

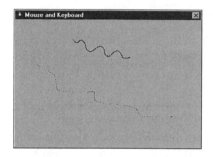

Tip

In Windows, each color is specified as a very large number that combines three different values: the brightness levels for the red, green, and blue pixels in your computer display. Each pixel in your monitor display is actually made up of three different color pixels combined to create the color you actually see. The RGB function in your code is a macro that combines these three separate values into the single number that must be passed to the SetPixel function or to any other function that requires a color value. These three numbers can be any value between and including 0 and 255. 0 is the darkest that an individual pixel can be; 255 is the brightest.

To see how the three color values work to create a specific color, open an application icon in the icon editor and choose Adjust Colors from the Image menu. Experiment putting different values from 0 to 255 in the Red, Green, and Blue edit boxes.

C++ Sidebar: Using the AND and OR Binaries

In C++, the two categories of ANDs and ORs are logical and binary. The logical ANDs and ORs are used in logical or conditional statements, such as an if or while statement that is controlling the logic flow. The binary ANDs and ORs are used to combine two values on a binary level.

In C/C++ you can do bit-wise comparisons and combinations by using the bit-operators. The bit operators are listed in Table 4.2.

TABLE 4.2   C/C++ Bit Operators

Operator	Description
&	Bit-level AND
&&	Logical AND
|	Bit-level OR
||	Logical OR
^	Bit-level XOR (Exclusive OR)
~	Bit-level complement
>>	Shift Right (bit-level)
<<	Shift Left (bit-level)

The ampersand character (&) is used to denote AND. A single ampersand (&) is a binary AND, and a double ampersand (&&) is a logical AND. A logical AND works much like the word AND in Visual Basic or PowerBuilder. It can be used in an if statement to say "if this condition AND this other condition..." where both conditions must be true before the entire statement is true. A binary AND is used to set or unset bits. When two values are binary ANDed, only the bits that are set to 1 in both values remain as 1; all the rest of the bits are set to 0. To understand how this works, start with two eight-bit values such as the following:

Value 1	01011001
Value 2	00101001

If you binary AND these two values together, you wind up with the following value:

ANDed Value	00001001

All the bits that had 1 in one of the values, but not in the other value, were set to 0. All the bits that were 1 in both values remained set to 1. All the bits that were 0 in both values remained 0.

OR is represented by the pipe character (|), and as with AND, a single pipe (|) is a binary OR, whereas a double pipe (||) is a logical OR. As with AND, a logical OR can be used in conditional statements such as if or while statements to control the logical flow, much like the word OR in Visual Basic and PowerBuilder. It can be used in an if statement to say "if this condition OR this other condition..." and if either condition is true, the entire statement is true. You can use a binary OR to combine values on a binary level. With OR, if a bit is set to 1 in either value, the resulting bit is set to 1. With a binary OR, the only way that a bit is set to 0 in the resulting value is if the bit was already 0 in both values. Take the same two values that were used to illustrate the binary AND:

Value 1	01011001
Value 2	00101001

If you binary OR these two values together, you get the following value:

ORed Value	01111001

In this case, every bit that was set to 1 in either value was set to 1 in the resulting value. Only those bits that were 0 in both values were 0 in the resulting value.

XOR (eXclusive OR) is represented by a caret (^). This operator works only on the binary level. The way that it works, is that when you take two binary values, the XOR operator looks at each bit in both values and returns a 1 in the bits where only one of the two values had a 1. If both values have a 1 in a bit, the resulting bit is 0. Likewise, if both values have a 0 in a particular bit, it remains 0 in the resulting value. For instance, if you XOR together the same two values that you've been looking at,

Value 1	01011001
Value 2	00101001

you get the following value:

XORed Value	01110000

In this case, only those bits where only one of the original two values had a 1 resulted in a 1. Otherwise, the result was a 0.

The complement operator is represented by a tilde (~). This operator works on a single binary value. It simply flips the binary values of each bit in a value. If a bit is set to 1, complement sets the bit to 0, and vice versa. To see how this works, take the first of the values that you have been working with:

Value 1	01011001

The complement of this value is the following value:

Complement value	10100110

4

The last two bit-level operators are the shifting operators. These two operators are used to shift the bits in a value to the right or left of a specific number of bits. For instance, if you needed to shift the first value to the right 3 bits, you would notate that as follows:

```
val2 = val1 >> 3;
```

How this would work is that the value

    Value 1   01011001

would be shifted to the right three bits, resulting in the following value:

    Shifted Value   00001011

Likewise, if this same value were shifted to the left three bits, you would notate that as follows:

```
val2 = val1 << 3;
```

How this would work is that the value

    Value 1   01011001

would be shifted to the left three bits, resulting in the following value:

    Shifted Value   11001111

Notice that the end bit is sometimes duplicated to fill in the missing bits that have to be added to either end of the value, depending on the system. As a result, bit-shifting is usually accompanied by masking the resulting value to zero-out the new bits. You would do this on the left-shifting example by enclosing the shifting in an AND mask:

```
val2 = (val1 << 3) & 0xF8;
```

The result of this operation would be the following value:

    Shifted Value   11001000

C++ Sidebar: Binary Attribute Flags

Binary ANDs and ORs are used in C++ for setting and reading attribute flags. Attribute flags are values where each bit in the value specifies whether a specific option is turned on or off. This enables programmers to use defined flags. A defined flag is a value with only one bit set to 1 or a combination of other values in which a specific combination of bits is set to 1 so that multiple options are set with a single value. The flags controlling various options are ORed together, making a composite flag specifying which options should be on and which should be off.

If two flags that specify certain conditions are specified as two different bits in a byte, those two flags can often be ORed together as follows:

Flag 1	00001000
Flag 2	00100000
Combination	**00101000**

This is how flags are combined to specify a number of settings in a limited amount of memory space. In fact, this is what is done with most of the true/false (on/off) settings on the window and control properties dialogs. These on/off settings are ORed together to form one or two sets of flags that are examined by the Windows operating system to determine how to display the window or control and how it should behave.

On the flip side of this process, when you need to determine if a specific flag is included in the combination, you can AND the combination flag with the specific flag that you are looking for as follows:

Combination	00101000
Flag 1	00001000
Result	**00001000**

The result of this operation can be compared to the flag that you used to filter the combined flag. If the result is the same, the flag was included. Another common approach is to check whether the filtered combination flag is nonzero. If the flag being used for filtering the combination hadn't been included, the resulting flag would be zero. As a result, you could have left the comparison out of the if statement in the preceding code, leaving you with an if statement that looks like the following:

```
if (nFlags & MK_LBUTTON)
```

You can modify this approach to check whether a flag isn't in the combination as follows:

```
if (!(nFlags & MK_LBUTTON))
```

You might find one of these ways of checking for a flag easier to understand than the others. You'll probably find all of them in use.

MFC Note: The Device Context

In Windows, you never directly interact with the display or other devices attached to the computer. Instead, you interact with what is known as the Device Context. This is an abstraction of the user display, or any other output device currently in use. This enables you to use the same drawing code to draw on the screen for the user display, or to the printer when printing the output of your program.

The device context is encapsulated in the CDC class, which is inherited by the CClientDC class in Listing 4.1. The CDC class provides you with functionality for drawing lines, filling in shapes, and any other base-level drawing functionality that you might need. The CClientDC class provides some housekeeping functionality that needs to perform before drawing, and clean-up functionality after finishing drawing around the CDC class.

You can't just declare an instance of the CDC or CClientDC classes and begin to draw. You need to get the device context for where you want to draw. In Listing 4.1, the constructor of the CClientDC class is passed this as its only argument. The variable this in this situation refers to the dialog window. What you're actually doing is passing a pointer to the dialog window to the constructor of the CClientDC class, which initializes the instance of the CClientDC class with the current device context of the dialog window. In future days, you'll learn a lot more about the device context and how you can use it to draw various figures on windows.

C++ Sidebar: Constructors and Destructors

In each C++ class are two methods that are always members of the class. These are the constructor and destructor methods. The constructor method always has the same name as the class (CMyClass), whereas the destructor method always has the class name, preceded with a tilde (~) as its name (~CMyClass). The constructor is automatically called when an instance of the class is created, and the destructor is automatically called when an instance of the class is destroyed. You needn't create either method if you don't need them, because the compiler will provide default methods if one or both methods are left out of your code.

You can create multiple constructors for a class, each with different set of parameters to pass. There are two methods of passing these parameters to the constructor, depending on whether you are creating an instance in the variable declaration or an instance that's assigned to a pointer. If you are creating an instance in the variable declaration, you pass the parameters to the variable in the declaration as follows:

```
CMyClass foo(param);
```

If you are creating a new instance of a class and storing it in a pointer, pass the parameters following the variable type declaration as follows:

```
CMyClass *pFoo;
pFoo = new CMyClass(param);
```

You can never have more than one `destructor`, and it never has any parameters.

C++ Sidebar: Dynamically Creating and Destroying Objects

Sometimes you need to dynamically create and destroy objects in your applications. Yes, you can do this by declaring them as variables, but there are many situations in which you need something more dynamic. This is when you use the `new` and `delete` keywords.

The `new` keyword is used in C++ to create an instance of a data type or class. The `delete` keyword is used to delete variables or objects that were created using the `new` keyword. You are responsible for keeping track of all objects and variables that you create using the `new` keyword and destroy them using the `delete` keyword. If you don't destroy all that you create, you end up with an application that has a memory leak. While you may not notice the memory leak during development and testing, if the application is run for long enough, it will eventually use up all of the memory available on the system, bringing all applications to a halt.

The syntax for the `new` keyword is to follow the keyword with the data type or class that you want to create. The return value is a pointer to the data type or class that was created. For instance, the way that the `new` keyword is used to create an integer is as follows:

```
int *pInt;
pInt = new int;
```

Likewise, to create an instance of a class, you'd use it as follows:

```
CMyClass *pMyClass;
pMyClass = new CMyClass;
```

If the class constructor requires parameters be passed to it, you need to pass them as follows:

```
pMyClass = new CMyClass(param1, param2,...);
```

If you don't add parenthesis after the class name, the default constructor for the class is called.

The syntax for the `delete` operator is just as simple. You follow the delete keyword with a pointer that is pointing to the variable or class instance that you want to delete, as follows:

```
delete pInt;
delete pMyClass;
```

If you allocate an array to a pointer, as follows:

```
int *pInt = new int[8];
```

You have to delete the memory allocated with the square brackets between the delete operator and the pointer, as follows:

```
delete [] pInt;
```

If you don't include the square brackets, not all of the memory allocated will be released.

> **Caution**
>
> After you delete a variable or class instance, don't try to access that variable or class instance again. Attempting to do so will result in a General Protection Fault in your application. Your application will halt immediately, losing any and all work that the user has done.

> **Tip**
>
> It's good coding practice to always initialize pointers to NULL as soon as the variable is created. Also, once objects allocated to the pointer are deleted, the pointer should be reset to NULL. Then, whenever you use the pointer, you should perform a check to make sure that the pointer is valid with a simple
>
> ```
>     if (pointer)   // If true, the pointer is valid
> ```
> or
> ```
>     if (!pointer)   // If true, the pointer is NOT valid
> ```
> This simple check can go a long way toward protecting your applications from causing any GPFs.

Improving the Drawing Program

If you ran your program, you probably noticed a small problem. To draw a solid line, you need to move the mouse very slowly. How do other painting programs solve this problem? Simple, they draw a line between two points drawn by the mouse. Although this seems a little like cheating, it's how computer drawing programs work.

As you move the mouse across the screen, your computer checks the location of the mouse every few clock ticks. Because your computer doesn't have a constant trail of where your mouse has gone, it has to make some assumptions. The way your computer makes these assumptions is by taking the points that the computer does know about and drawing lines between them. When you draw lines with the freehand tool in Paint, your computer is playing connect the dots.

All the major drawing programs draw lines between each pair of points. So, what do you do to adapt your application so it uses this same technique? First, you need to keep track of the previous position of the mouse. This means you need to add two variables to the dialog window to maintain the previous X and Y coordinates. You can do this by following these steps:

1. Select the Class View pane.

2. Select the dialog class—in this case, the CMouseDlg class.

3. Right-click the mouse and select Add and then Add Variable from the context menu.

4. Enter **int** as the Variable Type and **m_iPrevY** as the Variable Name, and specify private for the access in the Add Member Variable dialog (see Figure 4.3).

FIGURE 4.3

The Add Member Variable dialog.

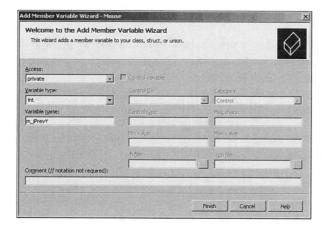

5. Click Finish to add the variable.

6. Repeat steps 3–5, specifying the Variable Name as **m_iPrevX** to add the second variable.

After you add the variables needed to track the previous mouse position, you can make the necessary modifications to the OnMouseMove function, as shown in Listing 4.2.

LISTING 4.2 The Revised OnMouseMove Function

```
void CMouseDlg::OnMouseMove(UINT nFlags, CPoint point)
{
    // TODO: Add your message handler code here and/or call default

    // Check to see if the left mouse button is down
    if ((nFlags & MK_LBUTTON) == MK_LBUTTON)
```

LISTING 4.2   continued

```
    {
            // Get the Device Context
            CClientDC dc(this);

            // Draw a line from the previous point to the current point
            dc.MoveTo(m_iPrevX, m_iPrevY);
            dc.LineTo(point.x, point.y);

            // Save the current point as the previous point
            m_iPrevX = point.x;
            m_iPrevY = point.y;
    }

    CDialog::OnMouseMove(nFlags, point);
}
```

Look at the code that draws the line from the previous point to the current point:

```
dc.MoveTo(m_iPrevX, m_iPrevY);
dc.LineTo(point.x, point.y);
```

You see that you need to move to the first position and then draw a line to the second point. The first step is important because without it, there is no telling where Windows might think the starting position is. If you compile and run your application, it draws a bit better. However, it now has a peculiar behavior. Every time you press the left mouse button to begin drawing some more, your application draws a line from where you ended the last line you drew (see Figure 4.4).

> **Tip**
>
> You could substitute a single CPoint variable for the two integer variables. This would allow you to simplify the code by setting the value of the variable as follows:
>
> ```
> m_pPrevPoint = point;
> ```
>
> and perform the drawing as follows:
>
> ```
> dc.MoveTo(m_pPrevPoint);
> dc.LineTo(point);
> ```

FIGURE 4.4

The drawing program with a peculiar behavior.

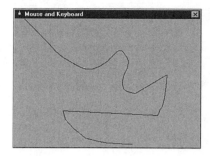

Adding the Finishing Touches

Your application is doing all its drawing on the mouse move event when the left button is held down. Initializing the previous position variables with the position of the mouse when the left button is pressed should correct this application's behavior. Let's try this approach by following these steps:

1. Using the Messages mode of the Properties pane, add a function for the WM_LBUTTONDOWN message on the dialog object. The dialog messages are available only if the dialog is in the resource editor and is selected and active.

2. Edit the OnLButtonDown function that you just created, adding the code in Listing 4.3.

LISTING 4.3 The OnLButtonDown Function

```
void CMouseDlg::OnLButtonDown(UINT nFlags, CPoint point)
{
    // TODO: Add your message handler code here and/or call default

    // Set the current point as the starting point
    m_iPrevX = point.x;
    m_iPrevY = point.y;

    CDialog::OnLButtonDown(nFlags, point);
}
```

INPUT

When you compile and run your application, you should find that you can draw much like you would expect with a drawing program (see Figure 4.5).

4

Figure 4.5

The finished drawing program.

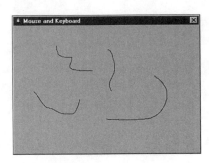

Capturing Keyboard Events

Reading keyboard events is similar to reading mouse events. As with the mouse, there are event messages for when a key is pressed and when it's released. These events are listed in Table 4.3.

Table 4.3   Keyboard Event Messages

Message	Description
WM_KEYDOWN	A key has been pressed down.
WM_KEYUP	A key has been released.
WM_SYSKEYDOWN	F10 or Alt has been pressed down with another key.
WM_SYSKEYUP	F10 or Alt key combination has been released.

The keyboard obviously has fewer messages than the mouse does. Then again, there are only so many things that you can do with the keyboard. These event messages are available on the dialog window object and are only triggered if there are no enabled controls on the window. Any enabled controls that are on the window have input focus, so all keyboard events go to them. That's why you remove all controls from the main dialog for your drawing application.

Changing the Drawing Cursor

To get a good idea of how you can use keyboard-related event messages, why don't you use certain keys to change the mouse cursor in your drawing application? Make the A key change the cursor to the default arrow cursor, which your application starts with. Then you can make B change the cursor to the I-beam and C change the cursor to the hourglass. You'll also make the X key exit the application. To get started adding this functionality, follow these steps:

1. Using the Messages mode of the Properties pane, add a function for the WM_KEY-DOWN message on the dialog object. The dialog messages are available only if the dialog is in the resource editor and the dialog is selected and active.

2. Edit the OnKeyDown function that you just created, adding the code in Listing 4.4.

LISTING 4.4 The OnKeyDown Function

```
void CMouseDlg::OnKeyDown(UINT nChar, UINT nRepCnt, UINT nFlags)
{
    // TODO: Add your message handler code here and/or call default

    char cChar;          // The current character being pressed
    HCURSOR hCursor = 0;     // The handle to the cursor to be displayed
    HCURSOR hPrevCursor = 0; // The handle to the previous cursor
    // Convert the key pressed to a character
    cChar = char(nChar);

    // Is the character "A"
    if (cChar == 'A')
    {
        // Load the arrow cursor
        hCursor = AfxGetApp()->LoadStandardCursor(IDC_ARROW);
        // Set the screen cursor
        hPrevCursor = SetCursor(hCursor);
    }

    // Is the character "B"
    if (cChar == 'B')
    {
        // Load the I beam cursor
        hCursor = AfxGetApp()->LoadStandardCursor(IDC_IBEAM);
        // Set the screen cursor
        hPrevCursor = SetCursor(hCursor);
    }

    // Is the character "C"
    if (cChar == 'C')
    {
        // Load the hourglass cursor
        hCursor = AfxGetApp()->LoadStandardCursor(IDC_WAIT);
        // Set the screen cursor
        hPrevCursor = SetCursor(hCursor);
    }

    // Destroy the previous cursor to free up the resources
    if (hPrevCursor)
        DestroyCursor(hPrevCursor);
```

INPUT

4

LISTING 4.4   continued

```
// Is the character "X"
if (cChar == 'X')
{
    // Load the arrow cursor
    hCursor = AfxGetApp()->LoadStandardCursor(IDC_ARROW);
    // Set the screen cursor
    hPrevCursor = SetCursor(hCursor);
    // Destroy the previous cursor to free up the resources
    if (hPrevCursor)
        DestroyCursor(hPrevCursor);
    // Exit the application
    OnOK();
}

CDialog::OnKeyDown(nChar, nRepCnt, nFlags);
}
```

In the function definition, you see three arguments to the OnKeyDown function. The first, nChar, is the key that was pressed. This argument is the character code of the character, which needs to be converted into a character in the first line of your code. Once you convert the character, you can perform straight-ahead comparisons to determine which key was pressed:

```
void CMouseDlg::OnKeyDown(UINT nChar, UINT nRepCnt, UINT nFlags)
```

The second argument to the OnKeyDown function, nRepCnt, is the number of times that the key is pressed. Normally, if the key is pressed and then released, this value is 1. If the key is pressed and held down, however, the repeat count rises for this key. In the end, this value tells you how many times that Windows thinks the key has been pressed.

The third argument to the OnKeyDown function, nFlags, is a combination flag that can be examined to determine whether the Alt key was pressed at the same time as the key or whether the key being pressed is an extended key. This argument doesn't tell you whether the shift or control keys were pressed.

Note   You don't have to check for both upper- and lowercase characters because the WM_KEYDOWN event message gives you only the uppercase character code. The Shift and Caps Lock keys are passed as separate key codes. If you need to know whether a character is upper- or lowercase, you are responsible for keeping track of when the Shift or Caps Lock key is pressed and released.

As soon as you determine that a specific key was pressed, you change the cursor to whichever cursor is associated with that key. There are two steps to this process. The first step is to load the cursor into memory. You accomplish this step with the LoadStandardCursor function, which loads one of the standard Windows cursors and returns a handle to the cursor.

> **Note**
>
> A sister function, LoadCursor, can be passed the file or resource name of a custom cursor so that you can create and load your own cursors. If you design your own cursor in the resource editor in Visual C++, you can pass the cursor name as the only argument to the LoadCursor function. For example, if you create your own cursor and name it IDC_MYCURSOR, you can load it with the following line of code:
>
> ```
>     lhCursor = AfxGetApp()->LoadCursor(IDC_MYCURSOR);
> ```
>
> After you load your own cursor, you can set the mouse pointer to your cursor using the SetCursor function, as with a standard cursor.

After the cursor is loaded into memory, the handle to that cursor is passed to the SetCursor function, which switches the cursor to the one the handle points to. SetCursor returns the handle to the previous cursor. You can destroy the previous cursor by using the DestroyCursor function. If you compile and run your application, you should be able to press one of these keys and get the cursor to change (see Figure 4.6). However, the moment you move the mouse to do any drawing, the cursor switches back to the default arrow cursor. The following section explains how to make your change stick.

4

FIGURE 4.6

Changing the cursor with specific keys.

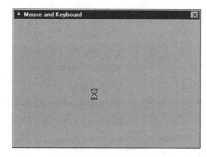

MFC Note: The `AfxGetApp` Function

In Listing 4.4, you see the `AfxGetApp` function being called along with the `LoadStandardCursor` function, as follows:

```
lhCursor = AfxGetApp()->LoadStandardCursor(IDC_ARROW);
```

Because this function is using a pointer to call the `LoadStandardCursor` function, you can safely assume that it's returning a pointer to some class. The `AfxGetApp` function is a global function that returns the instance of the application class for the current application. The application class is the descendent class of the `CWinApp` class that is in the current application. For this application, this is the `CMouseApp` class. When you need to access functionality that is encapsulated in the `CWinApp` class, or its current descendent, you can use the `AfxGetApp` function to get a pointer to it.

If you dig around in your source code, you'll find a globally declared variable for your application class, as follows:

```
CMouseApp theApp;
```

Despite this variable declaration existing in the code, you can't directly use or reference this variable. You have to use the `AfxGetApp` function to call or reference the application object.

C++ Sidebar: Using Quotation Marks

In Listing 4.4, you used the following code to compare the key that was pressed with individual characters:

```
if (lsChar == 'A')
```

Something important to note here is the use of quotes around the character. Single quotes (`'`) are being used because you are comparing a single character to another single character. This isn't a string comparison, but a character comparison. If the character being compared were enclosed in double quotes (`"`), the compiler would see it as a string and throw an error on this line of code. You can't compare a single character to a string, only to other single characters. When a single character is enclosed with single-quotes, the compiler recognizes it as a single character and compares the binary value of the character to the binary value of the character variable.

Making the Change Stick

The problem with your drawing program is that the cursor is redrawn every time you move the mouse. There must be some way of turning off this behavior.

Each time the cursor needs to be redrawn—because the mouse has moved, because another window that was in front of your application has gone away, or because of whatever other reason—a WM_SETCURSOR event message is sent to your application. If you override the native behavior of your application on this event, the cursor you set remains unchanged until you change it again. To do this, follow these steps:

1. Add a new variable to the CMouseDlg class, as you did for the previous position variables. This time, declare the type as BOOL, name the variable m_bCursor, and specify the access as private (see Figure 4.7).

FIGURE 4.7

Defining a class member variable.

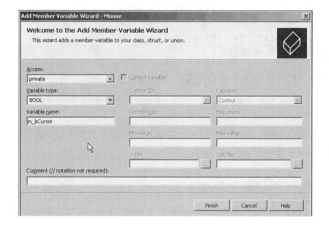

2. Initialize the m_bCursor variable in the OnInitDialog with the code in Listing 4.5.

LISTING 4.5   The OnInitDialog Function

```
BOOL CMouseDlg::OnInitDialog()
{
    CDialog::OnInitDialog();

    // Add "About..." menu item to system menu.

    // IDM_ABOUTBOX must be in the system command range.
    ASSERT((IDM_ABOUTBOX & 0xFFF0) == IDM_ABOUTBOX);
    ASSERT(IDM_ABOUTBOX < 0xF000);

    CMenu* pSysMenu = GetSystemMenu(FALSE);
    if (pSysMenu != NULL)
    {
        CString strAboutMenu;
        strAboutMenu.LoadString(IDS_ABOUTBOX);
        if (!strAboutMenu.IsEmpty())
        {
```

LISTING 4.5 continued

```
                pSysMenu->AppendMenu(MF_SEPARATOR);
                pSysMenu->AppendMenu(MF_STRING, IDM_ABOUTBOX, strAboutMenu);
        }
    }

    // Set the icon for this dialog.  The framework does this automatically
    //  when the application's main window is not a dialog
    SetIcon(m_hIcon, TRUE);             // Set big icon
    SetIcon(m_hIcon, FALSE);        // Set small icon

    // TODO: Add extra initialization here
```

INPUT

```
    // Initialize the cursor to the arrow
    m_bCursor = FALSE;

    return TRUE;  // return TRUE  unless you set the focus to a control
}
```

3. Alter the OnKeyDown function to set the m_bCursor flag to TRUE when you change the cursor (see Listing 4.6).

LISTING 4.6 The OnKeyDown Function

```
void CMouseDlg::OnKeyDown(UINT nChar, UINT nRepCnt, UINT nFlags)
{
    // TODO: Add your message handler code here and/or call default

    char cChar;         // The current character being pressed
    HCURSOR hCursor = 0;    // The handle to the cursor to be displayed
    HCURSOR hPrevCursor = 0;  // The handle to the previous cursor
    // Convert the key pressed to a character
    cChar = char(nChar);
```

INPUT

```
    // Is the character "A"
    if (cChar == 'A')
        // Load the arrow cursor
        hCursor = AfxGetApp()->LoadStandardCursor(IDC_ARROW);

    // Is the character "B"
    if (cChar == 'B')
        // Load the I beam cursor
        hCursor = AfxGetApp()->LoadStandardCursor(IDC_IBEAM);

    // Is the character "C"
    if (cChar == 'C')
        // Load the hourglass cursor
        hCursor = AfxGetApp()->LoadStandardCursor(IDC_WAIT);
```

LISTING 4.6 continued

```
        // Is the character "X"
        if (cChar == 'X')
        {
            // Load the arrow cursor
            hCursor = AfxGetApp()->LoadStandardCursor(IDC_ARROW);
            // Set the cursor flag
            m_bCursor = TRUE;
            // Set the screen cursor
            hPrevCursor = SetCursor(hCursor);
            // Destroy the previous cursor to free up the resources
            if (hPrevCursor)
                DestroyCursor(hPrevCursor);
            // Exit the application
            OnOK();
        }
        else
        {
            // Set the screen cursor
            if (hCursor)
            {
                hPrevCursor = SetCursor(hCursor);
                // Set the cursor flag
                m_bCursor = TRUE;
                // Destroy the previous cursor to free up the resources
                if (hPrevCursor)
                    DestroyCursor(hPrevCursor);
            }
        }

    CDialog::OnKeyDown(nChar, nRepCnt, nFlags);
}
```

4. Using the Messages mode of the Properties pane, add a function for the WM_SETCURSOR message on the dialog object. The dialog messages are only available if the dialog is in the resource editor and is selected and active.

5. Edit the OnSetCursor function that you just created, adding the code in Listing 4.7.

LISTING 4.7 The OnSetCursor Function

```
BOOL CMouseDlg::OnSetCursor(CWnd* pWnd, UINT nHitTest, UINT message)
{
    // TODO: Add your message handler code here and/or call default

    if (m_bCursor)
        // return TRUE
        return TRUE;
```

INPUT

LISTING 4.7   continued

```
        return CDialog::OnSetCursor(pWnd, nHitTest, message);
}
```

The OnSetCursor function needs to always return TRUE or else call the base function. The base function resets the cursor and does need to be called when the application first starts. Because of this, you need to initialize your variable to FALSE so that until the user presses a key to change the cursor, the default OnSetCursor processing is executed. Once the user changes the cursor, you want to bypass the default processing and return TRUE instead. This allows the user to draw with whichever cursor the user has selected, including the hourglass (see Figure 4.8).

FIGURE 4.8

Drawing with the hourglass cursor.

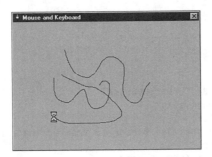

> **Note**
>
> The most common cursor change that you are likely to use in your programs is setting the cursor to the hourglass while your program is working on something that might take a while. There are actually two functions available in MFC that you can use to handle this task. The first is BeginWaitCursor, which displays the hourglass cursor for the user. The second function is EndWaitCursor, which restores the cursor to the default cursor. Both of these functions are members of the CCmdTarget class, from which all the MFC window and control classes are derived.
>
> If you have a single function controlling all the processing during which you need to display the hourglass and you don't need to display the hourglass after the function has finished, declare a variable of the CWaitCursor class at the beginning of the function. This automatically displays the hourglass cursor for the user. As soon as the program exits the function, the cursor will be restored to the previous cursor.

Summary

In this chapter, you learned how you can capture mouse event messages and perform some simple processing based upon these events. You used the mouse events to build a simple drawing program that you could use to draw freehand figures on a dialog window.

You also learned how to grab keyboard events and determine which key is being pressed. You used this information to determine which cursor to display for drawing. For this to work, you had to learn the default cursor drawing in MFC applications and how to integrate your code with this behavior to make your application behave the way you want it.

From here, you will learn how to use the Windows timer to trigger events at regular intervals. You will also learn how to use additional dialog windows to get feedback from the user so that you can integrate that feedback into how your application behaves. After that, you will learn how to create menus for your applications.

Q&A

Q. How can I change the type of line that I am drawing? I want to be able to draw a larger line with a different color.

A. When you use any of the standard device context commands to draw on the screen, you are drawing with what is known as a pen, much like the pen you use to draw on a piece of paper. To draw bigger lines, or different color lines, you need to select a new pen. You can do this by adapting the code in the OnMouseMove function, starting where you get the device context. The following code enables you to draw with a big red pen:

```
// Get the Device Context
CClientDC dc(this);

// Create a new pen
CPen lpen(PS_SOLID, 16, RGB(255, 0, 0));

// Use the new pen
dc.SelectObject(&lpen);

// Draw a line from the previous point to the current point
dc.MoveTo(m_iPrevX, m_iPrevY);
dc.LineTo(point.x, point.y);
```

4

Q. **How can you tell whether the Shift or Ctrl keys are being held down when you receive the WM_KEYDOWN message?**

A. You can call another function, `::GetKeyState`, with a specific key code to determine whether that key is being held down. If the return value of the `::GetKeyState` function is negative, the key is being held down. If the return value is not negative, the key isn't being held down. For instance, if you want to determine whether the Shift key is being held down, you can use this code:

```
if (::GetKeyState(VK_SHIFT) < 0)
    MessageBox("Shift key is down!");
```

A number of virtual key codes are defined in Windows for all the special keys. These codes let you look for special keys without worrying about OEM scan codes or other key sequences. You can use these virtual key codes in the `::GetKeyState` function and pass them to the `OnKeyDown` function as the `nChar` argument. Refer to the Visual C++ documentation for a list of the virtual key codes.

Workshop

The Workshop provides quiz questions to help you solidify your understanding of the material covered and exercises to provide you with experience in using what you've learned. The answers to the quiz questions are provided in Appendix A, "Answers to Quiz Questions."

Quiz

1. What are the possible mouse messages that you can add functions for?

2. How can you tell if the left mouse button is down on the WM_MOUSEMOVE event message?

3. How can you prevent the cursor from changing back to the default cursor after you set it to a different one?

Exercises

1. Modify your drawing program so that the left mouse button can draw in red, defined as RGB(255, 0, 0), and the right mouse button can draw in blue, defined as RGB(0, 0, 255).

2. Extend the OnKeyDown function in Listing 4.4 to add some of the following standard cursors:

    - IDC_CROSS

    - IDC_UPARROW

    - IDC_SIZEALL

- IDC_SIZENWSE
- IDC_SIZENESW
- IDC_SIZEWE
- IDC_SIZENS
- IDC_NO
- IDC_APPSTARTING
- IDC_HELP

4

DAY 5

Working with Timers

You may often find yourself building an application that needs to perform a specific action regularly. The task can be something simple, such as checking for e-mail messages every 30 minutes or writing a recovery file every five minutes. Both actions are regularly performed by applications that you probably use daily. Other actions that you might need to perform include checking specific resources regularly, like a resource monitor or performance monitor does. These examples are just a few of the situations where you want to take advantage of the availability of timers in the Windows operating system.

Today you will learn how to

- Control and use timers in your Visual C++ applications
- Set multiple timers, each with a different recurrence interval
- Know which timer has triggered
- Incorporate this important resource into all your Visual C++ applications

Understanding Windows Timers

 Windows *timers* are a mechanism that let you set one or more events to be triggered at a specific number of milliseconds. If you set a timer to be triggered at a 1000 millisecond interval, it triggers every second. When a timer triggers, it sends a WM_TIMER message to your application. You can use the Class Wizard to add a function to your application to handle this timer message.

Timer events are placed in the application event queue only if that queue is empty and the application is idle. Windows doesn't place timer event messages in the application event queue if the application is already busy. If your application has been busy and has missed several timer event messages, Windows places only a single timer message in the event queue. Windows doesn't send your application all the timer event messages that occurred while your application was busy. It doesn't matter how many timer messages your application may have missed; Windows still places only a single timer message in your queue.

When you start or stop a timer, you specify a timer ID, which can be any integer value. Your application uses this timer ID to determine which timer event has triggered, as well as to start and stop timers. You'll get a better idea of how this process works as you build your application for today.

Placing a Clock on Your Application

In the application that you will build today, you will use two timers. The first timer maintains a clock on the window that runs as long as the application is running. The second timer is configurable to trigger at whatever interval the user specifies in the dialog. Users can start and stop this timer at will.

Creating the Project and Application

You will build today's sample application in three phases:

1. Add all the controls necessary for the entire application.
2. Add the first of the two timers. This first timer will control the clock on the application dialog.
3. Add the second timer, which the user can tune, start, and stop as desired.

To create today's application, follow these steps:

1. Create a new MFC Application Visual C++ project named Timers.
2. Specify this project to be a dialog-based application in the MFC Application Wizard.
3. Use the default settings in the MFC Application Wizard.
4. Lay out the dialog window as shown in Figure 5.1, using the control properties in Table 5.1.

FIGURE 5.1

The Timers application dialog layout.

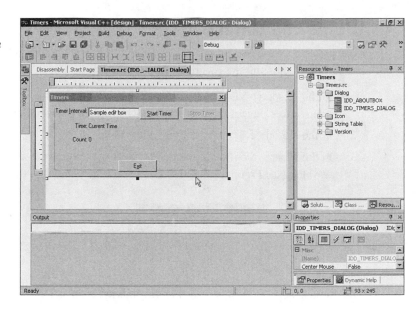

TABLE 5.1 Control Property Settings

Object	Property	Setting
Static Text	Caption	`Timer &Interval:`
Edit Box	ID	`IDC_EINTERVAL`
Button	ID	`IDC_BSTARTTIME`
	Caption	`&Start Timer`
Button	ID	`IDC_BSTOPTIMER`
	Caption	`S&top Timer`
	Disabled	TRUE
Static Text	Caption	`Time:`
Static Text	ID	`IDC_STATICTIME`
	Caption	`Current Time`
Static Text	Caption	`Count:`
Static Text	ID	`IDC_STATICCOUNT`
	Caption	`0`
Button	ID	`IDC_BEXIT`
	Caption	`E&xit`

5. Set the tab order as you learned on Day 3, "Using Controls in Your Application."

6. Add code to the Exit button to close the application, as you did on Day 3.

Adding the Timer IDs

Because you will use two timers in this application, you should add two IDs to your application to represent the two timer IDs. Follow these steps:

1. On the Resource View pane, right-click the Timers.rc folder at the top of the resource tree. Select Resource Symbols from the pop-up menu.

2. On the Resource Symbols dialog, click New.

3. On the New Symbol dialog, enter **ID_CLOCK_TIMER** as the symbol name and **1** as the value (see Figure 5.2). Click OK to add the symbol to the project.

FIGURE 5.2

Adding a new resource symbol.

4. Repeat steps 2 and 3, specifying **ID_COUNT_TIMER** as the symbol name and **2** as the value.

5. Click Close to close the Resource Symbols dialog. The two timer IDs are now in your application and ready for use.

Starting the Clock Timer

To start the clock timer, you need to edit the OnInitDialog function, as you did the previous two days. Add the new code in Listing 5.1.

LISTING 5.1   The OnInitDialog Function

```
BOOL CTimersDlg::OnInitDialog()
{
    CDialog::OnInitDialog();

    // Add "About..." menu item to system menu.

    // IDM_ABOUTBOX must be in the system command range.
    ASSERT((IDM_ABOUTBOX & 0xFFF0) == IDM_ABOUTBOX);
    ASSERT(IDM_ABOUTBOX < 0xF000);

    CMenu* pSysMenu = GetSystemMenu(FALSE);
    if (pSysMenu != NULL)
    {
        CString strAboutMenu;
        strAboutMenu.LoadString(IDS_ABOUTBOX);
        if (!strAboutMenu.IsEmpty())
        {
            pSysMenu->AppendMenu(MF_SEPARATOR);
```

LISTING 5.1   continued

```
                pSysMenu->AppendMenu(MF_STRING, IDM_ABOUTBOX, strAboutMenu);
        }
    }

    // Set the icon for this dialog. The framework does this automatically
    // when the application's main window is not a dialog
    SetIcon(m_hIcon, TRUE);            // Set big icon
    SetIcon(m_hIcon, FALSE);          // Set small icon

    // TODO: Add extra initialization here
```

INPUT
```
    // Start the clock timer
    SetTimer(ID_CLOCK_TIMER, 1000, NULL);
```

```
    return TRUE;  // return TRUE  unless you set the focus to a control
}
```

In this listing, you started the clock timer with the SetTimer function. The first argument that you passed to SetTimer is the clock timer's ID. The second argument specifies how often you want to trigger the event. In this case, the clock timer event is triggered every 1,000 milliseconds, or about every second. The third argument is the address of an optional callback function that you can specify to bypass the WM_TIMER event. If you pass NULL for this argument, the WM_TIMER event is placed in the application message queue.

Note

> A *callback* function is one you create that's called directly by the Windows operating system. Callback functions have specific argument definitions, depending on which subsystem calls the function and why. After you get past the function definition, however, you can do whatever you want or need to do in the function.
>
> A callback function works by passing the function's address as an argument to a Windows function that accepts callback functions as arguments. After you pass the function address to Windows, your function is called directly every time circumstances occur that require Windows to call the callback function.

5

Handling the Clock Timer Event

Now that you've started a timer, you need to add the code to handle the timer event message. Follow these steps:

1. Add a variable to the IDC_STATICTIME control of type CString named m_sTime.

2. Add a function to handle the WM_TIMER message for the CTimersDlg object.

3. Edit the OnTimer function, adding the code in Listing 5.2.

LISTING 5.2   The OnTimer Function

```
void CTimersDlg::OnTimer(UINT nIDEvent)
{
    // TODO: Add your message handler code here and/or call default
    // Get the current time
    CTime curTime = CTime::GetCurrentTime();

    // Display the current time
    m_sTime = curTime.Format("%H:%M:%S");

    // Update the dialog
    UpdateData(FALSE);

    CDialog::OnTimer(nIDEvent);
}
```

INPUT

The code in Listing 5.2 declares an instance of the CTime class, initializing it to the current system time. Next, it sets the m_sTime string to the current time, using the Format method to format the time in the familiar HH:MM:SS format. Finally, the code updates the dialog with the current time. If you compile and run your application now, you should see a clock running in the middle of your dialog (see Figure 5.3).

FIGURE 5.3

*A running clock
on your application
dialog.*

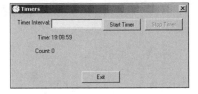

MFC Note: The CTime Class

The CTime class encapsulates much of the date/time functionality that you might need in your applications. CTime is built around the coordinated universal time (UTC), which is the same as Greenwich Mean Time (GMT). This enables you to easily work with both the local time(based on your computer's configuration) and the GMT.

Creating and Initializing the Date and Time

If you create a CTime object with just a simple declaration, you end up with an empty CTime object that can't be used until you've initialized it with a time. As such, this isn't a very practical method for creating a CTime object. There are actually several methods for creating a CTime object, initializing it when it's created. One method is used in Listing 5.2:

```
CTime curTime = CTime::GetCurrentTime();
```

Here, the code takes the `GetCurrentTime` method, which returns a `CTime` object, to initialize the new instance with the current date and time. Another method of creating and initializing the `CTime` object is to use the following version of the constructor:

```
CTime(int iYear, int iMonth, int iDay, int iHour, int iMin,
      int iSec, int iDst);
```

This version of the constructor passes values for the year, month, day, hour, minute, and second with which you want to initialize the object. The last parameter, *iDst*, specifies whether to use Daylight Savings Time. If *iDst* is 0, standard time is in effect; if *iDst* is greater than 0, Daylight Savings Time is in effect; if *iDst* is less than zero (the default if you choose not to provide this parameter), whether Daylight Savings Time is in effect is determined automatically based on the computer's configuration.

Getting the Date and Time

After you create and initialize a `CTime` object, you need to be able to retrieve the date and time out of the object. Table 5.2 lists several functions for doing this.

TABLE 5.2 CTime Date/Time Retrieval Functions

Function	Description
GetYear	Returns the year.
GetMonth	Returns the month.
GetDay	Returns the day of the month.
GetHour	Returns the hour.
GetMinute	Returns the minute.
GetSecond	Returns the second.
GetDayOfWeek	Returns the day of the week (1 = Sunday, 7 = Saturday).
Format	Returns a `CString` of the local time, formatted as specified in the format string passed to this function as a parameter. Table 5.3 lists the format codes.
FormatGmt	Returns a `CString` of the GMT time, formatted as specified in the format string passed to this function as a parameter. Table 5.3 lists the format codes.

TABLE 5.3 CTime Date/Time Formatting Codes

Format Code	Description
%a	The abbreviated weekday name.
%A	The full weekday name.
%b	The abbreviated month name.

5

TABLE 5.3 continued

Format Code	Description
%B	The full month name.
%c	The date and time standard format for the configured location.
%d	The day of the month.
%D	The total days in the CTime.
%H	The hour in 24-hour time format.
%I	The hour in 12-hour time format.
%j	The day of the year.
%m	The month as an integer.
%M	The minute.
%p	The AM/PM indicator.
%S	The seconds.
%U	The week of the year as a number, with Sunday as the first day of the week.
%w	The weekday as a number.
%W	The week of the year as a number, with Monday as the first day of the week.
%x	The date in the standard local format.
%X	The time in the standard local format.
%y	The year without the century (2-digit).
%Y	The year with the century.
%z, %Z	The time zone name or abbreviation.
%%	A percent sign.

Adding a Second Timer to Your Application

As you've seen, adding a single timer to an application is pretty simple. All it takes is calling the SetTimer function and then placing the timer code in the OnTimer function. However, sometimes you need more than one timer running simultaneously in the same application. Then things get a little bit more involved.

Adding the Application Variables

Before you add the second timer to your application, you need to add a few variables to the controls. With the clock timer, you needed only a single variable for updating the clock display. Now you need to add a few other variables for the other controls, as listed in Table 5.4

While adding the variable for the IDC_INTERVAL control, follow these steps:

1. Specify a Minimum Value of 1 and a Maximum Value of 100000 in the two edit boxes (see figure 5.4).

TABLE 5.4   Control Variables

Object	Name	Category	Type
IDC_STATICCOUNT	m_sCount	Value	CString
IDC_BSTARTTIME	m_cStartTime	Control	CButton
IDC_BSTOPTIMER	m_cStopTime	Control	CButton
IDC_EINTERVAL	m_iInterval	Value	int

FIGURE 5.4

Specifying a range for a variable.

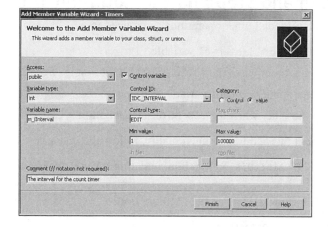

2. On the Class View pane, add a member variable to the CTimersDlg class as you learned yesterday. Specify the variable type as int, the variable name as m_iCount, and the access as Private.

3. Add a function on the EN_CHANGE event message for the IDC_EINTERVAL control ID (the edit box). Edit the function and add the code in Listing 5.3.

LISTING 5.3   The OnEnChangeEinterval Function

```
void CTimersDlg::OnEnChangeEinterval()
{
    // TODO:  If this is a RICHEDIT control, the control will not
    // send this notification unless you override the
    // CDialog::OnInitDialog()function and call
    // CRichEditCtrl().SetEventMask() with the ENM_CHANGE flag ORed
    // into the mask.
```

5

Listing **5.3**　continued

```
        // TODO:  Add your control notification handler code here
        // Update the variables
        UpdateData(TRUE);
    }
```

INPUT

When you specify a value range for the timer interval variable, Visual C++ automatically prompts the user, stating the available value range if the user enters a value outside of the specified range. This prompt is triggered by the `UpdateData` function call in the `OnEnChangeEinterval` function. The last variable added through the workspace pane is used as the actual counter, which is incremented with each timer event.

Starting and Stopping the Counting Timer

To make your second timer operational, you need to

- Initialize the `m_iInterval` variable.
- Start the timer when the `IDC_BSTARTTIME` button is clicked.
- Increment the `m_iCount` variable and update the dialog on each timer event.
- Stop the timer when the `IDC_BSTOPTIMER` button is clicked.

To implement this additional functionality, follow these steps:

1. Edit the `OnInitDialog` function, updating the code as in Listing 5.4.

Listing **5.4**　The Updated `OnInitDialog` Function

```
BOOL CTimersDlg::OnInitDialog()
{
    CDialog::OnInitDialog();
...
        // TODO: Add extra initialization here
        // Initialize the counter interval
        m_iInterval = 100;

        // Update the dialog
        UpdateData(FALSE);

        // Start the clock timer
        SetTimer(ID_CLOCK_TIMER, 1000, NULL);

        return TRUE;  // return TRUE  unless you set the focus to a control
    }
```

INPUT

2. Add a function to the BN_CLICKED message on the IDC_BSTARTTIME button. Edit the OnBnClickedBstarttime function as in Listing 5.5.

LISTING 5.5   The OnBnClickedBstarttime Function.

```
void CTimersDlg::OnBnClickedBstarttime()
{
    // TODO: Add your control notification handler code here
    // Update the variables
    UpdateData(TRUE);

    // Initialize the count
    m_iCount = 0;
    // Format the count for displaying
    m_sCount.Format("%d", m_iCount);

    // Update the dialog
    UpdateData(FALSE);
    // Start the timer
    SetTimer(ID_COUNT_TIMER, m_iInterval, NULL);
}
```

INPUT

3. Add a function to the BN_CLICKED message on the IDC_BSTOPTIMER button. Edit the OnBnClickedBstoptimer function as follows:

```
void CTimersDlg::OnBnClickedBstoptimer()
{
    // TODO: Add your control notification handler code here
    // Stop the timer
    KillTimer(ID_COUNT_TIMER);
}
```

INPUT

4. Edit the OnTimer function, updating the code as in Listing 5.6.

LISTING 5.6   The Updated OnTimer Function

```
void CTimersDlg::OnTimer(UINT nIDEvent)
{
    // TODO: Add your message handler code here and/or call default
    // Get the current time
    CTime curTime = CTime::GetCurrentTime();

    // Which timer triggered this event?
    switch (nIDEvent)
    {
        // The clock timer?
    case ID_CLOCK_TIMER:
        // Display the current time
```

INPUT

5

LISTING 5.6   continued

```
        m_sTime = curTime.Format("%H:%M:%S");
        break;
        // The count timer?
    case ID_COUNT_TIMER:
        // Increment the count
        m_iCount++;
        // Format and display the count
        m_sCount.Format("%d", m_iCount);
        break;
    }

    // Update the dialog
    UpdateData(FALSE);

    CDialog::OnTimer(nIDEvent);
}
```

To the OnInitDialog function, you added the initialization of the m_iInterval variable, starting it at 100. This initialization is reflected on the dialog window by calling the UpdateData function.

The OnBnClickedBstarttime function first synchronizes the variables with the control values, allowing you to get the current setting of the m_iInterval variable. Next, it initializes the m_iCount variable, setting it to 0, and formats the value in the m_sCount CString variable, which is updated in the dialog window. Finally, it starts the timer, specifying the ID_COUNT_TIMER ID and using the interval from the m_iInterval variable.

In the OnBnClickedBstoptimer function, all you need to do is to stop the timer by calling the KillTimer function, passing the timer ID as the only argument.

It's in the OnTimer function that things begin to get interesting. Here, you still see the code for handling the clock timer event. To add the functionality for the counter timer, you need to determine which timer triggered this function. The only argument to the OnTimer function just happens to be the timer ID, which you can use in a switch statement to determine which timer has called this function and to control which set of code is executed. The clock timer code is still the same as it was in Listing 5.2. The counter timer code is placed into its spot in the switch statement, incrementing the counter and then updating the m_sCount variable with the new value. You can compile and run your application at this point and specify a timer interval and start the timer running (see Figure 5.5).

FIGURE 5.5

A running counter on your application dialog.

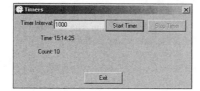

Caution

There is a "bug" in the application. If you enter an out-of-range value in the edit control, a warning message will pop up to inform you of this. While the message box is open, the clock timer will fire, trying to update the dialog controls. Because this results in the UpdateData function being called to update the controls while it's still in the process of updating the variables from the controls, it results in a reentrant conflict, crashing the program. To correct this problem, add a Boolean variable to the dialog class that you use to prevent the timer event from updating the controls until the edit control change event has completed.

The resulting OnEnChangeEinterval function would look like the following

```
void CTimersDlg::OnEnChangeEinterval()
{
...
    // TODO:  Add your control notification handler code here
    // Prevent updating the screen
    m_bPreventUpdate = TRUE;
    // Update the variables
    UpdateData(TRUE);
    // Allow updating the screen
    m_bPreventUpdate = FALSE;
}
```

INPUT

and the OnTimer function would look like this:

```
void CTimersDlg::OnTimer(UINT nIDEvent)
{
...
    // Can the display be updated?
    if (!m_bPreventUpdate)
        // Update the dialog
        UpdateData(FALSE);

    CDialog::OnTimer(nIDEvent);
}
```

INPUT

Finally, you'll want to prevent the timer from being started, so the OnBnClickedBstarttime function would look like this:

```
void CTimersDlg::OnBnClickedBstarttime()
{
    // TODO: Add your control notification handler code here
```

5

INPUT
```
                        // Prevent updating the screen
                        m_bPreventUpdate = TRUE;
    // Update the variables
    UpdateData(TRUE);
    // Allow updating the screen
    m_bPreventUpdate = FALSE;
    // Prevent going any further if the value is out of range
    if ((m_iInterval < 1) || (m_iInterval > 100000))
        return;
    ...
}
```

Enabling the Stop Button

If you run your application, you'll find that it works well except for one small problem.
Once you start your second timer, you can't stop it. When you specified all the control
properties, you disabled the Stop Timer button. Before you can stop the timer, you need
to enable this button.

What makes the most sense is enabling the stop button and disabling the start button
once the timer starts. Then you reverse the situation once the timer stops again. You can
do this in the same way you enabled and disabled controls on Day 3, or you can modify
your approach just a little.

Remember that when you added variables to the controls, you added variables to the start
and stop buttons. These weren't normal variables, but control variables. Rather than get a
pointer to these controls using their IDs, you can work directly with the control variables.
Try that now by updating the OnBnClickedBstarttime and OnBnClickedBstoptimer
functions as in Listing 5.7.

LISTING 5.7   The Revised OnBnClickedBstarttime and OnBnClickedBstoptimer Functions

```
void CTimersDlg::OnBnClickedBstarttime()
{
    // TODO: Add your control notification handler code here
    // Update the variables
    UpdateData(TRUE);

    // Initialize the count
    m_iCount = 0;
    // Format the count for displaying
    m_strCount.Format("%d", m_iCount);

    // Update the dialog
    UpdateData(FALSE);
```

LISTING 5.7 continued

```
    // Start the timer
    SetTimer(ID_COUNT_TIMER, m_iInterval, NULL);
```

INPUT
```
    // Enable the Stop Timer button
    m_cStopTime.EnableWindow(TRUE);
    // Disable the Start Timer button
    m_cStartTime.EnableWindow(FALSE);
}

void CTimersDlg::OnBnClickedBstoptimer()
{
    // TODO: Add your control notification handler code here
    // Stop the timer
    KillTimer(ID_COUNT_TIMER);
```

INPUT
```
    // Disable the Stop Timer button
    m_cStopTime.EnableWindow(FALSE);
    // Enable the Start Timer button
    m_cStartTime.EnableWindow(TRUE);
}
```

Now when you compile and run your application, it looks more like Figure 5.6, where you can start and stop the counter timer. This enables you to play with the timer interval, putting in various time intervals and observing the difference, with the clock ticking above the counter for reference.

FIGURE 5.6

The finished application.

5

Summary

Today you learned how to use the timers built into the Windows operating system to trigger your application at various time intervals that you can control. You learned how to use multiple timers in the same application, running them simultaneously and triggering different actions.

In the coming days, you'll learn how to use additional dialog windows to get user feedback so that you can integrate that feedback into how your application behaves. After that, you will learn how to a create menus for your applications. Then you will learn how you can work with text and fonts in your applications.

Q&A

Q. **What's the interval range that I can set for timers in my applications?**

A. The available range that you can set for timers in your applications is around 55 milliseconds on the short end to $2^{32} - 1$ milliseconds, or around 49 1/2 days, on the long end.

Q. **How many timers can I have running at the same time in my application?**

A. That depends. A limited number of timers are available to all applications in the Windows operating system. Although the available number should be more than sufficient for all running applications using no more than a handful of timers, if an application goes overboard and begins hogging the timers, the operating system may run out. Your application could be denied the use of some timers, or other applications won't have any to use. As a general rule, if you use more than two or three timers at the same time, you might want to reconsider your application design and determine if there's another way to design and build your application so that it can work with fewer timers.

Q. **Is there any way to trigger my application to perform some work when it's idle, rather than use a timer to trigger the work when I think my app might be idle?**

A. Yes, there is. All Windows applications have an `OnIdle` function that can be used to trigger idle processing. `OnIdle` is discussed on Day 17, "Implementing Multitasking in Your Application."

Workshop

The Workshop provides quiz questions to help you solidify your understanding of the material covered and exercises to provide you with experience in using what you've learned. The answers to the quiz questions and exercises are provided in Appendix A, "Answers to Quiz Questions."

Quiz

1. What did you accomplish by adding the two timer IDs to the resource symbols?

2. What's another way to add these two IDs to the application?

3. How can you tell two timers apart in the `OnTimer` function?

4. How many timer events does your application receive if the timer is set for one second and your application has been busy for one minute, preventing it from receiving any timer event messages?

Exercise

Update your application so that when the counter timer is started, the clock timer is reset to run at the same interval as the counter timer. When the counter timer is stopped, return the clock timer to a one-second interval.

5

Day 6

Adding Dialogs to Your Application for User Feedback

With most applications that you might use, there are numerous situations where the application asks you for information—how you want the application configured or whether you want to save your work before exiting, for example. In most of these situations, the application opens a new window to ask these questions. These windows are called *dialog boxes*.

Dialog boxes typically have one or more controls and some text explaining what information the program needs from you. Dialog boxes typically don't have a large blank work area, as you find in the main windows of a word processor or a programming editor. All the applications that you've built in the preceding days have been dialog boxes, and your projects will continue to be dialog boxes for the next few days.

All the dialogs that you've created up to now have been single-window dialog applications. Today you will learn how to

- Use dialog boxes more flexibly
- Call other dialog boxes and take the information entered by users in these dialogs back to the main application window for use in the application
- Use both standard dialogs, such as the message boxes you used in previous days and custom dialogs that you've created

Using Pre-existing (or System) Dialog Boxes

The Windows operating system provides a number of pre-existing dialog boxes. Simple dialog boxes, also known as *message boxes*, present users with a message and provide one to three buttons to click. More complex dialogs, such as the File Open, Save, or Print dialogs, are also provided with Windows. These system (or common) dialogs are created and used with a combination of a variable declaration of a C++ class and a series of interactions with the class instance.

Using Message Boxes

As you learned in previous days, using message boxes is as simple as making a single function call, passing the message text as the only argument. This results in a message box that displays the message with or without an icon and gives users one button to click to acknowledge the message. As you probably know from using other Windows software, you have a whole range of other message box possibilities with various button combinations and various icons that can be displayed.

The `MessageBox` Function

As you've seen in previous days, you can pass to the `MessageBox` function one, two, or three arguments. The first argument is the message to be displayed to users. The second argument, which is completely optional, is displayed in the message box's title bar. You can use a third argument, which is also optional, to specify the buttons to be presented to users and the icon to be displayed beside the message. In addition to this third argument, the `MessageBox` function returns a result value that indicates which button the users clicked. Through the combination of the third argument and the return value, the `MessageBox` function can provide a whole range of functionality in your Visual C++ applications.

Note If you use the third argument to the MessageBox function to specify the buttons or the icon to be presented to users, the second argument (the message box title) is no longer optional. You must provide a value for the title bar of the message box.

The button combinations you can use in the MessageBox function are limited. You don't have the freedom to make up your own button combination. If you get to the point where you need to make up your own, you have to create a custom dialog that looks like a message box. Table 6.1 lists the button combinations you can use.

TABLE 6.1 MessageBox Button Combination IDs

ID	Buttons
MB_ABORTRETRYIGNORE	Abort, Retry, Ignore
MB_OK	OK
MB_OKCANCEL	OK, Cancel
MB_RETRYCANCEL	Retry, Cancel
MB_YESNO	Yes, No
MB_YESNOCANCEL	Yes, No, Cancel
MB_CANCELTRYCONTINUE	Cancel, Try Again, Continue

To specify the icon to be displayed, you can OR the icon ID with the button combination ID. Table 6.2 lists the available icons. If you want to specify either the icon or the button combination and want to use the default for the other, you can specify just the one ID that you want to use.

TABLE 6.2 MessageBox Icon IDs

ID	Icon
MB_ICONINFORMATION	Informational icon
MB_ICONQUESTION	Question mark icon
MB_ICONSTOP	Stop sign icon
MB_ICONEXCLAMATION	Exclamation mark icon

6

When you do specify a button combination, you want to capture the return value so you can determine which button the users clicked. The return value is defined as an integer data type; Table 6.3 lists the return value IDs.

TABLE 6.3   MessageBox Return Value IDs

ID	Button Clicked
IDABORT	Abort
IDRETRY	Retry
IDIGNORE	Ignore
IDYES	Yes
IDNO	No
IDOK	OK
IDCANCEL	Cancel
IDTRYAGAIN	Try Again
IDCONTINUE	Continue

Note   The MessageBox function is a member of the CWnd class, and thus is available only to descendents of that class. This means that this function can be called only from a window or control class. If you need to open a message box from a class that isn't a descendent of CWnd, use another version of this function called AfxMessageBox. For this second message box function, you don't have the parameter for specifying the title on the message box, only the message to be displayed and the icon/button parameters.

Creating a Dialog Application

To get a good understanding of how you can use the MessageBox function in your applications to get information from users, you will build a simple application that uses the MessageBox function in a couple of different ways. Your application will have two separate buttons that call two different versions of the MessageBox function, so you can see the differences and similarities between the various options of the function. Later in the day, you will add a standard File Open dialog, so you can see how the standard dialogs can be used to allow users to specify a filename or perform other standard functions. Finally, you will create a custom dialog that allows users to enter a few different types of values, and you will see how you can read these values from the main application dialog after users close the custom dialog.

To start this application, follow these steps:

1. Create a new MFC Application Visual C++ project, naming it **Dialogs**.

2. Choose the same settings as for the previous days' applications.

3. Lay out the main application dialog as shown in Figure 6.1, using the properties in Table 6.4.

FIGURE 6.1

*The application main
dialog layout.*

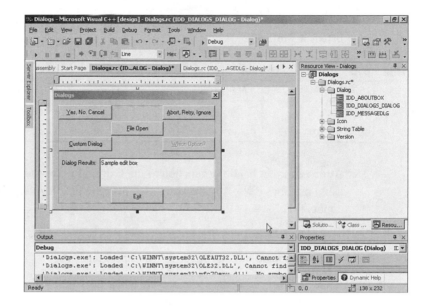

TABLE 6.4 Control Property Settings

Object	Property	Setting
Command Button	ID	IDC_BYESNOCANCEL
	Caption	&Yes, No, Cancel
Command Button	ID	IDC_BABORTRETRYIGNORE
	Caption	&Abort, Retry, Ignore
Command Button	ID	IDC_BFILEOPEN
	Caption	&File Open
Command Button	ID	IDC_BCUSTOMDIALOG
	Caption	&Custom Dialog
Command Button	ID	IDC_BWHICHOPTION
	Caption	&Which Option?
	Disabled	Checked
Command Button	ID	IDC_BEXIT
	Caption	E&xit
Static Text	Caption	Dialog Results:
Edit Control	ID	IDC_ERESULTS
	Multiline	True
	Auto Vscroll	True

6

4. By using the method you learned on Day 3, attach variables to the controls as listed in Table 6.5.

TABLE 6.5 Control Variables

Object	Name	Category	Type	Access
IDC_ERESULTS	m_strResults	Value	CString	public
IDC_BWHICHOPTION	m_cWhichOption	Control	CButton	public

5. Attach an event handling function to the Exit button for the BN_CLICKED event, as on previous days. Add the code used over the past few days to close the application.

Coding the Message Box Dialogs

For the first command button (the Yes, No, Cancel button):

6. Create a function on the clicked event using the Control Events section of the Properties pane, just as you did on previous days. Edit the function on this button, adding the code in Listing 6.1.

LISTING 6.1 The OnBnClickedByesnocancel Functions

```
void CDialogsDlg::OnBnClickedByesnocancel(void)
{
    // TODO: Add your control notification handler code here
    int iResults; // This variable will capture the button selection

    // Ask the user
    iResults = MessageBox("Press the Yes, No, or Cancel button",
                "Yes, No, Cancel Dialog",
                MB_YESNOCANCEL | MB_ICONINFORMATION);

    // Determine which button the user clicked
    // Give the user a message showing which button was clicked
    switch (iResults)
    {
    case IDYES:     // The Yes button?
        m_strResults = "Yes! Yes! Yes!";
        break;
    case IDNO:      // The No button?
        m_strResults = "No, no, no, no, no.";
        break;
    case IDCANCEL:     // The Cancel button?
        m_strResults = "Sorry, canceled.";
        break;
    }
```

INPUT

LISTING 6.1   continued

```
    // Update the dialog
    UpdateData(FALSE);
}
```

If you compile and run your application, you can see how selecting the different buttons on the message box can determine the next course of action in your application.

7. Add a function to the clicked event of the Abort, Retry, Ignore button using the Class Wizard and enter the same code as in Listing 6.1, substituting the MB_ABORTRETRYIGNORE and MB_ICONQUESTION values and changing the prompts and messages.

You can see how this other button combination can be used in the same way.

ANALYSIS   Both control event functions are virtually the same. In each function, an integer variable is declared to capture the return value from the MessageBox function. Next, the MessageBox function is called with a message to be displayed to users, a title for the message box, and a combination of a button combination ID and an icon ID.

When the return value is captured from the MessageBox function, that value is passed through a switch statement to determine which value was returned. A message displayed to users indicates which button was clicked on the message box. You can just as easily use one or two if statements to control the program execution based on user selection, but the return value being an integer lends itself to using a switch statement.

If you compile and run your application at this point, you can click either of the top two buttons and see a message box, as in Figure 6.2. When you click one of the message box buttons, you see a message in the edit box on the main dialog, indicating which button you selected, as in Figure 6.3.

FIGURE 6.2

The MessageBox with three choices.

FIGURE 6.3

A message is displayed based on which button was clicked.

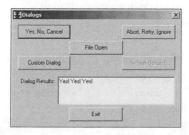

6

C++ Sidebar: The `switch` Statement

If you've used other programming languages, odds are that you've seen and used similar flow-control statements to the C/C++ `switch` statement. The `switch` statement is used when you have multiple values for a single variable where different processing logic needs to be performed, depending on what the variable value happens to be. There is one major difference between the C/C++ `switch` statement and similar statements in other languages (such as the `select case` statement in Visual Basic). In the C/C++ `switch` statement, all values to be compared have to be numeric in nature. You can't use strings to control the logic flow, or the return value of functions that return anything other than integer values. The value being evaluated must be a numeric value, and each case must also be a numeric value.

> **C++ Rule**
>
> The `switch` statement can compare only numeric values for controlling processing flow. Single characters can be compared by using the `switch` statement because the ASCII (or Unicode) value of the character used in performing the comparison.

The syntax for the `switch` statement is as follows:

```
switch (value)
{
case 0:
    processing logic
    break;
case 1:
    processing logic
    break;
default:
    processing logic
    break;
}
```

The `switch` statement is followed by the value to be used in the comparisons. This value is always enclosed in parentheses. Next, all cases to be checked are enclosed within a pair of braces (`{}`). The `case` keyword designates each individual value that corresponds to a unique set of processing logic, followed by the numeric value that signals that this set of logic should be executed, followed with a colon (`:`). After each set of processing logic is completed, you need to add the `break` statement to leave the `switch` statement. If you don't use the `break` statement, processing will continue with the processing logic of the next `case` in the statement. This behavior of C/C++ enables you to use multiple values to qualify for a single set of processing logic, as follows:

```
switch (value)
{
case 0:
    processing logic
    break;
case 1:
case 2:
case 3:
    processing logic
    break;
default:
    processing logic
    break;
}
```

In this example, if the value equals 1, 2, or 3, the second set of logic will be performed. The `default` keyword designates any programming logic that should be performed if none of the other cases apply. The `default` keyword should always come at the end of the switch statement, after all other cases.

Tip

If you are declaring any variables in the processing logic of a case, it's recommended that you enclose all processing logic of that case within a code block using braces ({}). This will make the variables local to that case, and prevents any compile errors if you use the same variable names in another set of processing logic.

Note

It's common practice to use the `#define` preprocessor directive to declare constants used in the `switch` statement instead of numeric values. This enables you to use readable constant names in terms of what the value being checked corresponds to, in terms of functionality. In Listing 6.1, defined constants are being used in this way. However, in this case, the constants were already defined, so you didn't have to do the work.

6

C++ Sidebar: The break Statement

The break statement that you use to end each case in the switch statement is a statement that you can use to leave the current level of processing logic. You also can use break to leave a for loop. For instance, if the following logic were used,

```
for (x=0; x < 10; x++)
```

```
{
    for (y=0; y < 10; y++)
    {
        if (x == y)
            break;
        //do something here
        ...
    }
}
```

every time the counters in both loops are equal, the processing would break out of the inner loop, skipping all the processing logic in that loop. Because break is in the inner loop, the outer loop is never broken and will continue looping. If in the processing logic, you output the values of both of the counters, the output would look something like this:

```
x = 1    y = 0
x = 2    y = 0
x = 2    y = 1
x = 3    y = 0
x = 3    y = 1
x = 3    y = 2
x = 4    y = 0
x = 4    y = 1
x = 4    y = 2
x = 4    y = 3
x = 5    y = 0
x = 5    y = 1
x = 5    y = 2
x = 5    y = 3
x = 5    y = 4
x = 6    y = 0
...
x = 9    y = 8
```

You also can use the break statement to leave do and while loops, both of which will be introduced in later days.

Using Common Dialogs

Using common dialogs isn't quite as simple and easy as using the MessageBox function, but it's still quite easy. The Microsoft Foundation Classes (MFC) provides several C++ classes for common Windows dialogs. These classes are listed in Table 6.6.

TABLE 6.6 Common Dialog Classes

Class	Dialog Type
CFileDialog	File selection
CFontDialog	Font selection

TABLE 6.6 continued

Class	Dialog Type
CColorDialog	Color selection
CPageSetupDialog	Page setup for printing
CPrintDialog	Printing
CFindReplaceDialog	Find and Replace

The common dialogs encapsulated in these classes are the standard dialogs that you use every day in most Windows applications to open and save files, configure printing options, print, perform find and replace on documents, and so on. In addition to these choices, a series of OLE common dialog classes provide several common functions to OLE or ActiveX components and applications.

All these dialogs are used in the same manner, although the individual properties and class functions vary according to the dialog functionality. To use one of these dialogs, follow these steps:

1. Declare a variable of the class type.
2. Set any properties that need to be configured before displaying the dialog to users.
3. Call the DoModal method of the class to display the dialog to users.
4. Capture the return value of the DoModal method to determine whether the users clicked OK or Cancel.
5. If users click OK, read any properties that they may have set when using the dialog.

To better understand how this works, add the CFileDialog class to your application. To do this, add a function to the clicked message on the File Open button. Edit this function, adding the code in Listing 6.2.

LISTING 6.2 The OnBnClickedBfileopen Function

```
void CDialogsDlg::OnBnClickedBfileopen()
{
    // TODO: Add your control notification handler code here
    CFileDialog ldFile(TRUE);

    // Show the File Open dialog and capture the result
    if (ldFile.DoModal() == IDOK)
    {
        // Get the file name selected
        m_strResults = ldFile.GetFileName();
```

INPUT

6

LISTING 6.2 continued

```
        // Update the dialog
        UpdateData(FALSE);
    }
}
```

ANALYSIS This code first declares an instance of the `CFileDialog` class. This instance is passed `TRUE` as an argument to the class constructor, which tells the class that it's a File Open dialog. If you pass it `FALSE`, it displays as a File Save dialog. There's no real functional difference between these two, only a visual difference. You can pass many more arguments to the constructor, specifying the file extensions to show, the default starting file and location, and filters to use when displaying the files. All the rest of these constructor arguments have default values, so you don't have to supply any of them.

After creating the instance of the File Open dialog, the code in Listing 6.2 calls its `DoModal` function. This is a member function of the `CDialog` ancestor class, and it's available in all dialogs. The `DoModal` function displays the File Open dialog to users (see Figure 6.4). The `DoModal` function's return value is examined to determine which button the users clicked. If the users click the Open button, the `IDOK` value is returned, as with the `MessageBox` function. This is how you can determine whether your application needs to take any action on what users selected with the dialog box.

FIGURE 6.4

The File Open dialog.

Note Depending on which operating system you are using, the File Open dialog may look different from the one shown in Figure 6.4. All screenshots in this book were taken on Windows 2000. If you are using a different OS, the standard dialogs that appear will be the standard dialogs available in that version of Windows.

To display the name of the selected file, set the m_strResults variable to the return value from the GetFileName method of the CFileDialog class. This method returns only the filename without the directory path or drive name (see Figure 6.5). You can use other class methods for getting the directory path (GetPathName) or file extension (GetFileExt).

FIGURE 6.5

Displaying the selected filename.

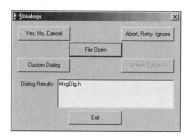

> **Note**
>
> You can display a dialog box to users in two modes: modal and modeless. A *modal* dialog halts all other user interaction while it's displayed. Users can't do anything else in the application until the dialog is closed. A good example of a modal dialog is a message box where users can't continue working with the application until they click a button in the message box.
>
> A *modeless* dialog can be open while users do something else in the application; it doesn't prevent users from performing other tasks while the dialog is visible. Good examples of modeless dialogs are the Find and Find and Replace dialogs in Microsoft Word. You can leave these dialogs open onscreen while you are still editing the document that you are searching.

MFC Note: The CFileDialog Class

The CFileDialog class encapsulates the functionality of the Open and Save File dialogs built into the Windows operating system. These enable you to provide users of your application with the same dialogs for finding and specifying files used in most other Windows applications. Table 6.7 lists the primary functions that you'll use with the CFileDialog class.

TABLE 6.7 Primary CFileDialog Member Functions

Function	Description
GetPathName	Returns the full path of the specified file
GetFileName	Returns the specified filename

6

TABLE 6.7 continued

Function	Description
GetFileExt	Returns the extension of the specified file
GetFileTitle	Returns the name of the file without the extension (for instance, if you selected the file "MyFile.txt", this function would return "MyFile")

 Note All methods listed in Table 6.7 shouldn't be called until after the DoModal method is called and returned with the IDOK return value. This same rule applies to all methods listed on the other common dialogs in the next few tables, unless otherwise specified.

MFC Note: The CFontDialog Class

The CFontDialog class encapsulates the standard font selection dialog built into Windows. This class enables you to provide your application users with a standard font selection dialog that they will be familiar with through use in other Windows applications. Table 6.8 lists the primary member methods for the CFontDialog class.

TABLE 6.8 Primary CFontDialog Member Functions

Function	Description
GetFaceName	Returns the name of the selected font.
GetStyleName	Returns the style of the selected font (a font style may have multiple fonts available).
GetSize	Returns the size specified for the selected font.
GetColor	Returns the color specified for the selected font.
GetWeight	Returns the weight specified for the selected font.
IsStrikeOut	Returns a Boolean value specifying whether the selected font was specified with the Strike Out attribute selected.
IsUnderline	Returns a Boolean value specifying whether the selected font was specified with the Underline attribute selected.
IsBold	Returns a Boolean value specifying whether the selected font was specified with the Bold attribute selected.
IsItalic	Returns a Boolean value specifying whether the selected font was specified with the Italic attribute selected.

MFC Note: The `CColorDialog` Class

The `CColorDialog` class encapsulates the standard color-picker dialog used in many Windows applications. This dialog is used to get the RGB value for the specified color, which can then be passed into any GDI method that requires a color value (you'll learn more about this in a couple of days). Table 6.9 lists the common methods used with the `CColorDialog` class.

TABLE 6.9 Primary `CColorDialog` Member Functions

Function	Description
GetColor	Returns the selected color.
GetSavedCustomColors	Returns an array of colors that users created.
SetCurrentColor	Specifies the current color selection. Call this method before calling the DoModal method.

MFC Note: The `CPageSetupDialog` Class

The `CPageSetupDialog` class encapsulates the Page Setup dialog that's often used with printing functionality. It can be called to allow users to specify the printer to be used, page size, and margins of the printed output. Table 6.10 lists the common methods used with the `CPageSetupDialog` class.

TABLE 6.10 Primary `CPageSetupDialog` Member Functions

Function	Description
CreatePrinterDC	Returns a device context that can be used for printing.
GetDeviceName	Returns the name of the selected printer.
GetDevMode	Returns a structure containing information about the selected printer and its capabilities (i.e. color or black and white).
GetMargins	You pass this method two pointers to either a CRect class or a RECT structure, and it populates the class or structures with the dimensions of the margins and print area.
GetPaperSize	This method returns a CSize class, which specifies the current paper size.
GetDriverName	Returns the name of the selected printer driver.
GetPortName	Returns the name of the selected output port.

6

MFC Note: The `CPrintDialog` Class

The `CPrintDialog` class encapsulates the standard Print dialog used in most Windows applications. This class contains most of the methods in the `CPageSetupDialog`, except for `GetPaperSize` and `GetMargin`. All the rest of the functions in Table 6.10 are available in the `CPrintDialog` class. Table 6.11 lists the other primary functions in this class.

TABLE 6.11   Primary `CPrintDialog` Member Functions

Function	Description
GetCopies	Returns the number of copies specified to be printed.
GetFromPage	Returns the starting page number when a range of pages have been specified to be printed.
GetToPage	Returns the ending page number when a range of pages have been specified to be printed.
GetPrinterDC	Returns a handle to the device context for the printer specified.
PrintAll	Returns a Boolean value specifying whether to print all pages of the current document.
PrintCollate	Returns a Boolean value specifying whether users requested that the printed output be collated.
PrintRange	Returns a Boolean value specifying whether users specified a range of pages to be printed.
PrintSelection	Returns a Boolean value specifying whether to print only the selected items or pages.

Note   Unlike with the `CPageSetupDialog`, you can call the `CreatePrinterDC` method without having called the `DoModal` method. In fact, you don't have to show the dialog at all, but you can use the class just to get the printer information and device context, so you can print to the current printer without displaying a dialog.

MFC Note: The `CFindReplaceDialog` Class

The `CFindReplaceDialog` class encapsulates the standard find/replace dialog used in many Windows applications. Unlike the other common dialogs, this dialog isn't modal, but instead enables users to interact with the parent window the entire time it's visible. Because of this difference, you don't call the `DoModal` method to display this dialog, but instead call the `Create` method.

The Create method requires two parameters but can take up to five parameters:

- The first parameter, a Boolean value, specifies whether the dialog is a find-only dialog or a find-and-replace dialog. If TRUE is passed as the first parameter, a find-only dialog is displayed. If FALSE is passed in this parameter, a find-and-replace dialog is displayed.

- The second parameter is the string to be searched for.

- The third parameter (which is optional) is the replacement string.

- The fourth parameter specifies which direction to search. The default direction is down, which is specified with the FR_DOWN constant. The up direction is specified by passing 0 in the fourth parameter.

- The final parameter is a pointer to the parent window.

Tip

The coding concepts required for using the CFindReplaceDialog class are more advanced than the other common dialog classes. If you are new to the C++ programming language, you might find this easier to understand after reading much more of this book. If you have trouble understanding how to use this dialog class, mark this section and come back to it after completing at least Day 14.

Because CFindReplaceDialog is a non-modal dialog, it requires a different usage in your application. First, don't declare a CFindReplaceDialog variable, but instead declare a pointer to a CFindReplaceDialog instance, and then use the new keyword to create the instance of the dialog:

```
// In the class header declaration (a class-level variable,
// declared in the header file)
CFindReplaceDialog *m_pFRDlg;
...
// In the class source code (prior to first use, somewhere in
// the source code file)
m_pFRDlg = new CFindReplaceDialog;
```

Second, you need to register parent window to receive the messages from the CFindReplaceDialog. Near the top of the source code file for the class that will be receiving the messages, you need to declare a message ID variable:

```
static UINT WM_FINDREPLACE = ::RegisterWindowMessage(FINDMSGSTRING);
```

After you register the message from the CFindReplaceDialog, add the function to receive and handle those messages. First, you need to add the function to your class that will be receiving the messages. The function should be defined as returning a long data

6

type, have `protected` access, and take two parameters: `WPARAM` for the data type and the `LPARAM` data type. After you add the function to your class, open the class definition (in the header file) and add the `afx_msg` keyword in front of the function definition. The class header definition for this function should look something like the following:

```
class CMyClass : public CWnd
{
...
protected:
    afx_msg long OnFindReplace(WPARAM wParam, LPARAM lParam);
        // Some other afx_msg functions here that the MFC Wizards added
    DECLARE_MESSAGE_MAP()
...
};
```

INPUT

Finally, to set up your class for receiving message from the `CFindReplaceDialog` class, add an entry in the message map near the top of your source code file. When you look at the message map, you'll find many entries that have been already added by the MFC Wizards. You'll add a new entry using the `ON_REGISTERED_MESSAGE` macro, as follows:

```
BEGIN_MESSAGE_MAP(CMyClass, CWnd)
    ...
    ON_REGISTERED_MESSAGE(WM_FINDREPLACE, OnFindReplace)
END_MESSAGE_MAP()
```

INPUT

Now your class is ready to receive and process event messages from the `CFindReplaceDialog` class. The way this works is that event messages are sent out from the Find/Replace dialog whenever users perform an action such as clicking the Find Next or Replace buttons. These messages are routed to the message map, through the `ON_REGISTERED_MESSAGE` macro, to the function you defined to handle these messages (see Figure 6.6).

In your message handling function, the primary member functions of the `CFindReplaceDialog` class that you'll be calling to determine what action users are taking are found in Table 6.12.

TABLE 6.12 Primary `CFindReplaceDialog` Member Functions

Function	Description
`FindNext`	Returns a Boolean value indicating whether users want to find the next occurrence of the specified string.
`GetFindString`	Returns the string entered by users to be found.
`GetReplaceString`	Returns the string users entered to replace the find string.
`IsTerminating`	Returns a Boolean value specifying whether users have chosen to close the Find/Replace dialog.

TABLE 6.12 continued

Function	Description
MatchCase	Returns a Boolean value specifying whether users want to match the case of the find string.
MatchWholeWord	Returns a Boolean value indicating whether users want to find whole-word matches of the find string.
ReplaceAll	Returns a Boolean value indicating whether users want to replace all occurrences of the find string.
ReplaceCurrent	Returns a Boolean value indicating whether users want to replace the current occurrence of the find string.
SearchDown	Returns a Boolean value indicating whether users want to search down from the current position in the data.

FIGURE 6.6

Find/Replace message routing.

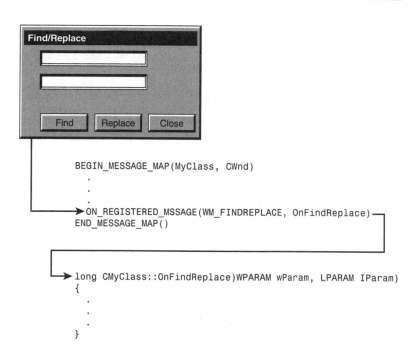

```
BEGIN_MESSAGE_MAP(MyClass, CWnd)
        .
        .
        .
   ON_REGISTERED_MSSAGE(WM_FINDREPLACE, OnFindReplace)
END_MESSAGE_MAP()


   long CMyClass::OnFindReplace)WPARAM wParam, LPARAM IParam)
   {
        .
        .
        .
   }
```

6

Creating Your Own Dialog Boxes

Now you have an understanding of using standard dialogs. What if you need to create a custom dialog? This task is simple because it combines the process that you've already used to create and use the main dialogs in all your applications and the methods you employed to use the common dialogs. You have to work through a few additional steps, but you should be comfortable with them.

Creating the Dialog Box

For the custom dialog that you will add to your application, you will provide users with an edit box in which to enter some text and a group of radio buttons from which users can select one. When users click OK, your application will display the text they entered in the display area of the main application dialog. Users will be able to click another button to display which radio button was selected. This exercise enables you to see how you can use custom dialogs to gather information from users and how you can read user selections after the dialog box is closed.

To create a custom dialog for your application, you need to

- Add another dialog to your application resources
- Design the dialog box layout
- Declare the base class from which the dialog will be inherited
- Attach variables to the controls on the dialog

After doing these things, your custom dialog will be ready for your application. Now, follow these steps:

1. Select the Resource View pane.
2. Right-click the Dialogs folder and select Insert Dialog.
3. Change the object ID for the new dialog to IDD_MESSAGEDLG.
4. When editing the new dialog, don't delete the OK and Cancel buttons. Move them to the location shown in Figure 6.7.
5. Design the rest of the window by using the object properties in Table 6.13.

TABLE 6.13   The Custom Dialog Control Property Settings

Object	Property	Setting
Dialog (entire window)	Caption	Message and Option Dialog
Static Text	Caption	Enter a &message:
Edit Control	ID	IDC_EMESSAGE
	Multiline	True
	Auto Vscroll	True
Group Box	Caption	Select an Option
Radio Button	ID	IDC_ROPTION1
	Caption	&Option 1
	Group	True

TABLE 6.13 continued

Object	Property	Setting
Radio Button	ID	IDC_ROPTION2
	Caption	O&ption 2
Radio Button	ID	IDC_ROPTION3
	Caption	Op&tion 3
Radio Button	ID	IDC_ROPTION4
	Caption	Opt&ion 4

FIGURE 6.7

The custom dialog layout.

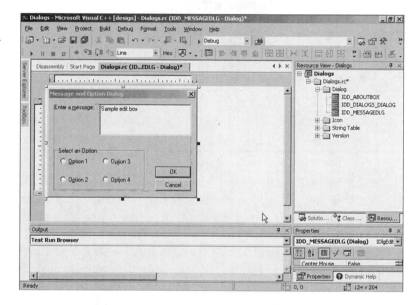

6. After you design the dialog, select the main dialog, right-click, and choose Add Class from the context menu.

7. Enter the class name **CMsgDlg** into the Name field, and make sure the Base Class is set to CDialog (see Figure 6.8).

9. Click Finish, leaving the other settings on this dialog at their defaults.

10. When the new class is created, attach the variables to the controls on the new dialog as specified in Table 6.14.

6

FIGURE 6.8

*The MFC Class Wizard
dialog.*

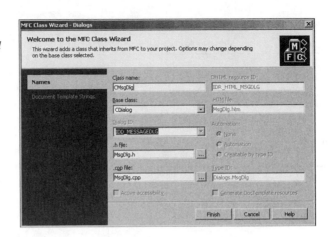

TABLE 6.14   Control Variables

Object	Name	Category	Type	Access
IDC_EMESSAGE	m_strMessage	Value	CString	public
IDC_ROPTION1	m_iOption	Value	int	public

Notice two things in the way you configured the control properties and variables in the custom dialog. First, you should have selected the Group property on only the first of the radio buttons. This designates that all the radio buttons following that one belong to a single group, where only one of the radio buttons may be selected at a time. If you select the Group property on all radio buttons, they are all independent of each other, allowing you to select all the buttons simultaneously. This property makes them behave somewhat like check boxes, but the primary difference is that users would find it difficult to uncheck one of these controls due to the default behavior where one radio button in each group is always checked. The other difference is in their appearance; the radio buttons have round selection areas instead of the square areas of check boxes.

Tip

If you have other controls following the group of radio buttons, it's a good idea to also mark the group option on the first of the controls after the radio buttons as TRUE. This makes it clear that none of the other controls are part of the group of radio buttons.

Also notice that you declared a single integer variable for the one radio button with the Group property checked. This variable value is controlled by which radio button is selected. The first radio button causes this variable to have a value of 0, the second sets this variable to 1, and so on. Likewise, if you want to automatically select a particular radio button, you can set this variable to one less than the sequence number of the radio button in the group of radio buttons.

Note

Because this is the C++ programming language, all numbering begins with 0, not 1. Therefore, the first position in an array or a set of controls is position 0. The second position is position 1. The third position is number 2, and so on.

You've now finished all that you need to do to the second dialog to make it ready for use. You would expect to need an UpdateData or two in the code behind the dialog, but because you didn't remove the OK and Cancel buttons from the dialog, the UpdateData call is already performed when users click OK. As a result, you don't have to touch any code in this second dialog, only in the first dialog.

Using the Dialog in Your Application

Now that your custom dialog is ready for your application, using it is similar to the way that you use the built-in Windows common dialogs:

1. Declare an instance of the custom dialog class, which calls the class constructor and creates an instance of the class.
2. Call the dialog's DoModal method and capture the return value of that function.
3. Read the values of the variables that you associated with the controls on the dialog.

The following sections explain these steps in more detail.

Creating the Dialog Instance

Before you can use your custom dialog in your application, you have to make your main dialog aware of the custom dialog, its variables, and methods and how your main dialog can interact with your custom dialog. You accomplish this by including the header file for your custom dialog in the main source file for your main application dialog. Follow these steps:

1. Select the Solution Explorer pane.
2. Expand the Dialog Files and Source Files folders.
3. Double-click the DialogsDlg.cpp file. This opens the source code file for the main application dialog in the editing area of Visual Studio.

6

4. Scroll to the top of the source code file where the #include statements are located, and add an include for the MsgDlg.h file before the DialogsDlg.h file, as in Listing 6.3.

LISTING 6.3   The Header File Includes

```
// DialogsDlg.cpp : implementation file
//

#include "stdafx.h"
#include "Dialogs.h"
#include "MsgDlg.h"
#include "DialogsDlg.h"
```

It's important that you place the #include statement for the MsgDlg.h file before the #include statement for the DialogsDlg.h file. You will be adding a variable declaration for your custom dialog to the main dialog class in the main dialog's header file. If the MsgDlg.h header file is included after the header file for the main dialog, the compiler will complain loudly and will refuse to compile your application until you move the #include of the MsgDlg.h file above the #include of the DialogsDlg.h file.

Note

The #include statement is what is known as a *pre-compiler directive* in the C and C++ programming languages. It tells the pre-compiler to read the contents of the file named into the source code being compiled. It's used to separate class, structure, and function declarations into a file that can be included in any source code that needs to be aware of the information in the header file. For more information on how the #include statements work, and why you use them, refer to Day 2.

Now that you've made your main application dialog aware of the custom dialog that you created, you need to declare a variable of your custom dialog. Follow these steps:

1. Select the Class View pane.
2. Right-click the CDialogsDlg class.
3. Select Add and then Add Variable from the context menu.
4. Specify the Variable Type as **CMsgDlg**, the Variable Name as **m_dMsgDlg**, and the Access as Private. Click Finish to add the variable to your main dialog.

If you expand the CDialogsDlg class in the tree view, you should see the instance of your custom dialog as a member of the main application dialog class. This means you are ready to begin using the custom dialog in your application.

Calling the Dialog and Reading the Variables

Now that you've added your custom dialog to the main application dialog as a variable that's always available, not just as a local variable available only within a single function (as with the CFileDialog variable), you can add code to use the dialog. Follow these steps:

1. Add a function to the clicked event message (BN_CLICKED) of the IDC_BCUSTOMDIA-LOG button.

2. Add a function for the clicked event message (BN_CLICKED) for the IDC_BWHICHOP-TION button.

3. Edit the OnBnClickedBcustomdialog function, adding the code in Listing 6.4.

LISTING 6.4   The OnBnClickedBcustomdialog Function

```
void CDialogsDlg::OnBnClickedBcustomdialog()
{
    // TODO: Add your control notification handler code here
    // Show the message dialog and capture the result
    if (m_dMsgDlg.DoModal() == IDOK)
    {
        // The user checked OK, display the message the
        // user typed in on the message dialog
        m_strResults = m_dMsgDlg.m_strMessage;
        // Update the dialog
        UpdateData(FALSE);
        // Enable the Which Option button
        m_cWhichOption.EnableWindow(TRUE);
    }
}
```

4. Edit the OnBnClickedBwhichoption function, adding the code in Listing 6.5.

LISTING 6.5   The OnBnClickedBwhichoption Function

```
void CDialogsDlg::OnBnClickedBwhichoption()
{
    // TODO: Add your control notification handler code here
    // Determine which radio button was selected, and display
    // a message for the user to show which one was selected.
    switch(m_dMsgDlg.m_iOption)
    {
    case 0:     // Was it the first radio button?
        m_strResults = "The first option was selected.";
        break;
```

6

LISTING 6.5   continued

```
        case 1:      // Was it the second radio button?
            m_strResults = "The second option was selected.";
            break;
        case 2:      // Was it the third radio button?
            m_strResults = "The third option was selected.";
            break;
        case 3:      // Was it the fourth radio button?
            m_strResults = "The fourth option was selected.";
            break;
        default:     // Were none of the radio buttons selected?
            m_strResults = "No option was selected.";
            break;
    }

    // Update the dialog
    UpdateData(FALSE);
}
```

The code in Listing 6.4 calls the DoModal method of the custom dialog, which displayed the dialog for the users, waiting for users to click one of two buttons in the dialog (see Figure 6.9). If users click OK, the function copies the message they typed in the custom dialog into the edit box variable to be displayed. After updating the dialog display with the new variable values, the function enables the Which Option button (see Figure 6.10). If the users click the Cancel button, none of this is done, and the dialog display isn't changed.

FIGURE 6.9

This custom dialog enables users to enter a message.

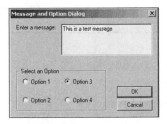

FIGURE 6.10

The message entered on the custom dialog is displayed for users.

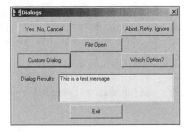

When the users click the Which Option button, the radio button variable on the custom dialog is passed to a `switch` statement, selecting a message that tells users which radio button was selected (see Figure 6.11). Notice that in both functions, you can access the control variables on the custom dialog directly from the main dialog. That is because the variables associated with controls were defined as `public`, making them completely accessible outside the dialog class. You can change this by placing a `private:` access specifier, where the `public:` access specifier is in the class header file.

FIGURE 6.11

The option selected on the custom dialog is displayed for users.

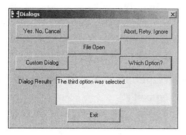

Summary

Today you learned how you can use additional dialogs in your application to provide interactive experience for your users. You learned about the options available to you with the simple `MessageBox` function, how you can provide your users a variety of button combinations, and how you can determine which button the users select. You saw how you can use this information to determine which path to take in your application logic.

You also learned about some of the common dialogs built into the Windows operating systems and how they've been encapsulated into C++ classes in the MFC class library. You learned how you can use the File Open dialog to present users with the standard file selection dialog and how you can determine which file users selected.

Finally, you learned how you can design your own additional dialogs that you can add to your applications to get information from users and how you can capture that information and use it in your application.

Q&A

Q. No code was added to the custom dialog. Do I have to design my custom dialogs this way, or can I add code to them?

A. The custom dialogs are no different from the main dialogs that you've used in all your applications so far. If you need to control the behavior of the dialog interactively, you can put as much code into the dialog as needed. You didn't add any code to the custom dialog today because there wasn't any need to add any. The only functionality that the dialog needed to perform was calling the UpdateData function before closing, which is done automatically by the OnOK function. Because you didn't delete the OK and Cancel buttons, you already had this functionality built in.

Q. What happens if I specify two or more button combinations in the same MessageBox function call?

A. Your application compiles just fine, but when the MessageBox function is called, sometimes nothing happens, sometimes one of the button combinations selected is displayed. Keep in mind that only one set of buttons will be displayed, so there's no reason to OR two or more sets of buttons together.

Q. How can I integrate the File Open dialog into my application where it opens in a specific directory that I specify?

A. The CFileDialog class has a public property called m_ofn. This property is a structure that contains numerous attributes of the File Open dialog, including the initial directory. This structure is defined as the OPENFILENAME structure in Listing 6.6.

LISTING 6.6   The OPENFILENAME Structure

```
typedef struct tagOFN { // ofn
        DWORD           lStructSize;
        HWND            hwndOwner;
        HINSTANCE       hInstance;
        LPCTSTR         lpstrFilter;
        LPTSTR          lpstrCustomFilter;
        DWORD           nMaxCustFilter;
        DWORD           nFilterIndex;
        LPTSTR          lpstrFile;
        DWORD           nMaxFile;
        LPTSTR          lpstrFileTitle;
        DWORD           nMaxFileTitle;
        LPCTSTR         lpstrInitialDir;
        LPCTSTR         lpstrTitle;
        DWORD           Flags;
        WORD            nFileOffset;
        WORD            nFileExtension;
        LPCTSTR         lpstrDefExt;
        DWORD           lCustData;
        LPOFNHOOKPROC   lpfnHook;
        LPCTSTR         lpTemplateName;
    } OPENFILENAME;
```

You can set any of these attributes before calling the DoModal class method to control the behavior of the File Open dialog. For instance, if you set the starting directory to C:\Temp before calling the DoModal method, as in Listing 6.7, the File Open dialog opens in that directory.

LISTING 6.7   The Revised OnBnClickedBfileopen Function

```
void CDialogsDlg::OnBnClickedBfileopen(void)
{
    // TODO: Add your control notification handler code here
    CFileDialog ldFile(TRUE);

    // Set the current directory
    ldFile.m_ofn.lpstrInitialDir = "C:\\Temp\\";

    // Show the File Open dialog and capture the result
    if (ldFile.DoModal() == IDOK)
    {
        // Get the file name selected
        m_strResults = ldFile.GetFileName();
        // Update the dialog
        UpdateData(FALSE);
    }
}
```

INPUT

Tip

> If you are confused by the use of the double backslashes used in the string containing the directory name in the above listing, refer to Table 2.3 on Day 2 for an explanation of special characters in C/C++ strings.

Workshop

The Workshop provides quiz questions to help you solidify your understanding of the material covered and exercises to provide you with experience in using what you've learned. The answers to the quiz questions are provided in Appendix A, "Answers to Quiz Questions."

6

Quiz

1. What possible return codes might your application receive from the MessageBox function call when you specify the MB_RETRYCANCEL button combination?

2. What common dialogs built into the Windows operating system are defined as MFC classes?

3. What's the difference between modal and modeless dialogs?

4. How can you display a File Save dialog for users instead of the File Open dialog that you have in your application?

5. Why didn't you need to create any functions and add any code to your custom dialog?

Exercises

1. Modify your application so that it includes the directory with the filename in the application. (*Hint:* The GetPathName function returns the path and filename that was selected in the File Open dialog.)

2. Add a button on the custom dialog that calls the MessageBox function with a Yes or No selection. Pass the result back to the main application dialog.

DAY 7

Creating Menus for Your Application

Most Windows applications use pull-down menus to provide users with a number of functions without having to provide buttons on the window. This enables you to provide your users a large amount of functionality while preserving most of your valuable screen real estate for other stuff.

Today you will learn how to

- Create menus for your Visual C++ application
- Attach a menu to your application's main dialog window
- Call application functions from a menu
- Create a pop-up menu that can be triggered with the right mouse button
- Set up accelerator keys for keyboard shortcuts to menus

Understanding Menus

Back when the first computer terminals were introduced and users began using computer software, even on large mainframe systems, software developers found the need to provide users with some sort of menu of the functions the software could perform. By today's standards, these early menus were crude and difficult to use and navigate. Menus have progressed since then; they've become standardized in how they are used and easy to learn.

The software designers who first came up with the idea of a graphical user interface (GUI) planned to make computer systems and applications easier to learn by making everything behave consistently. Menus used for selecting application functionality were one part of the GUI design that could be more easily learned if they all worked the same. As a result, a number of standard menu styles were developed.

Menu Styles

The first standardized menu styles were the pull-down and cascading menus. These menus have the categories all listed in a row across the top of the application window. If you select one of the categories, a list drops down below the category, with a number of entries that can be selected to trigger various functions in the application.

NEW TERM A variation on this menu style is the *cascading menu*, which has another submenu that opens to the right of a menu entry. This submenu is similar to the pull-down menu, with a number of entries that trigger application functions. Menu designers placed no limit on how many cascading menus could be strung together, but it quickly became clear to most developers that more than two cascading levels are a little unwieldy.

NEW TERM Eventually, a third style of menu was developed—a *pop-up menu*, which pops up underneath the mouse cursor, floating freely above the application work area. This is also called a *context menu* because the specific menu that pops up depends on the selected object or workspace area where the cursor or mouse pointer is.

Keyboard Shortcut-Enabling Menus

When users began working with keyboard-intensive applications, such as word processors, they discovered that taking their hands off the keyboard to use the mouse to make menu selections dramatically reduced productivity. Software designers decided that they needed to add keyboard shortcuts for the various menu entries, especially the most frequently used menu options. For this reason, keyboard shortcuts (*accelerators*) and hotkeys were added.

NEW TERM *Hotkeys* are the underlined letters in each menu entry. If you press the Alt key followed by the underlined letter, you can select the menu entry that contains the underlined letter. This is a means of navigating application menus without taking your hands off the keyboard.

> **Note**
>
> On newer versions of Windows, the underline doesn't normally show until you press the Alt key.

 For more advanced users, application designers added keyboard shortcuts, or *accelerators*. An accelerator is a single key combination that you can press to trigger an application function rather than have to navigate through the application menus. This enables advanced users to avoid the overhead of using menus for the most common application functions. To enable users to learn what accelerators are available in an application, the key combination is placed on the menu entry that it can be used to replace, positioned at the right edge of the menu window.

Menu Standards and Conventions

Although there are no standards in how menus are designed, there are a number of conventions for how they are designed and organized. All these conventions are available in *Microsoft Windows User Experience*, published by Microsoft Press for use by Windows software developers. The purpose of this publication is to facilitate the development of consistent application behaviors, which will help accomplish one of the primary goals behind the development of GUI systems. The conventions are as follows:

- Use single-word menu categories across the top menu bar. A two-word category can easily be mistaken for two one-word categories.

- The File menu is located as the first menu on the left. It contains all file-oriented functions (such as New, Open, Save, Print, and so on), as well as the Exit command. The Exit command is at the bottom of the menu, separated from the rest of the menu entries by a separator line.

- The Edit menu is next to and to the right of the File menu. The Edit menu contains all editing functions such as Copy, Cut, Paste, Undo, Redo, and so on.

- The View menu contains menu entries that control and affect the appearance of the application work area.

- The Window menu is used in Multiple Document Interface (MDI) style applications. This has commands for controlling the child windows, selecting the current window, and altering the layout. This menu is always the next-to-last menu from the right end of the menu bar.

- The Help menu is the final menu on the right. It contains entries that provide instruction or documentation on the application. If the application has any copyrighted or corporate information available for viewing, this should be located as the final entry on this menu, labeled About *<application name>*.

7

- Any application specific menus are normally located between the View and Window menus.

Note

> Not all these standard menus are included in every application. These are guidelines for where to place each menu if they belong in your application. If the area of functionality in any of these menus doesn't belong in a particular application, the menu doesn't belong and shouldn't be included.

Designing Menus

Menus are defined as a resource in Visual C++ applications. Because they are a resource, you can design menus in the Visual C++ editor through the Resource View tab on the workspace pane. When you first create a dialog-style application, there won't be a menu folder in the resource tree, but you can change that.

Note

> Various aspects of Windows applications are considered to be resources, including dialog window layouts, menus, toolbars, images, text strings, accelerators, and so on. All these features are organized in what is known as a *resource file*, which is used by the Visual C++ compiler to create these objects from their definitions. The resource file is a text file with an .rc filename extension and contains a textual description of all the various objects, including IDs, captions, dimensions, and so on.
>
> Some resources, such as images and sounds, can't be described in text, but have to be stored in a binary format. These resources are stored in individual files, with the filenames and locations included in the resource file.
>
> While the resource file is intended for storing all these application resources, it's not necessary to store all the application resources in the file. Menus can be created dynamically, and dialog windows can be drawn using external templates or skins.
>
> One benefit of using resource files is that they can be included in DLLs, and then used to localize your application. By placing all the text used in your application in the string table in the resource file, you can produce multiple DLLs containing the string table in different languages. This would enable you to distribute your application to different countries by including the DLL containing the appropriate language in the string table.

Creating a Menu

Creating a menu isn't difficult. You follow several general steps:

1. Create the application that will house the menu.

2. Add a menu resource to your project.

3. Customize the menu resource to include the menu items for your application.

4. Add functionality to your menu by connecting routines to your menu items.

Creating the Application

For this chapter's example, you will create a simple dialog-style application that contains a single button and a menu:

1. Create a new MFC Application Visual C++ project, naming the project Menus.

2. Select the default Application Wizard settings as on previous days.

3. After the Application Wizard generates your application shell, delete all the controls from the dialog.

4. Add a single button to the dialog. Name (ID property) the button IDC_EXIT, and specify the caption as E&xit.

5. Add a function to the exit button's BN_CLICKED event. Change the code in this function to call OnOK. (Remember, the OnOK function causes the application to close.)

 Note

If you don't remember how to add the OnOK function, review the section "Closing the Application" on Day 3, "Using Controls in Your Application," for an example.

Adding and Customizing a Menu

Now that you've built the basic application, you can start creating a menu for it. To create a menu, first add a menu resource to your project. When you add the resource, Visual C++ automatically invokes the Menu Designer, which allows you to customize the menu. Follow these steps to add and customize a menu:

1. Select the Resource View pane.

2. Select the project resources folder at the top of the tree; in your example, this is Menus.

3. Right-click to open a context menu, and then select Add and then Add Resource.

4. In the Add Resource dialog, select Menu from the list of available resources (see Figure 7.1). Click the New button.

7

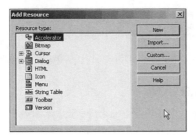

The Menu Designer opens in the editing area of Developer Studio. The first menu spot is highlighted (see Figure 7.2).

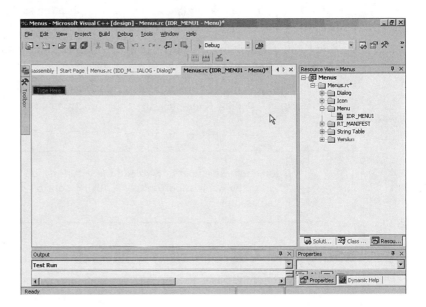

At this point, you've created the menu resource and are ready to customize it by adding menu items. Continue with these steps:

1. Click the highlighted area to be able to enter text into the menu position.
2. Enter the menu item's Caption. For this example, enter **&File**.

Note

When defining menu entries in Visual C++.NET, you type the text to be displayed to users in the menu position. You can't access any properties until you enter a menu entry name in the menu position. Because the Pop-up check box is set to true on the top-level menu entries that you add (by default on any menu items on the top-level menu bar), this menu element doesn't trigger any application functionality and thus doesn't need to have an object ID assigned to it.

3. The first drop-down menu location is highlighted. To add this menu item, click the highlighted area again and enter the text **&Hello**.

4. If you right-click and select Edit IDs, you'll see that the menu ID has already been initialized to ID_FILE_HELLO. Right-click and deselect Edit IDs to restore the menu.

At this point, you've created a menu with a single menu item. You can continue to add menu items by repeating preceding steps 3 and 4 for each highlighted area. You can also add separator lines onto the menu. To add a separator, select the highlighted area where you want the separator to be placed. In the example you just created, the second drop-down menu location should be highlighted. Right-click and select Insert Separator from the context menu (see Figure 7.3). You could also just type - to designate that the menu entry should be a separator.

FIGURE 7.3

Specifying a menu separator.

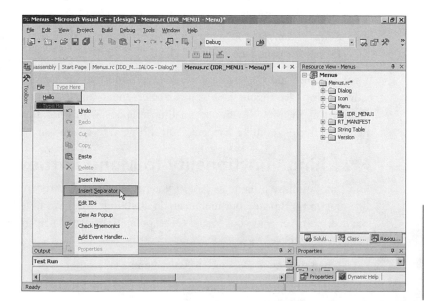

7

To complete your sample program, follow the same steps I just described to add an Exit item to your File menu and a second menu called Help with one menu item called About Menus. The following steps, which resemble the preceding steps, walk you through adding these additional items:

1. Click in the third drop-down location and enter the text **E&xit** for the menu entry caption.

2. Click in the second top-level menu location. Specify the caption as **&Help**.

3. Click in the first location below the Help top-level menu. Enter the text **&About Menus** for the menu entry caption.

At this point, your menu is created; however, it isn't attached to your application.

Attaching the Menu to Your Dialog Window

You now have a menu that you can use in your application. If you compile and run your application at this point, however, the menu doesn't appear. You still need to attach the menu to your dialog window by following these steps:

1. Open the dialog painter by double-clicking the primary application dialog in the Dialog folder in the Resource pane. For this example, double-click IDD_MENUS_DIALOG.

2. Select the entire dialog window, making sure that no controls are selected (what you are doing is preparing to set the properties for the dialog window itself, not for any of the controls that might be on the window).

3. Select the menu you've designed from the Menu drop-down list box in the Properties pane (see Figure 7.4).

If you compile and run your application, you find that the menu is attached to the application dialog (see Figure 7.5). You can select menu entries as you do with any other Windows application—with one small difference. At this point, when you select one of the menu entries, nothing happens. You still need to attach functionality to your menu.

Attaching Functionality to Menu Entries

Now that you have a menu as part of your application, it sure would be nice if it actually did something. Before your menu can do anything, you have to tell it what to do, just like everything else in your Visual C++ applications. To attach some functionality to your menu, follow these steps:

1. Open the Menu Designer to your menu.

2. Select the menu entry labeled Hello (under the File top-level menu).

FIGURE 7.4

Attaching the menu to the dialog window.

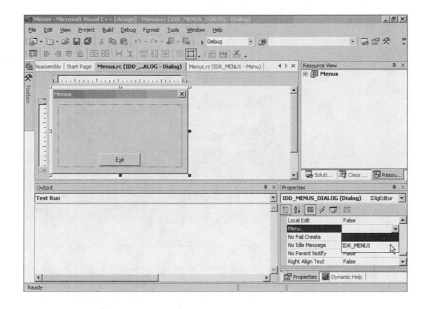

FIGURE 7.5

The menu is now part of the application dialog.

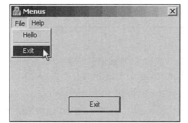

3. Right-click and select Add Event Handler from the context menu.

4. Select the COMMAND message type and the class that you want to have handle the event message. In this example, select the CMenusDlg class from the Class List (see Figure 7.6). Click the Add and Edit button to create the message handler function.

5. Edit the function that was created, adding the code in Listing 7.1.

LISTING 7.1 The OnFileHello Function

```cpp
void CMenusDlg::OnFileHello()
{
    // TODO: Add your control notification handler code here
    // Display a message for the user
    MessageBox("Hello there", "Hello");
}
```

INPUT

7

FIGURE 7.6

The Event Handler
Wizard dialog.

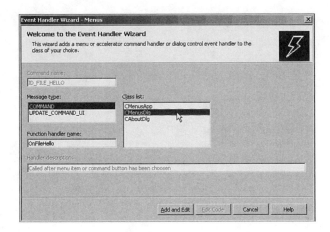

Note

The COMMAND event message is what's passed to the application window when a menu entry is selected. Placing a function on this event message has the same effect as placing a function on the menu entry selection. The actual event message is WM_COMMAND, but it's shortened for the Event Handler Wizard.

In previous versions of Visual C++, you could call existing event handlers from menu elements by adding the existing function to the menu COMMAND event. You can no longer do this in Visual C++.NET through the Event Handler Wizard. As a result, you have to add an event handler function for the menu, and then in that function call the other event handler function that you want to reuse.

To reuse the OnBnClickedExit function for the Exit menu element, follow these steps:

1. Reopen the Menu Designer and then select the Exit menu entry and add an event handler.

2. Add a function for the COMMAND event message. Accept the default function name presented to you by the Class Wizard and click Add and Edit.

3. Edit the function, adding the code in Listing 7.2 to call the Exit button's event handler.

LISTING 7.2   The OnFileExit Function

```
void CMenusDlg::OnFileExit()
{
    // TODO: Add your command handler code here
```

LISTING 7.2 continued

```
INPUT   // Call the exit button's event handler
        OnBnClickedExit();
}
```

4. To round out your example's functionality, add a function to the About menu entry on the COMMAND event message. Edit the function as in Listing 7.3.

LISTING 7.3 The OnHelpAbout Function

```
void CMenusDlg::OnHelpAboutmenus()
{
    // TODO: Add your command handler code here
INPUT   // Declare an instance of the About window
        CAboutDlg dlgAbout;

    // Show the About window
    dlgAbout.DoModal();
}
```

You attached the Exit entry to the File menu by using an existing function that closes the application. On File, Hello, you added a new function that called the MessageBox function to display a simple message. With Help, About Menus, you added another function that declared an instance of the About dialog window and called its DoModal method.

If you compile and run your application, you find that all the menu entries are working. If you select Help, About Menus (see Figure 7.7), you see the application About dialog (see Figure 7.8). If you select File, Hello, you see a Hello there message box (see Figure 7.9). And if you select File, Exit, your application closes.

FIGURE 7.7

The Help, About Menus menu entry.

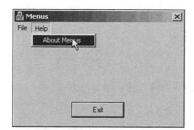

FIGURE 7.8

The About Menus dialog.

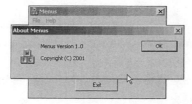

7

FIGURE 7.9

The Hello there message box.

MFC Note: The CMenu Class

The CMenu class encapsulates most of the menu functionality. However, most of the functionality it contains deals with building menus through your code, not for working with menus that you've created using the menu designer. However, some methods enable you to work with predefined menus.

Obviously, for the primary menu you'll be using in your application (or at least the first menu that users will see), you'll attach the menu to the main window and won't need to do any further processing of the menu. If you need to change the menu while your application is running, you'll need to tackle some coding of your own. The first method that you'll need to use for performing this task is LoadMenu. This method takes a single parameter—the resource ID of the menu you want to load. After you load the menu, you can use the CWnd class's SetMenu method on the window for which you want to change menus. The SetMenu method takes a pointer to the new menu as its only parameter. Performing this task would look something like the following:

```
// m_MyNewMenu is a class-level CMenu variable, in the window
// class for which you are wanting to set this as the new
// menu. It is NOT a local variable in the function that
// you are performing the switch.
m_MyNewMenu.LoadMenu(IDR_NEW_MENU);
// Remove the old menu by passing NULL in place of a CMenu pointer
SetMenu(NULL);
// Destroy the old menu using the handle
// m_hMenuHandle is also a class-level HANDLE variable in the
// window class.
// Get a pointer to the old menu
CMenu *pMenu = CMenu::FromHandle(m_hMenuHandle);
if (pMenu)
    // Destroy the menu, freeing any resources it's using
    pMenu->DestroyMenu();
// Add the new menu, passing the address for the CMenu variable
SetMenu(&m_MyNewMenu);
// Assign the new menu handle to the handle variable
m_hMenuHandle = m_MyNewMenu.m_hMenu;
```

In this code, after the old menu was no longer attached to the window, a pointer to the menu was retrieved from the menu handle, and then used to destroy it. This was done by using the FromHandle member function, which takes a CMenu handle as its only parameter and returns a pointer to the menu. After a pointer to the menu was returned, the

DestroyMenu method was called. This removes the old menu from memory, releasing any memory used by the old menu, and frees up any other resources being used by the menu. This could also have been accomplished by calling the Windows API DestroyMenu function, which takes the menu handle as its parameter:

```
// Destroy the old menu using the handle
::DestroyMenu(m_hMenuHandle);
```

You'll learn how to use two other member methods of the CMenu class in the next few pages. These are useful for creating context menus. The CMenu functions are the GetSubMenu function, which can be used to get a pointer to the drop-down portion of a menu, and TrackPopupMenu, which displays the menu as a context menu. You'll use these methods with the CWnd class's GetMenu function, which returns a pointer to the current menu in use by the window.

MFC Note: Menu Event Messages

When you assigned the event handler to your menu entries, you probably noticed two event messages for which you could assign handlers. The first event message, COMMAND, is obviously the event message passed to the window class to signal that the user has selected this particular menu entry. The other event message, UPDATE_COMMAND_UI, isn't quite as obvious as to what it signals. The UPDATE_COMMAND_UI event message is sent to the window class just before the menu entry is displayed for the user. This is the event where you need to add any processing to affect how the menu entry is displayed. If the menu entry should function like a check box and have a check-mark beside it, this is when you add that check mark. If a menu entry should be disabled, this is where you add that functionality. You'll work with this event message in much more detail on Day 10, "Creating SDI and MDI Applications."

Creating Context Menus

Most Windows applications have what are called either pop-up or context menus, which are triggered when users right-click an object. These are called *pop-up menus* because they pop up in the midst of the application area, not attached to a menu bar, the window frame, or anything else on the computer screen (not counting the mouse pointer). These menus are often referred to as *context menus* because the contents of a menu depend on the context in which they're opened; the elements available on the menu depend on what objects are currently selected in the application or what the mouse pointer is positioned over.

7

To provide a pop-up menu in your application, you have two approaches available. You can either design a menu specifically for use as a pop-up menu, or you can use one of the pull-down menus from the primary menu that you've already designed. If you design a menu specifically for use as a pop-up menu, you need to skip the top-level menu bar element by placing a space or some other text in the caption, knowing that it won't be seen (you might want to use a label that describes the context for the menu).

Every drop-down portion of a menu can also be used as a pop-up menu. To use it in this way, you must get a handle to the submenu (the drop-down part of the menu), and then call the TrackPopupMenu function on the submenu. The rest of the pop-up menu functionality is already covered in the other menu building and coding that you've already done. To add a pop-up menu to your application, follow these steps:

1. Using the Messages mode of the Properties pane, add a function for the WM_CONTEXTMENU event message in your dialog window.

> **Note**
>
> You can use two dialog event messages to trigger your context menu. The event you'd expect to use is WM_RBUTTONDOWN, which is triggered by right-clicking. The other event that can (and should) be used is WM_CONTEXTMENU, which is intended for use specifically to trigger a context menu. This event is triggered by a couple of user actions: the release of the right mouse button, and the pressing of the context menu button on one of the newer Windows-enabled keyboards.

2. Edit the function, adding the code in Listing 7.4. Be sure and uncomment the parameters being passed to the function.

LISTING 7.4   The OnContextMenu Function

```
void CMenusDlg::OnContextMenu(CWnd* pWnd, CPoint point)
{
    // TODO: Add your message handler code here
    CMenu *pMenu;

    // Get a pointer to the menu
    pMenu = GetMenu();
    // Get a pointer to the submenu
    pMenu = pMenu->GetSubMenu(0);
    // Open it as a context menu
    pMenu->TrackPopupMenu(TPM_CENTERALIGN | TPM_LEFTBUTTON,
        point.x, point.y, pWnd, NULL);
}
```

ANALYSIS Listing 7.4 first acquired a pointer to the dialog window's menu by using the GetMenu function. This pointer should always be a local pointer within the function where you are going to use it because the location (in memory) of the menu might change as the application runs. From the menu pointer, the code next gets a pointer to the first drop-down menu (submenu numbering begins with 0, like just about everything else in C/C++) by using the GetSubMenu function. After you have a pointer to the submenu, you can treat it as a regular CMenu class instance.

The final piece in this puzzle is the call to the CMenu member function, TrackPopupMenu. This function uses five arguments to determine where and how to show the pop-up menu. The first argument combines two flags. The first flag, TPM_CENTERALIGN, centers the pop-up menu on the mouse pointer. You can also use TPM_LEFTALIGN or TPM_RIGHTALIGN instead. These flags line up the left or right edge of the pop-up menu with the mouse position. The second part of this flag combination is TPM_LEFTBUTTON, which makes the pop-up menu trigger from the left mouse button. You can also use TPM_RIGHTBUTTON to make the menu trigger from the right mouse button.

The second and third arguments to the TrackPopupMenu function specify the screen position for the pop-up menu. This is the absolute position onscreen, not a relative position within the window area. The fourth argument is a pointer to the window that receives the menu command messages. The final argument is a rectangle that users can click without closing the pop-up menu. By passing NULL, you specify that if users click outside the pop-up menu, the menu closes. This code enables you to include a pop-up menu in your application (see Figure 7.10).

FIGURE 7.10

The pop-up menu in action.

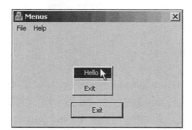

NEW TERM *Absolute position* and *relative position* are methods of specifying location onscreen. These positions are designated as horizontal position (x), and vertical position (y). The position is measured in pixels from the top left corner of the screen, for absolute position, or from the top left corner of the window for relative position. By combining absolute and relative position, you can determine where on the window the mouse pointer is located, and what item is beneath it. This way, you can open a context menu significant to the item under the mouse pointer.

7

Creating a Menu with Accelerators

One of the original keyboard shortcuts for selecting menu entries were accelerator keys. As mentioned earlier today, accelerator keys are specific key combinations, usually the Ctrl key combined with another key, or function keys, that are unique within the entire application. Each key combination triggers one menu event function.

Accelerator keys work similarly to the way menus work. They are also an application resource that's defined in a table in the workspace pane's resource tab. Each table entry has an object ID and a key code combination. After you define the accelerators, you can attach functionality to the object IDs. You can also assign accelerator entries the same object ID as the corresponding menu entry, so you have to define only a single entry in the application message map.

After you define all your accelerator keys, you can add the key combination to the menu entry so that users will know about the accelerator key combination. Add \t to the end of the menu entry caption, followed by the key combination. The \t is replaced in the menu display by a tab, which separates the menu caption from the accelerator key combination.

Note Unfortunately, accelerator keys don't work in dialog-style windows, so you can't add them to today's application. You will learn how to attach accelerator keys to menus in on Day 16 when you learn about using COM interfaces in MFC applications.

Summary

Today you learned about menus in Visual C++ applications. You learned how to use the tools in Visual Studio to create a menu for use in your application and then how to attach the menu to a window in your application. After you had the menu attached to your window, you learned how to attach functionality to the various menu entries. Later in the day, you learned how you can use a portion of your menu as a pop-up, or context, menu. Finally, you learned how accelerator keys are used in most applications. Tomorrow you will learn how to make use of the font capabilities built into Windows, so you can allow users to customize your application's appearance.

Q&A

Q. Do I have to name my menu items the same names everyone else uses? For example, a lot of applications use File and Help. Can I name my menus something else?

A. You can name your top-level menus anything you want. However, there are accepted menu name conventions that place all file-oriented functionality under a menu labeled File and all help-related functionality under a menu labeled Help. If you have a menu with entries such as Broccoli, Corn, and Carrots, you will probably want to call the menu Vegetables, although an equally valid label would be Food or Plants. In general, if you want to make your application easy for your users to learn, you will want to use menu labels that make sense for the entries on the pulldown portion of the menu.

Q. Why can't I specify a single character as an accelerator key?

A. The single character would trigger the WM_KEY messages, not the menu messages. When the designers of Windows were deciding how accelerator keys would work, they decided that single-character keys would most likely be input to the active application. If they had allowed single-character accelerators, Windows wouldn't be able to determine whether the character was input or a shortcut. By requiring a key combination (with the exception of function keys), the designers ensured that Windows won't have to make this determination.

Workshop

The Workshop provides quiz questions to help you solidify your understanding of the material covered and exercises to provide you with experience in using what you've learned. The answers to the quiz questions are provided in Appendix A, "Answers to Quiz Questions."

Quiz

1. What event message does a menu selection send to the window message queue?
2. How do you attach a menu to a dialog window?
3. Which existing class do you specify for handling event messages for the menu?
4. What event message should a pop-up menu be triggered by?

7

Exercises

1. Add a button to the main window and have it call the same function as the Hello menu entry.

2. Modify the context menu to your application, so it uses the Help drop-down menu as the pop-up menu.

WEEK 1

In Review

Well, you've made it through the first week. By this point, you've gotten a good taste for what's possible when building applications with Visual C++. Now it's time to look over what's been covered and what you should have learned up to this point.

What you might want to do at this point—to cement your understanding of how you can use these elements in your own applications—is try designing and building a couple of simple applications of your own. You can use various controls and add some more dialogs, just so you can make sure you understand and are comfortable with these topics. In fact, you might want to try all the topics that I've covered up to this point in small applications of your own design. That's the true test of your understanding. You might also want to dive into the MFC documentation to learn a little about some of the more advanced functionality that I haven't covered to see if you can figure out how you can use and incorporate it into your applications.

One of the most important things that you should understand at this point is how you can use controls and dialog windows in your applications to get and display information to the user. This is an important part of any Windows application because almost all applications interact with the user in some way. You should be able to place any of the standard controls on a dialog in your application and be able to incorporate them into your application without any problem. Likewise, you should be comfortable with using the standard message box and dialog windows provided to your application by the Windows operating system. You should also be able to create and incorporate your own custom dialog windows into any

1

2

3

4

5

6

7

application you might want to build. If you don't feel comfortable with any of these topics, you might want to go back and review Day 3, "Debugging Your Application," to get a better understanding of how to use controls and Day 6, "Adding Dialogs to Your Application for User Feedback," to understand how to incorporate standard and custom dialog windows in your applications.

Another key skill that you will use in most of your applications is the ability to build and incorporate menus into your applications. You need a firm understanding of how to design a good menu, how to ensure that there is no conflicting mnemonics, and how you can attach application functionality to the menu selections. At this point, you should be able to create your own customized menus, with entries for each of the various functions that your application performs, and integrate it with your application with no problems. If you aren't 100% comfortable with this topic, you might want to go back and study Day 7, "Creating Menus for Your Application," again.

You will find various situations in which you need to have some means of triggering actions regularly or in which you need to keep track of how long a process has been running. For both situations, as well as numerous others, you'll often find yourself turning to the use of timers in your application. If you are even slightly foggy on how you can integrate timers into your applications, you will definitely want to go back and review Day 5, "Working with Timers."

Depending on the nature of your application, capturing and tracking mouse and keyboard actions by the user can be very important. If you are building a drawing application, this is crucial information. If you are building an application that needs to include drag-and-drop capabilities, this is also important. There are many situations in which you'll want to include this functionality into your applications. By this point, you should understand how to capture the various mouse events and determine which mouse buttons are involved in the event. You should also be able to capture keyboard events in situations where the keyboard input isn't captured by any controls on the window. If you don't feel as though you have a complete grasp of this, take another look at Day 4, "Integrating Mouse and Keyboard to Allow User Interaction."

Finally, you should be familiar with the Visual C++ development environment—the Developer Studio. You should have a good understanding of what each area of the environment is for and how you can use the various tools and utilities in building your applications. You should be comfortable with using the workspace pane to navigate around your application project, locating and bringing into the various editors and designers any part of your application. You should be comfortable with locating and redesigning the icon that will be displayed to represent your application and with finding any member functions or variables in any of your application's classes. You should be comfortable with the Visual C++ debugger, and how it enables you to step through your code, watching to make sure that everything is working the way that you want it to work. Use the debugger on each of the examples that you build throughout this book. By the end of the 21 days, you should be quite experienced with the debugger.

By now you should be fairly comfortable working with Visual C++. If you feel you understand all the topics that I've covered so far, you are ready to move forward, learning more about the various things that you can do, and functionality that you can build, using Visual C++ as your programming tool. With that said, it's on to the second week...

WEEK 2

At a Glance

In the second week, you'll dive into several more involved topics. These topics are still very much core to building Windows applications. You'll find yourself using what you learn in this week, along with what you learned during the first week, in just about all applications that you build with Visual C++.

To start the week, on Day 8, "Working with Text and Fonts," you'll learn about the Windows font infrastructure and how you can access it in your Visual C++ applications. You'll see how to build a list of available fonts and how to display text in any of these fonts.

On Day 9, "Incorporating Graphics, Drawings, and Bitmaps," you'll learn how to draw graphics in a Windows application. You'll learn how to draw simple lines, rectangles, and ellipses. You'll also learn how to use the device context to draw your graphics without worrying about the graphics hardware your users might or might not have in their computers.

On Day 10, "Creating SDI and MDI Applications," you'll learn how to build a basic Single Document Interface (SDI) application. You'll learn about the Document/View architecture used with Visual C++ for building this style of application, and also how to use it to build your own applications. You'll also learn how you can apply what you learned about building SDI applications to building Multiple Document Interface (MDI) applications. You'll see how you can use the same Document/View architecture to create MDI applications, some of the most common styles of Windows applications available today.

8

9

10

11

12

13

14

On Day 11, "Adding Toolbars and Status Bars," you'll learn how to create and modify your own toolbars and status bars. You'll learn how to attach toolbar buttons to menus in your application and how to add more toolbars. You'll also learn how to place your own informational elements on the status bar at the bottom of most Windows applications and how to keep the status bar updated with the status of your application.

On Day 12, "Saving and Restoring Work," you'll see how you can use the structure provided for you by the Document/View architecture to save and restore the data created in your application. You'll learn how flexible this facility is and how you can store different data types in the same file, restoring them to your application just as they were when you first saved them.

On Day 13, "Updating and Adding Database Records Through ADO," you'll learn about Microsoft's latest database access technology, ActiveX Data Objects (ADO), and how to incorporate it into your Visual C++ applications to provide database access to your application's users.

Finally, rounding out the week on Day 14, "Sharing Functionality with Other Applications Through DLLs," you'll learn a different means of allowing other programmers to use your code by building DLLs. You'll learn how to build two different types of DLLs: those that can be used only by other Visual C++ applications and those that can be used by applications built with any other Windows development language or tool.

When you finish this week, you'll be well prepared for tackling most basic application development tasks with Visual C++. You might want to take a short break at that point to experiment a bit—try to build various types of applications, pushing your skills, and learning what your limits are (and aren't)—before jumping into the final week of more advanced topics.

DAY **8**

Working with Text and Fonts

In most Windows applications, you don't need to worry about specifying fonts, much less their weight, height, and so on. If you don't specify the font to be used, Windows supplies a default font for your application. If you do need to use a particular font, you can specify one to use for a particular dialog box through the dialog's properties. Sometimes, however, you want or need to control the font used in your application. You might need to change the font being used or to allow the user to select a font to use in a particular instance. It's for those circumstances that you will learn how to change and list fonts today. Among the things that you will learn are how to

- Build a list of available fonts
- Specify a font for use
- Change fonts dynamically

Finding and Using Fonts

One of the first things that you need to know when working with fonts is that not every system that your applications run on will have the same fonts installed. Fonts are specified in files that can be installed and removed from Windows systems with relative ease. All computer users can customize their systems with whatever combination of fonts they want. If you specify a font that doesn't exist on the system, Windows will choose either the system default font or what the operating system considers to be a reasonably close alternative font.

What you can do instead is ask the operating system what fonts are available. This method allows you to make your own decisions on which font to use or enables you to let the user make the decision. When you ask what fonts are available, you can limit the types of fonts that are listed, or you can choose to list them all and select various fonts based on various attributes.

Listing the Available Fonts

To get a list of all available fonts on a computer, you call the EnumFontFamiliesEx Windows API (Application Programming Interface) function. This function tells Windows that you want a list of the fonts on the system. Before you start using this function and expecting it to pass you a big list of available fonts, you need to understand how it gives you the list.

Callback Functions

NEW TERM   One key argument to the EnumFontFamiliesEx function is the address of another function. This second function is what's known as a *callback function*, which is called by the operating system. For almost every enumeration function in the Windows operating system, you pass the address of a callback function as an argument, because the callback function is called once for each element in the enumerated list. In other words, you have to include a function in your application to receive each individual font that's on the system, and then build the list of fonts yourself.

When you create this function to receive each font and build your list, you can't define your callback function in any way you want. All callback functions are already defined in the Windows API. You have to use a specific type of callback function to receive the font list. For getting a font list, the function type is EnumFontFamExProc. This function type specifies how your function must be defined, what its arguments must be, and what type of return value it must return. It doesn't specify what your function should be named or how it needs to work internally. These aspects are left completely up to you.

The `EnumFontFamiliesEx` Function

The `EnumFontFamiliesEx` function, which you call to request the list of available fonts, takes five arguments. A typical use of this function follows:

```
// Create a device context variable
CClientDC dc (this);
// Declare a LOGFONT structure
LOGFONT lLogFont;

// Specify the character set
lLogFont.lfCharSet = DEFAULT_CHARSET;
// Specify all fonts
lLogFont.lfFaceName[0] = NULL;
// Must be zero unless Hebrew or Arabic
lLogFont.lfPitchAndFamily = 0;
// Enumerate the font families
::EnumFontFamiliesEx((HDC) dc, &lLogFont,
(FONTENUMPROC) MyEnumFontFamExProc, (LPARAM) this, 0);
```

ANALYSIS The first argument is a device context, which can be an instance of the `CClientDC` class. Every application running within the Windows operating system has a device context, which provides a lot of necessary information from the operating system about what's available to the application and what isn't.

The second argument is a pointer to a `LOGFONT` structure. This structure contains information about the fonts that you want listed. You can specify in this structure which character set you want to list or whether you want all the fonts in a particular font family. If you want all the fonts on the system, you pass `NULL` in the place of this argument.

The third argument is the address of the callback function that will be used to build your font list. Passing the address of your callback function is a simple matter of using the function name as the argument. The Visual C++ compiler takes care of replacing the function name with the function address. You do, however, need to cast the function as the type of callback function that the function requires.

The fourth argument is a `LPARAM` value that will be passed to the callback function. This parameter isn't used by Windows but provides your callback function with a context in which to build the font list. In the example, the value being passed is a pointer to the window in which the code is being run. This way, the callback function can use this pointer to access any structures it needs to build the list of fonts. This pointer can also be the first node in a linked list of fonts or other such structure.

The final argument is always `0`. This reserved argument may be used in future versions of Windows, but for now, it must be `0` so that your application passes a value that won't cause the function to misbehave.

MFC Note: The LOGFONT Structure

The LOGFONT structure contains information about the font to be displayed. This information includes the height, width, weight, and whether the font is boldfaced or italicized. The LOGFONT structure is defined as follows:

```
typedef struct tagLOGFONT
{
    LONG        lfHeight;
    LONG        lfWidth;
    LONG        lfEscapement;
    LONG        lfOrientation;
    LONG        lfWeight;
    BYTE        lfItalic;
    BYTE        lfUnderline;
    BYTE        lfStrikeOut;
    BYTE        lfCharSet;
    BYTE        lfOutPrecision;
    BYTE        lfClipPrecision;
    BYTE        lfQuality;
    BYTE        lfPitchAndFamily;
    TCHAR       lfFaceName[LF_FACESIZE];
} LOGFONT;
```

The LOGFONT structure is the same as the parameters passed to the CreateFont function. Each structure member is discussed in detail shortly with the CreateFont function. The only real difference between the LOGFONT structure and the parameters to the CreateFont function is the last member, lfFaceName. With the CreateFont function, this last parameter is a pointer to a string that contains the name of the font. In the LOGFONT structure, the actual string is included, and it's limited in length to 32 characters, the value that LF_FACESIZE is currently defined as.

C++ Sidebar: Structures in C++

In C++, you hear a lot about classes and structures. Both seem very similar in how they work and how you interact with them. However, despite the similarities, the two are different. Structures originated with the C programming language. They are a way of defining a group of values that should always be kept together. Usually, a structure contains a number of member data elements that collectively describe something, which classes also do. One key difference between classes and structures is that structures rarely contain any functionality—they mostly contain only data elements. The technical difference between structures and classes is that the default access for structures is public, whereas the default access for classes is private. However, the real difference is in usage, as structures are primarily used only for holding data structures.

The basic syntax for defining a structure is as follows

```
struct MyStructure
{
    // Some data elements
};
```

or as follows:

```
struct
{
    // Some data elements
} MyStructure;
```

With this definition, you can declare an instance of this structure with the following variable declaration:

```
struct MyStructure msMyVariable;
```

C++ Sidebar: Defining Custom Data Types

When you are working with structures, you'll often want to declare a structure as a data type, so you can simplify the declaration and use of the structure throughout your application. This is done by adding the keyword `typedef` in front of your structure definition, as follows:

```
typedef struct tMySyructure
{
    // Some data elements
} MyStructure;
```

This enables you to simplify the variable declaration as follows:

```
MyStructure msMyVariable;
```

By declaring a data type of your structure, you no longer have to specify that it's a structure each time you need to declare an instance of that structure. You don't have to limit your data type declarations to structures, you can also define your own data types that are the same as other basic data types, as follows:

```
typedef long MyLong;
```

You'll normally do something like this when you have a consistently used data type that you want to reflect the purpose of the variable through the data type. This is how many Windows data types are defined, such as DWORD, HANDLE, and BYTE. All these standard variable types have been defined by using the `typedef` keyword.

You can also declare data types as pointers to other data types and structures by adding the asterisk just before the type name:

```
typedef long* PLONG;
```

In this instance, the PLONG data type is defined as a pointer to a long variable.

> **Note**
>
> It's common practice when you use typedef to declare a pointer data type that the data type name begin with "P" or "LP" (for Long Pointer, a holdover from 16-bit days), followed by the variable type, usually in all uppercase. For instance, if you declare a data type that's a pointer to a char data type, you would name the new data type as PCHAR. Extending this a little further, when you declare a data type as a pointer to a structure, the name is normally "P" followed by the structure name, all in uppercase (e.g. PMYSTRUCTURE would be a pointer to an instance of the MyStructure structure).
>
> This isn't to be confused with #define and const declarations, which typically are also all uppercase. These aren't the same, but the common practice in using all uppercase is used with all these situations.

The EnumFontFamExProc Function Type

Your callback function must be defined as an independent function, not as a member of any C++ class. A typical EnumFontFamExProc function declaration follows:

```
int CALLBACK MyEnumFontFamExProc(
LPENUMLOGFONTEX lpelf,
LPNEWTEXTMETRICEX lpntm,
DWORD nFontType,
long lParam)
{
    // Create a pointer to the dialog window
    CMyDlg* pWnd = (CMyDlg*) lParam;

    if (pWnd)
    {
        // Add the font name to the list box
        pWnd->m_ctlFontList.AddString(lpelf->elfLogFont.lfFaceName);
        // Return 1 to continue font enumeration
        return 1;
    }
    // NULL window pointer, stop the enumeration
    return 0;
}
```

ANALYSIS   The first argument to this function is a pointer to an ENUMLOGFONTEX structure. This structure contains information about the font's logical attributes, including the font name, style, and script. You may have numerous fonts listed with the same name but different styles. You can have one for normal, one for bold, one for italic, and one for bold italic.

The second argument is a pointer to a NEWTEXTMETRICEX structure. This structure contains information about the font's physical attributes, such as height, width, and space around the font. These values are all relative in nature because they need to scale as the font is made larger or smaller.

The third argument is a flag that specifies the type of font. This value may contain a combination of the following values:

- DEVICE_FONTTYPE
- RASTER_FONTTYPE
- TRUETYPE_FONTTYPE

Finally, the fourth argument is the value passed into the EnumFontFamiliesEx function. In the example, it was a pointer to the dialog on which the list of fonts is being built. If you cast this value as a pointer to the dialog, the function can access a list box control to add the font names.

The return value from this function determines whether the font listing continues. If this function returns 0, the operating system quits listing the available fonts. If 1 is returned, the operating system continues to list the available fonts.

MFC Note: The ENUMLOGFONTEX Structure

The ENUMLOGFONTEX structure contains information about enumerated fonts. The definition of this structure is as follows:

```
typedef struct tagENUMLOGFONTEX
{
    LOGFONT     elfLogFont;
    TCHAR       elfFullName[LF_FULLFACESIZE];
    TCHAR       elfStyle[LF_FACESIZE];
    TCHAR       elfScript[LF_FACESIZE];
} ENUMLOGFONTEX, FAR *LPENUMLOGFONTEX;
```

The elfLogFont member is a LOGFONT structure. It contains information about the specific font and its capabilities.

The elfFullName member is a string containing a unique name for the font, unless you are running on Windows 95/98/ME, in which it only specifies the unique name for TrueType fonts. For non-TrueType fonts on Windows 95/98/ME, the unique font name is in the lfFaceName member of the LOGFONT structure elfLogFont.

The elfStyle member contains a string that describes the style of the font. An example of this would be "Bold", "Italic", or "Bold Italic".

The elfScript member contains a string specifying the character set used by the font.

MFC Note: The NEWTEXTMETRICEX Structure

The NEWTEXTMETRICEX structure contains information about a font. All the information is contained in two other structures combined to make the NEWTEXTMETRICEX structure, as follows:

```
typedef struct tagNEWTEXTMETRICEX
{
    NEWTEXTMETRIC    ntmTm;
    FONTSIGNATURE    ntmFontSig;
}NEWTEXTMETRICEX;
```

The first of these two structures, NEWTEXTMETRIC, is defined as follows:

```
typedef struct tagNEWTEXTMETRIC
{
    LONG        tmHeight;
    LONG        tmAscent;
    LONG        tmDescent;
    LONG        tmInternalLeading;
    LONG        tmExternalLeading;
    LONG        tmAveCharWidth;
    LONG        tmMaxCharWidth;
    LONG        tmWeight;
    LONG        tmOverhang;
    LONG        tmDigitizedAspectX;
    LONG        tmDigitizedAspectY;
    TCHAR       tmFirstChar;
    TCHAR       tmLastChar;
    TCHAR       tmDefaultChar;
    TCHAR       tmBreakChar;
    BYTE        tmItalic;
    BYTE        tmUnderlined;
    BYTE        tmStruckOut;
    BYTE        tmPitchAndFamily;
    BYTE        tmCharSet;
    DWORD       ntmFlags;
    UINT        ntmSizeEM;
```

```
    UINT        ntmCellHeight;
    UINT        ntmAvgWidth;
} NEWTEXTMETRIC;
```

The NEWTEXTMETRIC structure contains information about the font, such as its size, average and maximum character width, and how much overhang (how far below the line all characters sit on do characters like g, q, and p go) it has.

The second structure, FONTSIGNATURE, is defined as follows:

```
typedef struct tagFONTSIGNATURE
{
    DWORD fsUsb[4];
    DWORD fsCsb[2];
} FONTSIGNATURE;
```

The two members of this structure point to information about what glyphs are supplied by this font. This information is key for knowing which languages can use a particular font. This is an element of making Windows portable to different languages and character sets.

NEW TERM — A *glyph* is the shape of a font character. The form that glyphs take depends on the font type. In raster fonts, a glyph is the bitmap used by the system to display each character or symbol in the font. In vector fonts, a glyph is the collection of points connected to draw the characters or symbols in the font (basically, each character is drawn by performing "connect-the-dots"). With TrueType and OpenType fonts, a glyph is a collection of line and curve drawing commands performed to draw the characters or symbols in the font.

Creating a Font for Use

To use a particular font in an application, you call an instance of the CFont class. By calling the CreateFont method, you can specify the font to be used, along with the size, style, and orientation. After you create a font, you can tell a control or window to use the font by calling the object's SetFont method. An example of this process follows:

```
CFont m_fFont;    // The font to be used

// Create the font to be used
m_fFont.CreateFont(12, 0, 0, 0, FW_NORMAL,
        0, 0, 0, DEFAULT_CHARSET, OUT_CHARACTER_PRECIS,
        CLIP_CHARACTER_PRECIS, DEFAULT_QUALITY, DEFAULT_PITCH |
        FF_DONTCARE, m_sFontName);

// Set the font for the display area
m_ctlDisplayText.SetFont(&m_fFont);
```

> **Note**
>
> The CFont variable used here should be declared as a member variable of the class in which this code is placed. It's declared here, where it's used to show how it's declared. This variable shouldn't be declared or used as a local variable in a function.

Seems simple enough—just two function calls—but that CreateFont function needs many arguments passed to it. It's these arguments that make the CreateFont method a flexible function with a large amount of functionality. After you create the font, using it is a simple matter of passing it to the SetFont method, which is a member of the CWnd class and thus available to all window and control classes in Visual C++. This means that you can use this technique on any visible object within a Visual C++ MFC application.

To understand how the CreateFont function works, look at the individual arguments that you have to pass to it. The function is defined as

```
BOOL CreateFont(
    int nHeight,
    int nWidth,
    int nEscapement,
    int nOrientation,
    int nWeight,
    BYTE bItalic,
    BYTE bUnderline,
    BYTE cStrikeOut,
    BYTE nCharSet,
    BYTE nOutPrecision,
    BYTE nClipPrecision,
    BYTE nQuality,
    BYTE nPitchAndFamily,
    LPCTSTR lpszFaceName);
```

 The first of these arguments, nHeight, specifies the height of the font to be used. This logical value is translated into a physical value. If the value is 0, a reasonable default value is used. If the value is greater or less than 0, the absolute height is converted into device units. It's key to understand that height values of 10 and –10 are basically the same.

The second argument, nWidth, specifies the average width of the font's characters. This logical value is translated into a physical value in much the same way as the height is.

The third argument, nEscapement, determines the angle at which the text will be printed. This value is specified counterclockwise in 0.1-degree units. If you want to print vertical text that reads from bottom to top, supply 900 as the value for this argument. For printing normal horizontal text that flows from left to right, supply 0 as this value.

8

The fourth argument, nOrientation, determines the angle of each individual character in the font. This works on the same basis as the previous argument, but it controls the output on a character basis, not a line-of-text basis. To print upside-down characters, set this value to 1800. To print characters on their backs, set this value to 900.

The fifth argument, nWeight, specifies the weight, or boldness, of the font. This can be any value from 0 to 1000, with 1000 being heavily bolded. You can use constants defined for this argument to control this value with ease and consistency. Table 8.1 lists these constants.

TABLE 8.1 Font Weight Constants

Constant	Value
FW_DONTCARE	0
FW_THIN	100
FW_EXTRALIGHT	200
FW_ULTRALIGHT	200
FW_LIGHT	300
FW_NORMAL	400
FW_REGULAR	400
FW_MEDIUM	500
FW_SEMIBOLD	600
FW_DEMIBOLD	600
FW_BOLD	700
FW_EXTRABOLD	800
FW_ULTRABOLD	800
FW_BLACK	900
FW_HEAVY	900

Note

You've already seen several sets of constant values and will see several more throughout this book. You might wonder about the naming convention of these constants. Notice that they all have a two- or three-letter prefix. This prefix usually indicates what the constant is used for, or is the initials of what use the constants are intended for. In this instance, all the constants have the initials FW, which is short for *font weight*. With all the sets of constants that you see throughout this book, and in the Windows API (as well as the MFC class library), look at the prefix and compare it to the use of the constant to determine what the prefix stands for.

The actual interpretation and availability of these weights depends on the font. Some fonts only have FW_NORMAL, FW_REGULAR, and FW_BOLD weights. If you specify FW_DONT-CARE, a default weight is used, just as with most of the rest of the arguments.

The sixth argument, bItalic, specifies whether the font is to be italicized. This is a Boolean value: 0 indicates that the font isn't italicized, and any other value indicates that the font is italicized.

The seventh argument, bUnderline, specifies whether the font is to be underlined. This value is also Boolean: 0 indicates that the font isn't underlined, and any other value indicates that the font is underlined.

> **Note**
>
> These values, while Boolean in nature, are declared as BYTE data types. Until the bool data type was introduced into the C++ standard, Boolean data types were defined as integers where 0 was FALSE, and any other value was TRUE. This is how Boolean expressions in conditional statements can function—by checking a pointer's value to determine whether the pointer is valid. If the pointer was initialized to NULL, any non-zero value means that the pointer has been set to point to something. It's this same form of Boolean values being used in these parameters. By treating them as Booleans, a 0 value is FALSE, and any other value is TRUE.

The eighth argument, cStrikeOut, specifies whether the characters in the font are displayed with a line through the character. This is another Boolean value using a nonzero value as TRUE and 0 as FALSE.

The ninth argument, nCharSet, specifies the font's character set. Table 8.2 lists the available constants for this value.

TABLE 8.2   Font Character Set Constants

Constant	Value
ANSI_CHARSET	0
DEFAULT_CHARSET	1
SYMBOL_CHARSET	2
SHIFTJIS_CHARSET	128
OEM_CHARSET	255

The system on which your application is running might have other character sets, and the OEM character set is system-dependent, making it different for systems from different manufacturers. If you are using one of these character sets, it's risky to try to manipulate the strings to be output, so it's best to just pass along the string to be displayed.

The 10th argument, nOutPrecision, specifies how closely the output must match the requested font's height, width, character orientation, escapement, and pitch. The available values for this argument are

- OUT_CHARACTER_PRECIS
- OUT_DEFAULT_PRECIS
- OUT_DEVICE_PRECIS
- OUT_OUTLINE_PRECIS
- OUT_RASTER_PRECIS
- OUT_STRING_PRECIS
- OUT_STROKE_PRECIS
- OUT_TT_ONLY_PRECIS
- OUT_TT_PRECIS

The OUT_DEVICE_PRECIS, OUT_RASTER_PRECIS, and OUT_TT_PRECIS values control which font is chosen if multiple fonts have the same name. For instance, if you use OUT_TT_PRECIS and specify a font with both a TrueType and raster version, the TrueType version is used. In fact, OUT_TT_PRECIS forces the system to use a TrueType font, even when the specified font doesn't have a TrueType version.

The 11th argument, nClipPrecision, specifies how to clip characters that are partially outside the display area. The values for this argument are

- CLIP_CHARACTER_PRECIS
- CLIP_DEFAULT_PRECIS
- CLIP_EMBEDDED
- CLIP_LH_ANGLES
- CLIP_MASK
- CLIP_STROKE_PRECIS
- CLIP_TT_ALWAYS

These values can be ORed together to specify a combination of clipping techniques.

The 12th argument, nQuality, specifies the output quality and how carefully the GDI (Graphics Device Interface) must attempt to match the logical font attributes to the physical font output. The available values for this argument are

- ANTIALIASED_QUALITY
- CLEARTYPE_QUALITY
- DEFAULT_QUALITY
- DRAFT_QUALITY
- NONANTIALIASED_QUALITY
- PROOF_QUALITY

The 13th argument, nPitchAndFamily, specifies the font's pitch and family. This value consists of two values ORed together to create a combination value. The first set of available values is

- DEFAULT_PITCH
- VARIABLE_PITCH
- FIXED_PITCH

This value specifies the pitch to be used with the font. The second set of available values specifies the font family to use. The available values for this portion of the argument are

- FF_DECORATIVE
- FF_DONTCARE
- FF_MODERN
- FF_ROMAN
- FF_SCRIPT
- FF_SWISS

The font family describes the general appearance of a font. You can use the font family value to choose an alternative font when a specific font doesn't exist on a system.

The final argument, lpszFacename, is a standard C-style string that contains the name of the font to be used. This font name comes from the font information received by the EnumFontFamExProc callback function.

Using Fonts

Today you will build an application that allows users to select from a list of available fonts to display. Users will be able to enter some text to display in the selected font, allowing them to see what the font looks like.

Creating the Application Shell

To begin today's application, follow these steps:

1. Create a new MFC Application Visual C++ project. Name the project TextFonts.

2. Use the same defaults that you have used for the previous day's projects, giving the application a title of Fonts.

3. Design the main dialog as in Figure 8.1 using the properties in Table 8.3.

FIGURE 8.1

The main dialog layout.

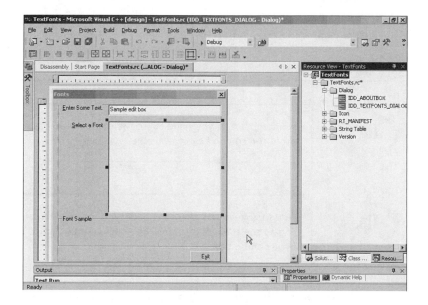

TABLE 8.3 Control Property Settings

Object	Property	Setting
Static Text	Caption	&Enter Some Text:
Edit Box	ID	IDC_ESAMPTEXT
Static Text	Caption	&Select a Font
List Box	ID	IDC_LFONTS
Group Box	Caption	Font Sample
Static Text (inside group box; size to fill the group box)	ID	IDC_DISPLAYTEXT
	Caption	Leave blank.
Command Button	ID	IDC_EXIT
	Caption	E&xit

4. Using the same actions as in previous days, add the variables in Table 8.4 to the dialog's controls.

TABLE 8.4   Control Variables

Object	Name	Category	Type
IDC_DISPLAYTEX	m_ctlDisplayText	Control	CStatic
(Static Text	m_strDisplayText	Value	CString
control inside the group			
box with no caption)			
IDC_LFONTS	m_ctlFontList	Control	CListBox
	m_strFontName	Value	CString
IDC_ESAMPTEXT	m_strSampText	Value	CString

Tip   Remember that you need to set the category first before selecting the type from the combo box of available types.

Tip   You may need to type in the data type for the variables that you are attaching to the static text control. The data types may not be available in the type combo box.

5. Attach a function to the IDC_EXIT button to close the application, as in yesterday's applications.

Building a List of Fonts

To be able to create your list of fonts, you need to add your callback function to get each font list and add it to the list box that you placed on the dialog window. To do this, edit the TextFontsDlg.h header file and add the function declaration in Listing 8.1 near the top of the file. This function can't be added through any of the tools available in Visual C++. You need to open the file and add it yourself.

LISTING 8.1   The Callback Function Declaration in the TextFontsDlg.h Header File

```
#pragma once
#include "afxwin.h"
```

LISTING 8.1 continued

```
INPUT    int CALLBACK MyEnumFontProc(ENUMLOGFONTEX* lpelf,
             NEWTEXTMETRICEX* lpntm, DWORD nFontType, long lParam);
```

After you add the function declaration to the header file, open the TextFontsDlg.cpp
source-code file, scroll to the bottom, and add the function definition in Listing 8.2.

LISTING 8.2 The Callback Function Definition in the TextFontsDlg.cpp Source File

```
int CALLBACK MyEnumFontProc(ENUMLOGFONTEX* lpelf,
    NEWTEXTMETRICEX* lpntm, DWORD nFontType, long lParam)
{
    // Create a pointer to the dialog window
    CTextFontsDlg* pWnd = (CTextFontsDlg*) lParam;

    if (pWnd)
    {
        // Add the font name to the list box
        pWnd->m_ctlFontList.AddString(lpelf->elfLogFont.lfFaceName);
        // Return 1 to continue font enumeration
        return 1;
    }
    return 0;
}
```

Note Although the portion that you need to enter in other code listings is boldfaced, no portion has been boldfaced in Listing 8.2. This is because you need
to enter the entire listing. No portion of this listing has already been added
by any of the code-generating wizards in the Visual C++ environment.

Now that you have the callback function defined, you need to add a function to request
the list of fonts from the operating system. To add this function, follow these steps:

1. Select the Class View pane.

2. Select the CTextFontsDlg class, right-click the mouse, and select Add and then
   Add Function from the context menu.

3. Specify the function type as void, the function name as FillFontList, and the
   access as Private. Click the Finish button to close the dialog and add the function.

4. Add the function definition as in Listing 8.3.

LISTING 8.3   The `FillFontList` Function

```
void CTextFontsDlg::FillFontList(void)
{
    LOGFONT lf;

    lf.lfCharSet = DEFAULT_CHARSET;
    // Specify all fonts
    lf.lfFaceName[0] = NULL;
    // Must be zero unless Hebrew or Arabic
    lf.lfPitchAndFamily = 0;

    // Clear the list box
    m_ctlFontList.ResetContent();
    // Create a device context variable
    CClientDC dc (this);
    // Enumerate the font families
    ::EnumFontFamiliesEx((HDC) dc, &lf,
        (FONTENUMPROC) MyEnumFontProc, (LPARAM) this, 0);
}
```

INPUT

5. Edit the `OnInitDialog` function to call the `FillFontList` function, as in Listing 8.4.

LISTING 8.4   The Edited `OnInitDialog` Function

```
BOOL CTextFontsDlg::OnInitDialog()
{
    CDialog::OnInitDialog();
...
    // Set the icon for this dialog.  The framework does this automatically
    //  when the application's main window is not a dialog
    SetIcon(m_hIcon, TRUE);              // Set big icon
    SetIcon(m_hIcon, FALSE);           // Set small icon

    // TODO: Add extra initialization here
    // Fill the font list box
    FillFontList();

    return TRUE;  // return TRUE  unless you set the focus to a control
}
```

INPUT

If you compile and run your application now, you should find that your list box is filled with the names of all available fonts on the system. However, there's one aspect of this list that you probably don't want in your application. Figure 8.2 shows many duplicate entries in the list of fonts in the list box. It would be nice if you could eliminate these duplicates and have only one line per font.

FIGURE 8.2

Listing all the fonts in the system.

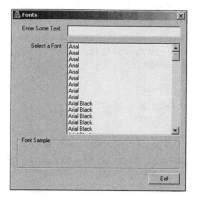

8

It just so happens that the EnumFontFamiliesEx function call is synchronous in nature. This means that it doesn't return until all the fonts in the system are listed in calls to your callback function. You can place code in the FillFontList function to remove all the duplicate entries once the list box is filled. To do this, modify the FillFontList function as in Listing 8.5.

LISTING 8.5   The Modified FillFontList Function

```
void CTextFontsDlg::FillFontList(void)
{
    int iCurCount;              // The current font
    CString strCurFont;             // The current font name
    CString strPrevFont = "";   // The previous font name
    LOGFONT lf;

    lf.lfCharSet = DEFAULT_CHARSET;
    // Specify all fonts
    lf.lfFaceName[0] = NULL;
    // Must be zero unless Hebrew or Arabic
    lf.lfPitchAndFamily = 0;

    // Clear the list box
    m_ctlFontList.ResetContent();
    // Create a device context variable
    CClientDC dc (this);
    // Enumerate the font families
    ::EnumFontFamiliesEx((HDC) dc, &lf,
        (FONTENUMPROC) EnumFontFamProc, (LPARAM) this, 0);
    // Loop from the last entry in the list box to the first,
    // searching for and deleting the duplicate entries
    for (iCurCount = m_ctlFontList.GetCount(); iCurCount > 0; iCurCount--)
    {
        // Get the current font name
```

INPUT

INPUT

LISTING 8.5 continued

```
        m_ctlFontList.GetText((iCurCount - 1), strCurFont);
        // Is it the same as the previous font name?
        if (strCurFont == strPrevFont)
        {
            // If yes, then delete it
            m_ctlFontList.DeleteString((iCurCount - 1));
        }
        else
        {
            // Set the previous font name to the current font name
            strPrevFont = strCurFont;
        }
    }
}
```

Notice that the for loop started at the end of the list and worked backward. This allowed you to delete the current entry without worrying about manipulating the loop counter to prevent skipping lines in the list box. If you compile and run your application, there shouldn't be any duplicate entries in the list of available fonts.

C++ Sidebar: Casting Pointers

One strength of C/C++ is its ability to cast pointers. When you declare a pointer as a certain data or class type, it will treat anything it points to as that type. If you declare a pointer as a pointer to a CWnd class, and it points to a CDialog class instance, you can only call the member functions and touch member variables of the CWnd class. What you can do is cast that pointer as a pointer to a CDialog class, enabling you to access the member functions and variables of the CDialog class. The same can be done with pointers to other data types where you can cast a pointer to a character as a pointer to an integer to access the ASCII value of the character.

You cast a pointer as a different type by enclosing within parentheses the data type that you want to cast the pointer as, along with an asterisk to signal that you are still casting it as a pointer to this new data type, as follows:

```
(NewType*)pPtr;
```

For instance, if you have a pointer to a CWnd class and need to set it to a pointer to a CDialog class, you would do it like this:

```
CDialog* pDlg = (CDialog*)pWndPtr;
```

You can also directly cast and call methods without setting the pointer to another pointer:

```
((CDialog*)pWndPtr)->DoModal();
```

Setting the Font Sample Text

Before you can display the font for users, you need to place some text into the display area. The edit box near the top of the dialog is where users enter text to be displayed in the font selected. To add the functionality, do the following:

1. Edit the OnInitDialog function to add code to initialize the edit box and display text, as in Listing 8.6.

LISTING 8.6 The Modified OnInitDialog Function

```
BOOL CTextFontsDlg::OnInitDialog()
{
    CDialog::OnInitDialog();

. . .

    // Set the icon for this dialog.  The framework does this automatically
    //  when the application's main window is not a dialog
    SetIcon(m_hIcon, TRUE);             // Set big icon
    SetIcon(m_hIcon, FALSE);            // Set small icon

    // TODO: Add extra initialization here
    // Fill the font list box
    FillFontList();
```

INPUT
```
    // Initialize the text to be entered
    m_strSampText = "Testing";
    // Copy the text to the font sample area
    m_strDisplayText = m_strSampText;
    // Update the dialog
    UpdateData(FALSE);

    return TRUE;  // return TRUE  unless you set the focus to a control
}
```

2. Using the Control Events mode of the Properties pane, add a function on the EN_CHANGE event message for the IDC_ESAMPTEXT edit box control.

3. Edit the function you just added, adding the code in Listing 8.7.

LISTING 8.7 The OnEnChangeEsamptext Function

```
void CTextFontsDlg::OnEnChangeEsamptext(void)
{
    // TODO:  If this is a RICHEDIT control, the control will not
    // send this notification unless you override the CDialog::OnInitDialog()
```

LISTING 8.7   continued

```
         // function and call CRichEditCtrl().SetEventMask()
         // with the ENM_CHANGE flag ORed into the mask.

         // TODO:  Add your control notification handler code here
         // Update the variables with the dialog controls
         UpdateData(TRUE);
         // Copy the current text to the font sample
         m_strDisplayText = m_strSampText;
         // Update the dialog with the variables
         UpdateData(FALSE);
     }
```

INPUT

If you compile and run your application, you should be able to type text into the edit box
and see it changed in the font display area in the group box below.

Selecting a Font to Display

Before you can start changing the font for the display area, you need to have a CFont
member variable of the dialog class that you can use to set and change the display font.
To add this variable, follow these steps:

1. In the Class View pane, right-click the CTextFontsDlg class and choose Add and
   then Add Variable.

2. Specify the variable type as CFont, the variable name as m_fSampFont, and the
   access as Private. Click the Finish button to close the dialog and add the variable.

When adding the code to use the selected font, you'll add it as a separate function that's
not attached to a control because you will eventually call this function from several different functions. To add the function to display and use the selected font, follow these
steps:

1. In the Class View pane, right-click the CTextFontsDlg class and choose Add and
   then Add Function.

2. Specify the function type as void, the function name as SetMyFont, and the access
   as Private. Click OK to close the dialog and add the function.

3. Edit the function to add the code in Listing 8.8.

LISTING 8.8   The SetMyFont Function

```
     void CTextFontsDlg::SetMyFont(void)
     {
         CRect rRect;          // The rectangle of the display area

         // Has a font been selected?
```

INPUT

8

LISTING 8.8 continued

```
    if (m_strFontName.GetLength() > 0)
    {
        // Get the dimensions of the font sample display area
        m_ctlDisplayText.GetWindowRect(&rRect);
        // Release the current font
        m_fSampFont.Detach();
        // Create the font to be used
        m_fSampFont.CreateFont((rRect.Height()- 5), 0, 0, 0, FW_NORMAL,
                0, 0, 0, DEFAULT_CHARSET, OUT_CHARACTER_PRECIS,
                CLIP_CHARACTER_PRECIS, DEFAULT_QUALITY, DEFAULT_PITCH |
                FF_DONTCARE, m_strFontName);

        // Set the font for the sample display area
        m_ctlDisplayText.SetFont(&m_fSampFont);
    }
}
```

4. Add a function to the LBN_SELCHANGE event message for the IDC_LFONTS list box. Edit the function, adding the code in Listing 8.9.

LISTING 8.9 The OnLbnSelchangeLfonts Function

```
void CTextFontsDlg::OnLbnSelchangeLfonts()
{
    // TODO: Add your control notification handler code here
    // Update the variables with the dialog controls
    UpdateData(TRUE);

    // Set the font for the sample
    SetMyFont();
}
```

INPUT

ANALYSIS In the SetMyFont function, you first checked to make sure a font had been selected. Next, you retrieved the area of the static text control that will display the font. This enables you to specify a font height just slightly smaller than the height of the area you have available to display the font. Finally, you created the selected font and told the static text control to use the newly created font.

In the OnLbnSelchangeLfonts function, you copy the control values to the attached variables and then call the SetMyFont function to use the selected font. If you compile and run your application, you should be able to select a font and see it displayed in the sample static text control, as in Figure 8.3.

Figure 8.3

Displaying the selected font.

Summary

Today you learned how to use fonts in Visual C++ applications. You learned how to get a list of the available fonts that are loaded on the system and then how to create a font for use on a display object. You learned how you can create and use callback functions to get a list of resources from the Windows operating system. You also learned how you can access controls from the callback function using a window pointer that you passed to the function requesting the resource list.

Q&A

Q. The CreateFont function has a lot of arguments to specify and pass. Is there any other alternative to using this function?

A. Yes, there is, although you still specify all the same information. A structure called LOGFONT contains all the same attributes that are passed to the CreateFont function. You can declare an instance of this structure, initializing the attributes to default values, and then pass this structure to the CreateFontIndirect function. If you make numerous font changes, this approach is preferable because you could use the same instance of the structure, modifying those attributes that are changing from the current settings and using it to create the various fonts.

The way you use this alternative way of creating the font is to declare an instance of the LOGFONT structure as a member of the dialog class, and then initialize all the attributes before calling the SetMyFont function. Modify the SetMyFont function as shown in Listing 8.10.

LISTING 8.10   The Modified SetMyFont Function

```
void CTextFontsDlg::SetMyFont()
{

    // Has a font been selected?
    if (m_strFontName,GetLength() > 0)
    {
        // Assume that the font size has already been initialized in the
        // m_lLogFont structure. This allows you to only have to specify
        // the font name.
        _tcscpy(m_lLogFont.lfFaceName, m_strFontName);
        // Release the current font
        m_fSampFont.Detach();
        // Create the font to be used
        m_fSampFont.CreateFontIndirect(&m_lLogFont);

        // Set the font for the sample display area
        m_ctlDisplayText.SetFont(&m_fSampFont);
    }
}
```

INPUT

Q. How can I limit the fonts in my list to just the TrueType fonts?

A. You can check the nFontType argument to your callback function to determine the font type. For instance, if you want to include only TrueType fonts in your list of fonts, you modify your callback function to mask the nFontType argument with the TRUETYPE_FONTTYPE constant and check to see if the resulting value equals the TRUETYPE_FONTTYPE value, as in the following listing:

```
int CALLBACK EnumFontFamProc(LPENUMLOGFONT lpelf,
LPNEWTEXTMETRIC lpntm, DWORD nFontType, long lParam)
{
    // Create a pointer to the dialog window
    CTextFontsDlg* pWnd = (CTextFontsDlg*) lParam;

    // Limit the list to TrueType fonts
    if (nFontType & TRUETYPE_FONTTYPE)
    {
        // Add the font name to the list box
        pWnd->m_ctlFontList.AddString(
                          lpelf->elfLogFont.lfFaceName);
    }
    // Return 1 to continue font enumeration
    return 1;
]
```

Workshop

The Workshop provides quiz questions to help you solidify your understanding of the material covered and exercises to provide you with experience in using what you've learned. The answers to the quiz questions are provided in Appendix A, "Answers to Quiz Questions."

Quiz

1. How can you specify that the text is to be underlined?

2. How can you print your text upside down?

3. How many times is the `EnumFontFamProc` callback function called by the operating system?

Exercises

1. Add a check box to switch between using the entered text to display the font and using the font name to display the font, as in Figure 8.4.

FIGURE 8.4

Displaying the selected font with the font name.

2. Add a check box to display the font sample in italic, as in Figure 8.5.

FIGURE 8.5

Displaying the selected font in italics.

DAY 9

Incorporating Graphics, Drawings, and Bitmaps

You've probably noticed that a large number of applications use graphics and display images. This adds a certain level of flash and polish to the application. With some applications, graphics are integral to their functionality. Having a good understanding of what's involved in adding these capabilities to your applications is a key to programming for the Windows platform. You've already learned on Day 4 how you can draw lines and string a series of these lines together to make a continuous drawing. Today, you will go beyond that capacity and learn how to add more advanced graphics capabilities to your applications. Today, you will learn how:

- Windows uses a device context to translate drawing instructions into graphics output.
- You can determine the level of control you have over the graphics output through different mapping modes.
- Windows uses pens and brushes to draw different portions of the graphics image.
- You can load and display bitmaps and other images dynamically.

Understanding the Graphics Device Interface

The Windows operating system provides you with a couple of levels of abstraction for creating and using graphics in your applications. During the days of DOS programming, you needed to exercise a great deal of control over the graphics hardware to draw any kind of images in an application. This control required an extensive knowledge and understanding of the various types of graphics cards that users might have in their computers, along with their options for monitors and resolutions. You could buy a few graphics libraries for your applications, but overall, it required fairly strenuous programming to add this capability to your applications.

With Windows, Microsoft has made the job much easier. First, Microsoft provides you with a virtual graphics device for all your Windows applications. This virtual device doesn't change with the hardware but remains the same for all possible graphics hardware that users might have. This consistency provides you with the capability to create whatever kind of graphics you want in your applications because you know that the task of converting them into something that the hardware understands isn't your problem.

Device Contexts

NEW TERM Before you can create any graphics, you must have the *device context* in which the graphics will be displayed. The device context contains information about the system, the application, and the window in which you are drawing any graphics. The operating system uses the device context to tell the application in which context a graphic is being drawn, how much of the area is visible, and where onscreen it's currently located.

When you draw graphics, you always draw them in the context of an application window. At any time, this window may be full view, minimized, partly hidden, or completely hidden. This status isn't your concern because you draw your graphics on the window using its device context. Windows keeps track of each device context and uses it to determine how much and what part of the graphics you draw to actually display for the user. In essence, the device context you use to display your graphics is the visual context of the window in which you draw them.

NEW TERM The device context uses two resources to perform most of its drawing and graphics functions. These two resources are *pens* and *brushes*. Much like their real-world counterparts, pens and brushes perform similar yet different tasks. The device context uses pens to draw lines and shapes, whereas brushes paint areas of the screen. It's the same idea as working on paper when you use a pen to draw an outline of an image and then pick up a paintbrush to fill in the color between the lines.

The Device Context Class

In Visual C++, the MFC device context class, CDC, provides numerous drawing functions for drawing circles, squares, lines, curves, and so on. All these functions are part of the device context class because they all use the device context information to draw on your application windows.

You create a device context class instance with a pointer to the window class that you want to associate with the device context. This enables the device context class to place all the code associated with allocating and freeing a device context in the class constructor and destructors.

Note

Device context objects, as well as all the various drawing objects, are classified as resources in Windows. The operating system has only a limited amount of these resources. Although the total number of resources is large in recent versions of Windows, it's still possible to run out of resources if an application allocates them and doesn't free them correctly. This loss is known as a *resource leak*, and much like a memory leak, it can eventually lock up a user's system. As a result, it's advisable to create these resources in the functions where they will be used and then delete them as soon as you are finished with them.

Following this advised approach to using device contexts and their drawing resources, you use them almost exclusively as local variables within a single function. The only real exception is when the device context object is created by Windows and passed into the event-processing function as an argument.

MFC Note: Important Device Context Drawing Functions

Many drawing functions are members of the CDC class. Plus, CDC is the base class for all the other device context classes, making all these drawing functions available no matter which context device class you are working with. The functions listed over the next several pages are just a small set of the functionality available, but is most appropriate for today's discussion.

Background and Foreground Colors

There are several functions for controlling the way text and figures are displayed. One key to controlling this is by specifying the foreground and background colors when you are putting text or other figures on a window. There are a group of functions in the CDC for controlling these aspects. The following functions are just some of the more commonly used.

GetBkColor and SetBkColor

When you are drawing text on a window, you need to worry about not only the color of the text itself, but also about the background color behind the text. That's what the GetBkColor and SetBkColor functions are all about. Both functions return a COLORREF (RGB, as in Red, Green, Blue; this is explained in a few pages when discussing pens) value that contains the current or previous background color. The SetBkColor function takes a COLORREF value as its only parameter. If an error occurs, the SetBkColor function returns the value 0x80000000 as the previous color.

GetBkMode and SetBkMode

Along with setting the background color, you also have to decide whether you want to use the background color, or whether you want whatever is behind the text to be seen. This is controlled with the GetBkMode and SetBkMode functions. There are only two background drawing modes in Windows: OPAQUE and TRANSPARENT. Obviously, the TRANSPARENT background mode doesn't fill in the background color, but enables whatever is behind the text to show through. The OPAQUE background mode does fill in the background color, hiding whatever is behind the text. These two values are the only return values from these two functions, as the current or previous background mode. These two values are also the only parameters that the SetBkMode function will accept.

GetTextColor and SetTextColor

When you need to draw text on a window, you may need to specify the color to use for the text. This is done through the use of the GetTextColor and SetTextColor functions. These two functions are just like their background color siblings, both returning a COLOR-REF value to specify the current or previous text color. And just like its background color sibling, SetTextColor takes a COLORREF value as its only argument.

Line-Drawing Functions

The next aspect of drawing that the CDC provides functionality for is the various line-drawing functions. Although the following are by no means all the available functions, they give you a basic idea of the type of functionality available.

GetCurrentPosition

Many line-drawing functions assume the current onscreen position as the starting point. This point may not be where you think it is, so you may need to check where it is from time to time. You can check this value by using the GetCurrentPosition function. The return value from this function is an instance of the CPoint class, which consists mainly of a particular point's X and Y coordinates.

MoveTo and LineTo

When you need to move around the drawing area, you can use the MoveTo and LineTo functions, which you first saw back on Day 4. Both functions can take either the X and Y coordinate values, or a CPoint object, depending on how you want to work with them.

Arc and ArcTo

If you need to draw a curve, the Arc and ArcTo functions may be more suitable to your needs. Both functions draw a curved line between two points. The arc's curve is defined by a bounding rectangle that encloses the beginning and ending points. The arc is drawn counter clockwise from the starting to the ending point. The arguments for both of these functions are as follows:

```
Arc(int x1, int y1, int x2, int y3, int x3, int y3, int x4, int y4);
ArcTo(int x1, int y1, int x2, int y3, int x3, int y3, int x4, int y4);
```

or

```
Arc(LPCRECT lpRect, POINT ptStart, POINT ptEnd);
ArcTo(LPCRECT lpRect, POINT ptStart, POINT ptEnd);
```

In the first syntax, the first four parameters are the upper-left and lower-right corners of the enclosing rectangle, which you can pass as a CRect class in the second syntax. The next two parameters in the first syntax are the starting point for the arc, passed as a CPoint in the second syntax. And finally, the last two parameters in the first syntax, and the last parameter in the second, is the arc's ending point. The difference between these two functions (Arc and ArcTo) is that the ArcTo function sets the current position to the ending point after it has drawn the arc.

Polyline and PolylineTo

The Polyline and PolylineTo functions take a series of points and draws a series of lines between them. Both functions take the same parameters:

```
Polyline(LPPOINT lpPoints, int iCount);
PolylineTo(LPPOINT lpPoints, int iCount);
```

The first parameter is a pointer to an array of CPoint objects. The second parameter is an integer specifying how many points are in the array. The PolylineTo function sets the current position to the last point in the array when the function returns.

Shape-Drawing Functions

Drawing lines is all nice and good, but sometimes you need to be able to draw an entire shape. A series of shape-drawing functions are included in the CDC. The following are some of the shape functions you might want to use in drawing graphics.

Ellipse

The `Ellipse` function draws an ellipse that's defined by a rectangle that encloses the ellipse. If the enclosing rectangle is a square, this function will draw a circle. Otherwise, the ellipse will be elongated according to the shape of the enclosing rectangle. The `Ellipse` function takes either a `CRect` object, or four integers as parameters to define the bounding rectangle. The ellipse is drawn using the current pen and brush (which you'll learn all about shortly).

Pie

The `Pie` function draws a pie-shaped wedge. This function takes the same parameters as the `Arc` and `ArcTo` functions. The arc at the outer end of the wedge is defined as the arc that would be drawn if the same values were passed to the `Arc` or `ArcTo` function. The point of the wedge is the center of the bounding rectangle.

Polygon

The `Polygon` function is similar to the `Polyline` and `PolylineTo` functions. They all take the same parameters and draw lines between the points in an array of points. The difference with the `Polygon` function is it completes the shape by drawing a final line between the last and first points.

Rectangle and RoundRect

The `Rectangle` and `RoundRect` functions both draw a rectangle shape. The `RoundRect` function draws rounded corners on the rectangle. These two functions take a `CRect` object as their parameter to define the rectangle to be drawn. The `RoundRect` function takes a second parameter, which is a `CPoint` object. The X coordinate of this point specifies the width of the ellipse used to draw the rounded corners, and the Y coordinate specifies the ellipse's height.

Bitmap Functions

There's also a series of functions in the CDC used to draw and display bitmap images. Most of these functions are for the purpose of transfering a bitmap from one display context in memory, to another onscreen. A couple of these functions are as follows.

BitBlt

The `BitBlt` function copies an image from one device context to another. The syntax for the `BitBlt` function is as follows:

```
BOOL BitBlt(int xDst, int yDst, int nWidth, int nHeight, CDC* pSrcDC,
    int xSrc, int ySrc, DWORD dwRop)
```

The first two parameters to the `BitBlt` function (`xDst` and `yDst`) are the X and Y coordinates for the upper-left corner of the image on the destination device context. The next two parameters, nWidth and nHeight, are the width and height of the image on the destination device context. The fifth parameter, pSrcDC, is a pointer to the compatible device context from where the image should be copied. The next two parameters, xSrc and ySrc, are the X and Y coordinates of the upper-left corner of the image in the device context that the image is being copied from. The last parameter, dwRop, is a flag indicating how the copy should be performed. Table 9.1 lists the possible values for this flag.

TABLE 9.1 BitBlt Option Flags

Option	Description
BLACKNESS	Causes all output to be black.
CAPTUREBLT	Includes any windows layered on top of the window in the resulting image (the default is to only include the image window).
DSTINVERT	Inverts the colors of the displayed image.
MERGECOPY	Causes the source image to be merged with the destination pattern using the Boolean AND operator.
MERGEPAINT	Causes the inverted source image to be combined with the destination image using the Boolean OR operator.
NOMIRRORBITMAP	Does not allow the bitmap to be mirrored.
NOTSRCCOPY	Copies the inverted source image to the destination output.
NOTSRCERASE	Inverts the merged image. It's like a combination of the MERGEPAINT and DSTINVERT options.
PATCOPY	Copies just the pattern to the destination image.
PATINVERT	Combines the pattern and the source image using the XOR operator.
PATPAINT	Combines the inverted source image with the pattern using the OR operator. The resulting image is combined with the destination image using the OR operator.
SRCAND	Combines the source and destination images using the AND operator.
SRCCOPY	Copies the source image to the destination image.
SRCERASE	Inverts the destination image, and then combines it with the source image using the AND operator.
SRCINVERT	Combines the source and destination images using the XOR operator.
SRCPAINT	Combines the source and destination images using the OR operator.
WHITENESS	Causes all output to be white.

StretchBlt

The StretchBlt function resizes, and then copies an image from one device context to another. The syntax for this function is as follows:

```
BOOL StretchBlt(int xDst, int yDst, int nWidth, int nHeight, CDC* pSrcDC,
    int xSrc, int ySrc, int nSrcWidth, int nSrcHeight, DWORD dwRop)
```

The first two parameters to the StretchBlt function, xDst and yDst, are the X and Y coordinates for the upper-left corner of the image on the destination device context. The next two parameters, nWidth and nHeight, are the width and height of the image on the destination device context. The fifth parameter, pSrcDC, is a pointer to the compatible device context from where the image should be copied. The next four parameters—xSrc, ySrc, nSrcWidth, and nSrcHeight—are the X and Y coordinates of the upper-left corner and the width and height of the image in the device context that the image is being copied from. The last parameter, dwRop, is a flag indicating how the copy should be performed. Table 9.1 lists the possible values for this flag.

Text Functions

Finally, there are several functions for putting text on the drawing surface. These functions use the selected font and color. Only two of these functions are discussed here.

TextOut

The TextOut function places text on the drawing surface and takes three parameters:

- The X coordinate for where the upper-left corner of the text should be located
- The Y coordinate for the upper-left corner
- A CString that contains the text to be displayed

GetTextExtent

The GetTextExtent function computes the size of the area that a string of text will take on the drawing area using the current font. This function takes a CString containing the text to be calculated, and the function returns a CSize object. The CSize class encapsulates the SIZE structure, which has two members: cx, which specifies the text's width, and cy, which specifies the text's height.

SelectObject

The SelectObject function is used to select pens, brushes, bitmaps, fonts, regions, and GDI (Graphical Device Interface) objects. It takes as its only parameter a pointer to the object to be selected for use by the device context, and returns a pointer to the previously selected object of the same type. In other words, when you call SelectObject to select a new pen for use in drawing, the function returns a pointer to the previously selected pen. When you select a new brush, it returns a pointer to the previously selected brush.

Once you select an object for use, every time that you call a device context function that uses the selected object in performing the drawing function requested, the new object is used. It is good programming practice to capture the previously selected object whenever you call SelectObject to select a new object for use. Then, when you are finished using the new object you selected, call SelectObject again, passing the previous object pointer to restore the device context to the state it was in prior to your changes.

MFC Note: The CPen Class

9

You've already seen how to use the pen class, CPen, to specify the color and width for drawing lines onscreen. CPen is the primary resource tool for drawing any kind of line onscreen. When you create an instance of the CPen class, you can specify the line type, color, and thickness. After you create a pen, you can select it as the current drawing tool for the device context, so it's used for all your drawing commands to the device context. To create a new pen, and then select it as the current drawing pen, use the following code:

```
// Create the device context
CDC dc(this);
// Create the pen
CPen pnPen(PS_SOLID, 1, RGB(0, 0, 0));
// Select the pen as the current drawing pen
// Capture the old pen so it can be reset once finished
// with the new pen
CPen* pOldPen = dc.SelectObject(&pnPen);
```

You can use a number of different pen styles. These pen styles all draw different patterns when drawing lines. Figure 9.1 shows the basic styles that can be used in your applications with any color.

FIGURE 9.1

Windows pen styles.

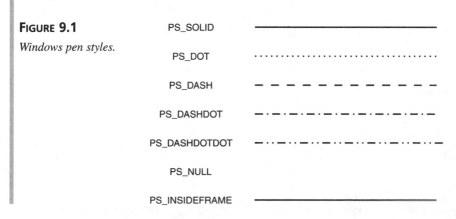

Note When you use any of these line styles with a pen thickness greater than 1, all the lines appear as solid lines. If you want to use any line style other than PS_SOLID, you need to use a pen width of 1.

Tip Whenever you select a new pen into the device context, you should always capture the previous pen so that you can reselect the previous pen into the device context after you are finished with the new pen.

Along with the line style that the pen should draw, you also have to specify the pen's width and color. The combinations of these three variables specify the appearance of the resulting lines. The line width can range from 1 on up, although when you reach a width of 32, it's difficult to exercise any level of precision in your drawing efforts.

You specify the color as an RGB value, which has three separate values for the brightness of the red, green, and blue color components of the pixels on the computer screen. These three separate values can range from 0 to 255, and the RGB function combines them into a single value in the format needed by Windows. Table 9.2 lists some of the more common colors.

TABLE 9.2 Common Windows Colors

Color	Red	Green	Blue
Black	0	0	0
Blue	0	0	255
Dark blue	0	0	128
Green	0	255	0
Dark green	0	128	0
Cyan	0	255	255
Dark cyan	0	128	128
Red	255	0	0
Dark red	128	0	0
Magenta	255	0	255
Dark magenta	128	0	128
Yellow	255	255	0
Dark yellow	128	128	0
Dark gray	128	128	128

TABLE 9.2 continued

Color	Red	Green	Blue
Light gray	192	192	192
White	255	255	255

MFC Note: The CBrush Class

9

The brush class, CBrush, enables you to create brushes that define how areas will be filled in. When you draw shapes that enclose an area and fill in the enclosed area, the outline is drawn with the current pen, and the interior of the area is filled by the current brush. Brushes can be solid colors (specified using the same RGB values as with the pens), a pattern of lines, or even a repeated pattern created from a small bitmap. If you want to create a solid-color brush, you need to specify the color to use:

```
CBrush brSolidBrush(RGB(255, 0, 0));
```

To create a pattern brush, you need to specify not only the color, but also the pattern to use:

```
CBrush brPatternBrush(HS_BDIAGONAL, RGB(0, 0, 255));
```

When you create a brush, you can select it with the device context object, just like you do with pens. After you select a brush, it's used as the current brush whenever you draw something that uses a brush.

Like with pens, you can select a number of standard patterns when creating a brush (see Figure 9.2). In addition to these patterns, an additional brush style, HS_BITMAP, uses a bitmap as the pattern for filling the specified area. This bitmap has to be at least 8 pixels by 8 pixels in size. You can create a bitmap brush by creating a bitmap resource for your application and assigning it an object ID. After you do this, you can create a brush with it by using the following code:

```
CBitmap bmpBitmap;

// Load the image
bmpBitmap.LoadBitmap(IDB_MYBITMAP);
// Create the brush
CBrush brBitmapBrush(&bmpBitmap);
```

Tip

If you want to create your own custom pattern for use as a brush, you can create the pattern as an 8 × 8 or larger bitmap and use the bitmap brush. This enables you to extend the number of brush patterns far beyond the limited number of standard patterns.

FIGURE 9.2

Standard brush patterns.

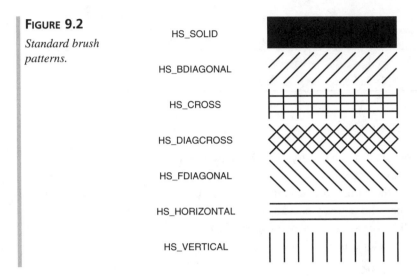

HS_SOLID

HS_BDIAGONAL

HS_CROSS

HS_DIAGCROSS

HS_FDIAGONAL

HS_HORIZONTAL

HS_VERTICAL

MFC Note: The CBitmap Class

When you want to display images in your applications, you have a couple of options. You can add fixed bitmaps to your application, as resources with object IDs assigned to them, and use a static picture control or an ActiveX control that displays images. You can also use the bitmap class, CBitmap, to exercise complete control over the image display. If you use the bitmap class, you can dynamically load bitmap images from files on the system disk, resizing the images as necessary to make them fit in the space you've allotted.

If you add the bitmap as a resource, you can create an instance of the CBitmap class using the resource ID of the bitmap as the image to be loaded. If you want to load a bitmap from a file, you can use the LoadImage API call to load the bitmap from the file. After you load the bitmap, you can use the handle for the image to attach the image to the CBitmap class, as follows:

```
// Load the bitmap file
HBITMAP hBitmap = (HBITMAP)::LoadImage(AfxGetInstanceHandle(),
                    m_strFileName, IMAGE_BITMAP, 0, 0,
                    LR_LOADFROMFILE | LR_CREATEDIBSECTION);
// Attach the loaded image to the CBitmap object.
bmpBitmap.Attach(hBitmap);
```

After you load the bitmap into the CBitmap object, you can create a second device context and select the bitmap into it. When you've created the second device context, you need to make it compatible with the primary device context before the bitmap is selected into it. Because device contexts are created by the operating system for a specific output device (screen, printer, and so on), you have to make sure the second device context is also attached to the same output device as the first.

```
// Create a device context
CDC dcMem;
// Make the new device context compatible with the real DC
dcMem.CreateCompatibleDC(dc);
// Select the bitmap into the new DC
dcMem.SelectObject(&bmpBitmap);
```

When you select the bitmap into a compatible device context, you can copy the bitmap into the regular display device context by using the BitBlt function:

```
// Copy the bitmap to the display DC
dc->BitBlt(10, 10, bm.bmWidth,
               bm.bmHeight, &dcMem, 0, 0,
               SRCCOPY);
```

You can also copy and resize the image by using the StretchBlt function:

```
// Resize the bitmap while copying it to the display DCz
dc->StretchBlt(10, 10, (lRect.Width() - 20),
               (lRect.Height() - 20), &dcMem, 0, 0,
               bm.bmWidth, bm.bmHeight, SRCCOPY);
```

By using StretchBlt, you can resize the bitmap so that it will fit in any area on the screen.

MFC Note: The CImage Class

Although bitmaps were once the primary format for images included with programs, this is no longer the case. Thanks in part to the popularity of the Internet, you find Web images formats more often than you find bitmaps these days. Now, you are more likely to find JPEG or PNG format images than bitmaps. Don't get me wrong, bitmaps still have a place in software, but you often find that you also need to be able to load and display other image formats as well.

In Visual C++, you can use two class libraries to build things. MFC is the one of these class libraries that you use to build applications. The other class library is the Active Template Library (ATL), which is primarily used to build components and services that run without any user interface. You'll work a little with the ATL library in the last few days of this book. When you need to build something, you have always had to choose between using the MFC library (if you needed to build applications), or the ATL library (if you needed to build components or applications without a user interface). It was all one or the other, with no middle ground. Beginning with Visual C++ .NET, a set of shared classes can be used in both the MFC and ATL class libraries. One of these shared classes is CImage.

The CImage class encapsulates functionality to read and write JPEG, GIF, BMP (bitmap), and PNG (Portable Network Graphics) images. One key difference with the CImage class from CBitmap (besides the obvious one with the image formats) is that CImage contains its own device context handle and can't be selected into another device context by using the SelectObject method. Instead, you just work directly with the CImage object, and then use its copy functions to copy an image to an output device context. This eliminates the process of selecting the image into a compatible device context, while still preserving the copy functions required to display the image.

Primary CImage Methods

The CImage class provides a full range of functionality for working with these various image formats. Although the functions listed here are by no means complete, they still will provide you with sufficient familiarity with the class functionality, so you can easily use it in your applications. However, before you try to use it in an application, you have to add the appropriate #include statement to your application:

```
#include <atlimage.h>
```

Because CImage isn't in the standard MFC class library, it's not automatically included in your application. This means that you need to add it yourself. However, you can't just include it anywhere, because it depends on other MFC class declarations that it uses. The atlimage.h header file must be included after the inclusion of the header file that contains the declaration of the CString class. The easiest thing to do is add this include statement at the bottom of the stdafx.h header file that's created as part of your application. The stdafx.h header file is created by the MFC Application Wizard, and consists primarily of include statements and constant definitions needed for MFC. Because the CImage class is part of the class library, this location makes the most sense for where to add the statement.

The Attach and Detach Functions

The Attach and Detach functions do pretty much what you might expect them to do. Attach attaches a loaded image to an instance of the CImage class, much in the same way you attach a bitmap to a CBitmap class with its Attach function. Attach takes two parameters, although just the first parameter is required. The first parameter is a handle to a bitmap that has been loaded into memory, just like the CBitmap Attach function. The second parameter is a flag that indicates the orientation of the DIB (Device-Independent Bitmap) in the image. The possible values for this flag are as follows:

Flag	Description
DIBOR_DEFAULT	The operating system determines the bitmap's orientation.
DIBOR_BOTTOMUP	The bitmap's lines start at the bottom of the image and go up to the top.
DIBOR_TOPDOWN	The bitmap's lines start at the top of the image and go down to the bottom.

The Detach function detaches the current image from an instance of the CImage class. This function takes no parameters and returns a handle to the image, if one was loaded.

The Create and Destroy Functions

To create your own image, use the Create function. Its syntax is as follows:

```
BOOL Create(int nWidth, int nHeight, int nBPP, DWORD dwFlags)
```

The first parameter, *nWidth*, specifies the width (in pixels) of the image to be created. The second parameter, *nHeight*, specifies the height of the image. The third parameter, *nBPP*, specifies the number of bits per pixel in the image. The number of bits per pixel determines the number of distinct colors that can be used in an image; the more bits per pixel, the more realistic the colors can be. The normal values for this parameter are 1 (for a monochrome image), 4 (16 colors), 8 (256 colors), 16, 24, or 32. The fourth parameter, *dwFlags*, is a flag value that specifies whether the image has what is called an alpha channel. The only values that can be passed in the flag are currently 0 or createAlphaChannel. An alpha channel is where the fourth byte in a 32-BPP image is used to specify a transparency factor. This enables whatever is behind the image to be seen through the image if the transparency factor is high enough. This flag can be used only with 32-BPP images.

The Destroy function takes no parameters and returns no result. It destroys the current image in the CImage class, freeing any memory or other resources currently being used by the image.

The GetHeight and GetWidth Functions

If you need to know the size of the image, use the GetHeight and GetWidth functions. Neither function takes any parameters, and both return an integer value. Another function along this line is GetBPP, which can be used to get the bits-per-pixel value of the image (also often called the image's depth).

The BitBlt, StretchBlt, and Draw Functions

When you are ready to display the image, you need to copy it to the output device context. There are several functions that you can use to do this. The BitBlt and StretchBlt functions work pretty much the same as the CDC versions, even taking the same parameters. The Draw function is basically the same as the StretchBlt function. It even takes the same parameters as the CDC StretchBlt function, without the final parameter (specifying how to copy the image). The difference is how it handles images that contain a transparent color or alpha channel (the StretchBlt function doesn't copy the transparency correctly). The syntax for the Draw function is as follows:

```
Draw(HDC hDestDC, int xDest, int yDest, int nDestWidth, int nDestHeight,
    int xSrc, int ySrc, int nSrcWidth, int SrcHeight);
```

The Load and Save Functions

When you need to load an image into an instance of the CImage class, you can use the Load function, which takes the filename as its only parameter. It determines the image format from the file extension and reads the file in as appropriate. The syntax for the Load function is as follows:

```
Load(LPCTSTR strFileName);
```

When you need to save an image, use the Save function. The syntax for the Save function is as follows:

```
Save(LPCTSTR strFileName, REFGUID guidFileType);
```

The Save function take two parameters: the filename (strFileName) and the image format to save the image in (guidFileType). The possible values for the image format are as follows:.

Flag	Description
GUID_NULL	The image formation is determined from the filename extension.
GUID_BMPFile	The image is saved as an uncompressed bitmap image.
GUID_PNGFile	The image is saved as a PNG image.
GUID_JPEGFile	The image is saved as a JPEG image.
GUID_GIFFile	The image is saved as a GIF image.

With the rich functionality encapsulated in the CImage Load and Save functions, you could easily write an image format conversion utility that consists of two primary lines of code:

```
// Read in the image
m_Image.Load(strInFile);
// Write out the image as a GIF file
m_Image.Save(strOutFile, GUID_GIFFile);
```

Mapping Modes and Coordinate Systems

When you are preparing to draw some graphics on a window, you can exercise much control over the scale you are using and the area in which you can draw. You can control these factors by specifying the mapping mode and drawing area.

By specifying the mapping mode, you can control how your specified coordinates are translated into locations onscreen. The different mapping modes translate each point into a different distance. You can set the mapping mode by using the `SetMapMode` device context function:

```
dc->SetMapMode(MM_ANSIOTROPIC);
```

Table 9.3 lists the available mapping modes.

TABLE 9.3 Mapping Modes

Mode	Description
MM_ANSIOTROPIC	Logical units are converted into arbitrary units with arbitrary axes.
MM_HIENGLISH	Each logical unit is converted into 0.001 inch. Positive x is to the right, and positive y is up.
MM_HIMETRIC	Each logical unit is converted into 0.01 millimeter. Positive x is to the right, and positive y is up.
MM_ISOTROPIC	Logical units are converted into arbitrary units with equally scaled axes.
MM_LOENGLISH	Each logical unit is converted into 0.01 inch. Positive x is to the right, and positive y is up.
MM_LOMETRIC	Each logical unit is converted into 0.1 millimeter. Positive x is to the right, and positive y is up.
MM_TEXT	Each logical unit is converted into 1 pixel. Positive x is to the right, and positive y is down.
MM_TWIPS	Each logical unit is converted into 1/20 of a point (approximately 1/1440 inch). Positive x is to the right, and positive y is up.

If you use the MM_ANSIOTROPIC or MM_ISOTROPIC mapping mode, you can use either the SetWindowExt or SetViewportExt functions to specify the drawing area where your graphics should appear.

Creating a Graphics Application

To get a good understanding of how you can put all this information to use, you'll build an application that incorporates much of what has been covered so far today. This application will have two independent windows, one with a number of options to choose for the shape, tool, and color to be displayed. The other window will act as a canvas, where all the selected options will be drawn. Users will be able to select whether to display lines, squares, circles, or a bitmap on the second window. Users will also be able to specify the color and choose whether to display the pen or brush for the circles and squares, as in Figure 9.3.

To build this application, you'll follow these general steps:

1. Create the application shell.
2. Design the main dialog.

FIGURE 9.3

The running graphics application.

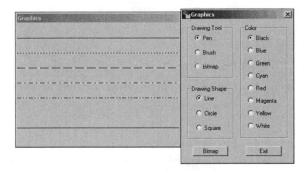

3. Add a second modeless dialog on which all drawing will be performed.
4. Add functionality for drawing lines on the second dialog.
5. Add functionality for drawing figures on the second dialog.
6. Add functionality for loading and displaying images on the second dialog.

Generating the Application Shell

As you've learned by now, the first step in building an application is generating the initial application shell. This shell provides the basic application functionality, displaying your first application dialog, along with all startup and shutdown functionality. For today's application, you need to start with a standard dialog-style application shell. Follow these steps:

1. Create a new MFC Application Visual C++ project. Name the project `Graphics`.
2. Use the same defaults that you've used for the previous projects.

Designing the Main Dialog

After you make your way through the MFC Application Wizard, you're ready to start designing your primary dialog. This window will contain three groups of radio buttons: to specify the drawing tool, to specify the drawing shape, and to specify the color. Along with these radio buttons, you'll have two buttons on the window: one to open a File Open dialog for selecting a bitmap to be displayed, and the other to close the application.

To add all these controls to your dialog, lay out the controls as shown in Figure 9.4 and specify the control properties listed in Table 9.4.

FIGURE 9.4

The main dialog layout.

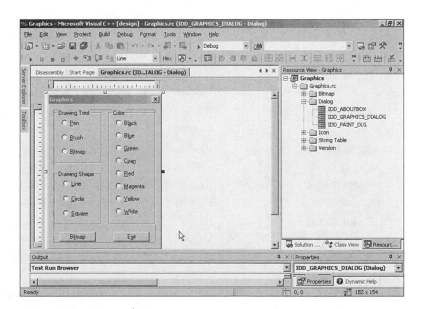

TABLE 9.4 Control Property Settings

Object	Property	Setting
Group Box	Caption	Drawing Tool
Radio Button	ID	IDC_RTPEN
	Caption	&Pen
	Group	True

TABLE 9.4 continued

Object	Property	Setting
Radio Button	ID	IDC_RTBRUSH
	Caption	&Brush
Radio Button	ID	IDC_RTBITMAP
	Caption	B&itmap
Group Box	Caption	Drawing Shape
Radio Button	ID	IDC_RSLINE
	Caption	&Line
	Group	True
Radio Button	ID	IDC_RSCIRCLE
	Caption	&Circle
Radio Button	ID	IDC_RSSQUARE
	Caption	&Square
Group Box	Caption	Color
Radio Button	ID	IDC_RCBLACK
	Caption	Bl&ack
	Group	True
Radio Button	ID	IDC_RCBLUE
	Caption	Bl&ue
Radio Button	ID	IDC_RCGREEN
	Caption	&Green
Radio Button	ID	IDC_RCCYAN
	Caption	Cya&n
Radio Button	ID	IDC_RCRED
	Caption	&Red
Radio Button	ID	IDC_RCMAGENTA
	Caption	&Magenta
Radio Button	ID	IDC_RCYELLOW
	Caption	&Yellow
Radio Button	ID	IDC_RCWHITE
	Caption	&White
Command Button	ID	IDC_BBITMAP
	Caption	Bi&tmap
Command Button	ID	IDC_BEXIT
	Caption	E&xit

After you finish designing your main dialog, you need to assign one variable to each group of radio buttons. To do this, assign one integer variable to the first radio button in each group. All the subsequent radio buttons in each group will be assigned to the same variable, with sequential values, in the order of the object ID values. For this reason, it's important to create all the radio buttons in each group in the order you want their values to be sequenced. If you didn't add the radio buttons in order, you can correct the problem by setting the tab order for the dialog.

To assign the necessary variables to the radio button groups in your application, add the following variables to the objects in your dialog by right-clicking the first radio button in each group and choosing Add Variable.

Object	Name	Category	Type	Access
IDC_RTPEN	m_iTool	Value	int	public
IDC_RSLINE	m_iShape	Value	int	public
IDC_RCBLACK	m_iColor	Value	int	public

After the variables are assigned to the radio buttons, add an event-handler function to the Exit button, calling the OnOK function in the code for this button. You can compile and run your application now, making sure you have all the radio button groups defined correctly, you can't select two or more buttons in any one group, and you can select one button in each group without affecting either of the other two groups.

Adding the Second Dialog

After you design the main dialog, you add the second window that you'll use as a canvas to paint your graphics on. This dialog will be modeless, which will remain open the entire time the application runs. You will put no controls on the dialog, providing a clean canvas for drawing.

To create this second dialog, follow these steps:

1. Go to the Resources tab in the workspace pane. Right-click the Dialogs folder in the resource tree and choose Insert Dialog.

2. When the new dialog is open in the window designer, remove all the controls from the window.

3. Select the dialog and go to the properties area. Set the System Menu option to FALSE to prevent users from closing this dialog without exiting the application.

4. Give this dialog an object ID that will describe its function. Specify the ID as IDD_PAINT_DLG.

5. Right-click the dialog and choose Add Class.

6. Specify the name of the new class as CPaintDlg, and make sure the base class is set to CDialog.

7. Click Finish to create the new class.

 Note

You need to make sure the new dialog is selected when you try to add the new class. If the dialog isn't selected, and you've switched to another object or even some code in your application, the New Class Wizard won't know that you need a class for the second dialog in your application.

Now that you've defined the second dialog, you need to add the code in the first dialog to open the second dialog. You can accomplish this by adding two lines of code to the OnInitDialog function in the first window's class:

- Create the dialog using the Create method of the CDialog class. This function takes two arguments: the object ID of the dialog and a pointer to the parent window, which will be the main dialog.

- Use the ShowWindow function, passing the value SW_SHOW as the only argument, to display the second dialog next to the first dialog.

You can implement this functionality by following these steps:

1. Select the Class View pane. Expand the class tree to show the CGraphicsDlg class.

2. Right-click the CGraphicsDlg class and choose Add, Add Variable.

3. Specify the variable type as CPaintDlg, the name as m_dlgPaint, and the access as Private. Click Finish to add the variable.

4. Expand the CGraphicsDlg node to show the methods. Double-click the OnInitDialog method. Add a couple of lines of variable initialization to make your OnInitDialog function resemble Listing 9.1.

LISTING 9.1 The OnInitDialog Function

```
BOOL CGraphicsDlg::OnInitDialog()
{
    CDialog::OnInitDialog();

. . .

    // Set the icon for this dialog.  The framework does this automatically
    //  when the application's main window is not a dialog
    SetIcon(m_hIcon, TRUE);            // Set big icon
    SetIcon(m_hIcon, FALSE);        // Set small icon

    // TODO: Add extra initialization here
```

LISTING 9.1 continued

```
INPUT    // Initialize the variables and update the dialog window
         m_iColor = 0;
    m_iShape = 0;
    m_iTool = 0;
    UpdateData(FALSE);

    // Create the second dialog window
    m_dlgPaint.Create(IDD_PAINT_DLG, this);
    // Show the second dialog window
    m_dlgPaint.ShowWindow(SW_SHOW);

    return TRUE;  // return TRUE  unless you set the focus to a control
}
```

9

Before you can compile and run your application, you'll need to include the header for the second dialog class in the source code for the first dialog. To include the header file in the first dialog, follow these steps:

1. Scroll to the top of the source code for the first dialog and add an #include statement, as in Listing 9.2.

LISTING 9.2 The Main Dialog's #include Statement

```
// GraphicsDlg.cpp : implementation file
//

#include "stdafx.h"
#include "Graphics.h"
INPUT   #include "PaintDlg.h"
        #include "GraphicsDlg.h"
```

2. Conversely, you need to include the header file for the main dialog in the source code for the second dialog. Edit the file, PaintDlg.cpp, making the include statements at the top of the file match those in Listing 9.2.

If you compile and run your application, you should see your second dialog open along with the first. Also notice that when you close the first dialog, and thus close the application, the second dialog also closes, even though you didn't add any code to make this happen. The second dialog is a child window to the first dialog. When you created the second dialog, you passed a pointer to the first dialog as the parent window for the second window (the "this" parameter). This set up a parent-child relationship between these two windows. When the parent closes, so does the child. This is the same relationship the first dialog has with all the controls you placed on it. Each control is a child window of the dialog. In a sense, what you've done is make the second dialog just another control on the first dialog.

Adding the Graphics Capabilities

Because all the radio button variables are declared as public, the second dialog can see and reference them as it needs to. You can place all the graphic drawing functionality into the second dialog class. However, you do need to place some functionality into the first dialog to keep the variables synchronized and to tell the second dialog to draw its graphics. Accomplishing this is simpler than you might think.

Whenever a window needs to be redrawn (it may have been hidden behind another window and come to the front, or minimized or off the visible screen and now in view), the operating system triggers the dialog's OnPaint function. You can place all the functionality for drawing your graphics in this function and make persistent the graphics you display.

Now that you know where to place your code to display the graphics, how can you cause the second dialog to call its OnPaint function whenever users change a selection on the first dialog? Well, you could hide and then show the second dialog, but that might look a little peculiar to users. Actually, a single function will convince the second window that it needs to redraw its entire dialog. This function, Invalidate, requires no arguments and is a member function of the CWnd class, so it can be used on any window or control. The Invalidate function tells the window, and the operating system, that the display area of the window is no longer valid and that it needs to be redrawn. You can trigger the OnPaint function in the second dialog at will, without resorting to any awkward tricks or hacks.

At this point, we have determined that all the radio buttons can use the same functionality on their clicked events. You can set up a single event-handler function for the clicked event on all the radio button controls. In this event function, you'll need to synchronize the class variables with the dialog controls by calling the UpdateData function and then tell the second dialog to redraw itself by calling its Invalidate function. You can write a single event handler that does these two things with the following steps:

1. Open the first dialog. Select the first radio button on the first dialog.

2. Add an event handler for the BN_CLICKED event message. Don't accept the default name for this function; enter the name **OnRSelection**.

3. Open the GraphicsDlg.cpp file, and locate the Message Map section for the CGraphicsDlg class. It should look like the following:

```
BEGIN_MESSAGE_MAP(CGraphicsDlg, CDialog)
    ON_WM_SYSCOMMAND()
    ON_WM_PAINT()
    ON_WM_QUERYDRAGICON()
    //}}AFX_MSG_MAP
    ON_BN_CLICKED(IDC_RTPEN, OnRSelection)
END_MESSAGE_MAP()
```

4. Copy the ON_BN_CLICKED macro, and paste it in the message map 13 more times. Edit these new copies of the ON_BN_CLICKED macro, replacing the ID for the first radio button with the IDs of the other 13 radio buttons. The final message map should look like Listing 9.3.

LISTING 9.3   The Modified Message Map

```
BEGIN_MESSAGE_MAP(CGraphicsDlg, CDialog)
    ON_WM_SYSCOMMAND()
    ON_WM_PAINT()
    ON_WM_QUERYDRAGICON()
    //}}AFX_MSG_MAP
ON_BN_CLICKED(IDC_RTPEN, OnRSelection)
ON_BN_CLICKED(IDC_RTBRUSH, OnRSelection)
ON_BN_CLICKED(IDC_RTBITMAP, OnRSelection)
ON_BN_CLICKED(IDC_RSLINE, OnRSelection)
ON_BN_CLICKED(IDC_RSSQUARE, OnRSelection)
ON_BN_CLICKED(IDC_RSCIRCLE, OnRSelection)
ON_BN_CLICKED(IDC_RCBLACK, OnRSelection)
ON_BN_CLICKED(IDC_RCBLUE, OnRSelection)
ON_BN_CLICKED(IDC_RCGREEN, OnRSelection)
ON_BN_CLICKED(IDC_RCCYAN, OnRSelection)
ON_BN_CLICKED(IDC_RCRED, OnRSelection)
ON_BN_CLICKED(IDC_RCMAGENTA, OnRSelection)
ON_BN_CLICKED(IDC_RCYELLOW, OnRSelection)
ON_BN_CLICKED(IDC_RCWHITE, OnRSelection)
END_MESSAGE_MAP()
```

5. Edit the OnRSelection function, adding the code in Listing 9.4.

LISTING 9.4   The OnRSelection Function

```
void CGraphicsDlg::OnRSelection()
{
    // TODO: Add your control notification handler code here
    // Synchronize the data
    UpdateData(TRUE);
    // Repaint the second dialog
    m_dlgPaint.Invalidate();
}
```

`INPUT`

Drawing Lines

You can compile and run your application at this point, and the second dialog redraws itself whenever you choose a different radio button on the main dialog, but you wouldn't notice anything happening. At this point, you are triggering the redraws, but you haven't told the second dialog what to draw, which is the next step in building this application.

The easiest graphics to draw on the second dialog will be different styles of lines because you already have some experience drawing them. What you'll want to do is create one pen for each of the different pen styles, using the currently selected color. After you create all the pens, you loop through the different pens, selecting each one in turn and drawing a line across the dialog with each one. Before you start this loop, you need to perform a few calculations to determine where each line should be on the dialog, with their starting and stopping points.

To begin adding this functionality to your application, you first add a color table, with one entry for each color in the group of available colors on the first dialog. To create this color table, follow these steps:

1. Add a new member variable to the second dialog class, CPaintDlg, and specify the variable type as COLORREF, the name as m_crColors, and the access as Public.

2. Open the CPaintDlg.h header file. Locate the declaration for the variable you just added, and modify it as in Listing 9.5.

LISTING 9.5   The Color Table Variable Declaration

```
public:
   static const COLORREF m_crColors[8];
};
```

3. Open the source code file for the second dialog class (PaintDlg.cpp), and add the color table in Listing 9.6 near the top of the file before the class constructor and destructor.

LISTING 9.6   The Color Table

```
INPUT    const COLORREF CPaintDlg::m_crColors[8] = {
         RGB(   0,   0,   0),    // Black
   RGB(   0,   0, 255),   // Blue
   RGB(   0, 255,   0),   // Green
   RGB(   0, 255, 255),   // Cyan
   RGB( 255,   0,   0),   // Red
   RGB( 255,   0, 255),   // Magenta
   RGB( 255, 255,   0),   // Yellow
   RGB( 255, 255, 255)    // White
};

// CPaintDlg dialog
```

With the color table in place, you can add a new function for drawing the lines. To keep the OnPaint function from getting too cluttered and difficult to understand, it makes more sense to place a limited amount of code in it to determine what should be drawn on the second dialog, and then call other more specialized functions to draw the various shapes. With this in mind, you need to create a new member function for the second dialog class for drawing the lines as follows:

1. In the Class View pane, select and right-click the CPaintDlg class. Choose Add, Add Function from the context menu.

2. Specify the return type as void, and specify the function name as DrawLine. Add the first parameters of type CPaintDC* and name pdc. Click the Add button to add the parameter. Add the second parameters of type int and name iColor. Click the Add button to add the second parameter. Specify the function access as Private.

3. Edit this function, adding the code in Listing 9.7.

LISTING 9.7 The DrawLine Function

```
void CPaintDlg::DrawLine(CPaintDC *pdc, int iColor)
{
    // Declare and create the pens
    CPen pnSolidPen (PS_SOLID, 1, m_crColors[iColor]);
    CPen pnDotPen (PS_DOT, 1, m_crColors[iColor]);
    CPen pnDashPen (PS_DASH, 1, m_crColors[iColor]);
    CPen pnDashDotPen (PS_DASHDOT, 1, m_crColors[iColor]);
    CPen pnDashDotDotPen (PS_DASHDOTDOT, 1, m_crColors[iColor]);
    CPen pnNullPen (PS_NULL, 1, m_crColors[iColor]);
    CPen pnInsidePen (PS_INSIDEFRAME, 1, m_crColors[iColor]);

    // Get the drawing area
    CRect rRect;
    GetClientRect(rRect);
    rRect.NormalizeRect();

    // Calculate the distance between each of the lines
    CPoint ptStart;
    CPoint ptEnd;
    int iDist = rRect.Height() / 8;
    CPen* pOldPen = NULL;
    // Specify the starting points
    ptStart.y = rRect.top;
    ptStart.x = rRect.left;
    ptEnd.y = ptStart.y;
    ptEnd.x = rRect.right;
    int i;
    // Loop through the different pens
    for (i = 0; i < 7; i++)
    {
```

LISTING 9.7 continued

```
// Which pen are we on?
switch (i)
{
case 0:    // Solid
    pOldPen = pdc->SelectObject(&pnSolidPen);
    break;
case 1:    // Dot
    pdc->SelectObject(&pnDotPen);
    break;
case 2:    // Dash
    pdc->SelectObject(&pnDashPen);
    break;
case 3:    // Dash Dot
    pdc->SelectObject(&pnDashDotPen);
    break;
case 4:    // Dash Dot Dot
    pdc->SelectObject(&pnDashDotDotPen);
    break;
case 5:    // Null
    pdc->SelectObject(&pnNullPen);
    break;
case 6:    // Inside
    pdc->SelectObject(&pnInsidePen);
    break;
}
// Move down to the next position
ptStart.y = ptStart.y + iDist;
ptEnd.y = ptStart.y;
// Draw the line
pdc->MoveTo(ptStart);
pdc->LineTo(ptEnd);
}
// Select the original pen
pdc->SelectObject(pOldPen);
}
```

The code in Listing 9.5 first declares several pen variables, one for each line style shown
earlier in Figure 9.1. Next, it determines the size of the drawing area, which is used to
calculate the distance between each line that you draw. After the starting position is
determined, the code begins looping through each pen style, selecting the next pen as the
current pen on each loop. Notice that you only captured the old pen the first time through
the loop, as that pen is the one you need to set the current pen back to when you complete the loop. After the switch statement is exited, the code moves down to the starting
point for the next line to be drawn, and draws the line, using the MoveTo and LineTo
methods. When the loop is completed, the original pen is reselected as the current pen.

Now you need to edit the OnPaint function so that the OnLine function is called when it needs to be called. Add this function as an event-handler function for the WM_PAINT message. Notice that the generated code for this function creates a CPaintDC variable instead of the normal CDC. The CPaintDC class is derived from the CDC. It automatically calls the BeginPaint and EndPaint API functions that all Windows applications must call before drawing any graphics during the WM_PAINT event message processing. It can be treated just like a regular device context object, calling all the same functions.

When you are in the OnPaint function, you need to get a pointer to the parent window, so you can check the values of the variables tied to the groups of radio buttons to determine the color, tools, and shapes to be drawn on the second dialog. This information tells you whether to call the DrawLine function or another function that you haven't written yet. To add this functionality to your application, follow these steps:

1. Add an event handler for the WM_PAINT message on the second dialog class (CPaintDlg).

2. Add the code in Listing 9.8 to the function created in your class.

LISTING 9.8 The OnPaint Function

```
void CPaintDlg::OnPaint()
{
    CPaintDC dc(this); // device context for painting

    // TODO: Add your message handler code here
    // Get a pointer to the parent window
        CGraphicsDlg *pWnd = (CGraphicsDlg*)GetParent();
    // Do we have a valid pointer?
    if (pWnd)
    {
        // Is the tool a bitmap?
        if (pWnd->m_iTool == 2)
        {
        }
        else    // No, we're drawing a shape
        {
            // Are we drawing a line?
            if (pWnd->m_iShape == 0)
                DrawLine(&dc, pWnd->m_iColor);
        }
    }
    // Do not call CDialog::OnPaint() for painting messages
}
```

INPUT

9

The function in Listing 9.8 first acquires a pointer to the parent window, the main dialog. With the pointer acquired, the code then determines what shape is to be drawn by checking first which tool is selected (to make sure users didn't specify to show the bitmap image, which is added later), and then to determine which shape is selected. After you determine that you need to draw lines, the code calls the DrawLine function, passing the device context and the currently selected color.

At this point, if you compile and run your application, you should be able to draw lines across the second dialog, as shown in Figure 9.5.

FIGURE 9.5

Drawing lines on the second dialog.

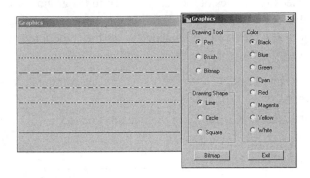

C++ Sidebar: The static and const Keywords

The static keyword is used on variables to indicate that they have a static lifetime (the life of the application). If a class member variable is declared as static, all instances of that class share the same instance of the variable, rather than have as many instances of the variable as there are instances of the class. Variables marked as static are created when the application starts and are destroyed when the application ends.

The const keyword is used on variables to indicate that they cannot be modified. If a variable is labeled with the const keyword, the value that the variable is initialized with is the only value that the variable will ever have. If an attempt is made to try and change the value of the variable, it will trigger a compile error. If the const keyword is used in a function parameter, it prevents that parameter from being modified within the function.

Drawing Circles and Squares

Now that you have the basic structure in place, and you can see how to change what's drawn on the second dialog at will, you are ready to add code to the second dialog to draw the circles and squares. To draw these figures, use the Ellipse and Rectangle device context functions. These functions will use the currently selected pen and brush to draw these figures at the specified location. With both functions, you pass a CRect object to specify the rectangle in which to draw the specified figure. The Rectangle function fills the entire space specified, and the `Ellipse` function draws a circle or ellipse where the middle of each side of the rectangle touches the edge of the ellipse. Because these functions use both the pen and brush, you'll need to create and select an invisible pen and invisible brush to enable users to choose either the pen or the brush. For the pen, you can use the null pen for this purpose, but for the brush, you'll need to create a solid brush the color of the window background (light gray).

When you calculate the position for each figure, you need to take a different approach from what you used with the lines. With lines, you could get the height of the window, divide it by 8, and then draw a line at each division from the left edge to the right. With ellipses and rectangles, you need to divide the dialog into eight even rectangles. The easiest way to do this is to create two rows of figures with four figures in each row. Leave a little space between each figure so users can see the different pens used to outline each figure.

To add this functionality to your application, do the following:

1. Add a new function to the second dialog class.
2. Specify the function type as `void`, the function name as `DrawRegion`, and add four parameters. The first parameter should be type `CPaintDC*` with the name `pdc`; the rest of the parameters should be type `int`, and have the names `iColor`, `iTool`, and `iShape`. Specify the function access as `Private`.
3. Edit the code in this function, adding the code in Listing 9.9.

LISTING 9.9 The `DrawRegion` Function

```
void CPaintDlg::DrawRegion(CPaintDC *pdc, int iColor, int iTool, int iShape)
{
    // Declare and create the pens
    CPen pnSolidPen (PS_SOLID, 1, m_crColors[iColor]);
    CPen pnDotPen (PS_DOT, 1, m_crColors[iColor]);
    CPen pnDashPen (PS_DASH, 1, m_crColors[iColor]);
    CPen pnDashDotPen (PS_DASHDOT, 1, m_crColors[iColor]);
    CPen pnDashDotDotPen (PS_DASHDOTDOT, 1, m_crColors[iColor]);
    CPen pnNullPen (PS_NULL, 1, m_crColors[iColor]);
    CPen pnInsidePen (PS_INSIDEFRAME, 1, m_crColors[iColor]);

    // Declare and create the brushes
    CBrush brSolidBrush(m_crColors[iColor]);
    CBrush brBDiagBrush(HS_BDIAGONAL, m_crColors[iColor]);
    CBrush brCrossBrush(HS_CROSS, m_crColors[iColor]);
    CBrush brDiagCrossBrush(HS_DIAGCROSS, m_crColors[iColor]);
    CBrush brFDiagBrush(HS_FDIAGONAL, m_crColors[iColor]);
    CBrush brHorizBrush(HS_HORIZONTAL, m_crColors[iColor]);
```

LISTING 9.9   continued

```
CBrush brVertBrush(HS_VERTICAL, m_crColors[iColor]);
CBrush brNullBrush(RGB(208, 208, 208));

// Calculate the size the the drawing regions
CRect rRect;
GetClientRect(rRect);
rRect.NormalizeRect();
int iVert = rRect.Height() / 2;
int iHeight = iVert - 10;
int iHorz = rRect.Width() / 4;
int iWidth = iHorz - 10;
CRect rDrawRect;
CPen *pOldPen = NULL;
CBrush *pOldBrush = NULL;
// Loop through all of the brushes and pens
for (int i = 0; i < 7; i++)
{
    if (i == 0)
    {
        // Determine the location for this figure.
        // Start the first row
        rDrawRect.top = rRect.top + 5;
        rDrawRect.left = rRect.left + 5;
        rDrawRect.bottom = rDrawRect.top + iHeight;
        rDrawRect.right = rDrawRect.left + iWidth;
    }
    else if (i == 4)
    {
        // Determine the location for this figure.
        // Start the second row
        rDrawRect.top = rDrawRect.top + iVert;
        rDrawRect.left = rRect.left + 5;
        rDrawRect.bottom = rDrawRect.top + iHeight;
        rDrawRect.right = rDrawRect.left + iWidth;
    }
    else
    {
        // Determine the location for this figure.
        rDrawRect.left = rDrawRect.left + iHorz;
        rDrawRect.right = rDrawRect.left + iWidth;
    }
    switch (i)
    {
    case 0:    // Solid
        // Select the appropriate pen and brush
        pOldPen = pdc->SelectObject(&pnSolidPen);
        pOldBrush = pdc->SelectObject(&brSolidBrush);
        break;
    case 1:    // Dot - Back Diagonal
        // Select the appropriate pen and brush
```

LISTING 9.9   continued

```
            pdc->SelectObject(&pnDotPen);
            pdc->SelectObject(&brBDiagBrush);
            break;
    case 2:    // Dash - Cross Brush
            // Select the appropriate pen and brush
            pdc->SelectObject(&pnDashPen);
            pdc->SelectObject(&brCrossBrush);
            break;
    case 3:    // Dash Dot - Diagonal Cross
            // Select the appropriate pen and brush
            pdc->SelectObject(&pnDashDotPen);
            pdc->SelectObject(&brDiagCrossBrush);
            break;
    case 4:    // Dash Dot Dot - Forward Diagonal
            // Select the appropriate pen and brush
            pdc->SelectObject(&pnDashDotDotPen);
            pdc->SelectObject(&brFDiagBrush);
            break;
    case 5:    // Null - Horizontal
            // Select the appropriate pen and brush
            pdc->SelectObject(&pnNullPen);
            pdc->SelectObject(&brHorizBrush);
            break;
    case 6:    // Inside - Vertical
            // Select the appropriate pen and brush
            pdc->SelectObject(&pnInsidePen);
            pdc->SelectObject(&brVertBrush);
            break;
    }
    // Which tool are we using?
    if (iTool == 0)
        pdc->SelectObject(brNullBrush);
    else
        pdc->SelectObject(pnNullPen);
    // Which shape are we drawing?
    if (iShape == 1)
        pdc->Ellipse(rDrawRect);
    else
        pdc->Rectangle(rDrawRect);
    }
    // Reset the original brush and pen
    pdc->SelectObject(pOldBrush);
    pdc->SelectObject(pOldPen);
}
```

Listing 9.9 basically follows the same logic as in the DrawLine function. First, it declares a set of pens, one for each line style, and then declares a set of brushes, one for each brush style. Next, the code determines the size of the drawing area, and the size for each

shape you can draw. Then the code loops through each brush and pen. The `switch` statement selects both the current pen and brush, and adjusts the drawing area rectangle for
the position of the next shape to be drawn. After the `switch` statement, the `DrawRegion`
function looks to see which tool the user is supposed to be using (the pen or the brush)
and sets the other to the `NULL` pen or brush. Finally, the code determines which shape you
are supposed to be drawing and calls the appropriate function to draw the shape, either
`Ellipse` or `Rectangle`. After the loop, the original pen and brush that were selected
when you entered this function are reselected.

Now that you can draw the circles and squares in the second dialog, you need to call this
function when the user has selected either of these two figures with either a pen or a
brush. To do this, add the two boldfaced lines in Listing 9.10 to the `OnPaint` function.

LISTING 9.10   The Modified `OnPaint` Function

```
void CPaintDlg::OnPaint()
{
    CPaintDC dc(this); // device context for painting

    // TODO: Add your message handler code here

    // Get a pointer to the parent window
    CGraphicsDlg *pWnd = (CGraphicsDlg*)GetParent();
    // Do we have a valid pointer?
    if (pWnd)
    {
        // Is the tool a bitmap?
        if (pWnd->m_iTool == 2)
        {
        }
        else    // No, we're drawing a shape
        {
            // Are we drawing a line?
            if (m_iShape == 0)
                DrawLine(&dc, pWnd->m_iColor);
            else    // We're drawing a ellipse or rectangle
                DrawRegion(&dc, pWnd->m_iColor, pWnd->m_iTool,
                    pWnd->m_iShape);
        }
    }
    // Do not call CDialog::OnPaint() for painting messages
}
```

Now you should be able to compile and run your application and display not only lines,
but also squares and circles, switching between displaying the outlines and the filled-in
figure without any outline, as shown in Figure 9.6.

FIGURE 9.6

Drawing rectangles on the second dialog.

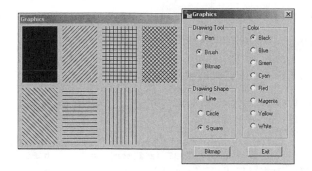

9

Loading Bitmaps

Now that you can draw various graphic images on the second dialog, all that's left is to add the functionality to load and display bitmaps. You could easily add the bitmaps to the resources in the application, give them their own object IDs, and then use the LoadBitmap and MAKEINTRESOURCE functions to load each bitmap into a CBitmap class object, but that isn't extremely useful when you start building your own applications. What's really useful is the capability to load bitmaps from files on the computer disk. To provide this functionality, use the LoadImage API function to load the bitmap images into memory and then attach the loaded image to the CBitmap object.

To do this in your application, attach a function to the bitmap button on the first dialog that displays the File Open dialog to users, enabling them to select a bitmap to be displayed. You'll want to build a filter for the dialog, limiting the available files to bitmaps that can be displayed in the second dialog. When users select a bitmap, you'll get the file and path name from the dialog and load the bitmap by using the LoadImage function. After you have a valid handle to the bitmap loaded into memory, you delete the current bitmap image from the CBitmap object. If a bitmap was loaded into the CBitmap object, you detach the CBitmap object from the now deleted image. After ensuring that there isn't already an image loaded in the CBitmap object, attach the image you just loaded into memory, using the Attach function. At this point, you'll want to invalidate the second dialog, so if it's displaying a bitmap, it'll display the newly loaded bitmap.

To support this functionality, you'll need to add a string variable to hold the bitmap name, and a CBitmap variable to hold the bitmap image, to the CGraphicsDlg class. Follow these steps:

1. Add the following variables to the CGraphicsDlg class:

Name	Type	Access
m_strBitmap	CString	Public
m_bmpBitmap	CBitmap	Public

2. Add an event-handler function to the clicked event of the Bitmap button.

3. Edit the new function, adding the code in Listing 9.11.

LISTING 9.11   The OnBnClickedBbitmap Function

```
void CGraphicsDlg::OnBnClickedBbitmap()
{
    // TODO: Add your control notification handler code here
        // Build a filter for use in the File Open dialog
        static char BASED_CODE szFilter[] = "Bitmap Files (*.bmp)|*.bmp||";
    // Create the File Open dialog
    CFileDialog dlgFile(TRUE, ".bmp", m_strBitmap,
        OFN_HIDEREADONLY | OFN_OVERWRITEPROMPT, szFilter);

    // Show the File Open dialog and capture the result
    if (dlgFile.DoModal() == IDOK)
    {
        // Get the filename selected
        m_strBitmap = dlgFile.GetPathName();
        // Load the selected bitmap file
        HBITMAP hBitmap = (HBITMAP) ::LoadImage(AfxGetInstanceHandle(),
            m_strBitmap, IMAGE_BITMAP, 0, 0,
            LR_LOADFROMFILE | LR_CREATEDIBSECTION);

        // Do we have a valid handle for the loaded image?
        if (hBitmap)
        {
            // Delete the current bitmap
            if (m_bmpBitmap.DeleteObject())
                // If there was a bitmap, detach it
                m_bmpBitmap.Detach();
            // Attach the currently loaded bitmap to the bitmap object
            m_bmpBitmap.Attach(hBitmap);
        }

        // Invalidate the second dialog window
        m_dlgPaint.Invalidate();
    }
}
```

INPUT

The code in Listing 9.11 first creates a filter for the Open File dialog with the following line:

```
static char szFilter[] = "Bitmap Files (*.bmp)|*.bmp||";
```

The filter for the Open File and Save File dialogs is a series of string pairs separated by the pipe (|) character. The first string in each pair is the file type description that users will see in the combo box where they are selecting the files type(s) to open or save. The second string in the pair is the extension that should be enabled for that selection. In this example, there is only a single pair, followed by an empty pair of strings. The empty string pair must always be there, no matter how many pairs are specified.After you created the file type filter, you created the Open File dialog with the CFileDialog class, using it to enable users to specify the image file to display. When users specify a file, the code retrieves the filename, complete with the full path to the file, using the GetPathName method.

After you have the filename, you use the LoadImage Windows API function to load the bitmap image and return a handle to the loaded image. The first parameter to the LoadImage function is the handle to the instance of the application. You can retrieve this by using the AfxGetInstanceHandle function. The second parameter is the filename to be loaded. The third parameter is the type of image to be loaded: IMAGE_BITMAP, IMAGE_CURSOR, or IMAGE_ICON. The fourth parameter is the desired width of the image, and the fifth parameter is the desired height of the image. Both can be set to 0 to use the actual image size. The sixth and final parameter is a flag that specifies how you want to load the image. Table 9.5 lists the various options.

TABLE 9.5   LoadImage Option Flags

Option	Description
LR_DEFAULTCOLOR	This default flag does nothing other than specify that the LR_MONO-CHROME flag isn't set.
LR_CREATEDIBSECTION	This flag is valid only with the IMAGE_BITMAP image type. It specifies to return a DIB section bitmap, that uses the colors in the bitmap for the color table (the selection of colors that are used in the bitmap). Without this flag, the bitmap would be loaded as a compatible bitmap, in which case the colors in the bitmap would be mapped to the current colors of the display device.
LR_DEFAULTSIZE	This flag specifies to use the system default sizes for icons and cursors. If this flag isn't set, and the desired width and height parameters are set to 0, then the actual size of the icon or cursor will be used.
LR_LOADFROMFILE	This flag indicates that the image name passed in the second parameter is the filename to be loaded. If this flag isn't set, then the image name is assumed to be the resource ID for images built into the application.
LR_LOADMAP3DCOLORS	This flag causes the color table of the image to be searched for three specific gray shades in the image that are replaced by system default 3-D colors for shadow, face, and light.

TABLE 9.5   continued

Option	Description
LR_LOADTRANSPARENT	This flag causes the color of the first pixel in the image to be interpreted as a transparent color. All other pixels in the image that are that same color are marked as transparent.
LR_MONOCHROME	This flag causes the image to be loaded as a black-and-white image.
LR_SHARED	If the image is to be loaded multiple times in the same application, this flag causes the application to use a single, shared handle to the image each time it's loaded. In other words, the image is loaded only one time, and each request to load the image is given a handle to the single instance of the image. Without this flag, each time the image is requested, a new copy is loaded.
LR_VGACOLOR	This flag causes the image to be loaded using true VGA colors.

After you've loaded the new bitmap, you need to clean up any previous bitmap that was loaded. To do this, the first thing you do is call the DeleteObject method, which removes the previous bitmap from memory. If a bitmap was loaded to be removed, the DeleteObject method returns TRUE. If a bitmap was loaded, you next need to detach that bitmap's handle from the CBitmap object by using the Detach method. When the previous image is unloaded and discarded, you can attach the new image to the CBitmap object using the Attach method, passing it the handle for the newly loaded bitmap.

Displaying Bitmaps

Now that you can load bitmaps into memory, you need to be able to display them for the users. You need to copy the bitmap from the CBitmap object to a BITMAP structure, using the GetBitmap function, which will get the width and height of the bitmap image. Next, you'll create a new device context that's compatible with the screen device context. You'll select the bitmap into the new device context and then copy it from this second device context to the original device context, resizing it as it's copied, using the StretchBlt function.

To add this functionality to your application, follow these steps:

1. Add a new member function to the second dialog class.
2. Specify the function type as void, the function name as ShowBitmap, and add one parameter. The parameter should be type CPaintDC* with name pdc. Specify the function access as Private.
3. Edit the function, adding the code in Listing 9.12.

> **Note**
>
> You've declared the window pointer being passed in as a pointer to a `CWnd` object, instead of the class type of your main dialog. To declare it as a pointer to the class type of the first dialog, you need to declare the class for the first dialog before the class declaration for the second dialog. Meanwhile, the first dialog requires that the second dialog class be declared first. This affects the order in which the include files are added to the source code at the top of each file. You can't have both classes declared before the other; one has to be first. Although there are ways to get around this problem, by declaring a forward reference for the second class before the declaration of the first class, it's easier to cast the pointer as a pointer to the first dialog class in the function in this instance.

9

LISTING 9.12 The `ShowBitmap` Function

```
void CPaintDlg::ShowBitmap(CPaintDC* pdc)
{
    // Convert the pointer to a pointer to the main dialog class
    CGraphicsDlg *pWnd = (CGraphicsDlg*)GetParent();
    BITMAP bm;
    CDC dcMem;
    CRect rRect;

    // Get the loaded bitmap
    pWnd->m_bmpBitmap.GetBitmap(&bm);
    // Create a device context to load the bitmap into
    dcMem.CreateCompatibleDC(pdc);
    // Select the bitmap into the compatible device context
    dcMem.SelectObject(pWnd->m_bmpBitmap);
    // Get the display area available
    GetClientRect(rRect);
    rRect.NormalizeRect();
    // Copy and resize the bitmap to the dialog window
    pdc->StretchBlt(10, 10, (rRect.Width() - 20), (rRect.Height() - 20),
        &dcMem, 0, 0, bm.bmWidth, bm.bmHeight, SRCCOPY);
}
```

This function first casts the pointer to the main dialog as a pointer to a `CGraphicsDlg` class, as in the `OnPaint` function. Next, it declares an instance of the `BITMAP` structure, and then passes it to the `CBitmap` object, so you could get the actual bitmap (which is needed for passing to the device context objects). The `BITMAP` structure contains information about the bitmap, as well as a pointer to the actual image.

After you have the bitmap, you create a compatible device context using the `CreateCompatibleDC` method. The compatible device context is a useful device that enables you to perform drawing and manipulation actions on a device context that's virtually the same as the display device context, only isn't attached to any output device. This means that you can use this second device context to manipulate the image in various ways in memory and then copy the finished image to the actual device context, displaying the image when you are finished. One primary advantage of this approach is that it's faster to manipulate an image in memory without having any display devices attached, than to manipulate the image with the display device attached, because the display hardware slows the manipulation process down considerably.

When you have the compatible device context, select the bitmap into it using the SelectObject method. After you have selected the bitmap into the compatible device context, you get the dimensions of the actual display area, and then use the StretchBlt method to resize and copy the image to the actual device context.

Now that you can display the currently selected bitmap on the dialog, you need to add the functionality to call this function to the OnPaint function in the second dialog. You can determine whether a bitmap has been specified by checking the value of the m_strBitmap variable on the first dialog. If this string is empty, no bitmap will be displayed. If the string isn't empty, you can call the ShowBitmap function. To add this last bit of functionality to this application, edit the OnPaint function, adding the boldfaced lines from Listing 9.13.

LISTING 9.13   The Modified OnPaint Function

```
void CPaintDlg::OnPaint()
{
    CPaintDC dc(this); // device context for painting

    // TODO: Add your message handler code here

    // Get a pointer to the parent window
    CGraphicsDlg *pWnd = (CGraphicsDlg*)GetParent();
    // Do we have a valid pointer?
    if (pWnd)
    {
        // Is the tool a bitmap?
        if (pWnd->m_iTool == 2)
        {
            // Is there a bitmap selected and loaded?
                if (pWnd->m_strBitmap.GetLength() >0)
            // Display it
            ShowBitmap(&dc);
        }
        else    // No, we're drawing a shape
        {
```

INPUT

```
                    // Are we drawing a line?
                    if (m_iShape == 0)
                        DrawLine(&dc, pWnd->m_iColor);
                    else    // We're drawing a ellipse or rectangle
                        DrawRegion(&dc, pWnd->m_iColor, pWnd->m_iTool,
                                        pWnd->m_iShape);
                }
            }
            // Do not call CDialog::OnPaint() for painting messages
        }
```

9

At this point, you should be able to select a bitmap from your system and display it in the second dialog (see Figure 9.7).

FIGURE 9.7

Showing a bitmap in the second dialog.

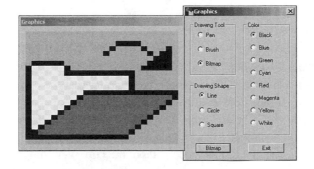

C++ Sidebar: Using Forward Class Definition

When one class needs to interact with another class, the first class needs to know what functions and variables are exposed in the second class. This is accomplished by including the header file in which the second class is declared before the first reference to the second class in the declaration or code of the first class. When a class has an instance of a second class as a member variable, or as a parameter in one of its member functions, that class needs to include the header of the second class before its own class declaration. But what if the second class has the same need to include the header for the first class prior to its class declaration? The declaration for one of the two classes has to be first, which means that the second class can't reference the first class until after its own class declaration unless some sort of placeholder can be used.

Well, it just so happens that there is such a placeholder that can substitute for the first class before the declaration of the second class in its own header file. This placeholder is called a Forward Reference. This enables the second class to wait until after its own declaration to include the header for the first class. In fact, the two classes don't even have to be in separate header files, they can both be in the same header file (or source code file). This is done is as follows:

```
// Declare a forward reference for the second class
class CClass2;

// Declare the first class
class CClass1
{
    // Declare a pointer to the second class
    CClass2 *pCls2;
};

// Declare the second class (for real this time)
class CClass2
{
    // Declare a pointer to the first class
    CClass1 *pCls1;
};
```

Essentially, the way this works is you are declaring that you will have a class, but you will define the class later. This satisfies the compiler that the class will exist, so it doesn't get upset when it finds references to it in the code before its declaration. Now, you do need to include the full class declaration before using the class in code, where the compiler needs to know about all the class methods and variables, but this lets you get past the declaration part and to your code without the compiler complaining.

Loading and Displaying JPG or PNG Images

The preceding functionality that you added is all nice and good, but how practical is it to display bitmaps these days? Thanks to the growth in popularity of Web image formats, it's becoming rare that you see bitmaps in frequent use. What's normally seen these days are the various Web image formats, such as JPEG and PNG. Because of this predominance, it makes sense to alter the code that you just added to use the CImage class instead of the CBitmap class.

With the CImage class, all the functionality required for loading and displaying the image can be performed by using only three member methods:

- You can load the image into the class instance with the Load method.
- You can display the image in the second dialog with the Draw method.
- When you need to load a second image, you can unload the previous image with the Destroy method.

To use the CImage class, you first have to add the appropriate include file to the project. Because CImage is a shared class between MFC and ATL, it's not automatically included with the MFC headers included in the stdafx.h header file. As a result, you need to add it to the stdafx.h header file as follows:

1. Open the stdafx.h file.

2. Add the boldfaced line in Listing 9.14 to include the appropriate shared class header file in the project. Add this line at the bottom of the stdafx.h header file.

LISTING 9.14 The Modified stdafx.h Include Directives

```
// stdafx.h : include file for standard system include files,
// or project specific include files that are used frequently,
// but are changed infrequently

#pragma once

. . .

#include <afxwin.h>         // MFC core and standard components
#include <afxext.h>         // MFC extensions
#include <afxdisp.h>        // MFC Automation classes

#include <afxdtctl.h>           // MFC support for Internet Explorer 4
➥Common Controls
#ifndef _AFX_NO_AFXCMN_SUPPORT
#include <afxcmn.h>               // MFC support for Windows Common Controls
#endif // _AFX_NO_AFXCMN_SUPPORT
]#include <atlimage.h>
```

INPUT

After you include the header file, you need to change the type declaration in the CGraphicsDlg class from CBitmap to CImage. To do this, make the following changes:

1. Open the GraphicsDlg.h file.

2. Comment out the declaration for the m_bmpBitmap variable and add a new one defining it as a CImage data type, as in Listing 9.15.

LISTING 9.15 The Modified GraphicsDlg.h Variable Declarations

```
public:
    afx_msg void OnRSelection();
    afx_msg void OnBnClickedBexit();
    CString m_strBitmap;
    //    CBitmap m_bmpBitmap;
        CImage m_bmpBitmap;
    afx_msg void OnBnClickedBbitmap();
```

INPUT

The next change that you need to make is to alter the OnBnClickedBbitmap function so that it loads a JPEG file as well as a bitmap file. To make this change, alter the OnBnClickedBbitmap function with the boldfaced code in Listing 9.16.

LISTING 9.16 The Modified OnBnClickedBbitmap Function

```
void CGraphicsDlg::OnBnClickedBbitmap(void)
{
    // TODO: Add your control notification handler code here
    // Build a filter for use in the File Open dialog
    static char szFilter[] =
            "JPEG Files (*.jpg)|*.jpg|Bitmap Files (*.bmp)|*.bmp||";
    // Create the File Open dialog
    CFileDialog dlgFile(TRUE, ".jpg", m_strBitmap,
        OFN_HIDEREADONLY | OFN_OVERWRITEPROMPT, szFilter);

    // Show the File Open dialog and capture the result
    if (dlgFile.DoModal() == IDOK)
    {
        // Get the filename selected
        m_strBitmap = dlgFile.GetPathName();
            // Delete the current image
                m_bmpBitmap.Destroy();
        // Load the new image
        m_bmpBitmap.Load(m_strBitmap);

        // Invalidate the second dialog window
        m_dlgPaint.Invalidate();
    }
}
```

The last change you need to make is in the ShowBitmap function, so it displays the image using the CImage Draw method. As in Listing 9.16, this will significantly simplify the ShowBitmap function by reducing the amount of code required. Now you will need to get only the drawing area dimensions, and then you can use the pointer to the device context passed into the function to draw the image. To make this change, alter the ShowBitmap function as indicated with the boldfaced code in Listing 9.17.

LISTING 9.17 The Modified ShowBitmap Function

```
void CPaintDlg::ShowBitmap(CPaintDC *pdc)
{
    // Convert the pointer to a pointer to the main dialog class
    CGraphicsDlg *pWnd = (CGraphicsDlg*)GetParent();
    CDC dcMem;
    CRect rRect;
```

LISTING 9.17 continued

```
        // Get the display area available
        GetClientRect(rRect);
        rRect.NormalizeRect();
```

```
        // Copy and resize the bitmap to the dialog window
            pWnd->m_bmpBitmap.Draw(pdc->m_hDC, rRect);
    }
```

9

Now if you compile and run the example application, you'll be able to find and display JPEG images, as shown in Figure 9.8, as well as bitmaps. You can alter the string specifying the file types to be available in the FileOpen dialog (in the `OnBnClickedBbitmap` function) to also enable your application to display PNG and GIF files.

> **Note**
>
> If the actual size of the JPEG image you are displaying is significantly different from the size of the display area you are viewing it in, the colors may look a little odd. The methods natively used in stretching and shrinking an image for display in Windows frequently don't handle maintaining fine details in the image. If the capability of displaying images in something other than their actual size is a need of yours, then you might need to write your own resizing routines rather than depending on the native Windows routines.

FIGURE 9.8

Showing a JPEG image in the second dialog.

Summary

You learned a lot today. You learned how Windows uses device context objects to enable you to draw graphics in the same way every time, without having to worry about what hardware users might have in their computers. You learned about some of the basic GDI objects, such as pens and brushes, and how they are used to draw figures on windows and dialogs. You also learned how you can load bitmaps from the system disk and display them on the screen for the user to see. You learned about the different pen and brush styles and how you can use these to draw the type of figure you want to draw. You also learned how you can specify colors for use with pens and brushes, so you can control how images appear to the user.

Q&A

Q. **Why do I need to specify both a pen and a brush if I'm just wanting to display one or the other?**

A. You are always drawing with both when you draw any object that's filled in. The pen draws the outline, and the brush fills in the interior. You can't choose to use one or the other; you have to use both. If you only want to display one or the other, you need to take special steps.

Q. **Why do all the pen styles become solid when I increase the pen width above 1?**

A. When you increase the pen width, you are increasing the size of the dot that's used to draw with. If you remember Day 4, "Integrating Mouse and Keyboard to Allow User Interaction," when you first tried to draw by capturing each spot the mouse covered, all you drew were a bunch of dots. Well, after you increase the size of the dots that you are drawing the line with, the gaps between the dots are filled in from both sides, providing an unbroken line.

Workshop

The Workshop provides quiz questions to help you solidify your understanding of the material covered and exercises to provide you with experience in using what you've learned. The answers to the quiz questions and exercises are provided in Appendix A, "Answers to Quiz Questions."

Quiz

1. What are the three values that are combined to specify a color?
2. What do you use to draw on windows without needing to know what graphics card the user has?
3. What size bitmap can you use to make a brush from it?
4. What event message is sent to a window to tell it to redraw itself?
5. How can you cause a window to repaint itself?

Exercises

1. Make the second dialog resizable, and make it adjust the figures drawn on it whenever it's resized. Hint: use the Border property and the WM_SIZE event message.

2. Add a bitmap brush to the set of brushes used to create the rectangles and ellipses.

9

DAY **10**

Creating SDI and MDI Applications

Today you will learn a different way of approaching application development with Visual C++ than you've used with the previous days' lessons. Today you will learn how to create Single Document Interface (SDI) and Multiple Document Interface (MDI) applications. An SDI application is a document-centric application that can work with only one document at a time, and can work with only one type of document. An MDI application is also a document-centric application that allows you to work on multiple documents at one time, switching between the windows of the application to do your work.

Some good examples of SDI applications are Notepad, WordPad, and Paint. All these applications can do only one type of task and can work on only one task at a time. WordPad is almost like an SDI version of Word. It's able to perform many of the same tasks as Word, but allows you to work on only one document at a time. Starting with Word 2000, the Word application became a combination of an SDI and an MDI application, looking like an MDI application when only a single document is open, with an MDI child window close button below the main window Title bar, but looking and acting like several SDI applications when more than one document is open.

Some of the things that you will learn today are

- The Document/View architecture that Visual C++ uses for creating SDI and MDI applications
- How to create an SDI and MDI application shell
- How to separate your data from the visual representation of the data
- How to encapsulate your data in its own C++ class
- How to create interaction between the data and the menus
- How to send multiple menu entries to a single event-handling function using a different approach than used earlier

Understanding the Document/View Architecture

When you create an SDI application, more classes are created for an SDI application than for a dialog-style application. Each class serves a specific purpose in how SDI applications operate. Ignoring the About window dialog class, four specific classes make up an SDI application:

- The CWinApp-derived class
- The CFrameWnd-derived class
- The CDocument-derived class
- The CView-derived class

The CWinApp class creates all the other components in the application. It's the class that receives all the event messages and then passes the messages to the CFrameWnd and CView classes.

The CFrameWnd class is the window frame. It holds the menu, toolbar, scrollbars, and any other visible objects attached to the frame. This class determines how much of the document is visible at any time. Very little (if any) of your programming efforts on SDI applications will require making any modifications or additions to either of these first two classes.

The CDocument class houses your document. This class is where you build the data structures necessary to house and manipulate the data that makes up your document. This class receives input from and passes display information to the CView class. CDocument is also responsible for saving and retrieving the document data from files.

The CView class displays the visual representation of your document for the users. This class passes input information to the CDocument class and receives display information from the CDocument class. Most of the coding that you will do for this class consists of drawing the document for users and handling user input. The CView class has several derived classes that you can use as the base for the view class; see Table 10.1.

TABLE 10.1 The CView Descendent Classes

Class	Description
CEditView	Provides the functionality of an edit box control. Can be used to implement simple text-editor functionality.
CFormView	The base class for views containing controls. Can be used to provide form-based documents in applications.
CHtmlView	Provides the functionality of a Web browser. This view directly handles the URL navigation, hyperlinking, and so on. Maintains a history list for browsing forward and backward.
CListView	Provides list-control functionality in the Document/View architecture.
CRichEditView	Provides character and paragraph formatting functionality. Can be used to implement a word-processor application.
CScrollView	Provides scrolling capabilities to a CView class.
CTreeView	Provides tree-control functionality in the Document/View architecture.

All four classes work together to make up the full functionality of an SDI application (see Figure 10.1). By taking advantage of this architecture, you can build powerful document-centric applications with relative ease.

FIGURE 10.1

The Document/View architecture.

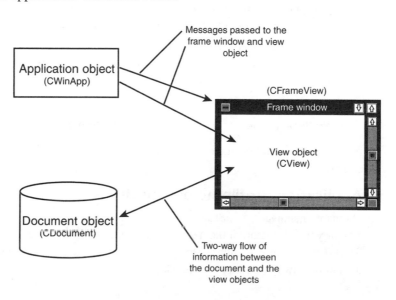

Note

> Don't let the term document mislead you. This doesn't mean that you can create only applications such as word processors and spreadsheets. In this situation, the term *document* refers to the data processed by your application, whereas *view* refers to the visual representation of that data. For instance, the Solitaire application could be implemented as a Document/View application, with the document being the cards and their position in the playing area. In this case, the view is the display of the cards, drawing each card where the document specifies it should be.

MFC Note: The CWinApp Class

The CWinApp class is the base class for the application startup functionality. It was mentioned on Day 1, "Building Your First Application in the Visual C++ Development Environment," and you've seen it in every one of your applications that you've built so far. You can use a series of global functions to interact with the CWinApp object, and the CWinApp class contains several functions that provide functionality you might need to use in your applications.

Global CWinApp-Related Functions

Four global functions can be used to interact with the application object:

- You've already seen and used AfxGetApp in previous days' examples. This function returns a pointer to the CWinApp class application object. In an MFC application, you can't directly access the CWinApp class. You have to use the AfxGetApp function to gain access to any CWinApp functionality needed.

- AfxGetInstanceHandle returns the application's handle. This handle can be used in situations where you need the application handle for passing to an API function that requires it.

- AfxGetResourceHandle returns the instance handle for the application resources.

- AfxGetAppName returns a null-terminated string containing the application name.

None of these functions take any parameters, and can be called anywhere in your application.

Application Profile Access Functions

On many instances you need to save configuration information about your application so that you can restore it the next time the application is run. Sometimes, on Windows 95/98/Me, this information is stored in .ini files, while on Windows NT/2000 systems it's almost always stored in the registry.

The CWinApp class contains the functionality necessary for reading and writing information to these configuration stores. These functions can be used to maintain the configuration settings in the registry.

To read configuration information, use the GetProfileString and GetProfileInt functions. The syntax for these functions is as follows:

```
CString GetProfileString(LPCTSTR lpszSection, LPCTSTR lpszEntry,
    LPCTSTR lpszDefault = NULL);
UINT GetProfileInt(LPCTSTR lpszSection, LPCTSTR lpszEntry,
    int iDefault);
```

The first parameter to both functions, lpszSection, is the configuration section or subkey for the configuration setting to be read with these functions. The second parameter, lpszEntry, is the name of the entry to be read from the configuration settings. This entry name value must be unique within the section. The third parameter, lpszDefault and iDefault, is the default value to be returned from these functions, in case the configuration setting isn't found in the registry or .ini file. If the third parameter is not provided to the GetProfileString function, an empty string is returned.

To write configuration information, use the WriteProfileString and WriteProfileInt functions. These two functions write the configuration settings to the registry or .ini file. The syntax for these functions are as follows:

```
BOOL WriteProfileString(LPCTSTR lpszSection, LPCTSTR lpszEntry,
    LPCTSTR lpszValue);
BOOL WriteProfileInt(LPCTSTR lpszSection, LPCTSTR lpszEntry,
    int iValue);
```

The first two parameters, lpszSection and lpszEntry, are the same as with the reading functions. The first parameter to both functions, lpszSection, is the configuration section or subkey for the configuration setting to be written with these functions. The second parameter, lpszEntry, is the name of the entry to be written to the configuration settings. The third parameter, lpszValue and iValue, is the value to be written to the registry.

Before you begin reading and writing to the registry, you need to take care of one detail in your application startup. In the application object, the class inherited from the CWinApp class (usually named C<your application name>), you need to find the SetRegistryKey function in the InitInstance function. Change the string passed to the SetRegistryKey function to the name that you want your application section to be located under. For example, the default for this section looks like Listing 10.1.

10

LISTING 10.1 A Typical `InitInstance` Function

```
BOOL CSDISquigApp::InitInstance()
{
    CWinApp::InitInstance();

. . .
    // Standard initialization
    // If you are not using these features and wish to reduce the size
    // of your final executable, you should remove from the following
    // the specific initialization routines you do not need
    // Change the registry key under which our settings are stored
    // TODO: You should modify this string to be something appropriate
    // such as the name of your company or organization
    SetRegistryKey(_T("Local AppWizard-Generated Applications"));
    LoadStdProfileSettings(4);  // Load standard INI file options
        ➥(including MRU)
...
```

Typically, you'll change the string being passed to the `SetRegistryKey` function from `"Local AppWizard-Generated Applications"` to your company name. This sets the key in the registry under `HKEY_CURRENT_USER/Software/`. Under this key will be a sub-key, which is the application name, followed by all the section keys used in the configuration reading and writing functions discussed earlier. For instance, if you modified the string to `"MyCompany"` as follows,

```
SetRegistryKey(_T("MyCompany"));
```

and your application name was MyApp, all your application configuration settings would be maintained under the following registry key:

```
HKEY_CURRENT_USER/Software/MyCompany/MyApp/
```

Icon and Cursor Functions

Along with the configuration functions, another set of functions that you might find yourself needing to use from the `CWinApp` class are the functions for loading cursors and icons. You used the `LoadStandardCursor` function on Day 4, "Integrating Mouse and Keyboard to Allow User Interaction," and the `LoadCursor` and `LoadIcon` functions work basically the same. The syntax for these two functions are as follows:

```
HCURSOR LoadCursor(UINT nIDResource);
HICON LoadIcon(UINT nIDResource);
```

In both functions, you pass the ID of the icon or cursor resource that you've compiled into your application (any you've created as part of your project are compiled into the application). Both functions return a handle to the cursor or icon that have been loaded.

MFC Note: The CFrameWnd Class

The CFrameWnd class is the base class from which the main window frame is inherited in SDI applications. Although it provides a good deal of vital functionality to the application, you will likely do relatively little with this class when building most applications.

Some functionality that you will most likely use in this class is actually inherited from base classes. This is the GetWindowPlacement and SetWindowPlacement functions. These functions can be used to get the location and size of a window for saving in the application configuration, and restoring of the window state upon application startup. Both functions take a pointer to a WINDOWPLACEMENT structure, which is defined as follows:

```
typedef struct tagWINDOWPLACEMENT {      /* wndpl */
    UINT   length;
    UINT   flags;
    UINT   showCmd;
    POINT  ptMinPosition;
    POINT  ptMaxPosition;
    RECT   rcNormalPosition;
} WINDOWPLACEMENT;
```

The first member of this structure, length, is the length in bytes of the structure itself. The second member, flags, contains information about the minimize and maximum options for the window (see Table 10.2). The third member, showCmd, specifies the state of the window. Table 10.3 lists the possible values for this member. The fourth member, ptMinPosition, is the position of the window's top-left corner when the window is minimized. The fifth member, ptMaxPosition, is the position of the top-left corner when the window is maximized. The last member, rcNormalPosition, specifies the position and size of the window in normal mode. You can retrieve the current state of the window as follows:

```
WINDOWPLACEMENT wndpl;
wndpl.length = sizeof(WINDOWPLACEMENT);
// gets current window position and iconized/maximized status
BOOL bRet = GetWindowPlacement(&wndpl);
```

And then you can restore the state of the window as follows:

```
// sets window's position and minimized/maximized status
BOOL bRet = SetWindowPlacement(&wndpl);
```

By saving the data in the WINDOWPLACEMENT structure to the registry, and then restoring it the next time the application is run, you can maintain the size and position of the application windows.

10

TABLE 10.2   The WINDOWPLACEMENT Flag Options

Option	Description
WPF_SETMINPOSITION	Specifies that the window's x and y positions can be set for when the window is minimized.
WPF_RESTORETOMAXIMIZED	Specifies that the window will be restored in its maximized state, regardless of the window's current state.
WPF_ASYNCWINDOWPLACEMENT	Specifies that, if multiple threads are running, the message is passed to the thread that owns the window. Other threads are prevented from blocking that thread from setting the window state. This option is only available on Windows 2000 or later OSs.

TABLE 10.3   The cmdShow Options

Command	Description
SW_HIDE	Hides the window.
SW_MAXIMIZE	Maximizes the window.
SW_MINIMIZE	Minimizes the window.
SW_RESTORE	Activates and shows the window in its normal position (same as SW_SHOWNORMAL).
SW_SHOW	Activates and shows the window in its current size and position.
SW_SHOWMAXIMIZED	Activates and maximizes the window.
SW_SHOWMINIMIZED	Activates and minimizes the window.
SW_SHOWMINNOACTIVE	Displays the window in the minimized state. Doesn't activate the window.
SW_SHOWNA	Displays the window in its current state and position. Doesn't activate the window.
SW_SHOWNOACTIVATE	Displays the window in its previous state and position. Doesn't activate the window.
SW_SHOWNORMAL	Activates the window and shows it in its normal size and position (not minimized or maximized).

C++ Sidebar: The sizeof function

The sizeof function can be called to get the size, in bytes, of a structure, class, or data type. It is typically used in situations where you need to get the size of a structure or data type, such as memory allocation situations, or for populating size parameters or structure members. The benefit of using this function is that you don't have to worry about the size of a structure yourself. This is important in those situations where a structure may be changing in size. For instance, some of the standard Windows structures have different sizes depending on the version of Windows the application is being run on. By using the sizeof function, you don't have to keep up with details like the version of Windows, and how that effects the size of particular structures.

MFC Note: The CDocument Class

The CDocument class is the base class for the data in your document. The document is the data used in your application, regardless of what form that data may take. It doesn't mean that you are limited to creating word processing or spreadsheet applications. It's merely a means of separating the data from the display. As such, it's expected that you'll create most of the functionality in your document class descendent, and only need supporting functionality from the CDocument class.

Most functions that you'll be working with in the CDocument class (see Table 10.4) are actually the functions that you'll be overriding for your own purposes.

TABLE 10.4 The Overridable CDocument Functions

Function	Description
DeleteContents	Called to delete the current contents of the document.
OnCloseDocument	Called when the document is being closed.
OnNewDocument	Called when a new document is being created for performing initialization for the new document.
OnOpenDocument	Called when an existing document is being opened.
OnSaveDocument	Called when the open document is being saved.

Whenever changes are made to the document data, you'll want to call the SetModifiedFlag function to mark the data as dirty. This will trigger the encapsulated functionality to ask users whether they want to save the document before closing it or the application.

MFC Note: The CView Classes

The CView class is linked to the CDocument class, in that it implements how the data in the CDocument class is displayed. You may have multiple instances of the CView class for each instance of the CDocument class in your running application. Like with the CDocument class, you'll be adding most of the functionality in the CView descendent class in your application. Most functionality will either be triggered by mouse or keyboard events, or from the overridable functions in the CView class. (Table 10.5 lists these overridable functions.). Several functions already have function shells in the default view class created by the Application Wizard for your application.

TABLE 10.5 The Overridable CView Functions

Function	Description
OnDraw	Called when the data in the document needs to be drawn on the window.
OnBeginPrinting	Called when beginning to print. This is where you perform any special actions that need to be performed before printing the document.
OnEndPrinting	Called when finishing printing. This is where you perform any clean-up necessary after printing the document.
OnPrint	Called when printing or print previewing the current document.
OnEndPrintPreview	Called when print preview mode is exited.
OnPreparePrinting	Called before printing. This is where you initialize the Print dialog box if your document requires special print configuration.
OnUpdate	Called to notify the view that the document has been updated.

Understanding MDI Applications

As far as coding an MDI application with Visual C++, there's little difference between creating an SDI and an MDI application. However, when you get deeper into the two application styles, you'll find quite a few differences. Although an SDI application allows users to work on only one document at a time, it also normally limits them to working on a specific type of document. MDI applications enable users to work not only on multiple documents at the same time, but also on multiple types of documents.

An MDI application uses a window-in-a-window style, where a frame window appears around one or more child windows. This is a common application style with many popular software packages, including older versions of Word and Excel.

Architecturally, an MDI application is similar to an SDI application. In fact, with a simple MDI application, the only difference is the addition of a second frame class to the other classes that the AppWizard creates (see Figure 10.2). As you can see, the Document/View architecture is still very much the approach you use for developing MDI applications as well as SDI applications.

FIGURE 10.2

*The MDI
Document/View
architecture.*

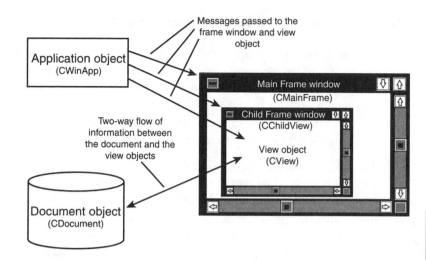

When you create an MDI application, you will create one more class than will be created with an SDI application. The MDI classes are

- The CWinApp-derived class
- The CMDIFrameWnd-derived class
- The CMDIChildWnd-derived class
- The CDocument-derived class
- The CView-derived class

The two MDI derived classes, CMDIFrameWnd (the CMainFrame class in your project) and CMDIChildWnd (the CChildFrame class in your project), are the only two classes that vary from the SDI application you created:

- The CMDIFrameWnd-derived CMainFrame class is the main frame of the application. It provides an enclosed space on the desktop within which all application interaction takes place. This frame window is the frame to which the menu and toolbars are attached.

- The CMDIChildWnd-derived CChildFrame class is the frame that holds the CView class. It's the frame that passes messages and events to the view class for processing or display.

In a sense, the functionality of the frame class in the SDI application has been split into these two classes in an MDI application. There is additional support for running multiple child frames with their own document/view class instances at the same time.

MFC Note: The `CMDIFrameWnd` and `CMDIChildWnd` Classes

The `CMDIFrameWnd` class is the outer frame window in an MDI application. This class is a descendent of the `CFrameWnd` class, so it contains much the same functionality as the SDI frame window. One member function that you'll use with this class is `MDIGetActive`, which returns a pointer to the currently active child window. Most other functions working with the child windows are encapsulated in the Window menu created with the MDI application shell by the Application Wizard.

The `CMDIChildWnd` class is the inner frame window in an MDI application. Like the `CMDIFrameWnd` class, the `CMDIChildWnd` class is also a descendent of the `CFrameWnd` class. Most specialized functions in this class have to do with setting the state of the child window within the parent frame: `MDIDestroy`, `MDIActivate`, `MDIMaximize`, and `MDIRestore`. None of them take any parameters or return any results. The one other member function, `GetMDIFrame`, returns a pointer to the `CMDIFrameWnd` parent window.

Creating an SDI Application

To get a good idea of how the Document/View architecture works, and of how you can use it to build applications, build a new version of the drawing application you created on Day 4. In this version, the user's drawing will be persistent, which means it's not erased each time another window is placed in front of the application. This version will also be able to save and restore drawings.

Building the Application Shell

To create the application shell for today's application, follow these steps:

1. Create a new MFC Application Visual C++ project. Name the project **SDISquig**.
2. In the Application Type area, select Single Document for the application type (see Figure 10.3).
3. In the Document Template Strings. area, enter a three-letter file extension for the files that your application will generate (for example, dhc or dvp), as in Figure 10.4.
4. In the Generated Classes area, you can choose the base class on which your view class will be based (see Figure 10.5). Leave the base class as `CView` and click Finish. The MFC Application Wizard will generate the application shell.

FIGURE 10.3

Specifying the application type.

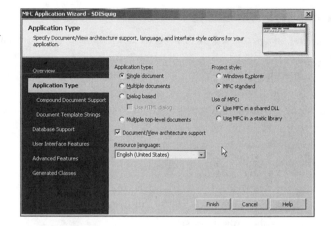

FIGURE 10.4

Specifying the document file extension.

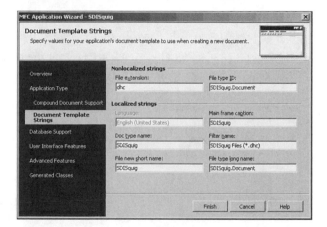

FIGURE 10.5

Specifying the view class to use.

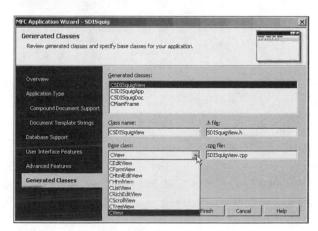

10

Creating a Line Class

One of the first issues that you will need to tackle is how to represent your data in the document class. For the drawing application, you have a series of lines, each consisting of starting and ending points. You might think that you can use a series of points for the data representation. If you do this, you also have to make special accommodations for where one series of lines between points ends and the next begins. It makes much more sense to represent the drawing as a series of lines. This allows you to store each individual line drawn on the window without having to worry where one set of contiguous lines ends and where the next begins.

Unfortunately, the Microsoft Foundation Classes (MFC) doesn't have a line object class, although it does have a point object class (CPoint). I guess you'll just have to create your own line class by following these steps:

1. In the Class View pane, select the top-level object in the tree (SDISquig classes). Right-click and select Add, Add Class from the context menu.

2. In the Add Class dialog, select Generic C++ Class for the class type (see Figure 10.6). Click Open to proceed to the next step in creating the class.

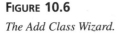

FIGURE 10.6

The Add Class Wizard.

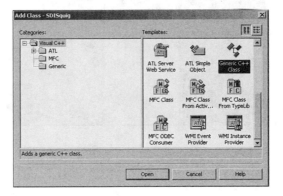

3. Enter CLine for the class name and CObject as the base class, leaving the class access as public (see Figure 10.7).

4. Click Finish to add the CLine class to your project.

Constructing the CLine Class

At this time, your CLine class needs to hold only two data elements—the two end points of the line that it represents. You want to add those two data elements and add a class constructor that sets both values when creating the class instance. To do this, follow these steps:

FIGURE 10.7

The Generic C++
Class Wizard.

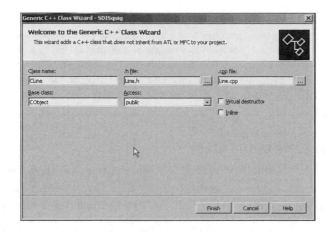

1. In the Class View pane, select the CLine class.

2. Right-click the CLine class and choose Add, Add Variable from the context menu.

3. Enter CPoint as the variable type and m_ptFrom as the variable name, and mark the access as private. Click Finish to add the variable.

4. Repeat steps 2 and 3, naming this variable m_ptTo.

5. Right-click the CLine class and choose Add, Add Function from the context menu.

6. Specify the function type as void, specify CLine as the function name, and add two parameters. Specify both parameters as CPoint for the parameter type and name them ptFrom and ptTo. Click Finish to add the function.

7. Edit the new function, adding the code in Listing 10.2.

LISTING 10.2   The CLine Constructor

```
CLine::CLine(CPoint ptFrom,  CPoint ptTo)
{
    //Initialize the from and to points
    m_ptFrom = ptFrom;
    m_ptTo = ptTo;
}
```

INPUT

In this object constructor, you are initializing the from and to points with the points passed in to the constructor.

> **Note**
>
> In other functions that you added, the return type was added in front of the function name. In this situation, the void return type wasn't included on the constructor definition name line. The return type of void wasn't included specifically because this is a class constructor. Class constructors and destructors never have a return type specified.

Drawing the CLine Class

To follow correct object-oriented design, your CLine class should be able to draw itself so that when the view class needs to render the line for users, it can just pass a message to the line object, telling it to draw itself. To add this functionality, follow these steps:

1. Add a new function to the CLine class by selecting Add, Add Function from the context menu.

2. Specify the function type as void and the function name as Draw. Specify one parameter with type CDC* and named pDC. Specify the function access as public.

3. Add the code in Listing 10.3 to the Draw function you just added.

LISTING 10.3   The CLine Draw Function

```
void CLine::Draw(CDC* pDC)
{
    // Draw the line
        pDC->MoveTo(m_ptFrom);
    pDC->LineTo(m_ptTo);
}
```

INPUT

This function is taken almost directly from the application you built on Day 4. It's a simple function that moves to the first point on the device context and then draws a line to the second point on the device context.

Implementing the Document Functionality

Now that you have an object to use for representing the drawings made by users, you can store these CLine objects on the document object in a simple dynamic array. To hold this array, add a CObArray member variable to the document class.

The CObArray object array class dynamically sizes itself to accommodate the number of items placed in it. It can hold any objects that are descended from the CObject class, and it's limited in size only by the amount of memory in the system.

To add the CObArray class to CSDISquigDoc, use the Add Member Variable Wizard and give it a name of m_oaLines. Specify the access as private.

MFC Note: The Array Classes

The MFC library includes several array classes for holding various data types. For the most part, all these array classes work the same, with the same functionality in all of them. The primary difference between them is the data type that each holds. Table 10.6 lists the array classes.

TABLE 10.6 The Array Classes

Class	Description
CArray	A template class for creating your own array classes.
CByteArray	An array of Byte data types.
CDWordArray	An array of DWORD data types.
CObArray	An array of classes derived from the CObject base class.
CPtrArray	An array of pointers (to any object or data type).
CStringArray	An array of CString objects.
CUIntArray	An array of UINT data types (unsigned integers).
CWordArray	An array of WORD data types.

Array Boundary Functions

You can use several functions to determine how many objects are currently in an array The obvious function is GetCount, which returns the number of elements in the array. This is actually a new function to the array classes. Before the newest version of MFC, the function you used to get the number of elements in the array was GetSize. You can still use GetSize, which is identical in functionality to the GetCount function.

A third function for determining how many elements are in an array is GetUpperBound. This function varies slightly from GetCount and GetSize in that it returns the number of the end position in the array, not the number of elements in the array.

Keep in mind that in C/C++, counting always begins with 0, not with 1, so if you wanted to create a loop that did something with each element in an array, you could use the GetCount function as follows:

```
int iMax = myArray.GetCount();
for (int i = 0; i < iMax; i++)
{
    // Do something here
}
```

Performing the same loop using the GetUpperBound function, you would write it as follows:

```
int iMax = myArray.GetUpperBound();
for (int i = 0; i <= iMax; i++)
{
    // Do something here
}
```

Notice that with the second version, you loop while i is less than or equal to iMax, not just while i is less than iMax. The reason for this is that the GetUpperBound function returns the array position of the last element in the array. This is usually one less than the total number of elements in the array because array position counting starts with 0.

One function, SetSize, controls the size of the array and how the array is grown. The syntax for SetSize is as follows:

```
void SetSize(int iNewSize, int iGrowBy);
```

The first parameter to the SetSize function, iNewSize, is the number of elements to have in the array at this time. If there are more than this number of elements in the array, the array will be truncated, and those elements will be lost. The second parameter, iGrowBy, specifies how many elements to add at a time when more elements are added to the array than it currently can hold. This function doesn't limit the array to the number of elements specified (unless you specified 0 for the iGrowBy parameter), it just specifies how to allocate new elements when the array needs to grow.

Array Element Access

Accessing the elements in the array can be done two different ways. You can use the GetAt function, where you pass the position number of the element and are returned the object at that position, or you can access the elements as you would with a normal C/C++ array by following the array variable name with the position in brackets ([ ]). In short, the following two methods have the same result:

```
pObject = myArray.GetAt(5);
pObject = myArray[5];
```

To set an element in an array, you can use the SetAt function. The syntax for SetAt is as follows:

```
void SetAt(int iIndex, datatype element);
```

The first parameter, iIndex, specifies the position in the array that you are setting. The second parameter, element, is the value to set in the specified position. The data type of the second parameter should be appropriate to the array class being used. The SetAt function doesn't grow the array so that it can hold additional elements. The position passed to this function must be an existing position in the array.

Adding and Removing Elements

When you need to add new elements to an array, you can use a couple of functions. The first of these functions is Add. The Add function takes the element to be added as its only parameter and adds the element to the end of the array. The second way to add new elements is with the InsertAt function. Whereas the Add function adds new elements to the end of the array, the InsertAt function will add new elements into the midst of the array. The syntax for InsertAt is as follows:

```
void InsertAt(int iIndex, datatype element);
```

The first parameter, iIndex, is the position in the array that the new element is to be added, and the second parameter is the element to be added. With both functions, the array will be grown if it doesn't currently have enough positions to hold the new elements being added.

When you need to remove some elements from the array, you can use the RemoveAt function, the syntax for which is as follows:

```
void RemoveAt(int iIndex, int iCount = 1);
```

The first parameter to this function, iIndex, is the position of the element to be removed from the array. The second parameter, iCount, specifies how many elements to remove from the array. The second parameter is optional, and defaults to 1 if you choose not to supply it.

If you need to remove all elements from an array, you can use the RemoveAll function, which deletes all objects from the array and resets the number of elements in the array to 0.

> **Caution**
>
> When you have a CObArray, or CPtrArray, the element isn't destroyed, only the pointer to the object is removed from the array. With the RemoveAt and RemoveAll functions, you need to be sure and delete the actual objects before removing them from the array.

Copying Arrays

If you need to copy or append one array to another, use the Copy or Append functions. Both functions take the array to be copied or appended as the only argument, and copy the array to the current array, or append the array data to the end of the current array.

With the CObArray and CPtrArray array classes, these functions only copy the pointers in the array, not the actual objects. As a result, changes to the values of some of the objects in one of the two arrays will change the values of the same objects in the other

10

array. Also, if one of the objects from one of the arrays is deleted, the pointer to that object in the other array is no longer valid.

Adding Lines

The first functionality that you need to add to the document class is the ability to add new lines. This should be a simple process of getting the from and to points, creating a new line object, and then adding it to the object array. To implement this function, follow these steps:

1. Add a new member function to the CSDISquigDoc class.

2. Specify the function return type as CLine*, the function name as AddLine, and two parameters. The two parameters should both be specified as CPoint for the variable type, and named ptFrom and ptTo. Specify the access as public.

3. Edit the function, adding the code in Listing 10.4.

LISTING **10.4**   The CSDISquigDoc AddLine Function

```
CLine* CSDISquigDoc::AddLine(CPoint ptFrom, CPoint ptTo)
{
    CLine* pLine = NULL;

    try
    {
        // Create a new CLine object
        pLine = new CLine(ptFrom, ptTo);
        // Add the new line to the object array
        m_oaLines.Add(pLine);
        // Mark the document as dirty
        SetModifiedFlag();
    }
    // Did we run into a memory exception?
    catch (CMemoryException* perr)
    {
        // Display a message for the user, giving him or her the
        // bad news
        AfxMessageBox("Out of memory", MB_ICONSTOP | MB_OK);
        // Did we create a line object?
        if (pLine)
        {
            // Delete it
            delete pLine;
            pLine = NULL;
        }
        // Delete the exception object
        perr->Delete();
    }
    return pLine;
}
```

INPUT

At first, this function is understandable. You create a new `CLine` instance, passing the from and to points as constructor arguments. Right before that, however, you have something interesting; the following flow control construct:

```
try
{
...
}.
catch (...)
{
...
}
```

What's this? This construct is an example of structured exception handling. Some code could fail because of a factor beyond your control, such as running out of memory or disk space; you can place a `try` section around the code that might have a problem. The `try` section should always be followed by one or more `catch` sections. If a problem occurs during the code in the `try` section, the program immediately jumps to the `catch` sections. Each `catch` section specifies what type of exception it handles (in the case of the `AddLine` function, it specifically handles memory exceptions only), and if there's a matching `catch` section for the type of problem that did occur, that section of code is executed to give the application a chance to recover from the problem. If there's no `catch` section for the type of problem that did occur, your program jumps to a default exception handler, which will shut down your application.

Within the `try` section, you add the new `CLine` instance to the array of line objects. Next, you call the `SetModifiedFlag` function, which marks the document as *dirty* (unsaved) so that if you close the application or open another file without saving the current drawing first, the application prompts you to save the current drawing (with the familiar Yes, No, Cancel message box).

In the `catch` section, you inform users that the system is out of memory and then clean up by deleting the `CLine` object and the exception object. You should always call the exception object's `Delete` method to delete the exception.

Finally, at the end of the function, you return the `CLine` object to the calling routine. This enables the view object to let the line object draw itself.

Before you can compile your application, you need to include the header file for the `CLine` class in the source code file for the document and view classes. Actually, you need to do this in every source file that includes the document class header, so it actually makes more sense to add the include statement to the document class header. To add this to your application, follow these steps:

1. Edit the SDISquigDoc.h file, adding the Line.h file include near the top of the file, as shown in Listing 10.5.

10

LISTING 10.5   The CSDISquigDoc includes

```
// SDISquigDoc.h : interface of the CSDISquigDoc class
//

#pragma once
#include "afxcoll.h"
#include "line.h"

class CSDISquigDoc : public CDocument
```

Getting the Line Count

Next, you will add a function to return the number of lines in the document. This functionality is necessary because the view object needs to loop through the array of lines, asking each line object to draw itself. The view object will need to be able to determine the total number of lines in the document and retrieve any specific line from the document.

Returning the number of lines in the document is a simple matter of returning the number of lines in the object array, so you can just return the return value from the GetCount method of the CObArray class. To implement this function, follow these steps:

1. Add a new member function to the CSDISquigDoc class.

2. Specify the function type as int and the function name as GetLineCount with public access.

3. Edit the function, adding the code in Listing 10.6.

LISTING 10.6   The CSDISquigDoc GetLineCount Function

```
int CSDISquigDoc::GetLineCount()
{
    // Return the array count
    return (int)m_oaLines.GetCount();
}
```

Note

You are casting the return value of the GetCount function as an integer. The reason for this is because the GetCount function returns an INT_PTR data type. The INT_PTR data type is a special instance of the integer data type. It is a special integer that is guaranteed to be the same size as a pointer, regardless of the pointer size or address space of a particular system. It is the recommended integer data type for use in situations where you are casting

> pointers as integer values. Because the compiler thinks it is a different data type than the standard int data type, we have to cast it as an int to prevent a warning from being generated.

Retrieving a Specific Line

Finally, you need to add a function to return a specific line from the document. This is a simple matter of returning the object at the specified position in the object array. To implement this function, follow these steps:

1. Add a new member function to the CSDISquigDoc class.

2. Specify the function type as CLine* and the function name as GetLine. Add a single parameter, specifying the parameter type as int and the parameter name as iIndex. Specify the function access as public.

3. Edit the function, adding the code in Listing 10.7.

LISTING 10.7 The CSDISquigDoc GetLine Function

```
CLine * CSDISquigDoc::GetLine(int iIndex)
{
    // Return a pointer to the line object
    //     at the specified point in the object array
    return (CLine*)m_oaLines[iIndex];
}
```

> **Note**
>
> The object being returned had to be cast as a pointer to a CLine object. Because the CObArray class is an array of CObjects, every element returned by the array is a CObject instance, not a CLine object instance.

Showing the Users

Now that you've built the capability into the document class to hold the drawing, you need to add the functionality to the view object to read the user's drawing input and to draw the image. The mouse events to capture user input are almost identical to those you created on Day 4. The second part of the functionality that you need to implement is drawing the image. You will make an addition to a function that already exists in the view object class.

Before adding these functions, you need to add a member variable to the `CSDISquigView` class to maintain the previous mouse point, just as you did on Day 4:

1. Add a member variable to the `CSDISquigView` class through the Class View pane.

2. Specify the variable type as `CPoint`, the name as `m_ptPrevPos`, and the access as `private`.

Adding the Mouse Events

To add the mouse events to capture the user's drawing efforts, follow these steps:

1. In the Class View, select the `CSDISquigView` class.

2. Using the Properties pane, add functions to the `CSDISquigView` class for the `WM_LBUTTONDOWN`, `WM_LBUTTONUP`, and `WM_MOUSEMOVE` messages.

3. Edit the functions as in Listing 10.8.

LISTING 10.8   The `CSDISquigView` Mouse Functions

```
void CSDISquigView::OnLButtonDown(UINT nFlags, CPoint point)
{
    // TODO: Add your message handler code here and/or call default
    // Capture the mouse, so no other application can
    //     grab it if the mouse leaves the window area
    SetCapture();
    // Save the point
    m_ptPrevPos = point;

    CView::OnLButtonDown(nFlags, point);
}

void CSDISquigView::OnLButtonUp(UINT nFlags, CPoint point)
{
    // TODO: Add your message handler code here and/or call default
    // Have we captured the mouse?
    if (GetCapture() == this)
    // If so, release it so other applications can
    // have it
    ReleaseCapture();

    CView::OnLButtonUp(nFlags, point);
}

void CSDISquigView::OnMouseMove(UINT nFlags, CPoint point)
{
    // TODO: Add your message handler code here and/or call default
    // Check to see if the left mouse button is down
    if ((nFlags & MK_LBUTTON) == MK_LBUTTON)
```

INPUT

INPUT

INPUT

LISTING **10.8** continued

```
    {
        // Have we captured the mouse?
        if (GetCapture() == this)
        {
            // Get the Device Context
            CClientDC dc(this);

            // Add the line to the document
            CLine *pLine = GetDocument()->AddLine(m_ptPrevPos, point);

            // Draw the current stretch of line
            pLine->Draw(&dc);

            // Save the current point as the previous point
            m_ptPrevPos = point;
        }
    }
    CView::OnMouseMove(nFlags, point);
}
```

10

ANALYSIS The first thing the OnLButtonDown function does is call the SetCapture function. This function "captures" the mouse, preventing any other applications from receiving any mouse events, even if the mouse leaves the window space of this application. This way, users can drag the mouse outside the application window while drawing and then drag the mouse back into the application window, without stopping the drawing. All mouse messages are delivered to this application until the mouse is released in the OnLButtonUp function, using the ReleaseCapture function. In the meantime, by placing the GetCapture function in an if statement and comparing its return value to this, you can determine whether your application has captured the mouse. If you capture the mouse, you want to execute the rest of the code in those functions; otherwise, you don't.

The OnMouseMove function does several things in a single line of code after it creates the device context:

```
CLine *pLine = GetDocument()->AddLine(m_ptPrevPos, point);
```

This line creates a new pointer to a CLine class instance. Next, it calls the GetDocument function, which returns a pointer to the document object. This pointer calls the document class's AddLine function, passing the previous and current points as arguments. The return value from the AddLine function is used to initialize the CLine object pointer. The CLine pointer can now be used to call the line object's Draw function.

Note

A *pointer* is the address of an object. It's used to pass an object more efficiently around a program. Passing a pointer to an object, instead of the object itself, is like telling someone that the remote control is "on the couch between the second and third cushion, beside the loose pocket change," instead of just handing the remote to the person. Actually, in programming terms, handing the remote to the person requires making an exact copy of the remote and handing the copy to the other person. It's obviously more efficient to tell the person where to find the remote than to manufacture an exact copy of the remote.

The notation `->` denotes that the object's functions or properties are accessed through a pointer, as opposed to directly through the object itself with the period (.) notation.

Drawing the Painting

In the view class, the function OnDraw is called whenever the image presented to users needs to be redrawn. Maybe another window was in front of the application window, the window was just restored from being minimized, or a new document was just loaded from a file. Why the view needs to be redrawn doesn't matter. All you need to worry about is adding the code to the OnDraw function to render the document that your application is designed to create. Do the following:

1. Locate the OnDraw function in the CSDISquigView class and add the boldfaced code in Listing 10.9. Be sure and uncomment the function parameter, as shown in the listing.

LISTING 10.9   The CSDISquigView OnDraw Function

```
void CSDISquigView::OnDraw(CDC* pDC)
{
    CSDISquigDoc* pDoc = GetDocument();
    ASSERT_VALID(pDoc);

    // TODO: add draw code for native data here
    // Get the number of lines in the document
        int iCount = pDoc->GetLineCount();

    // Are there any lines in the document?
    if (iCount)
    {
        int iPos;
        CLine *pLine = NULL;

        // Loop through the lines in the document
```

INPUT

LISTING 10.9 continued

```
        for (iPos = 0; iPos < iCount; iPos++)
        {
            // Get the line segment to be drawn
            pLine = pDoc->GetLine(iPos);
            // Draw the line
            pLine->Draw(pDC);
        }
    }
}
```

ANALYSIS This function first finds out how many lines are in the document to be drawn. If there aren't any lines, there's nothing to do. If there are lines in the document, it loops through the lines using a for loop, getting each line object from the document and then calling the line object's Draw function.

At this point, you should be able to compile and run your application, drawing figures in it as shown in Figure 10.8. If you minimize the window and then restore it, or if you place another application window in front of your application window, your drawing should still be there when your application window is visible again (unlike the application you built on day 4).

FIGURE 10.8

Drawing with your application.

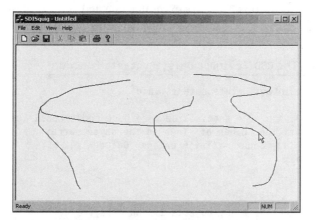

Saving and Loading the Drawing

Now that you can create drawings that don't disappear the moment you look away, it would be nice if you could make them even more persistent. If you play with the menus on your application, it appears that the Open, Save, and Save As entries on the File menu activate, but they don't seem to do anything. The printing menu entries all work, but the entries for saving and loading a drawing don't. Not even the New menu entry works! Well, you can do something to fix this situation.

Deleting the Current Drawing

If you examine the CSDISquigDoc class, you'll notice a OnNewDocument function that you can edit to clear out the current drawing. Wrong! This function is intended for initializing any class settings for starting work on a new drawing and not for clearing out an existing drawing. Instead, you need to add a function on the DeleteContents event message, which is intended for clearing the current contents of the document class. The way you add this function is as follows:

1. In the Class View, select the CSDISquigDoc class.

2. In the Properties pane, select the Overrides mode, as shown in Figure 10.9.

FIGURE 10.9

Adding base class function overrides.

3. Select the DeleteContents event function and add a new function.

4. Edit this new function, adding the code in Listing 10.10.

LISTING 10.10 The CSDISquigDoc DeleteContents Function

```
void CSDISquigDoc::DeleteContents(void)
{
    // TODO: Add your specialized code here and/or call the base class
    // Get the number of lines in the object array
        int iCount = (int)m_oaLines.GetCount();
    int iPos;

    try
    {
        // Are there any objects in the array?
        if (iCount)
        {
            //Loop through the array, deleting each object
            for (iPos = 0; iPos < iCount; iPos++)
                delete (CLine*)m_oaLines.GetAt(iPos);
            // Reset the array
            m_oaLines.RemoveAll();
        }
    }
    catch (CMemoryException* perr)
```

INPUT

LISTING 10.10 continued

```
    {
        // Display a message for the user, giving him or her the
        // bad news
        perr->ReportError();
        // Delete the exception object
        perr->Delete();
    }
    CDocument::DeleteContents();
}
```

ANALYSIS This function loops through the object array, deleting each line object in the array. After all the lines are deleted, the array is reset by calling its RemoveAll method. If you compile and run your application, you'll find that you can select File, New, and if you decide not to save your current drawing, your window is wiped clean.

Saving and Restoring the Drawing

NEW TERM Adding the functionality to save and restore your drawings is pretty easy to implement, but it might not be so easy to understand. That's okay; you'll spend the entire Day 12 on understanding saving and restoring files, also known as *serialization*. In the meantime, to add the ability to save and restore files follow these steps:

1. Find the Serialize function in the CSDISquigDoc class. The function should look something like

```
void CSDISquigDoc::Serialize(CArchive& ar)
{
    if (ar.IsStoring())
    {
        // TODO: add storing code here
    }
    else
    {
        // TODO: add loading code here
    }
}
```

2. Remove all contents of this function, and edit it so that it looks like Listing 10.11.

LISTING 10.11 The CSDISquigDoc Serialize Function

```
void CSDISquigDoc::Serialize(CArchive& ar)
{
        // Pass the serialization on to the object array
        m_oaLines.Serialize(ar);
}
```

INPUT

ANALYSIS This function takes advantage of the functionality of the CObArray class. This object array will pass down its array of objects, calling the Serialize function on each object. This means that you need to add a Serialize function to the CLine class:

1. Add a new function to the CLine class.

2. Specify the function return type as void, name the function Serialize, and add one parameter. The parameter type should be CArchive&, and the parameter name should be ar. The function access should be specified as public.

3. Edit the function, adding the code in Listing 10.12.

LISTING 10.12   The CLine Serialize Function

```
void CLine::Serialize(CArchive &ar)
{
    CObject::Serialize(ar);

    if (ar.IsStoring())
        ar << m_ptFrom << m_ptTo;
    else
        ar >> m_ptFrom >> m_ptTo;
}
```

INPUT

ANALYSIS This function follows the same flow that the original Serialize function would have followed in the CSDISquigDoc class. It uses the I/O stream functionality of C++ to save and restore its contents.

At this point, if you compile and run your application, you expect the save and open functions to work. Unfortunately, they don't—yet. If you run your application and try to save a drawing, a message box will tell you that the application was unable to save the file (see Figure 10.10).

FIGURE 10.10

Unable to save drawings.

You can't save your drawing because Visual C++ must be told that a class should be serializable. To do this, you add one line to the CLine class header file and one line to the CLine source code file:

1. Open the CLine header file (Line.h).

2. Add the DECLARE_SERIAL line in Listing 10.13 just after the first line of the class definition.

LISTING 10.13   The Line.h Edit for Serialization

```
class CLine :
    public CObject
{
    DECLARE_SERIAL (CLine)
    public:
    CLine(void);
```

INPUT

3. Next, open the CLine source code file (Line.cpp).

4. Add the IMPLEMENT_SERIAL line in Listing 10.14 just before the class constructor functions.

LISTING 10.14   The Line.cpp Edit for Serialization

```
#include "StdAfx.h"
#include "line.h"

IMPLEMENT_SERIAL (CLine, CObject, 1)

CLine::CLine(void)
: m_ptFrom(0)
, m_ptTo(0)
{
}
```

INPUT

10

Now if you compile and run your application, you should be able to draw your own self-portrait and save it for posterity, as in Figure 10.11.

FIGURE 10.11

My self-portrait.

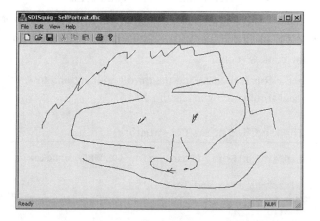

Interacting with the Menu

Now that you have a working drawing program, it would be nice if users could choose the color with which they want to draw. Adding this functionality requires making changes in the CLine class to associate the color with the line and to CSDISquigDoc to maintain the currently selected color. Finally, you need to add a pull-down menu to select the desired color.

Adding Color to the CLine Class

Making changes to the CLine class is fairly straightforward. Generally speaking, here is what you do:

1. Add another member variable to the CLine class to hold the color of each line.
2. Modify the class constructor to add color to the list of parameters to be passed in.
3. Modify the Draw function to use the specified color.
4. Modify the Serialize function to save and restore the color information along with the point information.

To do all this, follow these specific steps:

1. Select the CLine class in the Class View pane. Right-click and select Add Member Variable from the context menu.
2. Specify the variable type as COLORREF, the name as m_crColor, and the access as private. Click Finish to add the variable.
3. Right-click the custom CLine constructor that you created earlier in the Class View pane. Select Go to Definition from the context menu.
4. Add COLORREF crColor as a third argument to the constructor declaration.
5. Right-click the CLine constructor in the Class View tree. Select Go to Declaration from the context menu.
6. Modify the constructor to add the third argument and to set the m_crColor member to the new argument, as in Listing 10.15.

LISTING 10.15   The Modified CLine Constructor

```
CLine::CLine(CPoint ptFrom, CPoint ptTo, COLORREF crColor)
{
    //Initialize the from and to points
    m_ptFrom = ptFrom;
    m_ptTo = ptTo;
    m_crColor = crColor;
}
```

INPUT

7. Scroll down to the Draw function and modify it as in Listing 10.16.

LISTING 10.16 The Modified Draw Function

```
void, CLine::Draw(CDC * pDC)
{
        // Create a pen
           CPen lpen (PS_SOLID, 1, m_crColor);

    // Set the new pen as the drawing object
    CPen* pOldPen = pDC->SelectObject(&lpen);
    // Draw the line
    pDC->MoveTo(m_ptFrom);
    pDC->LineTo(m_ptTo);
    // Reset the previous pen
    pDC->SelectObject(pOldPen);
}
```

INPUT

10

8. Scroll down to the Serialize function and modify it as in Listing 10.17.

LISTING 10.17 The Modified Serialize Function

```
void  CLine::Serialize(CArchive &ar)
{
    CObject::Serialize(ar);

    if (ar.IsStoring())
        ar << m_ptFrom << m_ptTo << (DWORD) m_crColor;
    else
        ar >> m_ptFrom >> m_ptTo >> (DWORD) m_crColor;
}
```

Adding Color to the Document

The changes that you need to make to the CSDISquigDoc class are just slightly more extensive than those made to the CLine class. Again, here are the general steps:

1. Add a member variable to hold the current color and a color table to convert color IDs into RGB values.

2. Initialize the current color variable in the OnNewDocument function.

3. Modify the AddLine function to add the current color to the CLine constructor.

4. Add a function to return the current color.

That's all that you need to do for now until you start adding menu message handlers for setting the current color. To do these things, follow these detailed steps:

1. Select the CSDISquigDoc class in the Class View pane. Right-click and choose Add, Add Variable from the context menu.

2. Specify the variable type as UINT, the name as m_nColor, and the access as private. Click Finish to add the variable.

3. Open the SDISquigDoc.h header file.

4. Find one of the sections declared as public, and add the following variable declaration:

```
public:
```

INPUT

```
// Get the current drawing color
    static const COLORREF m_crColors[8];
```

5. Open the CSDISquigDoc source code (SDISquigDoc.cpp) and add the population of the m_crColors color table as in Listing 10.18.

LISTING 10.18   The Color Table Specification

```
END_MESSAGE_MAP()
```

INPUT

```
const COLORREF CSDISquigDoc::m_crColors[8] = {
       RGB(   0,   0,   0),    // Black
RGB(   0,   0, 255),    // Blue
RGB(   0, 255,   0),    // Green
RGB(   0, 255, 255),    // Cyan
RGB( 255,   0,   0),    // Red
RGB( 255,   0, 255),    // Magenta
RGB( 255, 255,   0),    // Yellow
RGB( 255, 255, 255)     // White
};
```

```
// CSDISquigDoc construction/destruction
```

6. Scroll down to the OnNewDocument function, and edit it as in Listing 10.19.

LISTING 10.19   The Modified OnNewDocument Function

```
BOOL CSDISquigDoc::OnNewDocument()
{
    if (!CDocument::OnNewDocument())
        return FALSE;

    // TODO: add reinitialization code here
```

INPUT

```
    // (SDI documents will reuse this document)
        // Initialize the color to black
    m_nColor = 0;

    return TRUE;
}
```

7. Scroll down to the AddLine function and modify it as in Listing 10.20.

LISTING 10.20 The Modified AddLine Function

```cpp
CLine * CSDISquigDoc::AddLine(CPoint ptFrom, CPoint ptTo)
{
    CLine* pLine = NULL;

    try
    {
        // Create a new CLine object
        pLine = new CLine(ptFrom, ptTo, m_crColors[m_nColor]);
        // Add the new line to the object array
        m_oaLines.Add(pLine);
        // Mark the document as dirty
        SetModifiedFlag();
    }
    // Did we run into a memory exception?
    catch (CMemoryException* perr)
    {
        // Display a message for the user, giving him or her the
        // bad news
        AfxMessageBox("Out of memory", MB_ICONSTOP | MB_OK);
        // Did we create a line object?
        if (pLine)
        {
            // Delete it
            delete pLine;
            pLine = NULL;
        }
        // Delete the exception object
        perr->Delete();
    }
    return pLine;
}
```

10

8. Add a new member function to the CSDISquigDoc class. Specify the function type as UINT, the function name as GetColor, and the access as public.

9. Edit the GetColor function, adding the code in Listing 10.21.

LISTING 10.21 The GetColor Function

```cpp
UINT CSDISquigDoc::GetColor(void)
{
    // Return the current color
    return ID_COLOR_BLACK + m_nColor;
}
```

INPUT

In the `OnNewDocument` and the `GetColor` functions, the color is added and subtracted from `ID_COLOR_BLACK`. This is the lowest numbered color menu ID when you add the menu entries. These calculations maintain the variable as a number between 0 and 7, but when working with the menus, they allow comparison with the actual menu IDs.

Modifying the Menu

Now comes the fun part: adding a new pull-down menu to the main menu, menu entries for all the colors in the color table, message handlers for all the color menu entries, and event handlers to check the menu entry that's the current color. To do all of this, follow these steps:

1. Select the Resource View pane. Expand the tree so that you can see the contents of the Menu folder. Double-click the menu resource.

3. Click the blank top-level menu (at the right end of the menu bar). Specify the menu as &Color.

2. Grab the new top-level menu (&Color) and drag it to the left, dropping it in front of the View menu entry.

4. Add submenu entries below the Color top-level menu. Specify the submenus in order, setting their captions as specified in Table 10.7.

5. After you set the labels for the menus, right-click and select Edit IDs. The menu IDs should all be set as in Table 10.7.

TABLE 10.7   Menu Property Settings

Object	Property	Setting
Menu Entry	ID	ID_COLOR_BLACK
	Caption	&Black
Menu Entry	ID	ID_COLOR_BLUE
	Caption	B&lue
Menu Entry	ID	ID_COLOR_GREEN
	Caption	&Green
Menu Entry	ID	ID_COLOR_CYAN
	Caption	&Cyan
Menu Entry	ID	ID_COLOR_RED
	Caption	&Red
Menu Entry	ID	ID_COLOR_MAGENTA
	Caption	&Magenta
Menu Entry	ID	ID_COLOR_YELLOW
	Caption	&Yellow
Menu Entry	ID	ID_COLOR_WHITE
	Caption	&White

6. Right-click and deselect Edit IDs. You should wind up with a menu looking like Figure 10.12.

FIGURE 10.12

The Color menu as designed.

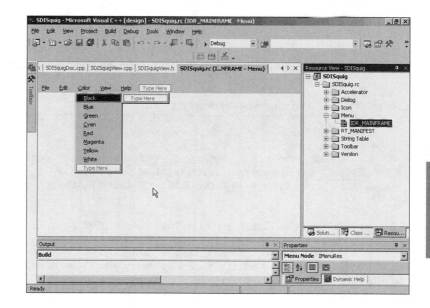

7. Open the Class View. Select the `CSDISquigDoc` class.

8. In the Properties pane, select the Events mode and scroll down until you find the menu IDs.

9. Click the plus sign to the left of each menu ID to show the menu events.

10. Add functions for both the `COMMAND` and `UPDATE_COMMAND_UI` event messages for all the color menu entries.

11. Edit the Black menu functions as in Listing 10.22.

LISTING 10.22 The Black Menu Functions

```
void CSDISquigDoc::OnColorBlack(void)
{
    // TODO: Add your command handler code here
    // Set the current color to black
        m_nColor = ID_COLOR_BLACK - ID_COLOR_BLACK;
}

void CSDISquigDoc::OnUpdateColorBlack(CCmdUI *pCmdUI)
{
    // TODO: Add your command update UI handler code here
    // Determine if the Black menu entry should be checked
        pCmdUI->Enable();
```

INPUT

INPUT

LISTING 10.22   continued

```
    pCmdUI->SetCheck(GetColor() == ID_COLOR_BLACK ? 1 : 0);
}
```

---

12. Edit the Blue menu functions as in Listing 10.23. Edit the remaining menu func-
    tions in the same way, substituting their menu IDs for ID_COLOR_BLUE.

LISTING 10.23   The Blue Menu Functions

```
void  CSDISquigDoc::OnColorBlue(void)
{
    // TODO: Add your command handler code here
    // Set the current color to blue
        m_nColor = ID_COLOR_BLUE - ID_COLOR_BLACK;
}

void CSDISquigDoc::OnUpdateColorBlue(CCmdUI *pCmdUI)
{
    // TODO: Add your command update UI handler code here
    // Determine if the Blue menu entry should be checked
        pCmdUI->Enable();
    pCmdUI->SetCheck(GetColor() == ID_COLOR_BLUE ? 1 : 0);
}
```

INPUT

INPUT

ANALYSIS

In the first of the two menu functions, the COMMAND function in Listing 10.22
(OnColorBlue), the current color variable is set to the new color. If you add the
menu entries in the correct order, their ID numbers are sequential, starting with
ID_COLOR_BLACK. Subtracting ID_COLOR_BLACK from the menu ID should always result in
the correct position in the color table for the selected color. For example, the Black color
is position 0 in the color table: ID_COLOR_BLACK – ID_COLOR_BLACK = 0. Blue is position
1 in the color table. Because ID_COLOR_BLUE should be one greater than
ID_COLOR_BLACK, ID_COLOR_BLUE – ID_COLOR_BLACK = 1.

The second function, UPDATE_COMMAND_UI in Listing 10.23 (OnUpdateColorBlue), may
need a little explaining. The UPDATE_COMMAND_UI event is called for each menu entry just
before it's displayed. You can use this event message function to check or uncheck the
menu entry, based on whether it's the current color. You can also use this event to enable
or disable menu entries or make other modifications as necessary. This code line

```
pCmdUI->SetCheck(GetColor() == ID_COLOR_BLUE ? 1 : 0);
```

does several things. First, the pCmdUI object that's passed in as the only argument is a
pointer to a menu object. The SetCheck function can check or uncheck the menu entry,

depending on whether the argument passed is 1 or 0 (1 checks, 0 unchecks). The argument portion for the SetCheck function is a flow-control construct that can be somewhat confusing if you haven't spent a large amount of time programming in C/C++. The first half

```
GetColor() == ID_COLOR_BLUE
```

is a simple Boolean conditional statement, resulting in a true or false result. The portion following this conditional statement

```
? 1 : 0
```

is basically an if...else statement in shorthand. If the conditional statement is true, then the value is 1, and if the statement is false, the value is 0. (This is a fancy way of placing an if..else flow control within the argument to another function.)

If you compile and run your application, you should be able to change the color you are drawing with. When you open the color menu, you should see the current drawing color checked on the menu, as in Figure 10.13.

10

FIGURE 10.13

Specifying the current color on the menu.

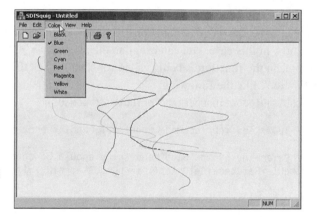

Summary

Whew, what a day! You learned quite a bit because this lesson was packed. You initially learned about the SDI style application and about a couple of standard applications that you've probably used that are SDI applications. You next learned about the Document/View architecture that Visual C++ uses for SDI applications. You learned to create a simple class of your own for use in your drawing application. You created a drawing application that can maintain the images drawn using it. You learned how you can save and restore documents in the Document/View architecture. You also learned about the CObArray object array class and how you can use it to create a dynamic object array for storing various classes. Finally, you learned how you can check and uncheck menu entries in MFC applications.

Q&A

Q. Is there any way that I can reduce the number of COMMAND and UPDATE_COMMAND_UI functions for my menus?

A. Yes, you can send all the color COMMAND events to the same function. From there, you can examine the nID value (which is passed as an argument) and compare it to the menu IDs to determine which menu is calling the function. As a result, you can write the COMMAND function for the color menus as follows:

```
void CSDISquigDoc::OnColorCommand(UINT nID)
{
    // TODO: Add your command handler code here

    // Set the current color to blue
    m_nColor = nID - ID_COLOR_BLACK;

}
```

For the UPDATE_COMMAND_UI functions, you can do the same thing, only slightly differently. In this case, you can examine the pCmdUI->m_nID value to determine which menu the function is being called for. This makes the UPDATE_COMMAND_UI function look like the following:

```
void CSDISquigDoc::OnUpdateColor(CCmdUI* pCmdUI)
{
    // TODO: Add your command update UI handler code here

    // Determine if the Blue menu entry should be checked
    pCmdUI->SetCheck(GetColor() == pCmdUI->m_nID ? 1 : 0);

}
```

The trick to this approach is that you can't use the wizards to implement it. You have to add the functions yourself, along with the message map entries. When you add the predecing two functions, specify their access as Protected. Next, add the message map entries in the source code file, near the top of the file (just above where you added the color table). If you look at the message map from the example application that you built today, it'll look something like the following:

```
BEGIN_MESSAGE_MAP(CSDISquigDoc, CDocument)
    ON_COMMAND(ID_COLOR_BLACK, OnColorBlack)
    ON_UPDATE_COMMAND_UI(ID_COLOR_BLACK, OnUpdateColorBlack)
    ON_COMMAND(ID_COLOR_BLUE, OnColorBlue)
    ON_UPDATE_COMMAND_UI(ID_COLOR_BLUE, OnUpdateColorBlue)
```

```
    ON_COMMAND(ID_COLOR_GREEN, OnColorGreen)
    ON_UPDATE_COMMAND_UI(ID_COLOR_GREEN, OnUpdateColorGreen)
    ON_COMMAND(ID_COLOR_CYAN, OnColorCyan)
    ON_UPDATE_COMMAND_UI(ID_COLOR_CYAN, OnUpdateColorCyan)
    ON_COMMAND(ID_COLOR_RED, OnColorRed)
    ON_UPDATE_COMMAND_UI(ID_COLOR_RED, OnUpdateColorRed)
    ON_COMMAND(ID_COLOR_MAGENTA, OnColorMagenta)
    ON_UPDATE_COMMAND_UI(ID_COLOR_MAGENTA, OnUpdateColorMagenta)
    ON_COMMAND(ID_COLOR_YELLOW, OnColorYellow)
    ON_UPDATE_COMMAND_UI(ID_COLOR_YELLOW, OnUpdateColorYellow)
    ON_COMMAND(ID_COLOR_WHITE, OnColorWhite)
    ON_UPDATE_COMMAND_UI(ID_COLOR_WHITE, OnUpdateColorWhite)
END_MESSAGE_MAP()
```

Rather than add all these entries for the individual menus, you'll add one entry for all the menus, as follows:

```
BEGIN_MESSAGE_MAP(CSDISquigDoc, CDocument)
    ON_COMMAND_RANGE(ID_COLOR_BLACK, ID_COLOR_WHITE, OnColorCommand)
    ON_UPDATE_COMMAND_UI_RANGE(ID_COLOR_BLACK, ID_COLOR_WHITE,
➥OnUpdateColorUI)
END_MESSAGE_MAP()
```

The normal message map macros have two arguments: the message ID and the event-handler function name that should be called for the event message. These new message map entries function in the same way, but they have two event ID arguments instead of one. The two event ID arguments mark the two ends of a range of event IDs that should be passed to the function specified. These two event IDs should be the first and last menu entries you created when building the color menu.

Q. What's the difference between SDI and MDI applications?

A. Although SDI applications can perform only one task, MDI (Multiple Document Interface) applications can have multiple documents open at the same time. Plus, in an MDI application, not all document types need be the same.

Q. Because it's basically the same code to create an MDI or SDI application, why would I want to create an SDI application? Why wouldn't I want to make all my applications MDI applications?

A. It depends on the application and how it will be used. You probably use both types of applications daily. If you are writing a memo or working on a spreadsheet, you are probably using an MDI application. If you are browsing the World Wide Web, your Web browser is most likely an SDI application. A simple text editor such as Notepad would probably be more difficult for users as an MDI style application, but as an SDI application, it's just about right (for the task it handles).

10

Certain applications make more sense implemented as an SDI application than as an MDI application. You need to think through how your application will be used and determine which model it's more suited for.

Q. Some entries on my color menu are changing to the wrong color. How can I determine the problem?

A. The problem is that the color menu IDs are probably not in sequential order or are out of order. You can check them by right-clicking the SDISquig resources in the Resource View tab of the workspace pane. Select Resource Symbols from the context menu to display a list of the IDs and the numbers assigned to them in alphabetical order. Start with the Black ID and make sure that the numbers increase by 1 without skipping any numbers. Be sure to check these IDs in the order that the colors appear on the menu (and in the color table in the SDISquigDoc.cpp file), not in the alphabetical order in which they are displayed in this list. If you find some errors, you have to close Visual C++ and open the Resource.h file in a text editor to renumber the IDs correctly. After you make the corrections (be sure to delete any duplicates), save them, restart Visual C++, and recompile your application. The color menu should work correctly.

Workshop

The Workshop provides quiz questions to help you solidify your understanding of the material covered and exercises to provide you with experience in using what you've learned. The answers to the quiz questions and exercises are provided in Appendix A, "Answers to Quiz Questions."

Quiz

1. What does SDI stand for?
2. What functionality is in the view class?
3. What function is called to redraw the document if the window has been hidden behind another window?
4. Where do you place code to clear out the current document before starting a new document?
5. What's the purpose of the document class?
6. What are the five base classes that are used in MDI applications?

Exercise

Add another pull-down menu to control the width of the pen used for drawing. Give it the following settings:

Menu Entry	Width Setting
Very Thin	1
Thin	8
Medium	16
Thick	24
Very Thick	32

 Tip

In the pen constructor, the second argument is the width.

10

DAY **11**

Adding Toolbars and Status Bars

When you create your SDI and MDI applications, they not only come with default menus already attached, but also with simple toolbars to go with the menus. These simple toolbars have the standard set of functions (New, Open, Save, Print, Cut, Copy, and Paste) that you find on the toolbars of most Windows applications. Most applications don't limit their toolbars to just this standard selection of functions but have customized toolbars that reflect the application's specific functionality.

In addition to the toolbars, SDI and MDI applications have a status bar at the bottom of the frame that provides textual descriptions of the toolbar buttons and menu entries. The status bar also has default areas that display whether the Caps Lock, Num Lock, and Scroll Lock keys are on.

Today, you will learn how to

- Design your own toolbar
- Attach your toolbar to the application frame
- Show and hide your toolbar with a menu entry

- Place a combo box on your toolbar
- Display descriptions of your toolbar entries in the status bar
- Add your own status bar elements

Understanding Toolbars, Status Bars and Menus

One driving intention behind the development of Graphical User Interfaces (GUI) such as Windows was the goal of making computers easier to use and learn. In the effort to accomplish this goal, GUI designers stated that all applications should use a standard set of menus and that the menus should be organized in a standardized manner. When Microsoft designed the Windows operating system, it followed this philosophy, using a standard set of menus, organized in a standard order, on most of its applications.

A funny thing happened when Windows became widely used. The application designers found that new users still had a difficult time learning new applications and that advanced users found the menus cumbersome. As a result, the application designers invented toolbars as one solution to both problems.

NEW TERM   A *toolbar* is a small band attached to the window frame or a dialog that floats independent of the application frame. This band (or dialog) has a number of small buttons containing graphic images that you can use in place of the menus. The application's designers place the most common functions on these toolbars and do their best to design graphical images that illustrate the functions the buttons serve.

As soon as advanced users learned what each toolbar button did, the toolbars were a hit. However, novice users still had problems learning what toolbar buttons did. As a result, the application designers went back to the drawing board to come up with ways to help new users learn how to use them.

One solution was to use the information bar that many of them had placed at the bottom of application windows to provide detailed descriptions of both menu entries and toolbar buttons. Another solution was to provide a little pop-up window with a short description of the button that appears whenever the mouse pointer is positioned over the button for more than a couple of seconds. The first of these solutions became known as the status bar, and the second became known as ToolTips. Both solutions are in common practice with most Windows applications today.

If you want to design and use your own toolbars and status bars in your applications, you might think that Visual C++ provides plenty of support for your efforts and even makes it easy to implement. After all, Microsoft's own application developers have been in the forefront of developing these elements, and most, if not all, Microsoft Windows applications are developed using its own Visual C++. Well, you are correct in making that assumption, and today, you'll learn how to create your own custom toolbars and status bars for your applications.

Designing a Toolbar

For learning how to create your own toolbar, you will modify the application that you created on Day 10, "Creating SDI and MDI Applications," the SDI drawing application, to add a toolbar for selecting the color to use in drawing.

 Note

> Before starting today's example, you need to make sure that you've completed yesterday's example, including all the exercise code at the end of the lesson. Today's example expects that functionality to be in place.

If all you want to do is add some buttons to the default toolbar, created by the MFC Application Wizard when you start a new SDI or MDI application, you can pull up the toolbar in the Visual C++ designer through the Resource View pane and begin adding new buttons. Just as in the Menu Designer, the end of the toolbar always has a blank entry, waiting for you to turn it into another toolbar button (see Figure 11.1). All you have to do is select the blank button, drag it to the right if you want a separator between it and the button beside it, or drag it to a different position if you want it moved. After you have the button in the desired location, you paint an icon on it to illustrate the function that the button will trigger. Finally, select the button in the toolbar view (the view showing all the buttons on the toolbar) to be able to access the button's properties, and give the button the same ID as the menu that it will trigger. The moment that you compile and run your application, you will have a new toolbar button that performs a menu selection that you chose. If you want to get rid of a toolbar button, just grab it on the toolbar view and drag it off the toolbar.

11

Creating a New Toolbar

To insert a new toolbar, right-click the Toolbar folder and select Insert Toolbar from the context menu. This creates an empty toolbar with a blank button. As you start drawing an icon on each blank button in the toolbar, another blank button is added on the end. To be able to select colors for use in drawing the button icon, you might need to right-click the toolbar button and select Show Colors Window from the context menu.

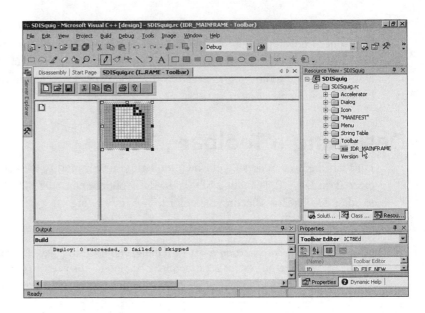

FIGURE 11.1

The toolbar designer.

For your drawing application, follow these steps:

1. Insert a new toolbar by selecting the Toolbar folder in the Resources View of the Workshop pane.

2. Fill eight buttons with the eight colors available in the drawing application.

3. After you draw icons on each button, click the first button in the toolbar view.

4. In the ID field of the Properties pane, enter (or select from the drop-down list) the ID of the menu that this toolbar button should trigger.

5. In the Prompt text box, enter the description that should appear in the status bar for this toolbar button. (If you entered a prompt for the menu, this text box is automatically populated with the menu description). At the end of the status bar description, add \n and a short description to appear in the ToolTips for the toolbar button.

For example, for the black button on the toolbar you are creating for your drawing application, enter an ID of **ID_COLOR_BLACK** and a prompt of **Black Drawing Color\nBlack** (see Figure 11.2).

After you finish designing your toolbar and have icons on all your buttons with properties set for each button, follow these steps to change the toolbar ID.

1. In the Resources View pane, select the new toolbar that you just added.

2. In the Properties pane, change the toolbar ID to a IDR_TBCOLOR.

Note

In C/C++, \n is shorthand notation for begin a new line. In the prompt for toolbar buttons and menu entries, this string separates the status bar descriptions of the menu entries and the ToolTips pop-up prompt that appears when the mouse pointer is held over a toolbar button for a few seconds. The first line of the prompt is used for the status bar description; the second line is used for the ToolTips description. The ToolTips description is used only with the toolbars, so there's no reason to add this for menu entries that won't have toolbar equivalents.

FIGURE 11.2

The toolbar button properties pane.

11

Attaching the Toolbar to the Application Frame

In the previous SDI application, you didn't add functionality that required you to touch the frame window. Because the toolbar is attached to the frame, you must begin adding and modifying code in that module. If you open the CMainFrame class to the OnCreate function, you can see where it's creating the existing toolbar, and then later in this function where the toolbar is being attached to the frame.

Before you can add your toolbar to the application frame, you need to add a variable to the CMainFrame class to hold the new toolbar. This variable of type CToolBar should be protected in accessibility.

To add your color toolbar to your draw application, follow these steps:

1. Right-click the CMainFrame class in the Class View pane and choose Add, Add Variable from the context menu.

2. Specify the variable type as CToolBar, the name as m_wndColorBar, and the access as protected.

After you add a variable for your toolbar, you need to add some code in the OnCreate function in the CMainFrame class to add the toolbar and attach it to the frame. Make the modifications in Listing 11.1 to add the color toolbar to your drawing application.

LISTING 11.1 The Modified `CMainFrame.OnCreate` Function

```
int CMainFrame::OnCreate(LPCREATESTRUCT lpCreateStruct)
{
    if (CFrameWnd::OnCreate(lpCreateStruct) == -1)
        return -1;

    if (!m_wndToolBar.CreateEx(this, TBSTYLE_FLAT, WS_CHILD |
➥WS_VISIBLE | CBRS_TOP
        | CBRS_GRIPPER | CBRS_TOOLTIPS | CBRS_FLYBY |
➥CBRS_SIZE_DYNAMIC) ||
        !m_wndToolBar.LoadToolBar(IDR_MAINFRAME))
    {
        TRACE0("Failed to create toolbar\n");
        return -1;      // fail to create
    }
```

INPUT
```
    // Add the color toolbar
        int iTBCtlID;
    int i;

    // Create the color toolbar
    if (!m_wndColorBar.CreateEx(this, TBSTYLE_FLAT, WS_CHILD |
            WS_VISIBLE | CBRS_TOP | CBRS_GRIPPER | CBRS_TOOLTIPS |
            CBRS_FLYBY | CBRS_SIZE_DYNAMIC) ||
            !m_wndColorBar.LoadToolBar(IDR_TBCOLOR))
    {
        TRACE0("Failed to create toolbar\n");
        return -1;    // fail to create
    }
    // Find the Black button on the toolbar
    iTBCtlID = m_wndColorBar.CommandToIndex(ID_COLOR_BLACK);
    if (iTBCtlID >= 0)
    {
        // Loop through the buttons, setting them to act as radio buttons
        for (i = iTBCtlID; i < (iTBCtlID + 8); i++)
            m_wndColorBar.SetButtonStyle(i, TBBS_CHECKGROUP);
    }
```

```
    if (!m_wndStatusBar.Create(this) ||
        !m_wndStatusBar.SetIndicators(indicators,
          sizeof(indicators)/sizeof(UINT)))
    {
        TRACE0("Failed to create status bar\n");
        return -1;      // fail to create
    }
    // TODO: Delete these three lines if you don't want the toolbar
➥to be dockable
    m_wndToolBar.EnableDocking(CBRS_ALIGN_ANY);
```

INPUT
```
        // Enable docking for the color toolbar
        m_wndColorBar.EnableDocking(CBRS_ALIGN_ANY);
    EnableDocking(CBRS_ALIGN_ANY);
    DockControlBar(&m_wndToolBar);
```

LISTING 11.1 continued

```
INPUT    // Dock the Color toolbar
            DockControlBar(&m_wndColorBar);
      return 0;
}
```

Creating the Toolbar

The first part of the code you added,

```
if (!m_wndColorBar.CreateEx(this, TBSTYLE_FLAT, WS_CHILD |
    WS_VISIBLE | CBRS_TOP | CBRS_GRIPPER | CBRS_TOOLTIPS |
    CBRS_FLYBY | CBRS_SIZE_DYNAMIC) ||
    !m_wndColorBar.LoadToolBar(IDR_TBCOLOR))
```

contains two separate functions necessary for toolbar creation. The first function, CreateEx, creates the toolbar itself, whereas the second, LoadToolBar, loads the toolbar that you designed in the toolbar designer. LoadToolBar requires a single argument, the ID for the toolbar that you want to create.

The CreateEx function has several arguments that you can pass with the function. The first (and only required) argument is a pointer to the parent window. In this case (which is normal), this argument is a pointer to the frame window to which the toolbar will be attached.

The second argument is the style of controls on the toolbar to be created. Several toolbar control styles are available for use (see Table 11.1), some of which have been introduced with the last few versions of Internet Explorer.

11

TABLE 11.1 Toolbar Control Styles

Style	Description
TBSTYLE_ALTDRAG	Enables users to move the toolbar by dragging it while pressing Alt.
TBSTYLE_CUSTOMERASE	Generates a NM_CUSTOMDRAW message when erasing the toolbar and button background, enabling you to choose when and whether to control the background erasing process.
TBSTYLE_FLAT	Creates a flat toolbar. Button text appears under the bitmap image.
TBSTYLE_LIST	Button text appears to the right of the bitmap image.
TBSTYLE_REGISTERDROP	Used in dragging and dropping objects onto toolbar buttons.
TBSTYLE_TOOLTIPS	Creates a ToolTip control that can be used to display descriptive text for the buttons.
TBSTYLE_TRANSPARENT	Creates a transparent toolbar.
TBSTYLE_WRAPABLE	Creates a toolbar that can have multiple rows of buttons.

The third argument is the style of the toolbar itself. This argument normally combines window and control bar styles. Normally, only two or three window styles are used, and the rest of the toolbar styles (see Table 11.2) are control bar styles.

TABLE 11.2 Toolbar Styles

Style	Description
WS_CHILD	The toolbar is created as a child window.
WS_VISIBLE	The toolbar will be visible when created.
CBRS_ALIGN_TOP	Enables the toolbar to be docked to the top of the view area of the frame window.
CBRS_ALIGN_BOTTOM	Enables the toolbar to be docked to the bottom of the view area of the frame window.
CBRS_ALIGN_LEFT	Enables the toolbar to be docked to the left side of the view area of the frame window.
CBRS_ALIGN_RIGHT	Enables the toolbar to be docked to the right side of the view area of the frame window.
CBRS_ALIGN_ANY	Enables the toolbar to be docked to any side of the view area of the frame window.
CBRS_BORDER_TOP	Places a border on the top edge of the toolbar when the toolbar isn't docked.
CBRS_BORDER_BOTTOM	Places a border on the bottom edge of the toolbar when the toolbar isn't docked.
CBRS_BORDER_LEFT	Places a border on the left edge of the toolbar when the toolbar isn't docked.
CBRS_BORDER_RIGHT	Places a border on the right edge of the toolbar when the toolbar isn't docked.
CBRS_FLOAT_MULTI	Enables multiple toolbars to be floated in a single miniframe window.
CBRS_TOOLTIPS	Causes ToolTips to be displayed for the toolbar buttons.
CBRS_FLYBY	Causes status bar message text to be updated for the toolbar buttons at the same time as the ToolTips.
CBRS_GRIPPER	Causes a gripper to be drawn on the toolbar.

The fourth argument, which you didn't provide in your code, is the size of the toolbar borders. This argument is passed as a standard CRect rectangle class to provide the length and height desired for the toolbar. The default value is 0 for all the rectangle dimensions, thus resulting in a toolbar with no borders.

The fifth and final argument, which you also didn't provide in your code, is the toolbar's child window ID. This defaults to AFX_IDW_TOOLBAR, but you can specify any defined ID that you need or want to use for the toolbar.

Setting the Button Styles

After you create the toolbar, there is a curious bit of code:

```
// Find the Black button on the toolbar
iTBCtlID = m_wndColorBar.CommandToIndex(ID_COLOR_BLACK);
if (iTBCtlID >= 0)
{
    // Loop through the buttons, setting them to act as radio buttons
    for (i= iTBCtlID; i < (iTBCtlID + 8); i++)
        m_wndColorBar.SetButtonStyle(i, TBBS_CHECKGROUP);
}
```

The first line in this code snippet uses the CommandToIndex toolbar function to locate the control number of the ID_COLOR_BLACK button. If you design your toolbar in the order of colors that you used on the menu, this should be the first control, with an index of 0. It's best to use the CommandToIndex function to locate the index of any toolbar button that you need to alter, just in case it's not where you expect it to be. This function returns the index of the toolbar control specified, and you use this as a starting point to specify the button style of each color button.

Where you loop through each of the eight color buttons on the toolbar, you use the SetButtonStyle function to control the toolbar buttons' behavior. The first argument to this function is the index of the button that you are changing. The second argument is the style that you want for the specified toolbar button. In this case, you are specifying that each button be a TBBS_CHECKGROUP button, which makes them behave like radio buttons, where only one of the buttons in the group can be selected at any time. Table 11.3 lists the available button styles.

TABLE 11.3 Toolbar Button Styles

Style	Description
TBBS_AUTOSIZE	Calculates the button's width based on the button's text.
TBBS_BUTTON	Creates a standard push button.
TBBS_CHECKBOX	Creates a button that acts like a check box, toggling between selected and deselected state.
TBBS_CHECKGROUP	Creates a button that acts like a radio button, remaining in the selected state until another button in the group is selected. This is actually the combination of the TBSTYLE_CHECK and TBSTYLE_GROUP button styles.

11

TABLE 11.3   continued

Style	Description
TBBS_DROPDOWN	Creates a drop-down list button.
TBBS_GROUP	Creates a button that remains selected until another button in the group is selected.
TBBS_NOPREFIX	Doesn't associate an accelerator prefix with the button text.
TBBS_SEPARATOR	Creates a separator, making a small gap between the buttons on either side.

Docking the Toolbar

The last thing that you do in the code added to the OnCreate function in the CMainFrame class is the following:

```
// Enable docking for the Color Toolbar
m_wndColorBar.EnableDocking(CBRS_ALIGN_ANY);

EnableDocking(CBRS_ALIGN_ANY);   // (AppWizard generated line)

// Dock the Color Toolbar
DockControlBar(&m_wndColorBar);
```

In the first of these lines, you called the EnableDocking toolbar function, which enables the toolbar to dock with the frame window. The value passed to this toolbar function must match the value passed in the following EnableDocking function called for the frame window. Table 11.4 lists the available values for these functions. These functions enable the borders of the toolbar, and the frame window, for docking. If these functions aren't called, you can't dock the toolbar with the frame window. If a specific side is specified in these functions for use in docking, and the sides don't match, you can't dock the toolbar with the frame.

TABLE 11.4   Toolbar Docking Sides

Style	Description
CBRS_ALIGN_TOP	Docks the toolbar to the top of the view area of the frame window.
CBRS_ALIGN_BOTTOM	Docks the toolbar to the bottom of the view area of the frame window.
CBRS_ALIGN_LEFT	Docks the toolbar to the left side of the view area of the frame window.
CBRS_ALIGN_RIGHT	Docks the toolbar to the right side of the view area of the frame window.
CBRS_ALIGN_ANY	Docks the toolbar to any side of the view area of the frame window.
CBRS_FLOAT_MULTI	Floats multiple toolbars in a single miniframe window.
0	Doesn't allow the toolbar to dock with the frame.

The final function you added was a frame window function, DockControlBar, which is passed the address of the toolbar variable. This function physically docks the toolbar to the frame window. Because all this code appears in the OnCreate function for the frame window, the toolbar is docked before users see either the window or the toolbar.

Now, after adding all this code to the OnCreate function of the CMainFrame class, if you compile and run your application, you'll find a working color toolbar that you can use to select the drawing color (see Figure 11.3).

FIGURE 11.3

The color toolbar on the drawing program.

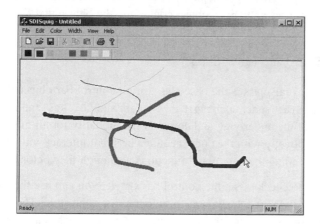

11

MFC Note: The CToolBar Class

The CToolBar class encapsulates the functionality of the toolbar controls. You might need to use a lot of functionality in this class. You're also likely to need some functionality in the ancestor class, CControlBar. You've already learned about the creation functionality, including the CreateEx, LoadToolbar, CommandToIndex, and SetButtonStyle functions. You might need to use several other functions from time to time.

Getting Information About a Toolbar Button

When working with the buttons on a toolbar, you occasionally have to walk through the toolbar's buttons to find the one you need. You can use the GetItemID function to retrieve the command ID for a particular button. You pass this function the button number on the toolbar (starting from the left with number 0), and it returns the button's ID.

If you need to get a button's location and dimensions, use the GetItemRect function. You pass GetItemRect the button number on the toolbar and a pointer to a CRect object, and it then populates the CRect object with the position and dimensions of the button.

If you need to check a button's style, use a corresponding function to the SetButtonStyle function, GetButtonStyle. You pass GetButtonStyle the button number that you want to check, and it returns an integer value that can be compared to the styles listed earlier in Table 11.3.

Getting and Setting Toolbar Text

On occasions when you need to add a text prompt to a toolbar button, you can use the `SetButtonText` function. You pass this function the button number and the string containing the button text. If you need to retrieve the text from a button, you can use the `GetButtonText` function. You pass just the button number to the `GetButtonText` function, and it returns a `CString` object containing the button text.

MFC Note: The `CControlBar` Class

The `CControlBar` class is the base class for all control bar object classes, including `CToolBar`, `CStatusBar`, `CControlBar`, `CReBar`, and `COleResizeBar`. `CControlBar` provides a lot of the underlying and common functionality for all these controls. You usually don't work directly with the `CControlBar` class, but interact with the derived class (like `CToolBar`), calling the base class' functions as though they belong to the derived class.

If you need to check or set the control bar's style, you can use the `GetBarStyle` function to check the style, and `SetBarStyle` function to set the style. The `GetBarStyle` returns a `DWORD` variable, specifying the style. The `SetBarStyle` takes a single `DWORD` parameter, specifying the style. Refer to Table 11.2 for the possible styles.

One handy member function to determine how many elements are on a toolbar is `GetCount`, which returns an integer specifying how many buttons and separators are on the toolbar. Another good informational function is `IsFloating`, which returns a Boolean value specifying whether the toolbar is currently floating.

If you need to get a pointer to the frame window where the toolbar is docked, call the `GetDockingFrame` function, which returns a pointer to the frame window. The last function, `EnableDocking`, you've already learned about.

Controlling Toolbar Visibility

Now that you have your color toolbar on the frame of your drawing application, it would be nice to show and hide the default toolbar and status bar through the View menu. This functionality is simple enough to add, but it doesn't necessarily work the way you might expect it to.

You first need to add a menu entry to toggle the visibility of the color bar. Follow these steps:

1. In the Menu Designer, add a new menu entry on the View menu.

2. Specify the menu properties as follows:

Property	Setting
ID	`ID_VIEW_COLORBAR`
Caption	`&Color Bar`
Prompt	`Show or hide the Color Bar\nToggle Color Bar`

Updating the Menu

To determine whether the toolbar is visible or hidden, you can get the toolbar's current style and mask out for the `WS_VISIBLE` style flag. If the flag is in the current toolbar style, the toolbar is visible. By placing this evaluation into the `SetCheck` function in the `UPDATE_COMMAND_UI` event message handler, you can check and uncheck the color bar menu entry as needed. You can also call the IsVisible function, which will return a Boolean value that specifies whether the toolbar is visible.

To add this functionality to your drawing program, follow these steps:

1. Add an event handler for the `UPDATE_COMMAND_UI` event message on the `ID_VIEW_COLOR` menu. Be sure to add this event-handler function into the `CMainFrame` class. (You're still making all your coding changes so far in the frame class.)

2. Edit the event-handler function, adding the code in Listing 11.2.

LISTING 11.2 The Modified `CMainFrame.OnUpdateViewColorbar` Function

```
void CMainFrame::OnUpdateViewColorbar(CCmdUI *pCmdUI)
{
    // TODO: Add your command update UI handler code here
    // Check the state of the color toolbar
    pCmdUI->SetCheck(m_wndColorBar.IsVisible());
}
```

INPUT

Toggling Toolbar Visibility

Because the `CToolBar` class is derived from the `CWnd` class (via the `CControlBar` class), you might think that you could call the `ShowWindow` function on the toolbar itself to show and hide the toolbar. Well, you can, but the background for the toolbar won't be hidden along with the toolbar. All users would notice is the toolbar buttons appearing and disappearing. (Of course, this might be the effect you're after, but your users might not like it.)

Instead, you use a frame window function, `ShowControlBar`, to show and hide the toolbar. This function takes three arguments:

- The address for the toolbar variable
- A Boolean specifying whether to show the toolbar (`TRUE` shows the toolbar; `FALSE` hides the toolbar)
- A Boolean specifying whether to delay showing the toolbar (`TRUE` delays showing the toolbar; `FALSE` shows the toolbar immediately)

When a toolbar is toggled on or off, you need to call another frame window function, `RecalcLayout`. This function causes the frame to reposition all toolbars, status bars, and anything else within the frame area. This function causes the color toolbar to move up and down if you toggle the default toolbar on and off.

To add this functionality to your drawing program, follow these steps:

1. Add an event handler for the `COMMAND` event message on the `ID_VIEW_COLOR` menu. Be sure to add this event-handler function into the `CMainFrame` class. (You're still making all your coding changes so far in the frame class.)

2. Edit the event-handler function, adding the code in Listing 11.3.

LISTING **11.3**   The Modified `CMainFrame.OnViewColorbar` Function

```
void CMainFrame::OnViewColorbar()
{
    // TODO: Add your command handler code here
    // Toggle the color bar
    ShowControlBar(&m_wndColorBar, !m_wndColorBar.IsVisible(), FALSE);
    // Reshuffle the frame layout
    RecalcLayout();
}
```

INPUT

At this point, after compiling and running your application, you should be able to toggle your color toolbar on and off from the View menu.

Adding a Combo Box to a Toolbar

It's commonplace to use applications that have more than just buttons on toolbars. The Visual Studio toolbars, for example, include combo boxes that enable you to select which build mode to work in. So how do you add a combo box to a toolbar? It's not available in the toolbar designer; all you have there are buttons that you can paint icons on. You can't add a combo box to any toolbar by using any of the Visual C++ wizards. You have to write some C++ code to do it.

To learn how to add a combo box to a toolbar, you'll add a combo box to the color tool-bar you just created. The combo box will be used to select the width of the pen the user will use to draw images. (If you haven't added the support for different drawing widths from the exercise at the end of Day 10, you might want to go back and add that now.)

Editing the Project Resources

To add a combo box to your toolbar, you first need to do what, until recently, Visual C++ was designed to prevent you from having to do—edit the resource file yourself. You can't do this through the Visual C++ Developer Studio visual tools. If you try to open the resource file in the Resource pane, you will be editing the resource file through the various resource editors and designers. No, you'll have to edit this file in another editor.

Go to the Solution Explorer pane and find the .rc file. Select this file and right click the mouse. Select Open with... from the menu. You'll be presented with a list of possible editors. Select Source Code (Text) Editor, and click Open. After you open this file, scroll down until you find the toolbar definitions. (You can search for the word toolbar.) When you've found the toolbar definitions, go to the end of the Color toolbar definition and add two separator lines at the bottom.

To make these changes to your drawing application, follow these steps:

1. Go to the Solution Explorer.
2. Find and select the SDISquig.rc file. Right-click the mouse and select Open With from the context menu.
3. Select Source Code (Text) Editor from the Open With dialog, as shown in Figure 11.4. Click Open to edit the resource file. If you have the Resource View pane open, or any of the resource editors, then you'll be asked if you want to close it. If asked this question, click Yes.

FIGURE 11.4

Choosing an editor for the project resource file.

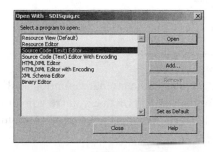

4. Search for the toolbar section, and then add two SEPARATOR lines just before the end of the IDR_TBCOLOR section, as shown in Listing 11.4.

5. After you add the SEPARATOR lines, save the file, then click the × just above the top-right of the editor area to close the project resource file.

LISTING 11.4   Toolbar.rc: The Modified Project Resource File

```
/////////////////////////////////////////////////////////////////////////////
//
// Toolbar
//

IDR_MAINFRAME TOOLBAR  16, 15
BEGIN
        BUTTON        ID_FILE_NEW
        BUTTON        ID_FILE_OPEN
        BUTTON        ID_FILE_SAVE
        SEPARATOR
        BUTTON        ID_EDIT_CUT
        BUTTON        ID_EDIT_COPY
        BUTTON        ID_EDIT_PASTE
        SEPARATOR
        BUTTON        ID_FILE_PRINT
        BUTTON        ID_APP_ABOUT
        SEPARATOR
        BUTTON        ID_VIEW_COLORBAR
END

IDR_TBCOLOR TOOLBAR  16, 15
BEGIN
        BUTTON        ID_COLOR_BLACK
        BUTTON        ID_COLOR_BLUE
        BUTTON        ID_COLOR_GREEN
        BUTTON        ID_COLOR_CYAN
        BUTTON        ID_COLOR_RED
        BUTTON        ID_COLOR_MAGENTA
        BUTTON        ID_COLOR_YELLOW
        BUTTON        ID_COLOR_WHITE
        SEPARATOR
        SEPARATOR
END
```

INPUT

You added these two SEPARATOR lines in the toolbar definition so that the second separator can act as a placeholder for the combo box that you are going to add to the toolbar. You had to make this edit by hand and not use the Visual C++ toolbar designer for two reasons:

- The toolbar designer wouldn't allow you to add more than one separator to the end of the toolbar.

- If you don't add anything else on the end of your toolbar after the separator, the toolbar designer decides that the separator is a mistake and removes it for you. In other words, the Visual C++ toolbar designer doesn't allow you to add the place-holder for the combo box to your toolbar.

Next, you need to add the text strings that you will load into your combo box. To add these strings, you need to open the string table in the Resource View of the workspace pane. Here you find all the strings that you entered as prompts in various properties dialogs. This table has a number of IDs, the values of those IDs, and text strings associated with those IDs (see Figure 11.5). You'll need to add the strings to be placed into your toolbar combo box in the string table; each line in the drop-down list must have a unique ID and entry in the strings table.

FIGURE 11.5

The string table editor.

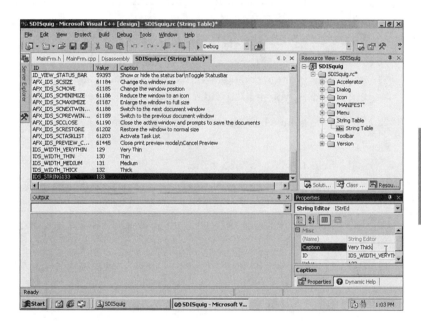

To add the strings for the combo box that you will add to the color toolbar:

1. Insert a new string by choosing New String from the Insert menu or by right-clicking the string table and selecting New String. You can also scroll down to the bottom of the list and select the blank entry at the bottom.

2. In the string properties, specify a string ID and then enter the string to appear in the drop-down list. For the strings in the Width combo box that you will add to the color toolbar, add the following strings:

ID	Caption
IDS_WIDTH_VERYTHIN	Very Thin
IDS_WIDTH_THIN	Thin

ID	Caption
IDS_WIDTH_MEDIUM	Medium
IDS_WIDTH_THICK	Thick
IDS_WIDTH_VERYTHICK	Very Thick

Tip

While entering the strings in the string table, pay attention to the Value assigned to the strings. The values need to be sequential, from Very Thin as the lowest value, to Very Thick as the highest value.

Creating the Toolbar Combo Box

Before you can add the combo box to the color toolbar, you need to create a variable that you can use for the combo box. Because you can't add this combo box through any of the designers, you need to add it as a variable to the CMainFrame class.

To add the combo box variable to the main frame class for the color toolbar, follow these steps:

1. Select the Class View pane.

2. Right-click the CMainFrame class and select Add, Add Variable from the context menu.

3. Specify the variable type as CComboBox, the name as m_ctlWidth, and the access as protected.

After you add the combo box variable to the main frame class, you need to perform a series of actions, all after the toolbar is created:

- Set the width and the ID of the combo box placeholder on the toolbar to the width and ID of the combo box.

- Get the position of the toolbar placeholder, and use it to size and position the combo box.

- Create the combo box, specifying the toolbar as the parent window of the combo box.

- Load the strings into the drop-down list on the combo box.

To organize this so that it doesn't get too messy, it's advisable to move the creation of the color toolbar to its own function that can be called from the OnCreate function of the main frame class. To create this function, follow these steps:

1. Right-click the CMainFrame class in the workspace pane and select Add, Add Function from the context menu.

2. Specify the function type as BOOL, the function description as CreateColorBar, and the access as public.

3. Edit the new function, adding the code in Listing 11.5.

LISTING **11.5** The CMainFrame CreateColorBar Function

```
BOOL CMainFrame::CreateColorBar(void)
{
    // Add the color toolbar
        int iTBCtlID;
    int i;

    // Create the color toolbar
    if (!m_wndColorBar.CreateEx(this, TBSTYLE_FLAT, WS_CHILD |
            WS_VISIBLE | CBRS_TOP | CBRS_GRIPPER | CBRS_TOOLTIPS |
            CBRS_FLYBY | CBRS_SIZE_DYNAMIC) ||
            !m_wndColorBar.LoadToolBar(IDR_TBCOLOR))
    {
        TRACE0("Failed to create toolbar\n");
        return FALSE;     // fail to create
    }
    // Find the Black button on the toolbar
    iTBCtlID = m_wndColorBar.CommandToIndex(ID_COLOR_BLACK);
    if (iTBCtlID >= 0)
    {
        // Loop through the buttons, setting them to act as radio buttons
        for (i = iTBCtlID; i < (iTBCtlID + 8); i++)
            m_wndColorBar.SetButtonStyle(i, TBBS_CHECKGROUP);
    }
    // Add the combo
    int nWidth = 100;
    int nHeight = 125;

    // Configure the combo place holder
    m_wndColorBar.SetButtonInfo(9, IDC_CBWIDTH, TBBS_SEPARATOR, nWidth);

    // Get the colorbar height
    CRect rect;
    m_wndColorBar.GetItemRect(9, &rect);
    rect.bottom = rect.top + nHeight;

    // Create the combo box
    m_ctlWidth.Create(WS_CHILD | WS_VISIBLE | WS_VSCROLL |
            CBS_DROPDOWNLIST, rect, &m_wndColorBar, IDC_CBWIDTH);

    // Fill the combo box
    CString strStyle;
    if (strStyle.LoadString(IDS_WIDTH_VERYTHIN))
        m_ctlWidth.AddString((LPCTSTR)strStyle);
```

INPUT

11

LISTING **11.5**   continued

```
    if (strStyle.LoadString(IDS_WIDTH_THIN))
        m_ctlWidth.AddString((LPCTSTR)strStyle);
    if (strStyle.LoadString(IDS_WIDTH_MEDIUM))
        m_ctlWidth.AddString((LPCTSTR)strStyle);
    if (strStyle.LoadString(IDS_WIDTH_THICK))
        m_ctlWidth.AddString((LPCTSTR)strStyle);
    if (strStyle.LoadString(IDS_WIDTH_VERYTHICK))
        m_ctlWidth.AddString((LPCTSTR)strStyle);

    // Select the first entry in the combo box
    m_ctlWidth.SetCurSel(0);

    return TRUE;
}
```

In Listing 11.5, you specify that the combo box should be created by using the object ID IDC_CBWIDTH:

```
m_ctlWidth.Create(WS_CHILD | WS_VISIBLE | WS_VSCROLL |
        CBS_DROPDOWNLIST, rect, &m_wndColorBar, IDC_CBWIDTH);
```

This object ID identifies the combo box when the combo box sends an event message to the application or when you need to specify what list entry is displayed in the edit field. However, this object ID doesn't exist in your application. Before you can compile the application, you'll need to add this ID to the project resource IDs, just as you did on Day 5, "Working with Timers." To add this ID to your project, follow these steps:

1. Select the Resource view in the workspace pane.
2. Select the top of the resource tree, right-click it, and select Resource Symbols from the context menu.
3. Add the object ID IDC_CBWIDTH.
4. Make sure you add the new object ID with a unique numerical value so that it won't conflict with any other objects used in your application.

Configuring the Placeholder

After creating the toolbar and configuring all the toolbar buttons, you need to configure the separator that's acting as the placeholder for the combo box you are about to create. You do this with the SetButtonInfo toolbar function:

```
m_wndColorBar.SetButtonInfo(9, IDC_CBWIDTH, TBBS_SEPARATOR, nWidth);
```

This function takes four arguments:

- The current index of the control in the toolbar, in this case, the tenth control in the toolbar (eight color buttons and two separators, and remember that counting starts with 0 in C/C++).
- The new ID of the toolbar control. This ID will be placed in the event message queue when a control event occurs.
- The type of toolbar control this control should be.
- The final argument is the new index of the control in the toolbar, according to the function documentation. This is the position where the control will be moved. However, this argument is somewhat deceptive. If the control is a separator, this argument specifies the control's width and doesn't move it anywhere. Because this toolbar control is a separator, this argument effectively sets the control's width to be as wide as the combo box you're going to create.

Getting the Toolbar Combo Box Position

Now that you've configured the toolbar separator as the placeholder for the combo box, you need to get the position of the combo box placeholder on the toolbar so that you can use it to set the position of the combo box:

```
m_wndColorBar.GetItemRect(9, &rect);
rect.bottom = rect.top + nHeight;
```

In the first line, you called the toolbar function GetItemRect to get the position and size of the placeholder for the combo box. In the next line, you added the height of the drop-down list to the height that the combo box will eventually be.

Creating the Combo Box

Now that you've sized a placeholder correctly and have the combo box's position and size, you can create the combo box. You do this with the Create combo box function:

```
m_ctlWidth.Create(WS_CHILD | WS_VISIBLE | WS_VSCROLL |
    CBS_DROPDOWNLIST, rect, &m_wndColorBar, IDC_CBWIDTH);
```

The first argument to the combo box Create function is the combo box style. Normally, several style flags are combined to create a combination style value. Table 11.5 lists the flags that you can use in this value.

TABLE 11.5 Combo Box Styles

Style	Description
WS_CHILD	Designates this as a child window (required).
WS_VISIBLE	Makes the combo box visible.

TABLE 11.5 continued

Style	Description
WS_DISABLED	Disables the combo box.
WS_VSCROLL	Adds vertical scrolling to the drop-down list.
WS_HSCROLL	Adds horizontal scrolling to the drop-down list.
WS_GROUP	Groups controls.
WS_TABSTOP	Includes the combo box in the tabbing order.
CBS_AUTOHSCROLL	Automatically scrolls the text in the edit control to the right when a user types a character at the end of the line. This enables users to enter text wider than the edit control into the combo box.
CBS_DROPDOWN	Similar to CBS_SIMPLE, but doesn't display the list unless users select the icon next to the edit control.
CBS_DROPDOWNLIST	Similar to CBS_DROPDOWN, but replaces the edit control with a static-text item displaying the currently selected item in the list.
CBS_HASSTRINGS	Makes the list box owner responsible for drawing the list box contents. The list box items consist of strings.
CBS_OEMCONVERT	Converts text entered in the edit control from ANSI to the OEM character set and then back to ANSI.
CBS_OWNERDRAWFIXED	Makes the list box owner responsible for drawing the list box contents. The list contents are fixed in height.
CBS_OWNERDRAWVARIABLE	Makes the list box owner responsible for drawing the list box contents. The list contents vary in height.
CBS_SIMPLE	Displays the list box at all times.
CBS_SORT	Automatically sorts the strings in the list box.
CBS_DISABLENOSCROLL	Displays a disabled scrollbar when the list doesn't have enough items to require scrolling.
CBS_NOINTEGRALHEIGHT	Specifies that the combo box is exactly the size specified.

The second argument is the rectangle that the combo box will occupy. This argument is the position within the parent window—in this case, the toolbar—that the combo box will stay in. It will move with the parent window (the toolbar), staying in this position the entire time.

The third argument is a pointer to the parent window—in this example, the address of the color toolbar variable. The fourth argument is the object ID for the combo box.

Populating the Combo Box

Finally, you can populate the drop-down list with the available items that users can select from. You do this with the combination of two functions:

```
if (strStyle.LoadString(IDS_WIDTH_VERYTHIN))
    m_ctlWidth.AddString((LPCTSTR)strStyle);
```

The first function, LoadString, is a CString function that takes a string ID and loads the string matching the ID from the string table. The second function, AddString, is a combo box function that adds the string passed in as an argument to the drop-down list. By calling this function combination for each element in the drop-down list, you can populate the combo box from the application string table.

Updating the OnCreate Function

After moving all the code to create the color toolbar to a separate function, you can update the OnCreate function so that it calls the CreateColorBar function, where it's used to create the color toolbar (see Listing 11.6).

LISTING 11.6 The Modified CMainFrame.OnCreate Function

11

```
int CMainFrame::OnCreate(LPCREATESTRUCT lpCreateStruct)
{
    if (CFrameWnd::OnCreate(lpCreateStruct) == -1)
        return -1;

    if (!m_wndToolBar.CreateEx(this, TBSTYLE_FLAT, WS_CHILD |
        WS_VISIBLE | CBRS_TOP | CBRS_GRIPPER | CBRS_TOOLTIPS |
        CBRS_FLYBY | CBRS_SIZE_DYNAMIC) ||
        !m_wndToolBar.LoadToolBar(IDR_MAINFRAME))
    {
        TRACE0("Failed to create toolbar\n");
        return -1;      // fail to create
    }

    // Add the color toolbar
        if (!CreateColorBar())
    {
        TRACE0("Failed to create color toolbar\n");
        return -1;      // fail to create
    }

    if (!m_wndStatusBar.Create(this) ||
        !m_wndStatusBar.SetIndicators(indicators,
          sizeof(indicators)/sizeof(UINT)))
    {
```

INPUT

LISTING 11.6   continued

```
        TRACE0("Failed to create status bar\n");
        return -1;        // fail to create
    }
    // TODO: Delete these three lines if you don't want the toolbar
➡to be dockable
    m_wndToolBar.EnableDocking(CBRS_ALIGN_ANY);
    // Enable docking for the color toolbar
    m_wndColorBar.EnableDocking(CBRS_ALIGN_ANY);
    EnableDocking(CBRS_ALIGN_ANY);
    DockControlBar(&m_wndToolBar);

    // Dock the Color toolbar
    DockControlBar(&m_wndColorBar);
    return 0;
}
```

Now, when you compile and run your application you should have a combo box on the end of your color toolbar (see Figure 11.6). However, the combo box doesn't do anything yet.

FIGURE 11.6

The color toolbar with a width combo box.

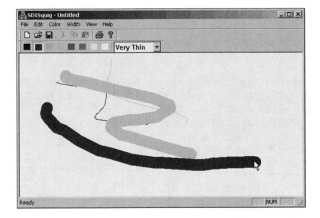

Handling Toolbar Combo Box Events

Before you can add the event handling functionality for the combo box, you need to add one small but significant function to the document class: SetWidth. To add this function, follow these steps:

1. Select the CSDISquigDoc class in the Class View, right-click it, and select Add, Add Function from the context menu.

2. Specify the function return type as void, the function name as SetWidth, and add one parameter. The parameter type should be unsigned int, and the parameter name should be nWidth.

3. Edit the function, adding the code in Listing 11.7.

LISTING 11.7 The SetWidth Function

```
void CSDISquigDoc::SetWidth(unsigned int nWidth)
{
    // Set the current width
    m_nWidth = nWidth;
}
```

INPUT

Adding an event handler for the combo box is fairly simple, although it does have to be done by hand (because the Class Wizard doesn't even know that the combo box exists). You have to add an ON_CBN_SELCHANGE entry into the message map and then add the actual message-handler function into the CMainFrame class. To start with, follow these steps:

1. Add the message-handler function by selecting the CMainFrame class in the workspace pane and selecting Add, Add Function from the context menu.

2. Enter the function type as afx_msg void, the function name as OnSelChangeWidth, and the access as protected.

3. Edit the new function as in Listing 11.8. Be sure and remove the afx_msg from the first line of the function implementation (this should only be in the function declaration in the header file).

LISTING 11.8 The OnSelChangeWidth Function

```
void CMainFrame::OnSelChangeWidth(void)
{
    // Get the new combo selection
    int iIndex = m_ctlWidth.GetCurSel();
    if (iIndex == CB_ERR)
        return;

    // Get the active document
    CSDISquigDoc* pDoc = (CSDISquigDoc*)GetActiveDocument();
    // Do we have a valid document?
    if (pDoc)
        // Set the new drawing width
        pDoc->SetWidth(iIndex);
}
```

11

In Listing 11.8, this function first gets the current selection from the combo box. Remember that the entries were added in order, and the CBS_SORT flag wasn't specified in the combo box creation, so the selection index numbers should correspond to the document widths. As a result, you can get a pointer to the current document instance, using the GetActiveDocument function, and then pass the new width to the document using its SetWidth function.

For the combo box selection changes to call this message-handler function, you need to add the appropriate entry to the CMainFrame message map. Scroll to the top of the CMainFrame source code until you find the message map section. Add the boldfaced line in Listing 11.9 to the message map.

LISTING 11.9   The Modified CMainFrame Message Map

```
// CMainFrame

IMPLEMENT_DYNCREATE(CMainFrame, CFrameWnd)

BEGIN_MESSAGE_MAP(CMainFrame, CFrameWnd)
    ON_WM_CREATE()
    ON_UPDATE_COMMAND_UI(ID_VIEW_COLORBAR, OnUpdateViewColorbar)
    ON_COMMAND(ID_VIEW_COLORBAR, OnViewColorbar)
    ON_CBN_SELCHANGE(IDC_CBWIDTH, OnSelChangeWidth)
    END_MESSAGE_MAP()
```

INPUT

The message map entry that you just entered specifies, that on combo box selection change events with the object ID of the color toolbar combo box, the OnSelChangeWidth function should be called. Now if you compile and run your application, you should be able to change the drawing width with the combo box on the color toolbar.

At this point, your application will not compile without errors. The reason for this is because you are referencing the document class in the main frame code, but you haven't included the header file for the document class in the main frame source code yet.

4. Scroll to the top of the CMainFrame.cpp source code file.

5. Just after the last #include directive, add another #include for the SDISquigDoc.h header file.

Updating the Toolbar Combo Box

The one remaining problem with the combo box is that it needs to be updated if users select a new value from the menu instead of the combo box. One of the most efficient methods of doing this is to set the current selection in the combo box when any menu selections are triggered. This requires a function in the main frame class that can be called from the document class to accomplish this action. All the function in the main frame needs to do is to set the current selection in the combo box.

To implement this function in the main frame, follow these steps:

1. Add a new member function to the CMainFrame class.

2. Specify the function type as void, the name as UpdateWidthCB, and add a parameter. Specify the parameter type as int, and the parameter name as iIndex. Specify the function access as public.

3. After you add this function, edit it as in Listing 11.10.

LISTING 11.10 The CMainFrame.UpdateWidthCB Function

```
void CMainFrame::UpdateWidthCB(int iIndex)
{
    // Set the new selection in the combo box
    m_ctlWidth.SetCurSel(iIndex);
}
```

INPUT

This function uses a single combo box function, SetCurSel, to set the current selection in the combo box drop-down list to the entry specified with the index number. The combo box's edit control is updated with the new selected list entry. If an index number that doesn't exist in the drop-down list is supplied to the combo box, the function returns an error.

On the document side, you need to call this function in the main frame whenever the appropriate menu event-handling functions are called. Because this could occur in several functions, it makes the most sense to enclose the necessary functionality in a single function. This function needs to get a pointer to the view associated with the document and then, through the view, get a pointer to the frame, which can then be used to call the UpdateWidthCB function that you just added to the main frame class.

To add this function to your application, follow these steps:

1. Select the CSDISquigDoc class in the Class View pane, and select Add, Add Function from the context menu.

2. Specify the function type as void, the name as UpdateColorbar, and add a parameter. Specify the parameter type as int and the parameter name as nIndex. Specify private as the function access.

3. Edit the function as in Listing 11.11.

11

LISTING **11.11**   The `CSDISquigDoc.UpdateColorbar` Function

```
void CSDISquigDoc::UpdateColorbar(int iIndex)
{
    // Get the position of the first view
        POSITION pos = GetFirstViewPosition();
    // Did we get a valid position?
    if (pos != NULL)
    {
        // Get a pointer to the view in that position
        CView* pView = GetNextView(pos);
        // Do we have a valid pointer to the view?
        if (pView)
        {
            // Get a pointer to the frame through the view
            CMainFrame* pFrame = (CMainFrame*)pView->GetTopLevelFrame();
            // Did we get a pointer to the frame?
            if (pFrame)
                // Update the combo box on the color toolbar
                // through the frame
                pFrame->UpdateWidthCB(iIndex);
        }
    }
}
```

INPUT

This function traces through the path that you have to follow to get to the application frame from the document class. It first gets the position of the first view associated with the document, using the `GetFirstViewPosition` function. A document might have multiple views open at the same time, this function returns the position of the first of those views.

The next function, `GetNextView`, returns a pointer to the view specified by the position. This function also updates the position variable to point to the next view in the list of views associated with the current document.

When you have a pointer to the view, you can call the window function `GetTopLevelFrame`, which returns a pointer to the application frame window. You have to call this function through the view because the document isn't descended from the `CWnd` class, although the view is.

When you have a pointer to the frame window, you can use this pointer to call the function you created earlier to update the combo box on the toolbar. Now if you call this new function from the Width menu command event handlers, as in Listing 11.12, the combo box you placed on the color toolbar is automatically updated to reflect the currently selected drawing width, whether or not the width was selected from the combo box or the pull-down menu.

To make this change, edit all the width menu event handlers in the `CSDISquigDoc` class, adding the two boldfaced lines in Listing 11.12.

LISTING 11.12 An Updated Width Menu Command Event Handler

```
void CSDISquigDoc::OnWidthVthin()
{
    // TODO: Add your command handler code here
    // Set the new width
    m_nWidth = 0;
    // Update the combo box on the color toolbar
        UpdateColorbar(m_nWidth);
}
```

INPUT

Once again, your application will not compile without errors. The reason for this is because you are referencing the main frame class in the document class code, but you haven't included the header file for the main frame class in the document class source code yet.

4. Scroll to the top of the CSDISquigDoc.cpp source code file.

5. Just after the last #include directive, add another #include for the MainFrm.h header file.

11

Adding a New Status Bar Element

Earlier today, you learned how to specify status bar messages and ToolTips for toolbar buttons and menus. What if you want to use the status bar to provide the user with more substantial information? What if, as in the Visual C++ Developer Studio, you want to provide information about what the user is doing, where he is in the document he is editing, or the mode that the application is in? This information goes beyond the Caps Lock, Num Lock, and Scroll Lock keys that Visual C++ automatically reports on the status bar.

It's actually easy to add panes to the status bar, as well as take away panes that are already there. To learn just how easy this change is, you will add a new pane to the status bar in your drawing application that will display the color currently in use.

Adding a New Status Bar Pane

Before you add a new status bar pane, you need to add a new entry to the application string table for use in the status bar pane. This string table entry will perform two functions for the status bar pane:

- The first function will provide the object ID for the status bar pane. You will use this ID for updating the pane when you need to update the text in the pane.

- The second function will size the pane. To size the pane correctly, you need to provide a caption for the string table entry that's at least as wide as the widest string placed in the status bar pane.

To add a new string to your application string table, follow these steps:

1. Use the same steps you used earlier in the "Editing the Project Resources" section to add the text for the combo box you placed on the color toolbar.

2. Specify the string ID as ID_INDICATOR_COLOR and the caption as MAGENTA (the widest string that you will put into the status bar pane).

A small section in the first part of the main frame source code defines the status bar layout. This small table contains the object IDs of the status bar panes as table elements, in the order in which they are to appear from left to right on the status bar. To add the color pane to the status bar, add the ID of the pane to the status bar indicator table definition, just after the message map in the source-code file for the main frame. Place the color pane ID in the table definition in the position that you want it to be on the status bar, as in the boldfaced line of Listing 11.13.

LISTING 11.13 A Modified Status Bar Indicator Table Definition

```
// CMainFrame

IMPLEMENT_DYNCREATE(CMainFrame, CFrameWnd)

BEGIN_MESSAGE_MAP(CMainFrame, CFrameWnd)
    ON_WM_CREATE()
    ON_UPDATE_COMMAND_UI(ID_VIEW_COLORBAR, OnUpdateViewColorbar)
    ON_COMMAND(ID_VIEW_COLORBAR, OnViewColorbar)
    ON_CBN_SELCHANGE(IDC_CBWIDTH, OnSelChangeWidth)
END_MESSAGE_MAP()

static UINT indicators[] =
{
    ID_SEPARATOR,              // status line indicator
    ID_INDICATOR_COLOR,
        ID_INDICATOR_CAPS,
    ID_INDICATOR_NUM,
    ID_INDICATOR_SCRL,
};
```

INPUT

If you want to drop any of the lock key indicators from the status bar, just remove them from the indicators table definition. If you examine the OnCreate function, where the status bar is created (just after the toolbars are created), you'll see where this table is used to create the status bar with the following code:

```
if (!m_wndStatusBar.Create(this) ||
   !m_wndStatusBar.SetIndicators(indicators,
     sizeof(indicators)/sizeof(UINT)))
```

As soon as the status bar is created, the SetIndicators function is called on the status bar to add the panes as they are defined in the indicators table. The strings associated with the IDs in the indicators table are used to initialize the panes and set their size. If you compile and run your application at this point, you see the new color pane on the status bar with the caption from the string table displayed within.

Setting a Status Bar Pane Text

After you add the pane to the status bar, you can let the UPDATE_COMMAND_UI event do all the pane updating. All you need to do is add an event handler for this event on the pane's object ID, and use this event to set the pane text. Because the status bar is always visible, the UPDATE_COMMAND_UI event for status bar panes is triggered every time the application is idle. This means that it's triggered after the application is finished processing just about every keystroke and mouse movement. In almost a week—on Day 17, "Implementing Multitasking in Your Application"—you will learn more about how often tasks are performed when the application is idle and when they are triggered.

In the event handler, you need to create a string containing the name of the current color (or whatever other text you want to display in the status bar pane). Next, you have to make sure that the pane is enabled. Finally, you need to set the text of the pane to the string that you've created.

To implement this in your application, you need to create an UPDATE_COMMAND_UI event handler. Again, the Class Wizard doesn't know about the status bar pane, so you have to create the message handler and add it to the message map yourself, as follows:

1. Add a new member function to the document class (CSDISquigDoc) with a type of afx_msg void, a name of OnUpdateIndicatorColor, a single parameter of type CCmdUI* and named pCmdUI, and an access of protected.

2. Edit the newly created function, adding the code in Listing 11.14.

LISTING 11.14   The OnUpdateIndicatorColor Function

```
void CSDISquigDoc::OnUpdateIndicatorColor(CCmdUI* pCmdUI)
{
    CString strColor;

    // What is the current color?
    switch (m_nColor)
    {
```

11

INPUT

LISTING 11.14   continued

```
        case 0:     // Black
            strColor = "BLACK";
            break;
        case 1:     // Blue
            strColor = "BLUE";
            break;
        case 2:     // Green
            strColor = "GREEN";
            break;
        case 3:     // Cyan
            strColor = "CYAN";
            break;
        case 4:     // Red
            strColor = "RED";
            break;
        case 5:     // Magenta
            strColor = "MAGENTA";
            break;
        case 6:     // Yellow
            strColor = "YELLOW";
            break;
        case 7:     // White
            strColor = "WHITE";
            break;
        }
        // Enable the status bar pane
        pCmdUI->Enable(TRUE);
        // Set the text of the status bar pane
        // to the current color
        pCmdUI->SetText(strColor);
    }
```

The function in Listing 11.14 followed three steps exactly: it created a string with the current color name, made sure that the pane was enabled, and set the pane text to the string that you had created.

Now, to make sure that your new message handler is called when it's supposed to be, add an ON_UPDATE_COMMAND_UI entry to the message map at the top of the document source code file, as specified in Listing 11.15.

LISTING 11.15   The Modified CSDISquigDoc Message Map

```
// CSDISquigDoc

IMPLEMENT_DYNCREATE(CSDISquigDoc, CDocument)

BEGIN_MESSAGE_MAP(CSDISquigDoc, CDocument)
    ON_COMMAND(ID_COLOR_BLACK, OnColorBlack)
```

LISTING 11.15   continued

```
ON_UPDATE_COMMAND_UI(ID_COLOR_BLACK, OnUpdateColorBlack)
ON_COMMAND(ID_COLOR_BLUE, OnColorBlue)
ON_UPDATE_COMMAND_UI(ID_COLOR_BLUE, OnUpdateColorBlue)
ON_COMMAND(ID_COLOR_GREEN, OnColorGreen)
ON_UPDATE_COMMAND_UI(ID_COLOR_GREEN, OnUpdateColorGreen)
ON_COMMAND(ID_COLOR_CYAN, OnColorCyan)
ON_UPDATE_COMMAND_UI(ID_COLOR_CYAN, OnUpdateColorCyan)
ON_COMMAND(ID_COLOR_RED, OnColorRed)
ON_UPDATE_COMMAND_UI(ID_COLOR_RED, OnUpdateColorRed)
ON_COMMAND(ID_COLOR_MAGENTA, OnColorMagenta)
ON_UPDATE_COMMAND_UI(ID_COLOR_MAGENTA, OnUpdateColorMagenta)
ON_COMMAND(ID_COLOR_YELLOW, OnColorYellow)
ON_UPDATE_COMMAND_UI(ID_COLOR_YELLOW, OnUpdateColorYellow)
ON_COMMAND(ID_COLOR_WHITE, OnColorWhite)
ON_UPDATE_COMMAND_UI(ID_COLOR_WHITE, OnUpdateColorWhite)
ON_COMMAND(ID_WIDTH_VERYTHIN, OnWidthVerythin)
ON_UPDATE_COMMAND_UI(ID_WIDTH_VERYTHIN, OnUpdateWidthVerythin)
ON_COMMAND(ID_WIDTH_THIN, OnWidthThin)
ON_UPDATE_COMMAND_UI(ID_WIDTH_THIN, OnUpdateWidthThin)
ON_COMMAND(ID_WIDTH_MEDIUM, OnWidthMedium)
ON_UPDATE_COMMAND_UI(ID_WIDTH_MEDIUM, OnUpdateWidthMedium)
ON_COMMAND(ID_WIDTH_THICK, OnWidthThick)
ON_UPDATE_COMMAND_UI(ID_WIDTH_THICK, OnUpdateWidthThick)
ON_COMMAND(ID_WIDTH_VERYTHICK, OnWidthVerythick)
ON_UPDATE_COMMAND_UI(ID_WIDTH_VERYTHICK, OnUpdateWidthVerythick)
ON_UPDATE_COMMAND_UI(ID_INDICATOR_COLOR, OnUpdateIndicatorColor)
END_MESSAGE_MAP()
```

INPUT

11

After adding the message handler and message map entry, you should now be able to
compile and run your application and see the color status bar pane automatically updated
to reflect the current drawing color (see Figure 11.7).

FIGURE 11.7

The drawing applica-
tion with the current
color displayed in the
status bar.

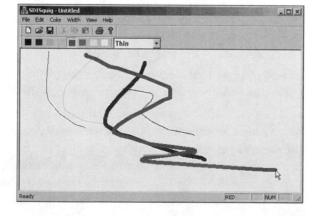

Summary

You learned quite a bit today. (Is this becoming a trend?) You learned how to design and create your own toolbars. Along with learning how to design toolbars, you learned how to specify status bar prompts for the toolbar buttons and menus, along with ToolTip text that will display after holding the mouse pointer over toolbar buttons for a couple of seconds. You learned how to create these toolbars and how to attach them to the application frame. You also learned how to control whether the toolbar is visible from a menu entry.

Next you learned how to place a combo box on a toolbar so that you can provide your application users with the same level of convenience that you have when using many popular software packages. In learning how to add this combo box to the toolbar, you saw how to create a combo box in code, without having to depend on the dialog designers to create combo boxes, and how to populate the combo box drop-down list with text entries. Then, you saw how to tie the combo box into your application by adding event handlers for the combo box events and how to update the combo box to reflect changes made through the application menus.

Finally, you learned how to add your own panes to the status bar and how you can update the pane to reflect the current status of the application.

Q&A

Q. In some applications, toolbars have the option of showing text, as in Internet Explorer. How can I add text to my toolbar buttons?

A. Unfortunately, the toolbar designer provides no way to add text to the toolbar buttons. This means you have to add the text to the buttons in your application code, similar to specifying all the color toolbar buttons to behave as radio buttons. Use the SetButtonText function to set the text on each toolbar button individually. This function takes two arguments: the button's index number and the button's text. If you really want to place text on the toolbar buttons, you also have to resize the toolbar to allow room for the text to be displayed.

Q. I made some changes to the color toolbar in the toolbar designer, and now I get an assertion error every time I try to run my application. What happened?

A. The problem is the toolbar designer found the separators you added to the resource file as placeholders for the combo box. The toolbar designer assumed that these were mistakes and removed them for you. The error occurs because you are trying to work with a control in the color toolbar that doesn't exist. To fix this problem, reopen the resource file in the text editor and add the two separators again, at the end of the color toolbar definition. Then, recompile the application.

Q. **The combo box on my toolbar looks too big. How can I get it to fit within the toolbar a little better?**

A. To make the combo box fit within the toolbar like the combo boxes in the Visual C++ Developer Studio, you need to do a couple of things:

1. Lower the top of the combo box by 3; this places a small border between the top of the combo box and the edge of the toolbar.

2. Set the font in the combo box to a smaller size that will fit better within the toolbar. You can experiment with fonts and pitches until you have a font that you like for the combo box in the toolbar.

Q. **How can I set the text in the first section of the status bar other than by using menu and toolbar prompts?**

A. You can use `SetWindowText` to set the text in the first pane of the status bar. As a default setting, the first pane is a separator that automatically expands to fill the width of the status bar with the other panes right-justified on the bar. The `SetWindowText` function, called on the status bar variable, sets the text in the first pane only. If you want to set the text in any other pane, at any other time than in the `ON_UPDATE_COMMAND_UI` event handler, you can use the `SetPaneText` function. There are two ways that you can set the text in the main part of the status bar. The first is

```
CString myString = "This is my string"
m_wndStatusBar.SetWindowText(myString);
```

The other method is

```
CString myString = "This is my string"
m_wndStatusBar.SetPaneText(0, myString);
```

Workshop

The Workshop provides quiz questions to help you solidify your understanding of the material covered and exercises to provide you with experience in using what you've learned. The answers to the quiz questions and exercises are provided in Appendix A, "Answers to Quiz Questions."

Quiz

1. How do you tie a toolbar button to a menu entry that triggers that same function?
2. How do you make sure that a toolbar can be docked with the frame window?
3. How can you remove the Num Lock status indicator from the status bar?
4. Why do you have to edit the resource file to add a combo box to a toolbar?

Exercises

1. Add another pane to the status bar to display the current width selected.

2. Add a button to the main toolbar that can be used to toggle the color toolbar on and off (see Figure 11.8).

FIGURE 11.8.

The color toolbar on/off button.

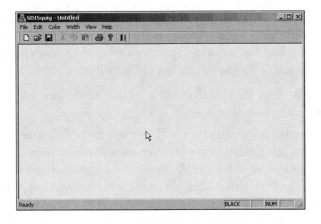

DAY **12**

Saving and Restoring Work

Most applications provide users the option of saving what has been created. The creation can be a word-processing document, a spreadsheet, a drawing, or a set of data records. Today, you will see how Visual C++ provides you with the means to implement this functionality easily. You will learn

- How Visual C++ uses C++ streams to save information about your application
- How to store your application data in binary files
- How to make your application objects "serializable"
- How you can store variables of differing data types into a single file

Understanding Serialization

NEW TERM There are two parts of serialization. When application data is stored on the system drive in the form of a file, it's called *serialization*. When the application state is restored from the file, it's called *deserialization*. The combination of these two parts makes up the serialization of application objects in Visual C++.

The CArchive and CFile Classes

Serialization in Visual C++ applications is accomplished through the CArchive class, which is designed to act as an input/output (I/O) stream for a CFile object (see Figure 12.1). It uses C++ streams to enable efficient data flow to and from the file that stores the application data. CArchive can't exist without a CFile class object to which it's attached.

FIGURE **12.1**

The CArchive *class stores application data in a* CFile *object.*

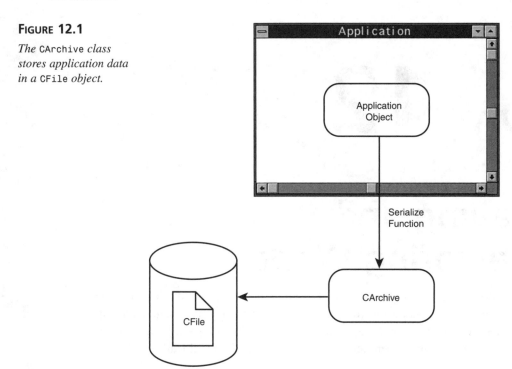

The CArchive class can store data in a number of types of files, all of which are descendants of the CFile class. By default, the AppWizard includes all the functionality to create and open regular CFile objects for use with CArchive. If you want or need to work with one of these other file types, you might need to add additional code to your application to enable the use of these different file types.

The Serialize Function

The CArchive class is used in the Serialize function on the document and data objects in Visual C++ applications. When an application is reading or writing a file, the document object's Serialize function is called, passing the CArchive object used to write to or read from the file. In the `Serialize` function, the typical logic to follow is to determine whether the archive is being written to or read from by calling the `CArchive` `IsStoring` or `IsLoading` functions. The return value from either function determines whether your application needs to be writing to or reading from the `CArchive` class's I/O stream. Listing 12.1 shows a typical `Serialize` function in the document, class.

LISTING 12.1 A Typical `Serialize` Function

```
void   CAppDoc::Serialize(CArchive& ar)
{
    // Is the archive being written to?
    if (ar.IsStoring())
    {
        // Yes, write my variable
        ar << m_MyVar;
    }
    else
    {
        // No, read my variable
        ar >> m_MyVar;
    }
}
```

You can place a `Serialize` function in any classes you create so that you can call their `Serialize` function from the document `Serialize` function. If you place your custom objects into an object array, such as the `CObArray` that you used in your drawing application for the past two days, you can call the array's `Serialize` function from the document's `Serialize` function. The object array will, in turn, call the `Serialize` function of any objects stored in the array.

Making Objects Serializable

When you created the `CLine` class on Day 10, "Creating SDI and MDI Applications," you had to add two macros before you could save and restore your drawings. These two macros, DECLARE_SERIAL and IMPLEMENT_SERIAL, include functionality in your classes necessary for the `Serialize` function to work correctly.

Including the DECLARE_SERIAL Macro

You must include the DECLARE_SERIAL macro in your class declaration (see Listing 12.2). This macro takes a single argument, the class name. It automatically adds to your class some standard function and operator declarations necessary for serialization to work correctly.

12

LISTING 12.2   Including the DECLARE_SERIAL Macro in the Class Declaration

```
class CMyClass : public  CObject
{
    DECLARE_SERIAL (CMyClass)
public:
    virtual void Serialize(CArchive &ar);
    CMyClass();
    virtual ~CMyClass();
};
```

> **Caution**
>
> The DECLARE_SERIAL changes the access scope to public. If you add ele-
> ments to your class declaration after the DECLARE_SERIAL macro, you need
> to explicitly declare the access for the elements, and not depend on the
> default access of private.

Including the IMPLEMENT_SERIAL Macro

You need to add the IMPLEMENT_SERIAL macro to the implementation of your class. This macro needs to appear outside any other class functions because it adds the code for the class functions that were declared with the DECLARE_SERIAL macro.

The IMPLEMENT_SERIAL macro takes three arguments:

- The class name, as in the DECLARE_SERIAL macro.
- The name of the base class, from which your class is inherited.
- A version number you can use to determine whether a file is the correct version for reading into your application. The version number, which must be a positive number, should be incremented each time the class's serialization method is changed in any way that alters the data being written to or read from a file.

Listing 12.3 shows a typical usage of the IMPLEMENT_SERIAL macro.

LISTING 12.3   Including the IMPLEMENT_SERIAL Macro in the Class Implementation

```
#include "stdafx.h"
#include "MyClass.h"

IMPLEMENT_SERIAL (CMyClass, CObject, 1)

CMyClass::CMyClass()
{
}
```

LISTING 12.3   continued

```
CMyClass::~CMyClass()
{
}
```

Defining the `Serialize` Function

Along with the two macros, you need to include a `Serialize` function in your class. This function should be declared as a `void` function with a single argument of type `CArchive&` with the name `ar`, public access, and the virtual check box selected—producing the function declaration in Listing 12.2. When you implement `Serialize` for your class, you typically use the same approach as that used in the document class in Listing 12.1, where you check to determine whether the file is being written to or read from.

MFC Note: The `CFile` Class

The `CFile` class is the primary class that you will use to read and write files. It uses several descendent classes to read and write to specific types of files, some of which aren't files at all. Some, like `CSocketFile`, allow you to perform network communications by using the same functionality that you use to read and write to files on a disk drive. You don't have to use the `CArchive` class with the `CFile` class, reading and writing files through serialization (the main topic of today), but can work directly with the `CFile` class to read and write files in whatever format you need.

Opening and Closing Files

You have a couple of options for opening files. You can open the file when you create the `CFile` object, or after you create it. If you want to open the file when you create the `CFile` object, you need to declare a pointer to a `CFile` object, and then call the `CFile` constructor with the open information as follows:

```
CFile *pComFile = new CFile(strFile, CFile::modeRead);
```

If you will be serializing the file, then you'll want to declare an instance of the CFile object instead of using a pointer, as follows:

```
CFile fComFile(strFile, CFile::modeRead);
```

The first parameter that you pass to this version of the `CFile` constructor is the filename and path. The second parameter is the set of flags that control how the file is opened. You can use more than one flag, `OR`'d together. Table 12.1 lists the possible flag settings for this parameter.

12

TABLE **12.1**   CFile Open Mode Flags

Flag	Description
CFile::modeCreate	Creates a new file. If the file already exists, it's erased (more commonly called *truncated*).
CFile::modeNoTruncate	Specifies that if the file already exists, it shouldn't be erased. Normally used with the CFile::modeCreate flag.
CFile::modeRead	Causes the file to be opened for reading only.
CFile::modeReadWrite	Causes the file to be opened for both reading and writing.
CFile::modeWrite	Causes the file to be opened for writing only.
CFile::modeNoInherit	Prevents the file from being inherited by child processes.
CFile::shareDenyNone	Allows other processes to open the file while you have it open.
CFile::shareDenyWrite	Prevents other processes from opening the file in writing mode (other processes can still open the file in reading mode).
CFile::shareDenyRead	Prevents other processes from opening the file in reading mode (other processes can still open the file in writing mode).
CFile::shareExclusive	Prevents other processes from opening the file while you have the file open.
CFile::typeText	Specifies that the file be opened in "text" mode, meaning that you can't read or write binary data to or from the file. Not used in the CFile class, but is used in derived classes.
CFile::typeBinary	Specifies that the file be opened in "binary" mode, meaning that you can read or write binary data to or from the file. Not used in the CFile class, but is used in derived classes.
CFile::osNoBuffer	Specifies that the file be opened without any buffering or cache.
CFile::osWriteThrough	Specifies that the system write directly to the disk, bypassing any cache.
CFile::osRandomAccess	Specifies that the file will be accessed randomly. This is a signal to the OS that any cache should be optimized for random file access.
CFile::osSequentialScan	Specifies that the file will be accessed sequentially from beginning to end. This is a signal to the OS that any cache should be optimized for sequential file access.

If a problem occurs in opening the file with this method of opening it, a CFileException type exception is thrown. Therefore, you always want to enclose this method of opening a file within a try...catch framework:

```
CFile *pComFile;
try
{
```

```
    pComFile = new CFile(strFile, CFile::modeRead);
...
}
catch (CFileException *e)
{
...
    e->Delete();
}
```

or

```
try
{
    CFile fComFile(strFile, CFile::modeRead);
...
}
catch (CFileException *e)
{
...
    e->Delete();
}
```

The other method for opening files is to use the Open method, which has the following syntax:

```
BOOL Open(LPCTSTR strFile, UINT iOpenFlags, CFileException* pErr);
```

The first two parameters, *strFile* and *iOpenFlags*, are the same as with the first method of opening the file. The third parameter, *pErr*, is a pointer to a CFileException instance that will receive any error that occurs while attempting to open the file. This approach varies from the first method, as with this method of opening the file, you don't have to use try...catch exception handling to catch any errors that occur. Instead, you need to check the return value to see if the file was opened successfully, and if not, check the exception object that you passed to the Open function to determine what the problem might have been.

12

When you are ready to close the file, use the Close function. Close has no parameters and doesn't return a result, but can throw a CFileException exception if any problems occur with closing the file. For those occasions where you need to close the file, regardless of the situation and conditions, ignoring any possible exception conditions, you can use the Abort method. Abort also doesn't take any parameters and doesn't return a result, but doesn't—under any circumstances—raise any exceptions.

Reading From and Writing To Files

When you need to read and write to and from open files, you can use the Read and Write functions. The Read function has the following syntax:

```
UINT Read(void* lpBuf, UINT iCount);
```

The first parameter, *lpBuf*, is a pointer to a buffer into which you want to read the file. The second parameter, *iCount*, is the size of the buffer. The Read function returns the number of bytes read into the buffer. A common way of using this function is as follows:

```
char buf[100];
int iRead;

iRead = file.Read(buf, 100);
```

If any problems are encountered while reading from the file, such as the end of the file is reached, a CFileException will be thrown. Because of this, you need to enclose the Read function within a try...catch structure.

When you need to write data to a file, use the Write function, which is basically the same as the Read function. The syntax for Write is as follows:

```
void Write(const void* lpBuf, UINT iCount);
```

The primary difference between Read and Write is that Write doesn't return the number of bytes written. The first parameter is a pointer to a buffer that contains the data to be written, and the second parameter specifies how much data in the buffer should be written. If there are any problems writing all the data to the file, a CFileException is thrown.

Navigating Around Files

From time to time, depending on how your application works with files, you may need to navigate around in the file. This is common with files that have a header section which describes the file with information like how many records are in the file, or other information about what's in the file. Also, sometimes you need to read and write specific values from the file. In these situations, you don't read or write the file from the beginning to the end. Instead, you read some data at one position in the file, go to another point in the file and read some more information, and then go to yet another position to write some data. This is how databases typically work, with the database program navigating around in a very large file to read specific records and values from the file.

The first functions that you'll need to use for this type of functionality will provide you with information that you'll need. The first information that you'll need is the size of the file. You can get this with the GetLength function, which returns the size, in bytes, of the file that you have open. The next function, GetPosition, returns your current position within the file. The position returned is in bytes from the beginning of the file.

There are three functions for navigating around within the file: Seek, SeekToBegin, and SeekToEnd. The Seek function takes two parameters, as follows:

```
long Seek(long lOff, UINT iFrom);
```

The first parameter, *lOff*, is the number of bytes to move, either in a positive or negative direction (negative values will move close to the beginning of the file, while positive values will move towards the end of the file). The second parameter, *iFrom*, is the location in the file to use as the starting point for the move. Table 12.2 lists the possible values for this parameter.

TABLE 12.2 CFile Seek Starting Position Values

Value	Description
CFile::begin	Moves the specified number of bytes from the beginning of the file. The first parameter must be a positive value with this starting position.
CFile::current	Moves the specified number of bytes from the current position within the file.
CFile::end	Moves the specified number of bytes from the end of the file. The first parameter must be negative to seek within the file with this starting position. If the value is positive, you will move past the end of the file.

The return value from the Seek function is the current position in the file.

The other two functions, SeekToBegin and SeekToEnd, move the current position within the file to the file's beginning or end, respectively. These functions take no parameters. SeekToBegin positions you at the beginning of the file and doesn't return any result value. SeekToEnd positions you at the end of the file and returns the total length of the file as it's return value.

Any functions used for navigating within the file, as well as getting information about the file size and position in the file, may throw a CFileException if an error occurs. As a result, it's advisable to enclose all file navigation within a try...catch structure.

Managing Files

If you need to manage files with your application, a couple of functions can help perform basic operations. These functions are static, and aren't used with an active instance of the CFile class, but are used independently.

If you need to rename a file, you can use the Rename function, as follows:

```
CString strOldName, strNewName;

CFile::Rename(strOldName, strNewName);
```

The first parameter to the Rename function is the file's current name. The second parameter is the new name for the file. This function doesn't return a result, but if it encounters a problem, it will throw a CFileException exception. This function doesn't work on directories; it works only on files.

12

If you need to delete a file, call the Remove function, as follows:

```
CString strName;
```

```
CFile::Remove(strName);
```

The only parameter the Remove function takes is the name of the file to be deleted. Like the Rename function, the Remove function doesn't return a result, but will throw a CFileException exception if a problem is encountered.

MFC Note: The CFileException Class

If an exception occurs while working with the CFile class, a CFileException exception is thrown. Most functionality that you want to use is actually part of the ancestor CException class, but a couple of functions specific to the CFileException class might be of interest.

CException Functions

You will likely use three member functions of the CException ancestor object in most exception situations. The first of these functions is the GetErrorMessage function, the syntax for which is as follows:

```
BOOL GetErrorMessage(LPTSTR pstrError, UINT iMaxErr);
```

The first parameter, pstrError, is a pointer to a character array that will receive the error message. The second parameter, iMaxErr, is the size of the character array. The way that you would use this is as follows:

```
CFile *pComFile;
try
{
    pComFile = new CFile(strFile, CFile::modeRead);
...
}
catch (CFileException *e)
{
    char pMsg[255];

    if (e->GetErrorMessage(pMsg, 255))
        AfxMessageBox(pMsg);
...
    e->Delete();
}
```

The ReportError function provides the functionality of the GetErrorMessage and AfxMessageBox functions in a single function. The syntax for the ReportError function is as follows:

```
int ReportError(UINT iType, UINT iMsgID);
```

Both parameters for this function are completely optional. The first parameter, *iType*, is the message box type flags for how to display the message box that's shown to the user. The second parameter, *iMsgID*, is the resource ID of a string in the string table to use as a default message if the exception that occurred doesn't have it's own error message. The return value from this function is the same as the return value from the `MessageBox` or `AfxMessageBox` functions, the ID of the selected button.

The last function for the `CException` ancestor object is `Delete`, which should always be called to delete any exception object after you are finished with it. The `Delete` function doesn't take any parameters, and performs the appropriate clean-up of the exception object, where using the `delete` operator may not perform the appropriate clean-up, depending on how the object was created.

CFileException Members

With the `CFileException` object, you can access a couple of class members to determine what problem occurred. The first of these members is m_cause. You can compare this value to several constants to determine what the problem is, and what action needs to be taken as a result of the exception. Table 12.3 lists the possible values for the m_cause variable.

TABLE 12.3 CFileException Cause Values

Value	Description
CFileException::none	There was no error.
CFileException::generic	An unspecified error occurred.
CFileException::fileNotFound	The file couldn't be found.
CFileException::badPath	The path specified for the file isn't valid.
CFileException::tooManyOpenFiles	Too many files are open.
CFileException::accessDenied	The file couldn't be accessed.
CFileException::invalidFile	The file handle used isn't valid. This usually occurs when you try to read or write to a file that wasn't successfully opened.
CFileException::removeCurrentDir	The current directory can't be removed.
CFileException::directoryFull	The directory is full.
CFileException::badSeek	An error occurred while trying to set the file pointer position.
CFileException::hardIO	There was a hardware problem.

12

TABLE 12.3 continued

Value	Description
CFileException::sharingViolation	There was a sharing problem with the file.
CFileException::lockViolation	An attempt was made to lock an already locked region.
CFileException::diskFull	The disk is full.
CFileException::endOfFile	The end of the file was reached.

Another member of the CFileException class that might be of interest is m_strFileName, which contains the filename in which the exception occurred.

MFC Note: The CArchive Class

If you want to automate a lot of the reading and writing of objects to a file and don't need a specific data format in the file, it's often more efficient to use the CArchive class to perform the reading and writing. You've already used CArchive to read and write data files in SDI and MDI applications, but in these instances, the MFC framework provided all the creation and management functionality for you. All you had to really provide was the serialization functionality in each class that would be stored in the file.

Creating and Closing a CArchive Instance

The key for working with a CArchive object is how the object is created. You must have already opened a file using the CFile class before creating your instance of the CArchive class. The syntax for creating a CArchive object is as follows:

```
CArchive(CFile* pFile, UINT iMode, int iBufSize, void* pBuf);
```

The first parameter, *pFile*, is a pointer to the CFile object for the file to be read or written. The second parameter, *iMode*, specifies whether the CArchive object will be used for reading from or writing to the open file. Table 12.4 lists the possible values for this flag.

TABLE 12.4 CArchive Mode Values

Mode	Description
CArchive::load	Reads data from the file.
CArchive::store	Writes data to the file.

TABLE 12.4   continued

CArchive::bNoFlushOnDelete	Use this flag with care. It prevents the CArchive object from automatically flushing all pending data writes to the disk before destroying the CArchive object. If you use this flag, you have to provide the code to make sure that all data is flushed to the disk before destroying the CArchive object.

The third parameter, *iBufSize*, specifies the size of the data buffer to use. The default value for this parameter is 4096. You only need to provide this parameter if you need a different buffer size. (If you are reading and writing very large files, this is one instance where you might want to use a larger buffer, for efficiency purposes). The final parameter, *pBuf*, also optional, is a pointer to a buffer if you want or need to supply your own buffer for use in reading and writing by the CArchive object.

When you need to close a CArchive object, you can use the Close method. Both the Close and constructor functions can throw either a CFileException or CArchiveException exception. The constructor might also throw a CMemoryException (out-of-memory) exception. If you need to close a CArchive, ignoring any possible exceptions, you can use the Abort function.

Reading and Writing

You've already used the IsStoring function to determine whether the file is being read from or written to. You've also written and read from the file using I/O Streams (although you may not have realized that you were doing it) with the >> and << operators. There is also the IsLoading function, which is the opposite from the IsStoring function, and gives you the same information. The CArchive class also has Read and Write functions that are basically the same as the ones in the CFile class. What the CArchive class does have that you might want to take advantage of are the ReadString and WriteString functions.

The WriteString function writes a single line of text to the file. The syntax for this function is as follows:

```
void WriteString(LPCTSTR strText);
```

If an error occurs, it throws a CFileException exception. The ReadString function reads a single line of text, as follows:

```
BOOL ReadString(CString& strText);
```

12

This function reads a line of text from the file and places it into the CString variable that was passed as the parameter to the function. If an error occurs, it throws a CArchiveException exception.

MFC Note: The CArchiveException Class

The CArchiveException class provides the m_cause member variable, just like the CFileException class. It also provides all the ancestor CException functionality. Table 12.5 lists the possible values of the m_cause variable.

TABLE 12.5 CArchiveException Cause Values

Value	Description
CArchiveException::none	No error occurred.
CArchiveException::generic	An unspecified error occurred.
CArchiveException::readOnly	An attempt was made to write to an archive that was opened for loading.
CArchiveException::endOfFile	The end of the file was reached.
CArchiveException::writeOnly	An attempt was made to read from an archive that was opened for writing.
CArchiveException::badIndex	The file has an invalid format.
CArchiveException::badClass	An attempt was made to read an object into the wrong class.
CArchiveException::badSchema	An attempt was made to read an object with a different version number.

C++ Sidebar: I/O Streams

In Day 4, "Integrating Mouse and Keyboard to Allow User Interaction," you learned how you can use the >> and << operators to shift bits to the left and right. In the last few days, you've used these operators to read and write variables to files through the CArchive class.

This second use of these operators was introduced with I/O streams when the C++ programming language was first invented. At that time, most C++ applications were for a command-line interface, without any GUI aspects to deal with. The idea was to simplify input and output greatly over what had been necessary with the C programming language. With C++, you could write messages to the screen with the << operator by placing the standard out (stdout, also known as the terminal screen) to the left of the operator, and the variable that you wanted to print on screen to the right of the operator. You could even string multiple variables together by placing a series of the << operator between the variables. As long as the output destination was on the left end of the line, everything was fine.

The opposite was done to read user input from the keyboard. The >> operator was used with the input source, usually standard in (stdin, also known as the keyboard), on the left of the operator, and the variable to take the input on the right. As long as whatever users entered made sense for the variable type into which it was being placed, everything worked fine.

Since the three primary input/output sources and destinations—stdin, stdout, and standard-error (stderr)—are just special case file handles, this same use of the << and >> operators was also available for reading and writing to files. In fact, most means of reading or writing to and from any other device—whether it be a file, a network connection to a program on another computer, or writing to a device like a printer—can often be performed by using these operators. There are constraints around when and where these operators can be used in this way, as the objects with which you are trying to use these operators do need to understand them and be able to accept input and produce output using them.

Implementing a Serializable Class

When you begin designing a new application, one of the first things you need to design is a method to store the data in the document class on which your application will create and operate. If you are creating a data-oriented application that collects sets of data from users, much like a contact database application, how will you hold that data in the application memory? What if you are building a word processor application—how will you hold the document being written in the application memory? Or a spreadsheet? Or a painting program? Or…you get the idea.

Once you determine how you will design the data structures on which your application will operate, you can determine how best to serialize your application and classes. If you hold all data directly in the document class, all you need to worry about is writing the data to and reading the data from the CArchive object in the document's Serialize function. If you create your own class to hold your application data, you need to add the serialization functionality to your data classes so that they can save and restore themselves.

In the application that you build today, you will create a simple, flat-file database application that illustrates how you can combine data types into a single data stream in the

12

application serialization. Your application will display a few fields of data, some of which are variable-length strings, and others that are integer or Boolean, and will save and restore them in a single data stream to and from the CArchive object.

Creating a Serialized Application

You can create your own classes, which can also be serialized, for use in an SDI or MDI application. In short, any application that works with any sort of data, whether a database or a document, can be serialized.

 Note

A *flat-file database* is one of the original types of databases. It's a simple file-based database, with the records sequentially appended to the end of the previous record. It has none of the fancy relational functionality that's standard in most databases today. The database that you will build today is closer to an old dBASE or Paradox database, without any indexes, than to databases such as Access or SQL Server.

Creating the Application Shell

To get your application started, follow these steps:

1. Create a new MFC Application Visual C++ project. Name the project **Serialize**.

2. In the Application Type area, select Single Document for the application type.

3. In the Document Template Strings area, enter a three-letter file extension for the files that your application will generate (for example, ser for serialize or fdb for flat-file database).

4. In the Generated Classes area, specify the base class as CFormView (see Figure 12.2) and click Finish. The MFC Application Wizard will generate the application shell.

   When you specify the CFormView as your base class for the view class, you will be presented with the informational dialog in Figure 12.3. This message informs you that the shell created won't have support for printing already built into the application. If you need to provide printing capability, you'll have to add it yourself.

5. After you finish making your way through the Application Wizard, open the IDD_SERIALIZE_FORM dialog. You will see a large window canvas in the dialog designer as though you had created a dialog-style application, only without the OK and Cancel buttons (see Figure 12.4).

FIGURE 12.2

Specifying the view class to use.

FIGURE 12.2

Specifying the view class to use.

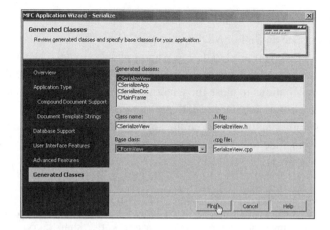

FIGURE 12.3

The Application Wizard informing you that the application shell won't have support for printing.

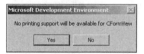

FIGURE 12.4

The window designer for an SDI application.

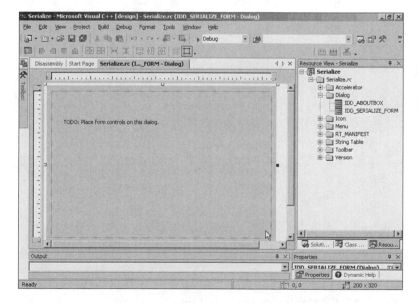

12

Designing Your Application Window

After you create an SDI or MDI application where the view class is based on the `CFormView` class, you need to design your application view. Designing the view is much like designing the window layout for a dialog window, but you don't need to worry about including any buttons to close the window while either saving or canceling the work done by users. With an SDI or MDI application, the functionality to save and exit the window is traditionally located on the application menus or on the toolbar. As a result, you need to include only the controls for the function that your application window will perform.

Note

If you are building dialog-style applications, the AppWizard doesn't provide any serialization code in your application shell. If you need to serialize a dialog-style application, you need to add all this code yourself.

For the sample application that you are building today, lay out controls on the window canvas (see Figure 12.5), using the control properties listed in Table 12.6.

FIGURE 12.5

The sample application window layout.

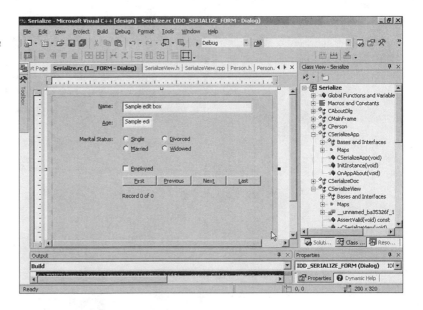

TABLE 12.6　Control Property Settings

Object	Property	Setting
Static Text	Caption	&Name:
Edit Control	ID	IDC_ENAME

TABLE 12.6 continued

Object	Property	Setting
Static Text	Caption	&Age
Edit Control	ID	IDC_EAGE
Static Text	Caption	Marital Status:
Radio Button	ID	IDC_RSINGLE
	Caption	&Single
	Group	True
Radio Button	ID	IDC_RMARRIED
	Caption	&Married
Radio Button	ID	IDC_RDIVORCED
	Caption	&Divorced
Radio Button	ID	IDC_RWIDOW
	Caption	&Widowed
Check Box	ID	IDC_CBEMPLOYED
	Caption	Empl&oyed
Button	ID	IDC_BFIRST
	Caption	F&irst
Button	ID	IDC_BPREV
	Caption	&Previous
Button	ID	IDC_BNEXT
	Caption	Nex&t
Button	ID	IDC_BLAST
	Caption	&Last
Static Text	ID	IDC_SPOSITION
	Caption	Record 0 of 0

12

When you were developing dialog-style applications or windows, you attached variables to the controls on the window in the dialog class. However, with an SDI or MDI application, which class do you create the variables in? Because the UpdateData function is a member of the CWnd class, and the view class is descended from the CWnd class, although the document isn't, the view class is the most logical place to add the variables that you will attach to the controls you placed on the window.

To attach variables to the controls in your sample application, follow these steps:

1. Select a control, right-click it, and select Add Variable from the context menu.
2. Add the variables in Table 12.7 to the controls specified.

TABLE 12.7 Control Variables

Object	Name	Category	Type	Access
IDC_ENAME	m_sName	Value	CString	public
IDC_EAGE	m_iAge	Value	int	public
IDC_RSINGLE	m_iMaritalStatus	Value	int	public
IDC_CBEMPLOYED	m_bEmployed	Value	BOOL	public
IDC_SPOSITION	m_sPosition	Value	CString	public

If you examine the source code for the view class, notice that there's no OnDraw function. If you are using the CFormView ancestor class for your SDI or MDI application, you don't need to worry about the OnDraw function. Instead, you treat the view class very much as you would the dialog class in a dialog window or dialog-style application. The primary difference is that the data that you need to use to populate the controls on the window aren't in the view class, but in the document class. As a result, you need to build the interaction between these two classes to pass the data for the controls back and forth.

Creating a Serializable Class

When you create a form-based application, it's assumed that your application will hold multiple records in the form and that the user will be able to scroll through the records to make changes. Users will be able to add additional records or even remove records from the record set. The challenge at this point in building this application is how you represent this set of records, supporting all the necessary functionality.

One approach is to create a class that would encapsulate each record, and then hold these records in an array, much as you did with the drawing application that you created and enhanced over the past few days. This class would need to descend from the CObject class and would need to contain variables for all the control variables that you added to the view class, along with methods to read and write all these variables. Along with adding the methods to set and read all the variables, you need to make the class serializable by adding the Serialize function to the class, as well as the two macros that complete the serialization of the class.

Creating the Basic Class

As you may remember from Day 10, "Creating SDI and MDI Applications," when you want to create a new class, you can select the project in the Class View pane, right-click, and select Add, Add Class from the context menu.

In the Add Class dialog, you specify the type of class, whether it's an MFC class, a generic class, or other. To create a class that can contain one record's data, you most likely want to create a generic class. The other things that you need to do are give your class a name and specify the base class from which it will be inherited.

For your sample application, follow these steps:

1. Create a new class by right-clicking the project node in the Class View of the workspace pane and selecting Add, Add Class from the context menu.
2. Select Generic C++ Class for the class type. Click Open to open the Generic C++ Class Wizard.
3. Call your class CPerson. Specify CObject as the base class.
4. Click Finish to create the class.

After you create your new class, you need to add the variables for holding the data elements that will be displayed onscreen. Following good object-oriented design, these variables will all be declared as private variables, where they can't be directly manipulated by other classes. The variable types should match the types of the variables attached to the window controls in the view class.

With the sample application you are creating, continue with these steps:

1. Right-click the CPerson class node in the Class View of the workspace pane. Select Add, Add Variable from the context menu to add a new variable.
2. Add the variables in Table 12.8.

TABLE 12.8 Class Variables for the CPerson Class

Name	Type
m_bEmployed	BOOL
m_iAge	int
m_strName	CString
m_iMaritalStatus	int

12

Adding Methods for Reading and Writing Variables

After you create your class, you need to provide a means for reading and writing to the variables in the class. One of the easiest ways to provide this functionality is to add inline functions to the class definition. You create a set of inline functions to set each of the variables and then make another set for retrieving the current value of each variable.

> **Note**
>
> An *inline function* is a short C++ function in which, when the application is being compiled, the function body is copied in place of the function call. As a result, when the compiled application is running, the function code is

executed without having to make a context jump to the function and then jump back after the function completes. This reduces the overhead in the running application, increasing the execution speed slightly, but also makes the resulting executable application slightly larger. The more places the inline function is called, the larger the application will eventually get.

There are two ways to create inline functions. One, the entire function definition must be included in the class declaration itself. The other is through use of the `inline` keyword. If, when building release versions of your application, you have specified to optimize your application for size, some or all of your inline functions may be changed to regular functions.

To implement the Get and Set variable functions for your CPerson class in the sample application that you are building, follow these steps:

1. Edit the Person.h header file, adding the boldfaced lines in Listing 12.4.

LISTING 12.4   The Get and Set Inline Function Declarations

```
class CPerson :
    public CObject
{
public:
        // Functions for setting the variables
        void SetEmployed(BOOL bEmployed) { m_bEmployed = bEmployed;}
    void SetMaritalStatus(int iStat) { m_iMaritalStatus = iStat;}
    void SetAge(int iAge) { m_iAge = iAge;}
    void SetName(CString sName) {m_strName = sName;}
    // Functions for getting the current settings of the variables
    BOOL GetEmployed() { return m_bEmployed;}
    int GetMaritalStatus() { return m_iMaritalStatus;}
    int GetAge() { return m_iAge;}
    CString GetName() { return m_strName;}
    CPerson(void);
    ~CPerson(void);
private:
    // Is the person employed
    BOOL m_bEmployed;
    // The person's age
    int m_iAge;
    // The person's name
    CString m_strName;
    // The person's marital status
    int m_iMaritalStatus;
};
```

After you have the methods for setting and retrieving the values of the variables in your custom class, you'll probably want to make sure that the variables are initialized when the class is first created. The MFC Application Wizard does this for you in the class constructor by setting each variable to a default value, as in Listing 12.5.

LISTING 12.5   The CPerson Constructor

```
CPerson::CPerson(void)
: m_bEmployed(false)
, m_iAge(0)
, m_strName(_T(""))
, m_iMaritalStatus(0)
{
}
```

 Note
The automatic insertion of initialization code into the class constructor is new to the .NET version of Visual C++. If you are working with an earlier version of Visual C++, you'll need to add the initialization code yourself within the function itself by using C++ code to set the values of each variable. Also, not all variables you add to a class may be added to the automatic initialization in the class constructor. You need to check the constructor to see which variables have been added, and which still need adding to the constructor for initialization.

Serializing the Class

After you have your custom class with all variables defined and initialized, you need to make the class serializable. Making your class serializable involves three steps. The first step is adding the Serialize function to the class. This function writes the variable values to, and reads them back from, the CArchive object using C++ streams. The other two steps consist of adding the DECLARE_SERIAL and IMPLEMENT_SERIAL macros. After you add these elements, your custom class will be serializable and ready for your application.

To add the Serialize function to your custom class, follow these steps:

1. Add a member function through the Class View pane.

2. Specify the function type as void, the function name as Serialize, add one parameter of type CArchive& and named ar, specify the access as public, and check the Virtual check box.

3. Click the Finish button. This should add the Serialize function and place you in the editor, ready to flesh out the function code with Listing 12.6.

12

LISTING 12.6 The CPerson.Serialize Function

```
// The serialization function
void CPerson::Serialize(CArchive& ar)
{
    // Call the ancestor function
        CObject::Serialize(ar);

    // Are we writing?
    if (ar.IsStoring())
        // Write all of the variables, in order
        ar << m_strName << m_iAge << m_iMaritalStatus << m_bEmployed;
    else
        // Read all of the variables, in order
        ar >> m_strName >> m_iAge >> m_iMaritalStatus >> m_bEmployed;
}
```

Listing 12.6 first calls the ancestor's Serialize function. When you call the ancestor's function first, any saved foundation information is restored first, providing the necessary support for your class before the variables in your class are restored. Once you call the ancestor function, you need to determine whether you need to read or write the class variables. You can do this by calling CArchive's IsStoring method. This function returns TRUE if the archive is being written to and FALSE if it's being read from. If the IsStoring function returns TRUE, you can use C++ I/O streams to write all your class variables to the archive. If the function returns FALSE, you can use C++ streams to read from the archive. In both cases, you must be certain to put the variables in the same order for both reading and writing.

Once you have the Serialize function in place, you need to add the macros to your custom class. The first macro, DECLARE_SERIAL, needs to go in the class header and is passed the class name as its only argument.

To add the DECLARE_SERIAL macro to the custom CPerson class in your sample application, use these steps:

1. Open the Person.h header file.

2. Add the macro just below the start of the class declaration, where it will receive the default access for the class.

3. Specify the class name, CPerson, as the only argument to the macro (see Listing 12.7).

LISTING 12.7 The Serialized CPerson Class Declaration

```
class CPerson :
    public CObject
```

Listing 12.7 continued

```
    {
DECLARE_SERIAL (CPerson)
    public:
    // Functions for setting the variables
    void SetEmployed(BOOL bEmployed) { m_bEmployed = bEmployed;}
    void SetMaritalStatus(int iStat) { m_iMaritalStatus = iStat;}
    void SetAge(int iAge) { m_iAge = iAge;}
    void SetName(CString sName) {m_strName = sName;}
    // Functions for getting the current settings of the variables
    BOOL GetEmployed() { return m_bEmployed;}
    int GetMaritalStatus() { return m_iMaritalStatus;}
    int GetAge() { return m_iAge;}
    CString GetName() { return m_strName;}
    CPerson(void);
    ~CPerson(void);
private:
    // Is the person employed
    BOOL m_bEmployed;
    // The person's age
    int m_iAge;
    // The person's name
    CString m_strName;
    // The person's marital status
    int m_iMaritalStatus;
};
```

> **Note**
>
> The default access permission for functions and variables in C++ classes is private. All functions and variables declared before the first access declaration are private by default. You could easily add all the private class functions and variables in this area of the class declaration, but explicitly declaring the access permission for all functions and variables is better practice—that way, there's little to no confusion about the visibility of any class functions or variables.

> **Note**
>
> Most C++ functions need a semicolon at the end of the line of code. The two serialization macros don't, due to the C preprocessor, which replaces each macro with all the code before compiling the application. It doesn't hurt to place the semicolons there; they are simply ignored.

To complete the serialization of your custom class, you need to add the IMPLEMENT_SERIAL macro to the class definition. The best place to add this macro is before the constructor definition in the CPP file containing the class source code. This macro takes three

12

arguments: the custom class name, the base class name, and the version number. If you make any changes to the Serialize function, you should increment the version number argument to the IMPLEMENT_SERIAL macro. This version number indicates when a file was written using a previous version of the Serialize function and thus may not be readable by the current version of the application.

> **Note**
>
> In practice, if you read a file that was written using a previous version of the Serialize function in your class, your application will raise an exception, which you can then catch using standard C++ exception-handling techniques. This allows you to add code to your application to recognize and convert files created with earlier versions of your application.
>
> If you need to be able to read in multiple versions of your serialized class, so that you can read earlier versions, you can use the VERSIONABLE_SCHEMA constant OR'd with the current version number in the IMPLEMENT_SERIAL macro, as follows:
>
> ```
> IMPLEMENT_SERIAL(CMyObject, CObject, VERSIONABLE_SCHEMA | 1)
> ```
>
> Once you are in your Serialize function, you can call the CArchive class GetObjectSchema function to determine the class version, and can use the appropriate formats to read in the file, as follows:
>
> ```
> void CMyObject::Serialize(CArchive &ar)
> {
>     if (ar.IsLoading())
>     {
>         switch (ar.GetObjectSchema())
>         {
>         case 1:
>             // Read in version 1
>             break;
>         case 2:
>             // Read in version 2
>             break;
>         }
>     }
>     else
>         // Normal writing code
> }
> ```

To add the IMPLEMENT_SERIAL macro to your sample application, follow these steps:

1. Open the Person.cpp file and scroll to the top of the file.

2. Add the IMPLEMENT_SERIAL macro just before the CPerson class constructor.

3. Pass CPerson as the first argument (the class name), CObject as the second argument (the base class), and 1 as the version number, as in Listing 12.8.

LISTING 12.8   The IMPLEMENT_SERIAL Macro in the CPerson Code

```
#include "StdAfx.h"
#include "person.h"
```

INPUT   `IMPLEMENT_SERIAL (CPerson, CObject, 1)`

```
CPerson::CPerson(void)
: m_bEmployed(false)
, m_iAge(0)
, m_strName(_T(""))
, m_iMaritalStatus(0)
{
}
```

Building Support in the Document Class

When you build a form-based application, where the form on the window is the primary place for users to interact with the application, there is an unstated assumption that your application will allow users to work with a number of records. This means that you need to include support for holding and navigating these records. The support for holding the records can be as simple as adding an object array as a variable to the document class, as you did back on Day 10. This allows you to add record objects as needed. The navigation could be a number of functions for retrieving the first, last, next, or previous record objects. Finally, you need informational functionality so that you can determine what record in the set the user is currently editing.

To hold and support this functionality, the document class will probably need two variables, the object array and the current record number in the array. These two variables will provide the necessary support for holding and navigating the record set.

For your example, add to the CSerializeDoc class the following two variables, and specify private access for both.

Name	Type
m_iCurPosition	int
m_oaPeople	CObArray

To provide support in the document class for the record objects, you also need to make sure that the document knows about and understands the record object that it will be holding. You do this by including the custom class header file before the header file for the document class is included in the document class source code file. Because the document class needs to trigger actions in the view class, it's a good idea to also include the header file for the view class in the document class.

12

To include these header files in your sample application, follow these steps:

1. Open the source-code file for the document class, SerializeDoc.cpp, and add the `#include` statement as shown in Listing 12.9.

LISTING 12.9 Including the View Class in the Document Class Implementation

```
// SerializeDoc.cpp : implementation of the CSerializeDoc class
//

#include "stdafx.h"
#include "Serialize.h"

#include "SerializeDoc.h"
#include "SerializeView.h"

#ifdef _DEBUG
#define new DEBUG_NEW
#endif

// CSerializeDoc
```

INPUT

2. Open the header file for the document class, SerializeDoc.h, and add the `#include` statement as shown in Listing 12.10.

LISTING 12.10 Including the Custom Class in the Document Class Header

```
// SerializeDoc.h : interface of the CSerializeDoc class
//

#pragma once
#include "afxcoll.h"
#include "Person.h"

class CSerializeDoc : public CDocument
```

INPUT

Adding New Records

Before you can navigate the record set, you need to be able to add new records to the object array. If you add a private function for adding new records, you can add new records to the set dynamically as new records are needed. Because new records should present users with blank or empty data fields, you don't need to set any of the record variables when adding a new record to the object array, so you can use the default constructor.

Following the same logic that you used to add new line records on Day 10, you should add a new person record to the object array in your document class in today's sample application. Once you add a new record, you can return a pointer to the new record so that the view class can directly update the variables in the record object.

Once the new record is added, you will want to set the current record position marker to the new record in the array. This way, the current record number can easily be determined by checking the position counter.

If there are any problems in creating the new person record object, let users know that the application has run out of available memory and delete the allocated object, just as you did on Day 10.

To add this functionality to your sample application, follow these steps:

1. Add a new member function to the document class.

2. Specify the function type as a pointer to your custom class, CPerson*. Name the function AddNewRecord. This function needs no arguments. Specify the access for this function as private because it will only be accessed from other functions within the document class.

3. Click Finish to add the function. Edit the resulting function, adding the code in Listing 12.11.

LISTING 12.11 The CSerializeDoc.AddNewRecord Function

```
CPerson* CSerializeDoc::AddNewRecord(void)
{
    // Create a new CPerson object
        CPerson *pPerson = NULL;
    try
    {
        pPerson = new CPerson();
        // Add the new person to the object array
        m_oaPeople.Add(pPerson);
        // Mark the document as dirty
        SetModifiedFlag();
        // Set the new position mark
        m_iCurPosition = (m_oaPeople.GetSize() - 1);
    }
    // Did we run into a memory exception?
    catch (CMemoryException* perr)
    {
        // Display a message for the user, giving them the
        // bad news
        AfxMessageBox("Out of memory", MB_ICONSTOP | MB_OK);
        // Did we create a person object?
```

INPUT

12

LISTING 12.11 continued

```
        if (pPerson)
        {
            // Delete it
            delete pPerson;
            pPerson = NULL;
        }
        // Delete the exception object
        perr->Delete();
    }
    return pPerson;
}
```

Getting the Current Position

To aid users in navigating the record set, it's always helpful to provide a guide about where users are in the record set. To provide this information, you need to be able to get the current record number and the total number of records from the document to display for the user.

The functions to provide this information are both fairly simple. For the total number of records in the object array, all you need to do is get the size of the array and return that to the caller.

For your sample application, perform these steps:

1. Add a new member function to the document class.
2. Specify the function type as int, the function name as GetTotalRecords, and the access as public.
3. After you add the function, edit it using the code in Listing 12.12.

LISTING 12.12 The CSerializeDoc.GetTotalRecords Function

```
int CSerializeDoc::GetTotalRecords(void)
{
    // Return the array count
    return m_oaPeople.GetSize();
}
```

INPUT

Getting the current record number is almost just as simple. If you are maintaining a position counter in the document class, this variable contains the record number that the user is currently editing. As a result, all you need to do is return the value of this variable to the calling routine. Because the object array begins with position 0, you need to add 1 to the current position before returning to display for users.

To add this function to your sample application, follow these steps:

1. Add another new member function to the document class.

2. Specify the type as int, the function name as GetCurRecordNbr, and the access as public.

3. Edit the function using the code in Listing 12.13.

LISTING 12.13   The CSerializeDoc.GetCurRecordNbr Function

```
int CSerializeDoc::GetCurRecordNbr(void)
{
    // Return the current position
    return (m_iCurPosition + 1);
}
```

INPUT

Navigating the Record Set

To make your application really useful, you need to provide users with some way of navigating the record set. A base set of functionality for performing this navigation is a set of functions in the document class to get pointers to specific records in the record set. First is a function to get a pointer to the current record. Next are functions to get pointers to the first and last records in the set. Finally, you need functions to get the previous record in the set and the next record in the set. If users are already editing the last record in the set and attempt to move to the next record, you can automatically add a new record to the set and provide users with this new, blank record.

To add all this functionality, start with the function to return the current record. This function needs to check the value in the position marker to make sure that the current record is a valid array position. Once it has made sure that the current position is valid, the function can return a pointer to the current record in the array.

To add this function to your sample application, follow these steps:

1. Add a new member function to the document class.

2. Specify the function type as CPerson* (a pointer to the custom class), the function name as GetCurRecord, and the access as public.

3. Edit the function, adding the code in Listing 12.14.

LISTING 12.14   The CSerializeDoc.GetCurRecord Function

```
CPerson* CSerializeDoc::GetCurRecord(void)
{
```

12

LISTING **12.14** continued

```
INPUT    // Are we editing a valid record number?
             if (m_iCurPosition >= 0)
         // Yes, return the current record
         return (CPerson*)m_oaPeople.GetAt(m_iCurPosition);
     else
             // No, return NULL
             return NULL;
     }
```

The next function you might want to tackle returns the first record in the array. In this function, you need to first check to make sure that the array has records. If there are records in the array, set the current position marker to 0 and return a pointer to the first record in the array.

To add this function to your sample application, follow these steps:

1. Add a new member function to the document class.

2. Specify the function type as CPerson* (a pointer to the custom class), the function name as GetFirstRecord, and the access as public.

3. Edit the function, adding the code in Listing 12.15.

LISTING **12.15** The CSerializeDoc.GetFirstRecord Function

```
CPerson* CSerializeDoc::GetFirstRecord(void)
{
INPUT    // Are there any records in the array?
             if (m_oaPeople.GetSize() > 0)
     {
         // Yes, move to position 0
         m_iCurPosition = 0;
         // Return the record in position 0
         return (CPerson*)m_oaPeople.GetAt(0);
     }
     else
         // No records, return NULL
         return NULL;
 }
```

For the function to navigate to the next record in the set, you need to increment the current position marker and then check to see if you are past the end of the array. If you aren't past the end of the array, you need to return a pointer to the current record in the array. If you are past the end of the array, you need to add a new record to the end of the array.

To add this function to your sample application, follow these steps:

1. Add a new member function to the document class.

2. Specify the function type as `CPerson*` (a pointer to the custom class), the function name as `GetNextRecord`, and the access as public.

3. Edit the function, adding the code in Listing 12.16.

LISTING 12.16   The `CSerializeDoc.GetNextRecord` Function

```
CPerson*  CSerializeDoc::GetNextRecord(void)
{
    // After incrementing the position marker, are we
    //     past the end of the array?
    if (++m_iCurPosition < m_oaPeople.GetSize())
        // No, return the record at the new current position
        return (CPerson*)m_oaPeople.GetAt(m_iCurPosition);
    else
        // Yes, add a new record
        return AddNewRecord();
}
```

For the function to navigate to the previous record in the array, you need to make several checks. First, you need to verify that the array has records. If there are records in the array, you need to decrement the current position marker. If the marker is less than zero, you need to set the current position marker to equal zero, pointing at the first record in the array. After you make it through all of this, you can return a pointer to the current record in the array.

To add this function to your sample application, follow these steps:

1. Add a new member function to the document class.

2. Specify the function type as `CPerson*` (a pointer to the custom class), the function name as `GetPrevRecord`, and the access as public.

3. Edit the function, adding the code in Listing 12.17.

LISTING 12.17   The `CSerializeDoc.GetPrevRecord` Function

```
CPerson*  CSerializeDoc::GetPrevRecord(void)
{
    // Are there any records in the array?
    if (m_oaPeople.GetSize() > 0)
    {
        // Once we decrement the current position,
        // are we below position 0?
```

12

LISTING **12.17**   continued

```
        if (--m_iCurPosition < 0)
            // If so, set the record to position 0
            m_iCurPosition = 0;
        // Return the record at the new current position
        return (CPerson*)m_oaPeople.GetAt(m_iCurPosition);
    }
    else
        // No records, return NULL
        return NULL;
}
```

For the function that navigates to the last record in the array, you still need to check to make sure that there are records in the array. If the array does have records, you can get the current size of the array and set the current position marker to one less than the number of records in the array. This is actually the last record in the array because the first record in the array is record 0. After you set the current position marker, you can return a pointer to the last record in the array.

To add this function to your sample application, follow these steps:

1. Add a new member function to the document class.

2. Specify the function type as CPerson* (a pointer to the custom class), the function name as GetLastRecord, and the access as public.

3. Edit the function, adding the code in Listing 12.18.

LISTING **12.18**   The CSerializeDoc.GetLastRecord Function

```
CPerson*  CSerializeDoc::GetLastRecord(void)
{
    // Are there any records in the array?
        if (m_oaPeople.GetSize() > 0)
    {
        // Move to the last position in the array
        m_iCurPosition = m_oaPeople.GetUpperBound();
        // Return the record in this position
        return (CPerson*)m_oaPeople.GetAt(m_iCurPosition);
    }
    else
        // No records, return NULL
        return NULL;
}
```

INPUT

Serializing the Record Set

When filling in the `Serialize` functionality in the document class, there's little to do other than pass the `CArchive` object to the object array's `Serialize` function, just as you did on Day 10.

When reading data from the archive, the object array will query the `CArchive` object to determine what object type it needs to create and how many it needs to create. The object array will then create each object in the array and call its `Serialize` function, passing the `CArchive` object to each in turn. This enables the objects in the object array to read their own variable values from the `CArchive` object in the same order that they were written.

When writing data to the file archive, the object array will call each object's `Serialize` function in order, passing the `CArchive` object (just as when reading from the archive). This allows each object in the array to write its own variables into the archive as necessary.

For the sample application, edit the document class's `Serialize` function to pass the `CArchive` object to the object array's `Serialize` function, as in Listing 12.19.

LISTING 12.19   The `CSerializeDoc.Serialize` Function

```
void CSerializeDoc::Serialize(CArchive& ar)
{
    // Pass the serialization on to the object array
    m_oaPeople.Serialize(ar);
}
```

INPUT

12

Cleaning Up

Now you need to add the code to clean up the document as soon as the document is closed or a new document is opened. This consists of looping through all objects in the object array and deleting each and every one. After all the objects are deleted, the object array can be reset when you call its `RemoveAll` function.

To implement this functionality in your sample application, follow these steps:

1. Select the document class, `CSerializeDoc`, in the class view of the workspace pane, and select the Overrides mode of the properties pane.

2. Add an function override for the `DeleteContents` base function.

3. When editing the function, add the code in Listing 12.20.

LISTING 12.20   The CSerializeDoc.DeleteContents Function

```
void CSerializeDoc::DeleteContents()
{
    // TODO: Add your specialized code here and/or call the base class
    // Get the number of people in the object array
        int iCount = m_oaPeople.GetSize();
    int iPos;

    // Loop through the array, deleting each object
    for (iPos = 0; iPos < iCount; iPos++)
        delete (CPerson*)m_oaPeople.GetAt(iPos);
    // Reset the array
    m_oaPeople.RemoveAll();
    CDocument::DeleteContents();
}
```

INPUT

Opening a New Document

When a new document is started, you need to present users with an empty form, ready for new information. To make that empty record ready to accept new information, you need to add a new record into the object array, which is otherwise empty. This results in only one record in the object array. When the new record is added to the array, you must modify the view to show that a new record exists; otherwise, the view will continue to display the last record edited from the previous record set (and users will probably wonder why your application didn't start a new record set).

To implement this functionality, you need to edit the OnNewDocument function in your document class. This function is already in the document class, so you don't need to add it through the properties pane. You first add a new record to the object array. Then, you need to get a pointer to the view object. You use the GetFirstViewPosition function to get the position of the view object. Using the position returned for the view object, you can use the GetNextView function to retrieve a pointer to the view object. After you have a valid pointer, you can use it to call a function that you will create in the view class to tell the view to refresh the current record information being displayed in the form.

Note

When writing this code, keep in mind that you need to cast the pointer to the view as a pointer of the class of your view object. The GetNextView function returns a pointer of type CView, so you can't call any of your additions to the view class until you cast the pointer to your view class. Casting the pointer tells the compiler that the pointer is really a pointer to your view object class and thus does contain all the functions that you've added. If you don't cast the pointer, the compiler will assume that the view object doesn't contain any of the functions that you've added and won't allow you to compile your application.

To implement the functionality discussed above, follow these steps:

1. Locate the `OnNewDocument` function in the document class source code, and add the code in Listing 12.21.

> **Caution**
>
> Before you can compile your application, you need to add the `NewDataSet` function to the view class. If you try to compile the application after adding the code in Listing 12.21, you'll get an error message stating that the `NewDataSet` function is unknown. You'll be adding this function to the `View` class shortly.

LISTING 12.21   The `CSerializeDoc.OnNewDocument` Function

```
BOOL CSerializeDoc::OnNewDocument()
{
    if (!CDocument::OnNewDocument())
        return FALSE;

    // TODO: add reinitialization code here
    // (SDI documents will reuse this document)
    // If unable to add a new record, return FALSE
        if (!AddNewRecord())
        return FALSE;

    // Get a pointer to the view
    POSITION pos = GetFirstViewPosition();
    CSerializeView* pView = (CSerializeView*)GetNextView(pos);
    // Tell the view that it's got a new data set
    if (pView)
        pView->NewDataSet();

    return TRUE;
}
```

When opening an existing data set, you don't need to add any new records, but you still need to let the view object know that it needs to refresh the record being displayed for the user. As a result, you can add the same code to the `OnOpenDocument` function as you added to the `OnNewDocument`, only leaving out the first part where you added a new record to the object array.

2. Select the document class, `CSerializeDoc`, in the class view of the workspace pane, and select the Overrides mode of the properties pane.

3. Add an event-handler function for the `OnOpenDocument` event.

4. Once you add the function, edit it by adding the boldfaced code in Listing 12.22.

LISTING 12.22   The CSerializeDoc.OnOpenDocument Function

```
BOOL CSerializeDoc::OnOpenDocument(LPCTSTR lpszPathName)
{
    if (!CDocument::OnOpenDocument(lpszPathName))
        return FALSE;

    // TODO:  Add your specialized creation code here
    // Get a pointer to the view
        POSITION pos = GetFirstViewPosition();
    CSerializeView* pView = (CSerializeView*)GetNextView(pos);
    // Tell the view that it's got a new data set
    if (pView)
        pView->NewDataSet();

    return TRUE;
}
```

INPUT

Adding Navigating and Editing Support in the View Class

Now that you've added support for the record set to your document class, you need to add the functionality into the view class to navigate, display, and update the records. When you first designed your view class, you placed a number of controls on the window for viewing and editing the various data elements in each record. You also included controls for navigating the record set. Now you need to attach functionality to those controls to perform the record navigation and to update the record with any data changes the user makes.

Because of the amount of direct interaction that the form will have with the record object—reading variable values from the record and writing new values to the record—it makes sense that you want to add a record pointer to the view class as a private variable. For your example, follow these steps:

1. Add a new member variable to the CSerializeView class.

2. Specify the type as CPerson*, name it m_pCurPerson, and specify the access as private.

Displaying the Current Record

The first functionality that you will want to add to the view class is the functionality to display the current record. Because this functionality will be used in several different places within the view class, it makes the most sense to create a separate function to perform this duty. In this function, you get the current values of all the variables in the record object and place those values in the view class variables that are attached to the controls on the window. You also want to get the current record number and the total number of records in the set and display those for users to see their relative position within the record set.

In your sample application, follow these steps:

1. Add a new member function to the view class.

2. Specify the function type as void, name the function PopulateView, and specify the access as private.

3. Edit the function, adding the code shown in Listing 12.23.

LISTING 12.23   The CSerializeView.PopulateView Function

INPUT

```
void CSerializeView::PopulateView(void)
{
    // Get a pointer to the current document
        CSerializeDoc* pDoc = GetDocument();
    if (pDoc)
    {
        // Display the current record position in the set
        m_sPosition.Format("Record %d of %d", pDoc->GetCurRecordNbr(),
                pDoc->GetTotalRecords());
    }
    // Do we have a valid record object?
    if (m_pCurPerson)
    {
        // Yes, get all of the record values
        m_bEmployed = m_pCurPerson->GetEmployed();
        m_iAge = m_pCurPerson->GetAge();
        m_sName = m_pCurPerson->GetName();
        m_iMaritalStatus = m_pCurPerson->GetMaritalStatus();
    }
    // Update the display
    UpdateData(FALSE);
}
```

12

ANALYSIS   The function in Listing 12.23 gets a valid pointer to the document object. Then it formats the position text display with the current record number and the total number of records in the set, using the GetCurRecordNbr and GetTotalRecords functions added to the document class earlier. Next, if there's a valid pointer to a record object, all the view variables are set to the values of their respective fields in the record object. Once the values of all the view class variables are set, the function updates the window with the variable values.

Navigating the Record Set

If you added navigation buttons to your window when you were designing the form, adding navigation functionality is a simple matter of adding event-handler functions for each navigation button and calling the appropriate navigation function in the document. After the document navigates to the appropriate record in the set, you need to call the function in Listing 12.23 to display the current record. If the document navigation functions are returning pointers to the new current record object, you should capture that pointer before calling the function to display the current record.

To add this functionality to your sample application, follow these steps:

1. Add an event handler to the clicked event for the First button using the Class Wizard.

2. Edit the function as in Listing 12.24.

LISTING 12.24   The CSerializeView.OnBnClickedBfirst Function

```
void CSerializeView::OnBnClickedBfirst()
{
    // TODO: Add your control notification handler code here
    // Get a pointer to the current document
        CSerializeDoc* pDoc = GetDocument();
    if (pDoc)
    {
        // Get the first record from the document
        m_pCurPerson = pDoc->GetFirstRecord();
        if (m_pCurPerson)
        {
            // Display the current record
            PopulateView();
        }
    }
}
```

INPUT

The function in Listing 12.24 gets a valid pointer to the document object. It then calls the document object's GetFirstRecord function, capturing the returned object pointer in the view CPerson pointer variable. If it receives a valid pointer, the function calls the PopulateView function to display the record data.

ANALYSIS

For the Last button, use these steps:

1. Perform the same steps as for the First button, but call the document object's GetLastRecord function, as in Listing 12.25.

LISTING 12.25   The CSerializeView.OnBnClickedBlast Function

```
void CSerializeView::OnBnClickedBlast()
{
    // TODO: Add your control notification handler code here
```

LISTING 12.25 continued

```
INPUT    // Get a pointer to the current document
           CSerializeDoc* pDoc = GetDocument();
    if (pDoc)
    {
        // Get the first record from the document
        m_pCurPerson = pDoc->GetLastRecord();
        if (m_pCurPerson)
        {
            // Display the current record
            PopulateView();
        }
    }
}
```

2. For the Previous and Next buttons, repeat the same steps, but call the document object's GetPrevRecord and GetNextRecord functions.

This final step provides your application with all the navigation functionality necessary to move through the record set. Also, because calling the document's GetNextRecord on the last record in the set automatically adds a new record to the set, you also can add new records to the set as needed.

Saving Edits and Changes

When users enter changes to the data in the controls onscreen, these changes somehow need to make their way into the current record in the document. If you are maintaining a pointer in the view object to the current record object, you can call the record object's various set value functions, passing in the new value, to set the value in the record object.

To implement this in your sample application, follow these steps:

1. Add an event handler to the CLICKED event for the Employed check box using the Class Wizard.

2. Edit the function as in Listing 12.26.

3. Repeat these same steps for the other controls, calling the appropriate record object functions.

LISTING 12.26 The CSerializeView.OnBnClickedCbemployed Function

```
void CSerializeView::OnBnClickedCbemployed()
{
    // TODO: Add your control notification handler code here
    // Sync the data in the form with the variables
```

12

LISTING **12.26**   continued

```
             UpdateData(TRUE);
             // If we have a valid person object, pass the data changes to it
      if (m_pCurPerson)
          m_pCurPerson->SetEmployed(m_bEmployed);
    }
```

The function first calls the UpdateData to copy the values from the form to the view variables. It checks to make sure that it has a valid pointer to the current record
object, and then calls the appropriate Set function on the record object (in this
case, the SetEmployed function).

For the Name and Age edit boxes, the function uses an event handler on the EN_CHANGE
event and calls the SetName and SetAge functions. For the marital status radio buttons, it
uses an event handler for the BN_CLICKED event and calls the same event-handler function
for all four radio buttons. This function also calls the SetMaritalStat function in the
record object.

> **Note**
>
> In previous versions of Visual C++, you could use the Wizards to point multi-
> ple radio buttons, or other controls, to the same event handler function.
> However, it seems that Microsoft has changed this functionality for the new
> version. As a result, what you need to do to implement this functionality is
> add the event handler for the first radio button in the group, and then
> make copies of the message map entry, changing the control ID, as you did
> back on Day 9, "Incorporating Graphics, Drawings, and Bitmaps."

Displaying a New Record Set

The last functionality that you need to add is the function to reset the view whenever a
new record set is started or opened so that users don't continue to see the old record set.
You will call the event handler for the First button, forcing the view to display the first
record in the new set of records.

To implement this functionality in your sample application, follow these steps:

1. Add a new member function to the view class.

2. Specify the function type as void, the name as NewDataSet, and specify the access
   as public (so that it can be called from the document class).

3. In the function, add a call to the First button event handler, as in Listing 12.27.

LISTING 12.27 The CSerializeView.NewDataSet Function

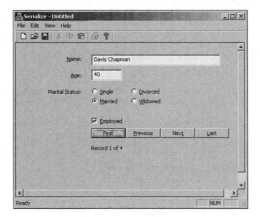

```
void CSerializeView::NewDataSet(void)
{
    // Display the first record in the set
    OnBnClickedBfirst();
}
```

INPUT

At this point, you can add, edit, save, and restore sets of records with your application. If you compile and run your application, you can create records of yourself and all your family members, your friends, and anyone else you want to include in this application. If you save the record set you create and then reopen the record set the next time that you run your sample application, you should find that the records are restored back to the state in which they were originally entered (see Figure 12.6).

FIGURE 12.6

The running serialization application.

Summary

Today, you learned quite a bit. You learned how serialization works and what it does. You learned how to make a custom class serializable and why and how to use the two macros that are necessary to serialize a class. You also learned how to design and build a form-based SDI application, maintaining a set of records in a flat-file database for use in the application. You learned how to use serialization to create and maintain the flat-file database and how to construct the functionality in the document and view classes to provide navigating and editing capabilities on these record sets.

12

Q&A

Q. **If I make any changes to one of the records in my record set after I save the record set and then close the application, or open a different set of records, my application doesn't ask if I want to save my changes. How do I get it to ask me? How do I get my application to prompt for saving when data has been changed?**

A. One function call in the `AddNewRecord` function in the document object is the key to this problem. After adding a new record to the object array, you call the `SetModifiedFlag` function. This function marks the document as "dirty." When you save the record set, the document is automatically set to a "clean" state (unless the application is unable to save the record set for any reason). What you need to do when saving the edits is set the document to the "dirty" state so that the application knows that the document has unsaved changes.

You can fix this by adding some code to each of your data control event handlers. Once you save the new value to the current record, get a pointer to the document object and call the document's `SetModifiedFlag` function, as in Listing 12.28. If you make this same addition to all the data change event handlers, your application will ask you whether to save the changes you made since the last time the record set was saved.

LISTING 12.28 The Modified `CSerializeView.OnCbemployed` Function

```
void CSerializeView::OnBnClickedCbemployed()
{
    // TODO: Add your control notification handler code here
    // Sync the data in the form with the variables
    UpdateData(TRUE);
    // If we have a valid person object, pass the data changes to it
    if (m_pCurPerson)
        m_pCurPerson->SetEmployed(m_bEmployed);
    // Get a pointer to the document
        CSerializeDoc * pDoc = GetDocument();
    if (pDoc)
        // Set the modified flag in the document
        pDoc->SetModifiedFlag();
}
```

INPUT

Q. **Why do I need to change the version number in the `IMPLEMENT_SERIAL` macro if I change the `Serialize` function in the record custom class?**

A. Whether you need to increment the version number depends on the type of change you make. For example, if you add a calculated field in the record class and you add the code to calculate this new variable from the values you read in the variables from the CArchive object, you don't really need to increment the version number because the variables and order of the variables that you are writing to and reading from the archive didn't change. However, if you add a new field to the record class and add the new field into the I/O stream being written to and read from the CArchive object, what you are writing to and reading from the archive will have changed, and you do need to increment the version number. If you don't increment the version number, reading files created using the previous version of your application will result in an Unexpected file format message instead of the file being read. Once you increment the version number and you read a file written with the old version number, you get the same message, but you have the option of writing your own code to handle the exception and redirecting the archive to a conversion routine to convert the file to the new file format.

Q. **How can I maintain the current position in the set of records from when I save the current set to when I restore it?**

A. You can modify the document class Serialize function to store and retrieve the current position variable before or after passing the CArchive object to the object array's Serialize function, as follows:

```
void CSerializeDoc::Serialize(CArchive& ar)
{
    // Are we writing?
    if (ar.IsStoring())
            ar << m_iCurPosition;
    else
            ar >> m_iCurPosition;

    // Pass the serialization on to the object array
    m_oaPeople.Serialize(ar);
}
```

You'll also need to modify the NewDataSet function in the view class to retrieve the current record instead of navigating to the first record.

Workshop

The Workshop provides quiz questions to help you solidify your understanding of the material covered and exercises to provide you with experience in using what you've learned. The answers to the quiz questions and exercises are provided in Appendix A, "Answers to Quiz Questions."

12

Quiz

1. What two macros do you have to add to a class to make it serializable?

2. How can you determine whether the CArchive object is reading from or writing to the archive file?

3. What arguments do you need to pass to the IMPLEMENT_SERIAL macro?

4. What class do you need to inherit the view class from to be able to use the dialog designer to create a form for the main window in an SDI or MDI application?

5. What type of file does the CArchive write to by default?

Exercise

Add a couple of radio buttons to the form to specify the person's sex, as shown in Figure 12.7. Incorporate this change into the CPerson class to make the field persistent.

FIGURE 12.7

The running serialization application with the person's sex.

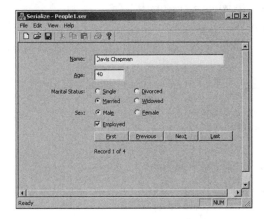

DAY 13

Updating and Adding Database Records Through ADO

Many applications use databases. Everything from personal organizers to large, corporate personnel systems use databases to store and maintain all records that the applications use and manipulate. Visual C++ provides you with four different technologies for using and accessing databases in your applications: Data Access Objects (DAO), ODBC (Open Database Connectivity), OLE DB (Object Linking and Embedding for Databases), and ActiveX Data Objects (ADO). Today, you'll learn about ADO—the latest Microsoft database access technology. Designed for use with all Microsoft programming and scripting technologies, ADO presents Visual C++ programmers with new challenges in database programming, while still keeping the functionality familiar. Today, you will learn

- How ADO works and how it uses the OLE DB technology for providing simple database access

- How to access and use the ADO objects to build a flexible database application
- How to use special ADO macros to build a custom recordset class for use in your database applications

Understanding Database Access

Most business applications work with data. They maintain, manipulate, and access records of data stored in databases. If you build business applications, odds are that you will need to access a database with your applications. The question is, which database?

A number of databases are on the market. If you need to create a single-user application that's self-contained on a single computer, you can use any of numerous PC-based databases, such as Microsoft Access, FoxPro, or Borland's Paradox. If you are building applications that need to access large, shared databases, you are probably using an SQL-based (Structured Query Language) database such as SQL Server or Oracle. All these databases provide the same basic functionality—maintaining records of data. Each allows you to retrieve several records or a single record, depending on your needs. They all let you add, update, or delete records as needed. Any of these databases can serve your application's needs, so you should be able to use any database for one application and then switch to another for the next application, based on the application's needs and which database is most suited for the specific application needs (or your employer's whim).

Note
Actually, numerous differences exist between the various databases available today. Each database has specific strengths and weaknesses, making one more suitable for a specific situation than another. However, a discussion of the differences between any of these databases is beyond the scope of this book. For the discussions of databases today and tomorrow, assume that all databases are functionally equal and interchangeable.

The problem that you will encounter when you switch from one database to another is that each database requires a different interface for accessing the database. This means you have to learn and use an entire new set of programming techniques and functions for each database that you need to work with. Interfaces such as ODBC and ADO were designed to correct this problem.

Understanding ADO

A few years ago, Microsoft designed a data access technology called OLE DB. This technology was intended as much more than just a way of getting data into and out of databases; it was intended to be the means of accessing data, regardless of where that data might be located. Through OLE DB, you could access mail messages, spreadsheets, files, and so on. Anything that might have data could possibly be accessed through OLE DB. This was one of the first technologies to be produced from the research and development of the object-oriented file system at the heart of Windows 2000, and now Windows XP.

As you can imagine, with the range of functionality that OLE DB must have to access data in all those different sources, working with it is complex. This is where ADO comes into play. ADO was designed as another layer on top of OLE DB, specifically for providing database access.

One goal in designing ADO was to create a control that could provide data access and control in Web pages, caching the data records on the client. Part of the reason for this goal was to allow Web browser users to access an entire set of data records, without having to pull down each record one at a time to navigate and change them. Because of this capability with ADO, the ADO control is distributed with Internet Explorer Web browser (version 4.0 and above).

ADO Objects

To make ADO as easy to use in scripting languages such as VBScript as it is in programming environments such as Visual Basic, Microsoft tried to keep the number of objects to a minimum. As a result, you have a small number of basic objects:

```
Connection              Parameter
Error                   Recordset
Command                 Field
```

Along with these objects, you have collection objects for containing collections of `Error`, `Parameter`, and `Field` objects.

The `Connection` Object

The `Connection` object is used to establish and maintain a connection to a database. This object is configured with the connection information, including database location, user ID, and password, before opening the connection. After all this information is appropriately configured, the connection object should have its `Open` method called to open the connection. When the `Connection` object goes out of scope, the connection is not automatically closed. You need to exercise control over closing the database connection by calling the `Connection` object's `Close` method to close the connection.

`Connection` is also the object through which any high-level connection functionality is controlled. This includes all transaction control through the object's `BeginTrans`, `CommitTrans`, and `RollbackTrans` methods.

13

Key `Connection` Object Properties

Many properties for the `Connection` object can be useful in working with databases. Table 13.1 lists some of the more useful ones.

Note

> In this and all following lists of properties and methods, ADO version 2.7 is being used. If you are working with an earlier version of ADO, all these properties and methods might not be available.

Note

> You don't access properties of COM objects, like all the ADO objects, as you would in Visual Basic. Each property has two possible syntaxes for accessing the property. For reading the value of the property, you add `Get` in front of the property name, and add an empty pair of parenthesis after the property name. For instance, if you wanted to read the value of a property named `Timeout`, you would read it as follows:
>
>   myVar = obj.GetTimeout();
>
> To set a property's value, add `Put` in front of the property name, and pass the new value as an argument to the property:
>
>   obj.PutTimeout(myVal);
>
> The reason for this is that, in C++, all object properties are actually functions.

TABLE 13.1   `Connection` Object Properties

Property	Description
CommandTimeout	The number of seconds that the ADO connection waits for any command to be executed. If your application will be executing SQL queries or *stored procedures* (SQL functions stored in the database) that could take a while to execute, you probably should tweak this value. The default is 30 seconds. If you set this property to 0, the ADO connection waits forever for all SQL commands and procedures to finish. Sometimes this is a good thing; other times, it's not.
ConnectionString	The string used to specify the database to connect to. It's similar to an ODBC connection string. The format of this string is a series of *argument=value* statements separated by semicolons, as in `Provider=MSDASQL.1;Data Source=STYVCDB`.

TABLE 13.1   continued

Property	Description
ConnectionTimeout	Like CommandTimeout, this property specifies the number of seconds to wait for the connection to the database to be established. If you are working with a database that's slow to respond, or is far away, you might need to adjust this property to allow more time for the connection to be made. The default value for this property is 15 seconds. If you set this property to 0, your application waits forever for the connection to be established.
CursorLocation	Specifies the location of the cursor (used for navigating through a set of records). This property has two possible settings: adUseClient and adUseServer. The cursor is located on either the client (your application) or the database server, depending on which setting you use. If you use a server side cursor, the cursor is implemented by the database, and uses the database cursor functionality. This prevents the use of OLE DB cursor service functionality, like disassociated Recordsets. However, using a server side cursor can enable you to see data changes made by other users and processes.
Mode	Specifies the mode in which you connect to the database. Table 13.2 lists the possible settings for this property. These settings normally only affect the mode in which you have specific records open in your recordsets. You can OR these mode settings together to specify your mode and the sharing mode.
State	Indicates the state of the connection to the database. Table 13.3 lists the possible values of this property.
Version	Specifies the ADO version number.

TABLE 13.2   Connection Mode Settings

Mode	Description
adModeRead	Read only
adModeReadWrite	Read and write permissions
adModeRecursive	Used with the "Share" modes to propagate permissions to any child records in the database
adModeShareDenyNone	Allows others to open the records in any mode
adModeShareDenyRead	Prevents others from opening the same records in read mode
adModeShareDenyWrite	Prevents others from opening the same records in write mode
adModeShareExclusive	Prevents others from opening the same records while you have them open

13

TABLE 13.2 continued

Mode	Description
adModeUnknown (default)	Indicates that the permissions are unknown and probably set by the database administrator
adModeWrite	Write-only permission

TABLE 13.3 Connection State Values

State	Description
adStateClosed	Database connection is closed.
adStateOpen	Database connection is open.
adStateConnecting	Database connection is being established.
adStateExecuting	Database is busy executing a command.
adStateFetching	Rows of data are being retrieved from the database.

Key Connection Methods

The Connection object has several useful methods, most of which don't require any parameters.

The Open method establishes the connection to the database. It takes parameters, as follows:

```
Open(_bstr_t ConnectionString, _bstr_t UserID, _bstr_t Password,
    long Options);
```

The first parameter for the Open method, ConnectionString, specifies the database to connect to. This parameter overrides the ConnectionString property. The second parameter, UserID, is the account name to use for connecting to the database. The third parameter, Password, is the database password for the account specified in the second parameter. (Although desktop databases such as Access often don't require user IDs and passwords for opening a connection, if you are working with a large SQL database, such as SQL Server or Oracle, you'll find that you almost always need to supply a user ID and password.) The final parameter, Options, specifies whether the database connection should be asynchronous or synchronous. (In other words, should this function return before the connection is established, or wait until the connection is either established or has timed out before returning?) The possible values for this last parameter are adAsyncConnect (to return right away) and adConnectUnspecified (the default setting, waits for the connection to be established before returning).

Note

So what's with this new data type, _bstr_t? Actually, it encapsulates the BSTR string type, which is the string data type. Most times, you can use a CString and cast it as an LPCTSTR data type when you need to provide a string to a COM method or property.

The other method that takes parameters is Execute. You can use the Execute method to execute any SQL command on the database. This can be a SQL query, DDL (Data-Definition Language used to build tables and indexes in the database) command, or a stored procedure. The syntax for the method is as follows:

```
_RecordsetPtr Execute(_bstr_t CommandText, VARIANT* RecordsAffected,
    long Options);
```

The first parameter for this method, CommandText, is the SQL command to be executed. The second parameter, RecordsAffected, is a pointer to a variant variable into which the number of records affected by the command are placed. The third parameter, Options, is a flag value specifying how the command should be interpreted and executed by the database. Table 13.4 lists the possible values. If the command produces a recordset, a pointer to a recordset is returned from this method.

TABLE 13.4 Execute Option Values

Option	Description
adCmdUnspecified	The command type is unspecified.
adCmdText	The command is evaluated as a textual definition of a command or stored procedure.
adCmdTable	The command is a table name where the entire table is to be returned.
adCmdStoredProc	The command is a stored procedure to be executed.
adCmdUnknown	The default value, the command type is unknown.
adCmdFile	The command is a filename of a stored recordset.
adAsyncExecute	The command should be executed asynchronously (the method won't wait for the command to be completed, but will return right away).
adAsyncFetch	The remaining rows after the initial quantity (limited by the CacheSize property) are retrieved asynchronously.
adExecuteNoRecords	The command doesn't return any rows of data. If it does return any data, the data is all discarded.
adExecuteRecord	The command returns only one row of data.
adOptionUnspecified	The command is unspecified.

13

The remaining methods for the `Connection` object don't take any parameters. They are listed in Table 13.5.

TABLE 13.5   Command Object Methods

Method	Description
Close	Closes the connection to the database.
Cancel	Cancels any asynchronous action currently executing, including connections, fetches, or command executions.
BeginTrans	Begins a transaction in the database.
CommitTrans	Commits a transaction, making all data changes permanent.
RollbackTrans	Rolls back a transaction, resetting all changed data to its values before beginning the transaction.

The `Error` Object

Whenever a database error occurs, the error information from the database is placed into an ADO `Error` object. The error information in the `Error` object is the database error information, not ADO error information. Whenever you encounter an error and need to look up the error information to determine what went wrong, you should examine the database error codes and descriptions, not the ADO error codes. Table 13.6 lists the properties of the `Error` object.

TABLE 13.6   Error Object Properties

Property	Description
Description	A string containing a description of the error.
NativeError	A long value giving a database provider specific error code. This value needs to be compared with the database vendor error codes to determine what can be done to correct the error.
Number	A long value specifying an ADO, OLE DB, or even OLE error.
Source	A string containing the name of the object or application that generated the error.
SQLState	A five-character string indicating the ANSI SQL standard for error codes. This code needs to be checked against the database documentation to determine what error occurred.

The `Command` Object

The `Command` object executes commands in the database. You can use it to run SQL statements or call stored procedures. Any time that a command returns rows of data, you need to attach the `Command` object to a `Recordset` object for the returned data to be stored in.

When you call a stored procedure, as with functions in any other programming language, you often need to pass parameters to the stored procedure. To pass these parameters, attach a series of `Parameter` objects to the `Command` object. Each `Parameter` object has the name of the parameter that it holds the value for, along with the value that should be passed to the database for that particular parameter.

Key `Command` Object Properties

Many properties for the `Command` object can be useful in working with databases. Table 13.7 lists some of the more useful ones.

TABLE 13.7   Command Object Properties

Property	Description
ActiveConnection	A pointer to the active `Connection` object to which this `Command` object is attached.
CommandText	A string containing the command to be executed by the database.
CommandTimeout	The number of seconds that the ADO connection waits for any command to be executed. If your application will be executing SQL queries or stored procedures that could take a while to execute, you probably should tweak this value. The default value is 30 seconds. If you set this property to 0, the ADO connection waits forever for all SQL commands and procedures to finish. Sometimes, this is a good thing; other times, it's not.
CommandType	The type of command being executed. Table 13.8 lists the possible values for this property.
State	The state of the connection to the database. Table 13.3, shown previously, lists the possible values of this property.

TABLE 13.8   Command Type Values

Option	Description
adCmdUnspecified	The command type is unspecified.
adCmdText	The command is evaluated as a textual definition of a command or stored procedure.
adCmdTable	The command is a table name where the entire table is to be returned.
adCmdStoredProc	The command is a stored procedure to be executed.
adCmdUnknown (default)	The command type is unknown.
adCmdFile	The command is a filename of a stored recordset.

13

Key Command Object Methods

Execute is the key method for the Command object. The syntax for this method is as follows:

```
_RecordsetPtr Execute(VARIANT* RecordsAffected, VARIANT* Parameters,
    long Options);
```

The first parameter to this function, RecordsAffected, is a VARIANT variable into which the number of records affected by the command is placed. The second parameter, Parameters, is an array of Parameter objects to be passed parameters to the command (if any are required). The third parameter, Options, specifies how the command should be executed. The possible values for this parameter are listed previously in Table 13.4.

Notice that no parameter exists for the command text. The actual command to be executed must already have been passed to the CommandText property before calling the Execute method.

You can use the CreateParameter method to create a parameter for passing with the Execute method. The syntax for this method is as follows:

```
_ParameterPtr CreateParameter(_bstr_t Name, DataTypeEnum Type,
    ParameterDirectionEnum Direction, long Size, _variant_t &Value);
```

The first parameter, Name, is the name for the parameter. The second parameter, Type, specifies the data type for the parameter. Table 13.9 lists the possible values for this parameter. The third parameter, Direction, specifies the parameter type. Table 13.10 lists the possible values for this parameter. The fourth parameter, Size, specifies the maximum length for the parameter value in either characters or bytes (depending on the data type). The final parameter, Value, is the actual value for the parameter object.

TABLE 13.9 Parameter Data Types

Data	Description
adBigInt	An 8-byte signed integer
adBinary	A binary value
adBoolean	A Boolean value
adBSTR	A null-terminated character string
adChar	A string value
adCurrency	A currency value (several databases have a currency data type)
adDate	A date value, stored as a double, indicating the number of days since December 30, 1899
adDBDate	A date value in the format *yyyymmdd*
adDBTime	A time value in the format *hhmmss*

TABLE 13.9   continued

Data	Description
adDBTimeStamp	A date-time stamp in the format *yyyymmddhhmmss*, plus a fraction indicating billionths of seconds
adDecimal	An exact numeric value with fixed precision and scale
adDouble	A double-precision floating-point value
adEmpty	No value
adError	A 32-bit error code
adFileTime	A 64-bit value specifying the number of 100-nanosecond intervals since January 1, 1601
adInteger	A 4-byte signed integer
adLongVarBinary	A long binary value (`Parameter` object only)
adLongVarChar	A long string value (`Parameter` object only)
adLongVarWChar	A long Unicode string value (`Parameter` object only)
adNumeric	An exact numeric value with fixed precision and scale
asSingle	A single-precision floating-point value
asSmallInt	A 2-byte signed integer
asTinyInt	A 1-byte signed integer
asUnsignedBigInt	An 8-byte unsigned integer
asUnsignedInt	A 4-byte unsigned integer
adUnsignedSmallInt	A 2-byte unsigned integer
adUnsignedTinyInt	A 1-byte unsigned integer
adUserDefined	A user-defined variable
adVarBinary	A binary value
adVarChar	A string value
adVarNumeric	A numeric value
adVarWChar	A Unicode string value
adWChar	A Unicode string value

13

TABLE 13.10   Parameter Types

Type	Description
adParamInput (default)	The parameter is an input parameter.
adParamInputOutput	The parameter is both an input and an output parameter.
adParamOutput	The parameter is an output parameter.

TABLE 13.10   continued

Type	Description
adParamReturnValue	The parameter represents the return value.
adParamUnknown	The type of parameter is unknown.

The final `Command` object method, `Cancel`, cancels any asynchronous action currently executing, including connections, fetches, or command executions.

The `Parameter` Object

The `Parameter` object passes variables for calling stored procedures or parameterized queries. These are attached to a `Command` object for use in calling the command programmed into the `Command` object. Table 13.11 lists the key properties for the `Parameter` object.

TABLE 13.11   Parameter Object Properties

Property	Description
Direction	Indicates whether the parameter is an Input, Output, or Return Value type of parameter. The possible values for this property are listed previously in Table 13.10.
Name	The name of the parameter object.
NumericScale	A byte value indicating the number of decimal places to which numeric values will be resolved.
Precision	A byte value indicating the number of digits used to represent numeric values.
Size	A long value indicating the maximum number of bytes or characters that can be used for the value of the `Parameter` object.
Type	The data type of the `Parameter` object. The possible values for this property are listed previously in Table 13.9.
Value	The actual value for the `Parameter` object.

The `Recordset` Object

The `Recordset` object contains a set of records from the database. The Recordset is the result of a command being sent to the database that results in a set of records being returned. You can navigate through the `Recordset`, much like you do with the `Recordset` objects for other database access technologies. You also can access the fields in each record in the Recordset through the `Field` objects that are associated with the Recordset.

You can update the records in the Recordset, and then use it to update the database. You also can insert new records into the Recordset, or delete records and have those changes made in the database.

Key `Recordset` Object Properties

Many properties for the `Recordset` object can be useful in working with databases. Table 13.12 lists some of the more useful ones.

TABLE 13.12 Recordset Object Properties

Property	Description
ActiveCommand	A pointer to the active `Command` object to which this `Recordset` object is attached.
ActiveConnection	A pointer to the active `Connection` object to which this `Recordset` object is attached.
BOF, EOF	Boolean values indicating whether the current position in the recordset is before the first record (`BOF`) or after the last record (`EOF`).
CursorType	The cursor type currently in use by the recordset. Table 13.13 lists the possible values that control how you can navigate and update the recordset.
EditMode	The editing status of the current record. The possible values are `adEditNone` (no edits have been made), `adEditInProgress` (data has been changed but not saved to the database), `adEditAdd` (the current record is a new record that hasn't been added to the database yet), and `adEditDelete` (the current record has been deleted).
Filter	A string value containing criteria used for filtering the records in the recordset.
LockType	The lock type being used when editing records in the recordset. Table 13.14 lists possible values for this property.
MaxRecords	The maximum number of records to be returned from a query to a recordset. This property limits the number of records that can be returned, regardless of how many records might match the SQL command criteria.
PageCount	The number of pages of data the recordset contains.
PageSize	The number of records that make up one page of data.
RecordCount	The number of records in a recordset.
Sort	A string value indicating one or more field names on which the recordset is sorted. The field names are followed by `ASC` for ascending order or `DESC` for descending order, and then separated by commas.
State	Indicates the state of the recordset. The possible values of this property are listed earlier in Table 13.3.

13

TABLE 13.13 Cursor Types

Type	Description
adOpenDynamic	Uses a dynamic cursor where additions, changes, and deletions by other users are visible, and all types of movement through the recordset is allowed.
adOpenForwardOnly	A read-only set of records that only can be scrolled from the first to the last record.
adOpenKeyset	Uses a keyset cursor. This is very similar to a dynamic cursor, except you can't see changes by other users.
adOpenStatic	A read-only set of records.
adOpenUnspecified	Doesn't specify the type of cursor in use.

TABLE 13.14 Lock Types

Type	Description
adLockBatchOptimistic	Indicates optimistic batch updates. Required for batch updates.
adLockOptimistic	Optimistic locking, in which individual records are locked when the Update method is called.
adLockPessimistic	Pessimistic locking, in which individual records are locked as soon as they are edited.
adLockReadOnly	Makes the data read-only so it can't be edited.
adLockUnspecified	No type of lock specified.

Key Recordset Object Methods

The largest amount of functionality is contained in the Recordset object because the primary reason you are working with a database is to work with the data stored in the database, and the Recordset object contains that data. Because of the amount of functionality contained in this object, it's easiest to break it down into different areas of functionality.

Opening and Closing Recordsets

Opening the recordset, can be accomplished through the Open method. The syntax for the Open method is as follows:

```
Open(_variant_t &Source, _variant_t &ActiveConnection,
    CursorTypeEnum CursorType, LockTypeEnum LockType, long Options);
```

The first parameter, Source, can be a Command object, SQL statement, table name, or stored procedure call. The second parameter, ActiveConnection, specifies the connection to the database to use. It can be either a Connection object or a connection string, specifying the database to connect to and retrieve the recordset from. The third parameter, CursorType, specifies the type of cursor to use. The possible values for this parameter are listed earlier in Table 13.13. The fourth parameter, LockType, specifies the locking scheme to use with the recordset. The possible values for this parameter are listed previously in Table 13.14. The final parameter, Options, specifies how the Source parameter should be evaluated by the database. The possible values for this parameter are listed earlier in Table 13.4.

After you are finished with a recordset, you can close it using the Close method. If you have any pending asynchronous operations, you can cancel them with the Cancel method. Neither method takes any parameters, and they don't return any result values.

Navigating Through Recordsets

When you have a set of records retrieved from the database, you need to navigate the set of records (unless the set has only one record). The Recordset object provides several functions for navigating the recordset, allowing you to move users to any record. Table 13.15 lists the functions that you use to navigate the recordset.

TABLE 13.15   Recordset Navigation Functions

Function	Description
MoveFirst	Moves to the first record in the set
MoveLast	Moves to the last record in the set
MoveNext	Moves to the next record in the set
MovePrevious	Moves to the previous record in the set
Move	Moves a specific number of records from the current record or from the first record in the set

Of all these navigation and informational functions, only one, Move, takes any arguments. The Move function takes two arguments:

- **The number of rows to move**—This number can be positive or negative; a negative number indicates a backward navigation through the recordset.

- **The starting location from where you will move through the set of rows**—This parameter can be either a bookmark or one of the defined bookmarks listed in Table 13.16.

13

TABLE 13.16 Move Starting Positions

Position	Description
adBookmarkCurrent	Moves the specified number of rows from the current row
adBookmarkFirst	Moves the specified number of rows from the first row
adBookmarkLast	Moves the specified number of rows from the last row

Updating Recordsets

Navigating a set of records from a database is only part of what you need to be able to do. You also need to add new records to the recordset, edit and update existing records, and delete records. These actions are all possible through the various functions that the Recordset object provides. Table 13.17 lists the functions you will use to provide this functionality to users.

TABLE 13.17 Recordset Editing Functions

Function	Description
AddNew	Adds a new record to the recordset. Takes two parameters: an array of field names and an array of values for the new record.
Delete	Deletes the current record from the recordset. Takes a single parameter to specify which records are affected by the delete operation; Table 13.18 lists the possible values.
Update	Saves the current changes to the database. Can take two optional parameters, an array of field names, and an array of values for the new record.
Requery	Reruns the current SQL query to refresh the recordset. Takes one parameter, which specifies how the requery is to be performed. The possible values for this parameter are listed previously in Table 13.4.

TABLE 13.18 Delete Affect Specifiers

Value	Description
adAffectAll	If there's no filter, all records in the recordset are affected. If there is a filter, only visible records are affected.
adAffectCurrent	Affects only the current record.
adAffectGroup	Affects only the records that satisfy the current Filter property setting.

To add a new record to the database, you can call the AddNew function. Next, set default values in any of the fields that require values, such as the key fields. After you add the new record to the recordset, you need to move to the last record in the recordset because this will be the new record that you've added.

When you need to delete the current record, call the `Delete` function. After you delete the current record, you need to navigate to another record so users aren't still looking at the just-deleted record. When you delete the current record, no current record exists until you navigate to another record.

The `Field` Object

The `Field` object represents a single column in the `Recordset`. Each `Field` object contains the column name, data value, and how the data value should be represented. Because ADO was designed to be used in Microsoft's scripting languages, and the only data type available in these scripting languages is the `Variant` data type, the `Field` objects always contain a `Variant` data value. The data value is automatically converted to the correct data type when updating to the database. While working with the ADO objects, you have to convert the value from a `Variant` to whatever data type you need it to be, as well as convert it back to a `Variant` when updating the value. Tale 13.19 lists the key properties for the `Field` object.

TABLE 13.19 Field Object Properties

Property	Description
ActualSize	The actual length of the field's value.
DefinedSize	The maximum possible length of the field's value.
Name	The name of the field object.
NumericScale	A byte value indicating the number of decimal places to which numeric values will be resolved.
OriginalValue	The original value of the field, before any changes to the value.
Precision	A byte value indicating the number of digits used to represent numeric values.
Status	The status of the field value. Table 13.20 lists the possible values for this property.
Type	The data type of the field. The possible values for this property are listed earlier in Table 13.9.
UnderlyingValue	The value in the database for this field.
Value	The current value of this field.

13

TABLE 13.20 Field Status Values

Status	Description
adFieldAlreadyExists	The field already exists.
adFieldBadStatus	An invalid status was passed from ADO to the OLE DB provider.
adFieldCannotComplete	The server couldn't complete the operation.
adFieldCannotConvertValue	The field can't be retrieved or stored without the loss of data.
adFieldCantCreate	The field can't be added because the provider exceeded some limitation.
adFieldDataOverflow	The data returned from the provider overflowed the data type of the field.
adFieldDefault	The default value for the field was used.
adFieldDoesNotExist	The field specified doesn't exist.
adFieldIgnore	This field was skipped when setting data values in the source.
adFieldIntegrityViolation	The field can't be set because it's a calculated or derived entity.
adFieldInvalidURL	The data source URL contains invalid characters.
adFieldIsNull	The field contains a NULL value, which indicates that a field, or column, doesn't contain a value.
adFieldOK (default)	The field was successfully added or deleted.
adFieldPendingChange	The field has been deleted and then re-added, possibly with a data type change.
adFieldPendingDelete	The field is deleted after the Update method is called.
adFieldPendingInsert	The field is added when the Update method is called.
adFieldPendingUnknown	The provider can't determine what operation caused the field status to be set.
adFieldPendingUnknownDelete	The provider can't determine what operation caused the field status to be set, and the field is deleted after the Update method is called.
adFieldPermissionDenied	The field can't be modified.
adFieldReadOnly	The field is defined as read-only.
adFieldResourceExists	The provider couldn't perform the operation because an object already exists and the provider can't overwrite the object.
adFieldResourceLocked	The provider couldn't perform the operation because the data source is locked.
adFieldResourceOutOfScope	The data source is outside the scope of the current record.

TABLE 13.20 continued

Status	Description
adFieldSchemaViolation	The value violated the constraints placed on the field.
adFieldSignMismatch	The data value returned by the provider was signed, but the field value is unsigned.
adFieldTruncated	A variable-length value was truncated when reading from the data source.
adFieldUnavailable	The value of the field couldn't be determined.
adFieldVolumeNotFound	The provider couldn't find the storage volume indicated in the URL.

Importing the ADO Dynamic Link Library (DLL)

If you look around in the MFC class hierarchy, you'll find no classes for use with ADO. You don't have to create the classes yourself because Microsoft has provided other means for you to create and use classes for each ADO object through the use of a C++ precompiler directive called #import.

You can use this directive to import an ActiveX Dynamic Link Library (DLL) that has been built with the IDispatch interface description included in the DLL. #import tells the Visual C++ compiler to import the specified DLL and to extract the object information from the DLL, creating a couple of header files that are automatically included in your project. These header files have the filename extensions .tlh and .tli and are in the output directory for your project (the Debug or Release directory, the same directory where you'll find the executable application after you've compiled your project). These two files contain definitions of classes for each object in the DLL that you can use in your code. The #import directive also tells the compiler to include the DLL as part of the project, eliminating the need to include the .lib file for the DLL in your project.

You can import the ADO DLL by placing the following code at the beginning of the header file in which you are defining any database objects:

```
#define INITGUID
#import "C:\Program Files\Common Files\System\ADO\msado15.dll"
        ➥rename_namespace("ADOCG") rename("EOF", "EndOfFile")
using namespace ADOCG;
#include "icrsint.h"
```

In these four lines of directives, the first line defines a constant that needs to be defined for ADO. The INITGUID constant controls how the DEFINE_GUID macro is defined, which is used for defining GUIDs (Globally Unique IDs) for various COM services and

13

objects. The second imports the ADO DLL, creating the two header files mentioned earlier. After the filename to be imported, this directive includes two attributes to the `#import` directive:

- `rename_namespace` renames the namespace into which the DLL has been imported. This is followed with the line following the `#import` directive, where the renamed namespace is specified as the one used.
- `rename` renames an element in the header files created with the `#import` directive. You rename elements in these header files to prevent conflicts with another element named elsewhere. If you examine the header file, the element specified isn't renamed in the file; however, the element is renamed when the compiler reads the file.

The final line includes the ADO header file, which contains the definition of some macros you will use when writing your ADO applications.

Connecting to a Database

Before you can use any of the ADO objects, you need to initialize the COM environment for your application. You can do this by calling the `CoInitialize` API (Application Programming Interface) function, passing `NULL` as the only parameter:

```
::CoInitialize(NULL);
```

This enables you to make calls to ActiveX objects. If you leave out this one line of code from your application, or don't put it before you begin interacting with the objects, you get a COM error whenever you run your application.

When you are finished with all ADO activity, you need to shut down the COM environment by calling the `CoUninitialize` function:

```
CoUninitialize();
```

This function cleans up the COM environment and prepares your application for shutting down.

As soon as you initialize the COM environment, you can create a connection to the database. The best way to do this isn't to declare a `Connection` object variable, but to declare a `Connection` object pointer, `_ConnectionPtr`, and use it for all interaction with the `Connection` object. After you declare a `Connection` object pointer, you can initialize it by creating an instance of the `Connection` object, calling the `CreateInstance` function, passing it the `UUID` of the `Connection` object as its only parameter, as follows:

```
_ConnectionPtr ptrConn;
ptrConn.CreateInstance(__uuidof(Connection));
```

Another way that you can do this is as follows:

```
_ConnectionPtr ptrConn("ADODB.Connection");
```

> **Note**
>
> When you work with these objects and functions, you need to use the correct number of underscore characters in front of the various object and function names. The _ConnectionPtr object has only a single underscore character, whereas the __uuidof function has two.

 The _ConnectionPtr object is what is known as a *smart pointer*. A smart pointer is a wrapper around a COM interface pointer. An interface pointer is a pointer to a COM interface. A smart pointer creates a wrapper around the interface via the interface pointer, enabling you to treat the interface pointer as a class instance. This simplifies working with a COM interface, but can be confusing when calling it an interface pointer while you don't interact with it like a normal C++ pointer.

After you create the object, you can call the Open function to establish the database connection. This function takes four parameters:

- The connection definition string, which defines the OLE DB data source for the database. It can be an ODBC OLE DB driver, where OLE DB is sitting on top of an ODBC data source, as you'll use in your sample application. If you are using SQL Server or Oracle databases, it can be a direct connection to the OLE DB interface provided by the database itself.
- The user ID for connecting to the database.
- The password for connecting to the database.
- The cursor type to use with the database. Cursor types are defined in the msado15.tlh header file created by the #import directive.

A typical use of the Open function to connect to an ODBC data source that doesn't need a user ID or password is similar to the following:

```
ptrConn->Open(L"Provider=MSDASQL.1;Data Source=STYVCDB", L"", L"",
    adConnectUnspecified);
```

Executing Commands and Retrieving Data

When you have the connection open, you can use a Command object to pass SQL commands to the database. This is the normal method of executing SQL commands with ADO. To create a Command object, follow the same process that you used to create a

13

Connection object. You declare a Command object pointer, _CommandPtr, and then create an instance of it using the UUID of the Command object, as follows:

```
_CommandPtr ptrCmd;
ptrCmd.CreateInstance(__uuidof(Command));
```

or

```
_CommandPtr ptrCmd("ADODB.Command");
```

After you create your Command object, assuming you've already established the connection to the database, you set the active connection property of the Command object to the open Connection object pointer, as follows:

```
ptrCmd->ActiveConnection = ptrConn;
```

Next, specify the SQL command to be executed by setting the CommandText property of the Command object:

```
ptrCmd->CommandText = "Select * from Addresses";
```

At this point, you have two options for how you execute this command and retrieve the records. The first is to call the Command object's Execute method, which returns a new Recordset object, which you'll want to set to a Recordset object pointer, as follows:

```
_RecordsetPtr ptrRs;
ptrRs = ptrCmd->Execute();
```

The other approach to running the command and retrieving the records is to specify that the Command object is the source for the records in the Recordset. This requires creating the Recordset object as follows:

```
_RecordsetPtr ptrRs;
ptrRs.CreateInstance(__uuidof(Recordset));
ptrRs->PutRefSource(ptrCmd);
```

or

```
_RecordsetPtr ptrRs("ADODB.Recordset");
ptrRs->PutRefSource(ptrCmd);
```

Now, you need to create two NULL variant values to pass as the first two parameters to the Recordset's Open method. The third parameter is the cursor type to use, followed by the locking method to use. Finally, the fifth parameter to the Recordset's Open method is an options flag that indicates how the database should evaluate the command being passed in. You do this with the following code:

```
// Create the variant NULL
_variant_t vNull;
vNull.vt = VT_ERROR;
vNull.scode = DISP_E_PARAMNOTFOUND;
```

```
// Open the recordset
ptrRs->Open(vNull, vNull, adOpenDynamic, adLockOptimistic, adCmdUnknown);
```

You could take another approach to accomplish all the preceding tasks with only a few lines of code. You skip the use of the Command and Connection objects altogether, placing all the necessary connection information in the Recordset's Open function. You can specify the SQL command as the first parameter and the connection information as the second parameter, instead of the two NULLs that you passed previously. This method reduces all the preceding code to the following few lines:

```
_RecordsetPtr ptrRs;
ptrRs.CreateInstance(__uuidof(Recordset));
ptrRs->Open(_T("Provider=MSDASQL.1;Data Source=STYVCDB"),
        _T("select * from Addresses"), adOpenDynamic,
        adLockOptimistic, adCmdUnknown);
```

Tip

Although placing all the command and connection information into the Recordset Open function is fine for a simple application, such as the one that you will build today, you are better off using the Connection object with any application that has more than a couple of database queries. This allows you to make a single connection to the database and use that connection for all database interaction.

Navigating the Recordset

After you retrieve a set of records from the database and are holding them in a Recordset object, you need to navigate the set of records. This functionality is available, just as you would expect, through the MoveFirst, MoveLast, MovePrevious, and MoveNext functions. None of these functions take any parameters because they perform the functions that you would expect them to perform.

Along with these functions, the Recordset object also has two properties—BOF and EOF (which you should normally rename to prevent a collision with the default definition of EOF)—which can be checked to determine whether the current record in the set is beyond either end of the set of records.

13

Note

The EOF constant stands for End Of File, and is a constant defined in the standard I/O functionality for the C/C++ languages. For use with database functionality, this constant needs to be redefined so that it can be used with the Recordset object to define the end of the recordset.

Accessing Field Values

Working with ADO in Visual C++ begins to get interesting when you need to begin
accessing the data values in each field. Because ADO is intended to be easy to use in
VBScript and JScript, which only have variant data types, all data elements that you'll
retrieve from fields in the ADO Recordset are variant values. They have to be converted into the data types that you need them to be.

You can do this in two ways. The first straightforward way is to retrieve the values into a
variant and then convert them, as in the following code:

```
_variant_t vFirstName;
CString strFirstName;
vFirstName = ptrRs->GetCollect(_variant_t("FirstName"));
vFirstName.ChangeType(VT_BSTR);
strFirstName = vFirstName.bstrVal;
```

The not-so-straightforward way is actually the better way, and in the long run, it's a lot
easier to work with. Microsoft provides a series of macros that perform the conversion
for you and maintain a set of variables of the records in the set. For the less straightforward way, you define a new class to use as the interface for your recordset. This class is
a descendent of the CADORecordBinding class defined in the icrsint.h header file, which
you included just after the #import directive. This class won't have any constructor or
destructor, but will have a series of macros, along with a number of variables. Each field
in the set of records has two variables, an unsigned long, which maintains the status of
the variable, and the field variable itself. These variables must be regular C variables,
and they can't be C++ classes such as CString. A simple example of this class
declaration is the following:

```
class CCustomRs :
    public CADORecordBinding
{
BEGIN_ADO_BINDING(CCustomRs)
    ADO_FIXED_LENGTH_ENTRY(1, adInteger, m_lAddressID, lAddressIDStatus,
        FALSE)
    ADO_VARIABLE_LENGTH_ENTRY2(2, adVarChar, m_szFirstName,
        sizeof(m_szFirstName), lFirstNameStatus, TRUE)
    ADO_FIXED_LENGTH_ENTRY(3, adDate, m_dtBirthdate, lBirthdateStatus,
        TRUE)
    ADO_FIXED_LENGTH_ENTRY(4, adBoolean, m_bSendCard, lSendCardStatus,
        TRUE)
END_ADO_BINDING()
public:
    LONG m_lAddressID;
    ULONG lAddressIDStatus;
    CHAR m_szFirstName[51];
    ULONG lFirstNameStatus;
```

```
    DATE m_dtBirthdate;
    ULONG lBirthdateStatus;
    VARIANT_BOOL m_bSendCard;
    ULONG lSendCardStatus;
};
```

After you define this record layout class to match the record layout that will be returned by your database query, you can declare a variable of this class for use in your application as follows:

```
CCustomRs m_rsRecSet;
```

Next, you need to create a pointer to an `IADORecordBinding` interface:

```
IADORecordBinding *picRs = NULL;
```

This pointer to a COM interface is part of the ADO `Recordset` object. When you retrieve the set of records, you need to retrieve the pointer to the `IADORecordBinding` interface and bind the custom recordset class to the `Recordset` object, as in the following code:

```
if (FAILED(ptrRs->QueryInterface(__uuidof(IADORecordBinding),
          (LPVOID *)&picRs)))
    _com_issue_error(E_NOINTERFACE);
picRs->BindToRecordset(&m_rsRecSet);
```

Now, as you navigate the records in the set, you just need to access the member variables of your custom record class to retrieve the current value for each field.

The BEGIN_ADO_BINDING and END_ADO_BINDING Macros

The key to the second method of accessing the data values in the recordset is in the macros used to define the record class. The macros start with `BEGIN_ADO_BINDING`, which takes the class name as its only parameter. This macro sets up the structure definition that's created with the rest of the macros that follow.

The set of macros is closed by `END_ADO_BINDING`. This macro doesn't take any parameters, and it wraps up the definition of the record-binding structure that's created in the class. The real work is done in the rest of the macros, which are used between these two.

The ADO_FIXED_LENGTH_ENTRY Macros

The `ADO_FIXED_LENGTH_ENTRY` macro is used for any database fields that are fixed in size. It can be used with a date or Boolean field, or even a text field that's a fixed size, with no option for any variation in the database. There are two versions of this macro; you add a 2 to the end of the name of the second version (`ADO_FIXED_LENGTH_ENTRY2`).

```
ADO_FIXED_LENGTH_ENTRY(Ordinal, DataType, Buffer, Status, Modify)
```

```
ADO_FIXED_LENGTH_ENTRY2(Ordinal, DataType, Buffer, Modify)
```

13

Both versions require the same first three and last parameters. The first version requires an additional parameter that's not required in the second version.

The first parameter, Ordinal, is the ordinal number of the field in the recordset. This is the position in the field order as returned by the SQL query run to populate the recordset. The second parameter, DataType, is the data type of the field; the available data types are defined in the header file created by the #import directive. The third parameter, Buffer, is the variable into which the data value is to be copied.

For the first version of the macro, the fourth parameter, Status, is the variable for the field status (the unsigned long that you defined with the variable for the actual value).

The last variable, Modify, is a Boolean that specifies whether this field can be modified.

The ADO_NUMERIC_ENTRY Macros

You use the ADO_NUMERIC_ENTRY macros with numeric fields only. They are similar to the ADO_FIXED_LENGTH_ENTRY macros in that there are two different versions of the macro, named in the same way. In these macros, the first five parameters are the same in both versions, along with the final parameter. Similar to the ADO_FIXED_LENGTH_ENTRY macros, the first version has an additional parameter that's not used in the second version.

```
ADO_NUMERIC_ENTRY(Ordinal, DataType, Buffer, Precision, Scale, Status,
       Modify)
```

```
ADO_NUMERIC_ENTRY2(Ordinal, DataType, Buffer, Precision, Scale, Modify)
```

The first three parameters for the ADO_NUMERIC_ENTRY macros are the same as those for the ADO_FIXED_LENGTH_ENTRY macros, as are the last parameter and the next-to-last parameter for the first version. The fourth and fifth parameters are unique to these macros. The fourth parameter, Precision, specifies the precision of the value in this field of the recordset; the fifth parameter, Scale, specifies the scale of the value. Both parameters are crucial in correctly converting the value to and from a variant data type.

The ADO_VARIABLE_LENGTH_ENTRY Macros

The final series of macros is ADO_VARIABLE_LENGTH_ENTRY. You use this series with database fields that will likely vary in length. With a SQL-based database, use this series of macros with any varchar (variable-length character string) columns.

This macro exists in four versions. In all four versions, the first four parameters are the same, and the final parameter is the same. The parameters between them vary, as follows:

```
ADO_VARIABLE_LENGTH_ENTRY(Ordinal, DataType, Buffer, Size, Status, Length,
       Modify)
```

```
ADO_VARIABLE_LENGTH_ENTRY2(Ordinal, DataType, Buffer, Size, Status, Modify)

ADO_VARIABLE_LENGTH_ENTRY3(Ordinal, DataType, Buffer, Size, Length, Modify)

ADO_VARIABLE_LENGTH_ENTRY4(Ordinal, DataType, Buffer, Size, Modify)
```

The first parameter, Ordinal, is the ordinal position of the column in the recordset as returned by the SQL query. The second parameter, DataType, is the data type. The third parameter, Buffer, is the variable in which the data value should be placed. The fourth parameter for all versions of the macro, Size, is the size of the variable into which the value is to be placed. This prevents the data from being written past the end of the variable that you defined for it to be placed in. As with the previous macros, the final parameter, Modify, specifies whether the field is updatable.

In the first version of this macro, there are two parameters between the fourth and final parameters. The second version of this macro only has the first of these two parameters, and the third version only has the second of these two parameters. The first of these two parameters, Status, is the status variable for use with this field. The second of these two parameters, Length, is the length of the field in the database. The preceding example used the second version of this macro.

Updating Records

When you need to update values in a record in the recordset, how you handle it depends on which of the two methods you used to retrieve the data elements from the recordset. If you retrieved each field and converted it from a variant yourself, you need to update each individual changed field. The update is done by using the Recordset object's Update method, which takes two variables: the field being updated and the new value for the field. You could make this update using the following code:

```
_variant_t vName, vValue;
vName.SetString("FirstName");
vValue.SetString("John");
ptrRs->Update(vName, vValue);
```

If you created your record class and bound it to the recordset, updating the record is a little simpler. After you copy the new values into the variables in the record class, you can call the record-bound version of the Update function, as in the following:

```
picRs->Update(&m_rsRecSet);
```

This updates the record in the Recordset object to be updated with the values in the record class that you've bound to the set.

13

Adding and Deleting

Adding and deleting records from an ADO recordset is similar to how you accomplish it in other database access technologies. However, how you perform the addition of new records involves some slight subtleties.

For deleting the current record, you can call the Recordset object's Delete method. This method requires a single parameter that specifies how the delete is supposed to be done. Most likely, you'll pass the adAffectCurrent value so that only the current record in the recordset is deleted, as in the following code:

```
ptrRs->Delete(adAffectCurrent);
ptrRs->MovePrevious();
```

As with any other database-access technology, after you delete the current record, there is no current record, so you need to navigate to another record before allowing users to do anything else.

When you add a new record, you can call the Recordset object's AddNew method. After you add a new record, the new record is the current record in the recordset. If you check the variables in the record class that you created, you'll find that they are all empty. However, you can't just begin entering data values into these fields. To allow users to immediately enter the various data elements in the new record, blank out the values in the record class and pass this variable as the only parameter to the AddNew method. You need to call it through the record-binding interface pointer, as in the following example:

```
m_rsRecSet.m_lAddressID = 0;
strcpy(m_rsRecSet.m_szFirstName, " ");
m_rsRecSet.m_dtBirthdate = NULL;
m_rsRecSet.m_bSendCard = VARIANT_FALSE;
picRs->AddNew(&m_rsRecSet);
```

This allows you to provide users with a blank record, ready for editing. After users enter all the various values in the record, copy all these values back to the record variable. Then, call the Update method to save the record.

Closing the Recordset and Connection Objects

After you finish working with a recordset, you close it by calling the Close method:

```
ptrRs->Close();
```

When you finish all database interaction for the entire application, close the connection to the database by calling the Connection object's Close method:

```
ptrConn->Close();
```

Building a Database Application with ADO

For the sample application that you will build today, you'll create an SDI application with no database support (with ADO, you add all the database support yourself). You'll use ADO to retrieve a set of records from an Access database, providing functionality to navigate the recordset. Users can make changes to the recordset's data, and those changes will be reflected in the database as well. Users also can add new records to the recordset and delete records as desired. You can do all this by using ADO as the means of accessing the database, which goes through the ODBC driver to communicate with the Access database.

Preparing the Database

Before you can begin building an application that uses a database, you need a database to use with your application. Almost every database that you can purchase for your applications comes with tools for creating a new database. You'll need to use these tools to create your database and then use the ODBC administrator to configure an ODBC data source for your new database.

For the sample application in this chapter, I used Access 95 to create a new database. I used the Access Database Wizard to create the database, choosing the Address Book database template as the database to be created. When the Database Wizard started, I selected the default set of fields for including in the database and selected the option to include sample data, as in Figure 13.1. I accepted the rest of the default settings offered in the Database Wizard.

FIGURE 13.1

*Include the sample
data in the database.*

> **Note**
>
> Access 95 was used to create the database because it had functionality to add sample data to the database that it created using the Database Wizard (a function that's not in Access 2000, nor in the new Access 2002). You can use any version of Access that you have. If you create a database with another version of Access, you'll need to modify the example code for the

> particular data fields included in the database you create. The database used for the example is available online with all of the example code at www.samspublishing.com (enter this book's ISBN—0672321971—in the search field to find all the downloads available for this book).

After you create the database, you need to configure an ODBC data source to point to the database you just created. Follow these steps:

1. Run the ODBC Administrator from the Windows Control Panel. If you are running Windows 2000, it's in the Administrative Tools folder off of the Start menu, and is called Data Sources (ODBC).

2. In the ODBC Administrator, add a new data source by clicking the Add button (see Figure 13.2).

FIGURE 13.2

Running the ODBC Data Source Administrator.

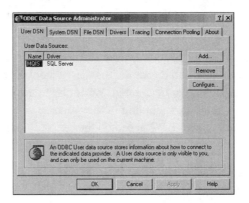

3. Select the database driver for the new data source (see Figure 13.3). For the sample application that you will build today, because the database was created using Access, select the Microsoft Access Driver.

4. Click the Finish button.

In the ODBC Microsoft Access Setup dialog box (see Figure 13.4), provide a short, simple name for the data source. Your application will use this name to specify the ODBC data source configuration to use for the database connection, so it should reflect the function that the database will be serving, or be similar to the name of the application that will be using this database.

FIGURE 13.3

The Create New Data Source dialog box.

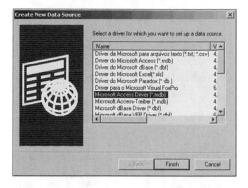

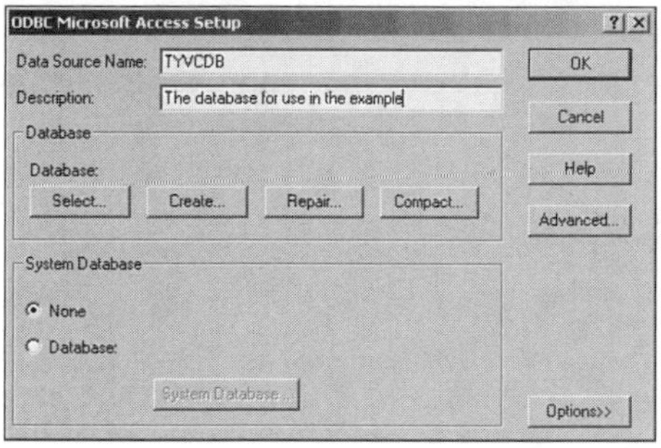

FIGURE 13.4

The ODBC Microsoft Access Setup dialog box.

Now, continue by following these steps:

1. Name your data source **STYVCDB** (for Sams Teach Yourself Visual C++ Database) and then enter a description for the database in the next field.

2. To specify where the database is, click the Select button, and then specify the Access database that you created.

3. After you finish configuring the ODBC data source for your database, click OK to add the new data source to the ODBC Administrator.

4. Click OK again to finish the task and close the ODBC Administrator.

You are now ready to turn your attention to building your application.

Creating the Application Shell

Today's application is an SDI-style application. As with several other sample applications that you build in the course of reading this book, everything you do in today's application is just as applicable to an MDI or dialog-style application. To start the application, use the MFC AppWizard to build the application shell, using most of the SDI-style application default settings:

13

1. Create a new MFC Application Visual C++ project. Name the project `AdoDatabase`.

2. In the Application Type area, select Single Document for the application type.

3. In the Database Support area, be sure to leave it at the default setting specifying No Database Support.

4. In the Generated Classes area, specify the base class as `CFormView`, and click Finish. The MFC Application Wizard generates the application shell.

5. After you finish creating your application shell, design the main dialog box form for use in your application. Add the standard controls for each field in the Addresses table from the database (or, if you created a different database, add controls for all the fields in the table that you choose from the database you created), as shown in Figure 13.5. Configure the controls using the properties listed in Table 13.21.

FIGURE 13.5

The main form layout.

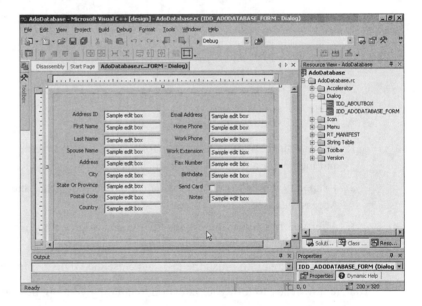

 Tip

If you want to save a little time when building the example, leave out most of the controls and database fields from the application. The key fields that you need to include onscreen are ID, First and Last Names, Birthdate, and Send Card. You also can leave out the other fields from the application. You need to include these fields in the `CCustomRs` class that you create today.

TABLE 13.21 Control Property Settings

Object	Property	Setting
Static Text	Caption	Address ID
Edit Control	ID	IDC_EADDRESSID
Static Text	Caption	First Name
Edit Control	ID	IDC_EFIRSTNAME
Static Text	Caption	Last Name
Edit Control	ID	IDC_ELASTNAME
Static Text	Caption	Spouse Name
Edit Control	ID	IDC_ESPOUSENAME
Static Text	Caption	Address
Edit Control	ID	IDC_EADDRESS
Static Text	Caption	City
Edit Control	ID	IDC_ECITY
Static Text	Caption	State Or Province
Edit Control	ID	IDC_ESTATEORPROVINCE
Static Text	Caption	Postal Code
Edit Control	ID	IDC_EPOSTALCODE
Static Text	Caption	Country
Edit Control	ID	IDC_ECOUNTRY
Static Text	Caption	Email Address
Edit Control	ID	IDC_EEMAILADDRESS
Static Text	Caption	Home Phone
Edit Control	ID	IDC_EHOMEPHONE
Static Text	Caption	Work Phone
Edit Control	ID	IDC_EWORKPHONE
Static Text	Caption	Work Extension
Edit Control	ID	IDC_EWORKEXTENSION
Static Text	Caption	Fax Number
Edit Control	ID	IDC_EFAXNUMBER
Static Text	Caption	Birthdate
Edit Control	ID	IDC_EBIRTHDATE
Static Text	Caption	Send Card
Check Box	ID	IDC_CBSENDCARD
Static Text	Caption	Notes
Edit Control	ID	IDC_ENOTES

13

6. After you add all the controls to the form, attach variables to each of them as specified in Table 13.22. The variables should match the data types of the columns in the database that the control will display.

TABLE 13.22 Control Variables

Object	Name	Category	Type
IDC_EADDRESSID	m_lAddressID	Value	long
IDC_EFIRSTNAME	m_strFirstName	Value	CString
IDC_ELASTNAME	m_strLastName	Value	CString
IDC_ESPOUSENAME	m_strSpouseName	Value	CString
IDC_EADDRESS	m_strAddress	Value	CString
IDC_ECITY	m_strCity	Value	CString
IDC_ESTATEORPROVINCE	m_strStateOrProvince	Value	CString
IDC_EPOSTALCODE	m_strPostalCode	Value	CString
IDC_ECOUNTRY	m_strCountry	Value	CString
IDC_EEMAILADDRESS	m_strEmailAddress	Value	CString
IDC_EHOMEPHONE	m_strHomePhone	Value	CString
IDC_EWORKPHONE	m_strWorkPhone	Value	CString
IDC_EWORKEXTENSION	m_strWorkExtension	Value	CString
IDC_EFAXNUMBER	m_strFaxNumber	Value	CString
IDC_EBIRTHDATE	m_oledtBirthdate	Value	COleDateTime
IDC_CBSENDCARD	m_bSendCard	Value	BOOL
IDC_ENOTES	m_strNotes	Value	CString

Building a Custom Record Class

Before you go any further in building your application, you need to create the custom record class that you will bind to the recordset. This class needs public variables for each column in the database table that you are selecting, as well as status variables for each column. You'll also build the set of macros to exchange the column values between the recordset and the class variables. To create this class, follow these steps:

1. Create a new class using the same method you used in previous days, specifying it as a generic class.

2. Name the class CCustomRs, and specify the base class as CADORecordBinding with public access.

3. Delete the constructor and destructor functions from both the header and source-code files for the new class.

4. Edit the header file for your new class, importing the ADO DLL and filling in the macros and variables, as in Listing 13.1.

LISTING 13.1 The Custom Record Class

```
#define INITGUID
#import "C:\Program Files\Common Files\System\ADO\msado15.dll"
    rename_namespace("ADOCG") rename("EOF", "EndOfFile")
using namespace ADOCG;
#include "icrsint.h"
class CCustomRs :
    public CADORecordBinding
{
    BEGIN_ADO_BINDING(CCustomRs)
        ADO_FIXED_LENGTH_ENTRY(1, adInteger, m_lAddressID, lAddressIDStatus,
        FALSE)
    ADO_VARIABLE_LENGTH_ENTRY2(2, adVarChar, m_szFirstName,
        sizeof(m_szFirstName), lFirstNameStatus, TRUE)
    ADO_VARIABLE_LENGTH_ENTRY2(3, adVarChar, m_szLastName,
        sizeof(m_szLastName), lLastNameStatus, TRUE)
    ADO_VARIABLE_LENGTH_ENTRY2(4, adVarChar, m_szSpouseName,
        sizeof(m_szSpouseName), lSpouseNameStatus, TRUE)
    ADO_VARIABLE_LENGTH_ENTRY2(5, adVarChar, m_szAddress,
        sizeof(m_szAddress), lAddressStatus, TRUE)
    ADO_VARIABLE_LENGTH_ENTRY2(6, adVarChar, m_szCity, sizeof(m_szCity),
        lCityStatus, TRUE)
    ADO_VARIABLE_LENGTH_ENTRY2(7, adVarChar, m_szStateOrProvince,
        sizeof(m_szStateOrProvince), lStateOrProvinceStatus, TRUE)
    ADO_VARIABLE_LENGTH_ENTRY2(8, adVarChar, m_szPostalCode,
        sizeof(m_szPostalCode), lPostalCodeStatus, TRUE)
    ADO_VARIABLE_LENGTH_ENTRY2(9, adVarChar, m_szCountry,
        sizeof(m_szCountry), lCountryStatus, TRUE)
    ADO_VARIABLE_LENGTH_ENTRY2(10, adVarChar, m_szEmailAddress,
        sizeof(m_szEmailAddress), lEmailAddressStatus, TRUE)
    ADO_VARIABLE_LENGTH_ENTRY2(11, adVarChar, m_szHomePhone,
        sizeof(m_szHomePhone), lHomePhoneStatus, TRUE)
    ADO_VARIABLE_LENGTH_ENTRY2(12, adVarChar, m_szWorkPhone,
        sizeof(m_szWorkPhone), lWorkPhoneStatus, TRUE)
    ADO_VARIABLE_LENGTH_ENTRY2(13, adVarChar, m_szWorkExtension,
        sizeof(m_szWorkExtension), lWorkExtensionStatus, TRUE)
    ADO_VARIABLE_LENGTH_ENTRY2(14, adVarChar, m_szFaxNumber,
        sizeof(m_szFaxNumber), lFaxNumberStatus, TRUE)
    ADO_FIXED_LENGTH_ENTRY(15, adDate, m_dtBirthdate, lBirthdateStatus,
        TRUE)
    ADO_FIXED_LENGTH_ENTRY(16, adBoolean, m_bSendCard, lSendCardStatus,
        TRUE)
    ADO_VARIABLE_LENGTH_ENTRY2(17, adLongVarChar, m_szNotes,
```

13

LISTING 13.1 continued

```
            sizeof(m_szNotes), lNotesStatus, TRUE)
    END_ADO_BINDING()
    public:
        LONG m_lAddressID;
            ULONG lAddressIDStatus;
        CHAR m_szFirstName[51];
        ULONG lFirstNameStatus;
        CHAR m_szLastName[51];
        ULONG lLastNameStatus;
        CHAR m_szSpouseName[51];
        ULONG lSpouseNameStatus;
        CHAR m_szAddress[256];
        ULONG lAddressStatus;
        CHAR m_szCity[51];
        ULONG lCityStatus;
        CHAR m_szStateOrProvince[21];
        ULONG lStateOrProvinceStatus;
        CHAR m_szPostalCode[21];
        ULONG lPostalCodeStatus;
        CHAR m_szCountry[51];
        ULONG lCountryStatus;
        CHAR m_szEmailAddress[51];
        ULONG lEmailAddressStatus;
        CHAR m_szHomePhone[31];
        ULONG lHomePhoneStatus;
        CHAR m_szWorkPhone[31];
        ULONG lWorkPhoneStatus;
        CHAR m_szWorkExtension[21];
        ULONG lWorkExtensionStatus;
        CHAR m_szFaxNumber[31];
        ULONG lFaxNumberStatus;
        DATE m_dtBirthdate;
        ULONG lBirthdateStatus;
        VARIANT_BOOL m_bSendCard;
        ULONG lSendCardStatus;
        CHAR m_szNotes[65536];
        ULONG lNotesStatus;
    };
```

INPUT

5. After you create this class, add a variable to the document class, specifying the variable type as CCustomRs, the name as m_rsRecSet, and the access as private.

You also need to provide a way for the view to get a pointer to the record class from the document class. This function should return a pointer to the record class variable. To add this function to your application, follow these steps:

1. Add a new member function to the document class, specifying the function type as CCustomRs*, the function name as GetRecSet, and the function access as public.

2. Edit this function, adding the code in Listing 13.2.

LISTING 13.2 The `CAdoDatabaseDoc GetRecSet` Function

```
CCustomRs* CAdoDatabaseDoc::GetRecSet(void)
{
    // Return a pointer to the record object
    return &m_rsRecSet;
}
```

One last piece of functionality that you'll add before getting to the real heart of ADO programming is the function for reporting ADO and database errors. This function displays a message to users, reporting that an error occurred and displaying the error code and error message. To add this function to your application, continue with these steps:

1. Add a new member function to your document class. Specify the function type as void, specify the function name as GenerateError, and add two parameters. Specify the first parameter type as HRESULT and the name as hr, the second parameter type as PWSTR and the name as pwszDescription. Specify the function access as public.

> **Note**
>
> The PWSTR data type is a pointer to a UNICODE string.

2. Edit the function, entering the code in Listing 13.3.

LISTING 13.3 The `CAdoDatabaseDoc GenerateError` Function

```
void* CAdoDatabaseDoc::GenerateError(HRESULT hr, PWSTR pwszDescription)
{
    CString strError;
    // Format and display the error message
    strError.Format("Run-time error '%d (%x)'", hr, hr);
    strError += "\n\n";
    strError += pwszDescription;

    AfxMessageBox(strError);
}
```

Connecting and Retrieving Data

You can perform all the database connecting and recordset retrieving in the document class's OnNewDocument function. Before you can add this functionality, you need to add a

13

few more variables to the document class: a Recordset object pointer, an IADORecordBinding interface pointer, a couple of string variables for holding the database connection string, and the SQL command to execute to populate the recordset. Add all these variables to the document class as specified in Table 13.23.

TABLE 13.23 Document Class Member Variables

Name	Type	Access
m_ptrRs	_RecordsetPtr	Private
m_piAdoRecordBinding	IADORecordBinding*	Private
m_strConnection	CString	Private
m_strCmdText	CString	Private

The OnNewDocument function performs a series of steps for connecting and retrieving the recordset. First, it sets the strings for the database connection and the SQL command to be run. Next, it initializes the COM environment and the two pointers so that they are both NULL. To create the Recordset object, OnNewDocument uses the CreateInstance function. It opens the Recordset, connecting to the database and running the SQL command at the same time. It binds the record class to the recordset by using the IADORecordBinding interface pointer. Finally, the function tells the view class to refresh the bound data, displaying the initial record for the user using a view class function that you'll add in a little while.

To add all this functionality, edit the OnNewDocument function in the document class, adding the boldfaced code in Listing 13.4.

LISTING 13.4 The CAdoDatabaseDoc OnNewDocument Function

```
BOOL* CAdoDatabaseDoc::OnNewDocument()
{
    if (!CDocument::OnNewDocument())
        return FALSE;
    // TODO: add reinitialization code here
    // (SDI documents will reuse this document)
    // Set the connection and SQL command strings
    m_strConnection = _T("Provider=MSDASQL.1;Data Source=STYVCDB");
    m_strCmdText = _T("select * from Addresses");

    // Initialize the Recordset and binding pointers
    m_ptrRs = NULL;
    m_piAdoRecordBinding = NULL;
    // Initialize the COM environment
    ::CoInitialize(NULL);
```

INPUT

LISTING 13.4   continued

```
        try
        {
            // Create the recordset object
            m_ptrRs.CreateInstance(__uuidof(Recordset));

            // Open the recordset object
            m_ptrRs->Open((LPCTSTR)m_strCmdText, (LPCTSTR)m_strConnection,
                adOpenDynamic, adLockOptimistic, adCmdUnknown);
            // Get a pointer to the record-binding interface
            if (FAILED(m_ptrRs->QueryInterface(__uuidof(IADORecordBinding),
                    (LPVOID *)&m_piAdoRecordBinding)))
                _com_issue_error(E_NOINTERFACE);
            // Bind the record class to the recordset
            m_piAdoRecordBinding->BindToRecordset(&m_rsRecSet);

            // Get a pointer to the view
            POSITION pos = GetFirstViewPosition();
            CAdoDatabaseView* pView = (CAdoDatabaseView*)GetNextView(pos);
            if (pView)
                // Sync the data set with the form
                pView->RefreshBoundData();
        }
        // Any errors?
        catch (_com_error &e)
        {
            // Display the error
            GenerateError(e.Error(), e.Description());
        }

        return TRUE;
}
```

In Listing 13.4, you specified to use the MSDASQL provider to use the Access database. This is the ODBC provider for the OLE DB technology that ADO is built on. If you were going directly to a SQL Server 2000 database, you could use the SQLOLEDB provider. Other providers can be determined in the documentation provided with the database.

Before continuing, make sure you add all the code necessary to clean up after yourself as your application closes. You need to close the recordset and release the pointer to the record-binding interface. You also need to shut down the COM environment. To add all this functionality to your application, follow these steps:

1. Add an override function to the DeleteContents function in the document class, as in the previous few days.

2. Edit this function, adding the code in Listing 13.5.

13

LISTING **13.5**   The CAdoDatabaseDoc DeleteContents Function

```
void CAdoDatabaseDoc::DeleteContents()
{
    // TODO: Add your specialized code here and/or call the base class
    // Close the recordset
        if (m_ptrRs)
        m_ptrRs->Close();
    // Do we have a valid pointer to the record binding?
    if (m_piAdoRecordBinding)
        // Release it
        m_piAdoRecordBinding->Release();
    // Set the recordset pointer to NULL
    m_ptrRs = NULL;

    // Shut down the COM environment
    CoUninitialize();
    CDocument::DeleteContents();
}
```

INPUT

Populating the Form

To display the record column values, add a function for copying the values from the record class to the view variables. This function first needs to get a pointer to the record class from the document class. Next, the function checks the status of each individual field in the record class to make sure that it's okay to copy, and then it copies the value. After all values are copied, you can call UpdateData to display the values in the controls on the form. To add this functionality to your application, follow these steps:

1. Add a new member function to the view class. Specify the function type as void, the function name as RefreshBoundData, and the access as public.

2. Edit this new function, adding the code in Listing 13.6.

LISTING **13.6**   The CAdoDatabaseView RefreshBoundData Function

```
void CAdoDatabaseView::RefreshBoundData(void)
{
    CCustomRs* pRs;
        // Get a pointer to the document object
    pRs = GetDocument()->GetRecSet();

    // Is the field OK
    if (adFldOK == pRs->lAddressIDStatus)
        // Copy the value
        m_lAddressID = pRs->m_lAddressID;
    else
```

INPUT

LISTING **13.6**   continued

```
            // Otherwise, set the value to 0
            m_lAddressID = 0;
    // Is the field OK
    if (adFldOK == pRs->lFirstNameStatus)
            // Copy the value
            m_strFirstName = pRs->m_szFirstName;
    else
            // Otherwise, set the value to 0
            m_strFirstName = _T("");
    // Is the field OK
    if (adFldOK == pRs->lLastNameStatus)
            // Copy the value
            m_strLastName = pRs->m_szLastName;
    else
            // Otherwise, set the value to 0
            m_strLastName = _T("");
    // Is the field OK
    if (adFldOK == pRs->lSpouseNameStatus)
            // Copy the value
            m_strSpouseName = pRs->m_szSpouseName;
    else
            // Otherwise, set the value to 0
            m_strSpouseName = _T("");
    // Is the field OK
    if (adFldOK == pRs->lAddressStatus)
            // Copy the value
            m_strAddress = pRs->m_szAddress;
    else
            // Otherwise, set the value to 0
            m_strAddress = _T("");
    // Is the field OK
    if (adFldOK == pRs->lCityStatus)
            // Copy the value
            m_strCity = pRs->m_szCity;
    else
            // Otherwise, set the value to 0
            m_strCity = _T("");
    // Is the field OK
    if (adFldOK == pRs->lStateOrProvinceStatus)
            // Copy the value
            m_strStateOrProvince = pRs->m_szStateOrProvince;
    else
            // Otherwise, set the value to 0
            m_strStateOrProvince = _T("");
    // Is the field OK
    if (adFldOK == pRs->lPostalCodeStatus)
            // Copy the value
            m_strPostalCode = pRs->m_szPostalCode;
    else
```

13

LISTING 13.6   continued

```
        // Otherwise, set the value to 0
        m_strPostalCode = _T("");
// Is the field OK
if (adFldOK == pRs->lCountryStatus)
    // Copy the value
    m_strCountry = pRs->m_szCountry;
else
    // Otherwise, set the value to 0
    m_strCountry = _T("");
// Is the field OK
if (adFldOK == pRs->lEmailAddressStatus)
    // Copy the value
    m_strEmailAddress = pRs->m_szEmailAddress;
else
    // Otherwise, set the value to 0
    m_strEmailAddress = _T("");
// Is the field OK
if (adFldOK == pRs->lHomePhoneStatus)
    // Copy the value
    m_strHomePhone = pRs->m_szHomePhone;
else
    // Otherwise, set the value to 0
    m_strHomePhone = _T("");
// Is the field OK
if (adFldOK == pRs->lWorkPhoneStatus)
    // Copy the value
    m_strWorkPhone = pRs->m_szWorkPhone;
else
    // Otherwise, set the value to 0
    m_strWorkPhone = _T("");
// Is the field OK
if (adFldOK == pRs->lWorkExtensionStatus)
    // Copy the value
    m_strWorkExtension = pRs->m_szWorkExtension;
else
    // Otherwise, set the value to 0
    m_strWorkExtension = _T("");
// Is the field OK
if (adFldOK == pRs->lFaxNumberStatus)
    // Copy the value
    m_strFaxNumber = pRs->m_szFaxNumber;
else
    // Otherwise, set the value to 0
    m_strFaxNumber = _T("");
// Is the field OK
if (adFldOK == pRs->lBirthdateStatus)
    // Copy the value
    m_oledtBirthdate = pRs->m_dtBirthdate;
else
```

LISTING 13.6　continued

```
            // Otherwise, set the value to 0
            m_oledtBirthdate = 0L;
    // Is the field OK
    if (adFldOK == pRs->lSendCardStatus)
            // Copy the value
            m_bSendCard = VARIANT_FALSE == pRs->m_bSendCard ? FALSE : TRUE;
    else
            // Otherwise, set the value to 0
            m_bSendCard = FALSE;
    // Is the field OK
    if (adFldOK == pRs->lNotesStatus)
            // Copy the value
            m_strNotes = pRs->m_szNotes;
    else
            // Otherwise, set the value to 0
            m_strNotes = _T("");

    // Sync the data with the controls
    UpdateData(FALSE);
}
```

Saving Updates

When you need to copy changes back to the recordset, you reverse the process of copying data from the controls on the form to the variables in the record class. You could take the approach of copying all values, whether or not their values have changed, or you could compare the two values to determine which have changed and need to be copied back. Call the function that does this before navigating to any other records in the recordset so that any changes that the user has made are saved to the database. To add this functionality to your application, follow these steps:

1. Add a new member function to the view class. Specify the function type as void, the function name as UpdateBoundData, and the access as private.

2. Edit the function, adding the code in Listing 13.7.

LISTING 13.7　The CAdoDatabaseView UpdateBoundData Function

```
void CAdoDatabaseView::UpdateBoundData(void)
{
    CCustomRs* pRs;
            // Get a pointer to the document
    pRs = GetDocument()->GetRecSet();

    // Sync the controls with the variables
```

INPUT

13

LISTING **13.7**   continued

```
UpdateData(TRUE);
// Has the field changed? If so, copy the value back
if (m_lAddressID != pRs->m_lAddressID)
    pRs->m_lAddressID = m_lAddressID;
// Has the field changed? If so, copy the value back
if (m_strFirstName != pRs->m_szFirstName)
    strcpy(pRs->m_szFirstName, (LPCTSTR)m_strFirstName);
// Has the field changed? If so, copy the value back
if (m_strLastName != pRs->m_szLastName)
    strcpy(pRs->m_szLastName, (LPCTSTR)m_strLastName);
// Has the field changed? If so, copy the value back
if (m_strSpouseName != pRs->m_szSpouseName)
    strcpy(pRs->m_szSpouseName, (LPCTSTR)m_strSpouseName);
// Has the field changed? If so, copy the value back
if (m_strAddress != pRs->m_szAddress)
    strcpy(pRs->m_szAddress, (LPCTSTR)m_strAddress);
// Has the field changed? If so, copy the value back
if (m_strCity != pRs->m_szCity)
    strcpy(pRs->m_szCity, (LPCTSTR)m_strCity);
// Has the field changed? If so, copy the value back
if (m_strStateOrProvince != pRs->m_szStateOrProvince)
    strcpy(pRs->m_szStateOrProvince, (LPCTSTR)m_strStateOrProvince);
// Has the field changed? If so, copy the value back
if (m_strPostalCode != pRs->m_szPostalCode)
    strcpy(pRs->m_szPostalCode, (LPCTSTR)m_strPostalCode);
// Has the field changed? If so, copy the value back
if (m_strCountry != pRs->m_szCountry)
    strcpy(pRs->m_szCountry, (LPCTSTR)m_strCountry);
// Has the field changed? If so, copy the value back
if (m_strEmailAddress != pRs->m_szEmailAddress)
    strcpy(pRs->m_szEmailAddress, (LPCTSTR)m_strEmailAddress);
// Has the field changed? If so, copy the value back
if (m_strHomePhone != pRs->m_szHomePhone)
    strcpy(pRs->m_szHomePhone, (LPCTSTR)m_strHomePhone);
// Has the field changed? If so, copy the value back
if (m_strWorkPhone != pRs->m_szWorkPhone)
    strcpy(pRs->m_szWorkPhone, (LPCTSTR)m_strWorkPhone);
// Has the field changed? If so, copy the value back
if (m_strWorkExtension != pRs->m_szWorkExtension)
    strcpy(pRs->m_szWorkExtension, (LPCTSTR)m_strWorkExtension);
// Has the field changed? If so, copy the value back
if (m_strFaxNumber != pRs->m_szFaxNumber)
    strcpy(pRs->m_szFaxNumber, (LPCTSTR)m_strFaxNumber);
// Has the field changed? If so, copy the value back
if (((DATE)m_oledtBirthdate) != pRs->m_dtBirthdate)
    pRs->m_dtBirthdate = (DATE)m_oledtBirthdate;
// Has the field changed? If so, copy the value back
if (m_bSendCard == TRUE)
    pRs->m_bSendCard = VARIANT_TRUE;
```

LISTING 13.7 continued

```
    else
        pRs->m_bSendCard = VARIANT_FALSE;
    // Has the field changed? If so, copy the value back
    if (m_strNotes != pRs->m_szNotes)
        strcpy(pRs->m_szNotes, (LPCTSTR)m_strNotes);
}
```

> **Caution**
>
> The preceding code does not take into account strings that are longer than the field lengths defined in the database. For this you would need to add some length checking code to truncate strings that exceed the length of the database field into which it will be stored. You may also make use of the strncpy function where you pass a third parameter specifying the number of characters to copy from the second string to the first.

Navigating the Recordset

For navigating the recordset, add a series of menus for each of the four basic navigation choices: first, previous, next, and last. Because the Recordset object and record-binding interface pointers are in the document object, the event messages for these menus must be passed to the document class to update the current record and then to navigate to the selected record. However, the view class needs to receive the event message first because it needs to copy back any changed values from the controls on the form before the update is performed. When the navigation is complete, the view also needs to update the form with the new record's column values. Looking at the sequence of where the event message needs to be passed, it makes the most sense to add the event message handler to the view class, and from there, call the event message handler for the document class.

To add this functionality to your application, follow these steps:

1. Add the four menu entries for navigating through the recordset (First, Previous, Next, and Last) and the corresponding toolbar buttons.

2. Add an event-handler function to the view class for the command event for all four of these menus.

3. Edit the event function for the Move First menu, adding the code in Listing 13.8.

13

LISTING 13.8 The CAdoDatabaseView OnDataFirst Function

```
void CAdoDatabaseView::OnDataFirst()
{
    // TODO: Add your command-handler code here
```

LISTING 13.8 continued

```
          // Update the current record
INPUT         UpdateBoundData();
       // Navigate to the first record
       GetDocument()->MoveFirst();
       // Refresh the form with the new record's data
       RefreshBoundData();
    }
```

Now add the `MoveFirst` function to the document class and perform all the actual recordset functionality for this function:

1. Add a member function to the document class in your application. Specify the function type as `void`, the name as `MoveFirst`, and the access as public.

2. Edit this function, adding the code in Listing 13.9.

Listing 13.9 The `CAdoDatabaseDoc` `MoveFirst` Function

```
void CAdoDatabaseDoc::MoveFirst(void)
{
    try
    {
        // Update the current record
        m_piAdoRecordBinding->Update(&m_rsRecSet);
        // Move to the first record
        m_ptrRs->MoveFirst();
    }
    // Any errors?
    catch (_com_error &e)
    {
        // Generate the error message
        GenerateError(e.Error(), e.Description());
    }
}
```

3. Edit and add the same set of functions to the view and document classes for the `MovePrevious`, `MoveNext`, and `MoveLast` ADO functions.

After you add all these functions, you should be ready to compile and run your application. Your application will be capable of opening the Addresses database table and presenting you with each individual record, which you can edit and update, as in Figure 13.6.

FIGURE 13.6

*The running
application.*

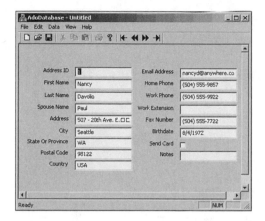

Adding New Records

Now that you can retrieve and navigate the recordset in the database table, it would be nice if you could add some new records to the table. You can add this functionality in exactly the same fashion that you added the navigation functionality: add a menu, trigger an event function in the view class from the menu, update the current record values back to the recordset, call a function in the document class, and refresh the current record from the recordset.

As far as the menu and the view class are concerned, the only difference between this functionality and any of the navigation menus and functions is the ID of the menu and the name of the functions that are called, just as with the different navigation functions. In the document function, things begin to diverge just a little.

In the document class function for adding a new record, after you update the current record, you need to make sure that adding a new record is an option. If it is, you can build an empty record and add it to the recordset. After you add the empty record, navigate to the last record in the set because this will be the new record. At this point, you can exit this function and let the view class refresh the form with the data values from the new, empty record.

To add this functionality to your application, follow these steps:

1. Add a new menu entry for adding a new record (Add).

2. Add an event-handler function to the view class for this new menu, adding the same code to the function as you did with the navigation functions, but call the AddNew function in the document class.

13

3. Add the AddNew function to the document class. Add a new member function to the document class, specifying the type as void, the name as AddNew, and the access as public.

4. Edit the AddNew function, adding the code in Listing 13.10.

LISTING **13.10**   The CAdoDatabaseDoc AddNew Function

```
void CAdoDatabaseDoc::AddNew(void)
{
    try
        {
        // Update the current record
        m_piAdoRecordBinding->Update(&m_rsRecSet);
        // Can we add a new record?
        if (m_ptrRs->Supports(adAddNew))
        {
            // Create a blank record
            CreateBlankRecord();
            // Add the blank record
            m_piAdoRecordBinding->AddNew(&m_rsRecSet);
            // Move to the last record
            m_ptrRs->MoveLast();
        }
    }
    // Any errors?
    catch (_com_error &e)
    {
        // Generate an error message
        GenerateError(e.Error(), e.Description());
    }
}
```

Now you'll add the function that creates the blank record. In this function, you'll set each field variable in the record class to an almost empty string. To add this function to your class, follow these steps:

1. Add a new member function to the document class. Specify its type as void, its name as CreateBlankRecord, and its access as private.

2. Edit this new function, adding the code in Listing 13.11.

LISTING **13.11**   The CAdoDatabaseDoc CreateBlankRecord Function

```
void CAdoDatabaseDoc::CreateBlankRecord(void)
{
    // Set each of the values in the record object
        m_rsRecSet.m_lAddressID = 0;
```

LISTING 13.11   continued

```
    strcpy(m_rsRecSet.m_szFirstName, " ");
    strcpy(m_rsRecSet.m_szLastName, " ");
    strcpy(m_rsRecSet.m_szSpouseName, " ");
    strcpy(m_rsRecSet.m_szAddress, " ");
    strcpy(m_rsRecSet.m_szCity, " ");
    strcpy(m_rsRecSet.m_szStateOrProvince, " ");
    strcpy(m_rsRecSet.m_szPostalCode, " ");
    strcpy(m_rsRecSet.m_szCountry, " ");
    strcpy(m_rsRecSet.m_szEmailAddress, " ");
    strcpy(m_rsRecSet.m_szHomePhone, " ");
    strcpy(m_rsRecSet.m_szWorkPhone, " ");
    strcpy(m_rsRecSet.m_szWorkExtension, " ");
    strcpy(m_rsRecSet.m_szFaxNumber, " ");
    m_rsRecSet.m_dtBirthdate = NULL;
    m_rsRecSet.m_bSendCard = VARIANT_FALSE;
    strcpy(m_rsRecSet.m_szNotes, " ");
}
```

If you compile and run your application, you should be able to insert and edit new records in the database table.

Deleting Records

The final piece of functionality to add to your application is the capability to delete the current record from the set. This function can follow the same form as all the navigation and add functions with a menu entry calling an event-handler function in the view class. The function in the view class can even follow the same set of code that you used in these previous functions, updating the current record, calling the corresponding function in the document class, and then refreshing the current record to the form.

In the document class function, the record deletion should follow almost the same path you took for adding a new record. You'll update the current record, check to determine whether it's possible to delete the current record, check with users to verify that they want to delete the current record, call the Delete function, and then navigate to another record in the set. To add this functionality to your application, follow these steps:

1. Add a new menu entry for the Delete function and then attach an event-handler function for the menu's command event in the view class.

2. Edit this function, adding the same code as in the navigation and add record functions, and calling the Delete function in the document class.

3. Add a new member function to the document class. Specify the new function's type as void, the name as Delete, and the access as public.

4. Edit this function, adding the code in Listing 13.12.

13

LISTING 13.12   The `CAdoDatabaseDoc` Delete Function

```
void CAdoDatabaseDoc::Delete(void)
{
    try
    {
        // Update the current record
        m_piAdoRecordBinding->Update(&m_rsRecSet);
        // Can we delete a record?
        if (m_ptrRs->Supports(adDelete))
        {
            // Make sure the user wants to delete this record
            if (AfxMessageBox(
                    "Are you sure you want to delete this record?",
                    MB_YESNO | MB_ICONQUESTION) == IDYES)
            {
                // Delete the record
                m_ptrRs->Delete(adAffectCurrent);
                // Move to the previous record
                m_ptrRs->MovePrevious();
            }
        }
    }
    // Any errors?
    catch (_com_error &e)
    {
        // Generate an error message
        GenerateError(e.Error(), e.Description());
    }
}
```

When you compile and run your application, you should be able to delete any records from the set that you want. If you delete all of the records in the recordset, an error will be produced on the move to the previous record. You need to check to see if there are any records remaining in the recordset prior to calling this method.

Summary

Today you learned about Microsoft's latest database access technology, ActiveX Data Objects. You learned how you can import the DLL, providing a rich set of data-access functionality that you can use and control in your applications. You learned how you can retrieve a set of data, manipulate the records in the set, and save your changes back in the database. You learned two different ways of accessing and updating the data values in a record in the recordset and how you can do a little more work upfront to save a large amount of work in the midst of the application coding.

Q&A

Q. Because Visual C++ doesn't support ADO with its wizards, why would I want to use it?

A. ADO is the database-access technology direction for Microsoft. It'll gradually become the data access technology for use with all programming languages and applications. Eventually, the wizards may be added to build some of the database access functionality for you.

Q. If ADO uses ODBC to get to my database, why wouldn't I want to just go straight to the ODBC interface to access my database?

A. ADO can use ODBC to access those databases that don't have a native OLE DB interface. If you are using either SQL Server or Oracle, OLE DB interfaces are available, in which case ADO wouldn't go through ODBC to get to the database. In these cases, using ADO gives your application better performance than using the ODBC interface.

Workshop

The Workshop provides quiz questions to help you solidify your understanding of the material covered and exercises to provide you with experience in using what you've learned. The answers to the quiz questions and exercises are provided in Appendix A, "Answers to Quiz Questions."

Quiz

1. What does ADO stand for?
2. What does ADO use for database access?
3. What are the objects in ADO?
4. How do you initialize the COM environment?
5. How do you associate a `Connection` object with a `Command` object?
6. How do you associate a `Command` object with and populate a `Recordset` object?

Exercise

Enable and disable the navigation menus and toolbar buttons based on whether the recordset is at the beginning of file (`BOF`) or end of file (`EOF`, renamed to `EndOfFile`).

13

DAY 14

Sharing Functionality with Other Applications Through DLLs

Sometimes you need to build a set of application functionality to be used in an application that another programmer is building. Maybe the functionality will be used in a number of applications. Another possibility is that you want to separate some functionality from the rest of the application for organizational purposes. You might develop this separate set of functionality and then give a copy of the code to your friend to include in his application, but then every time you make any changes to your set of functionality, it has to be reincorporated into the other set of application code. It would be much more practical if you could give a compiled version of your functionality to the other programmer so that every time you update your part, all you need to hand over is a new compiled file. The new file replaces the previous version, without having to make any changes to the other programmer's code.

Often, a family of applications will have some functionality in common. When you place this shared functionality into DLLs instead of library modules, all the applications can use the same functionality with only a single copy of the functionality distributed in the form of DLLs, instead of duplicating the same functionality in each application. This method saves disk space on any systems where the applications are installed.

Today, you will learn

- How to create different types of DLLs with Visual C++ and how to determine which type best suits your needs
- How to build two types of DLLs and the difference in approach for the different DLL types
- How to use the functionality for both types of DLLs in a Visual C++ application
- How to determine when an application needs to be relinked when you modify a DLL used by the application

Designing Classes

You've already designed and built your own classes over the past few days, so the basics of creating a new class isn't a new topic. Why did you create these classes? Each new class that you created encapsulated a set of functionality that acted as a self-contained unit. These units consisted of both data and functionality that worked together to define the object.

Encapsulation

Object-oriented software design is the practice of designing software in the same way that everything else in the world is designed. For instance, you can consider your car built from a collection of objects: the engine, the body, the suspension, and so on. Each object consists of a bunch of other objects. For instance, the engine contains a carburetor or fuel injectors, the combustion chamber and pistons, the starter, the alternator, the drive chain, and so on. Again, each object consists of even more objects.

Each object performs a function. Each knows how to perform its own functions with little, if any, knowledge of how the other objects perform their functions. Each knows how it interacts with the other objects and how it is connected to the other objects, but that's about all each object knows about the others. How each object works internally is hidden from the other objects. The brakes on your car don't know anything about how the transmission works, but if you have an automatic transmission, the brakes do know how to tell the transmission that they are being applied, and the transmission decides how to react to this information. (Actually, the brakes just slow down the car, and the transmission itself decides how to handle the new state of the car's movement)

NEW TERM You need to approach designing new classes for your applications in the same way. The rest of the application objects don't need to know how your objects work; they need to know only how to interact with your objects. This principle, called *encapsulation*, is one of the basic principles of object-oriented software.

Inheritance

NEW TERM Another key principle of object-oriented software design is the concept of *inheritance*. An object can be inherited from another object. The descendent object inherits all the existing functionality of the base object. This allows you to define the descendent object in terms of how it's different from the base object.

Let's see how this could work with a thermostat. Suppose that you had a basic thermostat to use in just about any setting. You could set a temperature for it to maintain, and it would turn on the furnace or air conditioner as needed to maintain that temperature. Now say that you needed to create a thermostat for use in a freezer. You could start from scratch and build a customized thermostat, or you could take your existing thermostat and specify how the freezer version varies from the original. These differences might include that it's limited to turning on the air conditioning and could never turn on the heater. You would probably also put a strict limit on the range of temperatures to which the thermostat could be set, such as around and below 32° Fahrenheit, or 0° Celsius. Likewise, if you needed a thermostat for an office building, you would probably want to limit the temperature range to what's normally comfortable for people and not allow the temperature to be set to an extremely cold or hot setting.

With inheritance in creating your own classes, this method just described represents the same principle that you want to apply. If possible, you should start with an existing C++ class that has the basic functionality that you need and then program how your class varies from the base class from which you inherited. You can add new data elements, extend existing functionality, or override existing functionality as you see fit.

Visual C++ Class Types

In most application projects, when you are creating a new class, you have a few options on the type of class that you are creating:

- Generic
- MFC
- ATL

Which type of classes you choose to create depends on your needs and what your class will be doing. It also depends on whether your class needs to descend from any MFC classes.

14

Generic Class

You use a generic class for creating a class that's inherited from a class you've already created. This class type is intended for creating classes that aren't inherited from any MFC classes (although you've already seen where you can use it to create classes that are based on MFC classes). If you want to create a more specialized version of the CLine class—for instance, a CRedLine class—that only draws in red, you create it as a generic class because it's inherited from another class that you created.

MFC Class

If you want to make a reusable class based on an existing MFC class, such as an edit box that automatically formats numbers as currency, you want to create an MFC class. The MFC class type is for creating new classes that are inherited from existing MFC classes.

 Note

Prior to the new version of Visual C++, you were limited to certain MFC classes that you could use as base classes through the New MFC Class Wizard. If you needed to inherit from a MFC class that wasn't included in the Wizard, you had to create a generic class. The new version of Visual C++ has opened this up quite significantly, enabling you to use many more MFC classes as base classes. With the new version of Visual C++, you could have created your CLine class as an MFC class, using the CObject class as the base class. Prior to the newest version of Visual C++, you were limited to creating a generic class in this situation.

ATL Class

The ATL (Active Template Library) class type is used for creating components and services. It's an alternative class library to MFC, used to build components for use in applications, but not whole user-oriented applications (it can be used to create service applications, which users don't see). You'll learn about ATL and how to use it to build components and services on Day 20, "Building Components with ATL."

Why Create DLLs?

When you create new classes for your application, they can be used in other applications as well. Often, with a little thought and effort, classes you create can be made flexible enough so that they can be used in other applications. When this is the case, you need some way of packaging the classes for other applications without having to hand over all your source code. This is the issue that DLLs address. They allow you to compile your classes and modules into a compiled object code library that can be linked into any other Visual C++ application.

Microsoft introduced dynamic link libraries (DLLs) back in the early days of Windows. DLLs are similar to library modules in that they both contain sets of functionality packaged for use by applications. The difference is when the applications link to the library. With a library module (LIB), the application is linked to the functionality in the library during the compile and build process. The functionality contained in the library file becomes part of the application executable file. With a DLL, the application links to the functionality in the library file when the application is run. The library file remains a separate file referenced and called by the application.

There are several reasons for creating DLLs:

- You can reduce the size of the application's executable files by placing functionality used by multiple applications into DLLs shared by all applications.

- You can update and modify functionality in the DLLs without having to update the application executable (assuming that the exported interface for the DLL doesn't change).

- If you create the right type of DLL, you can use DLLs with just about any other Windows programming language, which makes your functionality available to a wider number of programmers, not just fellow Visual C++ programmers.

Creating and Using DLLs

DLLs are library files with compiled code that other applications can use. The DLLs expose certain functions and classes to these applications by exporting the function. When a function is exported, it's added to a table included in the DLL. This table lists the location of all exported functions contained in the DLL and is used to locate and call each function. Any functions not exported are not added to this table, nor can they be seen or called by any outside application or DLL.

An application can call the functions in the DLL in two ways. The more involved method of calling these functions is to look up the location of the desired function in the DLL and get a pointer to this function. The pointer can then be used to call the function.

The other, much easier way (and the only way that you'll use in any of the examples in this book) is to link the application with the LIB file created with the DLL. This file is treated by the linker as a standard library file. The LIB file contains stubs for each exported function in the DLL. A stub is a pseudo-function that has the same name and argument list as the real function. In the interior of the function stub is a small amount of code that calls the real function in the DLL, passing all the arguments that were passed to the stub. This way, you can treat the DLL's functions as though they were part of the application code and not as a separate file.

14

Note

> The LIB file is automatically created for the DLL during the DLL's compilation. You don't need to do anything extra to create it.

Tip

> Not only is it easier to create your applications using the LIB files for any DLLs that you will be using, but it also can be safer when running the application. When you use the LIB files, any DLLs used by your application are loaded into memory the moment the application is started. If any DLLs are missing, Windows automatically informs users of the problem, and your application doesn't run. If you don't use the LIB files, you are responsible for loading the DLL into memory and handling any errors that occur if the DLL can't be found.

You can easily create two types of DLLs using Visual C++: MFC extension DLLs and regular DLLs.

Note

> You can create other types of DLLs using Visual C++. All these other types of DLLs involve a significant amount of ActiveX functionality, so they are beyond the scope of this book. If you need to build ActiveX in-process server DLLs or other types of ActiveX DLLs, I recommend that you find an advanced book on Visual C++ that provides significant coverage for these topics.

MFC Extension DLLs

MFC DLLs are the easiest to code and create because you can treat them just like any other class collection. For any classes that you want to export from the DLL, the only thing that you need to add is the AFX_EXT_CLASS macro in the class declaration, as follows:

```
class AFX_EXT_CLASS CMyClass
{
...
};
```

This macro exports the class, making it accessible to Visual C++ applications. You need to include this macro in the header file used by the applications that will use the DLL, where it will import the class from the DLL so it can be used. The classes that don't include this macro in the class declaration are not exported, and thus not visible to applications using the DLL.

The one drawback to creating MFC extension DLLs is that they can't be used by any other programming languages. They can be used with other C++ compilers as long as the compiler supports MFC (such as with Borland's and Symantec's C++ compilers).

Regular DLLs

The other type of DLL is a regular DLL. This type of DLL exports standard functions from the DLL, not C++ classes. As a result, this type of DLL can require a little more thought and planning than an MFC extension DLL. Inside the DLL, you can use classes all you want, but you have to provide straight function calls to the external applications.

To export a function, you have to declare it as an export function by preceding the function name with

```
extern "C" function_type PASCAL EXPORT function_declaration
```

You need to include all this additional stuff in both the header file function prototype and the actual source code:

- The extern "C" portion declares that this is a standard C function call so that the C++ name mangler doesn't mangle the function name.
- PASCAL tells the compiler that all function parameters are to be passed in PASCAL order, which places the parameters on the stack in the reverse order from how they are normally placed.
- EXPORT tells the compiler that this function is to be exported from the DLL and can be called outside the DLL.

To export the functions from your DLL, you also need to add all the exported function names to the DEF file for the DLL project. This file builds the stub LIB file and the export table in the DLL. It contains the name of the DLL, or library, a brief description of the DLL, and the names of all functions to be exported. This file has to follow a specific format, so you shouldn't modify the default DEF file automatically created by the DLL Wizard other than to add exported function names. A typical DEF file follows:

```
LIBRARY      "mydll"
DESCRIPTION 'mydll Windows Dynamic Link Library'

EXPORTS
    ; Explicit exports can go here
    MyFunc1
    MyFunc2
```

You can eliminate the need for the DEF file by adding __declspec(dllexport) in front of your function declarations. This is a directive that was added to Visual C++ a few years back to ease the complexity involved in exporting functions in a DLL. The __declspec(dllexport) directive tells the compiler to export the following function in the DLL, just like including the function name in the DEF file does.

14

If you're using MFC classes in your regular DLLs, you need to call the
AFX_MANAGE_STATE macro as the first line of code in all exported functions. This is necessary to make the exported functions thread-safe, which allows your class functions to
be called simultaneously by two or more threads. The AFX_MANAGE_STATE macro takes a
single argument, a pointer to an AFX_MODULE_STATE structure, which can be retrieved by
calling the AfxGetStaticModuleState function. A typical exported function that uses
MFC looks like the following:

```
extern "C" void PASCAL EXPORT MyFunc(...)
{
    AFX_MANAGE_STATE(AfxGetStaticModuleState());
    // normal function body here
...
}
```

Designing DLLs

When designing your DLLs, be aware that any functions in them can be called simultaneously by multiple threads all running at the same time. As a result, all the functionality
in any DLLs that you create must be thread-safe.

All variables that hold any values beyond each individual function call must be held and
maintained by the application and not the DLL. Any application variables that must be
manipulated by the DLL should be passed in to the DLL as a function argument. Any
global variables manipulated within the DLL may be swapped with variables from other
application threads while the function is running, leading to unpredictable results, thus
any global variable manipulation must be protected using thread synchronization mechanisms, which will be covered on Day 17, "Implementing Multitasking in Your
Applications."

Creating and Using an MFC Extension DLL

To see how easy it is to create and use an MFC extension DLL, you'll create one that
contains two classes. The first class will be the CLine class that you first created on Day
10, "Creating SDI and MDI Applications." The second class will create the random
drawings on the drawing surface. This class will contain an object array of the CLine
objects that it will create and populate with each drawing effort. This second class will
also need functionality to save and restore the drawing, as well as to delete the existing
drawing so that a new drawing can be started. It will need to know the drawing area's
dimensions so that it can generate a drawing that will fit in the drawing area. After you
create this module, you'll see how you can use it in an application project. After you see
how easy it is to create MFC extension DLLs, you'll then re-implement the same functionality as a regular DLL so that you can get an understanding of the different approaches necessary with the two DLL styles.

Creating the MFC Extension DLL

To start the project for today's example, follow these steps:

1. Create a new project, specifying that it's an MFC DLL project (see Figure 14.1). Name the project ModArtDll, and click OK to create the project.

FIGURE 14.1

Specifying an MFC DLL project.

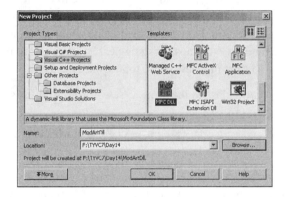

2. In the Application Settings area, specify MFC extension DLL (see Figure 14.2). Click Finish to create the project.

   After you create your project, you'll find yourself working with a project that has no classes. You've got a blank slate from which you can create whatever type of module you need.

FIGURE 14.2

Specifying the type of DLL to create.

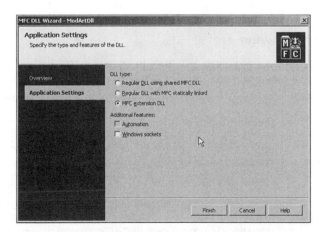

14

3. Because you already have the CLine class built, copy it (both Line.h and Line.cpp) from the Day 10 project area into the directory for today's project.

4. Add the header and source code files to today's project by choosing Add Existing Item from the Project menu. After you add both files to the project, you should see the CLine class appear in the Class View of your project.

Defining the Classes

Now that you have a basic project ready to go, it's time to begin adding the meat of the module. Using the CLine class is an easy way of reusing some functionality that you created earlier in another setting. However, this module's real functionality will be in its ability to generate random drawings, or squiggles. For this functionality, you'll need to create a new class. To start this new class, follow these steps:

1. Add a new generic class to the project (select Add, Add Class from the context menu) in the Class View tab.

2. Name the new class CModArt, the base class as CObject, and specify the access as public.

After you create your class, you need to add a couple of variables to it. First, you need somewhere to hold all the lines that will make up the drawing, so you'll add an object array. Second, you need to know the area of the drawing surface, so you'll want a CRect to hold the drawing area specification. Add both variables to your new class by using the following types and names:

Type	Name	Access
CRect	m_rDrawArea	Private
CObArray	m_oaLines	Private

Setting the Drawing Area

Before you can draw anything, you need to know the area that you have to draw within. You can add a public function to your class that will copy the passed in CRect to the member CRect variable. To add this function to your project, follow these steps:

1. Add a new member function to your new class.

2. Specify the function type as void, the name as SetRect, add a parameter of type CRect and named rDrawArea, and specify the access as public.

3. Edit the function as follows:

```
void CModArt::SetRect(CRect rDrawArea)
{
    // Set the drawing area rectangle
    m_rDrawArea = rDrawArea;
}
```

Creating a New Drawing

One key piece to this module is the ability to generate random squiggles on the drawing area. By generating a whole series of these squiggles, your module can create an entire drawing. By starting with the single squiggle, you can design a function that generates one squiggle and then calls this function numerous times to generate the entire drawing.

This first function, the squiggle generator, needs to determine how many lines will be in the squiggle, the color and width of the pen used, and the starting point. From this point, it could loop through the appropriate number of lines, generating a new destination to continue the squiggle from the previous destination point.

To add this functionality to your project, follow these steps:

1. Add a new member function to the drawing class.

2. Specify the function type as void, the name as NewLine, and the access as private (because this function will only be called by the master loop that's determining how many squiggles will be in the final drawing).

3. Edit the new function with the code in Listing 14.1.

LISTING 14.1   The CModArt NewLine Function

```
void CModArt::NewLine(void)
{
    int iNumLines;
    int iCurLine;
    int iCurColor;
    UINT nCurWidth;
    CPoint ptTo;
    CPoint ptFrom;

    static COLORREF crColors[8] = {
        RGB(   0,   0,   0),     // Black
        RGB(   0,   0, 255),     // Blue
        RGB(   0, 255,   0),     // Green
        RGB(   0, 255, 255),     // Cyan
        RGB( 255,   0,   0),     // Red
        RGB( 255,   0, 255),     // Magenta
        RGB( 255, 255,   0),     // Yellow
        RGB( 255, 255, 255)      // White
    };

    // Normalize the rectangle before determining the width and height
    m_rDrawArea.NormalizeRect();
    // get the area width and height
    int iWidth = m_rDrawArea.Width();
    int iHeight = m_rDrawArea.Height();
```

14

LISTING **14.1**   continued

```
// Determine the number of parts to this squiggle
iNumLines = rand() % 100;
// Are there any parts to this squiggle?
if (iNumLines > 0)
{
    // Determine the color
    iCurColor = rand() % 8;
    // Determine the pen width
    nCurWidth = (rand() % 8) + 1;
    // Determine the starting point for the squiggle
    ptFrom.x = (rand() % iWidth) + m_rDrawArea.left;
    ptFrom.y = (rand() % iHeight) + m_rDrawArea.top;
    // Loop through the number of segments
    for (iCurLine = 0; iCurLine < iNumLines; iCurLine++)
    {
        // Determine the end point of the segment
        ptTo.x = ((rand() % 20) - 10) + ptFrom.x;
        ptTo.y = ((rand() % 20) - 10) + ptFrom.y;
        // Create a new CLine object
        CLine *pLine = NULL;
        try
        {
            pLine = new CLine(ptFrom, ptTo, crColors[iCurColor],
                nCurWidth);
            // Add the new line to the object array
            m_oaLines.Add(pLine);
        }
        // Did we run into a memory exception?
        catch (CMemoryException* perr)
        {
            // Display a message for the user, giving him the
            // bad news
            AfxMessageBox("Out of memory", MB_ICONSTOP | MB_OK);
            // Did we create a line object?
            if (pLine)
            {
                // Delete it
                delete pLine;
                pLine = NULL;
            }
            // Delete the exception object
            perr->Delete();
        }
        // Set the starting point to the end point
        ptFrom = ptTo;
    }
}
}
```

The function in Listing 14.1 first makes the area available for drawing with the following lines:

```
m_rDrawArea.NormalizeRect();
int iWidth = m_rDrawArea.Width();
int iHeight = m_rDrawArea.Height();
```

The first of these lines normalizes the rectangle. This is necessary to guarantee that the width and height returned in the next two lines are both positive values. Because of the coordinate system used in Windows, getting the width by subtracting the left-side position from the right-side position can result in a negative number. The same can happen with the height. By normalizing the rectangle, you are guaranteeing that you'll get positive results for these two values.

After the drawing area is determined, the function determines the number of line segments you would use in this squiggle:

```
iNumLines = rand() % 100;
```

The rand function can return numbers in a wide range. By getting the modulus of 100, you guarantee that the resulting number will be between 0 and 100. This technique is common for generating random numbers within a certain range, using the modulus function with the upper limit of the value range (or the upper limit minus the lower limit, if the lower limit isn't equal to 0, and then adding the lower limit to the resulting number). You use the same technique to determine the color, width, and starting position for the squiggle:

```
iCurColor = rand() % 8;
nCurWidth = (rand() % 8) + 1;
ptFrom.x = (rand() % iWidth) + m_rDrawArea.left;
ptFrom.y = (rand() % iHeight) + m_rDrawArea.top;
```

Notice that when this code determines the starting position, it adds the left and top of the drawing area to the generated position. This guarantees that the starting position is within the drawing area. In the loop that generates all the line segments in the squiggle, the available area for the next destination is limited within 10 of the current position:

```
ptTo.x = ((rand() % 20) - 10) + ptFrom.x;
ptTo.y = ((rand() % 20) - 10) + ptFrom.y;
CLine *pLine = NULL;
pLine = new CLine(ptFrom, ptTo, crColors[iCurColor], nCurWidth);
m_oaLines.Add(pLine);
```

You can easily increase this distance to make the drawings more angular. After the next line segment, you create the line object and add it to the object array. Finally, you set the starting position to the ending position of the line segment you just generated:

```
ptFrom = ptTo;
```

14

Now you are ready to go through the loop again and generate the next line segment, until you've generated all line segments in this squiggle.

Now that you can generate a single squiggle, the rest of the process is easy. First, determine how many squiggles will be in the drawing. Next, loop for the number of squiggles that need to be generated and call the NewLine function once for each squiggle. To add this functionality to your project, follow these steps:

1. Add a new member function to the drawing class.

2. Specify the type as void, the name as NewDrawing, and the access as public.

3. Edit the function as in Listing 14.2.

LISTING 14.2   The CModArt NewDrawing Function

```
void CModArt::NewDrawing(void)
{
    int iNumLines;
    int iCurLine;

    // Determine how many lines to create
    iNumLines = rand() % 10;
    // Are there any lines to create?
    if (iNumLines > 0)
    {
        // Loop through the number of lines
        for (iCurLine = 0; iCurLine < iNumLines; iCurLine++)
        {
            // Create the new line
            NewLine();
        }
    }
}
```

Displaying the Drawing

To draw the set of squiggles on the drawing area, you can add a function that will loop through the object array, calling the Draw function on each line segment in the array. This function needs to receive the device context as the only argument and must pass it along to each line segment. To add this function to your project, follow these steps:

1. Add a new member function to the drawing class.

2. Specify the function type as void and the function name as Draw, add a parameter of type CDC* named pDC, and specify the access as public.

3. Edit the function as in Listing 14.3.

LISTING 14.3 The CModArt Draw Function

```
void CModArt::Draw(CDC* pDC)
{
    // Get the number of lines in the object array
    int iCount = m_oaLines.GetSize();
    int iPos;

    // Are there any objects in the array?
    if (iCount)
    {
        // Loop through the array, deleting each object
        for (iPos = 0; iPos < iCount; iPos++)
            ((CLine*)m_oaLines.GetAt(iPos))->Draw(pDC);
    }
}
```

Serializing the Drawing

Because you are using the line segment class that you created earlier and have already made serializable, you don't need to add the serialization macros to the drawing class. What you do need to add is a Serialize function that passes the archive object on to the object array, letting the object array and line segment objects do all the serialization work. To add this function to your project, follow these steps:

1. Add a new member function to the drawing class.

2. Specify the function type as void and the name as Serialize, add a parameter of type CArchive& named ar, and specify the access as public.

3. Edit the function as follows:

```
void CModArt::Serialize(CArchive &ar)
{
    // Pass the archive object on to the array
    m_oaLines.Serialize(ar);
}
```

Clearing the Drawing

To provide full functionality, you need to be able to delete a drawing from the drawing class so that a new drawing can be created or an existing drawing can be loaded. This is a simple matter of looping through the object array and destroying every line segment object and then resetting the object array. To add this functionality to your project, follow these steps:

1. Add a new member function to the drawing class.

2. Specify the type as void, the name as ClearDrawing, and the access as public.

3. Edit the function as in Listing 14.4.

14

LISTING 14.4 The `CModArt` `ClearDrawing` Function

```
void CModArt::ClearDrawing(void)
{
    // Get the number of lines in the object array
    int iCount = m_oaLines.GetSize();
    int iPos;

    // Are there any objects in the array?
    // Loop through the array, deleting each object
    for (iPos = 0; iPos < iCount; iPos++)
        delete m_oaLines.GetAt(iPos);
    // Reset the array
    m_oaLines.RemoveAll();
}
```

Completing the Class

Finally, to wrap up your drawing class, you need to initialize the random number generator. The random number generator function, `rand`, generates a statistically random number sequence based on a series of mathematical calculations. If the number generator starts with the same number each time, the sequence of numbers is the same each time. To get the random number generator to produce a different number sequence each time your application runs, you need to seed it with a value that varies each time. The typical way to do this is to feed the current system time into the `srand` function, which seeds the random number generator with a different time each time the application runs. This seeding of the number generator must be done only once each time the application is run. You can add this functionality by doing the following:

1. Edit the drawing class constructor with the following code:

```
CModArt::CModArt(void)
{
    // Initialize the random number generator
    srand((unsigned)time(NULL));
}
```

2. You also need to add the AFX_EXT_CLASS macro to the class declaration. To add this macro, open the header file (ModArt.h) containing the definition of the drawing class.

3. Add the macro to the class declaration as follows:

INPUT
```
class AFX_EXT_CLASS CModArt :
    public CObject
{
. . .
```

You've completed your DLL module. Before you go any further, you need to compile your project. As soon as you compile it, you can't run anything because you need to create an application that uses your DLL in order to run and test your code. To get ready for creating this test application, close the entire workspace so that you can start with a clean workspace for the test application.

Creating a Test Application

To be able to test your module, you need to create a test application that uses it. This plain application can contain just enough functionality to thoroughly test the module. All you want to do at this point is test all the module's functionality; you don't have to create a full-blown application.

When you create your test application, you need to include the header file for the drawing class in the relevant classes in your application. In a typical SDI or MDI application, this means including the header file in the document class at a minimum and probably the view and application class source files also. You also have to add the LIB file that was created with your DLL in the application project so that it will be linked into your application.

Creating the Test Application Shell

Creating a test application shell is a simple matter of creating a standard SDI or MDI application shell. For the purposes of keeping the test application as simple as possible, it's probably advisable to use an SDI application. However, if some functionality in your module is intended for use in an MDI application, that application style might be better selected as your test application.

For the test application for the sample module you created, follow these steps:

1. Create a new MFC Application Visual C++ project. Name the project TestApp.

2. In the Application Type area, select Single Document for the application type.

3. In the Document Template Strings area, enter a three-letter file extension for the files that your application will generate.

After you create the application shell, you need to add the library module to the project. You can do this by performing the following:

1. Select Add Existing Item from the Project menu.

2. Specify the file types as all files.

3. Navigate to the DLL project's debug directory to find the .LIB module that you created with the previous project. This typically requires moving up one directory level, finding the project directory for the module, and then navigating through it

14

to the debug directory. (If you are building the release version of the module and application, you want to navigate down to the release directory of the module project.) You should be able to find the library file for the module you created, as shown in Figure 14.3. Select this module and click OK to add it to the project.

14.3

Adding a library file to the project.

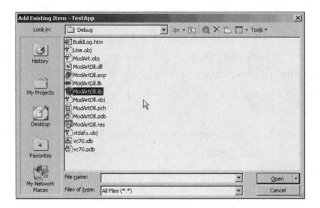

After you add the library file to the project, you also need to add the header files for any classes in the module that will be used into the appropriate application source code files. For the test application that you are building, continue with these steps:

1. Select Add Existing Item from the Project menu.

2. Navigate to the project directory of the DLL project.

3. Select the file ModArt.h and click OK to add it to the project.

Note

> You only need to add the header files for those classes in the DLL that have been exported, and that you'll be accessing in your project. If you add the header files for classes that have not been exported, you may run into link errors when you try and build your application.

The last thing that you need to do in preparing the application shell is to add a variable for any classes from the DLL that need to be included in any of the application classes. In the case of the test application that you are building, this is a variable in the document class of the drawing class that you created in the library module project. To add this variable to your application, perform these steps:

1. Add a new member variable to the document class.

2. Specify the variable type as CModArt, the name as m_maDrawing, and the access as private.

Creating a New Drawing

The first place where you want to put some of the functionality of your module is when you are creating a new document. This is the time to be generating a new drawing. As a result, you want to do two things:

- Get the drawing area of the view class, passing it along to the drawing object.
- Tell the drawing object to generate a new drawing.

This is all fairly straightforward. To add this functionality to your application simply edit the OnNewDocument function in the document class, adding the boldfaced lines in Listing 14.5.

LISTING 14.5   The `CTestAppDoc OnNewDocument` Function

```
BOOL CTestAppDoc OnNewDocument function:example code
CTestAppDoc::OnNewDocument()
{
    if (!CDocument::OnNewDocument())
        return FALSE;

    // TODO: add reinitialization code here
    // (SDI documents will reuse this document)
    // Get the position of the view
        POSITION pos = GetFirstViewPosition();
    // Did we get a valid position?
    if (pos != NULL)
    {
        // Get a pointer to the view
        CView* pView = GetNextView(pos);
        RECT rWndRect;
        // Get the display area rectangle
        pView->GetClientRect(&rWndRect);
        // Set  the drawing area
        m_maDrawing.SetRect(rWndRect);
        // Create a new drawing
        m_maDrawing.NewDrawing();
    }
    return TRUE;
}
```

INPUT

Saving and Deleting a Drawing

The other functionality that you want to add to the document class is to save and restore the drawing and to delete the current drawing. These tasks are the last of the document-related functionality of your library module.

14

To add the functionality to save and restore drawings to your application edit the Serialize function in the document class. Delete all the current contents of the function, replacing it with a call to the drawing object's Serialize function, as follows:

```
void CTestAppDoc::Serialize(CArchive& ar)
{
    // Serialize the drawing
    m_maDrawing.Serialize(ar);
}
```

To add the functionality to delete the current drawing so that a new drawing can be generated or a saved drawing can be loaded, you need to add the event handler for the DeleteContents function to the document class. In this function, you call the drawing object's ClearDrawing function. To add this functionality to your application, follow these steps:

1. Add an override function to the DeleteContents base function in the document class, as in the previous few days.

2. Edit this function, adding the following. code:

```
void CTestAppDoc::DeleteContents()
{
    // TODO: Add your specialized code here and/or call the base class
    // Delete the drawing
        m_maDrawing.ClearDrawing();

    CDocument::DeleteContents();
}
```

INPUT

Viewing a Drawing

You need to add one final set of functionality to your test application before you can test your DLL: the drawing functionality to the application. This functionality belongs in the view class because it's the object that knows when it needs to redraw itself. Before you can add this functionality to the view class, you need some way for the view class to access the drawing object. The easiest way to add this capability is to add another function to the document class that can be called to get a pointer to the drawing object. When the view has this pointer, it can call the drawing object's own Draw function.

To add the capability to get a pointer to the drawing object to your document class, follow these steps:

1. Add a new member function to the document class.

2. Specify the function type as CModArt*, the function name as GetDrawing, and the access as public.

3. Edit the function, adding the following code:

```
CModArt* CTestAppDoc::GetDrawing()
{
    // Return the drawing object
    return &m_maDrawing;
}
```

Adding the drawing functionality to the view class is a simple matter of editing the OnDraw function in the view class. In this function, you need to get a pointer to the drawing object and then call its Draw function. So edit the OnDraw function in the view class as follows:

```
void CTestAppView::OnDraw(CDC* pDC)
{
    CTestAppDoc* pDoc = GetDocument();
    ASSERT_VALID(pDoc);

    // TODO: add draw code for native data here
    // Get the drawing object
        CModArt* pDrawing = pDoc->GetDrawing();
    // Draw the drawing
    pDrawing->Draw(pDC);
}
```

INPUT

After you add all this functionality, you can compile your application to test the DLL's functionality. After you compile the test application, switch over to the file explorer, find the DLL in the debug subdirectory under the DLL project directory, and copy the DLL to the debug directory in the test application project directory.

Now you should be ready to run and test your application and DLL. Each time you select New from your application's File menu, a new drawing is created, as in Figure 14.4.

FIGURE 14.4

Creating random squiggle drawings.

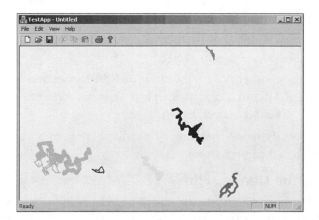

14

Creating and Using a Regular DLL

You might think that you broke the rules about using variables that aren't owned by the application in a DLL when you created and used the MFC extension DLL. Well, you didn't. The instance of the drawing class was a member of the document class in the test application. It was created and maintained by the application, not the DLL. Now that you are turning your attention to implementing the same functionality as a regular DLL, this will become clearer.

To convert the MFC extension DLL into a regular DLL, you have to convert the drawing class into a series of regular function calls. In the course of making this conversion, the object array must become a member variable of the application document class and must be passed as an argument to every exported function in the DLL.

Creating the Regular DLL

To convert the MFC extension DLL into a regular DLL, you have to start a new project. Visual C++ has to build a project that tells the compiler what type of file it's creating. You can create this new project using the same steps you used to create the MFC extension DLL project, but specify on the DLL Wizard that you are creating a regular DLL. (You can leave the wizard at the default settings.) After you create the project, you can copy the line and drawing class source code and header files into the project directory and add these files to the project. After you add these files to the project, you need to begin the process of converting the drawing class into a series of straight function calls.

To start the project for this example, follow these steps:

1. Create a new project, specifying that the project is an MFC DLL project. Name the project ModArtDll2 and click OK to create it.

2. In the Application Settings area, specify Regular DLL Using Shared MFC DLL. Click Finish to create the project.

3. Because you already have the CLine and CModArt classes built, copy them (Line.h, Line.cpp, ModArt.h, and ModArt.cpp) from the ModArtDll project area into the directory for this project.

4. Add both the header and source code files to this project by choosing Add Existing Item from the Project menu.

Altering the Header File

To start with, you need to radically alter the header file for the drawing class so that it will work for a regular DLL. You have to eliminate every trace of the actual class from the header file, leaving only the function calls. All these functions must be passed in any objects that they need to work with. (Every function will need to be passed the object array as one of its arguments.) Next, you need to slightly modify all the function names so that the compiler doesn't get mixed up and call a member function of any class by mistake (such as the Serialize function). Finally, each public function must be declared as exportable. To make these changes to the ModArt.h header file, open the file and then replace the entire class declaration with the following function prototypes:

```
extern "C" void PASCAL EXPORT ModArtNewDrawing(CRect* pRect,
    ➥CObArray* poaLines);
extern "C" void PASCAL EXPORT ModArtSerialize(CArchive& ar,
    ➥CObArray* poaLines);
extern "C" void PASCAL EXPORT ModArtDraw(CDC* pDC, CObArray* poaLines);
extern "C" void PASCAL EXPORT ModArtClearDrawing(CObArray* poaLines);
void NewLine(CRect* pRect, CObArray* poaLines);
```

Note

The object array is always passed as a pointer to each function. Because these functions are adding and removing objects from the array, they need to work with the actual array and not a copy of it.

Adapting the Drawing Generation Functions

Moving to the source-code file (ModArt.cpp), you need to make numerous small yet significant changes to these functions. Starting with the NewDrawing function, you need to pass in a pointer to the CRect object to get the drawing area. You dropped the function for setting the drawing area because you have no local variables in which you can hold this object. As a result, you are better off passing it to the drawing generation functions. The other change is where you pass in the object array as another argument to the function. You aren't doing anything with either argument in this function, just passing them along to the squiggle generating function. The other alteration in this function is the addition of the AFX_MANAGE_STATE macro as the first line in the body of the function. To make all these changes edit the NewDrawing function as in Listing 14.6.

LISTING 14.6   The ModArtNewDrawing Function

```
INPUT
        extern "C" void PASCAL EXPORT ModArtNewDrawing(CRect* pRect,
            ➥CObArray* poaLines)
        {
            AFX_MANAGE_STATE(AfxGetStaticModuleState());
            // normal function body here
            int iNumLines;
            int iCurLine;

            // Make sure that we have a valid pointer
            if (!poaLines) return;
```

14

LISTING 14.6 continued

```
INPUT    // Initialize the random number generator
            srand((unsigned)time(NULL));
    // Determine how many lines to create
    iNumLines = rand() % 10;
    // Are there any lines to create?
    if (iNumLines > 0)
    {
        // Loop through the number of lines
        for (iCurLine = 0; iCurLine < iNumLines; iCurLine++)
        {
            // Create the new line
            NewLine(pRect, poaLines);
INPUT       }
    }
}
```

Another change required in the NewDrawing function is the addition of the random number generator seeding in the following line:

```
srand((unsigned)time(NULL));
```

Because there's no class constructor any more, you can't seed the random number generator in it. Therefore, the next logical place to do this is in the NewDrawing function before any random numbers are generated.

On the NewLine function, the changes are more extensive.

- The CRect object and the object array are passed in as pointers.
- Because this isn't an exported function, you don't need to add the AFX_MANAGE_STATE macro.
- All the places where the CRect member variable is used must be changed to use the CRect pointer that's passed as an parameter to the function.
- When adding objects to the object array, you need to change this to use the object array pointer that was passed as an parameter.

To make these changes, simply edit the NewLine function, altering the code as in Listing 14.7.

LISTING 14.7 The NewLine Function

```
INPUT    void NewLine(CRect* pRect, CObArray* poaLines)
    {
    int iNumLines;
    int iCurLine;
```

LISTING 14.7   continued

```
        int iCurColor;
        UINT nCurWidth;
        CPoint ptTo;
        CPoint ptFrom;

        COLORREF crColors[8] = {
            RGB(   0,   0,   0),    // Black
            RGB(   0,   0, 255),    // Blue
            RGB(   0, 255,   0),    // Green
            RGB(   0, 255, 255),    // Cyan
            RGB( 255,   0,   0),    // Red
            RGB( 255,   0, 255),    // Magenta
            RGB( 255, 255,   0),    // Yellow
            RGB( 255, 255, 255)     // White
        };

        // Normalize the rectangle before determining the width and height
        pRect->NormalizeRect();
            // get the area width and height
    int iWidth = pRect->Width();
    int iHeight = pRect->Height();

        // Determine the number of parts to this squiggle
        iNumLines = rand() % 100;
        // Are there any parts to this squiggle?
        if (iNumLines > 0)
        {
            // Determine the color
            iCurColor = rand() % 8;
            // Determine the pen width
            nCurWidth = (rand() % 8) + 1;
            // Determine the starting point for the squiggle
            ptFrom.x = (rand() % iWidth) + pRect->left;
                ptFrom.y = (rand() % iHeight) + pRect->top;
            // Loop through the number of segments
            for (iCurLine = 0; iCurLine < iNumLines; iCurLine++)
            {
                // Determine the end point of the segment
                ptTo.x = ((rand() % 20) - 10) + ptFrom.x;
                ptTo.y = ((rand() % 20) - 10) + ptFrom.y;
                // Create a new CLine object
                CLine *pLine = NULL;
                try
                {
                    pLine = new CLine(ptFrom, ptTo, crColors[iCurColor],
                            nCurWidth);
                    // Add the new line to the object array
                        poaLines->Add(pLine);
                }
```

INPUT

INPUT

INPUT

14

LISTING 14.7   continued

```
                // Did we run into a memory exception?
                catch (CMemoryException* perr)
                {
                    // Display a message for the user, giving him the
                    // bad news
                    AfxMessageBox("Out of memory", MB_ICONSTOP | MB_OK);
                    // Did we create a line object?
                    if (pLine)
                    {
                        // Delete it
                        delete pLine;
                        pLine = NULL;
                    }
                    // Delete the exception object
                    // perr->Delete();
                }
                // Set the starting point to the end point
                ptFrom = ptTo;
        }
    }
}
```

Adapting the Other Functions

Making the necessary changes to the other functions is less involved than the changes to
the drawing generation functions. With the rest of the functions, you must add a pointer
to the object array as a function argument and then alter the uses of the array to use the
pointer instead of the no longer existing member variable. You also need to add the
AFX_MANAGE_STATE macro as the first line in each remaining function. To make these
changes, follow these steps:

1. Edit the remaining functions as shown in Listings 14.8, 14.9, and 14.10.

LISTING 14.8   The ModArtDraw Function

```
INPUT    extern "C" void PASCAL EXPORT ModArtDraw(CDC* pDC, CObArray* poaLines)
         {
         AFX_MANAGE_STATE(AfxGetStaticModuleState());
         // Make sure that we have a valid pointer
         if (!poaLines) return;

         // Get the number of lines in the object array
         int iCount = poaLines->GetSize();
         int iPos;

         // Loop through the array, deleting each object
```

LISTING 14.8   continued

```
            for (iPos = 0; iPos < iCount; iPos++)
                ((CLine*)poaLines->GetAt(iPos))->Draw(pDC);
INPUT   }
```

LISTING 14.9   The ModArtSerialize Function

```
INPUT   extern "C" void PASCAL EXPORT ModArtSerialize(CArchive& ar,
                    CObArray* poaLines)
    {
        AFX_MANAGE_STATE(AfxGetStaticModuleState());
        // Make sure that we have a valid pointer
        if (!poaLines) return;
        // Pass the archive object on to the array
        poaLines->Serialize(ar);
    }
```

LISTING 14.10   The ModArtClearDrawing Function

```
INPUT   extern "C" void PASCAL EXPORT ModArtClearDrawing(CObArray* poaLines)
    {
        AFX_MANAGE_STATE(AfxGetStaticModuleState());
        // Make sure that we have a valid pointer
        if (!poaLines) return;

        // Get the number of lines in the object array
        int iCount = poaLines->GetSize();
        int iPos;

        // Loop through the array, deleting each object
        for (iPos = 0; iPos < iCount; iPos++)
            delete poaLines->GetAt(iPos);
            // Reset the array
        poaLines->RemoveAll();
    }
```

2. Remove all code for the class constructor and destructor, along with the code for
    the SetRect function.

Building the Module Definition File

Before you compile the DLL, you need to add all the function names to the module definition file. You can find this file in the list of source-code files in the File View of the
workspace pane. When you open this file, you'll find that it briefly describes the module
that you are building in generic terms. You'll see a place at the bottom of the file where
you can add the exports for the DLL.

14

To add all the exportable functions, edit the ModArtDll2.def file as follows:

```
; ModArtDll2.def : Declares the module parameters for the DLL.

LIBRARY       "ModArtDll2"
DESCRIPTION   'ModArtDll2 Windows Dynamic Link Library'

EXPORTS
    ; Explicit exports can go here
    ModArtNewDrawing
    ModArtSerialize
    ModArtDraw
    ModArtClearDrawing
```

You are now ready to compile your regular DLL. After you compile it, copy it into the test application's debug directory.

Adapting the Test Application

To adapt the test application to use the new DLL that you've just created, you need to make a number of changes:

- Change the member variable of the document class from an instance of the drawing class to the object array.
- Remove the header file ModArt.h from the project, add the new ModArt.h header file to the project as an include directive in the document and view source code, and remove the include directive in the header for the document class.
- Drop the DLL LIB file and add the LIB file for the new DLL to the project. Change all the drawing class function calls to call functions in the new DLL instead.
- Change the GetDrawing function in the document class so that it returns a pointer to the object array, instead of the drawing object.

Start making these changes by deleting the LIB file from the test application project. Then follow these steps:

1. Add the LIB file for the new DLL to the project by selecting Add Existing Item from the Project menu.

2. Edit the source code for the document and view classes to add the include statement for the new ModArt.h header file, as follows:

```
// TestAppDoc.cpp : implementation of the CTestAppDoc class
//

#include "stdafx.h"
#include "TestApp.h"
```

```
#include "TestAppDoc.h"
#include "../ModArtDll2/ModArt.h"

#ifdef _DEBUG
#define new DEBUG_NEW
#endif
```

3. After you make all those changes, open the header file for the document class.

4. Edit the document class declaration: Change the function type of the GetDrawing function to return a pointer to an object array, remove the drawing class variable, and add an object array variable (see Listing 14.11). Make only these three changes; don't change anything else in the class declaration.

LISTING 14.11 The CTestAppDoc Class Declaration

```
class CTestAppDoc : public CDocument
{
protected: // create from serialization only
    CTestAppDoc();
    DECLARE_DYNCREATE(CTestAppDoc)

// Attributes
public:

// Operations
public:

// Overrides
    public:
    virtual BOOL OnNewDocument();
    virtual void Serialize(CArchive& ar);

// Implementation
public:
    virtual ~CTestAppDoc();
#ifdef _DEBUG
    virtual void AssertValid() const;
    virtual void Dump(CDumpContext& dc) const;
#endif

protected:

// Generated message map functions
protected:
    DECLARE_MESSAGE_MAP()
private:
//  // The drawing generator DLL
//    CModArt m_maDrawing;
        // The array of squiggles
    CObArray m_oaLines;
```

LISTING **14.11** continued

```
public:
    // Get a pointer to the object array
    CObArray* GetDrawing(void);
    virtual void DeleteContents();
};
```

Modifying the Document Functions

Now that you've made the general changes to the test application, it's time to start making functionality changes. All calls to a class method of the drawing object must be changed to the appropriate function call in the new DLL.

The changes necessary in the OnNewDocument function consist of dropping the function call to pass the CRect to the drawing object and replacing the NewDocument function call with the new DLL function—in this instance, ModArtNewDrawing, as shown in Listing 14.12.

LISTING **14.12** The CTestAppDoc OnNewDocument Function

```
BOOL CTestAppDoc::OnNewDocument()
{
    if (!CDocument::OnNewDocument())
        return FALSE;

    // TODO: add reinitialization code here
    // (SDI documents will reuse this document)
    // Get the position of the view
    POSITION pos = GetFirstViewPosition();
    // Did we get a valid position?
    if (pos != NULL)
    {
        // Get a pointer to the view
        CView* pView = GetNextView(pos);
        RECT rWndRect;
        // Get the display area rectangle
        pView->GetClientRect(&rWndRect);
        // Create a new drawing
        ModArtNewDrawing((CRect*)&rWndRect, &m_oaLines);
    }

    return TRUE;
}
```

INPUT

In the Serialize function, change the drawing object Serialize function call to the new DLL serialization function—in this case, ModArtSerialize, as follows:

```
void CTestAppDoc::Serialize(CArchive& ar)
{
    // Serialize the drawing
    ModArtSerialize(ar, &m_oaLines);
}
```

INPUT

For the DeleteContents function, you need to change the call to the ClearDrawing function to the new DLL function, ModArtClearDrawing, as follows:

```
void CTestAppDoc::DeleteContents()
{
    // TODO: Add your specialized code here and/or call the base class
    // Delete the drawing
    ModArtClearDrawing(&m_oaLines);

    CDocument::DeleteContents();
}
```

INPUT

For the GetDrawing function you need to change the function declaration to designate that it's returning a pointer to an object array, just as you did in the header file. Next, you need to change the variable being returned to the object array variable that you added to the header file, as follows:

```
CObArray* CTestAppDoc::GetDrawing()
{
    // Return the drawing object
    return &m_oaLines;
}
```

INPUT

Modifying the View Functions

Switching to the view class, you need to make only one simple change to the OnDraw function. In this function, change the type of pointer retrieved from the GetDrawing function from a drawing object to an object array object, as in Listing 14.13. Just after that, you need to call the DLL function, ModArtDraw, to perform the drawing on the window.

LISTING 14.13 The CTestAppView OnDraw Function

```
void CTestAppView::OnDraw(CDC* pDC)
{
    CModTestAppDoc* pDoc = GetDocument();
    ASSERT_VALID(pDoc);

    // TODO: add draw code for native data here
    // Get the drawing object
    CObArray* poaLines = pDoc->GetDrawing();
        // Draw the drawing
    ModArtDraw(pDC, poaLines);
}
```

INPUT

14

After making all these changes to the test application, you are ready to compile and test it. You should find that the application is working just as it did with the previous DLL. You can also play around with it, going back and changing the DLL, copying the new DLL into the debug directory for the test application, and seeing how the changes are reflected in the test application's behavior.

> **Caution**
>
> The particular example of a regular DLL that you developed in this exercise still isn't usable by other programming languages because you are passing MFC classes as the arguments for each DLL function. This still limits the usage to other applications built using MFC. To make this DLL truly portable, you need to pass the bare-bones structures instead of the classes (such as the RECT structure instead of the CRect class) and then convert the structures to the classes inside the DLL.

Summary

Today you learned about two ways to package your functionality for other programmers. You learned how you can easily package your classes as an MFC extension DLL and how easily it can be used by a Visual C++ application. You saw how you can make changes to the DLL without having to recompile the applications that use it. You also learned what's involved in creating a regular DLL that can be used with other, non-Visual C++ applications. You saw how you needed to convert the exported classes from the DLL into standard C-style functions and what's involved in adapting an application to use this style of DLL.

Q&A

Q. How can I convert a regular DLL so that it can be used by non-Visual C++ applications?

A. First, you have to make all arguments to the functions use the bare-bones struc-tures, instead of the MFC classes. For instance, to convert the ModArtNewDrawing function, you change it to receive the RECT structure instead of the CRect class and also to receive a generic pointer instead of a pointer to an object array. You have to make the conversions to the appropriate classes in the DLL, as in Listing 14.14.

LISTING 14.14 The ModArtNewDrawing Function

```
INPUT    extern "C" void PASCAL EXPORT ModArtNewDrawing(RECT* pRect,
            ➥LPVOID lpoaLines)
    {
```

LISTING 14.14 continued

```
        AFX_MANAGE_STATE(AfxGetStaticModuleState());
        CRect rRect;
            rRect.top = pRect->top;
    rRect.left = pRect->left;
    rRect.right = pRect->right;
    rRect.bottom = pRect->bottom;
    CObArray* poaLines = (CObArray*)lpoaLines;
    // Normal function body here
    int iNumLines;
    int iCurLine;

    // Initialize the random number generator
    srand((unsigned)time(NULL));
    // Determine how many lines to create
    iNumLines = rand() % 10;
    // Are there any lines to create?
    if (iNumLines > 0)
    {
        // Loop through the number of lines
        for (iCurLine = 0; iCurLine < iNumLines; iCurLine++)
        {
            // Create the new line
            NewLine(&rRect, poaLines);
        }
    }
}
}
```

INPUT

You also have to add functions to create and destroy the object array, with the application storing the object array as a generic pointer as follows:

```
extern "C" LPVOID PASCAL EXPORT ModArtInit()
{
    AFX_MANAGE_STATE(AfxGetStaticModuleState());
    // Create the object array
    return (LPVOID)new CObArray;
```

Once you've made these changes, the client applications could maintain a long variable that is passed to the DLL in place of the object array. This variable would hold a pointer to the object array that was instantiated by the DLL.

Q. When do I need to recompile the applications that use my DLLs?

A. Whenever you change any exported function calls. Changing, adding, or removing arguments to any of these functions would mean you need to recompile the applications that use the DLL. If you are working with an MFC extension DLL, the applications that use the DLL need to be recompiled if the public interface for the

14

exported classes change or a new function or variable is added or removed. It doesn't matter if the application isn't using any changed functions; it's still good practice to recompile the applications, just to be sure.

Workshop

The Workshop provides quiz questions to help you solidify your understanding of the material covered and exercises to provide you with experience in using what you've learned. The answers to the quiz questions and exercises are provided in Appendix A, "Answers to Quiz Questions."

Quiz

1. What kind of DLL do you have to create to make classes in the DLL available to applications?
2. What do you have to add to the class to export it from a DLL?
3. What kind of DLL can be used with other programming languages?
4. If you make changes in a DLL, do you have to recompile the applications that use the DLL?
5. What function does the LIB file provide for a DLL?

Exercises

1. Separate the line class into its own MFC extension DLL and use it with the second (regular) DLL.
2. Alter the line class DLL so that it uses a consistent line width for all lines.

WEEK 2

In Review

Now that you've finished the second week, you should be comfortable working with Visual C++. You should understand how you can use the MFC class hierarchy to provide a substantial amount of existing functionality in your applications. You should also understand how much supporting infrastructure your applications start with when you use the Visual C++ wizards to construct most of your application.

This is a good time to take a little break and try some of the things that you've learned on your own. Build an MDI application, using a custom document type that you've come up with yourself. See how you can save, restore, and maintain the document. Practicing on your own is key to cementing your understanding of what you've learned in this book. This will help you identify any areas that you need to study again, as well as those areas where you feel comfortable enough to not review.

Understanding how you can use text and fonts in your applications will allow you to build more flexibility into the appearance of your applications—to give your users the ability to customize the appearance as they want. You will be able to examine the available fonts on the computer on which your application is running and, if a font that you want to use in your application isn't available, choose another similar font to use instead. If you still have questions on how the font infrastructure in Windows works and how to use it in your applications, you'll want to go back and review Day 8, "Working with Text and Fonts."

By this time, you should have a good understanding of the Document/View architecture and how it is used to maintain the separation of the data from the representation of the data

8

9

10

11

12

13

14

that is displayed for the user. You've used this model for both Single Document Interface (SDI) and Multiple Document Interface (MDI) style applications, and you've used it for reading and writing files to the disk drive. This model is one of the main building blocks of MFC applications built with Visual C++. You should know where to place any initialization information for a new set of data and where to clean up when closing a set of data.

You should also have a good understanding of how the SDI and MDI application styles are similar and how they vary from each other and from the dialog application style. You should have a good idea of when an application you are building should use one of these styles and when it should use a different style. You should be able to create your own SDI and MDI applications as you need to, without any significant problems. If you have any questions about either of these areas, you might want to take another look at Day 10, "Creating SDI and MDI Applications," to review how the Document/View architecture works in both SDI and MDI style applications.

You should understand how, in SDI and MDI style applications, you can save and restore complex data structures in files on the system hard drive. You should be able to create mixed-type objects that you create and maintain in the document object in your applications, use the `Serialize` function with the `CArchive` object to write the objects to a file, and then restore the objects at a later time. If you have any trouble understanding how this works or are running into any problems trying to implement this functionality in your own applications, review Day 12, "Saving and Restoring Work."

Along with reading and writing files, you've also learned how to design and build toolbars for use in your SDI and MDI applications. At this point, you should be completely comfortable with designing and creating your own toolbars and using them in your applications. You should understand the importance of matching the toolbar button ID to the ID of the menu for which the toolbar will be used as a substitute. You should also have a basic understanding of creating and using your own customized status bar elements in SDI and MDI applications. You should understand how you can use the `UPDATE_COM-MAND_UI` event message to evaluate and alter the status of menu, toolbar, and status bar elements, relieving you of all the work of setting each element, and how to maintain their appearance and status yourself. If you aren't clear on how you can do any of these things, you might want to go back over Day 11, "Adding Toolbars and Status Bars," one more time.

You've seen how you can build a simple database application, pulling data from a database through the ADO interface. You should have a basic understanding of how you can build database applications by using this approach, how to maintain the data, how to add new records, and how to delete records. You should know how all the database interaction is directed through the record set class and how you can directly control the data through this object. If you're not sure of some of this, you might want to look back at Day 13, "Updating and Adding Database Records Through ADO," for a quick refresher.

You learned to share your functionality with other programmers by building DLLs. You learned how you can create two different types of DLLs: one that can be used only by other Visual C++ applications and one that can be used by any other application, regardless of what programming language was used to build it. You saw how you can create a DLL for use by other Visual C++ programmers without having to make any real changes to the way you design or code your modules. You also learned how you need to make dramatic changes to how your module is used and interacted with when creating DLLs that can be used by all programming languages. You learned how to provide straight function calls as an interface for use by other applications, with all necessary information to be passed in as parameters to the functions. You also learned how to build a definition file, with the names of all functions to be exported included in it. If you need any reminders of how you can do any of this, you'll want to look over Day 14, "Sharing Functionality with Other Applications Through DLLs," again.

Finally, you learned how to draw graphics on the windows of your applications. You learned how to draw lines, circles, and squares, using various pens and brushes. You even learned how you can make a customized brush from a bitmap. You learned how you can load a bitmap image from a file and display it for the user to see, as well as newer Internet image formats. But most importantly, you learned about the device context and how it's used to draw all these features on the windows of your applications. You should be able to use these and other figure drawing device context methods to draw any image you might want to draw on the window for the user to see and interact with. If you are unsure about how you can do this, you probably want to look back at Day 9, "Incorporating Graphics, Drawings, and Bitmaps," once more.

By this time, you've built quite a set of programming skills with Visual C++. You are probably ready to tackle most of the smaller programming tasks you might encounter—and maybe even a few not-so-small tasks. At this point, you are well on your way to becoming an accomplished Visual C++ programmer. That said, now is not the time to stop because there's still more to be learned. There's only one more week to go, so tally-ho!

WEEK 3

15

At a Glance

16

For this third and final week, you'll learn about several of the more advanced aspects of building applications with Visual C++. Some of these topics you'll use more than others, but if you do much work with Visual C++, odds are that you'll work with most, if not all, of these areas before long.

You'll begin the week on Day 15, "Building Your Own Widgets: Creating ActiveX Controls," by learning how to build your own controls that you can use in other applications or even in Web pages. You'll see how to define the properties and methods for your controls and how to trigger events in the containing application from your control.

17

On Day 16, "Adding Web Browsing Functionality to Your Applications," you'll learn how easy it is to incorporate Web browsing controls into your applications. You'll see how Visual C++ builds custom C++ classes around the controls you add to your project, enabling you to interact with an added control just as though it were another C++ object.

18

On Day 17, "Implementing Multitasking in Your Application," you'll learn how to enable your applications to be working on two or more separate tasks at the same time. You'll learn how to trigger some background processing whenever your application sits idle and how to spin off independent threads that continue to work even when your application is busy.

19

On Day 18, "Working with Internet Applications and Network Communications," you'll learn how Internet applications communicate with each other through the Winsock interface. You'll learn how to use this same interface to enable your applications to communicate over a network or even on the same machine.

20

21

On Day 19, "Working with Managed Code," you'll learn about building managed code applications. You'll learn the difference between standard C++ applications, and building managed code applications that are compiled to Microsoft's new Common Language Runtime (CLR). This can enable you to build applications that can be ported across multiple platforms without having to recompile or port any of your application functionality.

On Day 20, "Building Components with ATL," you'll dive into the world of Advanced Template Library (ATL) coding. ATL is used for building components and component-based applications that can run as services. These applications don't have a user-interface aspect, but can be called from Web pages or other applications.

Finally, on Day 21, "Interacting with Visual Basic and C# Components," you'll learn how to leverage CLR capabilities to easily interact with components and applications built in other languages like Visual Basic and Microsoft's new C# language. This will enable you to leverage the work of other developers working with other programming languages in your applications.

After you finish this final week, you'll be knowledgeable about many areas of Visual C++ programming. Although there will still be areas and technologies that require more in-depth study for you to master, you'll know and understand what those areas are all about. You'll be prepared to dive head first into all areas of Visual C++ programming; by then you might already have identified some areas that you want to learn more about than can be covered in this book.

You have only one week left to go, so dive in and get going.

DAY 15

Building Your Own Widgets: Creating ActiveX Controls

The software industry has seen a revolution over the past several years. How software is built and packaged has moved from a model in which all applications are large, monolithic pieces of executable code to a model in which most applications consist of small building blocks. These small building blocks, often called *components*, can be created using any of several different languages and can take many different forms. One of the most popular components is the ActiveX control. If you know how to create your own ActiveX controls, you can build your own components and provide them to other programmers. Today, you will learn

- How to use the Visual C++ wizards to build ActiveX controls
- How to add properties and methods to your controls using the Visual Studio Wizards
- How to test your control using the tools provided with Visual C++

What Is an ActiveX Control?

An ActiveX control is a software component that can be plugged into many different programs and used as though it were a native part of the program. It's similar to the concept of separate stereo components. If you buy a new tape deck, you can just plug it into the rest of your stereo and it works with everything else you already have. ActiveX controls bring this same type of interoperability to software applications.

ActiveX used to be called OLE 2.0, Microsoft's technology for combining two or more applications to make them work as one (or at least to switch between the various applications within the same application shell). OLE 2.0 was an expansion from the original OLE (Object Linking and Embedding) technology, which only enabled you to combine documents created with different applications into a single document. When revamping OLE technologies to work in a distributed environment (such as on the Internet), Microsoft decided to also revamp the name. Thus, ActiveX was born.

ActiveX controls provide a series of interfaces used by the container application to trigger the various sets of functionality contained in the control. Many of these interfaces are used for triggering events in the control or in the containing application. Others are for specifying the control's property page or for communicating whether the control has been activated. So many interfaces are built into most ActiveX controls that coding the functionality for each interface yourself would take quite some time. Luckily, the Visual C++ Wizards add much of this functionality for you, allowing you to focus on the specific functionality that the control is supposed to have.

Among the aspects of the control you create that you still must plan yourself are the properties, methods, and events you will expose for your control. You can add these elements to your control through the various Wizards, but if any of the properties or events requires special code on your part, you must add it yourself. As should be expected with any methods that you add to your controls, you have to supply all the code. The Add Method Wizard adds the surrounding structure and code to allow the containing application to see and call the method, just as it adds all the code necessary to call any event handlers for your applications.

ActiveX and the `IDispatch` Interface

The ActiveX technology is built on top of Microsoft's COM (Component Object Model) technology, using its interface and interaction model for making ActiveX control integration fairly seamless. The COM technology defines how ActiveX objects are constructed and how their interfaces are designed. The ActiveX technology defines a layer that's built on top of COM, what interfaces various objects should support, and how different types of objects should interact.

15

> **Note**
>
> Microsoft's COM technology defines how applications and components can interact via interfaces. An interface is like a function call into an ActiveX component. However, COM specifies how that function call must be built, called, and what supporting functionality must accompany the function call.
>
> Interfaces such as IUnknown are required in every COM object and used to query the component to find out what other interfaces the component supports. Each interface supports a specific set of functionality; you might have one interface to handle the control's visual appearance, another to control how its appearance interacts with the surrounding application, another that triggers events in the surrounding application, and so on.

NEW TERM One key technology in ActiveX controls is *Automation*. Automation enables an application embedded within another application to activate itself and control its part of the user interface or document, making its changes and then shutting itself down when the user moves on to another part of the application that isn't controlled by the embedded application.

This process is what happens when you have an Excel spreadsheet embedded within a Word document. If you click the spreadsheet, Excel becomes active and you can edit the spreadsheet using Excel, even though you're still working in Word. Then, after you finish making your changes to the spreadsheet, Excel closes itself down and you can continue working in Word.

NEW TERM One key to making Automation work is a special interface called IDispatch (also known as the *dispinterface*). This interface consists of a pointer to a table of available methods that can be run in the ActiveX control or embedded application. These methods have ID numbers, called DISPIDs, which are also loaded into a table that can be used to look up the ID for a specific method. When you know the DISPID for a specific method, you can call that method by calling the Invoke method of the IDispatch interface, passing the DISPID to identify the method to be run. Figure 15.1 shows how the IDispatch interface uses the Invoke method to run methods in the ActiveX object.

ActiveX Containers and Servers

NEW TERM To embed one ActiveX object within another ActiveX object, you have to implement the embedded object as an ActiveX *server*, and the object containing the first object must be an ActiveX *container*. Any ActiveX object that can be embedded within another is an ActiveX server, whether it's an entire application or just a small ActiveX control. Any ActiveX object that can have other ActiveX objects embedded within it is an ActiveX container.

FIGURE 15.1

The IDispatch ActiveX interface.

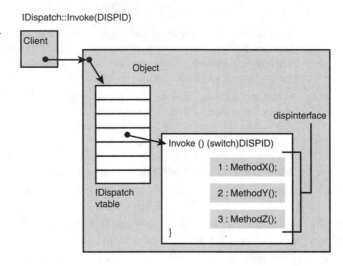

> **Note**
>
> Don't confuse the use of the terms *container* and *server* with the term *client* in Figure 15.1. The client is the object calling the other object's IDispatch interface. As you'll learn in a page or so, both the container and server call the other's IDispatch interfaces, making each one the client of the other.

These two types of ActiveX objects aren't mutually exclusive. An ActiveX server also can be an ActiveX container. A good example of this concept is Internet Explorer. Internet Explorer is implemented as an ActiveX server that runs within an ActiveX container shell (which also can house Word, Excel, PowerPoint, or any other ActiveX server application). At the same time that Internet Explorer is an ActiveX container running within the browser shell, it can contain other ActiveX controls.

ActiveX controls are special instances of an ActiveX server. Some ActiveX servers are also applications that can run on their own. ActiveX controls can't run on their own and must be embedded within an ActiveX container.

Most interaction between the ActiveX container and an ActiveX control takes place through three IDispatch interfaces. One of these IDispatch interfaces is on the control, and it's used by the container to make calls to the various methods that the ActiveX control makes available to the container.

The container provides two IDispatch interfaces to the control. The first of these IDispatch interfaces is used by the control to trigger events in the container application.

15

The second interface is used to set properties of the control, as shown in Figure 15.2. Most properties of an ActiveX control are actually provided by the container but are maintained by the control. When you set a property for the control, the container calls a method in the control to tell the control to read the properties from the container.

FIGURE 15.2

An ActiveX container and control interact primarily through a few IDispatch interfaces.

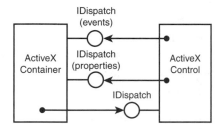

Properties

NEW TERM *Properties* are attributes of controls that are visible to, and often modifiable by, the container application. The four basic types of properties are ambient, extended, stock, and custom:

- The container application provides *ambient* properties—such things as background color or the default font—so that the control looks like part of the container application.

- *Extended* properties, such as tab order, aren't actually properties of the control but instead are provided and implemented by the container application. The control can extend these properties somewhat; for example, if the control contains two or more standard controls, it can control the tab order within the overall control, returning the tab order control to the application as soon as the control completes its internal tab order.

- The ActiveX control development kit implements *stock* properties, such as control font or control background color.

- You are most concerned with *custom* properties because they are specific to your control and are directly related to its functionality.

You can specify any properties you need in your control via the Add Property Wizard. When you add a new property to your control through this wizard, you'll specify several aspects of the property.

The first aspect is the external property name, which is shown to the containing application for the property. Another aspect that you can specify is the internal variable name, which is used in your code, but only if the property is implemented as a member variable. You also specify the variable type for the property.

If you specify that the property is to be implemented as a member variable (the property is a member variable of the control class), you can specify the name of the notification function, which is called when the property is changed by the containing application. If the property isn't a member variable of the control class, you need to specify that it's altered and viewed through Get and Set methods, where the containing application calls a Get method to get the current value of the property and calls a Set method to change the property's value. If the property is maintained through Get and Set methods, you can specify the names of these two methods (default names are provided).

For all these aspects of a property, the Add Property Wizard suggests appropriate names for everything after you enter the property's external name. If you want to accept the default names, you need to specify only the external name, the type, and whether the property is a member variable or uses Get and Set methods. If you choose a stock property from the list of available stock properties, the rest of the elements are automatically specified for you. After you specify this information, the Add Property Wizard adds all the necessary code and variables to your control project.

Methods

NEW TERM *Methods* are functions in the control that the container application can call. These functions are made available to other applications through the IDispatch interface, as discussed earlier. Because of the way the IDispatch works in calling the methods in a control, the variables passed to the method have to be packaged in a structure that's passed to the control. This structure is machine independent, so it doesn't matter whether your control is running with Windows 95/98 on an Intel Pentium III or on Windows NT/2000 with a MIPS or Alpha processor (assuming that Windows NT would still run on either processor, because those ports have been discontinued)—the structure will look the same. It's the responsibility of each side of the function call to convert the parameters as necessary to fit them into the structure correctly or to extract them from the structure. This process of packaging the method parameters is called *marshaling*.

When you add a new method to your control through the Add Method Wizard, the wizard adds all the necessary code to perform the marshaling of the parameters, as well as all other supporting functionality, including building the IDispatch interface and table.

When you add a new method to your control through the wizard, you're asked to provide the external name for the method called by the container application. Your method will get a default internal name, which you can override by entering your own internal name. Other aspects of your control methods that you have to specify are the method's return type and the parameters for the method. After you finish entering all this information, the Add Method Wizard adds all the necessary code to the control.

Events

NEW TERM *Events* are notification messages sent from the control to the container application. They are intended to notify the application that a certain event has happened, and the application can take action on that event if desirable. You can trigger two types of events from your control: stock or custom. Stock events are implemented by the ActiveX control development kit and are available as function calls within the control. These stock events enable you to trigger events in the container application for mouse or keyboard events, errors, or state changes.

You also can add your own custom events to be triggered in the container application. These events should be related to your control's specific functionality. You can specify arguments to be passed with the event to the container application so that the application can have the data it needs for reacting to the event message.

When you need to trigger any of these events, simply call the internal event function that fires the event, passing all the necessary parameters to the function. The Add Event Wizard will have added all the necessary code to trigger the event message from the internal function call.

Events are added through the Add Event Wizard. In the Add Event Wizard, you specify the event name, internal function name, and the parameters to be passed with the event to the container application.

Creating an ActiveX Control

The sample ActiveX control that you will build today is the squiggle drawing module that you packaged as DLLs on Day 14, "Sharing Your Functionality with Other Applications Through DLLs." In converting this module into an ActiveX control, you'll expose the maximum number of squiggles that the control will draw, as well as the maximum length of the squiggles, as properties that the container application can set. Every time the control is clicked, you'll program it to create a new squiggle drawing. You'll also add a method to load a squiggle drawing into the control that was created with the previous versions of the squiggle module. Finally, you'll have the control fire an event to let the container application know that the control has loaded the drawing.

Building the Control Shell

You've probably noticed by now that one of the Visual C++ Projects templates in the New Project dialog box is an MFC ActiveX control. This is another project wizard just like the MFC Wizards for creating application and DLL (Dynamic Link Library) projects. You can use it to build a shell for any ActiveX controls that you want to build. It creates all the necessary files and configures the project so that the compiler will build an ActiveX control when you compile.

NEW TERM When you start the Control Wizard, you're asked simple questions about your control project, such as whether the controls will have runtime licenses. *Runtime licenses* are a means of making sure that users of your control have purchased licenses to use it. Controls developed for selling to developers often have runtime licenses. The license prevents use of a control by users who haven't paid for it. When you use the control in an application, either the runtime license for the control is installed in the user's Registry by the install routine or the runtime license is compiled into the application. These means prevent someone from using the control to build new applications.

In another area of the Control Wizard, the questions get a little more involved, but are still fairly easy to answer. Here, you can click the Edit Names button to provide the control with descriptive names for the user. In a third area of the Control Wizard, a combo box lists a number of window classes that you can subclass in your control. If you want to create a special edit box that performs some special edits on anything the user types into the box, choose EDIT from the list of window classes in the drop-down portion of this combo box. In this same area of the wizard are questions about your project that require a fairly thorough understanding of ActiveX controls.

To begin the sample control project, follow these steps:

1. Start a new project, select the MFC ActiveX Control project template, and name the project Squiggle (see Figure 15.3).

FIGURE 15.3

Starting an ActiveX control project.

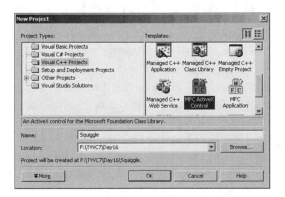

2. Click Control Names on the left side of the MFC ActiveX Control Wizard. Make sure the Control type name is sufficiently descriptive of the control, as in Figure 15.4. Leave the rest of the options with their default settings because you'll create only a single control today, and you won't need to include any runtime licensing. Click Finish to create the control project.

FIGURE 15.4

Checking the control type name.

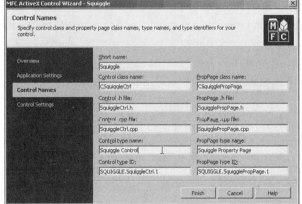

Modifying the CModArt Class

After you create the control shell, copy the Line and ModArt files from the MFC DLL project directory—the project you built on Day 14. Load all four files into the control project, adding the CLine and CModArt classes to the project.

Before you can use these files in your project, you have to remove the DLL class declaration from the ModArt.h header file:

1. With the ModArt.h header file open, remove the AFX_EXT_CLASS declaration from the class declaration, leaving the class declaration looking like the following:

```
class CModArt :
    public CObject
{
...
```

2. The primary changes that you need to make to the CModArt class for your control is setting the maximum number of squiggles and length of squiggles variables that can be exposed as control properties. To implement this, add two member variables to the CModArt class, one to control the length of the squiggles and the other to control the number of squiggles, as follows:

Name	Type	Access
m_iLength	int	private
m_iSegments	int	private

You need to provide a way for these variables to be retrieved and updated from the exposed properties. This means that you'll need functions for getting the current value, and for setting the new value, for each of these variables.

3. To add these functions for the m_iLength variable, add a member function to the CModArt class, specifying the type as int, the declaration as GetLength, and the access as public.

4. Edit the function with the code in Listing 15.1.

LISTING 15.1 The CModArt GetLength Function

```
int CModArt::GetLength(void)
{
    // Return the current value for the m_iLength variable
    return m_iLength;
}
```

INPUT

5. Add another member function to the CModArt class—specifying the function type as void and the name as SetLength—add one parameter of type int named iLength, and specify the access as public.

6. Edit this function, adding the code in Listing 15.2.

LISTING 15.2 The CModArt SetLength Function

```
void CModArt::SetLength(int iLength)
{
    // Set the current value for the m_iLength variable
    m_iLength = iLength;
}
```

INPUT

7. Add a similar pair of functions for the m_iSegments variable so that it also can be exposed as a property of the control. Call them GetSegments and SetSegments.

8. To make sure these two properties are initialized to reasonable values before the control is used, modify the CModArt constructor as in Listing 15.3.

15

LISTING 15.3   The Modified CModArt Constructor

```
CModArt::CModArt(void)
: m_iLength(200)
, m_iSegments(50)
{
    // Initialize the random number generator
    srand((unsigned)time(NULL));
}
```

Now modify the two functions that create the squiggle drawings so that they use these variables instead of the hard-coded values that they currently use. Follow these steps:

1. To modify the NewDrawing function, replace the maximum number of squiggles in the seventh line with the variable m_iSegments, as in Listing 15.4.

LISTING 15.4   The Modified CModArt NewDrawing Function

```
void CModArt::NewDrawing(void)
{
    int iNumLines;
    int iCurLine;

    // Determine how many lines to create
    iNumLines = rand() % m_iSegments;
    // Are there any lines to create?
    if (iNumLines > 0)
    {
        // Loop through the number of lines
        for (iCurLine = 0; iCurLine < iNumLines; iCurLine++)
        {
            // Create the new line
            NewLine();
        }
    }
}
```

2. Replace the maximum length of each squiggle with the m_iLength variable on the 28th line in the NewLine function, as in Listing 15.5.

LISTING 15.5   The Modified CModArt NewLine Function

```
void CModArt::NewLine()
{
    int lNumLines;
...
```

LISTING 15.5   continued

```
    // Determine the number of parts to this squiggle
    lNumLines = rand() % m_iLength;
    // Are there any parts to this squiggle?
...
}
```

You've made all the necessary modifications to the CModArt and CLine classes for your ActiveX control. Now you have to add an instance of the CModArt class to the control class as a member variable. To do so, simply add a new member variable to the control class, CSquiggleCtrl, specifying its type as CModArt, its name as m_maDrawing, and its access as private.

Adding Properties

Because the two variables that you added to the CModArt class aren't variables of the control class (CSquiggleCtrl), you will probably want to add Get and Set methods to set and retrieve the property value. If these two variables were members of the control class, you could add them through the Add Variable Wizard as member variables. You still know when and if the variables are changed because a notification method in the control class is called when the property values are changed. However, because they are members of an internal class, you'll want to exercise a little more control over their values.

 Tip

Even if the variables that you want to expose are member variables of the control class, you might still want to use the Get and Set methods for accessing the variables as control properties. Using Get and Set allows you to add validation on the new value for the properties so you can ensure that the container application is setting an appropriate value to the property.

To add these properties to your control, follow these steps:

1. Expand the SquiggleLib node in the Class View pane to expose the _DSquiggle interface node.

2. Select and right-click the _DSquiggle node. Select Add, Add Property from the context menu.

3. In the Add Property Wizard (see Figure 15.5), enter the external name that you want your property to have, SquiggleLength, and specify the type as SHORT (the int type isn't available, only SHORT and LONG). Select the Get/Set Methods radio button.

4. Click Finish to add this property.

FIGURE 15.5

The Add Property Wizard.

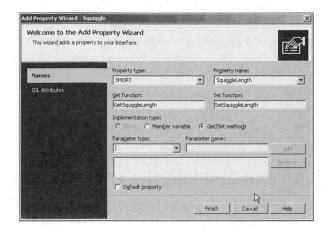

5. Expand the CSquiggleCtrl class in the Class View pane.

6. Double-click the GetSquiggleLength method to go to the function implementation. The SetSquiggleLength function implementation should follow immediately after the GetSquiggleLength implementation in the SquiggleCtrl.cpp file. In each method, call the Get and Set functions that you added to the CModArt class to control access to the length variable.

7. Edit these two methods as shown in Listing 15.6.

LISTING 15.6 The CSquiggleCtrl Get/SetSquiggleLength Functions

```
SHORT CSquiggleCtrl::GetSquiggleLength(void)
{
    AFX_MANAGE_STATE(AfxGetStaticModuleState());

    // TODO: Add your dispatch handler code here
    // Return the result from the GetLength function
    return m_maDrawing.GetLength();
}

void CSquiggleCtrl::SetSquiggleLength(SHORT newVal)
{
    AFX_MANAGE_STATE(AfxGetStaticModuleState());

    // TODO: Add your property handler code here
    // Set the new length value
    m_maDrawing.SetLength(newVal);

    SetModifiedFlag();
}
```

8. Add another property for the number of squiggles in a drawing by repeating steps 2–7, specifying `NumberSquiggles` as the property name, and calling the `Get/SetSegments` functions in your `CModArt` class.

9. One last property you might want to add to your control is a Boolean property that the container application could use to keep the control from creating any new drawings and to keep the current drawing visible. Add this property through the Add Property Wizard, name it `KeepCurrentDrawing`, and specify the type as `VARIANT_BOOL`. Leave it set as a member variable and click Finish. The Add Property Wizard automatically adds the variable to the control class, along with all the necessary code to maintain the variable.

Designing and Building the Property Page

You need to provide a property page with your control that developers can use when they work with your control. This property page provides users with a way to set the control's properties, even if their own development tools don't enable them to get to these properties in any way other than with code.

Adding a property page to your control is fairly easy. If you select the Resources View pane and expand the dialog folder, you'll see a dialog box for your control's property page already in the folder. Open this dialog box, and you'll find that it's a standard dialog window that you can design using the standard controls available in the dialog box designer. To design the property page for your sample control, lay out the property page dialog box as shown in Figure 15.6, using the property settings in Table 15.2.

FIGURE 15.6

The control property page layout.

TABLE 15.2   Control Property Settings

Object	Property	Setting
Static Text	Caption	Maximum Number of Squiggles:
Edit Box	ID	IDC_ENBRSQUIG
Static Text	Caption	Maximum Length of Squiggles:
Edit Box	ID	IDC_ELENSQUIG
Check Box	ID	IDC_CMAINTDRAW
	Caption	Maintain Current Drawing

Tip

If you resize the dialog box area for the property page, you need to pay close attention to the new size that you make it. The current size of the dialog box is displayed in the bottom-right corner of the Visual Studio environment. The size of the property page dialog box area needs to be either 62×250 or 110×250. Any other size is nonstandard for a property page and might cause problems—or at least warnings—when in use.

After you add all the controls and specify their properties, use the Add Member Variable Wizard to add variables for these controls. When you've added the variables for the controls on the property page dialog box, you can modify the data exchange to associate the property page variables with the control properties. Follow these steps:

1. Add variables to the controls on the property page for your control, tying them to the control's properties, as specified in Table 15.3.

TABLE 15.3 Control Variables

Object	Name	Category	Type	Access
IDC_CMAINTDRAW	m_bKeepDrawing	Value	BOOL	public
IDC_ELENSQUIG	m_iLenSquig	Value	int	public
IDC_ENBRSQUIG	m_iNbrSquiggles	Value	int	public

2. Open the SquigglePropPage.cpp source code file.

3. Locate the DoDataExchange function implementation. Modify it, changing the DDX functions to DDP functions, adding the property name to be associated with each of the variables, as in Listing 15.7.

LISTING 15.7 The Modified CSquigglePropPage DoDataExchange Function

```
void CSquigglePropPage::DoDataExchange(CDataExchange* pDX)
{
    DDP_Check(pDX, IDC_CMAINTDRAW, m_bKeepDrawing, _T("KeepCurrentDrawing"));
    DDX_Check(pDX, IDC_CMAINTDRAW, m_bKeepDrawing);
    DDP_Text(pDX, IDC_ELENSQUIG, m_iLenSquig, _T("SquiggleLength"));
    DDX_Text(pDX, IDC_ENBRSQUIG, m_iNbrSquiggles);
    DDP_Text(pDX, IDC_ENBRSQUIG, m_iNbrSquiggles, _T("NumberSquiggles"));
    DDX_Text(pDX, IDC_ELENSQUIG, m_iLenSquig);
    DDP_PostProcessing(pDX);
```

Note In previous versions of Visual C++, the Add Variable Wizard had an additional area where you specified the control class to which the property page should be attached. It eliminated steps 2 and 3, by automatically performing these actions for you. In the beta of Visual C++ that is being used to write this book, this functionality is not complete as of the time of my writing this. As a result, the Add Variable Wizard may have changed, adding back the functionality from the previous versions by the time that Visual C++.NET is released. If so, then on the Add Variable Wizard, specify `CSquiggleCtrl` as the control class to attach the property page variables to, and skip steps 2 and 3.

Adding Basic Control Functionality

The basic functionality that your control needs is the capability to respond to mouse clicks by generating a new drawing. To control this behavior, add a second Boolean variable to the control class so that the `OnDraw` function knows that a mouse click has been triggered. The easiest place to get the drawing area of the control is the `OnDraw` function, so this is where the new drawing needs to be generated. Do you want the control to generate a new drawing every time the user moves the application using your control in front of another application? Probably not. You will most likely want a greater amount of control over the behavior of the control, so it makes sense to add this second Boolean variable.

Add a member variable to the control class (`CSquiggleCtrl`), specifying the variable type as `BOOL`, the variable name as `m_bGenNewDrawing`, and the variable access as private.

Before you start adding the code to perform all the various tasks, you must initialize all the member variables in the control class. This consists of the member variable property, `m_keepCurrentDrawing`, and the member variable that you just added, `m_bGenNewDrawing`. You'll want your control to generate a new drawing right off the bat, and you probably don't want it to maintain any drawings, unless the container application explicitly specifies that a drawing is to be maintained. You'll set these two variable accordingly in the control class constructor, as shown in Listing 15.8.

LISTING 15.8 The `CSquiggleCtrl` Constructor

```
CSquiggleCtrl::CSquiggleCtrl()
    : m_bGenNewDrawing(TRUE)
    , m_KeepCurrentDrawing(FALSE)
{
    InitializeIIDs(&IID_DSquiggle, &IID_DSquiggleEvents);
    // TODO: Initialize your control's instance data here.
}
```

INPUT

Next, add the code to generate and display the squiggle drawings. The place to add this functionality is the OnDraw function in the control class. This function is called every time the control needs to draw itself, whether it was hidden or something triggered the redrawing by calling the Invalidate function on the control. In the OnDraw function, you'll determine whether you need to generate a new drawing or just draw the existing drawing. Also, keep in mind that you are responsible for drawing the entire area that the control occupies. This means you need to draw the background of the squiggle drawing—otherwise, the squiggles will be drawn on top of whatever was displayed in that same spot onscreen. (Who knows? That might be the effect you're looking for.)

To add all this functionality to your control, edit the OnDraw function in the control class (CSquiggleCtrl), adding the code in Listing 15.9.

LISTING 15.9   The CSquiggleCtrl OnDraw Function

```
void   CSquiggleCtrl::OnDraw(
            CDC* pdc, const CRect& rcBounds, const CRect& rcInvalid)
{
    // TODO: Replace the following code with your own drawing code.
    pdc->FillRect(rcBounds,
➥ CBrush::FromHandle((HBRUSH)GetStockObject(WHITE_BRUSH)));
    // pdc->Ellipse(rcBounds);
    // Do we need to generate a new drawing?
    if (m_bGenNewDrawing)
    {
        // Set the drawing area for the new drawing
        m_maDrawing.SetRect(rcBounds);
        // Clear out the old drawing
        m_maDrawing.ClearDrawing();
        // Generate the new drawing
        m_maDrawing.NewDrawing();
        // Reset the control flag
        m_bGenNewDrawing = FALSE;
    }
    // Draw the squiggle drawing
    m_maDrawing.Draw(pdc);
}
```

INPUT

Finally, you'll trigger the control to generate a new drawing whenever the control is clicked. This requires adding an event handler for the control's OnClick event. First, however, you'll add a stock method to the control to make sure that it receives the OnClick event message. Follow these steps to add this stock method:

1. Select the _DSquiggle interface node in the Class View pane.

2. Right-click and select Add, Add Method from the context menu.

LISTING **15.9** continued

3. Add a new method to the control class, selecting the `DoClick` method from the drop-down list of stock methods that can be added to your control (see Figure 15.7). Click Finish to add the method to your control.

FIGURE 15.7

The Add Method Wizard.

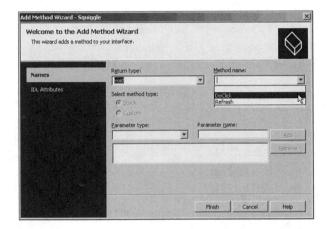

4. Select the `CSquiggleCtrl` class in the Class View pane.
5. Select the Overrides mode in the Properties pane.
6. Scroll down until you find the `OnClick` method. Click in the value area for this method, and select <Add> OnClick from the combo box.
7. Edit the code for the `OnClick` event handler, adding the code in Listing 15.10.

LISTING **15.10** The `CSquiggleCtrl OnClick` Function

```
void CSquiggleCtrl::OnClick(USHORT iButton)
{
    // TODO: Add your specialized code here and/or call the base class
    // Can we generate a new drawing?
    if (!m_KeepCurrentDrawing)
    {
        // Set the flag so a new drawing will be generated
        m_bGenNewDrawing = TRUE;
        // Invalidate the control to trigger the OnDraw function
        Invalidate();
    }
    COleControl::OnClick(iButton);
}
```

INPUT

ANALYSIS The `OnClick` function in Listing 15.10 checks to see whether it can generate a new drawing or maintain the current drawing. If you can generate a new drawing, the function sets the m_bGenNewDrawing flag to TRUE and invalidates the control, which triggers the OnDraw function.

Next, you need to add code for cleaning up when the control is closed. You need to override the control class' DestroyWindow function, calling the CModArt class' function for clearing the drawing and releasing all of the memory. To add this functionality:

1. Select the CSquiggleCtrl class in the Class View pane.

2. In the Properties pane, select Overrides mode, and add an override function for the DestroyWindow function.

3. Edit the new function, adding the code that follows:

```
BOOL CSquiggleCtrl::DestroyWindow()
{
    // TODO: Add your specialized code here and/or call the base class
    // Clear the drawing
    m_maDrawing.ClearDrawing();
    return COleControl::DestroyWindow();
}
```

Adding Custom Methods

Remember the functionality that you will give your control: One function is loading a squiggle drawing created with the version of the Squiggle module that you created on Day 14. To add this functionality, you add a method to the control that the container application can call to pass a filename to be loaded. You've already added a stock method to your application. Adding a custom method is similar, but you have to provide a little more information to the Add Method Wizard.

In the method to load an existing drawing, you create a CFile object for the filename passed as a parameter. The CFile constructor takes the filename and the flag CFile::modeRead to let it know that you're opening the file for reading only. After you create the CFile object, you create a CArchive object to read the file. The CArchive constructor takes the CFile object that you just created and the CArchive::load flag to tell it that it needs to load the file. At this point, you can pass the CArchive object to the drawing object's Serialize function and let it read and load the drawing. When the drawing is loaded, you need to display it by invalidating the control. Before you invalidate the control, make sure the m_bGenNewDrawing flag is set to FALSE so that the drawing you just loaded won't be overwritten.

To add this functionality to your control, follow these steps:

1. Select the _DSquiggle interface node in the Class View pane.

2. Right-click and select Add, Add Method from the context menu.

3. Specify the Method Name as LoadDrawing. The internal name is automatically generated based on the external name you entered. Next, specify the return type as VARIANT_BOOL so that you can let the container application know whether you were able to load the drawing. Finally, add one parameter to the parameter list, specify the parameter's name as sFileName and its type as BSTR (the CString type isn't available; the BSTR type is the COM interface string type) (see Figure 15.8).

4. Click Finish to add the method to your control.

5. Edit the new method, adding the code in Listing 15.11.

FIGURE 15.8

The Add Custom Method dialog box.

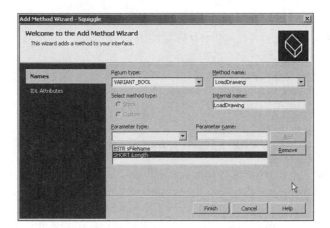

LISTING 15.11   The CSquiggleCtrl LoadDrawing Function

```
VARIANT_BOOL CSquiggleCtrl::LoadDrawing(LPCTSTR sFileName)
{
    AFX_MANAGE_STATE(AfxGetStaticModuleState());

    // TODO: Add your dispatch handler code here
    try
    {
        // Create a CFile object
        CFile fFile(sFileName, CFile::modeRead);
        // Create a CArchive object to load the file
        CArchive lArchive(&fFile, CArchive::load);
        // Load the file
        m_maDrawing.Serialize(lArchive);
        // Make sure that the loaded drawing won't be overwritten
        m_bGenNewDrawing = FALSE;
        // Draw the loaded drawing
        Invalidate();
```

INPUT

15

LISTING **15.11**   continued

```
    }
    catch (CFileException* perr)
    {
        // Report the error
        perr->ReportError();
        // Delete the exception
        perr->Delete();
        return VARIANT_FALSE;
    }
    return VARIANT_TRUE;
}
```

NEW TERM   The code in Listing 15.11 passes in a LPCTSTR data type to the function. A *BSTR* is a string type created as part of the OLE 2.0 specification. It's actually a pointer to a standard, NULL terminated, character array, usually UNICODE characters, with a twist. Although the BSTR pointer points to the first character in the array, if you back up a few bytes from the first character, you'll find a numeric value specifying the string's length. This standard string data type is used in Visual Basic and is the preferred string type for use in COM interfaces. Unfortunately, MFC doesn't work with BSTR strings easily, so it has to be converted to a CString before any real use. The CString constructor that can convert the BSTR to a CString requires the string to be cast as a wchar_t string, and also to be passed the length of the string. However, the Add Method Wizard added the code to perform the string conversion for you, providing you with a standard LPCTSTR string pointer, which you can pass directly to the CFile class constructor for the file name to be opened.

Adding Events

The final part of building your control is adding the events that your control will trigger in the container application. When using your control, users can add code to be triggered on these events. Adding these events to your control is done through the Add Events Wizard. If you want to add a stock event to be triggered by your control, right-click the control class, select Add, Add Event from the context menu, and then select a stock event from the drop-down list. If you need to add a custom event to your control, rather than select a stock event in the Add Event Wizard, you enter the name of your custom event. At the bottom of the Add Event Wizard is an area for adding parameters that you can pass from your control to the container application with the event.

For the sample control, add a custom event to let the application know that the drawing file specified has been loaded. Follow these steps:

1. Select the `CSquiggleCtrl` class in the Class View pane.

2. Right-click and select Add, Add Event from the context menu.

3. Enter the name for your custom event, `FileLoaded`. Notice that the Add Event dialog box automatically builds an internal name for the event—in this case, `FileLoaded` (see Figure 15.9). This internal name is the name for the function that you need to call in your code when you want to trigger this event.

4. Click Finish to add this event.

FIGURE 15.9

The Add Event Wizard.

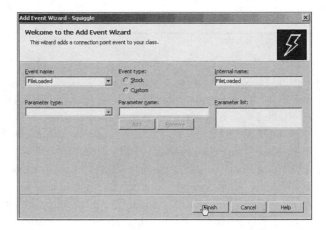

To add a stock event, select the desired stock event from the drop-down list of stock events, and click Finish.

Now that you've added your event to your control, you need to make the necessary changes to the code to trigger this event at the appropriate places. You'll trigger your event at the end of your `LoadDrawing` function, assuming that you can load the drawing correctly. Add this additional functionality to the `LoadDrawing` function, as shown in the boldfaced lines of Listing 15.12.

LISTING 15.12 The Modified `CSquiggleCtrl` `LoadDrawing` Function

```
VARIANT_BOOL CSquiggleCtrl::LoadDrawing(LPCTSTR sFileName)
{
    AFX_MANAGE_STATE(AfxGetStaticModuleState());

    // TODO: Add your dispatch handler code here
    try
    {
        // Create a CFile object
        CFile fFile(sFileName, CFile::modeRead);
```

LISTING 15.12   continued

```
            // Create a CArchive object to load the file
            CArchive lArchive(&fFile, CArchive::load);
            // Load the file
            m_maDrawing.Serialize(lArchive);
            // Make sure that the loaded drawing won't be overwritten
            m_bGenNewDrawing = FALSE;
            // Draw the loaded drawing
            Invalidate();
                // Fire the FileLoaded event
                FileLoaded();
        }
        catch (CFileException* perr)
        {
            // Report the error
            perr->ReportError();
            // Delete the exception
            perr->Delete();
            return VARIANT_FALSE;
        }
        return VARIANT_TRUE;
}
```

INPUT

Testing the Control

Now you are ready to compile and begin testing your control. Before you run to the store to pick up a copy of Visual Basic, you already have a tool just for testing ActiveX controls. On the Tools menu is an entry labeled ActiveX Control Test Container. This utility is designed specifically for testing ActiveX controls that you've built. After you compile your control, run the ActiveX Control Test Container to test your control.

> **Tip**
>
> If Visual C++ can't register your control, but can compile it, you might need to register your control yourself. Choose File, Register Control from the menu of the ActiveX Control Test Container. This allows you to find your compiled control and register it.

When you first start the test container, you see a blank area where your control will appear. Insert your control into this container area by selecting Edit, Insert New Control to open the Insert Control dialog box (see Figure 15.10). Select your control from the list of available controls and click OK to add the control to the container area.

FIGURE 15.10

The Insert Control dialog box.

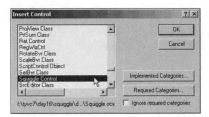

Now that your control is loaded into the test container, you can play with it, resize it, click it, and check when it generates a new drawing and when it just redraws the existing drawing. If you trigger any events for your control, you'll see the event that your control fired in the bottom pane of the test container so that you can watch as each of the events you added to your control are triggered.

Select your control and choose Edit, Properties to open the property page that you designed for your control (see Figure 15.11). Try modifying the control's various properties to determine whether they work correctly.

FIGURE 15.11

The Squiggle Control Properties page.

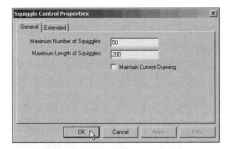

Finally, to test the methods that you added to your control, choose Control, Invoke Methods. In the Invoke Methods dialog box (see Figure 15.12), you can select from the list of available methods in your control, entering each parameter required for the methods, and then click the Invoke button to call that method. You can watch as your methods are called and your control responds.

Summary

Today, you learned how to use the tools and wizards in Visual C++ to build ActiveX controls with little effort on your part. You learned how to create the shell of the control project with the Control Wizard. You also learned how you can use the various Wizards to add properties, methods, and events to your control. You learned how to design a property page for your control and how to use the various wizards to attach the controls on this dialog box to the properties you defined for your control without having to add any code. Finally, you learned how to use the ActiveX Control Test Container to test your control, triggering all the functionality by using this utility's tools.

FIGURE 15.12

The Invoke Methods dialog box.

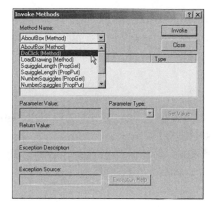

Q&A

Q. How do I change the icon that appears in the toolbox for my control?

A. In the Resource View tab of the workspace pane, open the Bitmap folder. You should find a single bitmap in this folder. This image is displayed in the toolbox for your control when you add it to a Visual C++ or Visual Basic project. Edit this bitmap so that it displays the image you want to represent your control.

Q. Why does my control have an About box?

A. If you're building ActiveX controls that other developers will use, whether you sell the control or give it away, you probably want to include some way of indicating that you wrote the control, and that you, or your employer, owns the control's copyright. This acts as a legal identification on the control so that whoever gets your control can't turn around and sell it as his creation.

Workshop

The Workshop provides quiz questions to help you solidify your understanding of the material covered and exercises to provide you with experience in using what you've learned. The answers to the quiz questions and exercises are provided in Appendix A, "Answers to Quiz Questions."

Quiz

1. What three aspects of a control are visible to the container application?
2. Why do you need to design a property page for your control?
3. What four types of properties might a control have?
4. What happens to the parameters passed to a control's methods?
5. What tool can you use to test your controls?

Exercises

1. Add a method to your control to enable the container application to trigger the generation of a new squiggle drawing.
2. Add a method to your control to save a squiggle drawing. Use the `CFile::modeWrite` and `CArchive::store` flags when creating the `CFile` and `CArchive` objects.

DAY 16

Adding Web Browsing Functionality to Your Applications

When Microsoft decided a few years ago to make all its applications Internet-enabled, it wasn't just talking about making Word read and write HTML pages. It wanted to make the Internet an integrated part of every application, in some way or another. Well, when it comes to development tools, making the editor double as an e-mail client isn't really a practical integration. However, making it easy for the users of development tools to build Internet-enabled applications is a very practical feature. And this is exactly what Microsoft did.

One of the capabilities that Microsoft made available to its application development tools is using Internet Explorer as an integrated part of any application. You can include Internet Explorer, and all its associated components, in your own applications. The possibilities extend far beyond providing your users Web browsing capability; your applications can also house, and interact with, Java applets. You can provide your users with not one, but two macro languages, VBScript and JScript (Microsoft's version of JavaScript). You can even interact with the HTML document that is displayed in the browser, modifying and reacting to the contents.

Today, you will learn

- How the Internet Explorer ActiveX Object Model enables you to integrate all the components into your applications
- How the CHtmlView view class encapsulates most of the Internet Explorer functionality in a ready-made class
- How to access the various COM Interfaces available in the Internet Explorer ActiveX Object Model
- How to use tools that are included with Visual C++ to build C++ wrappers around the COM interfaces
- How to build a simple Web browser using the CHtmlView class and Internet Explorer

The Internet Explorer ActiveX Model

To integrate ActiveX with its Web browser, Internet Explorer, Microsoft realized that it would need to re-engineer Internet Explorer to support the use of ActiveX controls. Well, the developers looked at what they would need to do, and what was possible, and decided to make Internet Explorer a lot more than just a Web browser.

Microsoft first separated the Web browser from the ActiveX objects that perform all the work. The results were the Internet Explorer application, which is little more than an ActiveX document container, and the Internet Explorer HTML viewer control, which ran as an ActiveX document server inside the application. This meant that the Internet Explorer application could host more than just Web pages; it could also be used to host Word documents, Excel spreadsheets, PowerPoint presentations, and any other ActiveX document that had an ActiveX document server installed on the same computer, as in Figure 16.1.

Within the HTML viewer component, Microsoft added the capability to host other controls, including scripting engines and ActiveX controls, as shown in Figure 16.2. This gave Microsoft the flexibility to add more scripting languages to Internet Explorer as they were requested and created. This also enabled Internet Explorer to host any ActiveX controls that developers might want to create.

In designing Internet Explorer this way, Microsoft not only gave itself a lot of flexibility for future expansion of the functionality supported by Internet Explorer, but it also made the entire workings of Internet Explorer available to any developer that wants to take advantage of it and integrate Internet Explorer into his or her applications.

FIGURE 16.1

The Internet Explorer ActiveX document model.

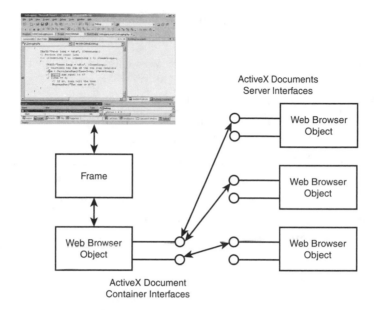

FIGURE 16.2

The Internet Explorer HTML viewer ActiveX object model.

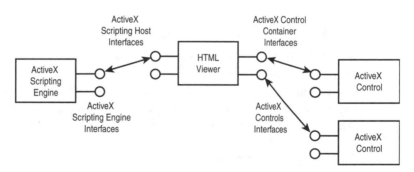

The `CHtmlView` Class

To make it easy to incorporate the Internet Explorer HTML viewer into Visual C++ applications, Microsoft wrapped it in the `CHtmlView` class. This class can be used as the base class for the view class in your SDI or MDI applications. You can easily create applications that have built-in Web browsing capabilities.

Navigating the Web

Several functions available in the `CHtmlView` class cover navigating the Web. There are functions for returning the browser to the starting page of the user or to taking the user to an Internet search page. There are also functions for taking the user to the previous or next pages or even to a remote Web page. All these functions are members of the

CHtmlView class and thus are member functions of your application view class (when using the CHtmlView class as the base class for your view class).

The navigation functions for the CHtmlView class are listed in Table 16.1.

TABLE 16.1   CHtmlView Navigation Functions

Function Definition	Description
GoBack()	Takes the user to the previous Web page.
GoForward()	Takes the user to the next Web page. (This assumes that the user has backed up from at least one Web page.)
GoHome()	Takes the user to the start page for Internet Explorer.
GoSearch()	Takes the user to an Internet search page.
Navigate(LPCTSTR URL)	Takes the user to the Web page specified in the URL variable.

The first four functions do not take any arguments and perform the exact same function as their toolbar equivalents in Internet Explorer. The final function does take arguments; the only required argument is the URL of the Web page to display.

Controlling the Browser

Along with the functions for navigating around the Web, you use some functions for controlling the browser. Two of these functions are Refresh(), which makes the HTML viewer control reload the current Web page, and Stop(), which halts a download in progress. As with most of the navigation functions, these functions do not take any arguments and work just like their equivalent toolbar buttons in Internet Explorer.

Getting the Browser Status

Another category of functions that are available in the CHtmlView class is informational in nature. You can use these functions to get information about the current state of the browser. For instance, if you want to get the current Web page in the browser, you can call GetLocationURL(), which returns a CString containing the URL. If you want to determine if the browser is busy with a download, you can call GetBusy(), which returns a Boolean value specifying whether the browser is busy.

Many more functions are available in the CHtmlView class, and some of them only work on Internet Explorer itself, not on the browser control.

Interacting with COM Interfaces

Although using the CHtmlView class to add Web browsing capabilities is nice, the real power is in all the COM interfaces available in the Internet Explorer Object Model.

With the new version of Visual C++, it's easier than ever to access and work with these COM interfaces.

MFC COM Interface Wrapper Base Classes

The MFC class library contains two classes used as base classes for COM Interface wrapper classes. These classes provide access to the IDispatch interface and provide support services that make the interfaces MFC friendly.

The COleDispatchDriver Class

The COleDispatchDriver class was created for use as a base for creating wrapper classes for COM IDispatch interfaces. This class provides access to the IDispatch interface via the m_lpDispatch member variable, which can be leveraged to call the QueryInterface function to get a pointer to any interface in the COM object.

When creating interface wrapper classes, the key COleDispatchDriver function to leverage is the InvokeHelper function. The InvokeHelper function is used to call the IDispatch Invoke method, which is used to access all properties and methods through the IDispatch interface. This function takes a series of parameters, as follows:

```
void InvokeHelper(DISPID dwDispID, WORD wFlags, VARTYPE atRet,
    void* pvRet, const BYTE* pbParamInfo, . . .);
```

The first parameter, *dwDispID*, is the ID of the method or property to be called. You can use the OLE/COM Object Viewer to determine the numeric value of the function or property that you want to call. After you find the interface, you examine the list of properties and methods until you find the one you want, and then use the ID number just above it, as seen in Figure 16.3.

FIGURE 16.3

Using the OLE/COM Object Viewer to retrieve method and property IDs.

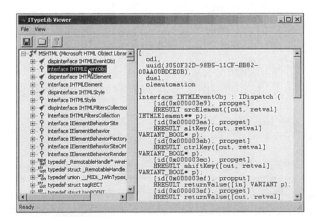

The second parameter, *wFlags*, specifies the context of the method call. The possible values for this parameter are listed in Table 16.2.

TABLE 16.2 InvokeHelper Context Flags

Flag	Description
DISPATCH_METHOD	Calls the IDispatch member as a method.
DISPATCH_PROPERTYGET	Calls the IDispatch member to retrieve a property value.
DISPATCH_PROPERTYPUT	Calls the IDispatch member to set a property value.
DISPATCH_PROPERTYPUTREF	Calls the IDispatch member to set a property value by reference assignment. This context is only useable on properties that accept a reference to an object.

The third parameter, *atRet*, specifies the return type of the method or property. The return type can be determined from the parameters labeled as out or retval in the interface specification seen in the OLE/COM Object Viewer. The possible values for this parameter are listed in Table 16.3.

TABLE 16.3 InvokeHelper Return Types

Parameter Value	Data Type
VT_EMPTY	void (no return value)
VT_I2	short
VT_I4	long
VT_R4	float
VT_R8	double
VT_CY	CURRENCY
VT_DATE	DATE
VT_BSTR	BSTR
VT_DISPATCH	LPDISPATCH (pointer to an IDispatch interface)
VT_ERROR	SCODE
VT_BOOL	BOOL
VT_VARIANT	VARIANT
VT_UNKNOWN	LPUNKNOWN (pointer to an IUnknown interface)

The fourth parameter, *pvRet*, is a pointer to the variable into which the return value will be placed. There is a twist to this parameter in that the COleDispatchDriver class converts BSTR return types into CString data types.

The fifth parameter, *pbParamInfo*, is an array of BYTES that specifies the data types of the parameters being passed to the methods or properties. The possible values for use in this array are listed in Table 16.4. You can create this parameter as follows:

```
static BYTE parms[] = VTS_BSTR;
```

This parameter is followed by any parameters that are being passed to the method or property. If there are no parameters to be passed, then a NULL needs to be passed as the final parameter (after the *pbParamInfo* parameter).

16

TABLE 16.4 InvokeHelper Parameter Types

Parameter Value	Data Type
VTS_I2	short
VTS_I4	long
VTS_R4	float
VTS_R8	double
VTS_COLOR	OLE_COLOR
VTS_CY	CURRENCY
VTS_DATE	DATE
VTS_BSTR	BSTR
VTS_DISPATCH	LPDISPATCH (pointer to an IDispatch interface)
VTS_FONT	IFontDispatch interface pointer
VTS_HANDLE	HANDLE
VTS_SCODE	SCODE
VTS_BOOL	BOOL
VTS_VARIANT	const VARIANT*
VTS_PVARIANT	VARIANT*
VTS_UNKNOWN	LPUNKNOWN (pointer to an IUnknown interface)
VTS_OPTEXCLUSIVE	OLE_OPTEXCLUSIVE
VTS_PICTURE	IPictureDisp interface pointer
VTS_TRISTATE	OLE_TRISTATE
VTS_XPOS_PIXELS	OLE_XPOS_PIXELS
VTS_YPOS_PIXELS	OLE_YPOS_PIXELS
VTS_XSIZE_PIXELS	OLE_XSIZE_PIXELS
VTS_YSIZE_PIXELS	OLE_YSIZE_PIXELS
VTS_XPOS_HIMETRIC	OLE_XPOS_HIMETRIC

TABLE 16.4   continued

Parameter Value	Data Type
VTS_YPOS_HIMETRIC	OLE_YPOS_HIMETRIC
VTS_XSIZE_HIMETRIC	OLE_XSIZE_HIMETRIC
VTS_YSIZE_HIMETRIC	OLE_YSIZE_HIMETRIC

When building a wrapper class, a typical use of the `InvokeHelper` class might be as follows:

```
CString CMyWrapper::get_designMode()
{
    CString result;
    InvokeHelper(0x3f6, DISPATCH_PROPERTYGET, VT_BSTR,
            (void*)&result, NULL);
    return result;
};

void CMyWrapper::put_designMode(CString newValue)
{
    static BYTE parms[] = VTS_BSTR ;
    InvokeHelper(0x3f6, DISPATCH_PROPERTYPUT, VT_EMPTY, NULL,
            parms, newValue);
};
```

The easiest way to create an instance of the `COleDispatchDriver` class descendant is to pass the constructor a pointer to the IDispatch interface for the COM interface that the class is a wrapper for, as follows:

```
CMyWrapper* pWrap = new CMyWrapper(ppvDisp);
```

or

```
CMyWrapper comWrap(ppvDisp);
```

The way that you get the pointer to the interface is through the use of the `QueryInterface` method through any interface pointer of the COM object. If you have a pointer to any IDispatch interface in the class, you can use it to get an IDispatch interface pointer for any other interface in the COM object, as follows:

```
void* ppvDisp;
```

```
pWrap1->m_lpDispatch->QueryInterface(IID_IHTMLDocument, &ppvDisp);
```

The CWnd Class

When you are working with ActiveX controls, you can use the `CWnd` class as a base class for some interfaces. If the interface wrapper class is derived from the `CWnd` class, then you can use the derived class as the variable type for the control placed on the application window. When used as the base class for a COM interface, the CWnd class has a member variable, m_pOuterUnknown, which is an interface pointer that can be used to call the QueryInterface method to get a pointer to any other interface in the control. If the control has no visible interface, then the CWnd class cannot be used as the base class.

Generating Interface Wrapper Classes

In previous editions of Visual C++, if you wanted to build a wrapper class for a COM interface, you had to do all the work yourself. This involved examining the interface using the OLE/COM Object Viewer and creating all the methods and property methods using either the COleDispatchDriver or CWnd classes. With the new version of Visual C++, wizards can create the wrapper classes for you. All you have to do is specify the ActiveX control or COM object, select the interfaces for which you want wrapper classes, and let the Wizard do the rest of the work.

Generating Interface Wrapper Classes for ActiveX Controls

You may have noticed when using the Add Class dialog, that there are two MFC templates for creating a new class from an ActiveX Control and from a TypeLib. These two new class templates open wizards that build wrapper classes for control and object interfaces. Selecting the MFC Class From ActiveX Control starts the Add Class From ActiveX Control Wizard, as in Figure 16.4.

FIGURE 16.4

The Add Class From ActiveX Control Wizard.

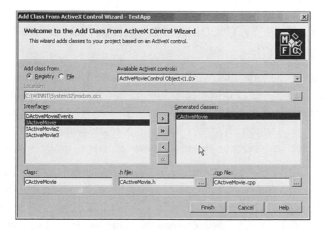

In the Add Class From ActiveX Control Wizard, you can specify whether you want to select a control already registered on your system, or specify the OCX file for the control. If you choose to select the control from the registered controls, you can select the control from a combo box containing all the ActiveX controls currently registered on your computer.

After you've selected a control, you will see a list of the available interfaces on the left side of the wizard. You have to select the interfaces for which you want wrapper classes, and press the right angle button (>) to add that interface to the list of wrapper classes to be generated. The generated class names, along with the filenames, are automatically generated from the interface name. If you want to rename any of these, edit the class and filenames in the edit controls on the bottom of the wizard. After you've selected all the interfaces that will have wrapper classes generated, press the Finish button to generate the classes, which will be added to your current project. Depending on the interface you selected, the generated wrapper class may be descended from the CWnd class, or the COleDispatchDriver class.

Generating Interface Wrapper Classes for COM Objects

If you choose to generate a wrapper class for a COM object, you'll select the MFC Class From TypeLib template. This opens the Add Class From Typelib Wizard. The Add Class From Typelib Wizard works basically the same as the Add Class From ActiveX Control Wizard, only you'll notice that there is one edit control for the filename for the wrapper class at the bottom of the dialog. This is because the wrapper classes generated from TypeLibs for COM controls are all derived from the COleDispatchDriver class, and are implemented as all inline functions within the class declaration. Because all the methods are declared in the class declaration, this wizard only generated a header file for the wrapper class.

Getting the IHTMLDocument Interface from the CHtmlView Class

By leveraging the tools that Visual C++ makes available, you can easily work with ActiveX controls and COM objects. All you have to do is select the object or control, generate the appropriate wrapper classes, and away you go. Well, almost away you go. You still have to acquire that first interface pointer from which you can get a pointer to the IDispatch interface for any of the other interfaces in the object or control.

If you're using an ActiveX Control, on a dialog, you can declare a control variable using the Add Variable Wizard. A default wrapper class is generated, based on the CWnd class, that provides you with little functionality. What it does provide is the m_pOuterUnknown member variable, which is a pointer to the IUnknown interface, and can then be used to get a pointer to any other interface desired.

If you are working with nonvisible ActiveX Controls, or other COM objects, you can get an interface pointer by creating an instance of the Interface with the object name, initializing it with the name of the interface, as follows:

```
IMyObjectPtr pMO(L"MyObject.MyInterface.1");
```

To use this approach, you'll need the #import directive to import the type library for the COM object prior to creating the interface pointer. You'll also need to have initialized the COM environment by calling the CoInitialize API function.

With the CHtmlView class, this is all greatly simplified. The view class has a member function, GetHtmlDocument, which returns a pointer to the IDispatch interface for the IHTMLDocument object. From this interface pointer, you can get interface pointers to any other COM object interface within the Internet Explorer object model.

Building a Web-Browsing Application

For an example of how you can integrate the Internet Explorer Web browser component into your own applications, you can build a simple Web browser application. You can create an SDI application using the CHtmlView class as the base for your own view class. You'll add a menu with functions for the back and forward navigation options. You can also add a dialog for getting from the user a URL that you will use to navigate the browser to the specified Web page.

Creating the Application Shell

To create a Web browser application, you can create a standard SDI or MDI application shell. Internet Explorer must be installed on the computer where your application will run. For your development computer, this is not a problem because the Visual C++ installation required you to install the latest version of Internet Explorer. On any computers where you run your application, however, you might need to be sure that Internet Explorer is installed, or install it yourself.

To create the shell of the application that you will build follow these steps:

1. Start a new MFC Application project. Name the project WebBrowse, and click OK to start the MFC Application Wizard.

2. In the Application Type area of the MFC Application Wizard, specify Single Document for the application type.

3. In the User Interface Features area of the MFC Application Wizard, specify Standard Docking and Browser Style under Toolbars.

4. In the Generated Classes area of the MFC Application Wizard, specify CHtmlView as the base class for the CWebBrowseView class.

5. Click Finish to generate the application shell.

After you finish generating the shell for your application, if you compile and run it while connected to the Internet, you'll find that you've already got a working Web browser, as in Figure 16.5. However, you do not have the capability to specify where your browser will take you, other than clicking links in the Web pages displayed.

FIGURE 16.5

The initial Web browsing application.

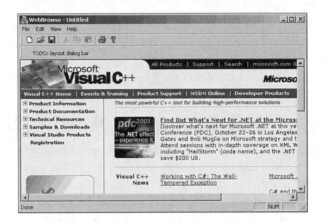

Adding Navigation Functionality

Now that you've got a working Web browser, it would be nice if you could control where it takes you. You need to add an edit control where the user can enter a URL. Looking at the toolbar of the running application, you notice there's a place to put this control.

Specifying a URL

You probably noticed when you ran your application that the second toolbar had some static text telling you to lay out the dialog bar. The dialog bar is different from what you have worked with before. It is a toolbar with dialog controls on it. You even design the bar in the dialog layout designer. When you look for this dialog bar in the resource tab, you won't find it in the toolbar folder; it's in the dialogs folder.

If you open the Dialog folder and double-click the IDR_MAINFRAME dialog to open it in the dialog designer, you'll see that it's the second toolbar in your application. You can place edit boxes, buttons, combo boxes, and check boxes on this toolbar. You can place any control that you can use on a dialog window on this toolbar.

1. For your Web browser, modify the static text control already on the dialog bar, and add an edit box, as shown in Figure 16.6.

2. Specify the ID for the edit box as IDC_EADDRESS.

Before you open the Class Wizard to begin adding variables and event functions to the dialog bar, be aware that the dialog bar automatically sends its events to the main frame class in your application. It is not necessary to create a dialog class for this toolbar because you can map all its events through the frame and from there feed them to the view or document classes.

FIGURE **16.6**

The dialog bar layout.

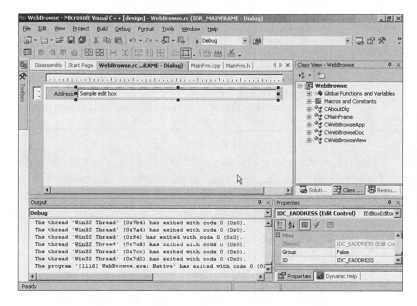

For this example, you don't even need to use the Event Handler Wizard to add any event handlers to the dialog bar. You need to trigger an action when the user finishes entering a URL into the edit box. The closest event available to you through the Class Wizard is the EN_CHANGED event, which triggers for each letter the user types. What you need is an event that will trigger when the user presses the Enter key. Fortunately, when the user types in the edit box on the dialog bar and presses the Enter key, the IDOK command ID is sent to the frame class. What you can do is add a command handler in the message map to call a function on the IDOK command.

In your command handler, you need to get the window text from the edit box on the dialog bar. You can pass this string to the Navigate function in the view class, making the browser go to the page specified by the user.

To add this functionality to your application:

3. Add a new member function to the CMainFrame class.

4. Specify the function return type as void, the function name as OnNewAddress, and the access as public.

5. Edit the new function, adding the code in Listing 16.1.

LISTING **16.1**   The CMainFrame OnNewAddress Function

```
void CMainFrame::OnNewAddress(void)
{
```

LISTING 16.1 continued

```
        CString strAddress;

        // Get the new URL
        m_wndDlgBar.GetDlgItem(IDC_EADDRESS)->GetWindowText(strAddress);
        // Navigate to the new URL
        ((CWebBrowseView*)GetActiveView())->Navigate(strAddress);
    }
```

In this function, the first line of code got the text in the edit box using the GetWindowText function, placing the text into the strAddress variable. The dialog bar was declared in the CMainFrame class as the m_wndDlgBar variable, so you were able to use the GetDlgItem function on the dialog bar variable to get a pointer to the edit box.

In the next line, you cast the return pointer from the GetActiveView function as a pointer to the CWebBrowseView class. This allowed you to call the Navigate function on the view class, passing it the URL that was entered into the edit box.

Now that you can take the URL that the user entered and tell the browser component to go to that Web page, how do you trigger this function? You have to add the message-map entry by hand because this is one that the Class Wizard can't add. In the message map, add the ON_COMMAND macro, specifying the IDOK command and your new function as the handler to be called, as in Listing 16.2.

LISTING 16.2 The CMainFrame Message Map

```
BEGIN_MESSAGE_MAP(CMainFrame, CFrameWnd)
    ON_WM_CREATE()
    ON_COMMAND(IDOK, OnNewAddress)
END_MESSAGE_MAP()
```

Before you can compile your application, you'll need to add #include directives to the main frame source code to include the header files for both the document and view classes, as in Listing 16.3.

LISTING 16.3 The CMainFrame #include Directives

```
// MainFrm.cpp : implementation of the CMainFrame class
//

#include "stdafx.h"
#include "WebBrowse.h"

#include "MainFrm.h"
```

LISTING 16.3 continued

```
#include "WebBrowseDoc.h"
#include "WebBrowseView.h"

#ifdef _DEBUG
#define new DEBUG_NEW
#endif
```

16

If you compile and run your application, you can enter a URL into the edit box on the toolbar and press the Enter key, and your application should browse to the Web page you specified, as in Figure 16.7.

FIGURE 16.7

Browsing to a specified URL.

Displaying the Current URL

When surfing the Web, you often follow links on Web pages that take you to other Web sites. When you do this, you don't know what Web site you accessed if your browser doesn't place the URL into the address box, indicating the site where you are and providing the opportunity to copy or modify the URL to find another page on the same site.

Getting the current URL from the browser is a simple matter of calling the GetLocationURL function and passing the result to the dialog bar. The problem is when to get the URL. It turns out that some event functions in the CHtmlView class can be overridden in your class. These functions are triggered on various events that are triggered by the browser control. There are event functions for starting the navigation, beginning a download, monitoring a download's progress, and, most important for your needs, indicating a download has finished.

To add the download-complete event handler to your application:

1. Select the CWebBrowseView class in the Class View pane.

2. Select the Overrides mode of the Properties pane.

3. Scroll down and locate the OnDocumentComplete function.

4. Click in the value side and select <Add> OnDocumentComplete from the combo box to create the override function.

5. Edit the function, adding the code in Listing 16.4.

LISTING 16.4 The CWebBrowseView OnDocumentComplete Function

```
void CWebBrowseView::OnDocumentComplete(LPCTSTR lpszURL)
{
    // TODO: Add your specialized code here and/or call the base class
    // Pass the new URL to the address bar
    ((CMainFrame*)GetParentFrame())->SetAddress(lpszURL);

    CHtmlView::OnDocumentComplete(lpszURL);
}
```

You'll notice in this function that you didn't need to call the GetLocationURL function after all. The URL that is downloaded is passed as an argument to this function. This allows you to pass the URL along to the frame, where you'll add another function to populate the edit box on the dialog bar with the URL.

To add the function to populate the dialog bar with the new URL:

6. Add a member function to the main frame class, CMainFrame.

7. Specify the function type as void, the function name as SetAddress, and add a single parameter of type LPCTSTR named lpszURL, and specify the function access as public.

8. Edit the function, adding the code in Listing 16.5.

LISTING 16.5 The CMainFrame SetAddress Function

```
void CMainFrame::SetAddress(LPCTSTR lpszURL)
{
    // Set the new URL in the address edit control
    m_wndDlgBar.GetDlgItem(IDC_EADDRESS)->SetWindowText(lpszURL);
}
```

In this function, you took the opposite path from the one you used to get the text from the edit box. You used the SetWindowText to change the text in the edit box to the URL that you are passing in.

9. Modify the #include directives in the CWebBrowseView class, adding one to include the header for the main frame class, as in Listing 16.6.

LISTING 16.6   The CWebBrowseView #include Directives

```
// WebBrowseView.cpp : implementation of the CWebBrowseView class
//

#include "stdafx.h"
#include "WebBrowse.h"

#include "WebBrowseDoc.h"
#include "WebBrowseView.h"
#include "MainFrm.h"

#ifdef _DEBUG
#define new DEBUG_NEW
#endif
```

When you run your application, the URL address on the dialog bar should change to reflect the Web page that you are viewing.

Back and Forth

Now that you can enter a URL into the dialog bar and have your application go to that Web site, and you can see the address of any Web sites that you view, it'd be nice if you could back up from where you are. This is a simple matter of calling the GoBack and GoForward functions on the view class in your application. You can call these functions from menu entries, which also allows you to attach toolbar buttons to perform the same calls.

To add this functionality:

1. Open the main menu in the Menu Designer.

2. Delete the Edit menu from the bar, and all the entries below it, because they are of no use in the application that you are building today.

3. Click in the blank menu entry on the bar, and give it a caption of Navi&gate.

4. Select the new menu and drag it to the left of the Help menu. This is the menu where all navigation functions will be located.

5. Add two menu entries, one for the GoBack function and one for the GoForward function. Specify the properties for these two menu entries as shown in Table 16.5.

16

TABLE 16.5 Menu Property Settings

Object	Property	Setting
Menu Entry	ID	ID_NAVIGATE_BACK
	Caption	&Back\tCtrl + B
	Prompt	Back to the previous page\nBack
Menu Entry	ID	ID_NAVIGATE_NEXT
	Caption	&Next\tCtrl + N
	Prompt	Go forward to the next page\nNext

After you add the menu entries, you can use the Handle Events Wizard to add functions to the view class on both of these menu events.

6. For the ID_NAVIGATE_BACK menu ID, add an event function on the COMMAND event message to the CWebBrowseView class. Edit the function, adding the code in Listing 16.7.

LISTING 16.7 The CWebBrowseView OnNavigateBack Function

```
void CWebBrowseView::OnNavigateBack()
{
    // TODO: Add your command handler code here
    // Go to the previous page
    GoBack();
}
```

7. Add an event-handler function for the ID_NAVIGATE_NEXT object ID on the COMMAND event message to the CWebBrowseView class. Edit this function with the code in Listing 16.8.

LISTING 16.8 The CWebBrowseView OnNavigateNext Function

```
void CWebBrowseView::OnNavigateNext()
{
    // TODO: Add your command handler code here
    // Go to the next page
    GoForward();
}
```

Now you can run your application and use the menus to back up to the previous Web pages on which you surfed and then trace your steps forward again. However, it's somewhat difficult using the menus, so what you need to do is add an accelerator for each of these menu entries.

16

If you open the accelerator table in the resources tree, you see a bunch of accelerators tied to menu IDs. Each of these accelerators consist of an ID and a key combination. If you right-click anywhere in the accelerator table, you see the option to add a new accelerator to the table. Choosing this option adds a new line to the bottom of the list where you can enter the accelerator information. First, in the left column, you need to specify the menu ID to which the accelerator will be tied. (As with toolbar buttons, accelerators are tied to menu entries.) In the third column, you can enter the key that will trigger the accelerator, or you can select a key from the drop-down list.

In the second column, you can select the modifiers for the key. Modifiers are the other keys that must be pressed in combination with the key that you've already specified for the accelerator to be triggered.

 Tip

It's recommended that you use either the Ctrl or Alt key as one of the modifier keys on all accelerators using standard keys. If you don't use one of these two keys as part of the accelerator, your application might get confused about when the user is typing information into your application and when the user is triggering an accelerator.

To add accelerators to the back and forward menus in your application:

1. Add a new accelerator and specify the ID as ID_NAVIGATE_BACK and the key as B and select the Ctrl modifier.

2. Add a second accelerator, specifying the ID as ID_NAVIGATE_NEXT and the key as N and select the Ctrl modifier.

Now when you run your application, you can use the Ctrl+B key combination to back up to the previous page and the Ctrl+N key combination to go forward. To really make your application work like most available Web browsers, you can add toolbar buttons for these two menu entries with arrows pointing to the left for back and to the right for forward.

Controlling the Browser

Often when browsing, you come across a Web page that you don't want to wait to download. Maybe you entered the wrong URL or maybe the download is taking too long. In any event, you'll want to stop the transfer part-way through. This is why the CHtmlView class has the Stop function. It cancels the download currently in progress. To add this functionality to your application, add a new menu entry to the Navigate menu in the Menu Designer. Specify the menu entry properties in Table 16.6.

TABLE 16.6   Menu Property Settings

Object	Property	Setting
Menu Entry	ID	ID_NAVIGATE_STOP
	Caption	&Stop
	Prompt	Stop the current transfer\nStop

Using the Event Handler Wizard, add an event-handler function to the CWebBrowseView class for this menu ID on the COMMAND event message. Edit the function with the code in Listing 16.9.

LISTING 16.9   The CWebBrowseView OnNavigateStop Function

```
void CWebBrowseView::OnNavigateStop()
{
    // TODO: Add your command handler code here
    // Stop the current download
    Stop();
}
```

If you run your application, you can use this menu entry to stop any download of a Web page that you don't want to wait for. It would be more convenient if you added a toolbar button for this menu ID.

Another control function that most browsers have is the capability to reload the current Web page. This function is handy for Web pages that contain dynamic elements that change each time the page is downloaded. It's also helpful for Web pages that your browser may have in its cache, preventing it from retrieving the newest version of the page. It's necessary to be able to force the browser to reload the page and not just display the cached version (especially if it's a Web page that you are in the process of creating). The browser component has the capability built in with the Refresh function. One call to this function means the current page is reloaded.

You can add this functionality to your application by adding another menu entry to the Navigate menu. Specify the properties for the new menu entry using the settings in Table 16.7. You can add a separator bar between the two navigate menu entries that were originally there, and the two new entries, to make your menu look like the one in Figure 16.8.

TABLE 16.7   Menu Property Settings

Object	Property	Setting
Menu Entry	ID ID_NAVIGATE_REFRESH	
	Caption	&Refresh
	Prompt	Refresh the current page\nRefresh

FIGURE 16.8

The modified Navigate menu.

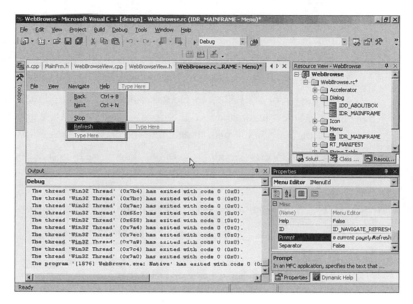

After you add the menu entry, use the Class Wizard to add an event-handler function to the CWebBrowseView class for the COMMAND event message for this menu entry. Edit the function, adding the code in Listing 16.10.

LISTING 16.10   The CWebBrowseView OnNavigateRefresh Function

```
void CWebBrowseView::OnNavigateRefresh()
{
    // TODO: Add your command handler code here
    // Reload the current page
    Refresh();
}
```

Now you can test this functionality by finding a Web site that returns a different page each time that you refresh the browser. As with the rest of the menu functions that you added to this application, this one should also be added to the toolbar.

Setting the Page Title to the Title Bar

The last thing that you'll do to your application requires generating a wrapper class for the IHtmlDocument2 Interface. You'll use the Title property, and the get_title property function to retrieve the page title and set it to the title bar of your application. To add this functionality to your application follow these steps:

1. Add a new class to your application.

2. On the Add Class dialog, select MFC Class From TypeLib for the class template to create. Click OK.

3. On the Add Class From Typelib Wizard, select the Microsoft HTML Object Library <4.0> in the Combo box of available type libraries.

4. In the list of available interfaces, scroll down and find the IHTMLDocument2 interface. Select it and add it to the list of Generated Classes by pressing the right angle button (>). Click Finish to generate the class.

5. In the view class, modify the OnDocumentComplete function, adding the highlighted code in Listing 16.12.

LISTING 16.11   The Modified CWebBrowseView OnDocumentComplete Function

```
void CWebBrowseView::OnDocumentComplete(LPCTSTR lpszURL)
{
    // TODO: Add your specialized code here and/or call the base class
    // Pass the new URL to the address bar
    ((CMainFrame*)GetParentFrame())->SetAddress(lpszURL);

    // Get an instance of the HTMLDocument2 interface
    CHTMLDocument2* pHDoc = new CHTMLDocument2(GetHtmlDocument());
    // Get the page title
    CString strTitle = pHDoc->get_title();
    // Get a pointer to the document class
    CWebBrowseDoc* pDoc = GetDocument();
    // Set the page title
    pDoc->SetTitle(strTitle);
    // Clean up
    delete pHDoc;

    CHtmlView::OnDocumentComplete(lpszURL);
}
```

6. Modify the #include directives in the CWebBrowseView class, adding one to include the header for the CHtmlDocument2 class, as in Listing 16.13.

LISTING 16.12   The Modified CWebBrowseView #include Directives

```
// WebBrowseView.cpp : implementation of the CWebBrowseView class
//

#include "stdafx.h"
#include "WebBrowse.h"

#include "WebBrowseDoc.h"
#include "WebBrowseView.h"
```

LISTING 16.12 continued

```
#include "MainFrm.h"
#include "CHtmlDocument2.h"

#ifdef _DEBUG
#define new DEBUG_NEW
#endif
```

16

Now you should be able to compile and run your application, seeing the Web page title added to the title bar of your application as you navigate from page to page.

Summary

Today you learned how Microsoft designed its Internet Explorer Web browser as a series of ActiveX components that could be used in other applications. You saw how Microsoft encapsulated the browser into the CHtmlView class, which can be used in SDI and MDI applications to provide Web browsing functionality to almost any application. You learned how you can use this view class to build a Web browser. You saw how you could use the dialog bar to place controls on a toolbar and how the events for these controls can be handled in the frame class for the application. Next, you learned how to add menus to your application to call the various functions of the Web browser to provide a complete surfing experience. Finally, you learned how you can use the Wizards included with Visual C++ to generate wrapper classes for ActiveX Controls and COM objects.

Q&A

Q. Why is Print Preview not included on the default menus when I choose CHtmlView as the base class for my view class?

A. The printing for the CHtmlView class is performed by the browser, not the view class. You don't have print preview because the browser doesn't support it.

Q. How can I get the HTML source code from the browser so that I can see or edit it?

A. The CHtmlView class has a member function, GetSource, that takes a CString variable as its only parameter. This CString parameter is populated with the HTML source code.

Workshop

The Workshop provides quiz questions to help you solidify your understanding of the material covered and exercises to provide you with experience in using what you've learned. The answers to the quiz questions and exercises are provided in Appendix A, "Answers to Quiz Questions."

Quiz

1. What does the `CHtmlView` class encapsulate for use in Visual C++ applications?

2. How can you get the URL for the current Web page from the `CHtmlView` class?

3. What command is triggered for the frame class when the user presses the Enter key in the edit box on the dialog bar?

4. What functions can you call to navigate the browser to the previous and the next Web pages?

5. How can you stop a download in progress?

Exercises

1. Add the `GoSearch` function to the menu and toolbar.

2. Add the `GoHome` function to the menu and toolbar.

3. Disable the Stop toolbar button and menu entry when the application is not downloading a Web page.

DAY 17

Implementing Multitasking in Your Applications

Sometimes letting your applications do more than one thing at a time is convenient. Your application could write a backup file or print in the background while a user is working on the same document. Maybe your application could perform calculations while a user enters new data, or draw multiple images simultaneously. You might want to add multitasking to your applications for many different reasons. Windows provides several facilities specifically for building this capability into applications.

Today, you will learn

- How tasks can be performed while an application is idle
- How tasks can run independently of the rest of the application
- How to coordinate access to resources that are shared between multiple independent tasks
- How to start and stop independently running tasks

Understanding Multitasking

NEW TERM In the days of Windows 3.*x*, all Windows applications were single-threaded, with only one path of execution at any one point in time. The version of multitasking that Windows 3.*x* offered is known as *cooperative multitasking*, in which each individual application makes the decision about when to give up the processor for another application to perform any processing that it might be waiting to perform. As a result, Windows 3.*x* was susceptible to an ill-behaved application that would hold other applications prisoner while it performed some long, winding process or even got itself stuck in some sort of loop.

With Windows NT/95, the nature of the operating system changed. No more cooperative multitasking—the new method was *preemptive multitasking*. With preemptive multitasking, the operating system decides when to take the processor away from the current application and give the processor to another application that's waiting for it. It doesn't matter whether the application that has the processor is ready to give it up; the operating system takes the processor without the application's permission. This is how the operating system enables multiple applications to perform computation-intensive tasks and still let all the applications make the same amount of progress in each task. Giving this capability to the operating system prevents a single application from holding other applications prisoner while hogging the processor.

> **Note**
>
> With the 16/32-bit structure of Windows 95/98/Me, it's still possible for an ill-behaved 16-bit application to lock up the system because a large amount of 16-bit code remains a core part of the operating system. The 16-bit code on Windows 95/98/Me is still a cooperative multitasking environment, so only one application can execute 16-bit code at a time. Because all the USER functions thunk down to the 16-bit version, and a good portion of the GDI functions thunk down to the 16-bit version, it's still possible for a single 16-bit application to lock up the entire system.
>
> On Windows NT, if all 16-bit applications run in a shared memory space, an ill-behaved application can lock up all of them, but it won't affect any 32-bit applications.

Performing Multiple Tasks at One Time

Along with the capability to allow multiple applications to run simultaneously comes the capability for a single application to execute multiple threads of execution at any one point in time. A thread is to an application what an application is to the operating system. If an application has multiple threads running, it's basically running multiple applications within the whole application. This lets the application accomplish more things simultaneously, such as when Microsoft Word checks your spelling at the same time you are typing your document.

Using Idle Processing Threads

NEW TERM One of the easiest ways to let your application perform multiple tasks at one time is to add some idle processing tasks. An *idle processing task* is performed when an application sits idle. Literally, a function in the application class is called when no messages are in the application message queue. The idea behind this function is that while the application is idle, it can perform work such as cleaning up memory (also known as *garbage collection*) or writing to a print spool.

The OnIdle function is a holdover from the Windows 3.*x* days. It's a member of the CWinApp class, from which your application class is inherited. By default, no processing in this function is added by the MFC Application Wizard, so if you want this function in your application, you must add it to your application class through the Class Property Overrides. (OnIdle is one of the available override functions for the App class in your applications.)

The OnIdle function receives one argument, which is the number of times the OnIdle function has been called since the last message was processed by your application. You can use this to determine how long the application has been idle and when to trigger any functionality that you need to run if the application is idle for more than a certain amount of time.

One of the biggest concerns in adding OnIdle processing to your applications is that any functionality you add must be small and must quickly return control to users. When an application performs any OnIdle processing, users can't interact with the application until the OnIdle processing finishes and returns control to them. If you need to perform some long, drawn-out task in the OnIdle function, break it up into many small and quick tasks so that control can return to users; then, you can continue your OnIdle task after the message queue is empty again. This means you also have to track your application's progress in the OnIdle task so that the next time the OnIdle function is called, your application can pick up the task where it left off.

Spawning Independent Threads

If you really need to run a long background task that you don't want interfering with the users, you should spawn an independent thread. A thread is like another application running within your application. It doesn't have to wait until the application is idle to perform its tasks, and it doesn't cause users to wait until it takes a break.

17

Both methods of creating an independent thread use the same function to create and start the thread. To create and start an independent thread, you call the AfxBeginThread function. You can choose to pass it a function to call for performing the thread's tasks, or you can pass it a pointer to the runtime class for an object derived from the CWinThread class. Both versions of the function return a pointer to a CWinThread object, which runs as an independent thread.

In the first version of the AfxBeginThread function, the first argument is a pointer to the main function for the thread to be started. The function pointed to is the equivalent of the main function in a C/C++ program. It controls the top-level execution for the thread. This function must be defined as a UINT function with a single LPVOID argument:

```
UINT MyThreadFunction( LPVOID pParam);
```

This version of AfxBeginThread also requires a second argument that's passed to the main thread function as that function's only argument. This argument can be a pointer to a structure containing any information that the thread needs to know to perform its job correctly.

The first argument to the second version of the AfxBeginThread function is a pointer to the runtime class of an object derived from the CWinThread class. You can get a pointer to the runtime class of your CWinThread class by using the RUNTIME_CLASS macro, passing your class as the only argument.

After these initial arguments, the rest of the arguments to AfxBeginThread are the same for both versions, and they are all optional. The first of these arguments is the priority to be assigned to the thread, with a default priority of THREAD_PRIORITY_NORMAL. Table 17.1 lists the available thread priorities.

TABLE 17.1   Thread Priorities

Priority	Description
0	The thread inherits the thread priority of the application creating the thread.
THREAD_PRIORITY_NORMAL	A normal (default) priority.
THREAD_PRIORITY_ABOVE_NORMAL	1 point above normal priority.
THREAD_PRIORITY_BELOW_NORMAL	1 point below normal priority.
THREAD_PRIORITY_HIGHEST	2 points above normal priority.
THREAD_PRIORITY_LOWEST	2 points below normal priority.
THREAD_PRIORITY_IDLE	Priority level of 1 for most threads (all non-real-time threads).
THREAD_PRIORITY_TIME_CRITICAL	Priority level of 15 for most threads (all non-real-time threads).

Note

Thread priority controls how much of the CPU's time the thread gets in rela-
tion to the other threads and processes running on the computer. If a thread
won't be performing any tasks that need to be completed quickly, you
should give the thread a lower priority when creating it. Giving a thread a
priority higher than normal isn't advisable unless it's vitally important that
the thread perform its tasks faster than other processes running on the
computer. The higher a thread's priority, the more CPU time that thread
will receive, and the less CPU time all other processes and threads on the
computer will receive.

The next argument to the AfxBeginThread function is the stack size to be provided for
the new thread. Each thread has it's own stack upon which parameters are passed to
functions, and local variables are created. The default value for this argument is 0, which
provides the thread the same size stack as the main application.

The next argument to AfxBeginThread is the thread-creation flag, which controls how
the thread is started and can contain one of two values. If CREATE_SUSPENDED is passed as
this argument, the thread is created in suspended mode, and the thread doesn't run until
the ResumeThread function is called for the thread. If you supply 0 (the default) as this
argument, the thread begins executing the moment it's created.

The final argument to AfxBeginThread is a pointer to the thread's security attributes. The
default value for this argument is NULL, which causes the thread to be created with the
same security profile as the application. Unless you are building applications to run on
Windows NT/2000/XP and need to provide a thread with a specific security profile, you
should always use the default value for this argument.

Building Structures

Imagine that you have an application running two threads, each parsing its own set of
variables at the same time. Imagine also that the application is using a global object array
to hold these variables. If the method of allocating and resizing the array consisted of
checking the current size and adding one position to the end of the array, your two
threads might build an array populated something like the one in Figure 17.1, where
array positions populated by the first thread are intermingled with those created by the
second thread. This could easily confuse each thread as it retrieves values from the array
for its processing needs because each thread is just as likely to pull a value that actually
belongs to the other thread. This would cause each thread to operate on wrong data and
return the wrong results.

17

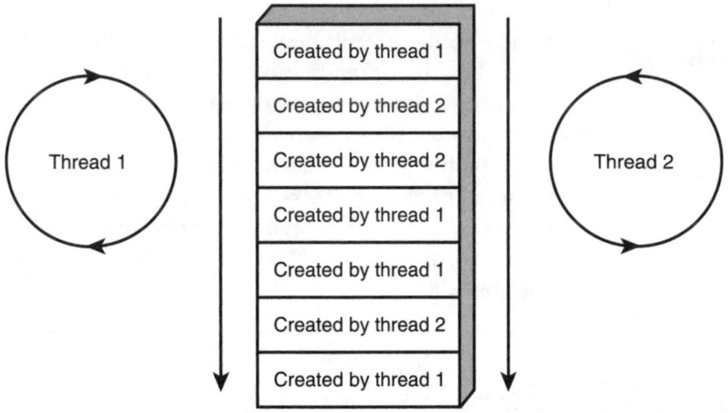

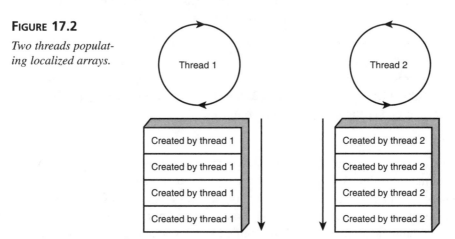

FIGURE 17.1

Two threads populating a common array.

If the application built these arrays as localized instead of global arrays, it could keep access to each array limited to only the thread that builds the array. Figure 17.2, for example, shows no intermingling of data from multiple threads. If you take this approach to using arrays and other memory structures, each thread can perform its processing and return the results to the client, confident that the results are correct because the calculations were performed on uncorrupted data.

FIGURE 17.2

Two threads populating localized arrays.

Managing Access to Shared Resources

Not all variables can be localized, and you will often want to share some resources between all the threads running in your applications. Such sharing creates an issue with multithreaded applications. Suppose that three threads all share a single counter, which is generating unique numbers. Because you don't know when control of the processor is going to switch from one thread to the next, your application might generate duplicate "unique" numbers, as shown in Figure 17.3.

FIGURE 17.3

Three threads sharing a single counter.

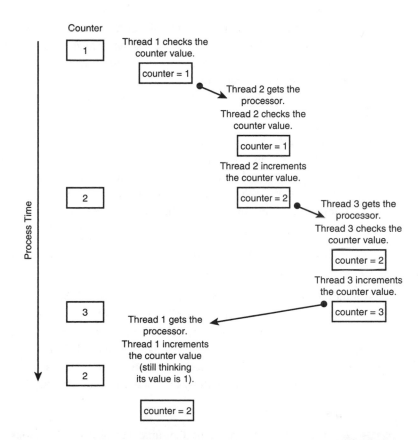

As you can see, this sharing doesn't work too well in a multithreaded application. You need a way to limit access to a common resource to only one thread at a time. In reality, there are four mechanisms for limiting access to common resources and synchronizing processing between threads, all of which work differently and whose suitability depends on the circumstances:

- Critical sections
- Mutexes
- Semaphores
- Events

Critical Sections

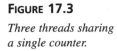 A *critical section* limits access to a certain resource to a single thread within an application. A thread enters the critical section before it needs to work with the specific shared resource and then exits the critical section after it finishes accessing the

resource. If another thread tries to enter the critical section before the first thread exits it, the second thread is blocked and doesn't take any processor time until the first thread exits and allows the second to enter. You use critical sections to mark sections of code in which only one thread should execute at a time. It doesn't prevent the processor from switching from that thread to another; it just prevents two or more threads from entering the same section of code.

If you use a critical section with the counter in Figure 17.3, you can force each thread to enter a critical section before checking the current value of the counter. If each thread doesn't leave the critical section until after it increments and updates the counter, you can guarantee that—no matter how many threads are executing and regardless of their execution order—truly unique numbers are generated (see Figure 17.4).

To use a critical section object in your application, create an instance of the CCriticalSection class. This object contains two methods, Lock and Unlock, which you can use to gain and release control of the critical section.

Another option that you can explore is the use of the CSingleLock class, which can be used to lock and unlock Critical Section objects. The CSingleLock class can be used with all of the synchronization objects discussed today for controlling access to the objects. Another synchronization class that can be used is the CMultiLock class, which works the same as the CSingleLock class, only can not be used with Critical Section objects (but can be used with all other synchronization objects).

Mutexes

NEW TERM *Mutexes* work in basically the same way as critical sections, but you use mutexes when you want to share the resource between multiple applications. By using a mutex, you can guarantee that no two threads running in any number of applications will access the same resource at the same time.

Because of their availability across the operating system, mutexes carry a lot more overhead than critical sections do. A mutex lifetime doesn't end when the application that created it shuts down. The mutex might still be in use by other applications, so the operating system must track which applications are using a mutex and then destroy that mutex when it's no longer needed. In contrast, critical sections have little overhead because they don't exist outside the application that creates and uses them. After the application ends, the critical section is gone.

To use a mutex in your applications, create an instance of the CMutex class. The constructor of this class has three available arguments:

- A Boolean value that specifies whether the thread creating the CMutex object is the mutex's initial owner. If so, this thread must release the mutex before any other threads can access it.

FIGURE 17.4

*Three threads using
the same counter,
which is protected by a
critical section.*

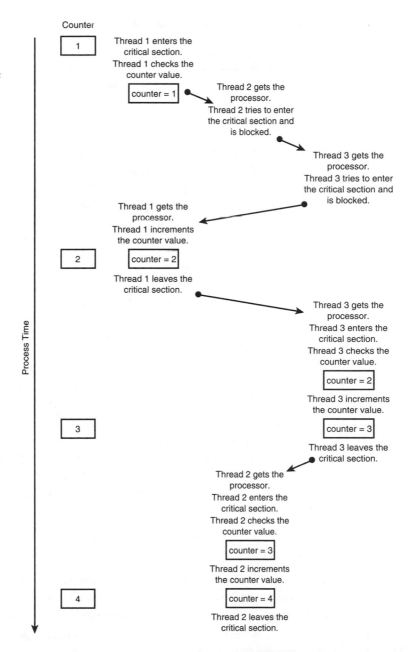

• The name of the mutex. All applications that need to share the mutex can identify
it by this textual name.

- A pointer to the mutex object's security attributes. If a NULL is passed for this pointer, the object uses the security attributes of the thread that created it.

When you create a CMutex object, you can lock and unlock it by using the Lock and Unlock member functions. This allows you to build in the capabilities to control access to a shared resource between multiple threads in multiple applications.

Semaphores

NEW TERM *Semaphores* work differently from critical sections and mutexes. You use semaphores with resources that aren't limited to a single thread at a time—a resource that should be limited to a fixed number of threads. A *semaphore* is a form of counter, and threads can increment or decrement it. The trick to semaphores is that they can't go any lower than zero. Therefore, if a thread tries to decrement a semaphore that's at zero, that thread is blocked until another thread increments the semaphore.

Suppose that you have a queue populated by multiple threads, and one thread removes the items from the queue and performs processing on each item. If the queue is empty, the thread that removes and processes items has nothing to do. This thread could go into an idle loop, checking the queue every so often to see whether something has been placed in it. The problem with this scenario is that the thread takes up processing cycles doing absolutely nothing. These processor cycles could go to another thread that does have something to do. If you use a semaphore to control the queue, each thread that places items into the queue can increment the semaphore for each item placed in the queue, and the thread that removes the items can decrement the semaphore just before removing each item from the queue. If the queue is empty, the semaphore is zero, and the thread removing items is blocked on the call to decrement the queue. This thread doesn't take any processor cycles until one of the other threads increments the semaphore to indicate that it has placed an item in the queue. Then, the thread removing items is immediately unblocked, and it can remove the item that was placed in the queue and begin processing it (see Figure 17.5).

To use a semaphore in your application, create an instance of the CSemaphore class. This class has four arguments that can be passed to the class constructor:

- The first two arguments are the starting usage count and the maximum usage count for the semaphore. You can use these two arguments to control how many threads and processes can have access to a shared resource at any one time.

- The name for the semaphore identifies it by all applications running on the system, just as with the CMutex class.

- The class also uses a pointer to the security attributes for the semaphore.

FIGURE 17.5

*Multiple threads plac-
ing objects into a
queue.*

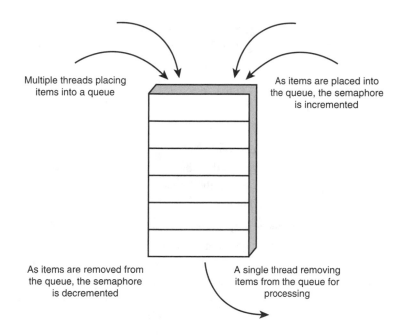

Multiple threads placing
items into a queue

As items are placed into
the queue, the semaphore
is incremented

As items are removed from
the queue, the semaphore
is decremented

A single thread removing
items from the queue for
processing

17

With the `CSemaphore` object, you can use the `Lock` and `Unlock` member functions to gain
or release control of the semaphore. When you call the `Lock` function, if the semaphore
usage count is greater than zero, the usage count is decremented and your program is
allowed to continue. If the usage count is already zero, the `Lock` function waits until the
usage count is incremented so that your process can gain access to the shared resource.
When you call the `Unlock` function, the usage count of the semaphore is incremented.

Events

As much as thread synchronization mechanisms are designed to control access to limited
resources, they are also intended to prevent threads from using unnecessary processor
cycles. The more threads running at one time, the slower each performs its tasks.
Therefore, if a thread doesn't have anything to do, block it and let it sit idle, allowing
other threads to use more processor time and thus run faster until the conditions are met
that provide the idle thread with something to do.

This is why you use events—to allow threads to be idle until the conditions are such that
they have something to do. Events take their name from the events that drive most
Windows applications, only with a twist. Thread synchronization events don't use the
normal event queuing and handling mechanisms. Rather than be assigned a number and
then wait for that number to be passed through the Windows event handler, thread synchronization events are actual objects held in memory. Each thread that needs to wait for
an event tells the event that it's waiting for it to be triggered and then it goes to sleep.

When the event is triggered, it sends wake-up calls to every thread that told it that it was waiting for it to be triggered. The threads pick up their processing at the exact point where they each told the event that they were waiting for it.

To use an event in your application, you need to create the CEvent object when you need to access and wait for the event. After the CEvent constructor is returned, the event has occurred and your thread can continue on its way.

The constructor for the CEvent class can take four arguments. The first argument is a Boolean flag to indicate whether the thread creating the event will own it initially. This value should be set to TRUE if the thread creating the CEvent object is the thread that will determine when the event has occurred.

The second argument to the CEvent constructor specifies whether the event is automatic or manual. A manual event remains in the signaled or unsignaled state until it's specifically set to the other state by the thread that owns the event object. An automatic event remains in the unsignaled state most of the time. When the event is set to the signaled state as soon as at least one thread has been released and has continued on its execution path, the event is returned to the unsignaled state.

The third argument to the event constructor is the name for the event. This name that will be used to identify the event by all threads that need to access the event. The fourth and final argument is a pointer to the security attributes for the event object.

The CEvent class has several member functions that you can use to control the state of the event (see Table 17.2).

TABLE 17.2 CEvent Member Functions

Function	Description
SetEvent	Puts the event into the signaled state.
PulseEvent	Puts the event into the signaled state and then resets the event back to the unsignaled state. A key aspect of this function is that only one of the waiting threads will be released.
ResetEvent	Puts the event into the unsignaled state.
Unlock	Releases the event object.

Building a Multitasking Application

To see how you can create your own multitasking applications, you'll create an application that has four spinning color wheels, each running on its own thread. Two spinners will use the OnIdle function; the other two will run as independent threads. This setup enables you to see the difference between the two types of threading, as well as learn how you can use each. Your application window will have four check boxes to start and stop each thread so you can see how much load is put on the system as each runs alone or in combination with the others.

Creating a Framework

For today's application, you need an SDI application framework, with the view class inherited from the CFormView class, so that you can use the dialog editor to lay out the few controls on the window. It will use the document class to house the spinners and the independent threads, whereas the view will have the check boxes and variables that control whether each thread is running or idle.

To start your application, follow these steps:

1. Create a new MFC Application Visual C++ project and name it Tasking.

2. In the Application Type area, select Single Document for the application type.

3. In the Generated Classes area, specify the base class as CFormView and click Finish. The MFC Application Wizard generates the application shell.

4. Remove the static text from the main application window, and add four check boxes at approximately the upper-left corner of each quarter of the window space (see Figure 17.6). Set the properties of the check boxes as in Table 17.3.

FIGURE 17.6

The main window design.

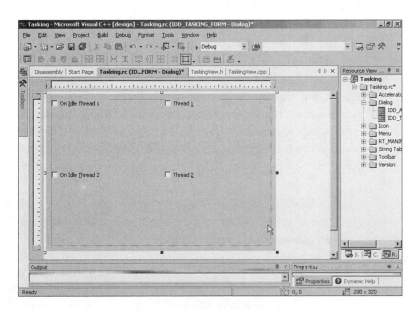

TABLE 17.3 Control Property Settings

Object	Property	Setting
Check Box	ID	IDC_CBONIDLE1
	Caption	On &Idle Thread 1
Check Box	ID	IDC_CBTHREAD1
	Caption	Thread &1
Check Box	ID	IDC_CBONIDLE2
	Caption	On Idle &Thread 2
Check Box	ID	IDC_CBTHREAD2
	Caption	Thread &2

5. Add a variable to each check box. Make all the variables BOOL, and give them names like the following:

Object	Name	Category	Type	Access
IDC_CBONIDLE1	m_bOnIdle1	Value	BOOL	public
IDC_CBONIDLE2	m_bOnIdle2	Value	BOOL	public
IDC_CBTHREAD1	m_bThread1	Value	BOOL	public
IDC_CBTHREAD2	m_bThread2	Value	BOOL	public

Designing Spinners

Before you can start adding threads to your application, you need to create the spinning color wheels that the threads will operate. Because these four color wheels will all spin independently of each other, it makes sense to encapsulate all functionality into a single class. This class tracks what color is being drawn, where in the spinning it needs to draw the next line, the size of the color wheel, and the location of the color wheel on the application window. It also needs a pointer to the view class so that it can get the device context in which it's supposed to draw itself. For the independent spinners, the class needs a pointer to the flag that controls whether the spinner is supposed to be spinning.

To start the spinner class, follow these steps:

1. Create a new generic class, inherited from the CObject base class.
2. Provide the new class with a name that describes what it will be doing. For this example, name the class CSpinner.

Setting Spinner Variables

After you create a new class for your spinner object, add some variables to the class. To follow good object-oriented design principles, you need to make all these variables private and add methods to the class to set and retrieve the values of each.

The variables you'll add are

- The current color
- The current position in the rotation of the color wheel
- The size of the color wheel
- The position on the application window for the color wheel
- The color table from which the colors are picked for drawing in the color wheel
- A pointer to the view object so that the spinner can get the device context that it will need for drawing on the window
- A pointer to the check box variable that specifies whether the thread should be running

Add all these variables to the CSpinner class by using the names and types specified in Table 17.4. Mark the access for all these as private.

TABLE 17.4 CSpinner Class Variables

Name	Type	Description
m_iColor	int	The current color from the color table.
m_iMinute	int	The position in the rotation around the wheel.
m_iRadius	int	The radius (size) of the wheel.
m_ptCenter	CPoint	The center point of the wheel.
m_crColors[8]	static COLORREF	The color table with all the colors to be drawn in the color wheel. You may have to add the static keyword by hand, as well as the array dimension.
m_pViewWnd	CWnd*	A pointer to the view object.
m_pbContinue	BOOL*	A pointer to the check box variable that specifies whether this thread should be running.

After you add all the necessary variables, you need to be sure that your class either initializes them or provides a suitable means of setting and retrieving the values of each. All integer variables can be initialized as zero, and they'll work their way up from that point. The pointers should be initialized with NULL. You can do all initialization in the class constructor, as in Listing 17.1.

LISTING 17.1 The CSpinner Constructor

```
CSpinner::CSpinner(void)
: m_iColor(0)
```

LISTING **17.1**   continued

```
, m_iMinute(0)
, m_iRadius(0)
, m_ptCenter(0)
, m_pViewWnd(NULL)
, m_pbContinue(NULL)
{
}
```

For those variables that you need to be able to set and retrieve, your spinner class is simple enough that you can write all the set and get functions as inline functions in the class declaration. The spinner object automatically calculates the color and position, so you don't need to add set functions for those two variables, but you do need to add set functions for the rest of the variables (not counting the color table). The only variables that you need to retrieve from the spinner object are the pointers to the view class and the check box variable.

Add all these functions to the CSpinner class declaration by opening the Spinner header file and adding the inline functions in Listing 17.2.

LISTING **17.2**   The CSpinner Class Declaration

```
class CSpinner :
    public CObject
{
public:
    CSpinner(void);
    ~CSpinner(void);
    BOOL* GetContinue() { return m_pbContinue;}
    void SetContinue(BOOL* pbContinue) { m_pbContinue = pbContinue;}
    CWnd* GetViewWnd() { return m_pViewWnd;}
    void SetViewWnd(CWnd* pWnd) { m_pViewWnd = pWnd;}
    void SetLength(int iLength) { m_iRadius = iLength;}
    void SetPoint(CPoint ptPoint) { m_ptCenter = ptPoint;}

private:
    // The current color from the color table
    int m_iColor;
    // The position in the rotation around the wheel
    int m_iMinute;
    // The radius (size) of the wheel
    int m_iRadius;
    // The center point of the wheel
    CPoint m_ptCenter;
    // The color table with all of the colors to be drawn in the color wheel
    static COLORREF m_crColors[8];
```

INPUT

LISTING 17.2   continued

```
    // A pointer to the view object
    CWnd* m_pViewWnd;
    // A pointer to the check box variable that specifies whether
    // this thread should be running
    BOOL* m_pbContinue;
};
```

Now that you've added all the support functions for setting and retrieving the necessary variables, you need to declare and populate the color table. This will look just like the color table definition you added to the drawing application on Day 10, "Creating SDI and MDI Applications." The color table consists of eight RGB values, with each value being either 0 or 255, with every combination of these two settings.

Add this table declaration to the spinner source code file, just before the class constructor, as in Listing 17.3.

LISTING 17.3   The CSpinner Color Table

```
#include "StdAfx.h"
#include "spinner.h"

COLORREF CSpinner::m_crColors[8] = {
    RGB(   0,   0,   0),    // Black
    RGB(   0,   0, 255),    // Blue
    RGB(   0, 255,   0),    // Green
    RGB(   0, 255, 255),    // Cyan
    RGB( 255,   0,   0),    // Red
    RGB( 255,   0, 255),    // Magenta
    RGB( 255, 255,   0),    // Yellow
    RGB( 255, 255, 255)     // White
};

CSpinner::CSpinner(void)
: m_crColor(0)
. ..
```

INPUT

Drawing the Spinner

Now comes the fun part: getting the spinner object to actually spin. To accomplish this, calculate the new position of the starting and ending points of each line, set the view port origination point, select the drawing color, and create a pen to draw in that color. When you have all of this, you can draw the line from the starting point to the ending point. After the line is drawn, you can restore the pen to what it was before drawing the line.

17

Next, you'll calculate the position of the next line to draw before exiting the function.

To add this functionality to your spinner object, follow these steps:

1. Add a member function to the CSpinner class. Specify the type as void, the name as Draw, and the access as public.

2. Edit the function, adding the code in Listing 17.4.

LISTING 17.4   The CSpinner Draw Function

```
void CSpinner::Draw(void)
{
    // Get a pointer to the device context
    CDC *pDC = m_pViewWnd->GetDC();
    // Set the mapping mode
    pDC->SetMapMode (MM_LOENGLISH);
    // Copy the spinner center
    CPoint org = m_ptCenter;
    CPoint ptStartPoint;
    // Set the starting point
    ptStartPoint.x = (m_iRadius / 2);
    ptStartPoint.y = (m_iRadius / 2);
    // Set the origination point
    org.x = m_ptCenter.x + (m_iRadius / 2);
    org.y = m_ptCenter.y + m_iRadius;
    // Set the viewport origination point
    pDC->SetViewportOrg(org.x, org.y);

    CPoint ptEndPoint;
    // Calculate the angle of the next line
    double nRadians = (double) (m_iMinute * 6) * 0.017453292;
    // Set the end point of the line
    ptEndPoint.x = (int) (m_iRadius * sin(nRadians));
    ptEndPoint.y = (int) (m_iRadius * cos(nRadians));


    // Create the pen to use
    CPen pen(PS_SOLID, 0, m_crColors[m_iColor]);
    // Select the pen for use
    CPen* pOldPen = pDC->SelectObject(&pen);

    // Move to the starting point
    pDC->MoveTo (ptEndPoint);
    // Draw the line to the end point
    pDC->LineTo (ptStartPoint);

    // Reselect the previous pen
    pDC->SelectObject(&pOldPen);
```

LISTING 17.4   continued

```
    // Release the device context
    m_pViewWnd->ReleaseDC(pDC);

    // Increment the minute
    if (++m_iMinute == 60)
    {
        // If the minutes have gone full circle, reset to 0
        m_iMinute = 0;
        // Increment the color
        if (++m_iColor == 8)
            // If we've gone through all colors, start again
            m_iColor = 0;
    }
}
```

17

ANALYSIS   That was quite a bit of code to type. What does it do? Well, to understand what this function is doing and how it will make your spinner draw a color wheel on the window, let's look more closely at the code.

To make efficient use of the spinner by the different threads, it'll only draw one line each time the function is called. This function is called 60 times for each complete circle, once for each "minute" in the clockwise rotation. Each complete rotation causes the spinner to switch to the next color in the color table.

One of the first things you need to do to perform any drawing on the window is to get the device context of the window. You do this by calling the GetDC function on the view object pointer:

```
CDC *pDC = m_pViewWnd->GetDC();
```

This function returns a CDC object pointer, which is an MFC class that encapsulates the device context.

When you have a pointer to the device context, you can call its member function, SetMapMode, to set the mapping mode:

```
pDC->SetMapMode (MM_LOENGLISH);
```

The mapping mode determines how the x and y coordinates are translated into positions onscreen. The MM_LOENGLISH mode converts each logical unit to 0.01 inch onscreen. There are several different mapping modes, each converting logical units to different measurements onscreen.

At this point, you start preparing to draw the current line for the color wheel. You start by calculating the starting point for the line that will be drawn. This point will be consistent for all lines drawn by the spinner object. After you calculate the starting point for the line, calculate the position of the viewport. The viewport is used as the starting point for the coordinates used for drawing.

 Note

> The starting point for the line to be drawn is calculated in an off-center position. If you want the starting point for the lines to be in the center of the color wheel, set both the x and y coordinates of the starting point to 0.

When the viewport origination point is calculated, use the `SetViewportOrg` function to set the viewport:

```
pDC->SetViewportOrg(org.x, org.y);
```

Now that you've specified the drawing area and the starting point for the line you will be drawing, you need to figure out where the other end of the line will be. You perform this calculation using the following code:

```
double nRadians = (double) (m_iMinute * 6) * 0.017453292;
ptEndPoint.x = (int) (m_iRadius * sin(nRadians));
ptEndPoint.y = (int) (m_iRadius * cos(nRadians));
```

The first of these calculations converts the minutes into degrees, which can then be fed into the sine and cosine functions to set the x and y coordinates to draw a circle. This sets the end point of the line that will be drawn.

Now that you've figured out the line's starting and ending points, create a pen to use in drawing the line:

```
CPen pen(PS_SOLID, 0, m_crColors[m_iColor]);
```

You've specified that the pen will be solid and thin, and you are picking the current color from the color table. When you create the pen to use, you select the pen for drawing, being sure to capture the current pen as the return value from the device context object:

```
CPen* pOldPen = pDC->SelectObject(&pen);
```

Now you are ready to draw the line, which is done using the `MoveTo` and `LineTo` functions that you're familiar with by now. After the line is drawn, you need to release the device context so that you don't have a resource leak in your application:

```
m_pViewWnd->ReleaseDC(pDC);
```

At this point, you've drawn the line, so all that's left to do is increment the minute counter, resetting it if you've made it all the way around the circle. Each time you complete a circle, you increment the color counter, until you've gone through all eight colors, at which time you reset the color counter.

To be able to use the trigonometric functions (sin and cos) in this function, you need to include the math.h header file in the Spinner class source file. To add this, simply scroll up to the top of the source code file and add another #include line, specifying the math.h header file as the file to be included:

```
#include "StdAfx.h"
#include <math.h>
#include "Spinner.h"
```

INPUT

Supporting the Spinners

Now that you've created the spinner class for drawing the spinning color wheel on the window, you need to add some support for the spinners. You can add an array to hold the four spinners in the document class, but you'd still need to calculate where each spinner should be placed on the application window and set all the variables in each spinner.

You can add all this code to the document class, starting with the array of spinners. To do so, add a member variable to the document class (in this instance, CTaskingDoc), specifying the type as CSpinner, the name as m_cSpin[4], and the access as private.

Calculating the Spinner Positions

One of the preparatory things that needs to happen while initializing the application is determining the locations of all four spinners. The window is roughly broken up into four quarters by the check boxes that will turn the spinner threads on and off, so it makes sense to divide the window area into four, quarter squares and place one spinner in each quarter.

To calculate the location of each spinner, it's easiest to create a function that calculates the location for one spinner, placing the spinner into the quarter square appropriate for the spinner number. If the function was passed a pointer to the spinner object, it could update the spinner object directly with the location.

To add this functionality to your application, follow these steps:

1. Add a new member function to the document class.
2. Specify the function type as void, the name as CalcPoint, and add two parameters. Specify the type of the first parameter as int and the name as iID. Specify the type of the second parameter as CSpinner* and the name as pSpin. Specify the function access as private.
3. Edit the function, adding the code in Listing 17.5.

17

LISTING **17.5** The `CTaskingDoc CalcPoint` Function

```cpp
void CTaskingDoc::CalcPoint(int iID, CSpinner* pSpin)
{
    RECT rWndRect;
    CPoint ptPos;
    int iLength;
    CTaskingView *pWnd;

    // Get a pointer to the view window
    pWnd = (CTaskingView*)pSpin->GetViewWnd();
    // Get the display area rectangle
    pWnd->GetClientRect(&rWndRect);
    // Calculate the size of the spinners
    iLength = rWndRect.right / 6;
    // Which spinner are we placing?
    switch (iID)
    {
    case 0:    // Position the first spinner
        ptPos.x = (rWndRect.right / 4) - iLength;
        ptPos.y = (rWndRect.bottom / 4) - iLength;
        break;
    case 1:    // Position the second spinner
        ptPos.x = ((rWndRect.right / 4) * 3) - iLength;
        ptPos.y = (rWndRect.bottom / 4) - iLength;
        break;
    case 2:    // Position the third spinner
        ptPos.x = (rWndRect.right / 4) - iLength;
        ptPos.y = ((rWndRect.bottom / 4) * 3) - (long)(iLength * 1.25);
        break;
    case 3:    // Position the fourth spinner
        ptPos.x = ((rWndRect.right / 4) * 3) - iLength;
        ptPos.y = ((rWndRect.bottom / 4) * 3) - (long)(iLength * 1.25);
        break;
    }
    // Set the size of the spinner
    pSpin->SetLength(iLength);
    // Set the location of the spinner
    pSpin->SetPoint(ptPos);
}
```

ANALYSIS This function first gets the pointer to the view window from the spinner object by calling the `GetViewWnd` function:

```cpp
pWnd = (CTaskingView*)pSpin->GetViewWnd();
```

Getting the pointer directly from the spinner object saves a few steps. It's a more direct route to get the information you need.

When you have a pointer to the view object, you can call the window's `GetClientRect` function to get the size of the available drawing area:

```
pWnd->GetClientRect(&rWndRect);
```

After you have the size of the drawing area, you can calculate a reasonable color wheel size by dividing the length of the drawing area by 6:

```
iLength = rWndRect.right / 6;
```

Dividing the drawing area by 4 will position you at the middle of the upper-left square. Subtract the size of the circle from this point, and you have the upper-left corner of the drawing area for the first spinner:

```
ptPos.x = (rWndRect.right / 4) - iLength;
ptPos.y = (rWndRect.bottom / 4) - iLength;
```

You can then include variations on this position, mostly by multiplying the center of the quadrant by 3 to move it to the center of the right or lower quadrant, and you can calculate the positions of the other three spinners.

After you calculate the length and position for the spinner, you call the `SetLength` and `SetPoint` functions to pass these values to the spinner for which they have been calculated:

```
pSpin->SetLength(iLength);
pSpin->SetPoint(ptPos);
```

Initializing the Spinners

Because you wrote the function in Listing 17.5 to calculate the location of each spinner on the window to work on only one spinner each time it's called, you need some routine that will initialize each spinner, calling the `CalcPoint` function once for each spinner. You need this function to get a pointer to the view object and pass that along to the spinner. You also need to get pointers to the check box variables for the spinners the independently running threads will use. Your code can do all this by just looping through the array of spinners, setting both pointers for each spinner, and then passing the spinner to the function you just finished.

To create this function for your application, follow these steps:

1. Add a new member function to the document class.
2. Specify the type as `void`, and name the function `InitSpinners`, and then specify the access as `private` because you'll only need to call this function once when the application is starting.
3. Edit the new function, adding the code in Listing 17.6.

LISTING 17.6   The CTaskingDoc InitSpinners Function

```
void CTaskingDoc::InitSpinners(void)
{
    int i;

    // Get the position of the view
    POSITION pos = GetFirstViewPosition();
    // Did we get a valid position?
    if (pos != NULL)
    {
        // Get a pointer to the view
        CView* pView = GetNextView(pos);

        // Loop through the spinners
        for (i = 0; i < 4; i++)
        {
            // Set the pointer to the view
            m_cSpin[i].SetViewWnd(pView);
            // Initialize the pointer to the continuation indicator
            m_cSpin[i].SetContinue(NULL);
            switch (i)
            {
            case 1:
                // Set the pointer to the first thread continuation indicator
                m_cSpin[i].SetContinue(&((CTaskingView*)pView)->m_bThread1);
                break;
            case 3:
                // Set the pointer to the second thread continuation indicator
                m_cSpin[i].SetContinue(&((CTaskingView*)pView)->m_bThread2);
                break;
            }
            // Calculate the location of the spinner
            CalcPoint(i, &m_cSpin[i]);
        }
    }
}
```

ANALYSIS   This function first goes through the steps of getting a pointer to the view class
from the document, as you did initially on Day 10. Once it has a valid pointer to
the view, it starts a loop to initialize each spinner in the array. You call the SetViewWnd
spinner function to set the spinner's pointer to the view window and then initialize the
spinner's pointer to the check box variable to NULL for all spinners. If the spinner is either
of the two that will be used by independent threads, you pass a pointer to the appropriate
check box variable. After you set all this, call the CalcPoint function from Listing 17.5
to calculate the spinner's location on the view window.

> **Note**
>
> Although you've seen several examples of using pointers, the way that you are passing a pointer to the check box variable to the spinner deserves a closer look:
>
>   m_cSpin[i].SetContinue(&((CTaskingView*)pView)->m_bThread1);
>
> In this statement, you take the pointer to the view object, pView, which is a pointer for a CView object, and cast it as a pointer to the specific view class that you've created in your application:
>
>   (CTaskingView*)pView
>
> Now that you can treat the pointer to the view object as a CTaskingView object, you can get to the check box variable, m_bThread1, which is a public member of the CTaskingView class:
>
>   ((CTaskingView*)pView)->m_bThread1
>
> After you access the m_bThread1 variable, you can get the address of this variable by placing an ampersand in front of this entire string:
>
>   &((CTaskingView*)pView)->m'_bThread1
>
> Passing this address for the m_bThread1 variable to the SetContinue function, you are, in effect, passing a pointer to the m_bThread1 variable, which can be used to set the pointer to this variable that the spinner object contains.

17

Now that you've created the routines to initialize all the spinners, you need to be sure that this routine is called when the application is started. Place this logic in the OnNewDocument function in the document class. This function is called when the application is started, so it's a logical place to trigger the initialization of the spinner objects.

So add the code in Listing 17.7 to the OnNewDocument function in the document class.

LISTING 17.7 The CTaskingDoc OnNewDocument Function

```
BOOL CTaskingDoc::OnNewDocument()
{
    if (!CDocument::OnNewDocument())
        return FALSE;

    // TODO: add reinitialization code here
    // (SDI documents will reuse this document)
    // Initialize the spinners
    InitSpinners();

    return TRUE;
}
```

INPUT

Spinning the Spinner

Once last thing that you'll add to the document class for now is a way to call the Draw function for a specific spinner from outside the document class. Because the array of spinners was declared as a private variable, no outside objects can get access to the spinners, so you need to add access for the outside objects. Follow these steps:

1. Add a function to provide this access by adding a new member function to your document class.

2. Specify the function type as void, specify the function name as DoSpin, and add a single parameter for the spinner number, specifying the parameter type as int and the parameter name as iIndex, and then specify the function's access as public.

3. Add the following code to the function to perform the actual call to the specified spinner:

```
void CTaskingDoc::DoSpin(int iIndex)
{
    // Spin the Spinner
    m_cSpin[iIndex].Draw();
}
```

Adding the OnIdle Tasks

Now that you have the supporting functionality in place, it's time to turn your attention to adding the various threads that turn the various spinners. You first add the threads that execute while the application is idle. You need to add a clicked event handler for the two On Idle check boxes so that you can keep the variables for these two check boxes in sync with the window. You also need to add the code to the application's OnIdle function to run these two spinners when the application is idle and the check boxes for these two spinner threads are checked.

 Note

> The use of the term *thread* in the preceding paragraph is slightly misleading. Any functionality that you place in the OnIdle function is running in the main application thread. All OnIdle processing that you add to the sample application won't run as an independent thread, but will be just functions that can be called from the main thread.

Starting and Stopping the OnIdle Tasks

The OnIdle function checks the values of the two check box variables that specify whether each should run, so all your application needs to do when either of these check boxes is clicked is be sure that the variables in the view object are synchronized with the controls on the window. To accomplish this, all you really need to do is call the UpdateData function when either control is clicked. To start and stop the OnIdle tasks, add a single event handler for both On Idle Thread check boxes and then call the UpdateData function in this event function.

To add this functionality to your application, follow these steps:

1. Open the main window dialog in the window painter.

2. Select one of the On Idle check boxes and add an event handler function for the BN_CLICKED event.

3. Add the following code:

```
void CTaskingView::OnBnClickedCbonidle1()
{
    // TODO: Add your control notification handler code here
    // Sync the variables with the dialog
    UpdateData(TRUE);
}
```

INPUT

4. Repeat steps 1–3 for the other On Idle check boxes.

Building the OnIdle Threads

If you examine the application class (CTaskingApp) source code, notice that the OnIdle function isn't there. All the functionality that OnIdle needs to perform by default is in the ancestor class of the application class created for your project. The only reason to have an OnIdle function in your application class is that your application needs some specific functionality to be performed during this event. As a result, you need to specifically add this event handler to your application using the Class Properties Overrides.

After you add the OnIdle function to your application class, what does it need to do?

1. It needs to get a pointer to the view so that it can check the status of the check box variables.

2. It needs to get a pointer to the document class so that it can call the DoSpin function to trigger the appropriate spinner object.

The key to both actions is getting pointers to each object. When you begin looking at what's necessary to get these pointers, you'll find that you have to reverse the order in which you get the pointers. You need to get a pointer to the document object to get a pointer to the view. However, to get a pointer to the document, you have to go through the document template, getting a pointer to the template before you can get a pointer to the document. Each step requires the same sequence of events, first getting the position of the first object and then getting a pointer to the object in that position. What you'll do is get the position of the first document template and then get a pointer to the document template in that position. Next, you'll use the document template to get the position of the first document and then use the document template to get a pointer to the document in that first position. Finally, you'll use the document to get the position of the first view and then use the document again to get a pointer to the view in the position specified. After you have a pointer to the view, you can check the value of the check boxes and call the appropriate spinner.

To add this functionality to your application, follow these steps:

1. Use the Class Properties Overrides to add a function to the OnIdle event message for the application class (CTaskingApp).

2. Add the code in Listing 17.8.

LISTING 17.8   The CTaskingApp OnIdle Function

```
BOOL CTaskingApp::OnIdle(LONG lCount)
{
    // TODO: Add your specialized code here and/or call the base class
    // Get the position of the first document template
    POSITION pos = GetFirstDocTemplatePosition();
    // Do we have a valid template position?
    if (pos)
    {
        // Get a pointer to the document template
        CDocTemplate* pDocTemp = GetNextDocTemplate(pos);
        // Do we have a valid pointer?
        if (pDocTemp)
        {
            // Get the position of the first document
            POSITION dPos = pDocTemp->GetFirstDocPosition();
            // Do we have a valid document position?
            if (dPos)
            {
                // Get a pointer to the document
                CTaskingDoc* pDocWnd =
                    (CTaskingDoc*)pDocTemp->GetNextDoc(dPos);
                // Do we have a valid pointer?
                if (pDocWnd)
                {
                    // Get the position of the view
                    POSITION vPos = pDocWnd->GetFirstViewPosition();
                    // Do we have a valid view position?
                    if (vPos)
                    {
                        // Get a pointer to the view
                        CTaskingView* pView =
                                (CTaskingView*)pDocWnd->GetNextView(vPos);
                        // Do we have a valid pointer?
```

INPUT

LISTING 17.8   continued

```
                    if (pView)
                    {
                        // Should we spin the first idle thread?
                        if (pView->m_bOnIdle1)
                            // Spin the first idle thread
                            pDocWnd->DoSpin(0);
                        // Should we spin the second idle thread?
                        if (pView->m_bOnIdle2)
                            // Spin the second idle thread
                            pDocWnd->DoSpin(2);
                    }
                }
            }
        }
    }
}

    // Call the ancestor's idle processing
    return CWinApp::OnIdle(lCount);
}
```

If you compile and run your application now, you should be able to check either of the On Idle Thread check boxes, and see the spinner drawing a color wheel (as in Figure 17.7), as long as you move the mouse. However, the moment you let the application become totally idle—no mouse movement or anything else—the spinner will stop spinning.

FIGURE 17.7

On Idle Thread draw-ing a color wheel.

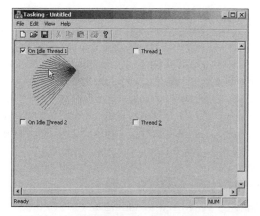

Making the `OnIdle` Tasks Continuous

It's not very practical to keep moving the mouse around to make your application contin-ue performing the tasks that it's supposed to do when the application is idle. There must be a way to get the application to continue to call the OnIdle function as long as the application is idle. Well, there is. If you look at the final line of Listing 17.8, notice that the OnIdle function returns the result value from the ancestor OnIdle function. It just so happens that this function returns FALSE as soon as there's no OnIdle functionality to be performed.

You want the OnIdle function to always return TRUE, to cause the OnIdle function to continue to be called over and over whenever the application is idle. If you move the call to the ancestor OnIdle function to the first part of the function and then return TRUE, as in Listing 17.9, you will get your spinner to continue turning, no matter how long the application sits idle.

LISTING 17.9   The Modified CTaskingApp OnIdle Function

```
BOOL CTaskingApp::OnIdle(LONG lCount)
{
    // TODO: Add your specialized code here and/or call the base class

    // Call the ancestor's idle processing
    CWinApp::OnIdle(lCount);

    // Get the position of the first document template
    POSITION pos = GetFirstDocTemplatePosition();
    // Do we have a valid template position?
    if (pos)
    {
...
    }
    return TRUE;
}
```

INPUT

INPUT

If you compile and run your application, you can turn on the OnIdle tasks and see them continue to turn, even when you aren't moving the mouse. However, if you activate any menus or open the About window, both tasks come to a complete stop (see Figure 17.8). The reason is that the open menus, and any open modal dialog windows, prevent the OnIdle function from being called. One limitation of OnIdle processing is that certain application functionality prevents it from being performed.

Adding Independent Threads

Now that you've seen what's involved in adding an OnIdle task, it's time to see what's involved in adding an independent thread to your application. To add a thread to your application, you need to add a main function for the threads. You also need to add the code to start and stop the threads. Finally, you add the code to the independent thread check boxes to start and stop each thread.

FIGURE 17.8

*On Idle Thread
stopped by the menu.*

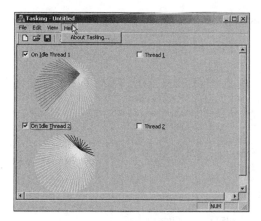

Creating the Main Thread Function

Before you can spin off any independent threads, the thread must know what to do. You will create a main thread function to be executed by the thread when it starts. This function acts as the main function for the thread, and the thread ends after the function ends. Therefore, this function must act as the primary control of the thread, keeping the thread running as long as the thread has work to do and then exiting after the thread's work is complete.

When you create a function to be used as the main function for a thread, you can pass a single parameter to this function. This parameter is a pointer to anything that contains all the information the thread needs to perform its tasks. For the application you've been building today, the parameter can be a pointer to the spinner that the thread will operate. Everything else that the thread needs can be extracted from the spinner object.

After the thread has a pointer to its spinner, it can get a pointer to the check box variable that tells it whether to continue spinning or stop itself. As long as the variable is TRUE, the thread should continue spinning. Once the thread is finished, it should call AfxEndThread to terminate and clean up after the thread. The AfxEndThread function takes two parameters, the first is the exit code for the thread, and the second is a Boolean specifying whether to release all resources held by the CWndThread class.

To add this function to your application, follow these steps:

1. Add a new member function to the document class in your application.

2. Specify the function type as UINT, the function name as ThreadFunc, add a single parameter of type LPVOID named pParam, check the static check box, and specify the access as private.

3. Edit the function with the code in Listing 17.10.

LISTING 17.10   The `CTaskingDoc ThreadFunc` Function

```
UINT CTaskingDoc::ThreadFunc(LPVOID pParam)
{
    // Convert the argument to a pointer to the
    // spinner for this thread
    CSpinner* pSpin = (CSpinner*)pParam;
    // Get a pointer to the continuation flag
    BOOL* pbContinue = pSpin->GetContinue();

    // Loop while the continue flag is true
    while (*pbContinue)
        // Spin the spinner
        pSpin->Draw();
    // End thread
    AfxEndThread(0, TRUE);
    return 0;
}
```

Starting and Stopping the Threads

Now that you have a function to call for the independent threads, you need some way to start and stop them. You need to be able to hold onto a couple of pointers for `CWinThread` objects, which will encapsulate the threads. You add these pointers as variables to the document object and then use them to capture the return variable from the `AfxBeginThread` function that you will use to start both threads.

To add these variables to your application, follow these steps:

1. Add a new member variable to your document class.
2. Specify the variable type as `CWinThread*`, the variable name as `m_pSpinThread[2]`, and the variable access as private. This provides you with a two-slot array for holding these variables. You may need to edit the header file to add the number of array positions that the variable holds.

Now that you have some place to hold the pointers to both threads, you'll add the functionality to start the threads. You can add a single function to start either thread, if it's not currently running, or to wait for the thread to stop itself, if it's running. This function needs to know which thread to act on and whether to start or stop the thread. To add this functionality, continue with these steps:

1. Add a new member function to the document class.
2. Specify the function type as `void`, the function name as `SuspendSpinner`, and add two parameters. Specify the first parameter type as `int` and name as `iIndex`. Specify the second parameter type as `BOOL` and name as `bRun`. Specify the function access as public.

3. Edit this function, adding the code in Listing 17.11.

LISTING 17.11   The CTaskingDoc SuspendSpinner Function

```cpp
void CTaskingDoc::SuspendSpinner(int iIndex, BOOL bRun)
{
    // if suspending the thread
    if (!bRun)
    {
        // Is the pointer for the thread valid?
        if (m_pSpinThread[iIndex])
        {
            // Get the handle for the thread
            HANDLE hThread = m_pSpinThread[iIndex]->m_hThread;
            // Wait for the thread to die
            ::WaitForSingleObject (hThread, INFINITE);
        }
    }
    else    // We are running the thread
    {
        int iSpnr;
        // Which spinner to use?
        switch (iIndex)
        {
        case 0:
            iSpnr = 1;
            break;
        case 1:
            iSpnr = 3;
            break;
        }
        // Start the thread, passing a pointer to the spinner
        m_pSpinThread[iIndex] = AfxBeginThread(ThreadFunc,
            (LPVOID)&m_cSpin[iSpnr]);
    }
}
```

17

ANALYSIS   This function first checks to see whether the thread is being stopped or started. If the thread is being stopped, it next checks to see if the pointer to the thread is valid. If the pointer is valid, it retrieves the thread's handle by reading the value of the handle property of the CWinThread class:

```cpp
HANDLE hThread = m_pSpinThread[iIndex]->m_hThread;
```

After it has the handle, the function uses it to wait for the thread to stop itself with the WaitForSingleObject function:

```cpp
::WaitForSingleObject (hThread, INFINITE);
```

The `WaitForSingleObject` Windows API function tells the operating system you want to wait until the thread, whose handle you are passing, has stopped. The second argument to this function specifies how long you are willing to wait. By specifying `INFINITE`, you tell the operating system that you will wait forever—until this thread stops. If you specify a timeout value and the thread doesn't stop by the time you specify, the function returns a value that indicates whether the thread has stopped. Because you specify `INFINITE` for the timeout period, you don't need to worry about capturing the return value because this function doesn't return until the thread stops.

If the thread is being started, you determine which spinner to use and then start that thread by calling the `AfxBeginThread` function:

```
m_pSpinThread[iIndex] = AfxBeginThread(ThreadFunc,
            (LPVOID)&m_cSpin[iSpnr]);
```

You passed the function to be called as the main function for the thread and the address of the spinner to be used by that thread.

Triggering the Threads from the View Object

Now that you have a means of starting and stopping each independent thread, you need to be able to trigger the starting and stopping from the check boxes on the window. When the check boxes are checked, you'll start each thread. When the check boxes are unchecked, each thread must be stopped. The second part of this is easy: As long as the variable tied to the check box is kept in sync with the control, once the check box is unchecked, the thread will stop itself. However, when the check box is checked, you need to call the document function that you just created to start the thread.

To add this functionality to the first of the two thread check boxes, follow these steps:

1. Open the main window dialog in the window painter.

2. Add an event handler function to the BN_CLICKED event for the first thread check box.

3. Edit the function with the code in Listing 17.12.

LISTING **17.12**   The `CTaskingView OnBnClickedCbthread1` Function

```
void CTaskingView::OnBnClickedCbthread1()
{
    // TODO: Add your control notification handler code here
    // Sync the variables with the dialog
    UpdateData(TRUE);
    // Get a pointer to the document
    CTaskingDoc* pDocWnd = GetDocument();
    // Did we get a valid pointer?
```

INPUT

LISTING 17.12 continued

```
    ASSERT_VALID(pDocWnd);

    // Suspend or start the spinner thread
    pDocWnd->SuspendSpinner(0, m_bThread1);
}
```

ANALYSIS This function first calls UpdateData to keep the variables in sync with the controls on the window. Next, it retrieves a pointer to the document. Once it has a valid pointer, it calls the document's SuspendSpinner function, specifying the first thread and passing the current value of the variable tied to this check box to indicate whether the thread is to be started or stopped.

To add this same functionality to the other thread check box, repeat the preceding steps, except add the code in Listing 17.13.

LISTING 17.13 The CTaskingView OnBnClickedCbthread2 Function

```
void CTaskingView::OnBnClickedCbthread2()
{
    // TODO: Add your control notification handler code here
    // Sync the variables with the dialog
    UpdateData(TRUE);
    // Get a pointer to the document
    CTaskingDoc* pDocWnd = GetDocument();
    // Did we get a valid pointer?
    ASSERT_VALID(pDocWnd);

    // Suspend or start the spinner thread
    pDocWnd->SuspendSpinner(1, m_bThread2);
}
```

INPUT

Now that you've added the capability to start and stop the independent threads, compile and run your application. You'll see that you can start and stop the independent threads with their check boxes, as well as the OnIdle tasks.

At this point, if you play around with your application for a while, notice a difference between the two thread types. If you have all threads running and are actively moving the mouse, you might notice the OnIdle spinners slowing down in their spinning (it can be difficult to notice this, because today most machines are too fast for this activity to have a sufficient effect on the OnIdle activity). The independent threads are taking a good deal of the processor time away from the main application thread, leaving less processor time to be idle. As a result, it's easier to keep your application busy. The other thing that you might notice is that if you activate the menus or open the About window, although the

17

OnIdle tasks come to a complete stop, the independent threads continue to run (see Figure 17.9). These two threads are completely independent processes running within your application, so they aren't affected by the rest of the application.

FIGURE 17.9

The menu doesn't affect the threads.

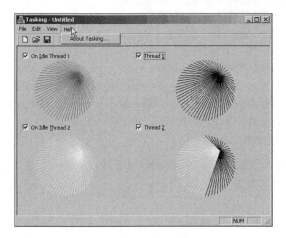

Shutting Down Cleanly

You might think that you are finished with this application—until you try to close the application while one or both of the independent threads is running. Then you'll see an unpleasant notification that you still have some work to do (see Figure 17.10). It seems that leaving the threads running when you closed the application cause it to crash.

FIGURE 17.10

Application error notification.

Although the application was closing, the threads continued to run. When these threads checked the value of the variable indicating whether to continue running or spin their spinners, they were trying to access a memory object that no longer existed. This problem causes one of the most basic and most fatal application memory errors, which you should eliminate before allowing anyone else to use the application.

What you need to do to prevent this error is stop both threads before allowing the application to close. The logical place to take this action is the OnDestroy event message processing in the view class. This event message is sent to the view class to tell it to clean up anything that it needs to before closing the application. You can add code to set both check box variables to FALSE so that the threads will stop themselves and then call the SuspendSpinner function for each thread to be sure that both threads have stopped before allowing the application to close. You don't need to call UpdateData to sync the variables with the controls because users don't need to see that you've changed the value of either check box.

To add this functionality to your application, follow these steps:

1. Add an event-handler function for the WM_DESTROY event message to the view class using the Class Properties Messages. This function doesn't normally exist in the view class created by the MFC Application Wizard, so you need to add it when it's needed in the descendent view class.

2. Edit the function, adding the code in Listing 17.14.

17

LISTING 17.14 The CTaskingView OnDestroy Function

```
void CTaskingView::OnDestroy()
{
    CFormView::OnDestroy();

    // TODO: Add your message handler code here
    // Is the first thread running?
    if (m_bThread1)
    {
        // Specify to stop the first thread
        m_bThread1 = FALSE;
        // Get a pointer to the document
        CTaskingDoc* pDocWnd = GetDocument();
        // Did we get a valid pointer?
        ASSERT_VALID(pDocWnd);

        // Suspend or start the spinner thread
        pDocWnd->SuspendSpinner(0, m_bThread1);
    }
    // Is the second thread running?
    if (m_bThread2)
    {
        // Specify to stop the second thread
        m_bThread2 = FALSE;
        // Get a pointer to the document
        CTaskingDoc* pDocWnd = GetDocument();
        // Did we get a valid pointer?
        ASSERT_VALID(pDocWnd);

        // Suspend or start the spinner thread
        pDocWnd->SuspendSpinner(1, m_bThread2);
    }
}
```

INPUT

ANALYSIS This function does exactly what it needs to do. It first checks one check box variable and then the other. If either is TRUE, it sets the variable to FALSE, gets a pointer to the document, and calls the SuspendSpinner function for that thread. Now when you close your application while the independent threads are running, your application will close without crashing.

Summary

You learned quite a bit today. You learned about the different ways you can make your applications perform multiple tasks at one time. You also learned about some of the considerations to take into account when adding this capability to your applications. You saw how you can make your application perform tasks when the application is sitting idle, along with some of the limitations and drawbacks associated with this approach. You also learned how you can create independent threads in your application that will perform their tasks completely independently of the rest of the application. You implemented an application that uses both approaches so that you could experience how each approach works.

 Tip

> When you start adding multitasking capabilities to your applications to perform separate tasks, be aware that this is an advanced aspect of Windows programming. You need to understand many factors and take into account far more than I can reasonably cover in a single day. If you want to build applications using this capability, get an advanced book on programming Windows applications with MFC or Visual C++. The book should include a substantial section devoted to multithreading with MFC and cover all synchronization classes in a lot more detail than I did here. Remember, you need a book that focuses on MFC, not the Visual C++ development environment. (MFC is supported by most commercial C++ development tools for building Windows applications, including Borland and Symantec's C++ compilers, so coverage for this topic extends beyond the Visual C++ environment.)

Q&A

Q. How can I use the other version of the AfxBeginThread to encapsulate a thread in a custom class?

A. First, the other version of AfxBeginThread is primarily for creating user-interface threads. The version that you used today is for creating what are called *worker threads* that immediately take off on a specific task. If you want to create a user-interface thread, you need to inherit your custom class from the CWinThread class.

Next, you need to override several ancestor functions in your custom class. After the class is ready to use, you use the RUNTIME_CLASS macro to get a pointer to the runtime class of your class and pass this pointer to the AfxBeginThread function, as follows:

```
CWinThread* pMyThread =
            AfxBeginThread(RUNTIME_CLASS(CMyThreadClass));
```

Q. Can I use SuspendThread and ResumeThread to start and stop my independent threads in my sample application?

A. Yes, but you need to make a few key changes to your application. First, in the OnNewDocument function, you initialize the two thread pointers to NULL, as in Listing 17.15.

LISTING 17.15 The Modified CTaskingDoc OnNewDocument Function

```
BOOL CTaskingDoc::OnNewDocument()
{
    if (!CDocument::OnNewDocument())
        return FALSE;

    // TODO: add reinitialization code here
    // (SDI documents will reuse this document)
    // Initialize the spinners
    InitSpinners();

    // Initialize the thread pointers
    m_pSpinThread[0] = NULL;
    m_pSpinThread[1] = NULL;

    return TRUE;
}
```

INPUT

Next, modify the thread function so that the thread doesn't stop itself when the check box variable is FALSE but continues to loop, as in Listing 17.16.

LISTING 17.16 The Modified CTaskingDoc ThreadFunc Function

```
UINT CTaskingDoc::ThreadFunc(LPVOID pParam)
{
    // Convert the argument to a pointer to the
    // spinner for this thread
    CSpinner* lpSpin = (CSpinner*)pParam;
    // Get a pointer to the continuation flag
    BOOL* pbContinue = lpSpin->GetContinue();
```

17

LISTING 17.16   continued

```
        // Loop while the continue flag is true
        while (TRUE)
            // Spin the spinner
        lpSpin->Draw();
    return 0;
}
```

Finally, modify the SuspendSpinner function so that if the thread pointer is valid, it calls the SuspendThread function on the thread pointer to stop the thread and the ResumeThread function to restart the thread, as in Listing 17.17.

LISTING 17.17   The Modified CTaskingDoc SuspendSpinner Function

```
void CTaskingDoc::SuspendSpinner(int iIndex, BOOL bRun)
{
    // if suspending the thread
    if (!bRun)
    {
        // Is the pointer for the thread valid?
        if (m_pSpinThread[iIndex])
        {
            // Suspend the thread
            m_pSpinThread[iIndex]->SuspendThread();
        }
    }
    else    // We are running the thread
    {
        // Is the pointer for the thread valid?
        if (m_pSpinThread[iIndex])
        {
            // Resume the thread
            m_pSpinThread[iIndex]->ResumeThread();
        }
        else
        {
            int iSpnr;
            // Which spinner to use?
            switch (iIndex)
            {
            case 0:
                iSpnr = 1;
                break;
            case 1:
                iSpnr = 3;
                break;
            }
```

LISTING 17.17 continued

```
        // Start the thread, passing a pointer to the spinner
        m_pSpinThread[iIndex] = AfxBeginThread(ThreadFunc,
            (LPVOID)&m_cSpin[iSpnr]);
    }
}
```

INPUT

```
    }
}
```

Workshop

The Workshop provides quiz questions to help you solidify your understanding of the material covered and exercises to provide you with experience in using what you've learned. The answers to the quiz questions and exercises are provided in Appendix A, "Answers to Quiz Questions."

Quiz

1. When is the OnIdle function called?

2. How can you cause the OnIdle function to be repeatedly called while the application is sitting idle?

3. What's the difference between an OnIdle task and a thread?

4. What are the four thread synchronization objects?

5. Why shouldn't you specify a higher than normal priority for the threads in your application?

Exercises

1. If you open a performance monitor on your system while the application that you built today is running, you'll find that even without any threads running, the processor usage remains 100 percent (see Figure 17.11). The OnIdle function is continuously being called even when there is nothing to be done.

   Modify the OnIdle function so that if there's nothing to be done, neither OnIdle task is active. Then, the OnIdle function won't continue to be called until one of these threads is active, at which time it should be continuously called until both threads are again turned off. This allows the processor to drop to a minimal utilization (see Figure 17.12).

2. When starting the independent threads, give one of the threads a priority of THREAD_PRIORITY_NORMAL and the other a priority of THREAD_PRIORITY_LOWEST

FIGURE 17.11

Processor utilization at 100 percent.

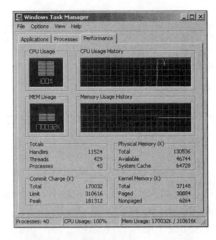

FIGURE 17.12

Processor utilization at normal levels.

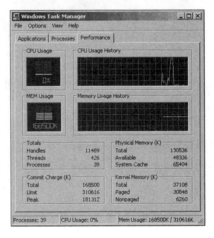

DAY **18**

Working with Internet Applications and Network Communications

Thanks in part to the Internet's popularity, more applications can communicate with other applications over networks, including the Internet. Since Microsoft started building networking capabilities into its operating systems with Windows NT and Windows 95, these capabilities have become commonplace in all sorts of applications.

Some applications perform simple networking tasks such as checking with a Web site to see whether there are any updates to the program and giving users the option of updating their copy of the program. Some word processing applications can format documents as Web pages, giving users the option of loading the pages onto the Web server. You have computer games that allow users to play against other users, halfway around the world, rather than just compete against the game itself.

Applications can have any number of networking functions and are built around the Winsock interface. If you know and understand how to program using the Winsock interface and the MFC Winsock classes, this entire realm of application programming is open to you, expanding your programming options considerably. Today, you will learn

- How applications use the Winsock interface to perform network communications between two or more computers
- The difference between a client and a server application and the role each plays in establishing a communications link
- How the MFC Winsock classes simplify the process of writing Internet applications
- How you can create your own Winsock class, descended from the MFC Winsock classes, to easily build an event-driven, networking application

Understanding How Network Communications Work

NEW TERM   Most applications that communicate over a network, whether it's the Internet or a small office network, use the same principles and functionality to perform their communication. One application sits on a computer, waiting for another application to open a communication connection. This application is *listening* for this connection request, much like you listen for the phone to ring if you are expecting someone to call.

Meanwhile, another application, most likely on another computer (but not necessarily), tries to connect to the first application. This attempt to open a connection is similar to calling someone on the telephone. You dial the number and hope that the other person is listening for the phone on the other end. As the person making the call, you have to know the phone number of the person you are calling. If you don't know the phone number, you can look it up using the person's name. Likewise, the application trying to connect to the first application has to know the network location, or address, of the first application.

When the connection is made between the two applications, messages can pass back and forth between them, much like you can talk to the person on the other end of the phone. This connection is a two-way communications channel, with both sides sending information (see Figure 18.1).

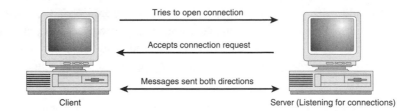

FIGURE 18.1

The basic socket connection process.

Tries to open connection

Accepts connection request

Messages sent both directions

Client | Server (Listening for connections)

Finally, after one or both sides finishes their side of the conversation, the connection is closed, much like when you hang up the phone after you finish talking to the person you called. When the connection is closed from one side, the other side can detect it and close its side, just like you can tell if the person on the other end of the phone has hung up on you or if you've been disconnected by some other means. This is a basic explanation of how network communications work between two or more applications.

> **Note**
>
> This is a basic description of how network communications work with TCP/IP, the primary network protocol used over the Internet. Many other network protocols use a subtle variation on this description. Other protocols, such as UDP, are more like radio broadcasts, where there's no connection between the two applications; one sends messages, and the other is responsible for making sure that it receives all the messages. These protocols are more involved than we have the luxury to discuss today. If you want to learn more about network protocols and how they work, many books cover this one topic and look at the various Internet applications and how they communicate over the connections they establish.

Sockets, Ports, and Addresses

NEW TERM The basic object that applications use to perform most network communications is called a *socket*. Sockets were first developed on UNIX at the University of California at Berkley. Sockets were designed so that most network communications between applications could be performed in the same way that these same applications would read and write files. Sockets have progressed quite a bit since then, but the basics of how they work are still the same.

During the days of Windows 3.*x*, before networking was built into the Windows operating system, you could buy the network protocols required for network communications from various companies. Each company had a slightly different way that an application performed network communications. As a result, any application that performed network communications had a list of the different networking software that the application would work with. Many application developers weren't happy with this situation. As a result, all the networking companies, including Microsoft, got together and developed the Winsock (Windows Sockets) API. This provided all the application developers with a consistent API to perform all network communications, regardless of the networking software used.

When you want to read or write a file, you must use a file object to point to the file. Although in most Visual C++ applications so far, this was hidden from you, with the ActiveX control you created a couple of days ago, you had to work through the steps of creating the file object for reading and writing. A socket is similar; it's an object used to read and write messages that travel between applications.

Making a socket connection to another application requires a different set of information than opening a file. To open a file, you need to know the file's name and location. To open a socket connection, you need to know the computer on which the other application is running and the port on which it's listening. A port is like a phone extension, and the computer address is like the phone number. If you call someone at a large office building, you might dial the main office number, but then you need to specify the extension number. Likewise, ports are used to route network communications (see Figure 18.2). As with the phone number, you can look up the port number if you don't already know what it is, but this requires your computer to be configured with the information about which port the connecting application is listening on. If you specify the wrong computer address or port number, you might connect to a different application; with making the phone call, someone other than the person you called might answer the phone call. You also might not get an answer at all if no application is listening at the other end.

> **Note**
>
> Only one application can listen on any specific port on a single computer. Although numerous applications can listen for connection requests on a single computer at the same time, each application must listen on a different port.

Initializing the Winsock Environment

Before you can use any Winsock MFC classes, you have to initialize the Winsock environment for your application. This is done with a single function call in the application instance initialization, `AfxSocketInit`. This function can take a single `WSADATA` structure as an optional parameter. If you supply this structure to this function, it will be populated with information about the version of Winsock currently in use on the computer on which your application is running. Unless you really need to know some of the information returned in this structure, you don't need to pass it as a parameter, as in the following:

FIGURE 18.2

Ports are used to route network communications to the correct application.

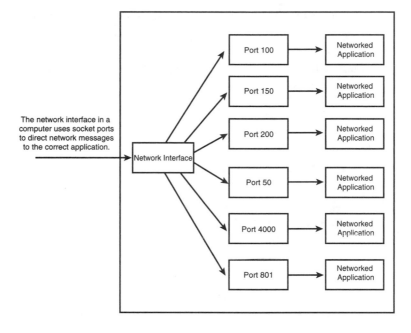

BOOL CSockApp::InitInstance()
{
    if (!AfxSocketInit())
    {
        AfxMessageBox(IDP_SOCKETS_INIT_FAILED);
        return FALSE;
    }
    ...
}

If you include this function in the instance initialization function, the Winsock environment will be correctly initialized and shut down by your application.

Tip

If you use the Visual C++ Wizards to create your project shell, and specify to include support for Winsock in your application shell, the AfxSocketInit function is automatically added to your application shell.

Creating a Socket

When you build applications with Visual C++, you use the MFC Winsock classes to add network communications capabilities with relative ease. The base class, CAsyncSocket, provides complete, event-driven socket communications. You can create your own descendent socket class to capture and respond to each event. The CSocket class is a descendant of the CAsyncSocket class, and encapsulates and simplifies some of the functionality of the base class. The CSocket class is primarily used for those instances when you need to use a blocking socket, where the socket functions don't trigger events, but instead wait until each function call is completed before returning control.

To create a socket that you can use in your application, you first need to declare a variable of CAsyncSocket (or your descendent class) as a class member for one of the main application classes:

```
class CMyDlg : public CDialog
{
...
private:
    CAsyncSocket m_sMySocket;
};
```

Before you can begin using the socket object, you must call its Create method. This actually creates the socket and prepares it for use. How you call the Create method depends on how you are using the socket. If you are using the socket to connect to another application as the one placing the call (the client), you don't need to pass any parameters to the Create method:

```
if (m_sMySocket.Create())
{
    // Continue on
}
else
    // Perform error handling here
```

However, if the socket will be listening for another application to connect to it (waiting for the call—the server), you need to pass at least the port number on which the socket should be listening:

```
if (m_sMySocket.Create(4000))
{
    // Continue on
}
else
    // Perform error handling here
```

You can include other parameters in the Create method call, such as the socket type to create, the events that the socket should respond to (CAsyncSocket only), and the address that the socket should listen on (in case the computer has more than one network card).

> **Note**
>
> You can create two types of sockets using the MFC Winsock classes: *streaming* (or TCP) and *datagram* (or UDP). Streaming sockets are connection-based and have guaranteed delivery functionality built in. Datagram sockets are connectionless, and require you to write the code to ensure that the packets are received and, in the receiving application, placed in the order that they were sent. If a particular packet isn't received, you also have to write the code to have the receiving application request that a particular packet be resent, and on the sending application, to resend the missing packet of data. To specify that a socket is to be streaming, pass SOCK_STREAM as the second argument to the Create method. To specify that a socket should be a datagram, pass SOCK_DGRAM as the second argument.

> **Note**
>
> If you are building a server application that might run on a computer with more than one network card installed, you might need to specify the network address that the socket will be listening on. This will tell the socket that it's listening for incoming connection requests only through a specific network card. To do this, pass the network address to bind the socket to as the last argument to the Create method. This will be the fourth argument for the CAsyncSocket class, and the third argument for the CSocket class. The network address should be passed as a string in the standard TCP/IP form:
>
>   "127.0.0.1"

18

Making a Connection

After you create a socket, you can open a connection with it. Three steps go along with opening a single connection: two take place on the server (the application listing for the connection), and the third takes place on the client (the one making the call).

For the client, opening the connection is a simple matter of calling the Connect method. The client has to pass two parameters to the Connect method: the computer name, or network address, and the port of the application to connect to. The Connect method could be used in the following two ways:

```
if (m_sMySocket.Connect("thatcomputer.com", 4000))
{
    // Continue on
}
else
    // Perform error handling here

if (m_sMySocket.Connect("127.0.0.1", 4000))
{
```

```
    // Continue on
}
else
    // Perform error handling here
```

After the connection is made, if you are using the `CAsyncSocket` class or a class that you derived from the `CAsyncSocket` class, an event is triggered to let your application know that it's connected or that problems occurred and the connection couldn't be made. (How these events work is covered later today in "Socket Events.") If you are using the `CSocket` class, the `Connect` function won't return until the connection is made, or an error has occurred that prevented the connection from being made.

For the server (or listening) side of the connection, the application first must tell the socket to listen for incoming connections by calling the `Listen` method. The `Listen` method takes only a single argument, which you don't need to supply. This parameter specifies the number of pending connections that can be queued, waiting for the connection to be completed. By default, this value is 5, which is the maximum. The `Listen` method can be called as follows:

```
if (m_sMySocket.Listen())
{
    // Continue on
}
else
    // Perform error handling here
```

Whenever another application tries connecting to the listening application, an event is triggered to let the application know that the connection request is there. To accept the connection request, the listening application must call the `Accept` method. This method requires the use of a second `CAsyncSocket` variable, which is connected to the other application. When a socket is placed into listen mode, it stays in that mode. Whenever connection requests are received, the listening socket creates another socket, which is connected to the other application. This second socket shouldn't have the `Create` method called for it because the `Accept` method creates the socket. You call the `Accept` method as follows:

```
if (m_sMySocket.Accept(m_sMySecondSocket))
{
    // Continue on
}
else
    // Perform error handling here
```

At this point, the connecting application is connected to the second socket on the listening application.

With the `CSocket` class, incoming connections are detected and accepted by calling the `Accept` function, as shown previously. When using the `CSocket` class, the `Accept` function won't return until a connection request is received and accepted.

Sending and Receiving Messages

Sending and receiving messages through a socket connection gets slightly involved. Because you can use sockets to send any kind of data, the functions to send and receive data expect to be passed a pointer to a generic buffer. For sending data, this buffer should contain the data to be sent. For receiving data, this buffer has the received data copied into it. As long as you send and receive strings and text, you can use fairly simple conversions to and from `CString`s with these buffers.

To send a message through a socket connection, use the `Send` method. This method requires two parameters and has a third, optional parameter that controls how the message is sent. The first parameter is a pointer to the buffer that contains the data to be sent. If your message is in a `CString` variable, you can use the `LPCTSTR` operator to pass the `CString` variable as the buffer. The second parameter is the length of the buffer. The method returns the amount of data sent to the other application. If an error occurs, the `Send` function returns `SOCKET_ERROR`. You can use the `Send` method as follows:

```
CString strMyMessage;
int iLen;
int iAmtSent;
...
iLen = strMyMessage.GetLength();
iAmtSent = m_sMySocket.Send(LPCTSTR(strMyMessage), iLen);
if (iAmtSent == SOCKET_ERROR)
{
    // Do some error handling here
}
else
{
    // Everything's fine
}
```

Note

If you are working with UNICODE strings, the `GetLength` function will return the length of the string itself, but this is not the length of the data to be sent. Because each character is represented by two bytes instead of one, the string length needs to be doubled to account for all of the data that is going to be sent. For the maximum portability of the data, you might want to convert the data into standard ASCII text prior to sending.

18

When data is available to be received from the other application, an event is triggered on the receiving application for the `CAsyncSocket` and descendent classes. This lets your application know it can receive and process the message. To get the message, the `Receive` method must be called. This method takes the same parameters as `Send` with a slight difference. The first parameter is a pointer to a buffer into which the message can be copied. The second parameter is the buffer size, which tells the socket how much data to copy (in case more is received than will fit into the buffer). Like the `Send` method, `Receive` will return the amount copied into the buffer. If an error occurs, `Receive` also returns `SOCKET_ERROR`. If your application is receiving a text message, it can be copied directly into a `CString` variable. This allows you to use the `Receive` method as follows:

```
char *pBuf = new char[1025];
int iBufSize = 1024;
int iRcvd;
CString strRecvd;

iRcvd = m_sMySocket.Receive(pBuf, iBufSize);
if (iRcvd == SOCKET_ERROR)
{
    // Do some error handling here
}
else
{
    pBuf[iRcvd] = NULL;
    strRecvd = pBuf;
    // Continue processing the message
}
```

Tip

> When receiving text messages, it's always a good idea to place a NULL in the buffer position just after the last character received to truncate the string, as in the preceding example. Otherwise, your application might interpret garbage characters in the buffer as part of the message.

As with most `CSocket` versions of these functions, the `Receive` function won't return until data is received from the connected application.

If you are using datagram sockets, you will want to use alternative versions of these two methods: `SendTo` and `ReceiveFrom`. These functions work the same as their streaming counterparts, only with the addition of the network address and port to send the data to (with the `SendTo` method), or variables to store the address of the application you are receiving from (for the `ReceiveFrom` method).

Closing the Connection

After your application finishes all communication with the other application, it can close the connection by calling the Close method. Close doesn't take any parameters, and you use it as follows:

m_sMySocket.Close();

> **Note** The Close function is one of the few CAsyncSocket and CSocket methods that doesn't return a status code. For all the previous member functions that today's lesson has examined, you can capture the return value to determine whether an error has occurred.

Sometimes you might want to shut down a socket before closing it. You can shut down a socket by using the ShutDown method. This method takes a single integer parameter, which specifies whether to shut down the sending or receiving of data over the socket. By default, ShutDown disables sending of data over a socket. You can specify which socket is disabled by passing the values shown in Table 18.1.

TABLE 18.1   Socket ShutDown Parameter Values

Value	Description
0	Prevents receiving of incoming data packets over the socket
1	Prevents the sending of data packets through the socket
2	Prevents both the sending and receiving of data packets through the socket

> **Note** Calling the ShutDown method on a socket doesn't close the connection or release any resources the socket is using. You still need to close the socket using the Close method.

Socket Events

You create your own descendent class of CAsyncSocket to capture the events triggered when messages are received, connections are completed, and so on. The CAsyncSocket class has a series of functions that are called for each of these various events. These functions all use the same definition—the function name is the only difference—and are intended to be overridden in descendent classes. All these functions are declared as protected members of the CAsyncSocket class and probably should be declared as protected in your descendent classes. The functions all have a single integer parameter, which is an error code that should be checked to make sure that no error has occurred. Table 18.2 lists these event functions and the events they signal.

TABLE 18.2   CAsyncSocket Overridable Event-Notification Functions

Function	Description
OnAccept	Called on a listening socket to signal that a connection request from another application is waiting to be accepted.
OnClose	Called to signal that the application on the other end of the connection has closed its socket or that the connection was lost. This should be followed by closing the socket that received this notification.
OnConnect	Called to signal that the connection with another application is completed and that the application can now send and receive messages through the socket.
OnOutOfBandData	Called when out-of-band data is received. Out-of-band data is sent over a logically independent channel, and is used to send urgent data that's not part of the regular communications between the two connected applications. The Send and Receive methods both have a third parameter, which can be passed a flag, MSG_OOB, to send and receive out-of-band data.
OnReceive	Called to signal that data has been received through the socket connection and that the data is ready to be retrieved by calling the Receive function.
OnSend	Called to signal that the socket is ready and available for sending data. This function is called right after the connection is completed. Usually, the other time that this function is called is when your application has passed the Send function more data than can be sent in a single packet. In this case, this signals that all data is sent, and the application can send the next buffer full of data.

In addition to these overridable event functions, the CSocket class provides another overridable function, OnMessagePending, which is called when messages are pending in the application event message queue. This way, you can look for particular Windows messages and respond to them in your CSocket class.

Controlling Event Triggering

By default, the CAsyncSocket class calls all the overridable functions in Table 18.2, whereas the CSocket class doesn't call any of them. So what if you want to have your descendant class somewhere in between, calling some of these functions while ignoring the others? Well, you're in luck. There are two ways of controlling which of these event functions are triggered.

The first way to specify which event functions are called is available only with the CAsyncSocket class and any custom classes directly descended from it. In the Create method, the third parameter that you can supply is a flag value that specifies which events to trigger. The CSocket class overrides this method, preventing you from providing this flag value. By default, the CAsyncSocket Create method combines all the event flag values, specifying that all event functions be triggered.

The second method of specifying which events to trigger, AsyncSelect, is available to the descendant classes of both CAsyncSocket and CSocket. This method takes only the combination flag to define which events to trigger. You can call AsyncSelect as follows:

```
iErr = m_sMySocket.AsyncSelect(FD_READ | FD_CONNECT | FD_CLOSE);
if (iErr == SOCKET_ERROR)
{
    // Do some error handling here
}
else
{
    // Continue processing
}
```

The default value for AsyncSelect's parameter is to specify that all event functions be triggered. As a result, if you want to turn all event triggering off and then back on, you first turn all events off by passing a zero as the flag value:

```
iErr = m_sMySocket.AsyncSelect(0);
```

To turn all event triggering back on, don't supply a value for the flag:

```
iErr = m_sMySocket.AsyncSelect();
```

Table 18.3 lists the flag values that you can supply for AsyncSelect and Create (CAsyncSocket only).

TABLE 18.3 Socket Event Notification Flags

Flag	Description
FD_READ	Triggers and calls the OnReceive function when data has arrived for reading.
FD_WRITE	Triggers and calls the OnSend function when the outbound Winsock buffers are available for sending data. This event function tells your application when it can send data.
FD_OOB	Triggers and calls the OnOutOfBandData function when out-of-band data is received and needs to be read.

18

TABLE 18.3 continued

FD_ACCEPT	Triggers and calls the OnAccept function to inform your application that there's an inbound connection request on your listening socket. Follow this with the Accept method to complete the connection.
FD_CONNECT	Triggers and calls the OnConnect function to inform your application that the connection request your application initiated with the Connect method is complete. This event will be immediately followed by the OnSend event function to inform your application that it can now send data to the connected application.
FD_CLOSE	Triggers and calls the OnClose function to inform your application that the socket connection was closed by the connected application.

Detecting Errors

Whenever any CAsyncSocket or CSocket member functions return an error—either FALSE for most functions or SOCKET_ERROR on the Send and Receive functions—you can call the GetLastError method to get the error code. This method returns only error codes, and you have to look up the translation yourself. All Winsock error codes are defined with constants, so you can use those constants in your code to determine the error message to display, if any. You can use the GetLastError function as follows:

```
int iErrCode;

iErrCode = m_sMySocket.GetLastError();
switch (iErrCode)
{
case WSANOTINITIALISED:
...
}
```

Getting Socket Information

At times you need to get information about the state of the sockets in your application, such as the address and port of the application on the other end of the connection, and whether the socket is waiting on a blocking function to complete. You also can set, or check, several options on your application's sockets.

Getting the Connected Address

When a socket is connected to another application, you can find out the other application's network address by calling the GetPeerName method, passing it a pointer to a CString and an unsigned integer. The address and port of the other application are returned in these two variables. You can call the GetPeerName method as follows:

```
CString sPeerAddress;
UINT iPeerPort;

iErr = m_sMySocket.GetPeerName(&sPeerAddress, &iPeerPort);
if (iErr == SOCKET_ERROR)
{
    // Do some error handling here
}
else
{
    cout << "Peer Network Address: " << sPeerAddress << "\n";
    cout << "Peer Port: " << iPeerPort << "\n";
    // Continue processing
}
```

Likewise, if you didn't bind your socket to a specific port or network address (which you usually don't unless your socket is listening for incoming connections), you can get the same information about your application's socket by calling the GetSockName method:

```
CString sMyAddress;
UINT iMyPort;

iErr = m_sMySocket.GetSockName(&sMyAddress, &iMyPort);
if (iErr == SOCKET_ERROR)
{
    // Do some error handling here
}
else
{
    cout << "My Network Address: " << sMyAddress << "\n";
    cout << "My Port: " << iMyPort << "\n";
    // Continue processing
}
```

Note

With the GetSockName method, you likely will get a network address of 0.0.0.0 as your application's network address. This is because your socket was never bound to a specific network address, and thus is using the default address (0.0.0.0) for its outbound connection requests. The Winsock interface translates this into the network address of your computer, so that even though your application sees your network address as all zeros, the application that you are connected to sees the actual computer network address.

Getting and Setting Options

You can set several options on a socket to affect how that socket behaves. You also can build most applications without needing to adjust any of these options. For those situations where you do need to adjust or check some of these settings, use the GetSockOpt and SetSockOpt methods.

The GetSockOpt method checks the current setting of various socket options. This method takes four parameters, of which the first three are required:

- The option you want the value of.
- A pointer to a buffer into which the current value of the option is to be copied.
- An integer pointer to a variable containing the size of the buffer into which the setting value is to be copied.
- Which level the option is defined for: socket or protocol. The default is the socket level, SOL_SOCKET, but one option is defined at the protocol level, IPPROTO_TCP. Table 18.4 lists the available socket options and their data types.

TABLE 18.4 Socket Options

Option	Data Type	Description
SO_ACCEPTCONN	BOOL	The socket is listening for an inbound connection request.
SO_BROADCAST	BOOL	The socket is configured for the transmission of broadcast messages.
SO_DEBUG	BOOL	Debugging is enabled on the socket.
SO_DONTLINGER	BOOL	Setting this option to TRUE disables the SO_LINGER option.
SO_DONTROUTE	BOOL	Routing is disabled.
SO_ERROR	int	Retrieve the error status and clears the status.
SO_KEEPALIVE	BOOL	Keepalives are being sent.
SO_LINGER	struct LINGER	Returns the current linger options.
SO_OOBINLINE	BOOL	Out-of-band data is being received in the normal data stream.
SO_RCVBUF	int	The buffer size used for receiving data.
SO_REUSEADDR	BOOL	The socket can be bound to an address (and port) that's already being used.
SO_SNDBUF	int	The buffer size used for sending data.
SO_TYPE	int	The type of socket (SOCK_STREAM or SOCK_DGRAM).
TCP_NODELAY	BOOL	Disables the Nagle algorithm for send coalescing.

To set or change any of these options, the SetSockOpt method takes the same four parameters with one small exception: The third parameter, the size of the buffer containing the value to set the option to, is passed as an integer, not as a pointer to an integer. Also keep in mind that you can use the SetSockOpt method to set or change the value of any options in Table 18.4 except for SO_ACCEPTCONN, SO_ERROR, and SO_TYPE, which are read-only.

To check and set the value of a particular option, you can use these two methods as follows:

```
BOOL bStatus;
int iStatusSize;

iStatusSize = sizeof(BOOL);
iErr = m_sMySocket.GetSockOpt(SO_KEEPALIVE, &bStatus, &iStatusSize);
if (iErr == SOCKET_ERROR)
{
    // Do some error handling here
}
else
{
    // Are we sending keep-alives?
    if (!bStatus)
    {
        // if not, then start sending them
        bStatus = TRUE;
        iErr = m_sMySocket.SetSockOpt(SO_KEEPALIVE, &bStatus, sizeof(BOOL));
        if (iErr == SOCKET_ERROR)
        {
            // Do some error handling here
        }
    }
    // Continue processing
}
```

Determining Whether a Socket Is Blocking

When you use the CSocket class, by default all socket communications functions block all thread processing until the function has completed. If you've called the Connect function on a socket, the function won't return control of the thread until the connection is completed, or the socket timeout has expired. The same thing is true for the Accept, Receive, and Send functions (along with the ReceiveFrom and SendTo functions). So what if you need to interrupt any of these functions before they return? Two methods in the CSocket class can be used for this purpose.

You first need to check to see whether the socket is blocking a thread (as well as additional operations). You can use the IsBlocking method to determine if a socket is in a blocking function. This method doesn't take any parameters and returns a Boolean value that tells you whether the socket is blocking.

After you determine that a socket is blocking a thread, you can cancel the blocking method by calling the CancelBlockingCall method. This method will cause the socket to abort the currently blocking function, causing the blocking function to return with an error condition of WSAEINTR.

 Caution

Using the CancelBlockingCall method to cancel any blocking function other than the Accept method can leave a socket unstable. The only socket method that you can call with any predictability after a blocking function is canceled is the Close method.

To determine if a socket is blocking, and if so, terminate it, you can do the following (in a second thread, of course):

```
if (m_sMySocket.IsBlocking())
    m_sMySocket.CancelBlockingCall();
```

Sockets and I/O Serialization

In those circumstances where the data to be passed between the two applications communicating through a socket connection is of a known format, and can easily be serialized, a specialized MFC class is designed to enable you to serialize the communications. This class is CSocketFile, which you can attach to an open CSocket class and then treat it just like a CFile class object.

When you connect a CSocket, you can attach a CSocketFile class object to the CSocket object, specifying whether to make the CSocketFile archive compatible:

```
CSocketFile sMySocketFile(&m_sMySocket, TRUE);
```

The first parameter that you need to pass to the CSocketFile constructor is a pointer to the CSocket object that's to be serialized. The second parameter is a Boolean value specifying whether to make the CSocketFile object compatible with a CArchive object. By passing TRUE as the second parameter, you can now take the CSocketFile object and associate it with a CArchive object:

```
CArchive lArchive(&sMySocketFile, CArchive::load);
```

From here, you can pass the CArchive object to the standard MFC Serialize function to read and write data to the socket connection.

Note Serializing socket communications requires both connected applications to be reading and writing the same data format to the socket. If one of the two connected applications isn't using the same serialized data format as the other, you'll end up sending and receiving garbage data.

Building a Networked Application

The sample application that you will build today is a simple dialog application that can function as either the client or server in a Winsock connection. This will allow you to run two copies of the sample application—one for each end of the connection—on the same computer or to copy the application to another computer so that you can run the two copies on separate computers and see how you can pass messages across a network. After the application establishes a connection with another application, you can enter text messages and send them to the other application. When the message is sent, it's added to a list of sent messages. Each received message is copied into another list of all received messages. This will allow you to see the complete list of what is sent and received. It will also allow you to compare what one copy of the application has sent and what the other has received (the two lists should be the same).

Creating the Application Shell

For today's sample application, just to keep things simple, you'll create a dialog-style application. Everything that you are doing in today's application can be done in an SDI or MDI application just as easily as with a dialog-style application. By using a dialog-style application today, we are getting everything that might distract from the basic socket functionality (such as questions about whether the socket variable belongs in the document or view class, how much of the application functionality belongs in which of these two classes, and so on) away from the sample application.

To start today's sample application, follow these steps:

1. Create a new MFC Application Visual C++ project and name it Sock.

2. In the Application Type area, select Dialog-Based for the application type.

3. In the Application Wizard's Advanced Features area, specify that the application should include support for Windows Sockets (see Figure 18.3).

4. Click Finish to create the application shell.

18

FIGURE 18.3

*Including sockets
support.*

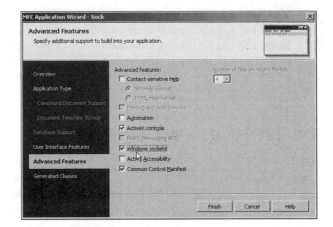

Implementing Window Layout and Startup Functionality

After you create your application shell, you can lay out the main dialog for your application. On this dialog, you need a set of radio buttons to specify whether the application is running as the client or server. You also need a couple of edit boxes for the computer name and port that the server will be listening on. Next, you need a command button to start the application listening on the socket, or opening the connection to the server, and a button to close the connection. You also need an edit box for entering the message to be sent to the other application and a button to send the message. Finally, you need a couple of list boxes into which you can add each message sent and received.

To lay out this dialog box, follow these steps:

1. Place all these controls on the dialog, as shown in Figure 18.4, setting all the control properties as specified in Table 18.5.

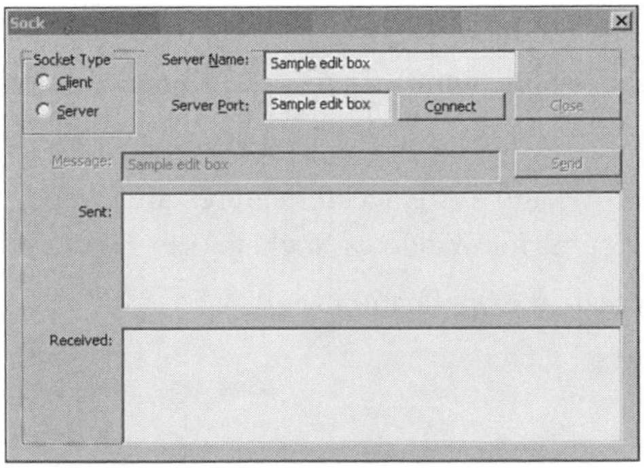

FIGURE 18.4

*The main dialog
layout.*

TABLE 18.5 Control Property Settings

Object	Property	Setting
Group Box	ID	IDC_STATICTYPE
	Caption	Socket Type
Radio Button	ID	IDC_RCLIENT
	Caption	&Client
	Group	True
Radio Button	ID	IDC_RSERVER
	Caption	&Server
Static Text	ID	IDC_STATICNAME
	Caption	Server &Name:
Edit Box	ID	IDC_ESERVNAME
Static Text	ID	IDC_STATICPORT
	Caption	Server &Port:
Edit Box	ID	IDC_ESERVPORT
Command Button	ID	IDC_BCONNECT
	Caption	C&onnect
Command Button	ID	IDC_BCLOSE
	Caption	C&lose
	Disabled	True
Static Text	ID	IDC_STATICMSG
	Caption	&Message:
	Disabled	True
Edit Box	ID	IDC_EMSG
	Disabled	True
Command Button	ID	IDC_BSEND
	Caption	S&end
	Disabled	True
Static Text	Caption	Sent:
List Box	ID	IDC_LSENT
	Tab Stop	False
	Sort	False
	Selection	None
Static Text	Caption	Received:
List Box	ID	IDC_LRECVD
	Tab Stop	False
	Sort	False
	Selection	None

18

2. After you design the dialog, attach variables to its controls, as specified in Table 18.6.

TABLE 18.6   Control Variables

Object	Name	Category	Type
IDC_RCLIENT	m_iType	Value	int
IDC_ESERVNAME	m_strName	Value	CString
IDC_ESERVPORT	m_iPort	Value	int
IDC_BCONNECT	m_ctlConnect	Control	CButton
IDC_EMSG	m_strMessage	Value	CString
IDC_LSENT	m_ctlSent	Control	CListBox
IDC_LRECVD	m_ctlRecvd	Control	CListBox

So that you can reuse the Connect button to also place the server application into listen mode, you need to add a function to the clicked event message for both radio buttons, changing the text on the command button depending on which of the two is currently selected. To add this functionality to your application:

1. Add a function to the BN_CLICKED event message for the IDC_RCLIENT control ID, naming the function OnBnClickedRType.

2. Open the SockDlg.cpp source code file and locate the Message Map section. Copy the ON_BN_CLICKED macro for the IDC_RCLIENT control ID, adding a new entry for the IDC_RSERVER control ID calling the same error handling function, as follows:

```
BEGIN_MESSAGE_MAP(CSockDlg, CDialog)
    ON_WM_SYSCOMMAND()
    ON_WM_PAINT()
    ON_WM_QUERYDRAGICON()
    //}}AFX_MSG_MAP
    ON_BN_CLICKED(IDC_RCLIENT, OnBnClickedRType)
    ON_BN_CLICKED(IDC_RSERVER, OnBnClickedRType)
END_MESSAGE_MAP()
```

3. Edit this function, adding the code in Listing 18.1.

LISTING 18.1   The CSockDlg OnBnClickedRType Function

```
void CSockDlg::OnBnClickedRType()
{
    // TODO: Add your control notification handler code here
    // Sync the controls with the variables
    UpdateData(TRUE);
```

INPUT

LISTING 18.1   continued

```
    // Which mode are we in?
    if (m_iType == 0)     // Set the appropriate text on the button
        m_ctlConnect.SetWindowText("C&onnect");
    else
        m_ctlConnect.SetWindowText("&Listen");
}
```

Now, if you compile and run the application, you should be able to select one radio button and then the other, and the text on the command button should change to reflect the part the application will play (see Figure 18.5).

FIGURE 18.5

Changing the button text.

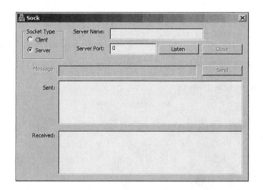

18

Inheriting from the CAsyncSocket Class

So that your application can capture and respond to socket events, you need to create your own descendent class from CAsyncSocket. This class will need its own versions of the event functions, as well as a means of passing this event to the dialog that the object will be a member of. So that you can pass each event to the dialog-class level, add a pointer to the parent dialog class as a member variable of your socket class. You'll use this pointer to call event functions for each socket event that's a member function of the dialog, after checking to make sure that no errors have occurred (of course).

To create this class in your application, follow these steps:

1. In the Class View, right-click the top (project) node.

2. Select Add, Add Class from the context menu.

3. In the Add Class dialog, select MFC in the tree view on the left, and MFC Class on the right (see Figure 18.6). Click the Open button.

4. Name your new class CMySocket, and select CAsyncSocket from the list of available base classes (see Figure 18.7). Click the Finish button to add this new class to your application.

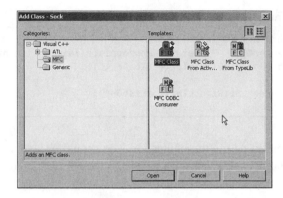

FIGURE 18.6

Specifying the class type to create.

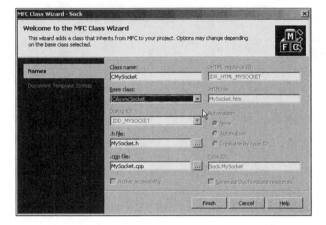

FIGURE 18.7

Specifying the MFC class to inherit from.

5. Add a member variable to the class to serve as a pointer to the parent dialog window. Specify the variable type as CDialog*, the variable name as m_pWnd, and the access as private.

6. Add a member function to your new socket class to set the pointer. Specify the function type as void, the name as SetParent, add one parameter of type CDialog* and named pWnd, and specify the function access as public.

7. Edit this new function, setting the pointer passed as a parameter to the member variable pointer, as follows:

```
void CMySocket::SetParent(CDialog *pWnd)
{
    // Set the member pointer
    m_pWnd = pWnd;
}
```

The only other thing you need to do to your socket class is add the event functions, which you use to call similarly named functions on the dialog class. To add a function for the OnAccept event function, follow these steps:

1. In the Properties Overrides area for the CMySocket class, add an override function for the OnAccept function.

2. Edit this function, adding the code in Listing 18.2.

LISTING 18.2 The CMySocket OnAccept Function

```
void CMySocket::OnAccept(int nErrorCode)
{
    // TODO: Add your specialized code here and/or call the base class
    // Were there any errors?
        if (nErrorCode == 0)
        // No, call the dialog's OnAcceptFunction
        ((CSockDlg*)m_pWnd)->OnAccept();

    CAsyncSocket::OnAccept(nErrorCode);
}
```

INPUT

18

3. Add similar override functions to your socket class for the OnConnect, OnClose, OnReceive, and OnSend functions, calling same-named functions in the dialog class, which you will add later.

4. Include the header file for your application dialog in your socket class, as in the bottom line of the following:

```
// MySocket.cpp : implementation file
//

#include "stdafx.h"
#include "Sock.h"
#include "MySocket.h"
#include "SockDlg.h"
```

After you add all the necessary event functions to your socket class, you need to add a variable of your socket class to the dialog class. For the server functionality, you need two variables in the dialog class: one to listen for connection requests and one to connect to the other application.

Because you need two socket objects, add two member variables to the dialog class (CSockDlg), specify the type of both variables as your socket class (CMySocket) and the access for both as private. Name one variable m_sListenSocket, to be used for listening for connection requests, and the other m_sConnectSocket, to be used for sending messages back and forth.

After you add the socket variables, you need to add the initialization code for all the variables. As a default, set the application type to client, the server name as `loopback`, and the port to 4000. Along with these variables, set the parent dialog pointers in your two socket objects so that they point to the dialog class. You can do so by adding the code in Listing 18.3 to the `OnInitDialog` function in the dialog class.

Note

The computer name `loopback` is in the TCP/IP network protocol to indicate the computer you are working on. It's an internal computer name resolved to the network address `127.0.0.1`. This computer name and address is commonly used by applications that need to connect to other applications running on the same computer. This is similar to the `localhost` special name used by the HTTP (Web) protocol. The `localhost` name was introduced with the Web protocols, and is now included as a default name in the system `hosts` file (a local file used to resolve host names, prior to checking with a DNS server), whereas the `loopback` name is used by the lower-level socket and networking infrastructure.

LISTING 18.3   The `CSockDlg OnInitDialog` Function

```
BOOL CSockDlg::OnInitDialog()
{
    CDialog::OnInitDialog();

    // Add "About..." menu item to system menu.

    // IDM_ABOUTBOX must be in the system command range.
    ASSERT((IDM_ABOUTBOX & 0xFFF0) == IDM_ABOUTBOX);
    ASSERT(IDM_ABOUTBOX < 0xF000);

    CMenu* pSysMenu = GetSystemMenu(FALSE);
    if (pSysMenu != NULL)
    {
        CString strAboutMenu;
        strAboutMenu.LoadString(IDS_ABOUTBOX);
        if (!strAboutMenu.IsEmpty())
        {
            pSysMenu->AppendMenu(MF_SEPARATOR);
            pSysMenu->AppendMenu(MF_STRING, IDM_ABOUTBOX, strAboutMenu);
        }
    }

    // Set the icon for this dialog. The framework does this automatically
    //  when the application's main window is not a dialog
    SetIcon(m_hIcon, TRUE);            // Set big icon
    SetIcon(m_hIcon, FALSE);           // Set small icon
```

LISTING **18.3**   continued

```
                  // TODO: Add extra initialization here
                  // Initialize the control variables
                      m_iType = 0;
         m_strName = "loopback";
         m_iPort = 4000;
         // Update the controls
         UpdateData(FALSE);
         // Set the socket dialog pointers
          m_sConnectSocket.SetParent(this);
         m_sListenSocket.SetParent(this);

         return TRUE;  // return TRUE  unless you set the focus to a control
     }
```

INPUT

Connecting the Application

When users click the Connect button, they disable all the top controls on the dialog. At this point, you don't want users to think that they can change the settings of the computer they're connecting to or change how the application is listening. You call the Create function on the appropriate socket variable, depending on whether the application is running as the client or server. Then you call either the Connect or Listen function to initiate the application's side of the connection.

To add this functionality to your application, follow these steps:

1. Add an event handler to the BN_CLICKED event message for the Connect button (ID IDC_BCONNECT).

2. Edit this function, adding the code in Listing 18.4.

LISTING **18.4**   The CSockDlg OnBnClickedBconnect Function

```
void CSockDlg::OnBnClickedBconnect()
{
    // TODO: Add your control notification handler code here
    // Sync the variables with the controls
    UpdateData(TRUE);
    // Disable the connection and type controls
    GetDlgItem(IDC_BCONNECT)->EnableWindow(FALSE);
    GetDlgItem(IDC_ESERVNAME)->EnableWindow(FALSE);
    GetDlgItem(IDC_ESERVPORT)->EnableWindow(FALSE);
    GetDlgItem(IDC_STATICNAME)->EnableWindow(FALSE);
    GetDlgItem(IDC_STATICPORT)->EnableWindow(FALSE);
    GetDlgItem(IDC_RCLIENT)->EnableWindow(FALSE);
    GetDlgItem(IDC_RSERVER)->EnableWindow(FALSE);
```

18

LISTING 18.4 continued

```
        GetDlgItem(IDC_STATICTYPE)->EnableWindow(FALSE);
        // Are we running as client or server?
        if (m_iType == 0)
        {
            // Client, create a default socket
            m_sConnectSocket.Create();
            // Open the connection to the server
            m_sConnectSocket.Connect(m_strName, m_iPort);
        }
        else
        {
            // Server, create a socket bound to the port specified
            m_sListenSocket.Create(m_iPort);
            // Listen for connection requests
            m_sListenSocket.Listen();
        }
    }
```

To complete the connection, add the socket event function to the dialog class for the OnAccept and OnConnect event functions. These are the functions your socket class is calling. They don't require any parameters and don't need to return any result code. For OnAccept, which is called for the listening socket when another application is trying to connect to it, you call the socket object's Accept function, passing in the connection socket variable. When you accept the connection, you can enable the prompt and edit box for entering and sending messages to the other application.

Follow these steps to add this function to your application:

1. Add a member function to the dialog class (CSockDlg).

2. Specify the function type as void, the name as OnAccept, and the access as public.

3. Edit the function, adding the following code:

```
void CSockDlg::OnAccept(void)
{
    // Accept the connection request
    m_sListenSocket.Accept(m_sConnectSocket);
    // Enable the text and message controls
    GetDlgItem(IDC_EMSG)->EnableWindow(TRUE);
    GetDlgItem(IDC_BSEND)->EnableWindow(TRUE);
    GetDlgItem(IDC_STATICMSG)->EnableWindow(TRUE);
}
```

For the client side, there's nothing to do after the connection is completed except enable the controls for entering and sending messages. You also need to enable the Close button so that the connection can be closed from the client side (but not the server side). To add this functionality to your application, follow these steps:

1. Add another member function to the dialog class (CSockDlg).

2. Specify the function type as void, the function name as OnConnect, and the access as public.

3. Edit the function, adding the following code:

```
void CSockDlg::OnConnect(void)
{
    // Enable the text and message controls
    GetDlgItem(IDC_EMSG)->EnableWindow(TRUE);
    GetDlgItem(IDC_BSEND)->EnableWindow(TRUE);
    GetDlgItem(IDC_STATICMSG)->EnableWindow(TRUE);
    GetDlgItem(IDC_BCLOSE)->EnableWindow(TRUE);
}
```

If you could compile and run your application now, you could start two copies, put one into listen mode, and then connect to it with the other. Unfortunately, you probably can't even compile your application now because your socket class is looking for several functions in your dialog class that you haven't added yet. So to add these missing functions, follow these steps:

1. Add three member functions to the dialog class (CSockDlg).

2. Specify all of them as void with public access. Specify the first function's name as OnSend, the second as OnReceive, and the third as OnClose.

You should now be able to compile your application. After you compile it, start two copies of it side by side. Specify that one be the server, and click the Listen button to put it into listen mode. Leave the other as the client and click Connect. You should see the connection controls disable and the message sending controls enable as the connection is made, as in Figure 18.8.

FIGURE 18.8

Connecting the two applications.

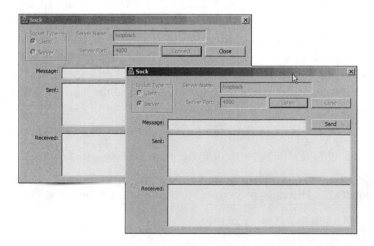

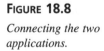

> **Tip**
>
> Be sure that the server application is listening before you try to connect to it with the client application. If you try to connect with the client before the server is listening for the connection, the connection will be rejected. Your application won't detect that the connection was rejected because you didn't add any error handling to detect this event.

> **Tip**
>
> To run these applications and get them to connect, you need TCP/IP running on your computer. If you have a network card in your computer, you may already have TCP/IP running. If you don't have a network card, and you use a modem to connect to the Internet, you will probably need to be connected to the Internet when you run and test these applications. When you connect to the Internet through a modem, your computer usually starts running TCP/IP as soon as the Internet connection is made. If you don't have a network card in your computer and don't have any means of connecting to the Internet or any other outside network that would allow you to run networked applications, you may not be able to run and test today's applications on your computer.
>
> Another option if you don't have any kind of network connection, is to install the loopback adapter. Check the documentation at the Microsoft Knowledge Base, on MSDN or the Microsoft Web site, to learn how to do this for your specific operating system.

Sending and Receiving

Now that you can connect the two running applications, you need to add functionality to send and receive messages. When a connection is established between the two applications, users can enter text messages in the edit box in the middle of the dialog window and then click the Send button to send the message to the other application. After the message is sent, it is added to the list of sent messages. To provide this functionality, when the Send button is clicked, your application needs to check whether a message needs to be sent, get the message's length, send the message, and then add the message to the list box. Follow these steps:

1. Add an event handler function to the clicked event of the Send (`IDC_BSEND`) button.

2. Edit this function, adding the code in Listing 18.5.

LISTING 18.5   The `CSockDlg` `OnBnClickedBsend` Function

```
void CSockDlg::OnBnClickedBsend()
{
```

LISTING 18.5   continued

```
    // TODO: Add your control notification handler code here
    int iLen;
    int iSent;

    // Sync the controls with the variables
    UpdateData(TRUE);
    // Is there a message to be sent?
    if (m_strMessage != "")
    {
        // Get the length of the message
        iLen = m_strMessage.GetLength();
        // Send the message
        iSent = m_sConnectSocket.Send(LPCTSTR(m_strMessage), iLen);
        // Were we able to send it?
        if (iSent == SOCKET_ERROR)
        {
        }
        else
        {
            // Add the message to the list box.
            m_ctlSent.AddString(m_strMessage);
            // Sync the variables with the controls
            UpdateData(FALSE);
        }
    }
}
```

When the `OnReceive` event function is triggered, indicating that a message has arrived, you retrieve the message from the socket using the `Receive` function. After you retrieve the message, you convert it into a `CString` and add it to the message-received list box. You can add this functionality by editing the `OnReceive` function of the dialog class to add the code in Listing 18.6.

LISTING 18.6   The `CSockDlg` `OnReceive` Function

```
void CSockDlg::OnReceive(void)
{
    char *pBuf = new char[1025];
    int iBufSize = 1024;
    int iRcvd;
    CString strRecvd;

    // Receive the message
    iRcvd = m_sConnectSocket.Receive(pBuf, iBufSize);
    // Did we receive anything?
    if (iRcvd == SOCKET_ERROR)
```

18

LISTING **18.6**   continued

```
        {
        }
        else
        {
            // Truncate the end of the message
            pBuf[iRcvd] = NULL;
            // Copy the message to a CString
            strRecvd = pBuf;
            // Add the message to the received list box
            m_ctlRecvd.AddString(strRecvd);
            // Sync the variables with the controls
            UpdateData(FALSE);
        }
    }
```

At this point, you should be able to compile and run two copies of your application, connecting them as you did earlier. After you establish the connection, you can send a message from one application to the other (see Figure 18.9).

FIGURE **18.9**

Sending messages between the applications.

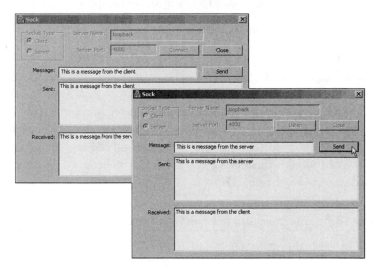

Ending the Connection

To end the connection between these two applications, the client application user can click the Close button. The server application will then receive the OnClose socket event. The same thing needs to happen in both cases. The connected socket needs to be closed, and the message sending controls need to be disabled. On the client, the connection controls can be enabled because the client could change some of this information and open a connection to another server application. Meanwhile, the server application continues to listen on the port that it was configured to listen to.

To add all this functionality to your application, simply edit the OnClose function, adding the code in Listing 18.7.

LISTING 18.7 The CSockDlg OnClose Function

```
void CSockDlg::OnClose(void)
{
    // Close the connected socket
    m_sConnectSocket.Close();
    // Disable the message sending controls
    GetDlgItem(IDC_EMSG)->EnableWindow(FALSE);
    GetDlgItem(IDC_BSEND)->EnableWindow(FALSE);
    GetDlgItem(IDC_STATICMSG)->EnableWindow(FALSE);
    GetDlgItem(IDC_BCLOSE)->EnableWindow(FALSE);
    // Are we running in Client mode?
    if (m_iType == 0)
    {
        // Yes, so enable the connection configuration controls
        GetDlgItem(IDC_BCONNECT)->EnableWindow(TRUE);
        GetDlgItem(IDC_ESERVNAME)->EnableWindow(TRUE);
        GetDlgItem(IDC_ESERVPORT)->EnableWindow(TRUE);
        GetDlgItem(IDC_STATICNAME)->EnableWindow(TRUE);
        GetDlgItem(IDC_STATICPORT)->EnableWindow(TRUE);
        GetDlgItem(IDC_RCLIENT)->EnableWindow(TRUE);
        GetDlgItem(IDC_RSERVER)->EnableWindow(TRUE);
        GetDlgItem(IDC_STATICTYPE)->EnableWindow(TRUE);
    }
}
```

18

Finally, for the Close button, call the OnClose function. Follow these steps:

1. Add an event handler to the clicked event for the Close button (IDC_BCLOSE).

2. Edit the function to call the OnClose function, as follows:

```
void CSockDlg::OnBnClickedBclose()
{
    // TODO: Add your control notification handler code here
    // Call the OnClose function
    OnClose();
}
```

If you compile and run your application, you can connect the client application to the server, send some messages back and forth, and then disconnect the client by clicking Close. You'll see the message-sending controls disable themselves in both applications, as in Figure 18.10. You can reconnect the client to the server by clicking Connect again and then pass more messages between the two, as though they had never been connected in the first place. If you start a third copy of the application, change its port number, designate it as a server and put it into listening mode. You can take your client back and forth between the two servers, connecting to one, closing the connection, changing the port number, and then connecting to the other.

FIGURE 18.10

Closing the connection between the applications.

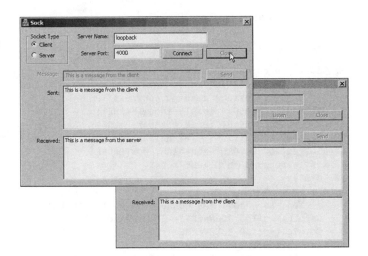

Summary

Today, you saw how to enable your applications to communicate with others across a network, or across the Internet, by using the MFC Winsock classes. You took a good look at the `CAsyncSocket` class and learned how to create your own descendent class from it that would provide your applications with event-driven network communications. You learned how to create a server application that can listen for and accept connections from other applications. You also learned how to build a client application that can connect to a server. You saw how to send and receive messages over a socket connection between two applications. Finally, you learned how to close the connection and how to detect that the connection is closed.

Q&A

Q. **How do Internet applications work?**

A. Most Internet applications use the same functionality that you created today. The primary difference is that the applications have a script of messages passed back and forth. The messages consist of a command and the data that needs to accompany that command. The server reads the command and processes the data appropriately, sending back a status code to let the client know the success or failure of the command. If you want to learn more about how Internet applications do this, several books cover this subject area in detail. You can also find the RFC documents that specify the communication protocol for various standardized applications at the Web site for the Internet Engineering Task Force at www.ietf.org. RFC documents are the specification documents for various applications, file formats, and other standards that are used throughout the Internet.

Q. How does a server application handle a large number of simultaneous connections from clients?

A. With a full-strength server, connection sockets aren't declared as class variables. The server instead uses some sort of dynamic allocation of sockets in an array or link-list to create sockets for the clients as the connection requests come in. Another approach often taken by servers is to spin off a separate thread for each connection request. This allows the application to have a single socket connection per thread, making keeping track of the sockets much easier. In any case, server applications don't normally have a single connection socket variable. Keep in mind, however, that if too many threads are running, then number of context switches will degrade server performance significantly, so the separate thread per connection may not be an appropriate approach for a heavy-load server application.

18

Workshop

The Workshop provides quiz questions to help you solidify your understanding of the material covered and exercises to provide you with experience in using what you've learned. The answers to the quiz questions and exercises are provided in Appendix A, "Answers to Quiz Questions."

Quiz

1. What two things must a client application know to be able to connect to a server application?

2. What CAsyncSocket function enables a server application to detect connection efforts by client applications?

3. What CAsyncSocket member function is called to signal that data has arrived through a socket connection?

4. What function is called to signal that a connection is established?

5. What function do you use to send a message through a socket connection to the application on the other end?

Exercise

The server application that you wrote can handle only a single connection at a time. If a second application tries to open a connection to it while it has an existing connection to an application, the server application will crash. The server tries to accept the second connection into the socket already connected to the first client application. Add a third socket object to the application that will be used to reject additional client connections until the first client closes the connection.

DAY 19

Working with Managed Code

Recently, Microsoft announced a new platform initiative called "dot-net" (.NET). At the announcement, Microsoft demonstrated several new devices that were part of the new platform, devices such as cellular phones with built-in color browsers and voice-recognition, tablet computers with handwriting recognition, and cars linked to all your communication devices (office and cell phones, computer e-mail, and so on). In all, these devices looked like something from a science-fiction movie, but they were all actual devices and technology that would start appearing on store shelves soon.

What Microsoft was actually demonstrating was the new .NET platform that it is in the process of building. With the .NET platform, you can have multiple computing devices tied together, sharing data and applications between them. It means that if you are in one place working on an application, and need to go somewhere else but still need to access the same application (and can't take your computer with you), you still can access and use that application using any other .NET device. If you were using your office computer, you can access the same application and data by using your cell phone, just to cite one possible scenario.

Today, you'll learn about the .NET platform, how it works and what you need to do to be able to write applications for it. Some of the topics that you'll learn are

- How Microsoft's .NET platform divides the processing responsibilities, merging the Web and client/server processing models to create what has been called the "Active Web" or "Active Internet"
- What the Common Language Runtime (CLR) is, and how it enables you to run your applications on any .NET device
- The difference between standard C++ and Managed C++, which is a new version of C++ that takes advantage of the Common Language Runtime
- How to port your existing MFC applications over to the CLR, making them usable on .NET devices
- How to build applications using Managed C++ for the .NET platform

Understanding Microsoft's .NET Platform and the Common Language Runtime

So, how does .NET and the CLR (Common Language Runtime) work, and what difference will it make to you as a software developer? There are a couple of key things that CLR and .NET will mean to you. First, you'll be able to write an application once and have it run on any .NET device. If you write a desktop application, you can run it on your PDA, or even on your digital television set-top box. It'll also mean that you need to use a different approach to designing and planning your applications from what you've seen up to this point. Your applications will need to be divided into portions to run on the server, and portions to run on the user device.

The .NET Architecture

The .NET architecture is the latest evolution in how the Web works. Initially, all functionality was located on the Web server, and the browser could do little beyond displaying pages and passing raw data to the server. Comparing this functionality to the client/server model for applications that preceded the Web, many users felt as though it was a large step backward for applications. Because all the functionality was located on the server, user interaction was nonexistent until the user would submit a request to the server.

In the client/server model, the application functionality was spread over multiple computers. The client (the user's computer) performed all user-interface functionality, presenting the data and interacting with the user. The database server housed the data and would occasionally perform business or processing logic on the data. In some client/server models, there was also a middleware server, which performed most of the heavy computing. The middleware server was where the business rules were housed, keeping the functionality most likely to change in a centralized location.

Going from the functionality-rich model of client/server to the bare-bones functionality of the Web, the consensus within the computer industry was that the Web solved some of the problems of the client/server model. The Web solved client/server problems such as client-software distribution and unsuitability for use over a wide-area network. At the same time, users didn't like the lack of interactivity on the front end. Because of the shortcomings, a series of additions and enhancements were made to the Web in an effort to bring it closer to the client/server, functionality-rich model. It began with scripting languages that would run in the browser, and then moved to Java applets and ActiveX components. At the same time, application servers were being built to improve functionality capabilities on the server side. The idea was to inch closer to client/server–type functionality while retaining the network-friendliness of the Web, bringing along the strengths that the Web has over client/server.

New Term   Several years down this road, we now have the latest arrival in this series of changes to the Web. This new arrival is known as Microsoft's .NET platform. The .NET platform consists of the next generation of several Microsoft technologies (COM+, ASP+, IIS, Passport, and so on) combined with several open standards (XML, SOAP, HTTP, and so on) and some new technologies and programming languages (CLR, C#, and so on) to create what has been called the *Active Web*. The resulting architecture of this combination looks like Figure 19.1. The server components do a lot of the heavy processing and data management, with direct connection to the database or any other data source. The client applications run within the Internet Explorer Web browser, or on any other .NET client device, with a rich functionality user experience. XML is used as the primary data format for all communications between client and server, as well as between components, over the HTTP Web protocol.

Server Components

New Term   On the server side, most application functionality is contained in *components*. Components are DLLs, they aren't part of one application, and can be called and used by many applications. These components don't have any user interface for interaction. They only have exposed functions that can be called to perform various processing tasks.

The server components normally have at least two responsibilities:

- To perform any business rules for the application
- To perform any interaction with the database

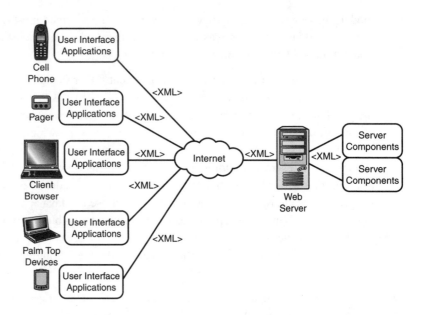

Figure 19.1

The basic .NET architecture.

One reason for maintaining this functionality on the server is because of its proximity to the database server, so that when large amounts of data are being processed, it's only moving across a short, high-speed network connection, instead of over the Internet. Another reason is that it's much easier to maintain and update the business rules if they are all on centralized servers, as opposed to having to get all users to upgrade their applications. A third reason is because it's much easier to buy large, powerful (fast) servers that all users use than to go through the expense and hassle of trying to maintain a minimum processing capability for each application user, especially within a large corporation.

NEW TERM A *business rule* refers to a piece of logic that has to be performed, or a rule that needs to be enforced. An example of this is rules your bank has to cash a check. First, it probably has a rule that your account must have sufficient money in it to cover the amount of the check. Next, it has a rule where your account needs to have the amount of the check removed, and given to the bearer of the check. Another example of a business rule is the calculation of tax on a purchase. Certain calculations must be performed using the amount of the items being purchased and the tax rate being charged. These are all simple examples of business rules.

Client Applications

The client portion of .NET applications will be running on many different devices. In a nutshell, the client application will all be running in what's essentially a version of

Microsoft's Internet Explorer Web browser. Because several devices that Microsoft is planning for .NET clients will have no common hardware platform, natively compiled applications won't be portable between devices, much like applications written for Windows haven't been usable on Windows CE devices. Instead, you've had to use a cross-compiler to make versions of the applications that will run on Windows CE devices.

NEW TERM A *cross-compiler* compiles applications for a different hardware platform than what it's running on. For instance, if you are working on a Windows machine and are building an application to run on a Windows CE device, you would use a cross-compiler to build the executable file that will run on that device. The resulting application won't run on the system on which you built it, but it will run on the system for which it was intended. Cross-compilers are common in shops that build applications that run on specialized hardware, such as the application that controls your microwave oven. The programmers responsible for that control program probably use either a Windows or UNIX system to code the application, and then use a cross-compiler to build the application, which is then burned into a ROM chip and placed into the microwave.

By using a Web browser as the primary interface, Microsoft can leverage and extend Web technologies to make the client interface for .NET applications portable across devices and platforms. To provide this portability, Microsoft has extended its ASP technology, adding much richer interactivity capabilities, as well as making it better able to interact with the server components. For the functionality provided through ActiveX controls, Microsoft has created the Common Language Runtime (CLR) to enable applications and controls run on any hardware device, something not possible with ActiveX prior to .NET.

SOAP and XML

Communication between the client and server portions of .NET applications is performed using XML (eXtensible Markup Language) and SOAP (Simple Object Access Protocol), two Internet standards for data and object communications. These are both markup languages, much like HTML (HyperText Markup Language). If you look at XML or SOAP files, they look like HTML taken to an extreme. The reason for this is that they are both text-based formats that use the same type of tags to describe and format the information that they are communicating. The reason they look alike is because they are all derived from the Standard Generalized Markup Language (SGML), which is a standard for specifying document layout and markup that precedes all of the Internet standards like HTML, XML, and so on.

The XML format is used to describe data and data objects. The SOAP format is used to describe objects and services available for use (SOAP is a specific application of XML).

19

By making use of these information formats for communication, all application communication can be performed between the client applications and the server components through the HTTP protocol. Standardized Web technologies are leveraged to enable rich-client functionality that used to only be practical on a local, closed network, over the Internet. If these applications can run over the Internet, they can run over any network.

 Note

> The topics of XML and SOAP are extensive and have entire books dedicated to them. If you want to understand how they work and what their formats are like, you should pick up a book dedicated to the subject.

The Common Language Runtime (CLR)

The Common Language Runtime is basically the same as the Java language's virtual machine. It's a binary machine-language for a computer processor that doesn't really exist. CLR is modeled after actual processors, but is designed more for translating the binary machine language into actual processor instructions. Microsoft took what they had learned from making one of the best Java Virtual Machines around and used that knowledge in designing and building its own Common Language Runtime.

The CLR's purpose is applications can be compiled for the CLR instead of a specific computer processor. The benefit is that any application can now run on any hardware for which a version of the CLR exists. With the proliferation of hand-held devices, and their various hardware configurations, this is important for making it easy to build applications that can run on as many devices as possible.

In reality, this is actually an old idea for Microsoft. Although it's likely that none of the actual developers that created the CLR were around at the time, Microsoft was using this same approach when it first started developing consumer applications, such as spreadsheets and word processors. These applications were compiled down to an intermediate binary format, and then run by a runtime engine on multiple platforms. If you really want to get picky, some people would even claim that this idea dates back to Microsoft's original product, Microsoft BASIC, because it enabled you to take the same application and run it on any computer that had Microsoft BASIC loaded. In fact, the remnants of this approach were still in evidence up until Visual Basic 5, when Microsoft finally gave programmers the option of compiling their VB applications to native executables.

NEW TERM While the idea is old, the CLR does have some new twists built into it. One twist is what's known as a *Just In Time (JIT) compiler*. The JIT recompiles the application from CLR to native executable when the application starts, eliminating the interpretation layer common to most virtual machines. This gives applications compiled to the CLR the ability to execute as fast as applications compiled to native machine code.

Another twist that the CLR is adding is that it will function as a replacement for COM. It will simplify working with COM significantly, and make interaction between components built in different programming languages more seamless than ever. The CLR contains a common set of object types used by all languages building applications for it.

Working with Managed C++

Part of the attraction of the C/C++ programming languages is that they compile down directly to machine code. For building fast and efficient applications, there is only one faster, more efficient programming language available—Assembler. With Assembler, you are essentially coding in machine code, with simple translations into machine code.

Another aspect of C/C++ that makes it a very desirable language is that there are no limits to what you can do with it. You can access all aspects of the computer on which your application is running, assuming that the OS allows access. This makes C/C++ ideal for building device drivers to control the interaction between the OS and any devices added to the computer, like sound and video cards.

Unfortunately, the level of access that C/C++ gives programmers to the computer goes against the whole idea behind the CLR. The idea behind the CLR is that applications are compiled to a virtual machine code, which is then converted to the actual machine code when the application is run. Second, the CLR performs all memory management for the applications that run on it. In C/C++, you are responsible for all memory management.

NEW TERM   *Memory management* is controlling how and when objects and variables are allocated from the available memory in the computer, as well as when and how that memory is returned to the pool of available memory. This task is performed in the C++ programming language with the `new` and `delete` keywords. When you allocate memory for a variable or object with the `new` keyword, you need to be sure to release that same memory with the `delete` keyword before the application exits. This task is hidden from the programmer in several programming languages, such as Visual Basic.

The solution that Microsoft came up with to solve this problem was two-fold. First, they designed and developed a new programming language, C# (pronounced C-sharp, a subject for another book), that is an adaptation of C++ with several lessons learned from Java and other object-oriented languages thrown in. The second solution was managed C++.

With managed C++, your application is compiled for the CLR, rather than compiled for native machine code. The memory management is still in place but requires new keywords for allocating and interacting with CLR objects.

19

Building Managed C++ Applications

You can build managed C++ applications and components in three ways:

- You can build a managed C++ application from scratch. Unfortunately, this may be the most difficult approach to building managed C++ applications, as Visual Studio doesn't provide you with any of the helpful wizards to piece together the application shell and functionality. This approach is the old-style of building C++ applications, before wizards and other code-generating tools. You'll build a simple application using this method later today.

- You can convert an existing C++ application to be a managed C++ application. This is probably the easiest method to create a managed C++ application. You'll also create a managed C++ application using this method later today.

- To create a managed C++ application or component, you can wrap the existing component in a managed C++ shell. This approach enables you to leave your existing C++ component untouched, with a CLR wrapper around it, exposing its functionality for use by other CLR controls and applications. This approach isn't practical for entire applications, but is very practical for components. You'll create an unmanaged component and wrap it with managed C++ tomorrow.

Managed Data Types

NEW TERM   There are two basic managed data types in managed C++: gc and `value`. The gc types are garbage collection types allocated on the CLR heap and managed by the CLR engine. The `value` types are short-lived types that are allocated on the stack or within other objects and don't justify the overhead of garbage collection. (*Garbage collection* refers to the automatic release of memory allocated to objects and variables.)

gc Classes and Structs

If you need to define a gc class in your project, you would make a simple addition to the class declaration of the __gc keyword as follows:

```
__gc class MyGCClass{
public:
   int i;
   int k;
...
}
```

In using this class in a managed C++ application, you would allocate an instance of the class using the new keyword, as follows:

```
MyGCClass* pMgc = new MyGCClass;
```

Although you don't have to call the `delete` keyword to release the memory allocated to this variable, you can if you want to force the memory deallocation to take place right then. However, you can't use the `delete` keyword on a gc class that doesn't have a user-defined destructor.

You have to follow a few rules when creating your own gc classes and structures:

- You can't inherit a gc class from an unmanaged class, or vice versa.
- A gc class can't be inherited from multiple classes.
- gc classes can't have friend classes or functions.
- You can't declare a copy constructor, or `new` and `delete` operators for a gc class.
- You can't use the `sizeof` or `offsetof` functions on a gc class.
- You can't have `const` or `volatile` modifiers in a member function of the gc class.
- Because all gc types must use the CLR built-in `new` operator, you can't declare an instance of a gc type, only a pointer to a gc type.

Note

The rules listed here mention several things that, if you didn't already know the C++ programming language before reading this book, you probably don't know about. These are the ability to create friend classes and functions, your own class operators, multiple inheritance, and copy constructors. These are all important aspects and capabilities of the C++ programming language but are beyond the scope of this book. While this book has tried to teach you the basics of the C++ programming language, it's not possible to cover all aspects of the language as a sidebar to the main topic. If you didn't already know the C++ programming language, you're probably becoming fairly comfortable with the basics by this point, and would be better served if you picked up a book on the language, which would go into all the aspects of the language mentioned here.

19

These are by no means all the rules that you need to follow when creating and working with gc classes. For a full list of rules, see the Managed Extensions for C++ Specification in the MSDN documentation that you received with your copy of Visual Studio or Visual C++.

`value` Classes and Structs

If you need to define a `value` class in your project, you would make a simple addition to the class declaration of the `__value` keyword as follows:

```
__value class MyValueClass{
public:
```

```
    int i;
    int k;
...
}
```

You can use `value` types by either declaring an instance of them, as follows

```
MyValueClass c;
```

or by treating them as an unmanaged object, where you have to be sure to deallocate the memory used by the object after you finish using it, like so:

```
MyValueClass* p = new MyValueClass;
...
delete p;
```

Like with the `gc` class and structures, you need to follow several rules for how `value` classes and structures are used:

- You can't inherit a `value` class from an unmanaged class, or vice versa.
- A `value` class can't be inherited from multiple classes.
- `value` classes can't have friend classes or functions.
- You can't declare a copy constructor, or `new` and `delete` operators for a `value` class.
- You can't use the `sizeof` or `offsetof` functions on a `value` class.
- You can't have `const` or `volatile` modifiers in a member function of the `value` class.
- A `value` class can't have any `virtual` methods.
- A `value` class can only inherit from a `gc` interface. A `value` class can't inherit from a `gc` class or other `value` classes.

 Note Like with the `gc` classes, these are nowhere close to all the rules that must be followed when creating and using `value` classes and structures. For a full list of the rules, see the specification in MSDN.

Managed Pointers

When an application runs under the CLR, which has built-in garbage collection, you might think that pointers go away, or at least are hidden as in Visual Basic. In reality, they became more complicated. You now have two types of pointers: unmanaged and garbage collected.

The unmanaged pointers are your standard C/C++ pointers, which you have to manage yourself. The managed pointers have two keywords that indicate whether the pointer can point to something on the CLR, garbage-collected heap. These keywords are __gc (garbage collected, discussed earlier) and __nogc (no garbage collection). One of these two keywords have to be placed just prior to the pointer operator (*), as follows:

```
G __gc* pG;
V __nogc* pV;
```

You can use the __gc keyword for pointers pointing at gc classes and structures allocated on the CLR heap. It can also be used to point to value classes or structures that are members of gc classes or structures, as follows:

```
__value struct Val {
    int x;
    int y;
}

__gc class Cgc
{
public:
    // The value structure Val is declared as a public member
    Val m_vMem;
}

// Later in the application code. . .
Cgc __gc* pCgc = new Cgc;
Val __gc* pVal = &(pCgc->m_vMem);
```

For any value classes or structures that aren't members of gc classes or structures, you have to use the __nogc keyword when creating pointers to them, as follows:

```
Val __nogc* pVal = new Val;
```

The purpose of gc pointers is so that the CLR can keep track of all references into the CLR heap. This is necessary for the CLR to perform proper garbage collection.

Managed String Literals

When you use string literals in a managed C++ application, a new, managed string literal is more efficient to use than a standard C++ string literal. The reason for this is because standard C++ string literals are made up of ASCII characters, which managed applications can't handle. Because of the incompatibility with managed objects and applications, standard C++ string literals would have to be converted into a form that managed objects could handle. You can avoid this overhead by using managed string literals instead.

19

To use managed string literals, you must specify that you are using the mscorlib.dll and System::String object, as follows:

```
#using <mscorlib.dll>
using System::String;
```

 Note

> The #using preprocessor directive and the using keyword are two new additions to C++ that will be explained in the upcoming section, "Using .NET Objects in Managed C++ Applications."

To create a managed string literal, you declare a pointer to the String type and assign the string literal to it, as follows:

```
String *s = "This is a managed string literal.";
```

You can also create a managed wide-character (UNICODE) string literal by adding the L prefix as follows:

```
String *s2 = L"This is a managed, wide-character string literal.";
```

For best performance, you can create a new type of string literal by using the new S prefix as follows:

```
String *s3 = S"This is a new, more efficient managed string literal.";
```

Managed C++ Keywords

Several other keywords have been introduced into the managed C++ extensions (see Table 19.1).

TABLE 19.1 Managed Extensions for C++ Keywords

Keyword	Description
__abstract	Placed in front of the class declaration to specify that the class is a base class and can't be directly instantiated. Only descendent classes of classes labeled as __abstract can be used in applications.
__box	Used to make a copy of a __value object and place it on the CLR heap.
__delegate	Used to declare a function pointer to a function in a __gc class.
__event	Used in a class declaration to declare an event method in the class.
__identifier	Used to access unmanaged C++ objects that use keywords as names (identifiers).
__pin	Used to declare a pointer to a managed, garbage collected object. This type of pointer specifies that the object it's pointing to can't be moved during garbage collection by the CLR.

TABLE 19.1 continued

Keyword	Description
__property	Used in the class declaration to identify properties of the class.
__sealed	Used in the class declaration. This keyword is used to mark a method in the class that can't be overridden in descendent classes, or to mark the entire class so that the class can't be inherited by other classes.
__try_cast	Used to specify that a variable should be cast as another object type. If the variable can't be cast as the specified type, an exception is thrown.
__typeof	Used to return the System::Type of an object passed to it.

Using .NET Objects in Managed C++ Applications

One benefit to building managed C++ applications is the built-in library of objects in the .NET platform. Your application can access an extensive list of objects. These built-in objects provide you with a significant amount of functionality that can be used in any .NET application, not just managed C++ applications.

However, you can't just start using these objects in your code. You need to be aware of a couple of details to be able to use these objects.

The #using Preprocessor Directive

Back on Day 13, you learned about the #import preprocessor directive that Microsoft added to Visual C++ to import COM objects into the project and make them available to your application. The #using preprocessor is basically the same, except that it can import only DLLs and objects compiled specifically for the CLR. Eventually, you'll even be able to use the #using directive to import executables that have been compiled for the CLR, but that capability isn't available yet.

The key DLL that you'll want to import for most of your managed C++ applications is mscorlib.dll, which contains many of the core objects that are part of the .NET platform. You use this directive at the beginning of your source code files, just as you would use the #import directive, as follows:

```
#using <mscorlib.dll>
```

The using namespace Directive

Whereas the #using preprocessor directive is new to managed C++, the using directive is part of the C++ language specification. The using directive allows you to specify a namespace, and nested namespace specifiers, to enable you to use objects from the namespace without having to use the fully qualified name of the objects. For example, take the following sample code:

19

```
#using <mscorlib.dll>
using namespace System
main()
{
    Console::Write("Hello World.");
}
```

If you left out the directive to use the System namespace, you would have to write this
code as follows:

```
#using <mscorlib.dll>
main()
{
    System::Console::Write("Hello World.");
}
```

The using directive doesn't have to be used at the beginning of the source code, but can
be used any where you want to use a namespace so that you can avoid having to fully
qualify the object names in that section of code.

The using Declaration

You'll also see the declaration form of using occasionally in managed C++ applications.
This use of the using keyword is also part of the C++ language, and not a new introduction by the managed extensions. The using declaration enables you to directly use an
object type or function within the context of where you specified to use it. An example of
this is the use of string literals, as follows:

```
#using <mscorlib.dll>
using System::String;
main()
{
    String *s = "This is a managed string literal.";
}
```

Without the using declaration, you would have had to code this as follows:

```
#using <mscorlib.dll>
main()
{
    System::String *s = "This is a managed string literal.";
}
```

Another use of the using declaration could be to access specific functions within a base
class from a descendent class, as follows:

```
class B
{
public:
    void f(char c);
};
```

```
class D : B
{
public:
   using B::f;
   void f(int i)
   {
      f('a');
   }
};

main ()
{
   D d;
   // Call the descendent method
   d.f(1);
   // Call the base method
   d.f('b');
}
```

Or to directly call a class method without having to specify the class, as follows:

```
class C
{
public:
   void f(char c);
};

void main()
{
   using C::f;

   f('a');
}
```

In all these situations, you are using the using declaration to create a shortcut to a specific object or method.

Some Standard .NET Objects

When you open up the MSDN documentation, and look at the .NET Framework Class Library, you'll see a list of almost 100 namespaces that you can use in your applications. In each namespace, you'll find several classes containing functionality for certain things that fall within the domain of the namespace. Most of the namespaces are fairly self-evident as to what type of functionality is contained within the classes enclosed. For instance, the System.Data group of namespaces contains classes for database functionality. To be more specific, the System.Data.OleDb namespace contains classes that encapsulate the OLEDB interface for accessing data sources. Table 19.2 lists some higher-level namespaces.

19

TABLE 19.2   .NET Framework Namespaces

Namespace	Contents
System	Base classes for commonly used resources, data types, events, interfaces, attributes, and exception processing.
System.Data	Classes that constitute the ADO.NET architecture.
System.Drawing	Classes that provide basic drawing functionality. This namespace encapsulates much of the Windows GDI functionality.
System.Net	Classes that provide network communications functionality.
System.Security	Classes that encapsulate much of the underlying CLR security, including permissions and access functionality.
System.Threading	Classes that encapsulate much of the threading functionality, including the synchronization objects.
System.Web	Classes that enable browser/server communication.
System.Xml	Classes used for working with XML data.

When you use a namespace in managed C++, although the documentation specifies the namespace domains separated by a period (.), you need to separate the namespace domains (as well as the classes within the namespace) by using the scope resolution operator (two colons, ::), as follows:

```
using namespace System::Net;
```

Using .NET Objects in MFC Applications

The easiest way to build GUI managed C++ applications is to build a MFC application, and then port it over to the CLR. This is a simple matter of changing some of the project compile options. To make these changes, follow these steps:

1. Open an existing MFC project.
2. In the Solutions Explorer pane, right-click the project node at the top of the files tree and select Properties from the context menu.
3. Select All Configurations from the Configuration combo box on top of the project properties dialog.
4. Select C/C++, General from the left side of the dialog, and for the Compile As Managed option, specify Assembly Support (/clr). For Debug Information Support, specify Program Database (/Zi), as shown in Figure 19.2.
5. Select C/C++, Code Generation from the left side of the dialog, and for the Basic Runtime Checks, specify Default. For the Enable Minimal Rebuild, specify No.

FIGURE 19.2

Specifying that a project be compiled for the CLR.

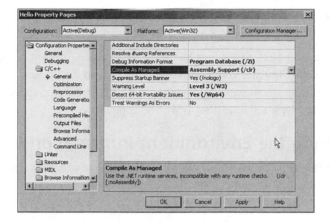

6. Click OK to apply these changes to your project, effectively converting your project to be compiled for the CLR.

When it comes time to add some .NET Foundation classes into your MFC application, you need to be aware of a small detail. The debug version of MFC redefines the new operator so that it can maintain track of allocated memory and can identify any memory leaks in your application. This is incompatible with the .NET objects. As a result, whenever you are creating instances of .NET objects or any other managed objects (including any garbage collected classes or structures that you've defined), you need to use the #pragma push_macro and pop_macro directives, along with the #undef directive, to unredefine the new operator for use with managed objects. This code would look something like the following:

```
#ifdef _DEBUG
#pragma push_macro("new")
#undef new
#endif

String* s;
s = new String("This is a managed string.");

#ifdef _DEBUG
#pragma pop_macro("new")
#endif
```

Writing a Managed C++ Application

For today's example, you will build a simple managed C++ application. This character-mode application extracts various information about the system on which the application is running and displays it. The application also asks the user to enter two numbers, and then adds the two numbers together.

19

To create the application shell for today's application, create a new Managed C++ Application project and name it ManagedEnv.

With today's project, you won't be presented with the Application Wizard that you're used to seeing. Instead, you'll be placed directly into the project with a few files already created. If you examine the ManagedEnv.cpp file, you'll find that the main function has been created with a simple "Hello World" application.

Creating the Environment Information Class

To start this application, you'll create a new, garbage collected class that will display environmental information about the computer and OS on which the application is running. To create this class, follow these steps:

1. Add a new generic class to the project using the same method that you used in previous days. Name the class CEnvironmentInfo.

2. Modify the class declaration, adding the __gc keyword as in Listing 19.1.

LISTING **19.1**　The CEnvironmentInfo Class Declaration

```
#using <mscorlib.dll>

using namespace System;

__gc class CEnvironmentInfo
{
public:
    CEnvironmentInfo(void);
    ~CEnvironmentInfo(void);
};
```

3. Add a new function to the CEnvironmentInfo class to display the OS version. Specify the return type as void, name the function ShowOSVersion, and specify the access as public.

4. Edit the ShowOSVersion function, adding the code in Listing 19.2.

LISTING **19.2**　The ShowOSVersion Function

```
void CEnvironmentInfo::ShowOSVersion(void)
{
    String* strLine;

    // Get the current OS version
    strLine = String::Concat(S"OS Version: ", Environment::get_OSVersion());
```

LISTING 19.2 continued

```
    // Display the OS version to the user
    Console::WriteLine(strLine);
}
```

ANALYSIS Listing 19.2 uses the get_OSVersion method of the Environment .NET class to get the OS version of the computer on which this application is running. OSVersion is actually specified as a property of the Environment class, so with other programming languages, you wouldn't directly call this method. However, this being the C++ language, the internals of class properties aren't hidden from you, so you have to call the actual method that provides the functionality for the property.

The display string is being built using the System.String class. This class doesn't have the concatenation operators that you've been using with the CString class. As a result, this is closer to standard C string functionality where you are calling the Concat method to combine the two strings into one.

After the display string is built, the WriteLine method from the Console class displays the string to the user. The Console class encapsulates much of the character-mode display functionality.

To add functionality to display more environment information, continue with these steps:

1. Add four more functions to the CEnvironmentInfo class to display additional environmental information. Use the function names, and call the Environment class methods (see Table 19.3). Specify that the access for all these functions is public, and their return types are void.

19

TABLE 19.3 Example Application Functions and Methods to Call

Function Name	Environment Property Method to Use
ShowCurDirectory	Environment::get_CurrentDirectory
ShowMachineName	Environment::get_MachineName
ShowUserName	Environment::get_UserName
ShowDomainName	Environment::get_UserDomainName

2. Add one final function to the CEnvironmentInfo class. Specify the return type as void, name the function ShowClrVersion, and specify that its access as public. Edit the function, adding the code in Listing 19.3.

LISTING 19.3 The ShowClrVersion Function

```
void CEnvironmentInfo::ShowClrVersion(void)
{
    String* strLine;

    // Get the CLR environment version
    Version* verClr = Environment::get_Version();
    // Format the CLR version information in a string
    strLine = String::Concat(S"CLR Version: ", verClr->ToString());
    // Display the CLR version for the user
    Console::WriteLine(strLine);
}
```

ANALYSIS This function creates an instance of the Version class by calling the get_Version property method of the Environment class. It then uses the ToString method of the Version class to convert this CLR information into a displayable string.

3. Modify the main function for the application, instantiating the CEnvironmentInfo class and then calling its methods to display the system information, as in Listing 19.4.

LISTING 19.4 The Modified Main Function

```
#include "stdafx.h"
#include "EnvironmentInfo.h"
#using <mscorlib.dll>
#include <tchar.h>
using namespace System;

// This is the entry point for this application
int _tmain(void)
{
    // TODO: Please replace the sample code below with your own.
    CEnvironmentInfo* eiInfo = new CEnvironmentInfo;

    // Show the current directory
    eiInfo->ShowCurDirectory();
    // Show the machine name
    eiInfo->ShowMachineName();
    // Show the OS version
    eiInfo->ShowOSVersion();
    // Show the user name
    eiInfo->ShowUserName();
    // Show the domain name
    eiInfo->ShowDomainName();
```

LISTING 19.4   continued

```
    // Show the CLR version
    eiInfo->ShowClrVersion();

    return 0;
}
```

You can now compile and run your application, displaying the system information as shown in Figure 19.3. You might want to run the application without debugging to get the application to stop upon completion and wait for you to press a key to close the window.

FIGURE 19.3

Displaying system information.

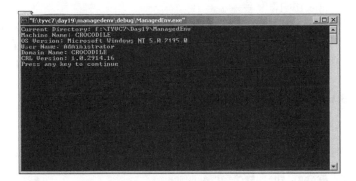

Creating the Number Addition Class

To add the input and addition portion of this application, you'll create a new, garbage collected class that will prompt the user to enter two numbers, which will then be added and the result displayed. To create this class, follow these steps:

1. Add a new class to the project using the same method that you used in previous days. Name the class CAddNumbers.

2. Modify the class declaration, adding the __gc keyword as in Listing 19.5.

LISTING 19.5   The CAddNumbers Class Declaration

INPUT
```
#using <mscorlib.dll>

using namespace System;

__gc class CAddNumbers
```

19

Listing 19.5   continued

```
{
public:
    CAddNumbers(void);
    ~ CAddNumbers(void);
};
```

To add class member variables to hold the two values entered by the user, continue with these steps:

1. Add two member variables to the CAddNumbers class. Specify the variable types as int, and the access as private, and name them m_iNumber1 and m_iNumber2, respectively.

2. Add a new function to the CAddNumbers class to get the first number from the user. Specify the return type as void, name the function GetFirstNumber, and specify the access as public. Edit the function, adding the code in Listing 19.6.

Listing 19.6   The GetFirstNumber Function

```
void CAddNumbers::GetFirstNumber(void)
{
    String* strIn;

    // Prompt the user for a number
    Console::Write(S"Enter a number: ");
    // Read the input from the user
    strIn = Console::ReadLine();
    // Convert the input into a number
    m_iNumber1 = Convert::ToInt32(strIn);
}
```

ANALYSIS   This function used the ReadLine method of the Console class to read what the user typed. When the user input is in a string, the Convert class's ToInt32 method converts the value entered into a number and stores it in the first of the member variables.

3. Add a new function to the CAddNumbers class to get the second number from the user. Specify the return type as void, name the function GetSecondNumber, and specify the access as public. Edit the function, adding the code in Listing 19.7.

Listing 19.7   The GetSecondNumber Function

```
void CAddNumbers::GetSecondNumber(void)
{
```

LISTING 19.7   continued

```
    String* strIn;

    // Prompt the user for a number
    Console::Write(S"Enter a number: ");
    // Read the input from the user
    strIn = Console::ReadLine();
    // Convert the input into a number
    m_iNumber2 = Int32::Parse(strIn);
}
```

ANALYSIS   This function uses the `Int32` class's `Parse` method to convert the user-entered string of digits into a number. Otherwise, this function is basically the same as one in Listing 19.6.

4. Add a new function to the `CAddNumbers` class to add the two numbers together and display the result. Specify the return type as `void`, name the function `AddNumbers`, and specify the access as `public`. Edit the function, adding the code in Listing 19.8.

LISTING 19.8   The `AddNumbers` Function

```
void CAddNumbers::AddNumbers(void)
{
    int iResult;
    String* strMsg;

    // Add the two numbers
    iResult = m_iNumber1 + m_iNumber2;
    // Prepare the first number entered to be displayed
    strMsg = String::Concat(S"First number entered: ",
            Convert::ToString(m_iNumber1));
    // Display the first number entered
    Console::WriteLine(strMsg);
    // Prepare the second number entered to be displayed
    strMsg = String::Concat(S"Second number entered: ",
            Convert::ToString(m_iNumber2));
    // Display the first number entered
    Console::WriteLine(strMsg);
    // Prepare the result to be displayed
    strMsg = String::Concat(S"Result of adding numbers: ",
            iResult.ToString());
    // Display the result of the addition
    Console::WriteLine(strMsg);
}
```

19

ANALYSIS   Listing 19.8 first adds together the two variables. Next, it displays the two numbers entered by the user. To convert these two numbers to strings, the `Convert`
class's `ToString` method passes the variable to be converted. It then builds the
string to display the result; however, we used the `Int32` class's `ToString` method to
show two different methods to convert from an integer to a string.

5. To finish the application, modify the main function, adding the boldfaced lines in
   Listing 19.9.

LISTING 19.9   The Modified Main Function

```
#include "stdafx.h"
#include "EnvironmentInfo.h"
#include "AddNumbers.h"

#using <mscorlib.dll>
#include <tchar.h>
using namespace System;

// This is the entry point for this application
int _tmain(void)
{
    // TODO: Please replace the sample code below with your own.
    CEnvironmentInfo* eiInfo = new CEnvironmentInfo;
    CAddNumbers* anNbrs = new CAddNumbers;

    // Show the current directory
    eiInfo->ShowCurDirectory();
    // Show the machine name
    eiInfo->ShowMachineName();
    // Show the OS version
    eiInfo->ShowOSVersion();
    // Show the user name
    eiInfo->ShowUserName();
    // Show the domain name
    eiInfo->ShowDomainName();
    // Show the CLR version
    eiInfo->ShowClrVersion();

    Console::WriteLine("");

    // Get the first number to add
    anNbrs->GetFirstNumber();
    // Get the second number to add
    anNbrs->GetSecondNumber();
    // Add the two numbers
    anNbrs->AddNumbers();
    return 0;
}
```

INPUT (appears beside `#include "AddNumbers.h"`)

INPUT (appears beside `CAddNumbers* anNbrs = new CAddNumbers;`)

INPUT (appears beside `Console::WriteLine("");`)

Now, if you compile and run your application, not only will it display information about your system, but it'll also request two numbers and add them together (see Figure 19.4).

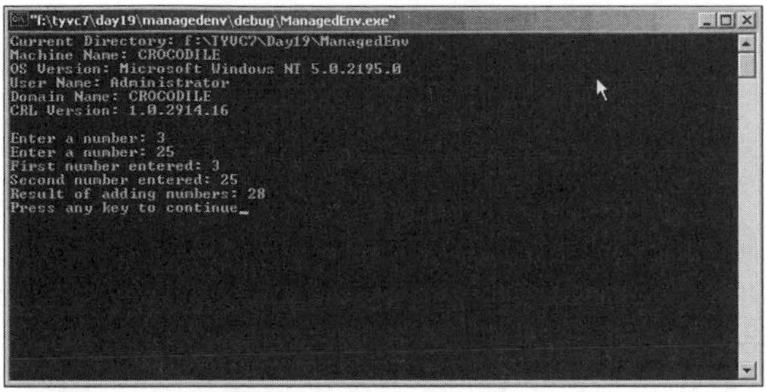

FIGURE 19.4

Displaying system information and adding two entered numbers.

Summary

Today you learned about how managed extensions for C++ can be used to create applications for the new Common Language Runtime that provides the platform portability aspect for Microsoft's .NET platform. You learned some of the new keywords, how to mark classes and structures for garbage collection, and how to use some of the CLR's built-in classes. You also learned how you can easily port your MFC applications over to run on the CLR, without having to make extensive code changes.

In the next two days, you'll learn how to use the Active Template Library (ATL) to construct components that can run on the server side of .NET applications, and how to put a managed C++ wrapper around these components. You'll also learn how to interact with components created in other CLR languages such as C# and Visual Basic.NET.

19

Q&A

Q. Why does building managed C++ applications feel like a step back in time to before all the tools and wizards to help build your applications were around?

A. The tools and wizards aren't available for helping you build managed C++ applications for a couple of reasons:

- Managed extensions for C++ were intended as a means of bringing existing applications and functionality to the .NET platform without having to rewrite the applications in a new language.

- ASP+ is the intended .NET tool for building user interfaces, relegating VB.NET, C#, and managed C++ to building server-side components. While this doesn't mean that you can't build GUI applications with these languages for the CLR, they are more intended for use on the server side. As such, a main reason for using C++ is for the native-executable speed. Although the CLR comes close to matching that speed, most developers will prefer to build their components in unmanaged C++, and then build a managed wrapper around the components for use with the CLR.

Q. How can I mix managed and unmanaged C++ in my applications?

A. In the same way that you use the project properties to mark the entire MFC project to be compiled for the CLR, you can mark individual files in the project. This enables you to mix parts of your application, marking some components to be managed, while keeping others as unmanaged. Usually, you'll want to add wrapper components in separate managed files, providing access to the unmanaged components by other CLR objects and applications. You'll learn how to do this in the next couple of days.

Workshop

The Workshop provides quiz questions to help solidify your understanding of the material covered and exercises to provide you with experience in using what you've learned. The answers to the quiz questions and exercises are provided in Appendix A, "Answers to Quiz Questions."

Quiz

1. How do you mark a class for garbage collection?
2. What two methods can you use to convert a managed string to an integer?
3. How do you mark a managed class or structure so that it doesn't have garbage collection performed on it?
4. What method do you use to print text for users in a DOS window?
5. How do you import a CLR DLL or object file for use in a managed C++ application?

Exercise

Modify today's application to allow users to specify whether to add or subtract the two numbers entered. *Hint:* You might want to use the System.String class's Equals method to perform the comparison.

DAY **20**

Building Components with ATL

In certain situations, using MFC to build applications or components just isn't appropriate. MFC is designed to make it easy to build GUI applications, but what if your application needs to run as a service, with no user interface? Or what about building business logic components that need to be called from multiple applications? What if you need to build a logic component that needs to be called from a Web page? These are all situations where using the Active Template Library (ATL) may be more appropriate than using MFC.

Today you'll learn about working with ATL to build components. Among the things that you'll learn today are

- How to determine when ATL may be the appropriate library to use
- The differences between ATL and MFC
- How ATL and Visual C++ relieve much of the drudgery of building COM components
- How you can build a component using ATL that can easily be wrapped with managed C++ so that it can be called from both managed and unmanaged applications

What Is ATL?

The Active Template Library (ATL) is a set of templates and classes designed for building components and services. The ATL doesn't provide any aid for drawing windows or graphics, and requires that most of your calls to services provided by Windows be made with the raw API calls. This makes it a less attractive tool for building GUI applications, but it has its advantages for building business logic components, because it doesn't carry around the overhead that MFC applications have.

ATL and COM

Several years ago, when Microsoft first came out with COM, there was only one way to create COM objects. That consisted of a lot of C/C++ code, a lot of effort, and an intimate knowledge of the Interface Definition Language (IDL). To say the least, it was complicated and took considerable effort. There were no tools and wizards to help.

Since that time, things have improved considerably. You can use MFC to build ActiveX controls, using the wizards provided to build all the IDL files needed to implement the COM interfaces. However, MFC isn't good at building COM components that don't have a user interface, or that need to be lightweight for use over the Internet. This is where ATL comes in.

Microsoft first created ATL several years ago for the purpose of enabling programmers to build lightweight ActiveX controls that were Internet-friendly (small). Microsoft also designed ATL in such a way to make it a good tool for building COM components that contained business logic, and didn't have any user interface. These components were ideal for loading into Microsoft's Transaction Server, COM+, or as extensions to Internet Information Server (IIS), Microsoft's Web server.

Now, by building ATL components that have the business logic separated from the COM interface, ATL is the perfect vehicle for creating dual-interface components that can be accessed via COM, or via CLR (Common Language Runtime) by .NET applications. You can use the ATL Wizards to define the COM interface and build the IDL files, and then you can easily create managed C++ wrappers to provide the CLR interface for the unmanaged component.

ATL Versus MFC

So, why choose ATL over MFC? Couldn't you build components using MFC? You can, but not without significant overhead that you might not want. MFC was designed for creating graphical objects and applications, not for components without a user-interface (although you can create them using MFC). Any object or application created using MFC requires mfc70.dll, a large DLL. You can choose to link the mfc70.dll in to your MFC application or component, eliminating the need to distribute the DLL, but that increases your component's size just as much.

> **Note**
>
> For previous editions of Visual C++, it was mfc42.dll that was required for use of any MFC applications. With the new edition, this has been updated to mfc70.dll, which is not backward-compatible with previous versions of MFC applications.

ATL was designed to be lightweight. Yes, it does have a runtime DLL that needs to be included with it, atl70.dll, but it's only a fraction of the size of mfc70.dll. The size difference in components created with MFC versus ATL makes ATL-based components much more Internet-friendly. However, the trade-off is that ATL doesn't abstract out any of the Win32 API functionality. This means that when you need to draw the user interface for the component, you have to make all the API calls, rather than rely on the MFC to do the work for you.

> **Note**
>
> Actually, ATL does have some helper templates for creating windows and dialogs. However, these templates are very slim in the functionality provided compared to the MFC classes for creating these same objects.

Another factor in the size issue is that, when you use MFC, you have to include the whole MFC library, even when you link it into your application (thus avoiding having to distribute the mfc70.dll). Because ATL is created using C++ templates, only what you use is linked into the application, keeping the size of your application or components down to what you actually use. ATL components still need a supporting DLL, atl70.dll, but it is much smaller than the MFC DLL.

20

C++ Sidebar: Working with Templates

In a sense, templates are like macros, only on a class level. They are a mechanism introduced as part of the C++ language, whereas macros were a holdover from C. Templates enable you to create a prototype class, with full functionality that can be used as a template for multiple classes of different data types.

An example of how this works could be the array classes from MFC. They all have the same functionality but work with different data types. You could implement a generic array class as a template, and then generate specific array classes to handle the different data types from the template.

To see how this works, implement your template class preceding the class declaration with the keyword template, followed by the key data elements needed for implementing specific instances of the class enclosed in angled brackets (<>) listed as parameters. Starting on the next line, you have a normal class declaration using the template parameter names, which is replaced with the actual variables or values when an actual class is derived from the template. This might look like the following:

```
template<class Tdatatype, int iMaxEntries>
class SimpleArray
{
private:
    int m_iCurrentNbr;
public:
    SimpleArray() { m_iCurrentNbr = 0;}
    ~SimpleArray() {}
    BOOL Add(Tdatatype value);
    Tdatatype Get(int iPos);
private:
    Tdatatype m_array[iMaxEntries];
};
```

This template class declaration is followed by the member function implementations, using the same format as follows:

```
template<class Tdatatype, int iMaxEntries>
BOOL SimpleArray<class Tdatatype, int iMaxEntries>::Add(Tdatatype value)
{
    if (m_iCurrentNbr < iMaxEntries)
    {
        m_array[m_iCurrentNbr++] = value;
        return TRUE;
    }
    return FALSE;
}

template<class Tdatatype, int iMaxEntries>
Tdatatype SimpleArray<class Tdatatype, int iMaxEntries>::Get(int iPos)
{
    if (iPos < m_iCurrentNbr)
        return m_array[iPos];
    return NULL;
}
```

When you need to create an actual class from this template, you just declare an instance of the class in your code, passing all the necessary parameters:

```
SimpleArray<long, 25> saMyLongArray;
```

You could even use it with your own classes, depending on how you implemented the template. For instance, the preceding sample template wouldn't work with a custom class of your own, but it would work with a pointer to your class, as follows:

```
SimpleArray<&CMyClass, 25> saMyClassArray;
```

You can also create function templates, if all you need is a simple function and not a whole class. The function templates work the same as the class templates, only for a single function. You can create your function as follows:

```
template<class Tdatatype>
void DoSomething(Tdatatype value, int iOtherParam)
{
    for (int i = 0; i < iOtherParam; i++)
    {
        // Do something to the value
    }
}
```

The function template creates the actual function when it's called in your code, replacing the data type placeholder with the data type of the value you pass to it:

```
int iMyInt;
double dbMyDouble;

DoSomething(iMyInt, 4);
DoSomething(dbMyDouble, 8);
```

C++ Sidebar: The Standard Template Library

As substantial as the class library for the ATL might be, sometimes you might still want or need to use something that isn't included. It just so happens that another substantial template library is available for use—the Standard Template Library (STL).

The STL is an extensive library of templates originally created by Hewlett-Packard and has since become part of the ISO C++ standard. It's far too extensive to cover in any depth here; there are plenty of books dedicated to using it. Table 20.1 lists some of the key templates included.

TABLE 20.1 Some Key Class Templates in the STL

Class	Description
allocator	Allocates memory for objects. This is the default `allocator` object for most STL templates.
iterator	Traverses arrays, linked lists, queues, and other memory structures. There are actually several `iterator` templates with different navigation characteristics, so you would be well advised to study the different `iterator` class templates to determine which would be appropriate for your needs.

20

TABLE 20.1 continued

Class	Description
vector	Performs functionality that closely resembles the array classes in MFC. The vector classes create a dynamically allocated and grown collection of objects that can be added to at the end of the collection but can easily be accessed randomly.
deque	Performs functionality similar to the vector class template, only you can add elements to both the end and the beginning of the collection.
queue	Implements an object queue, where new objects can be added to the end, and then objects can be removed from the front.
priority_queue	Implements a queue where elements can be ranked and given different priorities. Elements in the queue will be removed according to their priority.
list	Implements a list of objects where elements in the list can be added, removed, or accessed at any point in the list, not just at the end or beginning of the list.
map	Implements a collection of elements where each element has an associated key. Each key value must be unique and can occur in the map only once.
multimap	Works similarly to the map class template except that it allows multiple keys to have the same value.
set	Similar to the map class template, only there is no associated value, just the key.
multiset	Similar to the set class template, only it allows duplicate keys within the set.
stack	Implements a stack, where elements are added to and removed from the collection on the same end. This means that only the last element added to the stack can be removed (elements are removed in the opposite order from how they were added).
basic_string	Implements string functionality. This class template has been typedef'd as the string (ASCII) and wstring (UNICODE) types that can be used without touching the template class.

ATL Note: Debugging Macros

Just as the MFC class library isn't available for use in ATL projects, neither are the debugging macros that you learned back on Day 2. Instead, the ATL class library has its own series of macros that work the same as the MFC equivalents:

- The ATLASSERT macro verifies assumptions in your code. You pass it a Boolean expression that should always evaluate to TRUE, and it will alert you, while in debug mode, if the expression is ever not true. This is the same as the ASSERT macro in MFC applications.

- The ATLTRACE macro prints messages to an open debug output window. You can use standard C string formatting expressions in the parameters to this macro. This is the same as the TRACE macro in MFC applications.

- The ATLTRACENOTIMPL macro traces calls to unimplemented functions. You pass the function name to this macro, and it sends the string "*functionname* is not implemented" to the dump device.

Building a Simple ATL Component

Today, the example that you will build is a business object that calculates sales tax on purchased items. This component takes in a category for the purchased items, and the cost of the items being purchased, and calculates the amount of tax due. You initially wrap this component in a COM interface and build a simple C++ client to call the component. Finally, you add a managed wrapper around the component, mixing managed and unmanaged code, and build a managed C++ client to call the component.

The key to creating a dual-interface component like this is to keep the actual business logic separate from the interfaces. To do this, you place the tax calculation code into a generic class within the ATL component. You then add a simple ATL class to act as an external interface for the business logic class. Finally, you add a managed class to act as a second external interface for the business logic class.

Creating the ATL Component

The first thing to be done in building today's example will be to create the ATL project. This is a standard ATL project, so to create the project shell, follow these steps:

1. Start a new project. Select ATL Project from the C++ templates, and name the project TaxCalculations. Click OK to start the ATL Project Wizard.

2. In the ATL Project Wizard, click Finish to create the project using the default settings.

Creating the Business Logic Class

Now that you've created the project shell, you need to create the business logic class. You'll place this class in its own namespace and provide it with a single method for calculating the tax due. To create this class, follow these steps:

1. Add a generic C++ class to the TaxCalculations project following the steps used in previous days. Name the class CTaxCalculator.

2. Open the header file for the CTaxCalculator class and modify it as shown in Listing 20.1, adding a couple of standard C header includes, and encapsulating the class in a namespace called TaxCalcs.

20

LISTING 20.1 The `CTaxCalculator` Class Declaration

```
#pragma once
        #include <windows.h>
        #include <stdio.h>

namespace TaxCalcs
{
    class CTaxCalculator
    {
    public:
        CTaxCalculator(void);
        ~CTaxCalculator(void);
    };
}
```

INPUT

Namespaces are a conceptual means of organizing classes and objects into groupings of like functionality. While not necessary for this example, it's a concept that is used extensively in the .NET object library, as well as the C++ Standard Template Library (STL), so it's a good idea to get a little practice working with namespaces.

3. Open the source code file for the `CTaxCalculator` class and enclose it in the namespace `TaxCalcs` as in Listing 20.2.

LISTING 20.2 The `CTacCalculator` Class Implementation

```
#include "StdAfx.h"
#include "taxcalculator.h"

namespace TaxCalcs
{
    CTaxCalculator::CTaxCalculator(void)
    {
    }

    CTaxCalculator::~CTaxCalculator(void)
    {
    }
}
```

INPUT

INPUT

4. In the Class View pane, expand the tree and the `TaxCalcs` namespace to expose the `CTaxCalculator` class. Add a new method to the class, using the steps that you used in previous days.

5. Specify the return type for the new function as `BOOL`, name the function `CalculateTaxes`, specify the access as `public`, and add three parameters. Specify the type of the first parameter as `float`, and the name as `fPurchaseAmt`. Specify

the type of the second parameter as wchar_t*, and the name as wszCategory.
Specify the type of the third parameter as float*, and the name as pfTaxAmt. Click
Finish to add the method to your class.

6. Edit the new method, adding the code in Listing 20.3.

LISTING 20.3 The CalculateTaxes Function

```
BOOL TaxCalcs::CTaxCalculator::CalculateTaxes(float fPurchaseAmt,
         wchar_t* wszCategory, float* pfTaxAmt)
{
    // Declare the array of tax categories
    static const wchar_t *wszCategories[] =
             {L"food", L"clothing", L"music"};
    // Declare the array of tax rates
    static const float fRates[] = {0.0725, 0.0835, 0.081};
    // Loop through the categories
    for (int i = 0; i < 3; i++)
    {
        // Is this the category purchased?
        if (wcscmp(wszCategory, wszCategories[i]) == 0)
        {
            // Yes, calculate the taxes due
            *pfTaxAmt = fPurchaseAmt * fRates[i];
            // Return TRUE
            return TRUE;
        }
    }
    // Couldn't find the category purchased, return FALSE
    return FALSE;
}
```

ANALYSIS Because COM methods return a success/failure status, you have to return the calculation results through pointers passed in as parameters. Notice that all the strings used in this example are UNICODE strings, as COM is all UNICODE internally. Also, you are using a standard C string comparison function, wcscmp, to perform the string comparison. The C string comparison functions return 0 if the two strings match, or return either a negative or positive value that is the result of the comparison algorithm used to compare the two strings.

20

Tip

Normally, you would not allocate the categories and tax rates in the function itself as in this example. You would want to load them in on the class initialization from some form of dynamic storage, like a database or configuration file. They are implemented as arrays in the preceding function for purposes of brevity in the example.

Adding the COM Interface

The next step that you need to perform is to add the COM interface for your ATL component. You do this by adding a simple ATL class which contains a single method that mirrors the method of the class you already created. To add this class, follow these steps:

1. Add a new class to the TaxCalculations project, using the same steps you used in previous days. Select the ATL node on the left of the New Class dialog, and select ATL Simple Object in the templates on the right. Click Open to add the new class.

2. Specify the class name as GetTaxForPurchase in the Short Name field. Notice that this New Class dialog fills in the names for the COM interfaces as well as the file names. Click Finish to create the class.

3. Open the GetTaxForPurchase header file. Add an include for the TaxCalculation.h header file for your business logic class, as in Listing 20.4.

LISTING 20.4   The GetTaxForPurchase Header File

```
// GetTaxForPurchase.h : Declaration of the CGetTaxForPurchase

#pragma once
#include "resource.h"        // main symbols
      #include "TaxCalculator.h"

// IGetTaxForPurchase
```

4. Scroll down the header file and find the class declaration. Notice that the class constructor is implemented as an inline function within the header file. Add a private member pointer to your CTaxCalculation class just before the class constructor, and initialize it to point to a new instance of the CTaxCalculation class in the constructor, as in Listing 20.5. Delete the allocated pointer in the FinalRelease function, further down in the class declaration, to prevent memory leaks.

LISTING 20.5   The CGetTaxForPurchase Class Declaration

```
class ATL_NO_VTABLE CGetTaxForPurchase :
    public IGetTaxForPurchase
{
      private:
          TaxCalcs::CTaxCalculator* m_pTaxCalc;
public:
    CGetTaxForPurchase()
    {
          // Initialize the pointer to the calculation module
          m_pTaxCalc = new TaxCalcs::CTaxCalculator();
```

LISTING 20.5   continued

```
}
DECLARE_PROTECT_FINAL_CONSTRUCT()

HRESULT FinalConstruct()
{
    return S_OK;
}

void FinalRelease()
{
    delete m_pTaxCalc;
}
```

The ATL_NO_VTABLE macro that you see used in the class declaration is used to suppress the initialization of the virtual function table in the class construction and destructor. The virtual function table is a table of pointers to all virtual functions in a class. By suppressing the initialization of this table, the class is made even smaller and lighter than normal.

5. You need to add the exposed method that clients will use to access the business logic class in your component. Add a new method to the IGetTaxForPurchase interface. Be sure to add the method to the interface, and not to the class.

6. Specify the method name as GetPurchaseTaxes. You'll add three parameters to match the three parameters that have to be passed to the business logic class:

   - For the first parameter, select FLOAT for the parameter type, enter **fPurchaseAmt** for the parameter name, select the In check box, and click Add.

   - For the second parameter, select BSTR* for the parameter type, enter **bstrCategory** for the parameter name, select the In check box, and click Add.

   - For the third parameter, select FLOAT* for the parameter type, enter **pfTax** for the parameter name, select the Out check box, and click Add.

   The Add Method Wizard should look like Figure 20.1. Click Finish to add the method to the interface.

7. Edit the method, adding the code in Listing 20.6.

LISTING 20.6   The GetPurchaseTaxes Method

```
STDMETHODIMP CGetTaxForPurchase::GetPurchaseTaxes(FLOAT fPurchaseAmt,
            BSTR* bstrCategory, FLOAT* pfTax)
{
    // TODO: Add your implementation code here
```

20

LISTING 20.6 continued

```
        // Do we have a valid pointer to the variable
        // into which the tax due will be placed?
        if (!pfTax)
            return S_FALSE;
        // Calculate the taxes due
        if (m_pTaxCalc->CalculateTaxes(fPurchaseAmt, (wchar_t*)*bstrCategory,
                    pfTax))
            return S_OK;
        else
            return S_FALSE;
    }
```

FIGURE 20.1

The Add Method Wizard.

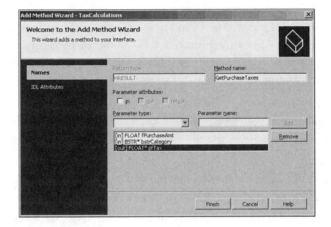

Creating the C++ Client

At this point, you should be able to compile your component, but you won't be able to use it yet. For this, you need to create a client application. The client application is a simple console application that passes a category string and purchase amount, and then displays the tax amount to charge that has been returned. To create the client application, follow these steps:

1. In the Solution Explorer pane, select and right-click the solution node at the top of the tree. Then select Add, New Project from the context menu.

2. Select Win32 Project from the Visual C++ Project templates. Name the project TaxCalcClient. Click OK.

3. In the Win32 Application Wizard, select the Application Settings area and specify Console application for the application type. Click Finish to create the project.

4. Open the TaxCalcClient.cpp code file. Edit it, adding the include for the atlbase.h header file, and import the DLL created by your ATL project, specifying the correct path for your project, as in Listing 20.7.

LISTING 20.7 The Client Includes and Import

```
// TaxCalcClient.cpp : Defines the entry point for the console application.
//

#include "stdafx.h"
#include "atlbase.h"
// TODO: Replace the path in the import directive with the correct
// path for your project
#import "..\TaxCalculations\Debug\TaxCalculations.dll"
```

INPUT

5. Edit the main function, adding the code in Listing 20.8.

LISTING 20.8 The Client Main Function

```
int _tmain(int argc, _TCHAR* argv[])
{
    // Startup the COM environment
    CoInitialize(NULL);
    {
        // Use the namespace of the Tax Calculations module
        using namespace TaxCalculations;
        // Get the interface pointer for the tax calculations module
        IGetTaxForPurchasePtr pGetTax(L"TaxCalculations.GetTaxForPurchase");

        // Create the string for the category being purchased
        CComBSTR bstrCat1(OLESTR("clothing"));
        float fPurchaseAmt, fTaxAmt;

        // Specify the purchase amount
        fPurchaseAmt = 45.0;
        // Get the amount of taxes to collect
        if (pGetTax->GetPurchaseTaxes(fPurchaseAmt, &bstrCat1, &fTaxAmt)
                == S_OK)
        {
            // add in the string conversion macros
            USES_CONVERSION;
            // Display the category being purchased
            printf("%s\n", W2A(bstrCat1));
            // Display the purchase amount
            printf("Purchase Amount = %9.2f\n", fPurchaseAmt);
            // Display the tax due
            printf("          Tax = %9.2f\n", fTaxAmt);
            // Display the total amount
            printf("    Total Due = %9.2f\n", fPurchaseAmt + fTaxAmt);
        }
    }
    // Shut down the COM environment
```

20

LISTING 20.8 continued

```
        CoUninitialize();
        return 0;
    }
```

ANALYSIS The code in Listing 20.8 first initializes the COM environment with the `CoInitialize` function call. At the other end of the main function, it shuts down the COM environment by using the `CoUninitialize` function.

By using the namespace for the component that you created earlier, you create an interface pointer for the COM interface you implemented. Everything between the `CoInitialize` and `CoUninitialize` functions is enclosed within braces so that the interface pointer is released by going out of scope before the COM environment is shut down. Next, a `CComBSTR` string specifies the category for the tax rate to be charged. `CComBSTR` is an ATL class that encapsulates the `BSTR` string type. After the function returns, you include the `USES_CONVERSION` macro to include the `BSTR` conversion macros, and then call the `W2A` macro to convert the category string to an ASCII string for displaying on the console. Because this is a DOS mode application, you use the C `printf` function to output text strings on the console window for users to see.

Before you try to compile and run the client application, you need to make a few configuration changes. To make these changes, follow these steps:

1. In the Solution Explorer pane, select and right-click the `TaxCalcClient` project. Select Properties from the context menu.

2. In the Configuration combo box, select All Configurations.

3. On the left side of the project properties dialog, select C/C++, General. Select the Additional Include Directories, and then enter **$(SolutionDir)\$(ConfigurationName)**. Click OK to close the Properties dialog box.

What you just configured was to include the directory where the current ATL component is being compiled in the list of directories being searched for header files, library files, and DLLs. The first half of this string, `$(SolutionDir)`, specifies the directory where the solution file is located. Because this project started with the ATL component project, that project directory is where the solution file also is located. The second half of the string, `$(ConfigurationName)`, specifies the directory matching the current build configuration. So, this entire string specifies to search the Debug directory under the ATL project directory for the ATL DLL when in debug mode, and the Release directory for the DLL when in release mode.

The last thing that you need to do before trying to compile and run the client application is to specify the client as the startup project. This tells Visual Studio that, when you select Start from the Debug menu, the client application should run. Follow these steps:

1. Select and right-click the TaxCalcClient project in the Solution Explorer pane. Select Set as Startup Project from the context menu.

2. Compile and run your project. You should see a DOS window displaying the amount purchased and the tax to charge (see Figure 20.2).

FIGURE 20.2

Running the client application.

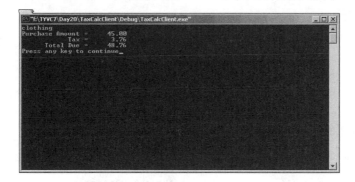

 Tip

If you start the project normally, using either the F5 key or the Debug, Start menu, the program will execute and close, preventing you from seeing the output in the console window (unless you look quickly). If you start the project without debugging (Ctrl + F5, or Debug, Start without debugging menu), it will stop after the application has completed, waiting for you to press a key to close the window and exit the application.

Adding the Managed C++ Wrapper

Now you need to add the managed wrapper around your business logic class. You'll add a new class to the ATL project, configuring the new class to be managed, and duplicate the functionality of the COM interface in this new, managed class. Follow these steps:

1. In the Class View pane, select the TaxCalculations project and add a new generic C++ class using the method you have been using for the past several days.

2. Specify the class name as MgdGetTaxForPurchase and click Finish to add it.

3. Open the MgdGetTaxForPurchase.h header file and modify it as shown in Listing 20.9. Include the header for the business logic class. Specify that the CLR mscorlib.dll should be used and configure the class as a garbage collected class. Add the same pointer to the business logic class that you added to the COM interface class. Finally, remove the declaration for the class destructor.

20

LISTING 20.9   The `MgdGetTaxForPurchase` Header File

```
#pragma once
#include "TaxCalculator.h"
#using <mscorlib.dll>
using namespace System;

public __gc class MgdGetTaxForPurchase
{
private:
    TaxCalcs::CTaxCalculator* m_pTaxCalc;
public:
    MgdGetTaxForPurchase(void);
};
```

4. Open the MgdGetTaxForPurchase.cpp source code file and modify the class constructor to initialize the class pointer, as in Listing 20.10.

LISTING 20.10   The `MgdGetTaxForPurchase` Class Constructor

```
MgdGetTaxForPurchase::MgdGetTaxForPurchase(void)
{
    // Initialize the pointer to the calculation module
    m_pTaxCalc = new TaxCalcs::CTaxCalculator();
}
```

5. Add a new function to this new class. The class is no longer visible in the Class View pane, so you can't add the function using the method you've used up until this point. Instead, reopen the header file, and add the function declaration, as in Listing 20.11.

LISTING 20.11   The Modified `MgdGetTaxForPurchase` Header File

```
#pragma once
#include "TaxCalculator.h"
#using <mscorlib.dll>
using namespace System;

public __gc class MgdGetTaxForPurchase
{
private:
    TaxCalcs::CTaxCalculator* m_pTaxCalc;
public:
    MgdGetTaxForPurchase(void);
    BOOL GetPurchaseTaxes(float fPurchaseAmt,
            System::String* pstrCategory, float* pfTax);
};
```

6. Reopen the source code file for the MgdGetTaxForPurchase class and add the definition for the new function, as in Listing 20.12.

LISTING 20.12 The GetPurchaseTaxes Function Definition

```
BOOL MgdGetTaxForPurchase::GetPurchaseTaxes(float fPurchaseAmt,
            System::String* pstrCategory, float* pfTax)
{
    wchar_t *pCat;
    int iLen;

    // Do we have a valid pointer to the variable into which
    // the tax due will be placed?
    if (!pfTax)
        return FALSE;
    // Convert the category from a managed string to a wchar_t
    __wchar_t pCategory __gc[] = pstrCategory->ToCharArray();
    iLen = pstrCategory->get_Length();
    pCat = new wchar_t[iLen + 1];
    for (int i = 0; i < iLen; i++)
    {
        pCat[i] = pCategory[i];
    }
    pCat[i] = NULL;
    // Calculate the taxes due
    if (m_pTaxCalc->CalculateTaxes(fPurchaseAmt, pCat, pfTax))
        return TRUE;
    else
        return FALSE;
}
```

You next need to configure one class in your ATL project to be compiled as managed C++. The first of these configuration changes is to mark the managed class as compiled for the CLR, with default debugging support. Second, you have to turn off use of precompiled headers for the entire project, as well as change the debug information format to just the program database. To make these configuration changes, follow these steps:

1. In the Solution Explorer pane, select and right-click the MgdGetTaxForPurchase.cpp file. Select Properties from the context menu.

2. In the Configuration combo box, select All Configurations so that the configuration changes you make will be applied for all build configurations, not just the current one.

3. On the left side of the Properties dialog, select C/C++, General, and then on the right side, for the Compile As Managed entry, select Assembly Support (/clr).

20

4. On the left side of the Properties dialog, select Code Generation. On the right side, for the Enable Minimal Rebuild entry, set it to No. For the Basic Runtime Checks, set it to Default.

5. Click the Apply button to apply these configuration changes and keep the Properties dialog open.

6. With the Properties dialog still open, click the TaxCalculations project node in the Solutions Explorer pane.

7. On the left side of the Properties dialog, select Precompiled Headers. On the right side of the dialog, set the Create/Use Precompiled Header entry to Not Using Precompiled Headers.

8. On the left side of the Properties dialog, select General. On the right side of the dialog, in the Debug Information Format entry, set it to Program Database (/Zi).

9. Click the Apply button to apply these configuration changes and keep the Properties dialog open.

10. With the Properties dialog still open, click the Stdafx.cpp file node under the TaxCalculations project in the Solutions Explorer pane.

11. On the left side of the Properties dialog, select Precompiled Headers. On the right side of the dialog, set the Create/Use Precompiled Header entry to Not Using Precompiled Headers.

> **Note**
>
> Precompiled headers are where the header files used in a project are stored in a file in a compiled form. This speeds up the time it takes to build the project as all the code contained in the project header files no longer needs compiling, only linking in to the project. Unfortunately, precompiled headers are stored in a binary form that can't be shared between managed and unmanaged C++ modules. As a result, in mixed mode projects, you can't use precompiled headers.

12. Click OK to apply the configuration changes and close the Properties dialog.

You should now be able to compile your project. If you run the project, you'll still be running the COM client, enabling you to see that the COM interface is still working.

Creating the Managed C++ Client

The last step in building today's example application is to create the managed C++ client. This client duplicates the functionality of the COM client, only as a managed C++ application, using the managed wrapper interface to your ATL component. To create this client, follow these steps:

1. In the Solution Explorer pane, select and right-click the solution node at the top of the tree. Then select Add, New Project from the context menu.

2. Select Managed C++ Project from the Visual C++ Project templates. Name the project MgdTaxCalcClient. Click OK.

3. Open the MgdTaxCalcClient.cpp file and make the additions shown in Listing 20.13.

LISTING 20.13 The GetPurchaseTaxes Function Definition

```
// This is the main project file for VC++ application project
// generated using an Application Wizard.

#include "stdafx.h"

#using <mscorlib.dll>
#using "TaxCalculations.dll"
#include <tchar.h>
using namespace System;

// This is the entry point for this application
int _tmain(void)
{
    // TODO: Please replace the sample code below with your own.
    // Get the interface pointer for the tax calculations module
    MgdGetTaxForPurchase* pGetTax = new MgdGetTaxForPurchase();

    float fPurchaseAmt, fTaxAmt, fTotalDue;

    // Create the string for the category being purchased
    String* pstrCategory = L"clothing";

    // Specify the purchase amount
    fPurchaseAmt = 45.0;
    // Get the amount of taxes to collect
    if (pGetTax->GetPurchaseTaxes(fPurchaseAmt, pstrCategory, &fTaxAmt))
    {
        // Calculate the total due
        fTotalDue = fPurchaseAmt + fTaxAmt;
        // Display the category being purchased
        Console::WriteLine(pstrCategory);
        // Display the purchase amount
        Console::Write("Purchase Amount = ");
        Console::WriteLine(fPurchaseAmt.ToString("c"));
        // Display the tax due
        Console::Write("            Tax = ");
        Console::WriteLine(fTaxAmt.ToString("c"));
        // Display the total amount
        Console::Write("      Total Due = ");
```

INPUT

INPUT

20

LISTING 20.13   continued

```
        Console::WriteLine(fTotalDue.ToString("c"));
    }
    return 0;
}
```

With the ToString method of the managed numeric variables, you passed a letter *c* as the only argument. This specified the formatting to use when converting the value to a string. The possible formatting values for this method are listed in Table 20.2.

TABLE 20.2   .NET ToString Numeric Formats

Format Character	Description
c, C	Currency format.
d, D	Decimal format.
e, E	Exponential (scientific) format.
f, F	Fixed-point format.
g, G	General format.
n, N	Number format.
r, R	Roundtrip format (guarantees that if the strings are converted back into numbers, the numbers will have the same value as the original numbers).
x, X	Hexadecimal format.

Finally, you need to configure the managed C++ client project for use in the ATL solution. You need to turn off the use of precompiled headers, and add a pre-build event to copy the ATL DLL into the build directory for the managed client. Finally, you need to specify that the Visual Studio compiler should look in the output directory for resolving any #using references. This is all so that the compiler can find the ATL DLL specified in the #using directive that you added to the managed client code.

To make these configuration changes, follow these steps:

1. In the Solution Explorer pane, select and right-click the MgdTaxCalcClient project. Select Properties from the context menu.

2. In the Configuration combo box, select All Configurations so that the configuration changes you make will be applied for all the build configurations, not just the current one.

3. On the left side of the Properties dialog, select C/C++, Precompiled Headers. On the right side of the dialog, set the Create/Use Precompiled Header entry to Not Using Precompiled Headers.

4. On the left side of the Properties dialog, select Build Events, Pre-Build Event. On the right side of the dialog, in the Command Line entry, enter

```
copy "$(SolutionDir)\$(ConfigurationName)\TaxCalculations.dll"
➥$(ConfigurationName)
```

This copies the DLL to the build directory for the managed client before building the managed client.

5. On the left side of the Properties dialog, select C/C++, General. On the right side of the dialog, in the Resolve #using References entry, enter **$(outdir)**. This tells the compiler to look in the build output directory for resolving any #using references in the project.

6. Click OK to apply the changes and close the Properties dialog.

7. Select and right-click the MgdTaxCalcClient project in the Solution Explorer pane. Select Set as Startup Project from the context menu.

At this point, you should be able to compile and run the managed C++ client for your ATL component. When you run the managed client, you should see a console window with the results of the call to the ATL component, as shown in Figure 20.3.

FIGURE 20.3

Running the managed client application.

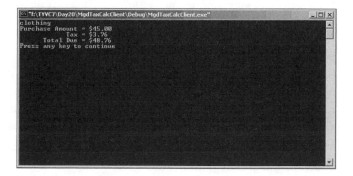

Summary

Today you learned about the Active Template Library, and how you can use it to build lightweight COM components to use with applications built in many different programming languages. You also learned how, if you keep the business logic separate from the COM interfaces in your ATL components, you can create a managed C++ wrapper around the component, making it available for use by any CLR application regardless of the language used to build the application. This provides a unique combination that can be leveraged to take advantage of the speed and capabilities of unmanaged C++ combined with the .NET architecture, enabling you to make these unmanaged components

20

available to any application on any platform. The flexibility of this approach allows you to decide which is more desirable for any component—managed or unmanaged execution?

To be honest, today was no more than an introduction to the world of ATL programming. This is an extensive topic on which entire books have been written. If this is an area of programming that you want to explore further, you would be well advised to pick up a book such as *Sams Teach Yourself ATL Programming in 21 Days* by Kenn Scribner (ISBN 0-672-31867-9).

Q&A

Q. When adding the parameters for the COM interface method, what were the check boxes (in, out, retval) above where the parameters were added used for?

A. Those check boxes added the direction for each parameter in the IDL definition of the COM interface. If you examine the IDL language in the header file for the COM interface class, you'll find the interface definition of the method contains `[in]` in front of the parameters that you checked the in box on, and `[out]` on the parameters that you checked the out box on. This specifies the direction and purpose for each of these parameters in the method. `[in]` specifies that a parameter is passed in to the method. `[out]` specifies that the parameter is replaced with a result value in the method that needs to be returned to the calling function. You can have both in and out specified for a parameter, signaling that the parameter's value is imported both when the method is being called, and when returning from the method. If you checked the retval box, this parameter signals that this parameter will be returned as the method result instead of the success or failure indicator.

Q. When I modified the managed interface wrapper, why did the class disappear from the Class View pane?

A. This is because the project was created as an unmanaged project. As such, it doesn't understand the managed C++ keywords used in the class declaration for the managed wrapper class. Any class, structure, or function that Visual Studio doesn't understand within the context of the project, it won't display in the Class View pane.

Workshop

The Workshop provides quiz questions to help solidify your understanding of the material covered and exercises to provide you with experience in using what you've learned. The answers to the quiz questions and exercises are provided in Appendix A, "Answers to Quiz Questions."

Quiz

1. What is a C++ class template?

2. What standard library of templates is available for use in any C++ application?

3. What is the key to creating an ATL component that you can provide with a managed C++ wrapper so that it can have both a COM and CLR interface?

4. Why do you have to turn off the use of precompiled headers after you add the managed wrapper to the project?

Exercise

Add a second method to your ATL class to return the tax rate for the specified category. Modify both interfaces for this new method, and modify both clients to request and display the tax rate.

20

DAY 21

Interacting with Visual Basic and C# Components

Something that Microsoft has been proclaiming as one of the benefits of the .NET platform and the CLR since the first announcement has been the ease and capability of interacting with objects created in other languages. Sure, with COM you could already do this, but that required creating COM objects in the various languages, and jumping through the hoops that COM forced you through. So the question remains, just how easy and effortless is it to interact with objects created in other languages? That's what you'll be exploring and learning about today. Today you'll learn how to

- Create managed C++ components that can be called from C# and VB.NET applications
- Call VB.NET and C# components from managed C++ applications
- Call CLR components from an unmanaged application

Mixing Languages: Realizing the Promise of the CLR

Yesterday you learned how you can create a COM component through ATL, and then wrap that component in a managed C++ wrapper to make it available to other CLR applications or objects. That provides you a path to making unmanaged C++ objects available for use in applications created with other CLR applications, but how does it really work? And can you go the other way, using .NET objects created in other languages in unmanaged C++ applications?

The quick answer is yes, you can use other .NET objects in unmanaged C++ applications, and you can create managed objects that can be used in other .NET languages. Although using objects created in managed C++ (or wrapped with managed C++) is much easier in other .NET languages, it's still possible to take it the other way, and use objects created in other .NET languages in both managed and unmanaged C++ applications.

Accessing and Using Managed C++ Objects in C# and VB.NET

Accessing objects created in other languages in C# and VB.NET projects is really very simple. If you've used previous versions of Visual Basic, you probably know how to add references to COM objects so that you can use those objects in your project. With VB.NET and C#, it's basically the same process that enables you to use other CLR objects, regardless of what language was used to create the objects, including managed C++.

When you create a C# (pronounced C-sharp, taken from musical notation) or VB.NET project in the Solution Explorer pane under the project node, you'll find a node labeled References. If you select and right-click this node, on the context menu you'll find the option Add Reference, which will open the Add Reference dialog (see Figure 21.1).

On the .NET page, you'll find the various registered .NET objects available for use in your application. On the COM page, you'll find all the COM objects registered on your computer, including the component you created yesterday (assuming that you did create the example application yesterday). On the Projects page, you'll find a list of projects in the current solution, plus you can browse to locate other objects in other projects.

After you select an object to reference, click the Select button to add it to the list of referenced objects in the bottom portion of the dialog. If you need to remove an object reference, select it in the bottom portion and click the Remove button. After you add references to all the objects you need, click OK to add all those objects as nodes below the References folder on the Solution Explorer pane.

FIGURE 21.1

The Add Reference dialog.

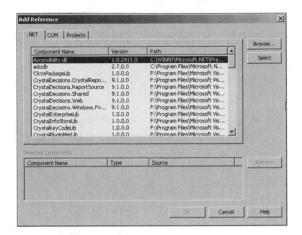

After you add references to the objects, you can freely include them in your VB.NET or C# code. For instance, if you added a reference to the component that you created yesterday into a C# project, you would use it as follows:

```
MgdGetTaxForPurchase pGetTax = new MgdGetTaxForPurchase();

if (pGetTax.GetPurchaseTaxes(fPurchaseAmt, pstrCategory, ref fTaxAmt))
...
```

If you're using the component in a VB.NET application, you'd use it as follows:

```
Dim pGetTax as MgdGetTaxForPurchase

pGetTax = New MgdGetTaxForPurchase()
if (pGetTax.GetPurchaseTaxes(fPurchaseAmt, pstrCategory, byref fTaxAmt))
...
```

Now, if you go back to yesterday's example and try to create C# and VB.NET clients for the component, you'll find that these don't quite work correctly. A few changes in yesterday's managed C++ wrapper need to be made before you can use it in C# or VB.NET applications:

- The amount of taxes to be calculated should be returned as a result, not passed in as a parameter.
- With the `float` variables, you need to use `Single` variable types in VB.NET. Another option is to use `double` variables instead of `float`.

After making these changes, your C# code would look like this:

```
MgdGetTaxForPurchase pGetTax = new MgdGetTaxForPurchase();

fTaxAmt = pGetTax.GetPurchaseTaxes(fPurchaseAmt, pstrCategory);
...
```

21

And the VB.NET code would look like this:

```
Dim pGetTax as MgdGetTaxForPurchase

pGetTax = New MgdGetTaxForPurchase()
sgTaxAmt = pGetTax.GetPurchaseTaxes(sgPurchaseAmt, pstrCategory)
...
```

The changes you need to make to your managed C++ wrapper look like the following:

```
float MgdGetTaxForPurchase::GetPurchaseTaxes(float fPurchaseAmt,
            System::String* pstrCategory)
{
    wchar_t *pCat;
    int iLen;
    float fTax;

    // Convert the category from a BSTR to a wchar_t
    __wchar_t pCategory __gc[] = pstrCategory->ToCharArray();
    iLen = pstrCategory->get_Length();
    pCat = new wchar_t[iLen + 1];
    for (int i = 0; i < iLen; i++)
    {
        pCat[i] = pCategory[i];
    }
    pCat[i] = NULL;
    // Calculate the taxes due
    if (m_pTaxCalc->CalculateTaxes(fPurchaseAmt, pCat, &fTax))
        return fTax;
    else
        return 0.0;
}
```

Accessing and Using C# and VB.NET Objects in Managed C++

Turning around the equation and trying to access objects created in C# and VB.NET from managed C++ applications is basically the same as the method you used yesterday to access the managed C++ wrapper around the COM object. You place a #using directive near the top of the source code, copy the DLL (or other object file that contains the objects) into the output directory, and then tell the compiler to use the output directory for resolving #using directives.

The biggest difference in the configuration is, if you are working with C# and VB.NET components that are part of the same project, you need to add a bin directory between the component project directory and the configuration name. For instance, if yesterday's component had been created by using C# instead ATL and managed C++, in the Pre-Build event command, instead of entering the command you did enter, you would enter the following:

```
copy "$(SolutionDir)\bin\$(ConfigurationName)\ProjectName.DLL"
➥ $(ConfigurationName)
```

The same string would have been entered if the component had been created using VB.NET. What this pre-build event does is make a copy of the DLL in which the component is packaged to the output directory of the client project. This is done before the client project is built, so that the client project can resolve its #using directive to the output directory.

Accessing and Using C# and VB.NET Objects in Unmanaged C++

Things get complicated when you try to access managed components from an unmanaged application. It's similar to putting a managed wrapper around your ATL COM component, only this time you're putting a managed C++ wrapper around the CLR components.

You have to create a managed C++ class as part of the unmanaged application. This managed C++ class functions as an interface between the CLR components, regardless of what language they were created with, and the rest of the unmanaged application. To keep things as simple as possible, you don't want your managed C++ class to be garbage collected, and you'll want to place all #using directives into the source code file (.cpp) instead of into the header file. This simplifies things because any other unmanaged C++ code in the application that needs to access the managed class will need to include the header file of the managed class. If the header file contains the #using directives or any managed extension keywords (such as the __gc keyword necessary to make the class garbage collected), those classes will also need to be compiled as managed C++ to understand those directives and keywords. The alternative is that you define all those by using the #define preprocessor directive, replacing those keywords with benign alternatives (such as white space).

Just as with the ATL component that you wrapped yesterday, you have to turn off the use of precompiled headers in your application, as well as the edit and continue while debugging capabilities. Depending on your unmanaged project, you may have to adjust some other configuration options. When you try to compile the project, if another option needs to be set to a different setting, the compiler will give you an error message showing the compiler option that needs to be set differently. It displays the compiler options in command-line form (the flags that would be passed to the compiler if you were invoking it from the DOS prompt), so you may have to search around the project properties dialog to find the option that needs to be set differently.

Another factor that needs to be taken into consideration is variable compatibility. One key variable type that may cause you problems is string type. For the most part, if the

21

CLR components that you are calling require a string variable as a parameter to a method, you can pass it a wchar_t array as follows:

```
wchar_t wszString[20];

pClrObject->SomeMethod(wszString);
```

Building a Managed C++ Component with a C# Client

Today, to illustrate how each different interaction scenario might work, you'll build not one, but three component/application combinations. The first one re-creates the component you built yesterday as a pure managed C++ component, and builds a C# and/or VB.NET client that accesses it. Next, you'll re-create the component using either C# or VB.NET, and access it using a managed C++ client. Finally, you'll access the C#/VB.NET component using an unmanaged C++ client.

Building the Managed C++ Component

To start the first of these projects, follow these steps:

1. Create a new Managed C++ Class Library project and name it MgdTaxCalc.

2. Open the MgdTaxCalc.h header file.

3. Replace the class name Class1 with the new class name, CTaxCalculator.

4. Add a new member function to the CTaxCalculator class (you'll need to expand the MgdTaxCalc namespace node in the Class View pane). Specify the function return type as double, the name as CalculateTaxes, and add two parameters. For the first parameter, specify the type as double and the name as dbPurchaseAmt. For the second parameter, specify the type as String* and the name as strCategory. Specify the function access as public.

5. Edit the function in the header file, adding the code in Listing 21.1.

LISTING 21.1   The CalculateTaxes Function

```
double CalculateTaxes(double dbPurchaseAmt, String* strCategory)
{
    // Declare the array of tax categories
    String* strCategories[] = {S"food", S"clothing", S"music"};
    // Declare the array of tax rates
    double dbRates[] = {0.0725, 0.0835, 0.081};
    // Loop through the categories
    for (int i=0; i < 3; i++)
```

LISTING 21.1 continued

```
    {
        // Is this the category purchased?
        if (strCategory == strCategories[i])
        {
            // Yes, calculate the taxes due
            return dbPurchaseAmt * dbRates[i];
        }
    }
    // Couldn't find the category purchased, return 0
    return 0;
}
```

That's all for the managed C++ component. The code is basically the same as the unmanaged component from yesterday, only uses managed strings and returns the amount of taxes to charge as the result value.

Building the C# or VB.NET Client

The next step in this example adds either the C# or VB.NET client application to this solution. The client application duplicates the functionality from the managed C++ client application that you implemented yesterday. To build this client, follow these steps:

1. In the Solution Explorer pane, select and right-click the solution node at the top of the tree. Select Add, New Project from the context menu.

2. Click either Visual Basic Projects or Visual C# Projects on the left side of the Add New Project dialog. Select Console Application on the right side of the dialog (this application type is available for both VB.NET and C# projects). If you are creating a Visual Basic project, name it VBClient. For a C# project, name it CSClient. Click OK to create the project.

3. In the Solution Explorer pane, select and right-click the References node in the new project you just created. Select Add Reference from the context menu.

4. In the Add Reference dialog, select the Projects tab. You should see your managed C++ component project (MgdTaxCalc) in the project list. Click the project and then click Select. Click OK to add the reference to the project.

5. If you created a C# project, open the Class1.cs file. If you created a VB project, open the Module1.vb file.

6. If you created a C# project, edit the main function, adding the code in Listing 21.2. If you created a VB project, edit the main function, adding the code in Listing 21.3.

21

LISTING 21.2   The C# Client Main Function

```
static void Main(string[] args)
{
    //
    // TODO: Add code to start application here
    //
    MgdTaxCalc.CTaxCalculator pGetTax = new MgdTaxCalc.CTaxCalculator();

    double dbPurchaseAmt, dbTaxAmt, dbTotalDue;

    // Create the string for the category being purchased
    String strCategory = "clothing";

    // Specify the purchase amount
    dbPurchaseAmt = 45.0;
    // Get the amount of taxes to collect
    dbTaxAmt = pGetTax.CalculateTaxes(dbPurchaseAmt, strCategory);
    if (dbTaxAmt > 0.0)
    {
        // Calculate the total due
        dbTotalDue = dbPurchaseAmt + dbTaxAmt;
        // Display the category being purchased
        Console.WriteLine(strCategory);
        // Display the purchase amount
        Console.Write("Purchase Amount = ");
        Console.WriteLine(dbPurchaseAmt.ToString("c"));
        // Display the tax due
        Console.Write("            Tax = ");
        Console.WriteLine(dbTaxAmt.ToString("c"));
        // Display the total amount
        Console.Write("      Total Due = ");
        Console.WriteLine(dbTotalDue.ToString("c"));
    }
}
```

LISTING 21.3   The VB.NET Client Main Function

```
Sub Main()
    Dim pGetTax As MgdTaxCalc.CTaxCalculator
    pGetTax = New MgdTaxCalc.CTaxCalculator()

    Dim dbPurchaseAmt As Double
    Dim dbTaxAmt As Double
    Dim dbTotalDue As Double

    ' Create the string for the category being purchased
    Dim strCategory As String
```

LISTING 21.3 continued

```
        strCategory = "clothing"

        ' Specify the purchase amount
        dbPurchaseAmt = 45
        ' Get the amount of taxes to collect
        dbTaxAmt = pGetTax.CalculateTaxes(dbPurchaseAmt, strCategory)
        If (dbTaxAmt > 0) Then
            ' Calculate the total due
            dbTotalDue = dbPurchaseAmt + dbTaxAmt
            ' Display the category being purchased
            Console.WriteLine(strCategory)
            ' Display the purchase amount
            Console.Write("Purchase Amount = ")
            Console.WriteLine(dbPurchaseAmt.ToString("c"))
            ' Display the tax due
            Console.Write("            Tax = ")
            Console.WriteLine(dbTaxAmt.ToString("c"))
            ' Display the total amount
            Console.Write("      Total Due = ")
            Console.WriteLine(dbTotalDue.ToString("c"))
        End If

    End Sub
```

7. In the Solution Explorer pane, select and right-click the client project that you created. Select Set as Startup Project from the context menu.

Now you should be able to compile and run your example application, producing the
output in Figure 21.2. You can also repeat these steps to build the client application,
using the other language than what you used, assuming that you have Visual Studio and
not just Visual C++ (so that you have both languages available for your use).

FIGURE 21.2

*The running
application.*

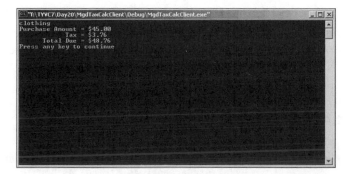

21

Building a C# Component with a Managed C++ Client

The next example reverses the situation from the previous example. For this example, you'll create the component using either VB.NET or C#, and then create a managed C++ client that accesses the component. Because of the macros that will be used in the managed C++ client, if you want to try building the component in the other language from the original one selected, you'll need to start a completely new solution.

Building the C# or VB.NET Component

To start this example project, follow these steps:

1. Select New and then Project from the File menu.

2. To create the component in C#, select Visual C# Projects on the left side of the new project dialog. To create the component in VB, select Visual Basic Projects on the left side of the dialog. For both component types, select Class Library on the right side of the dialog. If you are creating a C# component, name the project CSTaxCalc. If you are creating a VB component, name the project VBTaxCalc. If the previous example project is still open, be sure that the Close Solution radio button is selected. Click OK to create the new project.

3. If you created a C# project, open the Class1.cs file. If you created a VB project, open the Class1.vb file. Replace all occurrences of Class1 with CTaxCalculations.

4. If you want to rename the file in which the component is located, select the Class1.cs or Class1.vb file in the Solution Explorer pane. Press F2, and rename the file TaxCalculations, being sure to keep the file extension unchanged (for example, if it's a C# project, the new filename should be TaxCalculations.cs; if it's a VB project, the new filename should be TaxCalculations.vb).

5. If you are creating a Visual Basic component, edit the source code file, adding the function in Listing 21.4 (you don't have the capability to use the Add Function dialog with the Visual Basic component). You can skip the rest of the steps in this section, as the VB component is complete at this point.

LISTING **21.4**   The VB.NET CalculateTaxes Function

```
Public Class CTaxCalculations
    Public Function CalculateTaxes(ByVal fPurchaseAmt As Double, _
                    ByVal strCategory As String) As Double
        ' Declare the array of tax categories
```

LISTING 21.4   continued

```
            Dim strCategories() As String = {"food", "clothing", "music"}
            ' Declare the array of tax rates
            Dim fRates() As Double = {0.0725, 0.0835, 0.081}
            Dim i As Int32

            ' Preset the default return value
            CalculateTaxes = 0
            ' Loop through the categories
            For i = 0 To 2
                ' Is this the category purchased?
                If (strCategory = strCategories(i)) Then
                    ' Yes, calculate the taxes due
                    CalculateTaxes = fPurchaseAmt * fRates(i)
                End If
            Next
    End Function

End Class
```

If you are creating a C# component, select and right-click the `CTaxCalculations` class in the Class View pane. Select Add, Add Method from the context menu.

6. In the C# Method Wizard, specify the method access as `public`, the return type as `double`, the name as `CalculateTaxes`, and add two parameters. For the first parameter, specify the modifier as None, the parameter type as `double`, and the parameter name as `dbPurchaseAmt`. For the second parameter, specify the modifier as None, the parameter type as `string`, and the parameter name as `strCategory`. Click Finish to add this method.

7. Edit the method created, adding the code in Listing 21.5.

LISTING 21.5   The C# `CalculateTaxes` Function

```
public double CalculateTaxes(double dbPurchaseAmt, string strCategory)
{
    // Declare the array of tax categories
    String[] strCategories = {"food", "clothing", "music"};
    // Declare the array of tax rates
    double[] dbRates = {0.0725, 0.0835, 0.081};
    // Loop through the categories
    for (int i=0; i < 3; i++)
    {
        // Is this the category purchased?
        if (strCategory == strCategories[i])
        {
            // Yes, calculate the taxes due
```

21

LISTING 21.5   continued

```
                return dbPurchaseAmt * dbRates[i];
        }
    }
    // Couldn't find the category purchased, return 0
    return 0;
}
```

Building the Managed C++ Client

The next step in this example creates the managed C++ client application that accesses the component that you created using VB or C#. To create the client, follow these steps:

1. In the Solution Explorer pane, select and right-click the solution node at the top of the tree. Select Add, New Project if you are creating this example for the first time. Select Add, Existing Project if you are creating this example for the second time, using the other language to create the component, and then navigate to the project directory of the managed C++ client and select the project file.

2. If you are adding a new project, select Visual C++ Projects on the left side of the dialog, and select Managed C++ Application on the right side. Name the project MgdClient. Click OK to create the project.

3. If you created the component using C#, add the boldfaced code in Listing 21.6. If you created the component using VB, add the boldfaced code, substituting VBTaxCalc for CSTaxCalc every occurrence in Listing 21.6.

LISTING 21.6   The Managed C++ Client Main Function

```
// This is the main project file for VC++ application project
// generated using an Application Wizard.
```

INPUT
```
#include <tchar.h>

using namespace System;

// This is the entry point for this application
int tmain(void)
{
```

LISTING 21.6   continued

```
        // TODO: Please replace the sample code below with your own.
        CSTaxCalc::CTaxCalculations* pGetTax = new CSTaxCalc::CTaxCalculations();

    double dbPurchaseAmt, dbTaxAmt, dbTotalDue;

    // Create the string for the category being purchased
    String* pstrCategory = S"clothing";

    // Specify the purchase amount
    dbPurchaseAmt = 45.0;
    // Get the amount of taxes to collect
    dbTaxAmt = pGetTax->CalculateTaxes(dbPurchaseAmt, pstrCategory);
    if (dbTaxAmt > 0.0)
    {
        // Calculate the total due
        dbTotalDue = dbPurchaseAmt + dbTaxAmt;
        // Display the category being purchased
        Console::WriteLine(pstrCategory);
        // Display the purchase amount
        Console::Write("Purchase Amount = ");
        Console::WriteLine(dbPurchaseAmt.ToString("c"));
        // Display the tax due
        Console::Write("            Tax = ");
        Console::WriteLine(dbTaxAmt.ToString("c"));
        // Display the total amount
        Console::Write("      Total Due = ");
        Console::WriteLine(dbTotalDue.ToString("c"));
    }

    return 0;
}
```

INPUT

4. In the Solution Explorer pane, select and right-click the project node for the MgdClient project. Select Properties from the context menu.

5. On the Configuration combo box, select All Configurations.

6. On the left side of the Properties dialog, select Build Events, Pre-Build Events. On the right side of the dialog, in the Command Line entry, if you created the component using C#, enter:

```
copy "$(SolutionDir)\bin\$(ConfigurationName)\CSTaxCalc.dll"
    ➡$(ConfigurationName)
```

If you created the component using VB, enter:

```
copy "$(SolutionDir)\bin\VBTaxCalc.dll" $(ConfigurationName)
```

21

7. On the left side of the dialog, select C/C++, General. On the right side of the dialog, in the Resolve #using References section, enter

   `$(outdir)`

8. Click OK to accept the configuration changes and close the Properties dialog.

9. In the Solution Explorer pane, select and right-click the project node for the `MgdClient` project. Select Set as Startup Project from the context menu.

You are now ready to compile and run this example application. You should see the same output window that you saw for the previous example with the language roles reversed back in Figure 21.2.

Building an Unmanaged C++ Client

With the final example, things start to get really sticky. Creating the code to enable an unmanaged C++ application to access components created with C# and VB.NET is simple and fairly straightforward. It is with the configuration of the project where things start to get messy.

To create the project, follow these steps:

1. Select New and then Project from the File menu.

2. Select Visual C++ Projects on the left side of the New Project dialog, and Win32 Project on the right side. Name the project `UnmgdClient`. If the previous example project is still open, be sure that the Close Solution radio button is selected. Click OK to create the new project.

3. In the Win32 Application Wizard, select Application Settings on the left side, and then specify Console application for the application type. Click Finish to create the project.

Building the Managed C++ Interface

Creating the managed interface for the CLR components is similar to creating the managed wrapper for your ATL component. To create the interface, follow these steps:

1. Add a new generic class to the project, using the same method as in prior days. Name the new class `MgdClient`.

2. Add a new function to the `MgdClient` class. Specify the return value for the new function as `double`, the name as `GetTaxes`, the access as `public`, and add two parameters. Specify the first parameter type as `double` and the name as `dbPurchaseAmt`. Specify the second parameter type as `wchar_t*` and the name as `strCategory`.

3. Edit the new function as in Listing 21.7.

LISTING 21.7 The `GetTaxes` Function

```
double MgdClient::GetTaxes(double dbPurchaseAmt, wchar_t* strCategory)
{
    double dbTaxAmt;

    // Declare and create an instance of the CLR object
    CSTaxCalc::CTaxCalculations* pGetTax = new CSTaxCalc::CTaxCalculations();
    // Get the amount of taxes to collect
    dbTaxAmt = pGetTax->CalculateTaxes(dbPurchaseAmt, strCategory);
    // Return the result
    return dbTaxAmt;
}
```

4. If you are using the C# component, add the directives in Listing 21.8 at the top of the MgdClient.cpp file. If you are using the VB component, substitute the word `VBTaxCalc` for every occurrence of `CSTaxCalc` in both Listing 21.7 and 21.8.

LISTING 21.8 The `MgdClient` Directives

```
#include "StdAfx.h"
#include "mgdclient.h"

#using <mscorlib.dll>
#using "CSTaxCalc.dll"

using namespace System;
```

Coding and Configuring the Unmanaged C++ Client

Coding the main function for the unmanaged client is very similar to the main function in the COM client that you created yesterday. To add the code for the main function, follow these steps:

1. Open the UnmgdClient.cpp file.

2. Add the `#include` directives in Listing 21.9.

LISTING 21.9 The `UnmgdClient` Directives

```
// UnmgdClient.cpp : Defines the entry point for the console application.
//

#include "stdafx.h"
#include <windows.h>
#include <stdio.h>
#include "atlbase.h"
#include "mgdclient.h"
```

INPUT

21

3. Edit the main function, adding the code in Listing 21.10.

LISTING 21.10   The Main Function

```
int _tmain(int argc, _TCHAR* argv[])
{
    MgdClient* pGetTax = new MgdClient();

    double dbPurchaseAmt, dbTaxAmt, dbTotalDue;

    // Create the string for the category being purchased
    wchar_t pstrCategory[20];

    wcscpy(pstrCategory, L"clothing");

    // Specify the purchase amount
    dbPurchaseAmt = 45.0;
    // Get the amount of taxes to collect
    dbTaxAmt = pGetTax->GetTaxes(dbPurchaseAmt, pstrCategory);
    if (dbTaxAmt > 0.0)
    {
        // Calculate the total due
        dbTotalDue = dbPurchaseAmt + dbTaxAmt;
        // Display the category being purchased
        USES_CONVERSION;
        printf("%s\n", W2A(pstrCategory));
        // Display the purchase amount
        printf("Purchase Amount = %9.2f\n", dbPurchaseAmt);
        // Display the tax due
        printf("            Tax = %9.2f\n", dbTaxAmt);
        // Display the total amount
        printf("      Total Due = %9.2f\n", dbTotalDue);
    }
    return 0;
}
```

4. In the Solution Explorer pane, select and right-click the project node for the MgdClient.cpp file. Select Properties from the context menu.

5. On the Configuration combo box, select All Configurations.

6. On the left side of the properties dialog, select C/C++, General. On the right side, for the Compile As Managed entry, specify Assembly Support (/clr). For the Resolve #using References entry, enter **$(outdir)**.

7. Click the Apply button to apply the configuration changes without closing the Properties dialog.

8. In the Solution Explorer pane, select the stdafx.cpp file.

9. On the left side of the Properties dialog, select C/C++, Precompiled Headers. On the right side, in the Create/Use Precompiled Headers entry, select Not Using Precompiled Headers.

10. Click the Apply button to apply the configuration changes without closing the Properties dialog.

11. In the Solution Explorer pane, select the `UnmgdClient` project node.

12. On the left side of the Properties dialog, select Build Events, Pre-Build Events. On the right side, in the Command Line entry, if you are using the C# component, enter:

```
copy "..\CSTaxCalc\bin\$(ConfigurationName)
    ➥\CSTaxCalc.dll" $(ConfigurationName)
```

If you are using the VB component, enter:

```
copy "..\VBTaxCalc\bin\VBTaxCalc.dll"
    ➥$(ConfigurationName)
```

On your system, replace the relative path specified with the actual path to the project directories on your system if necessary. Because the solution file isn't located in the project directory for either component in this example, you can't use the `$(SolutionDir)` label.

13. On the left side of the Properties dialog, select C/C++, Precompiled Headers. On the right side, in the Create/Use Precompiled Headers section, select Not Using Precompiled Headers.

14. In the Configuration combo box, select Active(Debug). The settings you change from here on affect only the Debug builds.

15. On the left side of the Properties dialog, select C/C++, Code Generation. On the right side, for the Basic Runtime Checks entry, select Default. For the Runtime Library entry, select Multi-threaded Debug (/MTd). For the Enable Minimal Rebuild entry, select No.

16. On the left side of the dialog, select C/C++, General. On the right side, for the Debug Information Format, select Program Database (/Zi).

17. Click OK to apply the configuration changes and close the Properties dialog.

You should now be able to compile and run the unmanaged client application, accessing the C# or VB.NET component that you created in the previous example. Running the unmanaged client produces the output shown in Figure 21.3.

21

FIGURE 21.3

The unmanaged C++ client accessing CLR components created using C# or VB.NET.

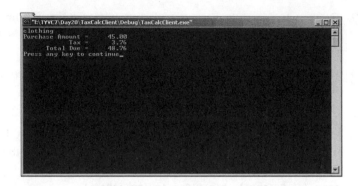

Summary

Today you learned how easy it is to access components created in other languages using managed C++, both in managed and unmanaged C++ applications. You also learned how you can easily access components created using managed C++ by other CLR languages such as VB.NET and C#. As other languages become available on the CLR platform, accessing components created using these other languages should be similarly simple.

You've accomplished a lot over the past 21 days. You spent the first week learning the basics of building Windows applications using Visual C++. You built on that knowledge during Week 2 by learning about more Windows programming topics that built on the knowledge you learned in the first week. Finally, in the Week 3, you built on all that you had learned in the first two weeks by diving into some advanced Windows programming topics. You finished off the third week by learning about some brand new topics that have been introduced with Microsoft's new .NET platform. At this point, you've got a good general knowledge of building applications with Visual C++. From here you might want to pick out some specific topics that you want to explore in more depth and pick up a more advanced book that focuses on those particular topics. Good luck!

Q&A

Q. What other languages are available for the CLR that can be accessed using managed C++?

A. Right now, Microsoft is only creating and distributing Visual Basic, C#, and managed C++. However, Microsoft has published the CLR specifications for other companies to create compilers for other languages. Several companies have pledged support for the platform and have announced plans to bring out compilers for various other programming languages. One of the first announced was by a company bringing out a COBOL compiler for the CLR. Any and all languages compiled for the CLR should be able to create objects that you can access using managed C++, or that you can create components using managed C++ that these languages can access.

Q. In the unmanaged C++ client, why couldn't I put the __gc modifier on the managed class?

A. The managed class in the unmanaged client has to be accessible by the unmanaged code in the application. When a managed class is marked for garbage collection, it can't be accessed by any unmanaged code. The reverse situation was seen yesterday, when you had a managed, garbage collected class accessing an unmanaged class. It seems that managed, garbage collected objects can reach outside the managed sandbox to access unmanaged objects. It's just that the garbage collected objects are located on the CLR managed heap, which can't be accessed from the outside. But objects on the managed CLR heap can use non-garbage collected pointers to access objects on the outside.

Workshop

The Workshop provides quiz questions to help solidify your understanding of the material covered and exercises to provide you with experience in using what you've learned. The answers to the quiz questions and exercises are provided in Appendix A, "Answers to Quiz Questions."

Quiz

1. What do you need to do to be able to access a managed component in a VB.NET or C# application?

2. What configuration changes do you need to make for a managed C++ application to access objects created in other CLR languages?

3. What data type can you pass from an unmanaged application to a managed string data type in a managed component?

4. Can you use precompiled headers in a mixed managed/unmanaged C++ project?

Exercise

Add a second method to your VB or C# component to return the tax rate for the specified category. Modify the managed C++ client to request and display the tax rate.

21

WEEK 3

In Review

You made it! You now have the skills to tackle most of the Windows programming tasks in Visual C++, with the exception of those that require specialized knowledge and understanding. Although there's still plenty for you to learn, you have covered the vast majority of the topics in a very short amount of time. From here you will probably want to delve into one or two more specialized areas of Windows programming—the type that an entire book can be written on—because at this point, you've got down just about all the general skills.

Just in case you don't have them all down, it's not a bad idea to take some time once again to come up with some of your own applications where you can apply the things you've learned. This will help pinpoint any areas that you might need to go back and review before jumping into any more advanced topics. Let's take a quick look back at what you should have learned during the past week, just to make sure.

You also learned how to share the functionality of your modules without sharing the code by packaging it as an ActiveX control. You can use the Control and Class Wizards to add in all the properties, methods, and events that you want to have in your control. You learned how to read and write the properties in your control. You saw how there are two different ways that the properties in your control can be implemented, and you now know how to determine which type is appropriate for each of your control's properties. You learned how you can raise events in the container application from your control by firing the event in your code. Along with all of this, you learned how you can use the ActiveX Control Test Container

15

16

17

18

19

20

21

utility to test your control, calling all its methods and triggering all the events that it's capturing. You saw how you can monitor the events that your control is firing in the containing application to make sure that they are being fired as and when they should. If you need any reminders of how all this works, you can look back at Day 15 for a refresher.

Next, you gained experience in incorporating the Microsoft Internet Explorer Web browser into your application without any effort whatsoever. You learned how you can control the browser by specifying the URL that it should load and display for the user and how you can display informational messages to the user to show what the browser is doing and when it's busy. You also learned how Visual C++ builds C++ classes around ActiveX controls and COM objects, enabling you to interact with controls and COM objects as if they were just another C++ object. You should have a good grasp of how to access any COM object interface (armed with the documentation for the control or object) in your application and interact with it in a seamless manner. You should be able to declare a variable for the control or object, call its methods, and react to the its events just as if it were a standard part of the Visual C++ development environment. If you need to look back at this to refresh your memory, you can go back to Day 16.

An important skill that you tackled was enabling your applications to perform more than one task at a time. This is an important piece of functionality, and more applications are requiring this capability every day. Not only did you learn how to make your applications perform multiple tasks at once, but you also learned two different ways to do so. First, you studied the `OnIdle` function and how you can hook into this function to trigger your own functionality to be run when the application is sitting idle. You learned about the shortcomings of using this approach to adding a second task to your application and how it can prevent your application from responding to the user. You need to slice the background task into little pieces that can be done quickly, which requires you to develop some elaborate way of keeping track of where the task is and where it needs to pick back up when the application is idle again.

The second way that you learned to give your applications a second or third task to do is by spinning off separate threads, which run completely independent of the main user-interface thread. You know how to create a call back function that controls the top level of execution for the threads and how to start and stop the thread as necessary. You also saw how these independent threads are completely independent from the rest of the application and how they'll continue to run, even when the rest of the application is also busy. If you feel the need to look at all this a second time, you might want to read Day 17 again.

Another area of growing importance that you learned about was how to build Internet applications using the Winsock interface classes. You learned how you can build one application that connects to another over a network and sends messages back and forth. You learned that, just like with a telephone, for one application to connect to another, the second application has to be listening for the connection. After the connection between the two applications has been made, you saw how easy it was to send messages and to be notified when a message has arrived. If you need to review some of this, you might want to look back at Day 18.

For the last three days you dove into the new world of .NET and managed C++. In the first of the three days, you studied managed extensions for C++, and how it changes your development. You learned how you can easily migrate your MFC applications to managed C++ easily, enabling them to run on any .NET client device. You also learned the basics of creating your own managed C++ application from scratch. If you need a refresher on how to do any of these tasks, take another look at Day 19.

On the second day of managed C++ topics, you also gained experience in using the ATL class library to build lightweight COM objects. You saw how you can design a COM object in a specific way so that it's easy to add a managed C++ interface onto the object, making it accessible from other CLR languages like VB.NET and C#. If you've got any questions on how to do any of this, check back in Day 20 to review this topic.

Finally, to end the week you learned how to build managed C++ objects that can be used in applications built in other languages, and how you can use objects built in other CLR languages in your managed C++ projects. You also learned how you could access and use CLR objects from unmanaged C++ applications using a managed wrapper for the objects. If you've got any questions on how to do any of these, you might want to read day 21 again.

That's it. You're done. You've covered a lot of ground and gained skill and knowledge in some advanced topics, especially over this last week. Now it's time to put this book down and get busy programming, building your own applications using what you've learned. Good luck. If you find that you need a little help or advice, a good place to turn is the Microsoft newsgroups on the Internet. They are full of people who are both knowledgeable and helpful.

Appendix A

Answers to Quiz Questions

Answers for Day 1

Quiz

1. How do you change the caption on a button?

   In the window layout editor, select the button to be changed. Change the value in the Caption field of the Properties pane.

2. What can you do with the MFC Application Wizard?

   You can use it to build a shell for your application, based on the type of application and the functionality needs of the application. The shell will have support for the desired functionality already built in.

3. How do you attach functionality to the click of a button?

   By using the Control Events mode of the Properties pane, you can create a function and attach it to an object for handling a specific Windows message. The Developer Studio creates the function, then you can use the

Class View of the workspace pane to take you right to the spot in the function's code to which you need add your own code.

Exercise

Add a second button to the About window in your application. Have the button display a different message from the one in the first window.

1. In the workspace pane, select the Resource View tab.
2. Expand the dialog tree branch and double-click the IDD_ABOUTBOX dialog, bringing it into the Developer Studio editor.
3. Click the button control on the toolbox.
4. Click and drag the mouse on the window to which you want the button to be placed.
5. In the Properties pane, change the ID and caption to describe the message to be displayed by the button.
6. Go into the Control Events mode of the Properties pane and add a new function for the clicked message (BN_CLICKED) for your new button.
7. Add the MessageBox function to display a message to the user.
8. Compile and run your application to test your new button.

Answers for Day 2

Quiz

1. What are the three primary stepping commands that are used when debugging code?

   Step Into, Step Over, and Step Out

2. What is the difference between the ASSERT and VERIFY macros?

   The ASSERT macro will strip out the condition code passed as a parameter when making a release build, while the VERIFY macro will leave the condition code in.

3. Why would you use the Spy++ tool?

   To see the event messages that are passed to a specific window or application. This will enable you to analyze what events are triggered, and which ones aren't. This information is key to understanding why some events aren't triggered when you expect them to be.

Exercise

Add ASSERT macros to validate the parameters being passed to the CalculateSum function. You need to make sure that the values passed in are greater than or equal to 0. Also add an ASSERT macro to verify that the iSum value is non-negative prior to returning it.

LISTING 2.A DEBUGGINGDLG.CPP—The CalculateSum Function

```cpp
int CDebuggingDlg::CalculateSum(int iLeftValue, int iRightValue)
{
    ASSERT(iLeftValue >= 0);
    ASSERT(iRightValue >= 0);
    int iSum;

    // Add the two parameters together
    iSum = iLeftValue - iRightValue;
    ASSERT(iSum >= 0);
    // Return the result
    return iSum;
}
```

Answers for Day 3

Quiz

1. Why do you need to specify the tab order of the controls on your application windows?

   By specifying the tab order of the controls on your application windows, you can control the order in which the user navigates the application window. If the user is using the keyboard to navigate around the application window, the two primary means of navigating between controls are the tab key and mnemonics that jump directly to specific controls. The tab order helps provide the user with a consistent and predictable experience when using your application.

2. How can you include a mnemonic that will take the user to the edit box or combo box?

   If you place a mnemonic in a static text control and then make sure that the static text control is just before the edit control associated with the static text in the tab order, the user can select the mnemonic in the static text control to jump directly to the edit box control.

3. Why do you need to give unique object IDs to the static text fields in front of the edit box and combo boxes?

A

The unique object IDs on the two static text controls were necessary because you need to manipulate those two controls with the check boxes that enable or disable and show or hide sets of controls.

4. Why do you need to call the UpdateData function before checking the value of one of the controls?

If the user has changed the value of the control on the screen, the UpdateData function must be called, passing it TRUE as the function argument, to copy the values from the controls on the window to the variables that are associated with those controls. If UpdateData isn't called, the values of the variables may not correctly reflect what the user has changed on the screen.

Exercises

1. Add code to the Default Message button to reset the edit box to say Enter a message here.

Using the Properties pane, add a function to the Default Message button's clicked event. In this function, add the code in Listing 3.A.

LISTING 3.A   CONTROLSDLG.CPP—Placing a Default Message in the Edit Box

```
void CControlsDlg::OnBnClickedDfltmsg()
{
    // TODO: Add your control notification handler code here
    // Set the message to a default message
    m_strMessage = "Enter a message here";

    // Update the screen
    UpdateData(FALSE);
}
```

`INPUT`

2. Add code to enable or disable and show or hide the controls used to select and run another application.

Add functions to the Enable and Show Program Action check boxes. In these functions, add the code in Listing B.X.

LISTING 3.B   CONTROLSDLG.CPP—Enabling or Disabling and Showing or Hiding the Run Program Controls

```
void CControlsDlg::OnBnClickedCkenblpgm()
{
    // TODO: Add your control notification handler code here
    // Get the current values from the screen
    UpdateData(TRUE);
```

`INPUT`

LISTING 3.B continued

```
        // Is the Enable Program Action check box checked?
        if (m_bEnablePgm == TRUE)
        {
            // Yes, so enable all controls that have anything
            // to do with running a program
            GetDlgItem(IDC_PROGTORUN)->EnableWindow(TRUE);
            GetDlgItem(IDC_RUNPGM)->EnableWindow(TRUE);
            GetDlgItem(IDC_STATICPGM)->EnableWindow(TRUE);
        }
        else
        {
            // No, so disable all controls that have anything
            // to do with running a program
            GetDlgItem(IDC_PROGTORUN)->EnableWindow(FALSE);
            GetDlgItem(IDC_RUNPGM)->EnableWindow(FALSE);
            GetDlgItem(IDC_STATICPGM)->EnableWindow(FALSE);
        }
    }

    void CControlsDlg::OnBnClickedCkshwpgm()
    {
        // TODO: Add your control notification handler code here
        // Get the current values from the screen
        UpdateData(TRUE);

        // Is the Show Program Action check box checked?
        if (m_bShowPgm == TRUE)
        {
            // Yes, so show all controls that have anything
            // to do with running a program
            GetDlgItem(IDC_PROGTORUN)->ShowWindow(TRUE);
            GetDlgItem(IDC_RUNPGM)->ShowWindow(TRUE);
            GetDlgItem(IDC_STATICPGM)->ShowWindow(TRUE);
        }
        else
        {
            // No, so hide all controls that have anything
            // to do with running a program
            GetDlgItem(IDC_PROGTORUN)->ShowWindow(FALSE);
            GetDlgItem(IDC_RUNPGM)->ShowWindow(FALSE);
            GetDlgItem(IDC_STATICPGM)->ShowWindow(FALSE);
        }
    }
```

INPUT

A

3. Extend the code in the OnBnClickedRunpgm function to allow the user to enter his program name to be run.

Modify the OnBnClickedRunpgm function as in Listing 3.C.

LISTING 3.C CONTROLSDLG.CPP—The Code to Run Any Program Name Typed into the Run Program Combo Box

```
void CControlsDlg::OnBnClickedRunpgm()
{
    // TODO: Add your control notification handler code here
    // Get the current values from the screen
    UpdateData(TRUE);

    // Declare a local variable for holding the program name
    CString strPgmName;

    // Copy the program name to the local variable
    strPgmName = m_strProgToRun;

    // Make the program name all uppercase
    strPgmName.MakeUpper();

    // Did the user select to run the Paint program?
    if (strPgmName == "PAINT")
        // Yes, run the Paint program
        WinExec("mspaint.exe ", SW_SHOW);

    // Did the user select to run the Notepad program?
    if (strPgmName == "NOTEPAD")
        // Yes, run the Notepad program
        WinExec("notepad.exe ", SW_SHOW);

    // Did the user select to run the Solitaire program?
    if (strPgmName == "SOLITAIRE")
        // Yes, run the Solitaire program
        WinExec("sol.exe ", SW_SHOW);
```

INPUT
```
    // Run any other program name typed into the combo box
    if ((lszPgmName != "PAINT") && (lszPgmName != "NOTEPAD") &&
        (lszPgmName != "SOLITAIRE"))
        // Yes, run the program typed into the combo box
        WinExec(lszPgmName, SW_SHOW);
}
```

Answers for Day 4

Quiz

1. What are the possible mouse messages that you can add functions for?

WM_LBUTTONDOWN, WM_LBUTTONUP, WM_LBUTTONDBLCLK, WM_RBUTTONDOWN, WM_RBUT-
TONUP, WM_RBUTTONDBLCLK, WM_MBUTTONDOWN, WM_MBUTTONUP, WM_MBUTTONDBLCLK,
WM_XBUTTONDOWN, WM_XBUTTONUP, WM_XBUTTONDBLCLK, WM_MOUSEMOVE, and
WM_MOUSEWHEEL.

2. How can you tell if the left mouse button is down on the WM_MOUSEMOVE event message?

You can mask the flags passed to the OnMouseMove function with the MK_LBUTTON flag, as follows:

```
((nFlags & MK_LBUTTON) == MK_LBUTTON)
```

3. How can you prevent the cursor from changing back to the default cursor after you set it to a different one?

Return TRUE in the OnSetCursor event function, preventing the base OnSetCursor function from being called.

Exercises

1. Modify your drawing program so that the left mouse button can draw in red, defined as RGB(255, 0, 0), and the right mouse button can draw in blue, defined as RGB(0, 0, 255).

Add a function for the WM_RBUTTONDOWN event message and write the code for it as follows:

```
void CMouseDlg::OnRButtonDown(UINT nFlags, CPoint point)
{
    // TODO: Add your message handler code here and/or call default

    // Set the current point as the starting point
    m_iPrevX = point.x;
    m_iPrevY = point.y;

    CDialog::OnRButtonDown(nFlags, point);
}
```

INPUT

Extend the OnMouseMove function as follows:

```
void CMouseDlg::OnMouseMove(UINT nFlags, CPoint point)
{
    // TODO: Add your message handler code here and/or call default

    // Check to see if the left mouse button is down
    if (((nFlags & MK_LBUTTON) == MK_LBUTTON) ||
        ((nFlags & MK_RBUTTON) == MK_RBUTTON))
    {
        // Get the Device Context
        CClientDC dc(this);
        CPen* pPrevPen = NULL; // Pointer to the previous pen
```

INPUT

A

```
if ((nFlags & MK_LBUTTON) == MK_LBUTTON)
    // Create a new pen
       CPen lpen(PS_SOLID, 16, RGB(255, 0, 0));

  if ((nFlags & MK_RBUTTON) == MK_RBUTTON)
      // Create a new pen
      CPen lpen(PS_SOLID, 16, RGB(0, 0, 255));

      // Use the new pen
      pPrevPen = dc.SelectObject(&lpen);

      // Draw a line from the previous point to the current point
      dc.MoveTo(m_iPrevX, m_iPrevY);
      dc.LineTo(point.x, point.y);

      // Save the current point as the previous point
      m_iPrevX = point.x;
      m_iPrevY = point.y;

      // Restore the previous pen
      dc.SelectObject(pPrevPen);
  }

  CDialog::OnMouseMove(nFlags, point);
}
```

2. Extend the OnKeyDown function in Listing 4.4 to add some of the following standard cursors:

- IDC_CROSS
- IDC_UPARROW
- IDC_SIZEALL
- IDC_SIZENWSE
- IDC_SIZENESW
- IDC_SIZEWE
- IDC_SIZENS
- IDC_NO
- IDC_APPSTARTING
- IDC_HELP

Your modified OnKeyDown function can look something like the following:

```
void CMouseDlg::OnKeyDown(UINT nChar, UINT nRepCnt, UINT nFlags)
{
    // TODO: Add your message handler code here and/or call default

    char cChar;          // The current character being pressed
```

```
HCURSOR hCursor = 0;     // The handle to the cursor to be displayed
HCURSOR hPrevCursor = 0;  // The handle for the previous cursor
// Convert the key pressed to a character
cChar = char(nChar);

// Is the character "A"
if (cChar == 'A')
    // Load the arrow cursor
    hCursor = AfxGetApp()->LoadStandardCursor(IDC_ARROW);
// Is the character "B"
if (cChar == 'B')
    // Load the I beam cursor
    hCursor = AfxGetApp()->LoadStandardCursor(IDC_IBEAM);
// Is the character "C"
if (cChar == 'C')
    // Load the hourglass cursor
    hCursor = AfxGetApp()->LoadStandardCursor(IDC_WAIT);
```

INPUT

```
// Is the character "D"
if (cChar == 'D')
    // Load the cross hair cursor
    hCursor = AfxGetApp()->LoadStandardCursor(IDC_CROSS);
// Is the character "E"
if (cChar == 'E')
    // Load the up arrow cursor
    hCursor = AfxGetApp()->LoadStandardCursor(IDC_UPARROW);
// Is the character "F"
if (cChar == 'F')
    // Load the size cursor
    hCursor = AfxGetApp()->LoadStandardCursor(IDC_SIZEALL);
// Is the character "G"
if (cChar == 'G')
    // Load the up/right-down/left size cursor
    hCursor = AfxGetApp()->LoadStandardCursor(IDC_SIZENWSE);
// Is the character "H"
if (cChar == 'H')
    // Load the up/left-down/right size cursor
    hCursor = AfxGetApp()->LoadStandardCursor(IDC_SIZENESW);
// Is the character "I"
if (cChar == 'I')
    // Load the left-right size cursor
    hCursor = AfxGetApp()->LoadStandardCursor(IDC_SIZEWE);
// Is the character "J"
if (cChar == 'J')
    // Load the up-down size cursor
    hCursor = AfxGetApp()->LoadStandardCursor(IDC_SIZENS);
// Is the character "K"
if (cChar == 'K')
    // Load the no cursor
    hCursor = AfxGetApp()->LoadStandardCursor(IDC_NO);
// Is the character "L"
if (cChar == 'L')
```

A

```
        // Load the app starting cursor
        hCursor = AfxGetApp()->LoadStandardCursor(IDC_APPSTARTING);
    // Is the character "M"
    if (cChar == 'M')
        // Load the help cursor
        hCursor = AfxGetApp()->LoadStandardCursor(IDC_HELP);
    if (cChar == 'X')
        // Load the arrow cursor
        hCursor = AfxGetApp()->LoadStandardCursor(IDC_ARROW);
    // Set the cursor flag
    m_bCursor = TRUE;
    // Set the screen cursor
    if (hCursor)
        hPrevCursor = SetCursor(hCursor);

    // Destroy the previous cursor to free up the resources
    if (hPrevCursor)
        DestroyCursor(hPrevCursor);
    // Is the character "X"
    if (cChar == 'X')
    {
        // Exit the application
        OnOK();
    }a

    CDialog::OnKeyDown(nChar, nRepCnt, nFlags);
}
```

Answers for Day 5

Quiz

1. What did you accomplish by adding the two timer IDs to the resource symbols?

   You defined the two IDs so that they were available as constants throughout the application.

2. What's another way to add these two IDs to the application?

   Add them as #define constants in the class header file (*TimersDlg.h*) or the source code file (TimersDlg.cpp):

   ```
   /////////////////////////////////////////////////////////////////////////////
   //
   // CTimersDlg dialog

   #define ID_CLOCK_TIMER 1
   #define ID_COUNT_TIMER 2

   class CTimersDlg : public CDialog
   {
   ...
   ```

3. How can you tell two timers apart in the OnTimer function?

   You use the timer ID to determine which timer triggered the event.

4. How many timer events does your application receive if the timer is set for one second and your application has been busy for one minute, preventing it from receiving any timer event messages?

   One.

Exercise

Update your application so that when the counter timer is started, the clock timer is reset to run at the same interval as the counter timer. When the counter timer is stopped, return the clock timer to a one-second interval.

To change the interval at which a timer is running, you need to first stop the timer and then restart it, as in Listing 5.A.

LISTING 5.A   The Revised OnBnClickedBstarttime and OnBnClickedBstoptimer Functions

```
void CTimersDlg::OnBnClickedBstarttime()
{
    // TODO: Add your control notification handler code here
    // Update the variables
    UpdateData(TRUE);

    // Initialize the count
    m_iCount = 0;
    // Format the count for displaying
    m_sCount.Format("%d", m_iCount);

    // Update the dialog
    UpdateData(FALSE);
    // Start the timer
    SetTimer(ID_COUNT_TIMER, m_iInterval, NULL);

    // Stop the clock timer
    KillTimer(ID_CLOCK_TIMER);
    // Restart the clock timer with the counter interval
    SetTimer(ID_CLOCK_TIMER, m_iInterval, NULL);

    // Enable the Stop Timer button
    m_cStopTime.EnableWindow(TRUE);
    // Disable the Start Timer button
    m_cStartTime.EnableWindow(FALSE);
}

void CTimersDlg::OnBnClickedBstoptimer()
{
```

INPUT

A

LISTING 5.A   continued

```
// TODO: Add your control notification handler code here
// Stop the timer
KillTimer(ID_COUNT_TIMER);
```

INPUT
```
// Stop the clock timer
KillTimer(ID_CLOCK_TIMER);
// Restart the clock timer with 1 second interval
SetTimer(ID_CLOCK_TIMER, 1000, NULL);
```

```
// Disable the Stop Timer button
m_cStopTime.EnableWindow(FALSE);
// Enable the Start Timer button
m_cStartTime.EnableWindow(TRUE);
}
```

Answers for Day 6

Quiz

1. What possible return codes might your application receive from the `MessageBox` function call when you specify the `MB_RETRYCANCEL` button combination?

   `IDRETRY` and `IDCANCEL`.

2. What common dialogs built into the Windows operating system are defined as MFC classes?

   The common Windows dialogs that are defined as MFC classes are

   - File selection
   - Font selection
   - Color selection
   - Page setup for printing
   - Printing
   - Find and replace

3. What's the difference between modal and modeless dialogs?

   A modal dialog stops all application processing until the users respond to the dialog. A modeless dialog allows users to continue working with the rest of the application while the dialog is open for use.

4. How can you display a File Save dialog for users instead of the File Open dialog that you have in your application?

In the class instance variable declaration, pass FALSE instead of TRUE. This makes the variable declaration look like this:

```
CFileDialog m_ldFile(FALSE);
```

5. Why didn't you need to create any functions and add any code to your custom dialog?

The only functionality that was needed on the custom dialog was calling UpdateData before closing the dialog. Because the OK and Cancel buttons were never deleted from the dialog, the OK button automatically performed this functionality.

Exercises

1. Modify your application so that it includes the directory with the filename in the application. (*Hint:* The GetPathName function returns the path and filename that was selected in the File Open dialog.)

Modify the OnBnClickedBfileopen function as follows:

```
void CDialogsDlg::OnBnClickedBfileopen()
{
    // TODO: Add your control notification handler code here
    CFileDialog ldFile(TRUE);

    // Show the File open dialog and capture the result
    if (ldFile.DoModal() == IDOK)
    {
        // Get the filename selected
        m_sResults = ldFile.GetPathName();
        // Update the dialog
        UpdateData(FALSE);
    }

}
```

INPUT

The GetPathName function returns the path and filename, so changing the function call from GetFileName to GetPathName alters the display to include the path with the filename.

2. Add a button on the custom dialog that calls the MessageBox function with a Yes or No selection. Pass the result back to the main application dialog.

Follow these steps:

1. Using the Class View, add a member variable to the CMsgDlg class. Specify the variable type as int, the name as m_iYesNo, and the access as public.

2. Using the Resource View, open the custom dialog in the editor area. Add a command button to the window, named IDC_BYESNO with a caption &Yes or No.

A

3. Using the Properties pane, add a function to the new button you just added and edit the function. Include the following code:

```
void CMsgDlg::OnBnClickedByesno()
{
    // TODO: Add your control notification handler code here
    // Ask the user
    m_iYesNo = MessageBox("Choose Yes or No", "Yes or No", MB_YESNO);
}
```

INPUT

4.Add a button to the main dialog named IDC_BYESNO with the caption Y&es or No.

5.Using the Properties pane, add a function to the new button, including the following code:

```
void CDialogsDlg::OnBnClickedByesno()
{
    // TODO: Add your control notification handler code here
    // What did the user answer
    switch (m_dMsgDlg.m_iYesNo)
    {
    case IDYES:     // Did the user answer YES?
        m_sResults = "Yes!";
        break;
    case IDNO:      // Did the user answer NO?
        m_sResults = "No!";
        break;
    }

    // Update the dialog
    UpdateData(FALSE);
}
```

INPUT

Answers for Day 7

Quiz

1. What event message does a menu selection send to the window message queue?

   COMMAND (actually WM_COMMAND, but COMMAND is what appears in the Event Handler Wizard).

2. How do you attach a menu to a dialog window?

   In the dialog designer, open the properties dialog for the window, and choose the menu from the drop-down list of menus. Another approach is to use the SetMenu function to attach the menu to the dialog.

3. Which existing class do you specify for handling event messages for the menu?

   The dialog class for the window on which the menu appears.

4. What event message should a pop-up menu be triggered by?

The WM_CONTEXTMENU event.

Exercises

1. Add a button to the main window and have it call the same function as the Hello menu entry.

Follow these steps:

1. Add a button to the dialog screen. Supply a button ID of IDC_HELLO and a caption of &Hello.

2. With the Class Wizard, add a function to the button. Accept the default name for the function, OnBnClickedHello.

3. In the OnBnClickedHello function, call the OnFileHello function.

2. Modify the context menu to your application , so it uses the Help drop-down menu as the pop-up menu.

Follow these steps:

1. Edit the OnContextMenu function, changing the highlighted code:

INPUT

```
void CMenusDlg::OnContextMenu(CWnd* pWnd, CPoint point)
{
    // TODO: Add your message handler code here
    CMenu *pMenu;

    // Get a pointer to the menu
    pMenu = GetMenu();
    // Get a pointer to the submenu
    pMenu = pMenu->GetSubMenu(1);
    // Open it as a context menu
    pMenu->TrackPopupMenu(TPM_CENTERALIGN | TPM_LEFTBUTTON,
        point.x, point.y, pWnd, NULL);
}
```

Answers for Day 8

Quiz

1. How can you specify that the text is to be underlined?

Pass 1 as the value for the bUnderline argument to the CreateFont function.

2. How can you print your text upside down?

Pass 1800 as the nEscapement argument to the CreateFont function.

A

3. How many times is the EnumFontFamProc callback function called by the operating
system?

The function is called once for each font that's available in the system, unless the
callback function returns 0 and stops the listing of fonts.

Exercises

1. Add a check box to switch between using the entered text to display the font and
using the font name to display the font, as in Figure 8.4.

Add the check box to the dialog. Set its properties as follows:

ID	IDC_CBUSETEXT
Caption	&Use Entered Text

Attach a variable to this control. Specify the variable type as a Boolean with the
name m_bUseText.

Add a function for the BN_CLICKED event message for the check box. Edit the function, adding the following code:

```
void CTextFontsDlg::OnBnClickedCbusetext(void)
{
    // TODO: Add your control notification handler code here
    // Update the variables with the dialog controls
    UpdateData(TRUE);
    // Using the font name for the font sample?
    if (!m_bUseText)
        // Using the font name
        m_strDisplayText = m_strFontName;
    else
        // Using the entered text
        m_strDisplayText = m_strSampText;

    // Update the dialog
    UpdateData(FALSE);
}
```

INPUT

Modify the OnInitDialog function to initialize the check box as follows:

```
BOOL CTextFontsDlg::OnInitDialog()
{
    CDialog::OnInitDialog();
...
    // TODO: Add extra initialization here
    // Fill the font list box
    FillFontList();

    // Initialize the text to be entered
    m_strSampText = "Testing";
```

```
             // Copy the text to the font sample area
             m_strDisplayText = m_strSampText;
```
INPUT
```
             // Initialize the check box
             m_bUseText = TRUE;
             // Update the dialog
             UpdateData(FALSE);

             return TRUE;  // return TRUE  unless you set the focus
                           // to a control
      }
```

Modify the OnLbnSelchangeLfonts function as follows:

```
void CTextFontsDlg::OnLbnSelchangeLfonts(void)
{
      // TODO: Add your control notification handler code here
      // Update the variables with the dialog controls
      UpdateData(TRUE);
```
INPUT
```
      // Using the font name for the font sample?
      if (!m_bUseText)
         {
             // Copy the font name to the font sample
             m_strDisplayText = m_strFontName;
             // Update the dialog with the variables
             UpdateData(FALSE);
         }
      // Set the font for the sample
      SetMyFont();
}
```

Finally, modify the OnEnChangeEsamptext function as follows:

```
void CTextFontsDlg::OnEnChangeEsamptext(void)
{
      // TODO:  If this is a RICHEDIT control, the control will not
      // send this notification unless you override the
CDialog::OnInitDialog()
      // function and call CRichEditCtrl().SetEventMask()
      // with the ENM_CHANGE flag ORed into the mask.

      // TODO:  Add your control notification handler code here
      // Update the variables with the dialog controls
      UpdateData(TRUE);
```
INPUT
```
      // Using the text for the font sample?
      if (m_bUseText)
         {
             // Copy the current text to the font sample
             m_strDisplayText = m_strSampText;
             // Update the dialog with the variables
             UpdateData(FALSE);
         }
}
```

A

2. Add a check box to display the font sample in italics, as in Figure 8.5.

Add the check box to the dialog. Set its properties as follows:

ID	IDC_CBITALIC
Caption	&Italic

Attach a variable to this control. Specify the variable type as a Boolean with the name m_bItalic.

Add a function for the BN_CLICKED event message for the check box. Edit the function, adding the following code:

```
void CTextFontsDlg::OnBnClickedCbitalic()
{
    // TODO: Add your control notification handler code here
    // Update the variables with the dialog controls
    UpdateData(TRUE);

    // Set the font for the sample
    SetMyFont();
}
```

Modify the SetMyFont function as in the following listing:

```
void CTextFontsDlg::SetMyFont()
{
    CRect rRect;          // The rectangle of the display area
    int iItalic = 0;      // Italicize the font?

    // Has a font been selected?
    if (m_strFontName != "")
    {
        // Get the dimensions of the font sample display area
        m_ctlDisplayText.GetWindowRect(&rRect);
        if (m_bItalic)
          iItalic = 1;
        // Release the current font
        m_fSampFont.Detach();
        // Create the font to be used
        m_fSampFont.CreateFont((rRect.Height() - 5), 0, 0, 0,
            FW_NORMAL, iItalic, 0, 0, DEFAULT_CHARSET,
                OUT_CHARACTER_PRECIS, CLIP_CHARACTER_PRECIS,
                DEFAULT_QUALITY, DEFAULT_PITCH |
                FF_DONTCARE, m_strFontName);

        // Set the font for the sample display area
        m_ctlDisplayText.SetFont(&m_fSampFont);
    }
}
```

INPUT

INPUT

INPUT

INPUT

Answers for Day 9

Quiz

1. What are the three values that are combined to specify a color?

    Red, green, and blue.

2. What do you use to draw on windows without needing to know what graphics card the user has?

    The device context.

3. What size bitmap can you use to make a brush from it?

    8 pixels by 8 pixels or larger.

4. What event message is sent to a window to tell it to redraw itself?

    The WM_PAINT message.

5. How can you cause a window to repaint itself?

    Use the Invalidate function on it.

Exercises

1. Make the second dialog resizable, and make it adjust the figures drawn on it whenever it's resized. Hint: use the Border property and the WM_SIZE event message.

    Open the second dialog in the dialog layout designer. Set the Border property to Resizing. Add an event-handler function for the WM_SIZE event message. Edit the function that you just created and call the Invalidate function, as in Listing 9.A.

LISTING 9.A   The OnSize Function

```
void CPaintDlg::OnSize(UINT nType, int cx, int cy)
{
    CDialog::OnSize(nType, cx, cy);

    // TODO: Add your message handler code here
    // Redraw the window
        Invalidate();
}
```

INPUT

A

2. Add a bitmap brush to the set of brushes used to create the rectangles and ellipses.

    Open the Resources View pane. Right-click the top folder of the resource tree. Select Add, Add Resource from the pop-up menu. Select Bitmap from the list of available resources to add. Paint a pattern on the bitmap that you just created.

Right-click the bitmap ID in the workspace pane. In the Properties pane, change the object ID to IDB_BITMAPBRUSH. Open the source code for the DrawRegion function. Add the bolded code in Listing 9.B, Increase the number of loops in the for statement.

LISTING 9.B The DrawRegion Function

```
void CPaintDlg::DrawRegion(CPaintDC *pdc, int iColor, int iTool, int iShape)
{
    // Declare and create the pens
...
    CBrush lVertBrush(HS_VERTICAL, m_crColors[iColor]);
    CBrush lNullBrush(RGB(192, 192, 192));

    CBitmap bmpBitmap;
        bmpBitmap.LoadBitmap(IDB_BITMAPBRUSH);
    CBrush brBitmapBrush(&bmpBitmap);

    // Calculate the size of the drawing regions
    CRect rRect;
    GetClientRect(rRect);
...
    // Loop through all of the brushes and pens
    for (int i = 0; i < 8; i++)
        {
        switch (i)
        {
...
            pdc->SelectObject(&brVertBrush);
            break;
        case 7:     // Null - Bitmap
                // Select the appropriate pen and brush
            pdc->SelectObject(&pnNullPen);
            pdc->SelectObject(&brBitmapBrush);
            break;
        }
        // Which tool are we using?
...
    pdc->SelectObject(pOldBrush);
    pdc->SelectObject(pOldPen);
}
```

INPUT

INPUT

INPUT

Answers for Day 10

Quiz

1. What does SDI stand for?

   Single Document Interface.

2. What functionality is in the view class?

   The view class is responsible for displaying the document for the user.

3. What function is called to redraw the document if the window has been hidden behind another window?

   The OnDraw function in the view class is called to redraw the document.

4. Where do you place code to clear out the current document before starting a new document?

   The DeleteContents function in the document class is where you place code to clear the current document.

5. What's the purpose of the document class?

   The document class is where the data is managed and manipulated. It maintains the abstract representation of the document being edited and processed.

6. What are the five base classes that are used in MDI applications?

   The CWinApp-derived class, the CMDIFrameWnd-derived class, the CMDIChildWnd-derived class, the CDocument-derived class, and the CView-derived class.

Exercise

Add another pull-down menu to control the width of the pen used for drawing. Give it the following settings:

Menu Entry	Width Setting
Very Thin	1
Thin	8
Medium	16
Thick	24
Very Thick	32

Follow these steps:

1. Select the CLine class in the Class View tab of the workspace pane. Right-click the mouse and select Add Member Variable from the pop-up menu.

A

2. Specify the variable type as UINT, the name as m_nWidth, and the access as private. Click Finish to add the variable.

3. Right-click the CLine constructor in the Class View tree. Select Go to Definition from the pop-up menu.

4. Add UINT nWidth as a fourth argument to the constructor declaration.

5. Right-click the CLine constructor in the Class View tree. Select Go to Declaration from the pop-up menu.

6. Modify the constructor to add the fourth argument.

7. Edit the constructor to set the m_nWidth member to the new argument, as in Listing 10.A.

LISTING 10.A   The Modified CLine Constructor

```
CLine::CLine(CPoint ptFrom, CPoint ptTo, COLORREF crColor, UINT nWidth)
{
    //Initialize the from and to points
    m_ptFrom = ptFrom;
    m_ptTo = ptTo;
    m_crColor = crColor;
    m_nWidth = nWidth;
}
```

INPUT

7. Scroll down to the Draw function and modify it as in Listing 10.B.

LISTING 10.B   The Modified Draw Function

```
void CLine::Draw(CDC * pDC)
{
    // Create a pen
    CPen lpen (PS_SOLID, m_nWidth, m_crColor);

    // Set the new pen as the drawing object
    CPen* pOldPen = pDC->SelectObject(&lpen);
    // Draw the line
    pDC->MoveTo(m_ptFrom);
    pDC->LineTo(m_ptTo);
    // Reset the previous pen
    pDC->SelectObject(pOldPen);
}
```

8. Scroll down to the Serialize function and modify it as in Listing 10.C.

LISTING 10.C   The Modified Serialize Function

```
void CLine::Serialize(CArchive &ar)
{
    CObject::Serialize(ar);

    if (ar.IsStoring())
        ar << m_ptFrom << m_ptTo << (DWORD) m_crColor << m_nWidth;
    else
        ar >> m_ptFrom >> m_ptTo >> (DWORD) m_crColor >> m_nWidth;
}
```

9. Select the CSDISquigDoc class in the Class View tab on the workspace pane. Right-click the mouse and choose Add Member Variable from the pop-up menu.

10. Specify the variable type as UINT, the name as m_nWidth, and the access as private. Click Finish to add the variable.

11. Open the CSDISquigDoc source code (SDISquigDoc.cpp), scroll down to the OnNewDocument function, and edit it as in Listing 10.D.

LISTING 10.D   The Modified OnNewDocument Function

```
BOOL CSDISquigDoc::OnNewDocument()
{
    if (!CDocument::OnNewDocument())
        return FALSE;

    // TODO: add reinitialization code here
    // (SDI documents will reuse this document)
    // Initialize the color to black
    m_nColor = 0;
    // Initialize the width to thin
    m_nWidth = ID_WIDTH_VTHIN - ID_WIDTH_VTHIN;

    return TRUE;
}
```

INPUT

12. Scroll down to the AddLine function, and modify it as in Listing 10.E.

LISTING 10.E   The Modified AddLine Function

```
CLine * CDay10Doc::AddLine(CPoint ptFrom, CPoint ptTo)
{
    static UINT nWidths[5] = { 1, 8, 16, 24, 32};
    CLine* pLine = NULL;

    try
```

INPUT

A

LISTING 10.E continued

```
    {
        // Create a new CLine object
        pLine = new CLine(ptFrom, ptTo,
            m_crColors[m_nColor], nWidths[m_nWidth]);
        // Add the new line to the object array
        m_oaLines.Add(pLine);
        // Mark the document as dirty
        SetModifiedFlag();
    }
    // Did we run into a memory exception?
    catch (CMemoryException* perr)
    {
        // Display a message for the user, giving him or her the
        // bad news
        AfxMessageBox("Out of memory", MB_ICONSTOP | MB_OK);
        // Did we create a line object?
        if (pLine)
        {
            // Delete it
            delete pLine;
            pLine = NULL;
        }
        // Delete the exception object
        perr->Delete();
    }
    return pLine;
}
```

13. Add a new member function to the SDISquigDoc class. Specify the function type as UINT, the function name as GetWidth, and the access as public.

14. Edit the GetWidth function, adding the code in Listing 10.F.

LISTING 10.F The GetWidth Function

```
UINT CSDISquigDoc::GetWidth()
{
    // Return the current width
    return ID_WIDTH_VTHIN + m_nWidth;
}
```

15. Select the Resource View tab in the workspace pane. Expand the tree so that you can see the contents of the Menu folder. Double-click the menu resource.

16. Click the blank top-level menu (at the right end of the menu bar). Specify the caption as &Width.

17. Grab the new menu (Width) and drag it to the left, dropping it in front of the View menu entry.

18. Add submenu entries below the Width top-level menu. Specify the submenus in order, setting their captions and IDs as specified in Table 10.G.

TABLE 10.G Menu Property Settings

Object	Property	Setting
Menu Entry	ID	ID_WIDTH_VTHIN
	Caption	&Very Thin
Menu Entry	ID	ID_WIDTH_THIN
	Caption	Thi&n
Menu Entry	ID	ID_WIDTH_MEDIUM
	Caption	&Medium
Menu Entry	ID	ID_WIDTH_THICK
	Caption	Thic&k
Menu Entry	ID	ID_WIDTH_VTHICK
	Caption	Very &Thick

19. Open the Class View. Select the CSDISquigDoc in the Class view.

20. Select the Events view in the Properties pane.

21. Add functions for both the COMMAND and UPDATE_COMMAND_UI event messages for all the width menu entries.

22. After you add the final menu entry function, edit the Very Thin menu functions as in Listing 10.H.

LISTING 10.H The Very Thin Menu Functions

```
void CSDISquigDoc::OnWidthVthin()
{
    // TODO: Add your command handler code here

    // Set the current width to very thin
        m_nWidth = ID_WIDTH_VTHIN - ID_WIDTH_VTHIN;
}

void CSDISquigDoc::OnUpdateWidthVthin(CCmdUI* pCmdUI)
{
    // TODO: Add your command update UI handler code here

    // Determine if the Very Thin menu entry should be checked
        pCmdUI->SetCheck(GetWidth() == ID_WIDTH_VTHIN ? 1 : 0);
}
```

INPUT

INPUT

A

23. Edit the Thin menu functions as in Listing 10.I. Edit the remaining menu functions in the same way, substituting their menu IDs for ID_WIDTH_THIN.

LISTING 10.I   The Thin Menu Functions

```
void CSDISquigidthThin()
{
    // TODO: Add your command handler code here

    // Set the current width to thin
        m_nWidth = ID_WIDTH_THIN - ID_WIDTH_VTHIN;
}

void CSDISquigpdateWidthThin(CCmdUI* pCmdUI)
{
    // TODO: Add your command update UI handler code here

    // Determine if the Thin menu entry should be checked
        pCmdUI->SetCheck(GetWidth() == ID_WIDTH_THIN ? 1 : 0);
}
```

> **INPUT**

> **INPUT**

Answers for Day 11

Quiz

1. How do you tie a toolbar button to a menu entry that triggers that same function?

    Give the toolbar button the same object ID as the menu entry.

2. How do you make sure that a toolbar can be docked with the frame window?

    Both must have docking enabled on the same sides (using the EnableDocking function) in the OnCreate function of the frame class.

3. How can you remove the Num Lock status indicator from the status bar?

    Remove the ID_INDICATOR_NUM from the indicators table near the top of the main frame source code file.

4. Why do you have to edit the resource file to add a combo box to a toolbar?

    You need to add a separator to the toolbar as a placeholder in the toolbar. The toolbar designer will do its best to prevent you from adding the separators, assuming that they are a mistake.

Exercises

1. Add another pane to the status bar to display the current width selected.

   Add an entry to the strings table with an ID of ID_INDICATOR_WIDTH and a caption of VERY THICK.

   Add another entry to the status bar indicators table at the beginning of CMainFrame.cpp:

```
static UINT indicators[] =
{
    ID_SEPARATOR,            // status line indicator
    ID_INDICATOR_WIDTH,
        ID_INDICATOR_COLOR,
    ID_INDICATOR_CAPS,
    ID_INDICATOR_NUM,
    ID_INDICATOR_SCRL,
};
```

INPUT

   Add a new member function to the CSDISquigDoc class. Specify the function type as afx_msg void, the function name as OnUpdateIndicatorWidth, one parameter of type CCmdUI* and named pCmdUI, and the function access as protected. Edit the function as follows:

```
void CSDISquigDoc::OnUpdateIndicatorWidth(CCmdUI *pCmdUI)
{
    CString strWidth;

    // What is the current width?
    switch (m_nWidth)
    {
    case 0:     // Very Thin
        strWidth = "VERY THIN";
        break;
    case 1:     // Thin
        strWidth = "THIN";
        break;
    case 2:     // Medium
        strWidth = "MEDIUM";
        break;
    case 3:     // Thick
        strWidth = "THICK";
        break;
    case 4:     // Very Thick
        strWidth = "VERY THICK";
        break;
    }
    // Enable the status bar pane
    pCmdUI->Enable(TRUE);
    // Set the text of the status bar pane
```

A

```
        // to the current width
        pCmdUI->SetText(strWidth);
}
```

Edit the `CSDISquigDoc` message map, adding the `ON_UPDATE_COMMAND_UI` message handler entry as follows:

```
// CSDISquigDoc

IMPLEMENT_DYNCREATE(CSDISquigDoc, CDocument)

BEGIN_MESSAGE_MAP(CSDISquigDoc, CDocument)
    ON_COMMAND(ID_COLOR_BLACK, OnColorBlack)
    ON_UPDATE_COMMAND_UI(ID_COLOR_BLACK, OnUpdateColorBlack)
    ON_COMMAND(ID_COLOR_BLUE, OnColorBlue)
    ON_UPDATE_COMMAND_UI(ID_COLOR_BLUE, OnUpdateColorBlue)
    ON_COMMAND(ID_COLOR_GREEN, OnColorGreen)
    ON_UPDATE_COMMAND_UI(ID_COLOR_GREEN, OnUpdateColorGreen)
    ON_COMMAND(ID_COLOR_CYAN, OnColorCyan)
    ON_UPDATE_COMMAND_UI(ID_COLOR_CYAN, OnUpdateColorCyan)
    ON_COMMAND(ID_COLOR_RED, OnColorRed)
    ON_UPDATE_COMMAND_UI(ID_COLOR_RED, OnUpdateColorRed)
    ON_COMMAND(ID_COLOR_MAGENTA, OnColorMagenta)
    ON_UPDATE_COMMAND_UI(ID_COLOR_MAGENTA, OnUpdateColorMagenta)
    ON_COMMAND(ID_COLOR_YELLOW, OnColorYellow)
    ON_UPDATE_COMMAND_UI(ID_COLOR_YELLOW, OnUpdateColorYellow)
    ON_COMMAND(ID_COLOR_WHITE, OnColorWhite)
    ON_UPDATE_COMMAND_UI(ID_COLOR_WHITE, OnUpdateColorWhite)
    ON_COMMAND(ID_WIDTH_VERYTHIN, OnWidthVerythin)
    ON_UPDATE_COMMAND_UI(ID_WIDTH_VERYTHIN, OnUpdateWidthVerythin)
    ON_COMMAND(ID_WIDTH_THIN, OnWidthThin)
    ON_UPDATE_COMMAND_UI(ID_WIDTH_THIN, OnUpdateWidthThin)
    ON_COMMAND(ID_WIDTH_MEDIUM, OnWidthMedium)
    ON_UPDATE_COMMAND_UI(ID_WIDTH_MEDIUM, OnUpdateWidthMedium)
    ON_COMMAND(ID_WIDTH_THICK, OnWidthThick)
    ON_UPDATE_COMMAND_UI(ID_WIDTH_THICK, OnUpdateWidthThick)
    ON_COMMAND(ID_WIDTH_VERYTHICK, OnWidthVerythick)
    ON_UPDATE_COMMAND_UI(ID_WIDTH_VERYTHICK, OnUpdateWidthVerythick)
    ON_UPDATE_COMMAND_UI(ID_INDICATOR_COLOR, OnUpdateIndicatorColor)
    ON_UPDATE_COMMAND_UI(ID_INDICATOR_WIDTH, OnUpdateIndicatorWidth)
END_MESSAGE_MAP()
```

INPUT

2. Add a button to the main toolbar that can toggle the color toolbar on and off, as in Figure 11.8.

Open the `IDR_MAINFRAME` toolbar in the toolbar designer. Paint an icon for the blank button at the end of the toolbar. Select the button to open its properties. Specify the button ID as `ID_VIEW_COLORBAR` and enter an appropriate prompt for the button. Recompile and run your application and the color toolbar toggle should be working on the main toolbar.

Answers for Day 12

Quiz

1. What two macros do you have to add to a class to make it serializable?

   `DECLARE_SERIAL` and `IMPLEMENT_SERIAL`.

2. How can you determine whether the CArchive object is reading from or writing to the archive file?

   You call the either the `IsLoading` or `IsStoring` functions.

3. What arguments do you need to pass to the `IMPLEMENT_SERIAL` macro?

   The class name, the base class name, and the version number.

4. What class do you need to inherit the view class from to be able to use the dialog designer to create a form for the main window in an SDI or MDI application?

   `CFormView`.

5. What type of file does the `CArchive` write to by default?

   `CFile`.

Exercise

Add a couple of radio buttons to the form to specify the person's sex, as in Figure 12.7. Incorporate this change into the `CPerson` class to make the field persistent.

In the window designer, add the two radio buttons and the static text prompt. Specify the control properties in Table 12.A.

TABLE 12.A Control Property Settings

Object	Property	Setting
Static Text	Caption	Sex:
Radio Button	ID	IDC_RMALE
	Caption	Mal&e
	Group	True
Radio Button	ID	IDC_RFEMALE
	Caption	&Female

A

Attach a variable to the new radio buttons as follows:

Object	Name	Category	Type
IDC_RMALE	m_iSex	Value	int

Increment the version number in the IMPLEMENT_SERIAL macro in the CPerson class. Add a new member variable to the CPerson class. Specify the type as int, the name as m_iSex, and the access as private. The CPerson constructor function should have been updated, adding the m_iSex variable to the initializations as in Listing 12.A.

LISTING 12.A   The Modified CPerson Constructor

```
CPerson::CPerson(void)
: m_bEmployed(false)
, m_iAge(0)
, m_sName(_T(""))
, m_iMaritalStatus(0)
, m_iSex(0)
{
}
```

INPUT

Add the inline functions to the CPerson class declaration to set and get the value of this new variable, as in Listing 12.B.

LISTING 12.B   The Modified CPerson Class Declaration

```
class CPerson :
    public CObject
{
    DECLARE_SERIAL (CPerson)
public:
    // Functions for setting the variables
    void SetEmployed(BOOL bEmployed) { m_bEmployed = bEmployed;}
    void SetMaritalStatus(int iStat) { m_iMaritalStatus = iStat;}
    void SetAge(int iAge) { m_iAge = iAge;}
    void SetSex(int iSex) { m_iSex = iSex;}
    void SetName(CString sName) {m_sName = sName;}
    // Functions for getting the current settings of the variables
    BOOL GetEmployed() { return m_bEmployed;}
    int GetMaritalStatus() { return m_iMaritalStatus;}
    int GetAge() { return m_iAge;}
    int GetSex() { return m_iSex;}
    CString GetName() { return m_sName;}
    CPerson(void);
    ~CPerson(void);
private:
```

INPUT

INPUT

LISTING 12.B continued

```
    // Is the person employed
    BOOL m_bEmployed;
    // The person's age
    int m_iAge;
    // The person's name
    CString m_sName;
    // The person's marital status
    int m_iMaritalStatus;
public:
    // The serialization function
    virtual void Serialize(CArchive& ar);
private:
    // The person's sex
    int m_iSex;
};
```

Update the Serialize function in the CPerson class to include the m_iSex variable as in Listing 12.C.

LISTING 12.C The Modified CPerson.Serialize Function

```
void CPerson::Serialize(CArchive& ar)
{
    // Call the ancestor function
    CObject::Serialize(ar);

    // Are we writing?
    if (ar.IsStoring())
        // Write all of the variables, in order
        ar << m_sName << m_iAge << m_iMaritalStatus << m_bEmployed
                << m_iSex;
        else
        // Read all of the variables, in order
        ar >> m_sName >> m_iAge >> m_iMaritalStatus >> m_bEmployed
                >> m_iSex;
}
```

INPUT

INPUT

A

Update the version number in the IMPLEMENT_SERIAL macro.

```
IMPLEMENT_SERIAL (CPerson, CObject, 2)
```

Modify the PopulateView function in the view object to include the Sex variable in the data exchange, as in Listing 12.D.

LISTING 12.D   The modified `CSerializeView.PopulateView` Function

```
void CSerializeView::PopulateView(void)
{
    // Get a pointer to the current document
    CSerializeDoc* pDoc = GetDocument();
    if (pDoc)
    {
        // Display the current record position in the set
        m_sPosition.Format("Record %d of %d", pDoc->GetCurRecordNbr(),
                pDoc->GetTotalRecords());
    }
    // Do we have a valid record object?
    if (m_pCurPerson)
    {
        // Yes, get all of the record values
        m_bEmployed = m_pCurPerson->GetEmployed();
        m_iAge = m_pCurPerson->GetAge();
        m_sName = m_pCurPerson->GetName();
        m_iMaritalStatus = m_pCurPerson->GetMaritalStatus();
        m_iSex = m_pCurPerson->GetSex();
    }
    // Update the display
    UpdateData(FALSE);
}
```

Add an event handler for the clicked event of both new radio buttons, using the same function for both event handlers. Update the record object's field using the `Set` function, as in Listing 12.E.

LISTING 12.E   The `CSerializeView.OnSex` Function

```
void CSerializeView::OnBnClickedRSex()
{
    // TODO: Add your control notification handler code here
    // Sync the data in the form with the variables
    UpdateData(TRUE);
    // If we have a valid person object, pass the data changes to it
    if (m_pCurPerson)
        m_pCurPerson->SetSex(m_iSex);
    // Get a pointer to the document
    CSerializeDoc* pDoc = GetDocument();
    if (pDoc)
        // Set the modified flag in the document
        pDoc->SetModifiedFlag();
}
```

Answers for Day 13

Quiz

1. What does ADO stand for?

   ActiveX Data Objects.

2. What does ADO use for database access?

   OLE DB.

3. What are the objects in ADO?

   `Connection`, `Command`, `Parameter`, `Error`, `Recordset`, and `Field`.

4. How do you initialize the COM environment?

   ```
   ::CoInitialize(NULL);
   ```

5. How do you associate a `Connection` object with a `Command` object?

   ```
   pCmd->ActiveConnection = pConn;
   ```

6. How do you associate a `Command` object with and populate a `Recordset` object?

   One of two ways:

   ```
   _RecordsetPtr ptrRs;
   ptrRs = pCmd->Execute();
   ```

   or

   ```
   _RecordsetPtr ptrRs;
   ptrRs.CreateInstance(__uuidof(Recordset));
   ptrRs->PutRefSource(pCmd);

   // Create the variant NULL
   _variant_t vNull;
   vNull.vt = VT_ERROR;
   vNull.scode = DISP_E_PARAMNOTFOUND;

   // Open the recordset
   ptrRs->Open(vNull, vNull, adOpenDynamic, adLockOptimistic, adCmdUnknown);
   ```

A

Exercise

Enable and disable the navigation menus and toolbar buttons based on whether the recordset is at the beginning of file (`BOF`) or end of file (`EOF`, renamed to `EndOfFile`).

1. Add event-handler functions to the document class for the navigation menu entries' `UPDATE_COMMAND_UI` event message.

2. Edit these functions, adding the code in Listing A.X to the functions for the First and Previous menus, and the code in Listing 13.A to the functions for the Last and Next menus.

LISTING 13.A   The CAdoDatabaseDoc OnUpdateDataFirst Function

```
void CAdoDatabaseDoc::OnUpdateDataFirst(CCmdUI* pCmdUI)
{
    // TODO: Add your command update UI handler code here
    // Does the recordset exist?
    if (m_ptrRs)
    {
        // Are we at the BOF?
        if (m_ptrRs->BOF)
            pCmdUI->Enable(FALSE);
        else
            pCmdUI->Enable(TRUE);
    }
}
```

LISTING 13.B   The CAdoDatabaseDoc OnUpdateDataLast Function

```
void CAdoDatabaseDoc::OnUpdateDataLast(CCmdUI* pCmdUI)
{
    // TODO: Add your command update UI handler code here
    // Does the recordset exist?
    if (m_ptrRs)
    {
        // Are we at the EOF?
        if (m_ptrRs->EndOfFile)
            pCmdUI->Enable(FALSE);
        else
            pCmdUI->Enable(TRUE);
    }
}
```

Answers for Day 14

Quiz

1. What kind of DLL do you have to create to make classes in the DLL available to applications?

   An MFC extension DLL.

2. What do you have to add to the class to export it from a DLL?

   The AFX_EXT_CLASS macro in the class declaration.

3. What kind of DLL can be used with other programming languages?

   A regular DLL.

4. If you make changes in a DLL, do you have to recompile the applications that use the DLL?

Normally, no. Only if changes were made in the exported interface for the DLL do you need to recompile the applications that use the DLL.

5. What function does the LIB file provide for a DLL?

The LIB file contains stubs of the functions in the DLL, along with the code to locate and pass the function call along to the real function in the DLL.

Exercises

1. Separate the line class into its own MFC extension DLL and use it with the second (regular) DLL.

Follow these steps:

1. Create a new project. Specify that the project is an MFC DLL project, and give the project a suitable name, such as LineDll.

2. Specify that the DLL will be an MFC extension DLL.

3. After generating the project skeleton, copy the line source code and header files into the project directory. Add these files into the project.

4. Edit the CLine class declaration, adding the AFX_EXT_CLASS macro to the class declaration.

5. Compile the DLL. Copy the DLL into the debug directory for the test application.

6. Open the regular DLL project. Delete the line source code and header files from the project in the File View of the workspace pane. Add the line DLL LIB file to the project. Edit the drawing functionality source-code file, changing the line class header include to include the version in the CLine DLL project directory, as follows:

```
#include "StdAfx.h"
#include "modart.h"
#include "..\LineDll\Line.h"
```

INPUT

7. Compile the project. Copy the DLL into the test application project debug directory.

8. Run the test application.

A

2. Alter the line class DLL so that it uses a consistent line width for all lines.
Follow these steps:

1. Open the line class DLL project that you created in the previous exercise. Edit the class constructor, replacing the initialization of the m_nWidth variable with a constant value, as follows:

INPUT

```
CLine::CLine(CPoint ptFrom, CPoint ptTo, COLORREF crColor, UINT
nWidth)
{
    m_ptFrom = ptFrom;
    m_ptTo = ptTo;
    m_nWidth = 1;
    m_crColor = crColor;
}
```

2. Compile the DLL. Copy the DLL into the test application project debug directory. Run the test application.

Answers for Day 15

Quiz

1. What three aspects of a control are visible to the container application?

Properties, methods, and events.

2. Why do you need to design a property page for your control?

To provide users with the ability to set the control's properties through a dialog.

3. What four types of properties might a control have?

Ambient, extended, stock, and custom.

4. What happens to the parameters passed to a control's methods?

They are marshaled into a standardized, machine-independent structure.

5. What tool can you use to test your controls?

The ActiveX Control Test Container.

Exercises

1. Add a method to your control to enable the container application to trigger the generation of a new squiggle drawing.

Add a new method to the _DSquiggle interface. Specify the method name as GenNewDrawing, and specify the return type as void. Click Finish to add the method. Edit the method, adding the code in Listing 15.A.

LISTING 15.A The CSquiggleCtrl GenNewDrawing Function

```
void CSquiggleCtrl:: GenNewDrawing()
{
    // TODO: Add your specialized code here and/or call the base class
    // Set the flag so a new drawing will be generated
    m_bGenNewDrawing = TRUE;
    // Invalidate the control to trigger the OnDraw function
    Invalidate();
}
```

INPUT

2. Add a method to your control to save a squiggle drawing. Use the
   CFile::modeWrite and CArchive::store flags when creating the CFile and
   CArchive objects.

   Add a new method to the _DSquiggle interface. Specify the method name as
   SaveDrawing, and specify the return type as VARIANT_BOOL so that you can let the
   container application know whether you loaded the drawing. Finally, add one
   parameter to the parameter list. Specify the parameter's name as sFileName and its
   type as BSTR. Click Finish to add the method. Edit the method, adding the code in
   Listing 15.B.

LISTING 15.B The CSquiggleCtrl SaveDrawing Function

```
BOOL CSquiggleCtrl::SaveDrawing(LPCTSTR sFileName)
{
    // TODO: Add your dispatch handler code here
    try
    {
        // Create a CFile object
            CFile lFile(sFileName, CFile::modeWrite);
        // Create a CArchive object to store the file
        CArchive lArchive(&lFile, CArchive::store);
        // Store the file
        m_maDrawing.Serialize(lArchive);
    }
    catch (CFileException* perr)
    {
        // Report the error
        perr->ReportError();
        // Delete the exception
        perr->Delete();
        return VARIANT_FALSE;
    }
    return VARIANT_TRUE;
}
```

INPUT

A

Answers for Day 16

Quiz

1. What does the `CHtmlView` class encapsulate for use in Visual C++ applications?

   The Internet Explorer Web browser.

2. How can you get the URL for the current Web page from the `CHtmlView` class?

   `GetLocationURL()`.

3. What command is triggered for the frame class when the user presses the Enter key in the edit box on the dialog bar?

   `IDOK`.

4. What functions can you call to navigate the browser to the previous and the next Web pages?

   `GoBack()` and `GoForward()`.

5. How can you stop a download in progress?

   With the `Stop()` function.

Exercises

1. Add the `GoSearch` function to the menu and toolbar.

   Add a menu entry to the Navigate menu. Specify the menu entry properties in Table 16.A.

TABLE 16.A   Menu Property Settings

Object	Property	Setting
Menu Entry	ID	ID_NAVIGATE_SEARCH
	Caption	&Search
	Prompt	Search the Web\nSearch

Using the Class Wizard, add an event-handler function to the view class on the `ID_NAVIGATE_SEARCH` ID for the `COMMAND` event message. Edit the code as in Listing 16.A.

LISTING 16.A   The `CWebBrowseView` `OnNavigateSearch` Function

```
void CWebBrowseView::OnNavigateSearch()
{
    // TODO: Add your command handler code here
```

LISTING 16.A continued

```
    // Go to the search page
    GoSearch();
}
```

Add a toolbar button for the menu ID ID_NAVIGATE_SEARCH.

2. Add the GoHome function to the menu and toolbar.

Add a menu entry to the Navigate menu. Specify the menu entry properties in Table 16.B.

TABLE 16.B Menu Property Settings

Object	Property	Setting
Menu Entry	ID	ID_NAVIGATE_START
	Caption	S&tart Page
	Prompt	Go to the start page\nHome

Using the Class Wizard, add an event-handler function to the view class on the ID_NAVIGATE_START ID for the COMMAND event message. Edit the code as in Listing 16.B.

LISTING 16.B The CWebBrowseView OnNavigateStart Function

```
void CWebBrowseView::OnNavigateStart()
{
    // TODO: Add your command handler code here
    // Go to the start page
    GoHome();
}
```

Add a toolbar button for the menu ID ID_NAVIGATE_START.

3. Disable the Stop toolbar button and menu entry when the application is not down-loading a Web page.

Using the Class Wizard, add an event handler to the view class for the ID_NAVI-GATE_STOP object ID on the UPDATE_COMMAND_UI event message. Edit the function, adding the code in Listing 16.C.

A

```
void CWebBrowseView::OnUpdateNavigateStop(CCmdUI* pCmdUI)
{
    // TODO: Add your command update UI handler code here
    // Enable the button if busy
    pCmdUI->Enable(GetBusy());
}
```

Answers for Day 17

Quiz

1. When is the `OnIdle` function called?

   When the application is idle and there are no messages in the application message queue.

2. How can you cause the `OnIdle` function to be repeatedly called while the application is sitting idle?

   Returning a value of TRUE causes the `OnIdle` function to continue to be called as long as the application remains idle.

3. What is the difference between an `OnIdle` task and a thread?

   An `OnIdle` task executes only when the application is idle and there are no messages in the message queue. A thread executes independently of the rest of the application.

4. What are the four thread synchronization objects?

   Critical sections, mutexes, semaphores, and events.

5. Why shouldn't you specify a higher than normal priority for the threads in your application?

   The rest of the threads and processes running on the computer will receive a greatly reduced amount of processor time.

Exercises

1. If you open a performance monitor on your system while the application that you built today is running, you'll find that even without any threads running, the processor usage remains 100 percent, as in Figure 17.11. The `OnIdle` function is continuously being called even when there is nothing to be done.

   Modify the `OnIdle` function so that if there's nothing to be done, neither of the `OnIdle` threads are active. Then, the `OnIdle` function won't continue to be called

until one of these threads is active, at which time it should be continuously called
until both threads are once again turned off. This allows the processor to drop to a
minimal utilization, as in Figure 17.12.

Edit the OnIdle function as in Listing 17.A.

LISTING 17.A The Modified CTaskingApp OnIdle Function

```
BOOL CTaskingApp::OnIdle(LONG lCount)
{
    // TODO: Add your specialized code here and/or call the base class
    // Call the ancestor's idle processing
    BOOL bRtn = CWinApp::OnIdle(lCount);
    // Get the position of the first document template
    POSITION pos = GetFirstDocTemplatePosition();
    // Do we have a valid template position?
    if (pos)
    {
        // Get a pointer to the document template
        CDocTemplate* pDocTemp = GetNextDocTemplate(pos);
        // Do we have a valid pointer?
        if (pDocTemp)
        {
            // Get the position of the first document
            POSITION dPos = pDocTemp->GetFirstDocPosition();
            // Do we have a valid document position?
            if (dPos)
            {
                // Get a pointer to the document
                CTaskingDoc* pDocWnd =
                    (CTaskingDoc*)pDocTemp->GetNextDoc(dPos);
                // Do we have a valid pointer?
                if (pDocWnd)
                {
                    // Get the position of the view
                    POSITION vPos = pDocWnd->GetFirstViewPosition();
                    // Do we have a valid view position?
                    if (vPos)
                    {
                        // Get a pointer to the view
                        CTaskingView* pView =
                          (CTaskingView*)pDocWnd->GetNextView(vPos);
                        // Do we have a valid pointer?
                        if (pView)
                        {
                            // Should we spin the first idle thread?
                            if (pView->m_bOnIdle1)
                            {
                                // Spin the first idle thread
                                pDocWnd->DoSpin(0);
```

INPUT

A

LISTING 17.A   continued

```
INPUT                                           bRtn = TRUE;
                                          }
                              // Should we spin the second idle thread?
                              if (pView->m_bOnIdle2)
                              {
                                  // Spin the second idle thread
                                  pDocWnd->DoSpin(2);
INPUT                                     bRtn = TRUE;
                              }
                          }
                      }
                  }
              }
          }
INPUT     return bRtn;
          }
```

2. When starting the independent threads, give one of the threads a priority of
   THREAD_PRIORITY_NORMAL and the other a priority of THREAD_PRIORITY_LOWEST.

   Edit the SuspendSpinner function as in Listing 17.B.

LISTING 17.B   The Modified CTaskingDoc SuspendSpinner Function

```
void CTaskingDoc::SuspendSpinner(int iIndex, BOOL bRun)
{
    // if suspending the thread
    if (!bRun)
    {
        // Is the pointer for the thread valid?
        if (m_pSpinThread[iIndex])
        {
            // Get the handle for the thread
            HANDLE m_hThread = m_pSpinThread[iIndex]->m_hThread;
            // Wait for the thread to die
            ::WaitForSingleObject (m_hThread, INFINITE);
        }
    }
    else     // We are running the thread
    {
        int m_iSpnr;
        int m_iPriority;
        // Which spinner to use?
        switch (iIndex)
        {
        case 0:
```

LISTING 17.B   continued

```
            m_iSpnr = 1;
            m_iPriority = THREAD_PRIORITY_NORMAL;
            break;
        case 1:
            m_iSpnr = 3;
            m_iPriority = THREAD_PRIORITY_LOWEST;
            break;
        }
        // Start the thread, passing a pointer to the spinner
        m_pSpinThread[iIndex] = AfxBeginThread(ThreadFunc,
            (LPVOID)&m_cSpin[m_iSpnr], m_iPriority);
    }
}
```

Answers for Day 18

Quiz

1. What two things must a client application know to be able to connect to a server application?

   The network address (or name) of the computer and the port on which the server is listening.

2. What `CAsyncSocket` function enables a server application to detect connection efforts by client applications?

   `Listen.`

3. What `CAsyncSocket` member function is called to signal that data has arrived through a socket connection?

   `OnReceive.`

4. What function is called to signal that a connection is established?

   `OnConnect.`

5. What function do you use to send a message through a socket connection to the application on the other end?

   `Send.`

Exercises

The server application that you wrote can handle only a single connection at a time. If a second application tries to open a connection to it while it has an existing connection to an application, the server application will crash. The server tries to accept the second

A

connection into the socket already connected to the first client application. Add a third socket object to the application that will be used to reject additional client connections until the first client closes the connection.

Follow these steps:

1. Add a member variable to the dialog class (CSockDlg). Specify the variable type as BOOL, the name as m_bConnected, and the access as private.

2. Initialize the variable as FALSE in the OnInitDialog function.

3. Set the variable to TRUE in the OnAccept dialog function when the connection is accepted.

4. Set the variable to FALSE in the OnClose dialog function.

5. Modify the OnAccept dialog function as in Listing 18.A.

LISTING 18.A   The Modified CSockDlg OnAccept Function

```
void CSockDlg::OnAccept()
{
    if (m_bConnected)
    {
        // Create a rejection socket
        CAsyncSocket sRjctSock;
        // Create a message to send
        CString strMsg = "Too many connections, try again later.";
        // Accept using the rejection socket
        m_sListenSocket.Accept(sRjctSock);
        // Send the rejection message
        sRjctSock.Send(LPCTSTR(strMsg), strMsg.GetLength());
        // Close the socket
        sRjctSock.Close();
    }
    else
    {
        // Accept the connection request
        m_sListenSocket.Accept(m_sConnectSocket);
        // Mark the socket as connected
        m_bConnected = TRUE;
        // Enable the text and message controls
        GetDlgItem(IDC_EMSG)->EnableWindow(TRUE);
        GetDlgItem(IDC_BSEND)->EnableWindow(TRUE);
        GetDlgItem(IDC_STATICMSG)->EnableWindow(TRUE);
    }
}
```

Answers for Day 19

Quiz

1. How do you mark a class for garbage collection?

   Add __gc in front of the class declaration.

2. What two methods can you use to convert a managed string to an integer?

   Convert::ToInt32() and Int32::Parse().

3. How do you mark a managed class or structure so that it doesn't have garbage collection performed on it?

   Add __value in front of the class or structure declaration.

4. What method do you use to print text for users in a DOS window?

   Console::WriteLine() or Console::Write().

5. How do you import a CLR DLL or object file for use in a managed C++ application?

   #using <somedll.dll>

Exercise

Modify today's application to allow the user to specify whether to add or subtract the two numbers entered. *Hint:* You might want to use the System.String class's Equals method to perform the comparison.

Modify the CAddNumbers class AddNumbers function as in Listing 19.A

LISTING 19.A The Modified AddNumbers Function

```
void CAddNumbers::AddNumbers(void)
{
    int iResult;
    String* strMsg;
    bool bAdd;

    // Prompt the user for which action to perform
    Console::Write(S"Enter + to add the numbers, or - to subtract: ");
    // Read the user's response
    strMsg = Console::ReadLine();
    // Determine if a plus sign was entered
    if (strMsg->Equals("+"))
    {
        // Add the two numbers
        iResult = m_iNumber1 + m_iNumber2;
        bAdd = true;
```

INPUT

A

LISTING 19.A   continued

```
        }
        else
        {
            // Subtract the two numbers
            iResult = m_iNumber1 - m_iNumber2;
            bAdd = false;
        }
        // Prepare the first number entered to be displayed
        strMsg = String::Concat(S"First number entered: ",
                Convert::ToString(m_iNumber1));
        // Display the first number entered
        Console::WriteLine(strMsg);
        // Prepare the second number entered to be displayed
        strMsg = String::Concat(S"Second number entered: ",
                Convert::ToString(m_iNumber2));
        // Display the first number entered
        Console::WriteLine(strMsg);
        // Prepare the result to be displayed
        if (bAdd)
            strMsg = String::Concat(S"Result of adding numbers: ",
                    iResult.ToString());
        else
            strMsg = String::Concat(S"Result of subtracting numbers: ",
                    iResult.ToString());
        // Display the result of the addition
        Console::WriteLine(strMsg);
    }
```

INPUT

Answers for Day 20

Quiz

1. What is a C++ class template?

   Templates are macros for entire classes.

2. What standard library of templates is available for use in any C++ application?

   The Standard Template Library (STL).

3. What is the key to creating an ATL component that you can provide with a managed C++ wrapper so that it can have both a COM and CLR interface?

   The business logic class(es) must be separate from the interface class(es).

4. Why do you have to turn off the use of precompiled headers after you add the managed wrapper to the project?

Because the precompiled headers are in a binary format that can't be shared between both managed and unmanaged code.

Exercise

Add a second method to your ATL class to return the tax rate for the specified category. Modify both interfaces for this new method, and modify both clients to request and display the tax rate.

To complete this exercise, follow these steps:

1. Add a new function to the CTaxCalculator class.

2. Specify the return type for the new function as BOOL, name the function GetTaxRate, specify the access as public, and add two parameters. Specify the type of the first parameter as wchar_t*, and the name as wszCategory. Specify the type of the second parameter as float*, and the name as pfTaxRate. Click Finish to add the method to your class.

3. Edit the new method, adding the code in Listing 20.A.

LISTING 20.A   The GetTaxRate Function

```
BOOL TaxCalcs::CTaxCalculator::GetTaxRate(wchar_t* wszCategory,
       float* pfTaxRate)
{
    // Declare the array of tax categories
    static const wchar_t *wszCategories[] = {L"food", L"clothing", L"music"};
    // Declare the array of tax rates
    static const float fRates[] = {0.0725, 0.0835, 0.081};
    // Loop through the categories
    for (int i = 0; i < 3; i++)
    {
        // Is this the category purchased?
        if (wcscmp(wszCategory, wszCategories[i]) == 0)
        {
            // Yes, return the tax rate charged
            *pfTaxRate = fRates[i];
            // Return TRUE
            return TRUE;
        }
    }
    // Couldn't find the category purchased, return FALSE
    return FALSE;
}
```

A

4. You need to add the exposed method that clients will use to access the business logic class in your component. Add a new method to the IGetTaxForPurchase interface. Be sure to add the method to the interface, and not to the class.

5. Specify the method name as GetTaxRate. You'll add two parameters to match the two parameters that have to be passed to the business logic class. For the first parameter, select BSTR* for the parameter type, enter **bstrCategory** for the parameter name, select the In check box, and click Add. For the second parameter, select FLOAT* for the parameter type, enter **pfTax** for the parameter name, select the Out check box, and click Add. Click Finish to add the method to the interface.

6. Edit the method, adding the code in Listing 20.B.

LISTING 20.B The GetTaxRate Method

```
STDMETHODIMP CGetTaxForPurchase::GetTaxRate(BSTR* bstrCategory, FLOAT* pfTax)
{
    // TODO: Add your implementation code here
    // Do we have a valid pointer to the variable into which the tax due
    // will be placed?
    if (!pfTax)
        return S_FALSE;
    // Get the tax rate
    if (m_pTaxCalc->GetTaxRate((wchar_t*)*bstrCategory, pfTax))
        return S_OK;
    else
        return S_FALSE;
}
```

7. Open the TaxCalcClient.cpp source code file, and add the boldface lines to the main function of the COM client in Listing 20.C.

LISTING 20.C The COM Client Main Function

```
int _tmain(int argc, _TCHAR* argv[])
{
    // Startup the COM environment
    CoInitialize(NULL);
    {
        // Use the namespace of the Tax Calculations module
        using namespace TaxCalculations;
        // Get the interface pointer for the tax calculations module
        IGetTaxForPurchasePtr pGetTax(L"TaxCalculations.GetTaxForPurchase");

        // Create the string for the category being purchased
        CComBSTR bstrCat1(OLESTR("clothing"));
        float fPurchaseAmt, fTaxAmt, fTaxRate;

        // Specify the purchase amount
        fPurchaseAmt = 45.0;
        // Get the amount of taxes to collect
```

LISTING 20.C continued

```
            if (pGetTax->GetPurchaseTaxes(fPurchaseAmt, &bstrCat1, &fTaxAmt)
                == S_OK)
            {
                // add in the string conversion macros
                USES_CONVERSION;
                // Display the category being purchased
                printf("%s\n", W2A(bstrCat1));
                // Display the purchase amount
                printf("Purchase Amount = %9.2f\n", fPurchaseAmt);
                // Display the tax due
                printf("            Tax = %9.2f\n", fTaxAmt);
                // Display the total amount
                printf("      Total Due = %9.2f\n", fPurchaseAmt + fTaxAmt);
            }
```

INPUT

```
                // Get the tax rate charged
                if (pGetTax->GetTaxRate(&bstrCat1, &fTaxRate) == S_OK)
                // Display the tax rate charged
                printf("Tax Rate Charged = %f\n", fTaxRate);
        }
        // Shut down the COM environment
        CoUninitialize();
        return 0;
    }
```

8. Select and right-click the `TaxCalcClient` project in the Solution Explorer pane. Select Set as Startup Project from the context menu.

9. Compile and run the application, using the COM interface.

10. Add a new function to the managed wrapper class (`MgdGetTaxForPurchase`). Open the header file and add the function declaration, as in Listing 20.D.

LISTING 20.D The Modified `MgdGetTaxForPurchase` Header File

```
#pragma once
#include "TaxCalculator.h"
#using <mscorlib.dll>
using namespace System;

public __gc class MgdGetTaxForPurchase
{
private:
    TaxCalcs::CTaxCalculator* m_pTaxCalc;
public:
    MgdGetTaxForPurchase(void);
    BOOL GetPurchaseTaxes(float fPurchaseAmt,
            System::String* pstrCategory, float* pfTax);
    BOOL GetTaxRate(System::String* pstrCategory, float* pfTax);
};
```

INPUT

A

11. Reopen the source code file for the `MgdGetTaxForPurchase` class and add the definition for the new function, as in Listing 20.E.

LISTING 20.E   The `GetTaxRate` Function Definition

```
BOOL MgdGetTaxForPurchase::GetTaxRate(System::String* pstrCategory,
    float* pfTax)
{
    wchar_t *pCat;
    int iLen;

    // Do we have a valid pointer to the variable into
    // which the tax due will be placed?
    if (!pfTax)
        return FALSE;
    // Convert the category from a BSTR to a wchar_t
    __wchar_t pCategory __gc[] = pstrCategory->ToCharArray();
    iLen = pstrCategory->get_Length();
    pCat = new wchar_t[iLen + 1];
    for (int i = 0; i < iLen; i++)
    {
        pCat[i] = pCategory[i];
    }
    pCat[i] = NULL;
    // Get the taxes rate
    if (m_pTaxCalc->GetTaxRate(pCat, pfTax))
        return TRUE;
    else
        return FALSE;
}
```

12. Open the MgdTaxCalcClient.cpp source code file and add the boldfaced lines in Listing 20.F to the main function of the managed client.

LISTING 20.F   The Managed Client Main Function

```
// This is the entry point for this application
int _tmain(void)
{
    // TODO: Please replace the sample code below with your own.
    // Get the interface pointer for the tax calculations module
    MgdGetTaxForPurchase* pGetTax = new MgdGetTaxForPurchase();

    float fPurchaseAmt, fTaxAmt, fTotalDue, fTaxRate;

    // Create the string for the category being purchased
    String* pstrCategory = L"clothing";
```

LISTING 20.F   continued

```
// Specify the purchase amount
fPurchaseAmt = 45.0;
// Get the amount of taxes to collect
if (pGetTax->GetPurchaseTaxes(fPurchaseAmt, pstrCategory, &fTaxAmt))
{
    // Calculate the total due
    fTotalDue = fPurchaseAmt + fTaxAmt;
    // Display the category being purchased
    Console::WriteLine(pstrCategory);
    // Display the purchase amount
    Console::Write("Purchase Amount = ");
    Console::WriteLine(fPurchaseAmt.ToString("c"));
    // Display the tax due
    Console::Write("            Tax = ");
    Console::WriteLine(fTaxAmt.ToString("c"));
    // Display the total amount
    Console::Write("      Total Due = ");
    Console::WriteLine(fTotalDue.ToString("c"));
}
```

INPUT
```
// Get the tax rate charged
if (pGetTax->GetTaxRate(pstrCategory, &fTaxRate))
{
    // Display the tax rate charged
    Console::Write("Tax Rate Charged = ");
    Console::WriteLine(fTaxRate.ToString());
}
```
```
    return 0;
}
```

13. Select and right-click the MgdTaxCalcClient project in the Solution Explorer pane. Select Set as Startup Project from the context menu.

14. Compile and run the application, using the managed C++ wrapper interface.

Answers for Day 21

Quiz

1. What do you need to do to be able to access a managed component in a VB.NET or C# application?

   Add a reference for the component to the project.

A

2. What configuration changes do you need to make for a managed C++ application to access objects created in other CLR languages?

Add a #using directive to use the component. Modify the pre-build event for the project, copying the component DLL to the output directory for the project. Add a #using directive resolution directory for the project output directory.

3. What data type can you pass from an unmanaged application to a managed string data type in a managed component?

wchar_t*

4. Can you use precompiled headers in a mixed managed/unmanaged C++ project?

No.

Exercise

Add a second method to your VB or C# component to return the tax rate for the specified category. Modify the managed C++ client to request and display the tax rate.

To perform this exercise, follow these steps:

1. If you built your component using VB, add the function in Listing 21.A. If you created your component using C#, add a new method to the CTaxCalculations class.

LISTING 21.A   The VB GetTaxRate Function

```
Public Function GetTaxRate(ByVal strCategory As String) As Double
    ' Declare the array of tax categories
    Dim strCategories() As String = {"food", "clothing", "music"}
    ' Declare the array of tax rates
    Dim dbRates() As Double = {0.0725, 0.0835, 0.081}
    Dim i As Int32

    ' Preset the default return value
    GetTaxRate = 0
    ' Loop through the categories
    For i = 0 To 2
        ' Is this the category purchased?
        If (strCategory = strCategories(i)) Then
            ' Yes, calculate the taxes due
            GetTaxRate = dbRates(i)
        End If
    Next
End Function
```

2. In the C# Method Wizard, specify the method access as public, the return type as double, the name as GetTaxRate, and add one parameters. For the first parameter,

specify the modifier as None, the parameter type as `string`, and the parameter name as `strCategory`. Click Finish to add this method.

3. Edit the method created, adding the code in Listing 21.B.

LISTING 21.B   The C# `GetTaxRate` Function

```csharp
public double GetTaxRate(string strCategory)
{
    // Declare the array of tax categories
    String[] strCategories = {"food", "clothing", "music"};
    // Declare the array of tax rates
    double[] dbRates = {0.0725F, 0.0835F, 0.081F};
    // Loop through the categories
    for (int i=0; i < 3; i++)
    {
        // Is this the category purchased?
        if (strCategory == strCategories[i])
        {
            // Yes, calculate the taxes due
            return dbRates[i];
        }
    }
    // Couldn't find the category purchased, return 0
    return 0;
}
```

4. Modify the managed C++ client application, adding the boldfaced code in Listing 21.C.

LISTING 21.C   The Modified Managed C++ Client Main Function

```cpp
// This is the entry point for this application
int _tmain(void)
{
    // TODO: Please replace the sample code below with your own.
    VBTaxCalc::CTaxCalculations* pGetTax = new VBTaxCalc::CTaxCalculations();

    double dbPurchaseAmt, dbTaxAmt, dbTotalDue, dbTaxRate;

    // Create the string for the category being purchased
    String* pstrCategory = S"clothing";

    // Specify the purchase amount
    dbPurchaseAmt = 45.0;
    // Get the amount of taxes to collect
    dbTaxAmt = pGetTax->CalculateTaxes(dbPurchaseAmt, pstrCategory);
    if (dbTaxAmt > 0.0)
```

A

LISTING 21.C continued

```
    {
        // Calculate the total due
        dbTotalDue = dbPurchaseAmt + dbTaxAmt;
        // Display the category being purchased
        Console::WriteLine(pstrCategory);
        // Display the purchase amount
        Console::Write("Purchase Amount = ");
        Console::WriteLine(dbPurchaseAmt.ToString("c"));
        // Display the tax due
        Console::Write("            Tax = ");
        Console::WriteLine(dbTaxAmt.ToString("c"));
        // Display the total amount
        Console::Write("      Total Due = ");
        Console::WriteLine(dbTotalDue.ToString("c"));
    }
```

INPUT
```
    // Get the tax rate charged
    dbTaxRate = pGetTax->GetTaxRate(pstrCategory);
    if (dbTaxRate > 0.0)
    {
        // Display the tax rate charged
        Console::Write("Tax Rate Charged = ");
        Console::WriteLine(dbTaxRate.ToString());
    }

    return 0;
}
```

INDEX

D

G

O

X